paralegal STUDIES

Hillary J. Michaud, Esq., CPA

Paralegal Program Coordinator and Professor of Law
Stevenson University

Boston Columbus Indianapolis New York San Francisco Upper Saddle River
Amsterdam Cape Town Dubai London Madrid Milan Munich Paris Montreal Toronto
Delhi Mexico City Sao Paulo Sydney Hong Kong Seoul Singapore Taipei Tokyo

Editorial Director: Vernon Anthony
Executive Acquisitions Editor: Gary Bauer
Editorial Assistant: Tanika Henderson
Director of Marketing: David Gesell
Marketing Manager: Stacey Martinez
Marketing Assistant: Les Roberts
Senior Managing Editor: JoEllen Gohr
Project Manager: Christina Taylor
Senior Operations Supervisor: Pat Tonneman
Senior Art Director: Diane Ernsberger

Text and Cover Designer: PreMediaGlobal
Manager, Visual Research: Mike Lackey
Photo Researcher: Kerri Wilson
Cover Art: ©Jurgen Vogt/Getty Images Inc.–Image Bank
Full-Service Project Management: PreMediaGlobal
Composition: PreMediaGlobal
Printer/Binder: Quebecor World Color/Versailles
Cover Printer: Lehigh Phoenix Color/Hagerstown
Text Font: Helvetica 9/15

Credits and acknowledgments borrowed from other sources and reproduced, with permission, in this textbook appear on appropriate pages within text. Credits for chapter openers and detailed contents pages are as follows: Chris Ryan/Alamy; Eric1513/Dreamstime; Jerric Ramos/Shutterstock; Konstantin L/Shutterstock; RubberBall/SuperStock; Imagesource/Imagesource/PhotoLibrary; Amy Dunn/Shutterstock; Sean Nel/Shutterstock; Stephen VanHorn/Shutterstock; Exactostock/SuperStock; Yuri Arcurs/Shutterstock; EdBockStock/Shutterstock.

Library of Congress Cataloging-in-Publication Data

Michaud, Hillary J.
  Paralegal studies / Hillary J. Michaud.
    p. cm.
  Includes bibliographical references and index.
  ISBN 978-0-13-705268-4 (pbk. : alk. paper)
  1. Legal assistants—United States. 2. Law—Vocational guidance—United States. I. Title.
  KF320.L4M53 2013
  340.023'73—dc23

                                                                    2011041945

10 9 8 7 6 5 4 3 2 1

ISBN 10:   0-13-705268-5
ISBN 13: 978-0-13-705268-4

To Katy, Davis, and Randy—who patiently wait for me while I write and write and write.

Brief Contents

CONTENTS

PREFACE

From the Author

I am grateful to Pearson Education for publishing this work, my second law textbook. It is a joy for me to express my "lawyering" and teaching experiences in these textbooks.

It might be helpful to provide a bit of my history, which, hopefully, qualifies me to write this introductory text. Before becoming a lawyer, I worked as a certified public accountant as an auditor for an international accounting firm. After receiving my Juris Doctor with Honors from the University of North Carolina at Chapel Hill School of Law in 1991, I worked as in-house legal counsel for The Coca-Cola Company at its world headquarters in Atlanta, Georgia, as well as at its Nordic Division headquarters in Oslo, Norway. Later I moved to Baltimore and spent several years working in private practice with downtown law firms before accepting a position as legal counsel for Baltimore City. During this period, I began to teach business law courses at a local community college in order to improve my public speaking skills, which were rarely used in those days. Quickly coming to love students and teaching law, I found myself working full-time as a lawyer as well as teaching as an adjunct law professor at Carroll Community College in Westminster, Maryland, and at Stevenson University, in Owings Mills, Maryland. Today I am program director for an ABA-approved bachelor's degree program in paralegal studies at Stevenson University, as well as a part-time administrative hearing officer in Baltimore City. I am thankful for and appreciate the variety of employers I have worked for over the years, as they gave me wonderful opportunities to both study and gain experience in the many sides of the practice of law.

Given my background as a lawyer who has worked as in-house counsel for a major corporation, in private practice for law firms, and in public service for the government, teaching and writing a textbook for an Introduction to Legal Studies course is a natural fit. In all my "attorney" positions, I have worked with and supervised paralegals. We have been on the same team throughout my legal career. I value the paralegal profession, and those who work in it. I am pleased to have the opportunity to educate and train the next generation of paralegals and pre-law students in my role as Paralegal Program Director at Stevenson University.

This text and its student supplements are designed to introduce students to all aspects of the practice of law and the "players" involved. Actual experiences of working paralegals are incorporated into the materials based on a series of paralegal interviews conducted in conjunction with the writing of the text and filmed as part of the accompanying video series. To provide students with a realistic view of the law office and the courts and to provide them with experience doing tasks they will be called on to perform in a law office, we have created the MyLegalStudiesLab Virtual Law Office Experience. This innovative book-specific online program allows students and instructors to confirm mastery of terminology and concepts and gain hands-on experience doing real work producing workplace documents for their portfolio.

I hope that you enjoy using this text. As an educator, I welcome feedback on any aspect of the textbook and its accompanying supplements. Feel free to contact me at hmichaud@stevenson.edu.

Hillary J. Michaud

Chapter Organization

The text covers the paralegal profession, the American legal system, legal ethics and professional responsibility for paralegals, paralegal skills, and important legal specialty areas for paralegal practice. Along with its supplementary resources, including the video series, the text is designed to be comprehensive in its discussion of topics, and some instructors may find it contains more information than they can or wish to cover in a three-credit introductory class. In that situation, instructors can pick and choose chapters or parts they want to include in their classes and refer students to the other chapters or parts for independent study and/or reference.

The text, containing 13 chapters, is organized into five parts. Part I contains an introduction to the paralegal profession, including the definition and role of a paralegal, qualifications to become a paralegal, and paralegal careers and career preparation. Part II examines the American legal system, including sources of American law, the civil and criminal law systems, the court systems, litigation, and alternative dispute resolution. Part III covers legal ethics and professional responsibility for paralegals, discussing the regulation of the paralegal profession, an introduction to legal ethics rules and their sources, a discussion of the three major legal ethics rules affecting paralegals, and a review of other legal ethics rules that may affect paralegals depending on their practices. Part IV develops paralegal skills for workplace success in conducting legal research and writing and briefing court cases, and in interviewing, investigation, and negotiation. Part V discusses important legal specialty areas for paralegal practice, including business-related legal specialty areas and "other" legal specialty areas not directly related to business.

Special Features

The text incorporates a variety of features designed to accommodate learning style diversity and to enhance its visual appeal and readability. Each chapter contains the following features.

Paralegal Viewpoint(s) highlight the practice of one or two working paralegals.

matters by preparing and processing legal documents. Many of California's LDAs have paralegal education, training, and experience. However, paralegals in California may not provide services directly to the public. Paralegals in California must be employed by an attorney, law firm, corporation, governmental agency, or other entity, and work under the direct supervision of a licensed attorney. In California, neither paralegals nor LDAs may engage in the practice of law.

The paralegal profession is the obvious profession most concerned with the unauthorized practice of law. Paralegals, by definition, perform certain substantive legal work for and delegated by a lawyer, under the lawyer's supervision and for which the lawyer is responsible. Other professions also face some risks regarding the unauthorized practice of law, though. For example, accountant, realtors, and bankers often use legal documents, including contracts, in their professional work. Many jurisdictions enact statutes and other rules to permit certain practices and activities by professionals who often deal with certain legal documents—such as realtors who routinely draft contracts for their clients to purchase and sell real estate. These special rules often provide for training of the nonlawyer in the

> *I always get the attorney involved in what I am doing early and often. I do not finalize any nonstandard legal document without first running it by the attorney for approval.*
> Susan Campbell

Attorneys who engage in the unauthorized practice of law (typically, by practicing outside the jurisdictions in which they are licensed) or who assist a nonlawyer, such as their paralegal, in the unauthorized practice of law, including by failing to properly supervise the nonlawyer, may face the same consequences as nonlawyers who engage in this conduct, as just noted. Courts may issue injunctions ordering a lawyer to stop engaging in the unauthorized practice of law, or in assisting a nonlawyer in engaging in the unauthorized practice of law. Attorneys may be cited for civil contempt as well. They can be prosecuted by the government if they violate the jurisdiction's criminal statutes on the unauthorized practice of law. Where a paralegal's unauthorized prac-

Paralegal Quotes from the practicing paralegals featured in the chapter opener appear throughout the textbook to reinforce concepts and application.

CASE on POINT

Harper v. Maverick Recording Co, 131 S. Ct. 590 (2010).

The U.S. Supreme Court heard this petition for *certiorari* out of the U.S. Court of Appeals for the Fifth Circuit. The case involved a 16-year-old girl who was found to have infringed the Maverick Recording Company's copyrights by downloading digital music files.

provided proper copyright notice on each of its works (the phonorecords from which the digital files were taken and made available through file-sharing), and the girl had access to the phonorecords. Further, the Fifth Circuit ruled that the infringer need not actually see a material object with a copy-

Cases on Point to be read, briefed, and discussed in class.

STATUTE on POINT

Cal. Bus. & Prof. Code §§ 6450-6456 (2010)

- The California statute states that a "paralegal" means a person who holds herself out to be a paralegal; who is qualified by education, training, or work experience; who contracts with or is employed by an attorney, law firm, corporation, governmental agency, or other organization; who performs substantial legal work specifically delegated to her by an active member of the State Bar of California or an attorney practicing in the federal courts in California; and whose work is performed under the direction and supervision of that attorney.

- A paralegal shall not give legal advice; represent a client in court; select, explain, draft, or recommend the use of any legal document to or for any person other than the attorney who supervises the paralegal; act as a "runner or capper"; contract with or be employed by a person other than an attorney to perform legal services; induce a person to make an investment in connection with providing paralegal services; or establish the fees to charge a client for the paralegal services.

- Every two years, a paralegal must complete four hours

Statutes on Point are examined and discussed as they relate to materials included in the text and end-of-chapter materials.

KEY Point

Role of the Paralegal

The role of the paralegal is to assist attorneys in the delivery of certain legal services.

Key Points highlight material for classroom discussion.

Tips for Conducting an Interview

Here are some tips for how to conduct an interview.

- Greet the interviewee and introduce yourself.
- If you are a paralegal, inform the interviewee that you are a paralegal and not an attorney (in compliance with legal ethics rules on the unauthorized practice of law).
- Practice the art of conversation and be friendly, courteous, and polite to establish rapport and build trust with the interviewee.
- Act professionally in greeting and questioning the interviewee.
- Explain the purpose of the interview—that is it to gather and record information.
- Demonstrate confidence, for you control how the

Interesting workplace tips provide practical guidance.

Reinforcement and Skill Building Exercises

End-of-chapter exercises reinforce mastery of concepts and build paralegal skills including:

- End-of-chapter questions for review
- Critical-thinking exercises
- Assignments and practical applications
- Technology resources and Internet exercises
- Ethical applications

MyLegalStudiesLab Virtual Law Office Experience for Paralegal Studies

The Paralegal Studies MyLegalStudiesLab Virtual Law Office Experience is a multi media course program (including an integrated ebook) designed to provide students with the tools they need to confirm their mastery of legal concepts and applications and then apply their knowledge and skills in a workplace context. Students watch realistic video scenarios, work with case files and documents, and use technology tools they will find in the law office to do the work a paralegal is asked to do in practice. Throughout the course, students build a portfolio of work that demonstrates they have the training and experience employers require.

- **Students engage in a workplace experience as a law office intern.**

- **Students see behind closed doors in practice and in the courts.**

- **Students build a comprehensive portfolio of workplace products to show potential employers.**

Within MyLegalStudiesLab, students can access a wealth of resources to complete assignments, including:

- *Ask the Law Librarian Instructional Videos* answer student's research and writing questions.

- *Ask Technical Support* provides technology and legal software support for students.

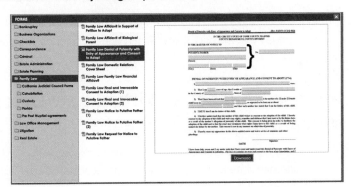

- *Forms File* contains hundreds of examples of commonly used legal documents, forms, and checklists for the major legal specialties.

- *Case Materials* contain all of the case information and documents needed to complete assignments.

ACCIDENT SCENE

Davis Hilary, a minor, by his Parent and guardian, Katy Hilary, Plaintiff

v.

Bobby Jones, Ronald Clemmons, Lower Council School District, Defendants

: No.: 24-1432

:

:

:

Attorney ID No. 124987

NOTICE OF INTENT TO SERVE A SUBPOENA TO PRODUCE DOCUMENTS AND THINGS FOR DISCOVERY PURSUANT TO RULE 4009.21

Defendants intend to serve a subpoena identical to the one that is attached to this notice. You have twenty (20) days from the date listed below in which to file of record and serve upon the undersigned an objection to the subpoena. If no objection is made, the subpoena may be served.

Date: September 14, 2011

John Morris
John Morris
Attorney for Defendants

Davis Hilary, a minor, by his Parent and guardian, Katy Hilary, Plaintiff

v.

Bobby Jones, Ronald Clemmons, Lower Council School District, Defendants

: No.: 24-1432

:

:

:

Attorney ID No. 124987

SUBPOENA TO PRODUCE DOCUMENTS OR THINGS FOR DISCOVERY PURSUANT TO RULE 4009.22

TO:

Downstate Medical Associates

Within twenty (20) days after service of this subpoena, you are ordered by the court to produce the following documents or things:

All medical records and billings for the treatment of Davis Hilary, a minor.

Date: September 14, 2011

John Morris

Attorney for Plaintiff

PROGRAM BENEFITS AND INSTRUCTOR RESOURCES FOR MYLEGALSTUDIESLAB VIRTUAL LAW OFFICE EXPERIENCE FOR PARALEGAL STUDIES

- MyLegalStudiesLab Virtual Law Office Experience makes it easy for you to confirm that students are achieving measurable outcomes for knowledge of the law, procedural knowledge, and administrative workplace skills.

- MyLegalStudiesLab Virtual Law Office Experience content is book-specific and available with or without a Pearson eText. If purchased with the integrated eText, all resource and quiz question responses link directly back to the textbook content providing immediate remediation and/or reinforcement of concepts.

- All course outcomes are assessed and include all AAFPE recommended learning objectives.

- Legal concept and legal application quiz questions feed an instructor's gradebook.

- Assessments for all Virtual Law Office Experience assignments include grading rubrics.

- Book-specific instructor supplements, including the Instructor's Manual, PowerPoint Lecture Screens, and MyTest have been upgraded and include the Virtual Law Office Assignment teaching notes and rubrics.

- All videos within MyLegalStudies Lab are also available on DVD in a high-resolution format for use in the classroom.

- For selected assignments, use of legal software is integrated into the MyLegalStudiesLab Virtual Law Office Experience to be assigned at the instructor's option.

A MyLegalStudiesLab Virtual Law Office Experience access code with or without the Pearson eText can be packaged with the print textbook at a value price or can be purchased standalone in a bookstore or online.

MyLegalStudiesLab Virtual Law Office Experience w/Pearson eText Packages

- To order *Paralegal Studies* print text value-packaged with a MyLegalStudiesLab Virtual Law Office Experience w/ eText for *Paralegal Studies* Access Code, order ISBN: 0-13-299299-X.

- Instant Access to the MyLegalStudiesLabs can be purchased by students online at www.mylegalstudieslab.com.

- Bookstores can order Standalone MyLegalStudiesLabs with eText Access Code with ISBN: 0-13-298897-6.

MyLegalStudiesLab Virtual Law Office Experience w/out eText Packages

- To preview MyLegalStudiesLab Virtual Law Office Experience courses go to www.mylegalstudieslab.com.

- For other packaging options and customized product packages, please contact your local representative.

Instructor's Resources for Paralegal Studies

Instructor's Manual for Paralegal Studies, by Hillary J. Michaud

Includes content outlines for classroom discussion, teaching suggestions, and answers to end-of-chapter questions from the text. It also includes guidelines for instructors on how to use the accompanying videos in course work.

Comprehensive Test Bank and MyTest for Paralegal Studies, by Hillary J. Michaud

The test bank is arranged by chapter, containing a variety of question formats such as true/false, multiple choice, completion, short answer, and essay. Many of these questions have been "vetted" through use in the author's intro classes over the last several years.

PowerPoint Lecture Presentations for Paralegal Studies, by Hillary J. Michaud

A PowerPoint presentation, organized by chapter, outlines and summarizes the major points covered in the text and corresponds with the organization of the text.

Paralegal Professional Videos Series for Paralegal Studies on DVD

The text is supplemented by a video series containing 13 interviews of working paralegals and 30 scenario-based videos for use in class. Videos cover a variety of topics and situations that paralegals will encounter on the job. The list of video segments is listed in the Video Case Study listing on page 319. The Instructor's Manual includes guidelines for instructors on how to use the videos in course work.

Movie Guide for Legal Studies, by Kent Kaufman

This guide contain a synopsis, key scenes, and discussion suggestions for 33 movies involving legal subjects. It is available for instructors as a resource and can be value-packed at no additional cost with this textbook.

ACKNOWLEDGMENTS

I wish to acknowledge and thank Alice Barr, my Pearson Prentice Hall representative, and Gary Bauer, my editor, for allowing me to continue to write for Pearson Prentice Hall. I also want to thank Christina Taylor for her help with manuscript review and revision. I thank Tom Goldman for inspiring me to write more than one law textbook—Tom, you continue to lead all of us who write for Pearson.

I also wish to thank the educators whose reviews of my manuscript provided valuable insights into its development. Many of their comments have been incorporated into the text. Reviewers include:

Pamela Gibson, Esq., Rockford Career College

Ara Hatamian, Platt College

Jennifer Jenkins, South College

Elaine S. Lerner, Kaplan University

Carol Brady, Milwaukee Area Technical College

Brian J. McCully, Fresno City College

Sheila M. Foglietta, Schenectady County Community College

Warren C. Hodges, Forsyth Technical Community College

John A. Plesa, West Virginia Northern Community College

Ernest Davila, San Jacinto College

MORE ABOUT THE AUTHOR

Hillary Michaud is a full-time law professor, instructor of the "Introduction to Legal Studies" course (among other courses), and director of an ABA-approved baccalaure-ate paralegal studies program at Stevenson University in Maryland. She is an active member of the Maryland State Bar Association and the State Bar of Georgia, and she maintains a part-time law practice as an administrative hearing officer. The author started her career as a certified public accountant for an international accounting firm before attending law school at the University of North Carolina at Chapel Hill School of Law, where she graduated with honors. As a lawyer, she has practiced as in-house legal counsel to The Coca-Cola Company, as well as for law firms and for Baltimore City.

At Stevenson University, the author directs a law clinic, performing pro bono legal services in tax and family law. In addition, she is a member of the Maryland State Bar Association's Special Committee on Paralegals, the American Association for Paralegal Education, and is a contributor to AAfPE's "The Paralegal Educator."

1

The Definition and Role of a Paralegal

Michele Shipley

PACE Registered Paralegal at Hyatt & Weber, P.A.

Michele became interested in the paralegal profession when she took a college course on the subject of the Supreme Court and religion. She became a paralegal by working as a legal secretary during the day and taking paralegal studies classes at night. Michele has worked as a paralegal for more than 15 years and for the same law firm for more than 18 years. Michele is a PACE Registered Paralegal. In November 2005, Michele sat for the PACE exam just to see if she could pass it, which she did. To maintain her registration, Michele completes at least 12 hours of continuing legal education every two years, with at least one hour in legal ethics.

Michele's practice is varied. She works in several areas of law, including foreclosure/bankruptcy, wills and estates, corporate law, and land use. She drafts legal documents, including pleadings, correspondence, and corporate law documents, such as LLC and incorporation documents and organizational agreements and minutes; files documents, with the Maryland State Department of Assessments and Taxation; and assists with sales of business transactions. She also represents creditors in bankruptcy matters and drafts proofs of claims and motions for relief from stays. In performing her work, Michele communicates directly with clients and meets regularly with her supervising attorneys. The main laws she uses in her practice are Maryland's state statutes, as well as administrative laws and regulations involving liquor licenses, land use, rezoning, and annexations. Michele prefers to use print materials for conducting legal research.

> *The most fulfilling part for me about being a paralegal is that is affords me the opportunity to work in a challenging and rewarding career . . . while also being able to maintain a healthy balance with my family life.*
> **Michele Shipley**

Michele adamantly supports regulation of the paralegal profession. She acknowledges that today there is no minimum standard of qualification to become a paralegal and that someone working as a paralegal might not have the education and/or training necessary to perform competently in the paralegal profession.

The full video interview is accessible from within both the New MyLegalStudiesLab Virtual Law Office Experience course and the Resources Website for Paralegal Studies.

The chapter will answer the following questions:

- What is a paralegal?
- Is there a difference between the terms "paralegal" and "legal assistant"?
- What titles may paralegals use?
- What is a paralegal's role in the American legal system?

- What are the qualifications and education necessary to become a paralegal?
- How do you distinguish the paralegal's role from the attorney's role?
- What paralegal associations exist that paralegals, and paralegal students, may join?

CHAPTER **INTRODUCTION**

This chapter defines the term "paralegal" and its commonly known synonym, "legal assistant". Other titles that paralegals may use are discussed. It provides students with a basic understanding of the role of the paralegal within the context of the American legal system and the qualifications necessary to become a paralegal. The role of the paralegal is distinguished from that of the attorney in the delivery of legal services. Professional paralegal associations are discussed. Our study begins with an examination of the definition of the term "paralegal".

DEFINITION OF PARALEGAL

To study the paralegal profession, the first question to be answered is, "What is a paralegal?" Interestingly, there is no universal definition. Organizations interested in the paralegal profession have their own definitions, some of which are very similar and some of which are not.

That said, most legal professionals agree that a **paralegal** is a person who performs certain substantive legal work for and delegated by a lawyer, under the lawyer's supervision and for which the lawyer is responsible. Some definitions refer to a person's qualifications as achieved through paralegal education, legal training, and work experience. Definitions may refer to places of paralegal employment, such as law firms, corporate law departments, and governmental agencies.

Note that the definition of "paralegal" references the kinds of work a paralegal performs—substantive legal work delegated by an attorney. Further, note that the kind of substantive legal work a nonlawyer, such as a paralegal, may perform is regulated by criminal statutes and legal ethics rules. This concept is examined thoroughly in Chapter 6.

You probably have heard the term "legal assistant" used to describe members of this profession. Is a legal assistant someone different than a paralegal? That question is answered next.

I went into this profession because I want to help people.
Julianne Ennis

> A **paralegal** is a person who performs certain substantive legal work for and delegated by a lawyer, under the lawyer's supervision and for which the lawyer is responsible.

RELATIONSHIP BETWEEN THE TERMS "PARALEGAL" AND "LEGAL ASSISTANT"

There is no real distinction between the terms "paralegal" and "legal assistant". Most legal professionals consider the terms synonymous, meaning interchangeable. Therefore, a **legal assistant** is a paralegal. Note that this is similar to the interchangeable use of the terms "attorney" and "lawyer" to mean a person licensed to practice law in a jurisdiction.

The National Association of Legal Assistants (NALA) is one of the premier paralegal associations in the United States. NALA has an interesting history on this point. In its definition of the profession, it uses both the terms "legal assistant" and "paralegal". Today, NALA uses the title "the

> *What I find most fulfilling about my work as a paralegal is client satisfaction. I find it rewarding when a client thanks us for our work, knowing that I contributed to the positive outcome.*
> Kristina Winter

Association of Legal Assistants–Paralegals" on its website, further demonstrating the interchangeability of these two terms.

That said, another major paralegal association prefers the term "paralegal" to the term "legal assistant". The National Federation of Paralegal Associations (NFPA), which is another premier paralegal association in the United States, prefers this designation in order to distinguish paralegals from legal secretaries. This is especially true more recently when the term "assistant" has become a common replacement for the term "secretary". A legal assistant in the "paralegal" sense is not a legal secretary, and a paralegal performs a significantly different role than administrative assistant, which is examined later in this chapter.

Besides "paralegal" and "legal assistant", are there other titles workers in this profession may use? That question is considered next.

A **legal assistant** is a paralegal.

WHAT TITLES PARALEGALS MAY USE

Historically, persons in this profession have used the titles "legal assistant" and "paralegal". However, they may use other titles, as well. For example, a person in this field could call herself a "lawyer's assistant" or a "nonlawyer paralegal". In fact, a person in this profession generally may use any title that does not potentially mislead a third party into believing that she is an attorney.

This is where the title debate is impacted by legal ethics rules and other laws. Legal ethics rules throughout the jurisdictions require that a person's paralegal status be disclosed to the person with whom the paralegal is dealing, typically the client. While the legal ethics rules directly bind only attorneys,

as discussed more fully in Part III of this text, a paralegal should disclose her status anytime her supervising attorney fails to do so. The reason for this is that the paralegal should not be mistaken for an attorney by a third party, particularly a client. In many jurisdictions, any person who misrepresents herself as an attorney has committed a misdemeanor, or even a felony, crime.

In selecting a title, a paralegal should avoid use of the term "associate". Accordingly, "legal associate" and "paralegal associate" are poor choices. This is so because law firms typically call their non-owner lawyer-employees "associate attorneys". Therefore, use of the term "associate" could easily mislead a third party into believing a non-attorney is actually an attorney. The distinction between the role of the paralegal and the role of the attorney is examined later in this chapter.

Throughout this text, the term "paralegal" will be used to reference members of this profession. Keep in mind that they can also be called "legal assistants" or any other title that appropriately identifies their role.

What is the role of the paralegal, then? How does a paralegal fit within the legal services delivery team? We examine the paralegal's role next.

THE PARALEGAL'S ROLE IN THE AMERICAN LEGAL SYSTEM

Paralegals today play a vital role in the delivery of legal services in the United States. That role has been developing for the last several decades.

As a profession, paralegalism first emerged in the United States in the late 1960s. It began when legal secretaries and law clerks, under the supervision of their employing attorneys, started performing many of the functions performed by today's paralegals to meet a societal demand for the provision of lower-cost legal services. In essence, they were trained on the job to perform more complex legal tasks. Regarding cost reduction, attorneys typically bill at a rate commensurate with their level of education (doctorate in jurisprudence), training (passing a bar exam and obtaining and maintaining one or more licenses), and experience (practicing law). Nonlawyers can perform some (but not all) of the functions performed by lawyers, under a lawyer's supervision, as required by law, to help reduce the cost of the legal services and to free up the lawyer to perform services only she can perform.

> *I would describe my role as a paralegal as the worker bee.*
> Michael Weiland

By the mid-1970s, the American Bar Association had begun approving paralegal education programs that met its guideline requirements. Currently there are more than a thousand paralegal education programs in the United States that offer certificates and a variety of degrees, as discussed later in this chapter.

Since the emergence of the paralegal career, the profession has seen explosive growth. That growth continues today. To review the U.S. Bureau of Labor Statistics' current information regarding the paralegal profession, perform the relevant exercise in the end-of-chapter materials.

I describe my role as a paralegal as an integral part of the effective representation of clients. By providing strong support to attorneys, paralegals can help attorneys represent their clients in a most efficient and cost-effective manner. As a paralegal, I provide support the attorney needs, as he directs, in order for him to be able to represent the clients efficiently and cost-effectively.
Sherry Myers

> **KEY Point**
>
> **Role of the Paralegal**
>
> The role of the paralegal is to assist attorneys in the delivery of certain legal services.

Specifically, the role of the paralegal is to assist attorneys in the delivery of certain legal services. Paralegals assist attorneys in a variety of ways. They may conduct interviews of clients and witnesses, prepare legal documents for filing with a court or for use in a legal transaction, conduct factual investigations, calendar and track deadlines, organize and maintain client files, attend legal proceedings, and perform many other tasks more fully discussed in Chapter 2. What paralegals and other nonlawyers may *not* do in the delivery of legal services is examined in Chapter 6.

While most paralegals perform this role in a law firm setting, paralegals may also work for corporate law departments, governmental agencies, courts, real estate or insurance companies, or any other types of entities that utilize legal services. The scope of employers that employ paralegals is also discussed more thoroughly in Chapter 2.

How, then, does one become a paralegal? That question is examined next.

QUALIFICATIONS AND EDUCATION REQUIRED TO BECOME A PARALEGAL

As discussed earlier, the paralegal profession emerged in the 1960s when, to meet a growing demand for lower-cost legal services, legal secretaries and law clerks began performing more complex legal tasks, for which they were trained on the job by the attorneys supervising them. There were no qualifications for entry into the profession in its early years.

My role is that of a communicator.
Tenae Smith

Within years of the emergence of the profession, colleges and universities began offering education programs in the field of paralegal studies. The early programs offered training courses, certificate programs, and associate degree programs. In the mid-1970s, the American Bar Association (ABA) began a voluntary approval process for high-quality paralegal education programs meeting the ABA's guideline requirements.

Today, there are a variety of education options for students who wish to become paralegals. One option is a certificate program. A certificate program provides a student with a certificate rather than a college degree on successful completion of the program.

There are two types of certificate programs. One is a paralegal certificate program. This type of program is for students who have earned a high school diploma or its equivalent and possibly have pursued some further education. From this type of program, a student earns a paralegal studies certificate, typically from a for-profit business or trade school. The other type of certificate program is a post degree certificate program. This type of program is for students who have already completed a degree program at a college or university. From this type of program, a student earns a post graduate paralegal studies certificate.

Many of these certificate programs take a year or less to complete, though some take more time (such as 15 months).

In addition to certificate programs, paralegal education programs are available for degree-seeking candidates. These programs are typically associate's degree and bachelor's degree programs. However, there are master's degree programs offered today as well.

Associate's degree programs offer two-year college degrees and are typically available at community colleges. Bachelor's degree programs offer four-year college degrees and are typically available from colleges and universities. In more recent years, a trend has developed toward obtaining a bachelor's degree in paralegal studies to begin a paralegal career, and the job market in some localities is beginning to demand it, at least for the highest-paying and more prestigious entry-level paralegal positions.

More and more master's degree programs in paralegal studies are being offered by colleges and universities. These programs are for students with bachelor's degrees, typically in other disciplines, who now desire to have a degree in paralegal studies to effectively enter the job market in this profession.

Whatever the type of educational program, paralegal education curriculums blend the study of both substantive and procedural law. **Substantive law** is law that defines the rights and duties of persons. It includes areas of law such as contracts, torts, business organizations, environmental, labor and employment, immigration, estates and trusts, constitutional, and

Paralegal Education Program Options
- Paralegal certificate programs
- Post-degree certificate programs
- Associate's degree programs
- Bachelor's degree programs
- Master's degree programs

so on. Most law courses are substantive law courses. **Procedural law** is law that sets forth the procedures, or methods, used to enforce a legal right by bringing a civil action or a criminal prosecution. The courses offered in the area of procedural law typically are civil procedure and criminal procedure.

The American Association for Paralegal Education (AAfPE) is a national organization that helps to establish curriculums and standards for paralegal education programs and paralegal educators. The American Bar Association also sets standards for paralegal education programs that desire to comply with the ABA's Guidelines for the Approval of Paralegal Education Programs and obtain ABA approval of their programs. Membership in either of these organizations is voluntary, though many paralegal education programs maintain memberships in one or both organizations, and a minority of paralegal education programs obtain and maintain ABA approval of their programs.

Remember the definition of "paralegal" studied earlier in this chapter. Note that many variations of this definition refer to education, training, and experience that qualify a person to work as a paralegal. That said, there are no mandatory qualification requirements for paralegals as there are for lawyers, as discussed below.

In almost all jurisdictions, there are no minimum education, training, or experience requirements necessary to become a paralegal—at least not yet. Without regulation and licensing of paralegals, which is being considered and/or implemented mostly on a voluntary (rather than compulsory) basis in a minority of jurisdictions at this time, the profession is open

Master's Degree versus *Juris Doctorate*

Both master's degrees and *juris doctorates* are postgraduate degrees, meaning academic degrees earned after a bachelor's degree has been awarded.

A master's degree is an academic degree awarded to a person who successfully completes a postgraduate course of study, usually completed in one to two years (full-time) in a specific area or field, such as in business administration (master's degree in business administration, or MBA) or paralegal studies.

A *juris doctorate* (J.D.) is a professional doctorate degree in law awarded to a person who successfully completes a doctoral course of study, usually completed in three years (full-time). It is a normal prerequisite to becoming a lawyer.

Substantive law is law that defines the rights and duties of persons.

Procedural law is law that sets forth the procedures, or methods, used to enforce a legal right by bringing a civil action or a criminal prosecution.

to anyone who wishes to participate in it, subject to qualifications set by the marketplace as applicants seek paralegal employment. In Chapter 5, the regulation of paralegals is discussed in detail. As part of the competitive process involved in seeking employment, legal employers choose from a pool of paralegal candidates who have different educational backgrounds and varying levels of training and experience. It is the marketplace, then, rather than laws and regulations, that currently sets the qualifications necessary to enter the paralegal profession in localities where paralegal degrees are offered. This is why a bachelor's degree is becoming the norm in paralegal education. Candidates with a bachelor's degree (or higher, such as a master's degree) have a competitive advantage in the marketplace over candidates possessing certificates or associate's degrees.

How does the role of a paralegal differ from the role of an attorney? These two different but related professions are compared and contrasted next.

DISTINGUISHING THE PARALEGAL'S ROLE FROM THE ATTORNEY'S ROLE

In the last section, we discussed qualifications to enter the paralegal profession. These qualifications differ dramatically from qualifications necessary to become an attorney. This difference and the reasons for it are the essence of the distinction between the role of the paralegal and the role of the attorney in the performance of legal services.

I describe my role as 'the right hand person' of the attorney. I perform a lot of preparation work for the attorney and am on the front line when dealing with both internal and external customers. This helps free up the attorney's time to make the more complicated legal decisions and perform negotiations. Mine is 'liaison-type' work.
Susan Campbell

We will begin with a discussion of qualifications necessary to be a practicing attorney in the United States. Attorneys are required by state law to be licensed. Every state and the District of Columbia sets its own requirements for those wishing to become attorneys licensed to practice law in that jurisdiction. Through licensing, the state and District of Columbia (D.C.) governments grant permission to persons to practice law in their jurisdictions. The practice of law by a nonlicensed person is illegal.

Remember that each state has its own specific licensing requirements. With few exceptions, these must be met before a person can practice law in that state. Generally speaking, there are three minimum requirements (and perhaps several other requirements) to obtain a license to practice law in a given jurisdiction: education, passing of a bar examination, and demonstration of good moral character. We will discuss each of these requirements more thoroughly.

First, in order to obtain a license to practice law, a person typically must earn a bachelor's degree from a college or university and must graduate from law school. Most states require that the law school be accredited by the American Bar Association. Law school is a three-year program of postgraduate study, and students successfully completing law school obtain a doctorate in jurisprudence, also called a J.D. (for "juris doctorate"). Note that graduating from law school is a step in the process of becoming a lawyer; it, alone, does not give a person the right to practice law. A license is needed.

Pro Hac Vice Admission

An exception to the requirement that an attorney must be licensed to practice law in the state where she is handling a matter is *pro hac vice* admission. With this type of admission, a court permits an attorney who is licensed but not in a certain foreign jurisdiction to work on a particular matter in that foreign jurisdiction. For example, an attorney licensed in Georgia may obtain *pro hac vice* admission to work on a matter in South Carolina.

See the end-of-chapter exercises for an assignment regarding *pro hac vice* admission and how it is obtained.

Next, a prospective attorney typically must apply to sit for the state's bar examination. This exam is called a bar examination because it is administered by the state's bar association. A bar association is an organization to which the lawyers in that jurisdiction are either required (called an "integrated" or "unified" bar association) or permitted (called a "nonintegrated" or "voluntary" bar association) to join as a law practitioner in that state. Application to sit for a bar examination does not automatically entitle one to take the examination. It is within the bar examiner's discretion to deny a candidate's application to take the bar examination, such as if it is determined that the candidate does not possess the necessary educational qualifications or if she was not truthful in her application. When a candidate is permitted to take the bar examination, she then must successfully pass it based on the grading criteria established by that state.

Finally, a person must pass an extensive personal background investigation to demonstrate that she possesses good moral character—good enough to permit her to have a license to practice law in that jurisdiction. The purpose of this investigation is to verify whether the person is qualified to engage in the legal profession and whether she is able to abide by its ethical rules for the conduct of lawyers. Some states publish standards for bad moral character. Examples of conduct that might constitute bad moral character and prohibit the success of an applicant are conviction of a crime or commission of unethical conduct like cheating on the bar examination. A body of case law exists providing guidance as to what specific conduct disqualifies a person from becoming a member of the bar because of a moral character issue. See the Case on Point for another example.

States may require additional steps to licensure as well. For example, a state may require a candidate who has passed the bar examination to then successfully complete a legal training course or a legal ethics course.[1] Many states require each can-

KEY Point

Three Typical Minimum Requirements to Obtain a License to Practice Law in a State

1. Education. Earn a bachelor's degree from a college or university and graduate from law school (many states require the law school be accredited by the American Bar Association).

2. Bar examination. Apply for, take, and pass the jurisdiction's bar examination.

3. Moral character. Successfully demonstrate good moral character.

CASE on POINT

In re Application of Blackwell, 880 N.E.2d 886 (Ohio 2007).

After Rahshann Blackwell had unsuccessfully taken the Ohio bar examination six times, the Ohio Board of Bar Examiners disqualified his application to take the bar examination a seventh time. The reason given by the Board of Bar Examiners for the disqualification was a recommendation given by the Board of Commissioners on Character and Fitness to disqualify Blackwell. The Board of Commissioners on Character and Fitness based their recommendation on a review of Blackwell's qualifications for admission to the state bar. On the last two bar examination attempts, Blackwell violated examination protocol by continuing to write answers on the examination after the allotted time—he was caught cheating on the bar exam, twice!

The Supreme Court of Ohio held that Blackwell failed to meet his burden of proof, by clear and convincing evidence, that he possessed the character, fitness, and moral qualifications necessary for admission to practice law in Ohio. The court said that Blackwell was not, at that time, "psychologically prepared for the rigors of practicing law."

didate to be "sworn in" at a ceremony conducted by a judge in court. At a swearing-in ceremony, the candidate takes an oath to practice law skillfully and ethically and to uphold the U.S. and state constitutions. States, through their bar associations, normally require the payment of dues, as well both for admission to practice law in the jurisdiction and to maintain one's license every year thereafter. In addition, for attorneys to maintain a license to practice law, many jurisdictions have continuing legal education requirements pursuant to which attorneys can stay current, through education, in the laws affecting their practice areas and in legal ethics.

A person may not hold himself out as an attorney or lawyer—the terms are synonymous—unless and until he has fulfilled all the requirements in a jurisdiction to obtain a license to practice law. Upon meeting the licensing requirements, a person can call himself a "lawyer" or "attorney" and can use the title "Esquire" or its abbreviation, "Esq." At this point, he can or must become a "member of the bar" by joining his state's bar association. An attorney *must* join his state's bar association if the state's bar association is integrated because bar membership is mandatory in such states. Alaska, Florida, and Texas are examples of states with integrated state bar associations. By being a member of an integrated bar association, a lawyer is regulated by that bar association. Further, he becomes subject to the rules of legal ethics enacted by that state and must pay annual dues. A lawyer *may* join his state's bar association if the state's bar association is nonintegrated. Iowa, Vermont, and Maryland are examples of states with nonintegrated state bar associations. In states where bar admission is voluntary, the state's highest court oversees regulation of attorneys, with regard to both bar admission and compliance with rules of legal ethics. In addition to state bar association membership, a lawyer may join the voluntary national bar association (the American Bar Association) or one or more local bar associations (such as regional, county, or city bar associations).

Note that each state has its own licensing requirements for attorneys. If an attorney wishes to move from New York to Florida, does his license transfer? The answer to that question is no. In most cases, to practice law in a jurisdiction, an attorney needs a license to practice in that jurisdiction. That means that he must meet the new state's licensing requirements. In most states, that means, at a minimum, applying for, taking, and passing that new state's bar examination and fulfilling any post–

"Member of the Bar"

To be a member of the bar means a person is licensed as an attorney to practice law in that state and can or must join that state's bar association, depending on whether the state's bar association is integrated (must join) or nonintegrated (can join).

Membership in a state bar association is a privilege earned by people meeting all the requirements to obtain a license to practice law in a jurisdiction.

Unauthorized Practice of Law

To hold oneself out as an attorney, lawyer, member of the bar, or Esquire, a person must have a license to practice law; otherwise, she has committed the unauthorized practice of law, which is a misdemeanor crime in most states, a felony crime in others.

"Waiver"

Some jurisdictions, including Illinois, Michigan, Minnesota, North Dakota, and the District of Columbia, permit admission to their bar associations without the taking of the bar examination. This is done through "waiver" into that state's bar association. The requirements for waiver vary by the jurisdiction permitting it. However, a common requirement is that the person applying for waiver must have passed another state's bar examination with a minimum score on the Multistate Bar Examination (MBE) and have subsequently been admitted to that state's bar association.

Where a person is "waived" into a state's bar association, though he may not have to take that state's bar examination, he will have to complete other formalities required to practice law in that jurisdiction (such as pay the licensing fee).

bar examination requirements, such as completing an ethics course. It is not uncommon for an attorney to possess licenses to practice law in more than one jurisdiction and to have taken and passed multiple bar examinations. Remember that the licensing of attorneys is done at the state, not national, level.

Also remember that attorneys need to obtain licenses in any state in which they practice. This somewhat limits their ability to move from jurisdiction to jurisdiction. The same is not true for paralegals. Because paralegals are not licensed, they can move freely from jurisdiction to jurisdiction without having to pass examinations, having background investigations conducted, and so on.

Now that we have discussed the qualifications necessary to become an attorney, we will compare those to qualifications necessary to become a paralegal, discussed in the preceding section. Remember that the marketplace dictates the level of education, training, and experience necessary to obtain a particular paralegal position. No mandatory licensing is required in any state (though there is debate in this area, and a minority of jurisdictions are considering regulation of paralegals or trying out new regulation schemes, as discussed in Chapter 5).

My job is to make sure my attorneys are properly informed and ready to manage their cases with competence.
Peg Hartley

Attorneys, on the other hand, must be licensed in every jurisdiction in which they practice. Why the difference?

The distinction in the qualifications required of attorneys and paralegals exists because of the nature of the work that they are, by law, allowed to perform. While paralegals can perform many of the more basic legal tasks also performed by attorneys (as long as they are performed under the supervision of an attorney), some aspects to the performance of legal services are reserved, by law, to licensed attorneys. Only attorneys may practice law. As you will see when we examine this topic more closely in Part III of this text, only attorneys may establish the attorney/client relationship, make court appearances, and give legal opinions and advice. Nonlawyers performing any of these tasks are engaging in illegal, often criminal, conduct. There is a good reason for this, too.

Consider the following. What if your hip was giving you chronic trouble and you needed hip replacement surgery? To whom do you go to have this surgery performed? You would go to an orthopedic surgeon, of course. What if an orthopedic nurse could perform the surgery less expensively? Or a hair stylist from a hair salon? Would you go to the nurse or hair stylist to have the surgery performed? No, you hopefully would not. First, it would be illegal for a nurse or hair stylist to perform orthopedic surgery on you. Like lawyers, medical doctors are licensed to practice medicine; and with today's complex and extensive body of medical knowledge, they are normally licensed in a specialized field, such as orthopedics. While a nurse may be able to perform surgery more cheaply, as a paralegal could give legal advice in comparison to an attorney, only surgeons should perform surgery because only they have the

> *Make sure you remain aware that someone else is . . . always on the line for your work.*
> **Shanae Golder**

education, training, and experience necessary to do so safely. Accordingly, only attorneys should give legal advice. Only they are educated (with doctoral degrees), trained (through licensing examinations and post-examination training courses), and experienced (through practice) to perform this specialized work. Doctors and lawyers are licensed in order to protect the public from the harm that can result if uneducated, untrained, and inexperienced persons take on certain tasks, such as performing orthopedic surgery or representing clients in court.

How does the difference in qualifications impact the difference between the roles of the paralegal and the attorney in the performance of legal services? The paralegal's role is to assist the attorney in the performance of legal services. The paralegal should always be working under the supervision of the lawyer who delegated the work. Further, the lawyer may never delegate certain tasks, including the establishing of the attorney/client relationship, making court appearances, and giving legal opinions or advice. These tasks may be performed only by lawyers licensed to practice law in that jurisdiction. Together, however, paralegals and lawyers may deliver legal services at a reduced cost to their clients through the lawyer's delegation of appropriate tasks to the paralegal, who often bills out at a lesser hourly rate. This delegation frees up the lawyer's time as well, permitting the lawyer to use her time on tasks that are more complex and/or that only she may, by law, perform.

Now that we have reviewed the distinction in roles between paralegals and attorneys, we will examine the role of paralegal associations in the enhancement of the paralegal profession.

PROFESSIONAL PARALEGAL ASSOCIATIONS

National, state, and local professional associations support and promote the paralegal profession. Some of the most prominent national associations include the National Association of Legal Assistants (NALA), the National Federation of Paralegal Associations (NFPA), the Association of Legal Administrators (ALA), the National Association of Legal Secretaries (NALS), the American Bar Association (ABA), and the American Association for Paralegal Education (AAfPE). Each of these national paralegal associations is discussed on the following page.

TABLE 1-1	Important Professional Paralegal Associations
NALA	The National Association of Legal Assistants
NFPA	The National Federation of Paralegal Associations
ALA	The Association of Legal Administrators
NALS	Formerly, the National Association of Legal Secretaries
ABA	The American Bar Association
AAfPE	The American Association for Paralegal Education

> *There are numerous benefits to joining a paralegal association. Joining a paralegal association can provide a way to obtain continuing legal education, keep up to date on trends in the profession, and provide numerous networking opportunities, both on the local and national level (most local associations are affiliated with a national 'parent' organization). Paralegal associations typically have a board of directors and numerous committees, job banks, offer continuing legal education, provide pro bono opportunities, offer professional development, and publish newsletters. Paralegal associations are always looking for new volunteers with fresh ideas and spare time.*
>
> Michele Shipley, President, Maryland Association of Paralegals, an NFPA chapter

The two main national-level professional associations specifically supporting the paralegal profession are the National Association of Legal Assistants (NALA) and the National Federation of Paralegal Associations (NFPA). In addition, most states have at least one state paralegal association and often have multiple ones in local cities or counties. Membership in paralegal associations is voluntary, rather than mandatory. Paralegal associations promote professionalism, adopt legal ethics codes and utilization guidelines for paralegals, and offer membership benefits. Membership benefits include providing networking opportunities, providing continuing legal education programs, offering certification programs, and providing job search assistance, as examples. Benefits specific to particular associations are set forth below.

The National Association of Legal Assistants (NALA) is a leading national professional association for paralegals/ legal assistants (remember our discussion of the synonymous use of the terms "paralegal" and "legal assistant" at the beginning of this chapter). Founded in 1975, NALA provides current information about the paralegal profession, networking opportunities, occupational survey results, manuals to help paralegals excel in the workplace, continuing education materials and seminars, and professional certification programs. NALA represents over 18,000 paralegals today as individual members or members of a state or local NALA-affiliated association (a local chapter). Its mission is to provide continuing education and professional development for all paralegals. NALA publishes a quarterly journal for paralegals called *Facts & Findings*.

As mentioned above, NALA offers a voluntary professional certification program for paralegals. It does this through its Certified Legal Assistant (CLA) program, which was established in 1976. This certification, while voluntary, establishes a national professional standard for legal assistants. To become a Certified Legal Assistant (now also called a Certified Paralegal, or CP, for those who prefer that term), a paralegal must be eligible to take the two-day CLA/CP exam by variously (1) graduating from a paralegal education program that is approved by the American Bar Association, an associate degree program, a post baccalaureate certificate program in paralegal studies, a bachelor's degree program in paralegal studies, or a legal assistant program with a minimum of 60 semester hours, of which at least 15 semester hours are substantive legal courses; (2) possessing a bachelor's degree in any field plus one year of work experience as a paralegal; or (3) possessing a high school diploma or its equivalent plus seven years of work experience as a paralegal and obtain a minimum of 20 hours of continuing legal education within the two-year period prior to the examination date. The examination is administered three times per year, and examinees must pay a fee. The exam tests basic skills such as grammar, writing proficiency, and analytical ability, as well as knowledge of the American legal system and various substantive areas of law. After passing the examination, the certification process is ongoing, with certification awarded for a period of five years. CLA/CP-designated paralegals must meet continuing legal education requirements to maintain and renew their certification as well as provide an affidavit of continuing good moral character. Currently, these continuing education requirements are 50 hours in a certification period, with at least five hours in legal ethics.

In addition, NALA offers an Advanced Paralegal Certification. This is a type of legal specialty certification. It is for CLA/CP-certified paralegals who successfully complete both an advanced paralegal certification course and a four-hour exam in a particular specialty area of law such as personal injury, business organizations, trial practice, or contract administration. This advanced certification allows a paralegal to use the title "CLA Specialist," or "CLAS".

The National Federation of Paralegal Associations (NFPA) is another leading national professional paralegal association. Its mission is to promote a global presence for the paralegal profession and leadership in the legal community. NFPA routinely monitors legislation, case law, and proposed changes to the rules of professional responsibility and legal ethics opinions that affect the paralegal profession. Founded in 1974, today it represents over 11,000 individual members and more than 50 state and local paralegal association members. NFPA publishes a quarterly journal for paralegals called the *National Reporter*.

Like NALA, since 1996 NFPA has offered its own voluntary certification program, this one for experienced paralegals only. NFPA's certification is for the designation PACE Registered Paralegal. To achieve this distinction, an applicant must apply to take the Paralegal Advanced Competency Exam (PACE). This examination is used to test the competency level of experienced paralegals; it is not an entry-level examination. To be eligible to apply to take this examination, an applicant must have at least two years of work experience as a paralegal and must meet specific educational requirements. This exam consists of questions on general legal issues and legal ethics, as well as questions on specialty areas of law. The exam takes four hours to complete and consists of 200 multiple choice questions. It is offered Monday through Saturday throughout the year and is administered at Sylvan Technology Centers' computerized testing facilities located throughout the United States. A fee similar in amount to that for NALA's CLA/CP examination is also charged. Once an applicant passes the PACE exam,

Profession Paralegal Certifications

NALA offers Certified Legal Assistant, Certified Legal Assistant Specialist, and Certified Paralegal certification. NFPA offers PACE Registered Paralegal certification.

While these certifications are voluntary and are not needed to participate in the paralegal profession, obtaining and maintaining them demonstrates a commitment to excellence in furtherance of one's profession and a commitment to continuing legal education. Plus, they enhance a paralegal's marketability, giving NALA- and NFPA-certified paralegals a competitive advantage in the job market.

she must obtain at least 12 hours of continuing legal education, including at least one hour in ethics, every two years.

Remember our discussion of paralegal education programs, specifically certificate programs. We discussed the two types of certificate programs, namely paralegal certificate programs and postdegree certificate programs. The CLA/CP, CLAS, and PACE certifications offered by NALA and NFPA are distinct from educational programs that offer certificates, as demonstrated by the requirements for those professional certifications, noted above.

The Association of Legal Administrators (ALA) is a professional association formed in 1971 to provide support to professionals involved in the management of law firms, corporate law departments, and governmental legal agencies. The mission of ALA is to promote and enhance the competence and professionalism of all members of the legal management team, to improve the quality of management in law firms and other legal service organizations, and to represent professional legal management and managers to the legal community and the community at large. Certified Legal Manager (CLM) certification is offered through ALA. This organization is relevant to paralegals because some of them become law office managers and/or paralegal managers, administering all or part of a law practice and/or supervising the practice's paralegals. Today, ALA has more than 10,000 individual members.

The National Association of Legal Secretaries (now NALS) was formed in 1929 and incorporated in 1949 as a professional organization for legal secretaries. (Note that at this time the paralegal profession did not yet exist.) Its mission was to enhance the careers of legal secretaries. As the legal secretary profession evolved so did the association. Today, the association has adopted the name NALS (and dropped the name "National

State Paralegal Certification Examinations

Some states, including California, Florida, North Carolina, Ohio, Texas, and Louisiana, offer paralegal certification exams. These exams are offered as part of voluntary certification programs in those jurisdictions.

Association of Legal Secretaries") and promotes itself as an association for legal professionals. It offers professional development through continuing legal education, certifications, career information, and training for people interested in a career in the legal services industry. Included in its membership are legal secretaries, paralegals, legal administrators, and law office managers.

The American Bar Association (ABA) is the largest voluntary professional association for lawyers in the world, with more than 400,000 members. Among other things, ABA provides law school accreditation, continuing legal education, information about the law, programs to assist lawyers and judges in their work, and initiatives to improve the legal system for the public. Its mission is to serve equally all members, the profession, and the public by defending liberty and delivering justice as the national representative of the legal profession. It was founded in 1878.

In addition to accrediting law schools, beginning in the middle 1970s, ABA began a process of approving high-quality paralegal education programs that volunteered to meet its Guidelines for the Approval of Paralegal Education Programs.

This approval is administered by the Approval Commission of ABA's Standing Committee on Paralegals. The mission of the Standing Committee on Paralegals is to develop and promote policies relating to the education, employment, training, and effective use of paralegals.

Finally, the American Association for Paralegal Education (AAfPE) is a national professional association that services the needs of paralegal educators and institutions offering paralegal education programs. Established in 1981, the mission of the organization is to assist in the development of higher-quality education for paralegal students. While AAfPE promotes high standards for paralegal education, it provides a forum for professional improvement for paralegal educators through the conduct of regional and national conferences. It also provides technical assistance and consultation services to institutions, educators, and employers.

These professional associations, individually and in combination, have, over the years, helped to develop and enhance the paralegal profession. They are valuable resources today to paralegals, paralegal educators, and their employers.

CHAPTER SUMMARY

- A paralegal is a person who performs certain substantive legal work for and delegated by a lawyer, under the lawyer's supervision and for which the lawyer is responsible. The terms "paralegal" and "legal assistant" are interchangeable.

- Paralegals may use any title that does not potentially mislead a third party into believing the paralegal is an attorney.

- The role of the paralegal is to assist attorneys in the delivery of certain legal services.

- In almost all jurisdictions there are no educational or other qualification requirements to become a paralegal, other than those dictated by marketplace hiring decisions. However, paralegals today typically complete a paralegal education program from either a certificate, associate's degree, bachelor's degree, or master's degree program, where students study both substantive and procedural law.

- Attorneys must be licensed to practice law in every state or jurisdiction in which they practice. There are no similar licensing requirements for paralegals. The difference is based on the nature of the work that each performs in the delivery of legal services. Only attorneys may establish the attorney/client relationship, make court appearances, and give legal opinions or advice. Paralegals, working under the supervision of an attorney, may assist the attorney in the performance of legal services by performing some of the more basic legal tasks that the attorney would otherwise perform. This helps reduce the cost of legal services for clients because paralegals bill out at a lesser amount than attorneys typically do, plus it allows for the lawyer to perform tasks that only she, by law, can perform.

- Important paralegal professional associations include NALA (the National Association of Legal Assistants), NFPA (the National Federation of Paralegal Associations), ALA (the Association of Legal Administrators), NALS (the National Association of Legal Secretaries), the ABA (the American Bar Association), and AAfPE (the American Association for Paralegal Education).

CONCEPT REVIEW AND REINFORCEMENT

Key Terms and Concepts

Paralegal
Legal assistant
Substantive law
Procedural law

Questions for Review

1. What is a paralegal?
2. Is there a difference between the terms "paralegal" and "legal assistant"? If so, what is that difference?

3. What titles may paralegals use?
4. What is a paralegal's role on the legal services delivery team?
5. What qualifications and education are necessary to become a paralegal?
6. How do you distinguish the paralegal's role from the attorney's role?
7. What paralegal associations exist that paralegals and paralegal students may join?

DEVELOPING YOUR PARALEGAL SKILLS

Critical Thinking Exercises

1. Write your own definition for the term "paralegal" based on your understanding of the profession. Discuss student definitions in class.
2. Consider the professional paralegal organizations discussed in this chapter. Which, if any, do you think offer something of value to you as a student and prospective paralegal? What is each organization's potential value to you?
3. In this chapter, the qualifications to become a paralegal and to become a lawyer were identified and distinguished. Do you think lawyers need to be licensed and go through all that is required to obtain a license in every jurisdiction where they practice? Why or why not? Do you think that paralegals should be licensed in a similar way? Note that there is an ongoing debate in this country as to whether and how the paralegal profession should be regulated and if paralegals should be required to obtain a license.

Assignments and Practical Applications

Using the Internet (recommended to obtain the most current definitions and because it makes the research part of this assignment quick and easy) or law library resources, research the definition of "paralegal" as used by the following four organizations: (1) ABA, (2) NALA, (3) NFPA, and (4) AAfPE. Compare and contrast these definitions. How are they similar? How are they different? Can you come up with a better, or different, definition?

Would you rather be a "paralegal" or a "legal assistant"? Do you prefer one title over the other? Does one seem more "professional" than the other? Is there yet another title you would prefer? Discuss your preferences and reasons, as well as title alternatives, as a class. Discuss whether members of the profession should be given a new, different title, and why or why not.

Research whether your state has any regulations regarding entry into or participation in the paralegal profession. If so, what are they? Is compliance with them voluntary or mandatory? Discuss your research results in class.

The chapter discussed the role of state bar associations in administering bar examinations to prospective attorneys. What other tasks do state bar associations typically perform? Perform factual research to answer this question. Discuss your answers in class.

The chapter discussed the licensing of attorneys and doctors. What other professions are licensed? In what way(s)? Do you think licensure is necessary for these professions? Why or why not?

Technology Resources and Internet Exercises

Using the Internet, research to see if there are any professional paralegal associations in your area. Are there any local chapters of NALA or NFPA? Do these associations accept student members? If so, how do you apply for membership, and what is the membership fee for student members? You may want to consider joining and taking advantage of membership benefits such as networking events.

The paralegal profession emerged in the United States during the 1960s as the result of a growing need for the provision of lower-cost legal services. In the late 1960s and early 1970s, the American Bar Association officially recognized the profession, and paralegal education programs began to develop. For a discussion of the profession and its qualifications, employment and advancement opportunities, job outlooks, projections, and wages, see the U.S. Department of Labor's Bureau of Labor Statistics' website, at http://www.bls.gov/oco/ocos114.htm.

Using the Internet, research *pro hac vice* admission, which allows an attorney licensed in another jurisdiction to handle a particular legal matter in a jurisdiction in which she is not licensed. How does an attorney apply for this type of admission? What is the scope of this admission? Who determines whether or not to grant this type of admission? Is the granting of this admission automatic, or within the deciding body's discretion?

Using the Cornell University Law School website for its Legal Information Institute, found at http://www.law.cornell.edu/, find your state's legal ethics code. Use it to answer the following Ethical Applications.

Ethical Applications

Maria Jones wishes to work as a paralegal. Finding an advertisement for a "litigation paralegal" opportunity with a local law firm, she submits her resume and cover letter. Maria has a bachelor's degree in business administration from a local university and has worked as an administrative assistant for a national mortgage company.

Under your state's legal ethics rules, can Maria work as a paralegal? Is she qualified to work as a paralegal? Should she even be applying for this position?

VIDEO CASE STUDIES

Video Interview of Michele Shipley

Paralegal case study videos to accompany this textbook are accessible from within both the New MyLegalStudiesLab Virtual Law Office Experience course and the Resources Website for Paralegal Studies.

ENDNOTES

[1]The author of this text completed a "Bridge the Gap" training course required in the state of Georgia and, an ethics course required in the state of Maryland, in order to obtain her licenses to practice law in both those states. These courses were required upon successful completion of the bar examination.

2

Paralegal Careers
and Career Preparation

Shanae Golder

Paralegal at Fedder and Garten Professional Association

Shanae works as a paralegal for the law firm of Fedder and Garten Professional Association. She found her position on a job database run by the career services office of the university where she was a paralegal student. She brought to her interview the professional portfolio she had prepared during her years in the paralegal education program. Shanae now practices in the areas of business law, corporate law, contract law, bankruptcy law and collections, and corporate litigation.

Shanae thinks the skills crucial to paralegal success are in communication, time management, technology, and research. Shanae says that both written and verbal communication skills are important because paralegals routinely have to communicate and correspond with other legal professionals, court staff, clients, and other third parties. Time management is important because paralegals must meet the deadlines set by their supervising attorneys. Also, paralegals must have the ability to manage various projects assigned by their supervisors. Shanae recognizes how important it is for paralegals to be comfortable working with computers and other technology, such as word processing, e-mail, the Internet, spreadsheets, electronic calendaring, computerized legal research, and online local court forms. She also notes that being able to perform legal and factual research is essential to the job performance of paralegals.

In her practice, Shanae regularly drafts documents such as correspondence, pleadings, motions, contracts, memorandums, deposition abstracts, and spreadsheets. She learned how to draft contracts while studying for her paralegal degree. Shanae also performs legal and factual research, assists in litigation preparation, indexes documents during discovery, reviews and edits contracts, as well as performs administrative tasks such as answering telephones, making copies, and filing.

The full video interview is accessible from within both the New MyLegalStudiesLab Virtual Law Office Experience course and the Resources Website for Paralegal Studies.

The chapter will answer the following questions:

- What do paralegals do?
- What are the major legal specialty areas in which paralegals work?

- Where do paralegals work?
- How are paralegals compensated?
- How does a person find employment as a paralegal?

This chapter identifies and describes the work performed by paralegals. It reviews the different legal specialty areas in which paralegals work and the varying employers who employ paralegals. Compensation, including the amount and methods of compensation, is reviewed. How to find a job as a paralegal is discussed at the end of the chapter. We begin this chapter with a study of the tasks that paralegals perform.

WHAT PARALEGALS DO

Paralegals assist attorneys in the delivery of legal services, as discussed in Chapter 1. What tasks do paralegals perform in the delivery of legal services? Paralegals can perform many of the legal tasks that attorneys perform, as long as these tasks are performed under the direct supervision of an attorney. However, there are certain legal tasks only a licensed attorney may perform; for any nonlawyer, including a paralegal, to perform them is the unauthorized practice of law.

© Orange Line Media/Shutterstock

Among the tasks that paralegals may perform are conducting factual investigations; arranging and conducting interviews of clients and witnesses; performing legal research; drafting legal documents such as contracts, wills, and legal memoranda; and reading, analyzing, and briefing cases. Other legal tasks that paralegals may perform include drafting corporate meeting minutes and maintaining corporate records. They may prepare disclosure reports for filing with governmental agencies. Paralegals may monitor corporate compliance with governmental regulations. These are just several examples of legal tasks that paralegals perform. So long as the task is not prohibited by law from being performed by a nonlawyer, a paralegal can perform any legal task reasonably delegated by a supervising attorney.

Take advantage of internships. Do not take any job for granted and be flexible about what your job tasks entail.
Peg Hartley

In addition, paralegals often perform some administrative tasks such as calendaring and tracking important deadlines (for example, litigation deadlines or trademark registration maintenance deadlines), maintaining client files, and organizing closings for transactions. Paralegals are required to use technology to perform these legal and administrative tasks.

As will be discussed in the material concerning where paralegals work, the smaller the law firm, the more administrative work a paralegal—and an attorney, for that matter—will

Paralegal Tasks

Paralegal tasks include:

- Conducting factual investigations
- Arranging and conducting interviews of clients and witnesses
- Performing legal research
- Drafting legal documents
- Reading, analyzing, and briefing cases
- Drafting corporate minutes
- Maintaining corporate records
- Preparing disclosure reports
- Monitoring corporate compliance
- Calendaring and tracking important deadlines
- Maintaining client files
- Organizing transaction closings
- Other legal tasks not reserved, by law, for attorneys
- Other administrative tasks

perform. This is because a smaller firm perhaps has fewer, if any, full-time administrative assistants. In a large firm a paralegal will have a secretary that she shares with other paralegals or an attorney. This will reduce the number of administrative tasks the paralegal needs to perform.

Because paralegals may be available in their offices more regularly than attorneys, who may be out of their offices with meetings, court appearances, and the like, a good task for attorneys to delegate to paralegals is to maintain regular communications with clients. As you will learn in the legal ethics study in Part III, attorneys must communicate regularly with their clients to keep them reasonably informed about the status of their matters. This communication can be delegated to paralegals so long as the communication is made under the attorneys' supervision.

Now that we have discussed what paralegals do, we will examine more closely the areas of law in which paralegals may perform their work. These are called legal specialty areas—and there are many.

I communicate directly with clients . . . usually through phone calls, e-mails, and meetings.
Kristina Winter

LEGAL SPECIALTY AREAS FOR PARALEGALS

Paralegals, like attorneys, often specialize in one area of law. What is a legal specialty area? A **legal specialty area** is a separate and distinct area of law in which a lawyer or paralegal practices. The body of U.S. law today is vast and often complex. Similar to the practice of medicine, where most doctors today specialize in one branch of medicine, such as cardiology or pediatrics, lawyers and paralegals often specialize in one area of law. There is no way to know and practice all of law, just as there is no way to know and practice all of medicine. Instead, paralegals, like lawyers, often practice in one "branch" of law that they know well, understand, and stay abreast of new developments. There are numerous specialized areas of law in which a lawyer or paralegal may practice, and these specialty areas grow and emerge as laws evolve to meet changes in society, technology, demographics, and the like. What, then, are some of these legal specialty areas?

In Part V, we closely examine the substantive laws for many of the most commonly practiced legal specialty areas today. In this chapter, these and other areas of law are introduced and discussed as they relate to paralegal employment, rather than the rules of law themselves.

The most commonly practiced legal specialty areas are litigation and corporate law, in that order. Other less common legal specialty practice areas for paralegals include criminal law, estate planning and probate administration, family law,

A **legal specialty area** is a separate and distinct area of law in which a lawyer or paralegal practices.

real estate law, securities law, bankruptcy law, environmental law, administrative law, labor and employment law, immigration law, banking law, elder law, and intellectual property law. Smaller law firms may specialize in one of these areas. Larger law firms and corporate law departments may practice in many of these areas, dividing their practices into departments by legal specialty area.

Litigation is the area of law that deals with the court system and the process of resolving legal disputes in the civil law system. Of all the legal specialty areas, most paralegals work in this one. In doing so, paralegals provide assistance to attorneys by helping them prepare cases for trial and even assist in certain tasks during and after the trial. Tasks performed by litigation paralegals include conducting factual investigations, interviewing

© Greg Kushmerek/Shutterstock

> *The knowledge and ability to prepare different legal documents is only an intermediate step that takes me to my real goal, which is to help clients.*
> Tatyana Bronzova

KEY Point
────────────────

Legal Specialty Areas

Common examples of legal specialty areas include:

- Litigation
- Corporate law
- Criminal law
- Estate planning and probate administration
- Family law
- Real estate law
- Securities law
- Bankruptcy law
- Environmental law
- Administrative law
- Labor and employment law
- Immigration law
- Banking law
- Elder law
- Intellectual property law

clients and witnesses, reviewing evidence including medical records and other relevant documents, conducting legal research, preparing documents for filing with the court, preparing discovery requests and responses, and assisting with trial preparation and/or appeal. Some litigation paralegals specialize even further, as do their supervising attorneys and firms, by representing only plaintiffs or only defendants. Litigation paralegals may specialize in certain types of cases. The most common of these litigation specialties is personal injury litigation.

Personal injury litigation is a type of civil litigation. Personal injury litigation paralegals typically work for law firms that specialize in this type of practice, perhaps representing only plaintiffs (called plaintiff's firms) or representing insurance companies defending the actions. These cases involve injuries to persons or their property caused by another's misconduct for which a legal remedy is sought—in other words, tort cases. Tort claims for negligence are a major portion of personal injury litigation practice.

Corporate law is a nonlitigation specialty area. **Corporate law** is transactional law dealing with laws that govern the formation, financing, merger, acquisition, operation, and termination of legal entities, as well as the rights and duties of those

Litigation is the area of law that deals with the court system and the process of resolving legal disputes in the civil law system.

Corporate law is transactional law dealing with laws that govern the formation, financing, merger, acquisition, operation, and termination of legal entities, as well as the rights and duties of those who own and manage those entities.

who own and manage those entities. Note that corporate law deals with legal entities, as opposed to human individuals, though human individuals often are involved in their ownership and operation. Paralegals who work in this legal specialty area typically work for medium- to large-sized law firms and corporate law departments. They may prepare documents for filing with the state agency responsible for forming and maintaining certain types of legal entities such as corporations, limited liability partnerships, and limited liability companies; prepare stock certificates; conduct legal research; organize and schedule shareholder meetings; draft minutes of shareholder and directors' meetings; and draft contracts concerning business operations.

© Brand X Pictures/Thinkstock

Criminal law is the system of law that deals with public wrongs, known as wrongs against society, for which punishment may be imposed. What conduct constitutes different crimes is typically defined by statute, often state statute. Governments, rather than private individuals (including humans and entities), bring criminal actions, called prosecutions, against persons accused of committing crimes. Paralegals who specialize in criminal practice may work for the government in prosecuting those accused of committing crimes. They may work for the government on the other side of the case as well, working for a public defender's office, where attorneys are paid by the government to defend indigent criminal defendants, meaning criminal defendants who cannot afford an attorney. They may work for criminal defense attorneys who are paid by their clients to defend them in criminal actions. Tasks paralegals in the legal specialty area of criminal law may perform include factual investigation, conducting legal research, drafting documents to be filed with a court, and drafting search or arrest warrants.

Estate planning and probate administration is that specialty area of law dealing with planning for and administering the disposition of a person's property upon his death. Estate planning involves deciding how to distribute a person's property upon death while he is living. Probate administration deals with the actual administration of the estate of a person after he has died. Paralegals working in this specialty area may draft wills; interview clients; perform factual investigations, including locating heirs and property; and perform legal research.

Family law, also called **domestic relations law**, is that legal specialty area dealing with prenuptial agreements, marriage, divorce, child custody and support, paternity, adoption, and the like. It is largely litigation practice. Many small law firms specialize in this area. Besides private firms, local government agencies and legal aid providers often have practices in this area, assisting people with family law issues. Paralegals working in this specialty area may draft documents to be filed with the court, draft discovery requests and responses, perform legal research, and perform factual investigations, among other tasks.

Real estate law is a legal specialty area dealing with transactions involving real property, which means land and anything permanently attached to it, such as buildings, fences, growing

Criminal law is the system of law that deals with public wrongs, known as wrongs against society, for which punishment may be imposed.

Estate planning and probate administration is that specialty area of law dealing with planning for and administering the disposition of a person's property upon his death.

Family law is that legal specialty area dealing with prenuptial agreements, marriage, divorce, child custody and support, paternity, adoption, and the like; it is also called **domestic relations law**.

Real estate law is a legal specialty area dealing with transactions involving real property.

crops, silos, and so on. The transfer of real estate is an important legal transaction in this practice area. Other important aspects of real estate law are lease transactions and the related landlord-tenant relationship. Some small law firms, departments of larger law firms, corporate law departments, title companies, banks, and other real estate–related companies perform legal work in this specialty area. Paralegals working in this area may draft contracts for the transfer of real estate, draft and record deeds, schedule transaction closings, record property transfers with relevant public offices, and attend closings where permitted by law.

Securities law is a legal specialty area dealing with the regulation of securities, such as stocks and bonds. It is a complex and sophisticated area of law. Typically, large law firms and corporate law departments for publicly traded companies have securities law practices. Disclosure is of particular importance under federal and state securities laws, and paralegals working in this field may prepare disclosure forms for filing with the government. Paralegals in this field may also work for state and federal government agencies, such as the Securities and Exchange Commission of the federal government.

Bankruptcy law is that legal specialty area dealing with federal judicial proceedings commenced when an entity or individual cannot pay debts. Bankruptcy law grants a debtor some debt relief. Small, **boutique firms**, meaning specialty firms, and large firms with bankruptcy law departments practice law in this area. Paralegals working in bankruptcy law may draft bankruptcy forms for filing with the court, interview debtors, and review creditors' claims.

Environmental law is that legal specialty area dealing with laws and regulations designed to protect the environment. State and federal laws that regulate air and water pollution, hazardous waste disposal, cleanup of toxic waste sites, and the management of natural resources are examples of environmental laws. Paralegals working in this legal specialty area may work for state or federal agencies, such as the Environmental Protection Agency of the federal government. They may work for large law firms with environmental law departments or corporate law departments in helping their clients with environmental law compliance and obtaining permits. A paralegal can work for a company as an environmental coordinator, monitoring and maintaining the company's compliance with local, state, and federal environmental rules and regulations.

> " *I enjoy the people factor. Especially in the area of family law, it is always interesting, sometimes stressful, and always enriching to interact with people who you are trying to help get through a very difficult time in their lives.* "
> **Sherry Myers**

Administrative law is the specialty area of law dealing with the administration and regulation of government agencies at the local, state, and federal levels. These agencies are delegated their powers from the jurisdiction's legislature (Congress, for federal agencies; state legislatures, for state governments; and councils or boards, for local governments) to act as agents for the jurisdiction's executive (the U.S. president for federal agencies, the governor for state agencies, and the mayor or executive for local governments such as cities and counties). Paralegals may work for the government in administrative agencies when practicing in this legal specialty area, such as for the Securities and Exchange Commission or the Environmental Protection Agency at the federal level of government and for the public service commission or the corrections department at the state government level.

Labor and employment law is a legal specialty area dealing with laws regulating the employment relationship, workplace safety, and collective bargaining. It includes the vast area of employment discrimination law and workplace harassment. Small, specialty law firms, large law firms with employment law departments, and corporate law departments practice law in this area. Many state and federal governmental employment opportunities exist in this area as well, such as with the Equal Employment Opportunity Commission and the Occupational Safety and Health Administration of the federal government.

Securities law is a legal specialty area dealing with the regulation of securities, such as stocks and bonds.

Bankruptcy law is that legal specialty area dealing with federal judicial proceedings commenced when an entity or individual cannot pay debts.

A **boutique firm** is a small law firm that specializes in a certain practice area, such as bankruptcy law or family law.

Environmental law is that legal specialty area dealing with laws and regulations designed to protect the environment.

Administrative law is the specialty area of law dealing with the administration and regulation of government agencies at the local, state, and federal levels.

Labor and employment law is a legal specialty area dealing with laws regulating the employment relationship, workplace safety, and collective bargaining.

Keep in mind that you might not land your "dream job" in the first go-round. You might have to work in a field that is not your first choice in order to obtain experience.
Julianne Ennis

Immigration law is another legal specialty area. **Immigration law** deals with laws and regulations regarding citizenship, the right to be and work in the United States, naturalization, deportation, and the like. Being bi- or multilingual can be an advantage for a paralegal who wants to work in this legal specialty area, where translation skills are important.

Banking law is a legal specialty area involving rules and regulations governing financial institutions, such as banks, savings and loan companies, and credit unions. Banking is a heavily regulated industry. Banking laws are complex and deal with such issues as establishing and operating financial institutions, meeting reporting and disclosure requirements, and maintaining capital and reserve requirements. Paralegals working in this area often are employed directly by banks.

Elder law is the legal specialty area dealing with laws serving the needs of elderly Americans. It can involve issues with Social Security, Medicare and Medicaid, health insurance, disability planning, living trusts and living wills, durable powers of attorney, long-term care placement in nursing care facilities, patient rights, fraud recovery, and elder abuse. This is an emerging legal specialty area as new legal needs arise with the growth of the elderly demographic in the United States.

Intellectual property law is the legal specialty area covering patents, copyrights, trademarks, and trade secrets. Intellectual property laws deal with products of the human mind that are protected by law. Paralegals who work in this legal specialty area may work for a law firm or a corporate law department. This is a high-paying legal specialty area (see the section below on compensation and the relevance of legal specialty area on paralegal compensation). Paralegal tasks in this field may include conducting research on existing patents, copyrights, and trademarks; drafting registration documents for patents, copyrights, and trademarks; and monitoring filing deadlines for document filings necessary to maintain trademark registrations. Intellectual property litigation is among the most expensive and time-consuming types of litigation, often requiring the use of expert witnesses. Intellectual property litigation is its own legal specialty area.

Now that we have examined many of the different legal specialty areas in which paralegals and attorneys may practice, we will discuss the types of employers who employ them.

> **Immigration law** deals with laws and regulations regarding citizenship, the right to be and work in the United States, naturalization, deportation, and the like.
>
> **Banking law** is a legal specialty area involving rules and regulations governing financial institutions, such as banks, savings and loan companies, and credit unions.
>
> **Elder law** is the legal specialty area dealing with laws serving the needs of elderly Americans.
>
> **Intellectual property law** is the legal specialty area covering patents, copyrights, trademarks, and trade secrets.

WHERE PARALEGALS WORK

Most paralegals, like most attorneys, work for law firms. In fact, more than 70 percent of all paralegals are employed by law firms.[1] A **law firm** is a for-profit organization whose business is the provision of legal services. Paralegals (and attorneys) may work for other types of employers as well, such as corporations, in their law department. However, because the majority of paralegals are employed by law firms, we begin our discussion of legal employers with a comprehensive review of law firms and their practices.

Law firms range in size, from employing one lawyer to thousands of them. Large law firms offer employment advantages in terms of higher salaries, more comprehensive employment benefits packages (employment benefits are discussed in the next section on paralegal compensation), more administrative assistance and other support, better technology and resources (such as library resources), greater opportunity for advancement or promotion, and more opportunities to specialize in a particular area of law. However, with large law firm practice

> A **law firm** is a for-profit organization whose business is the provision of legal services.

come certain disadvantages, including the requirement of specializing in one area of law and a more formal work environment. Importantly, large law firms have significant billable hours requirements for their attorneys and sometimes their paralegals, too. Legal professionals working for large law firms make a huge commitment of time to their employers.

Smaller law firms offer advantages in terms of providing more variety in work experience and tasks to perform, a less formal work environment, and perhaps greater flexibility within the work environment and billable hours requirements. However, compensation at smaller firms usually is less, sometimes much less, than compensation at large firms. In addition, employment benefits offered may be fewer or nonexistent. Usually smaller firms have less administrative and other support as well, so attorneys and paralegals working for small firms often perform more of their own administrative and clerical work.

© Eric1513/Dreamstime.com

Law firms are organized today in one of four major forms of business organization. These are sole proprietorships, partnerships, professional corporations, and limited liability corporations. We will discuss each of these in turn.

Sole proprietorships, as a form of business organization, are created when one person owns a business, in this case, a law firm. The owner of a sole proprietorship is called a **sole proprietor**. When the sole proprietorship is a law firm, its owner is often called a **solo practitioner**. As owner of the business, the sole proprietor is entitled to any profits from the business, but also bears the risk of loss if the law practice does not operate at a profit. Further, a sole proprietor is personally liable for the debts and obligations of the business, meaning the owner's personal assets, such as house, car, bank accounts, and other real and personal property, may be reached to satisfy debts and other obligations of the business.

When two or more people want to operate a law practice for profit, they often organize the business as some form of partnership. A **partnership** is an association of two or more persons who carry on, as co-owners, a business for profit. A **partner** is an owner of a partnership. Like sole proprietorships, partners are entitled to all the profits derived from the business if profits, rather than losses, occur. Also like sole proprietorships, generally speaking, in partnerships the partners can be held personally liable for the debts and obligations of the partnership, meaning their personal assets can be reached by the partnership's creditors.

Largely because of the unlimited personal liability of partners in partnerships, different forms of partnership organization have evolved over the years. The partnership just discussed details a general partnership. Today, by statute from state to state (as form of business organization is governed by state, rather than federal or local, law), many jurisdictions permit different forms of partnership, including limited

A **sole proprietorship** is a form of business organization created when a person goes into business by herself.

The owner of a sole proprietorship is called a **sole proprietor**.

When the sole proprietorship is a law firm, the sole proprietor may be called a **solo practitioner**.

A **partnership** is an association of two or more persons who carry on, as co-owners, a business for profit.

A **partner** is an owner of a partnership.

partnerships, limited liability partnerships, and limited liability limited partnerships. While these different forms of partnership do different things, they are all designed to protect partners, particularly from unlimited personal liability for the debts and obligations of the partnership. In doing so, however, they may require that a partner, such as a limited partner in a limited partnership, not participate in the management and operation of the partnership.

Owners of the partnership are called partners, as we discussed earlier. Management of the law firm is often delegated to a **managing partner** if the firm is a larger one where it is not practical for all the owners/partners to manage the business jointly. More than one managing partner may be named. Non-owner employees of the partnership who are also attorneys are called **associate attorneys**. Some law partnerships employ attorneys who are not on a partnership, meaning ownership, track. These attorneys are called **staff attorneys**. The partnership may also utilize **contract attorneys** who are not employees of the law firm, but rather are independent contractors who contract with the law firm to perform legal services on a project-by-project basis. Law school students who work for a law firm in the summer, or part-time while attending law school, are called **summer associates** or **law clerks**. These students may be hired, on a permanent basis, by the firm after graduating from law school and subject to passing the jurisdiction's bar examination and obtaining a license to practice law.

A **professional corporation** is a corporation formed by licensed professionals, such as doctors or lawyers. You may be familiar with its abbreviation, which often appears at the end of the firm name in a professional corporation—P.C. Professional corporations are organized under the statutory laws of the state of their formation. Their owners are called shareholders or stockholders. By law all the owners in a professional corporation are members of a particular profession. For law firms, the stockholders are all lawyers.

The major benefit to the corporate form of business organization is that owners of the business have limited liability for the debts and obligations of the business. Their liability is limited to the extent of their investment in the business, which means

Partnership "Players"

Partners are the owners of a partnership.

A managing partner is the partner chosen by the partnership to manage the operation of the law firm. There may be more than one.

Associate attorneys are the non-owner attorneys employed by the law firm.

Staff attorneys are attorneys employed by the law firm but who are not on a partnership track (they will not become owners—partners—in the firm).

Contract attorneys are attorneys who are not employed by the law firm, but who are independent contractors hired to perform legal work on a project-by-project basis.

Summer associates, also called law clerks, are law students who are temporary employees of a law firm who work for it during the summer, or part-time during the school year, in hopes of obtaining permanent employment as an associate attorney with the firm upon graduation from law school.

Paralegals are nonlawyers who assist lawyers in providing legal services, and are typically considered part of the law firm's professional staff.

Legal administrators, also called law office managers, are employees hired by larger law firms to run the day-to-day business operations of the firm.

Accounting personnel are employees who handle the law firm's billing and collection procedures.

Administrative assistants, also known as secretaries, are employees who perform administrative assistance for the lawyers and paralegals in the law firm.

Other technical and support personnel employees include receptionists, file clerks, bookkeepers, librarians, messengers, and others whose job functions support the provision of legal services and operation of the law firm.

A **managing partner** is a partner to whom management of the law firm is delegated.

Associate attorneys are non-owner employees of the law firm partnership who are also attorneys.

Staff attorneys are attorneys employed by the law firm partnership but who are not on a partnership, meaning ownership, track.

Contract attorneys are attorneys who are not employed by the law firm, but who are independent contractors hired to perform legal work on a project-by-project basis.

Summer associates are law school students who work for a law firm in the summer or part-time while attending law school; they are also called **law clerks**.

A **professional corporation** is a corporation formed by licensed professionals, such as doctors or lawyers.

Professional Corporation

A professional corporation is a corporation owned by members of a particular profession, such as all lawyers in a law firm. As required by state law, at the end of the firm name a professional corporation will affix "Professional Corporation" or "P.C."

Note that some states call these types of companies "professional service corporations," "service corporations," or "professional associations," with a different abbreviation such as "S.C." or "P.A." State statutes set forth each jurisdiction's rules and requirements for organizing and operating a corporation of such licensed professionals.

that the personal assets of the owners of the corporation cannot be reached by creditors to pay the debts and obligations of the business. However, there is a major disadvantage to the corporate form of business organization. Owners of corporations are taxed twice for profits earned and distributed. This is how. First, the corporation is taxed on its profits (if it has any). When the profits are distributed to shareholders in the form of dividends, the dividends are taxable income to the shareholders on their individual tax returns.

This tax treatment is different from taxation of sole proprietorships and partnerships. Sole proprietorships are not taxed as a business. Rather, any profits earned flow through to the owner and are reported on his individual tax return, where they are taxed. The same is true with partnerships. While partnerships do file tax returns, they are informational returns only. The partnership entity is not subject to income tax. Instead, any profits earned flow through to the partners and are reported on their individual income tax returns, where they are taxed.

Because of the major tax disadvantage of the corporate form of business organization, limited liability corporations, also called limited liability companies and abbreviated as LLCs, were created fairly recently by state statute throughout the states. A **limited liability corporation** is a hybrid form of business organization. It combines certain benefits of a partnership with the benefits of a corporation. Specifically, a limited liability corporation may file with the Internal Revenue Service an election to be taxed like a partnership. In doing so, it avoids the double taxation to which corporations are normally subject. Rather, any profits earned by the business flow through to the individual tax returns of its owners, called members, where members are taxed. In addition to this tax benefit, members of a limited liability corporation have limited liability for the debts and obligations

of the business. Therefore, creditors of the business may not reach the personal assets of the limited liability corporation's owners. Because the limited liability corporation is, in effect, the "best of both worlds," considering partnership and corporate form, the number of law firms organizing in this way is growing.

As noted in the beginning of this section, most paralegals work for law firms. Less than 30 percent of paralegals work for other types of employers. What are these other types of employers?

The two most important are corporations and governments. Each of these is discussed next.

Larger corporations may have their own corporate law departments. These departments are normally headed by the company's general counsel, who is the company's top lawyer. The law department may employ lawyers, paralegals, or both. It has administrative and other support, such as technology support, for its legal professionals as law firms do. While some corporate law departments are small, with one or only a few legal professionals, large corporations can have hundreds of lawyers working for them, called in-house counsel. A corporate law department may be subdivided further, according to legal specialty area.

Working for a company in its corporate law department has several advantages. Salaries are often higher than working for a law firm, and employment benefits packages may be better. While in-house lawyers and paralegals often track their time,

Nature of the Business

Note the distinction between employment with a law firm and with a different type of entity, such as a corporation or government. The business of a law firm is to provide legal services to clients. The business of corporations (other than law firms organized as corporations, of course) and governments is something other than providing legal services—such as manufacturing and selling soft drinks or sports apparel in the case of a corporation, or operating a city in the case of a government.

A **limited liability corporation**, also called a limited liability company and abbreviated "LLC," is a hybrid form of business organization authorized by state statute that permits the organization to elect to be treated like a partnership for income tax purposes while maintaining limited liability protection for its owners.

they do not bill their time to clients as lawyers and paralegals in law firms do. So while they do perform timekeeping, they may not have to meet billable hours requirements. Further, they may have more regular working hours. This is especially true for lawyers, who tend to work much longer hours than paralegals—in any employment setting. There may be more travel involved in working for a corporation, especially if it is a national or multinational company, which is an advantage or disadvantage depending on the employee's perspective.

Lawyers and paralegals are employed by the government as well. They are employed at all levels of government, including federal, state, and local government. They may work in legislative offices or in the courts. They may work in the area of criminal law, such as in prosecutors' or public defenders' offices. They may work in the government's law department, such as a city solicitor's office. Many legal professionals work for administrative agencies of the government, such as the Environmental Protection Agency or the Securities and Exchange Commission. Advantages of working for the government include regular (and often substantially fewer) work hours, competitive employment benefits packages, more time off from work, and perhaps employment stability. While lawyers and paralegals who work for the government may be required to perform timekeeping, no one is actually billed for that time, so there are no billable hours requirements. The major disadvantage of working as a lawyer or paralegal for the government is compensation, which may be much lower than compensation at a law firm, especially a larger one, or in a corporate law department.

Some lawyers and paralegals work for legal aid offices, providing legal services to the disadvantaged population at reduced or no charge. Employment satisfaction, in helping the poor, is a major advantage to this type of employment. Also, the opportunity for paralegals to represent clients before administrative agencies may be present with this type of employment (generally, only attorneys may represent clients in court, but there are exceptions with certain administrative agencies—this

is discussed more fully in Part III). Practitioners with legal aid offices may work in a variety of legal specialty areas as well, including tax law, bankruptcy law, debtor/creditor relations, domestic relations, and landlord/tenant law. However, a significant disadvantage to this type of employment is low compensation. A much lower salary would be earned compared to a law firm or other for-profit company.

Note that some of the titles given to employees in partnerships are the same as those used in professional corporation and limited liability corporation settings as well as in corporate law department and governmental settings. For example, the titles for associate attorneys, staff attorneys, contract attorneys, summer associates, paralegals, and legal administrators have the same meaning in all of these legal employment settings.

Besides law firms, corporate law departments, governments, and legal aid offices, paralegals today work in any kinds of settings where knowledge of the law and strong professional skills, such as critical thinking, communication, teamwork, and organization, are desired. They may work in law-related occupations, which include law libraries, court administration, legal software sales, legal publishing, contract administration, and corporate compliance. Paralegals may also work for insurance companies, banks, title companies, and nonprofit service providers.

Freelance Paralegals

Some paralegals own their own "freelance" businesses and work for themselves rather than being employed by a law firm or other legal services provider. They perform legal services on a contract basis for traditional legal services providers, mainly law firms. Advantages of working as a freelance paralegal include setting one's own hours and working from home. Disadvantages include the fact that one's income is dependent on obtaining projects, so freelance paralegals have to generate and promote their own businesses. There are no employment benefits for freelance paralegals because they are no one's employees.

What is of critical concern to freelance paralegals is that they work under the supervision of attorneys, despite the fact that they are not employees of a legal employer. They must be supervised by the attorney who contracts with them do to the work and who delegates the work. Otherwise they risk violating legal ethics rules regarding the unauthorized practice of law.

The knowledge that paralegals possess and the skills that paralegals develop, whether through education, training, and/or experience, make them suitable for a wide variety of types of employment in the private and public sectors.

Now that we have reviewed the places where paralegals work and who employs them, we will discuss paralegal compensation.

PARALEGAL COMPENSATION

What constitutes paralegal compensation? Salary or wages is the obvious answer. However, paralegal compensation also includes employment benefits. In addition, bonuses and overtime compensation are also included. After discussing the determination of amount of salary or wages, we will review what constitutes employment benefits. Whether or not a paralegal is eligible for a bonus or overtime compensation is discussed at the end of this section, with the topic of how paralegals are paid. We begin our review of paralegal compensation by examining how much paralegals earn.

How much a paralegal is compensated is affected by several factors. These factors include the type of employer, the size of the employer, the education of the paralegal, the experience of the paralegal, the geographic location of the employer, and the legal specialty practice area. Interestingly, as noted throughout the discussion of these factors, they impact attorney compensation in much the same way. We will examine the impact of each of these factors on compensation now.

The type of employer, whether it is a law firm, corporate law department, or government that employs the paralegal, impacts paralegal compensation. Large law firms and corporate law departments typically pay more to their employees, including their paralegals and attorneys, than do governments and legal aid providers—much more, in many cases. So the type of employer is critical in determining the amount of compensation.

The size of the employer is also relevant to the determination of amount of compensation. Particularly with regard to law firms as employers, larger firms typically pay more to their employees, including paralegals and lawyers, than do medium- and especially small-sized firms.

The educational background of the paralegal is relevant as well. This is particularly true for a paralegal new to the profession and recently graduated from a paralegal education program. The higher the degree and the more prestigious the institution from which it was obtained, the more money that paralegal is likely to command in the job market. Remember our earlier discussion in Chapter 1 about educational program options for paralegals. We discussed how there is a trend today, in some localities, toward students obtaining a bachelor's degree in paralegal studies from a university or college before entering the paralegal profession. A graduate of a bachelor's degree program will likely command more compensation in the job market than an associate's degree program graduate or certificate program graduate. Keep in mind that grades matter. The higher the grade point average of a student, the more opportunities she will have—regardless of the type of program attended. A high grade point average from a well-respected paralegal education program, particularly a bachelor's degree program, will best position a candidate for entry into the profession at a higher rate of pay.

Interestingly, educational background is the one factor in the determination of compensation that is not as relevant for attorneys. Attorneys have bachelor's degrees and doctorates in jurisprudence in order to obtain licenses to practice law. So their educational backgrounds are largely similar—and most states require that the law schools attended be accredited.

KEY Point

Factors in Determining the Amount of Paralegal Compensation

- Type of employer
- Size of employer
- Education of the paralegal
- Experience of the paralegal
- Geographic location of the employer
- Legal specialty practice area

Note that most of these factors also apply in determining the amount of attorney compensation.

nings Information	Current	
mal Gross	4,389.30	
uctions	0.00	
itions	0.00	Year to Date
rtime	0.00	
EARNINGS TOTAL	4,389.30	5,277.30
-Taxable Gross	351.14	418.18
able Gross	3,971.12	4,859.12

atutory & Other Deductions	Current	Year to Date
deral Withholding	311.17	311.17
ditional Federal Withholding	0.00	*****
ate Withholding	135.96	135.96
ditional State Withholding	0.00	*****
SDI	0.00	55.06
dicare	62.67	75.55
dicare Buyout	0.00	0.00
ate Disability Insurance	0.00	0.00
	351.14	351.14
RS	0.00	0.00
RS	0.00	
rnate Retirement	67.04	0.00

M /02

© Josh Randall/Shutterstock

Compensation for new attorneys entering the job market is likely to be about the same at a particular employer in a given year, probably regardless of the institution from which the student graduated. Going to a top school and getting great grades may help a new attorney obtain an associate attorney position at a large, prestigious firm. However, the firm will likely pay all its newly hired associate attorneys that year substantially the same salary. So for new attorneys, they all have doctoral degrees. Those with the best grades and/or from the best schools typically are hired by the most prestigious firms, at higher pay.

Prior work experience of the paralegal, particularly in the legal field, is another relevant factor in determining a paralegal's compensation. Obviously, the more relevant work experience in the field, the more compensation the paralegal will likely earn. The same holds true for attorneys; the more experience they have, the more pay they may command in the job marketplace.

Geographic location of the employer is another critical factor in paralegal compensation. Geography plays a major role in determining compensation in many professions. A paralegal or lawyer practicing in New York City will likely make substantially more compensation than one working in Mobile, Alabama. The difference in cost of living between those two locales demands it.

Finally, the legal specialty practice area of the paralegal or lawyer also impacts the amount of compensation she will earn. Certain legal specialties have fewer practitioners in them or are very complex areas in which to practice. These specialty areas can pay more. Consider mergers and acquisitions law

and intellectual property law as two examples. These legal specialty areas are very high-paying ones—much more, say, than real estate law or family law. Patent law, which requires practitioners to be specially licensed by the United States Patent and Trademark Office, by adding this additional requirement to practice, can also demand more compensation in the marketplace. So the nature of the work performed can impact a paralegal's or lawyer's compensation as well.

Next, we will define what constitutes employment benefits, for employment benefits are part of a paralegal's or attorney's overall compensation package. Employment benefits may be provided by employers, including legal employers, to their employees. Employment benefits can be provided free of charge or at a reduced cost, where the employer pays for or subsidizes that cost. Examples of customary employment benefits made available by employers, including legal employers, are medical and dental insurance, vision plans, group life insurance, retirement and/or savings plans, paid holidays, paid sick leave, vacation and personal time, and reimbursement for educational expenses. Having these benefits provided, especially at no or reduced cost, is a significant employment incentive and part of a paralegal's compensation package.

KEY Point

Employment Benefits

Employment benefit packages may include such employment benefits as medical and dental insurance, vision plans, group life insurance, retirement and/or savings plans, paid holidays, paid sick leave, vacation and personal time, and reimbursement for educational expenses.

Usually the larger the employer, including the legal employer, the more comprehensive and better the benefits package. Interestingly, government employers, because of their size, are known to offer great benefits packages. So while government-employer salaries are typically less than salaries in the private sector, such as with law firms, employment benefits packages from a government employer may be as good, or even better.

Remember that these employment benefits require an employment relationship. This means that paralegals and attorneys who are independent contractors and not employees are not eligible to receive employment benefits. Further, certain part-time employees are not eligible for employment benefits. Full-time workers in an employment relationship with an employer are the usual recipients of employment benefits as part of their compensation.

How, then, are paralegals paid the compensation they earn? Are they paid a salary? Are they paid hourly wages? If they are paid by the hour, are they entitled to overtime compensation for overtime hours worked? These questions are answered next.

KEY Point

Salary versus Hourly Wage

Paralegals paid an annual salary may be paid an annual bonus for strong overall performance and awarded at their employer's discretion.

Paralegals paid an hourly wage may be paid at least one and one-half times their regular wage rate for overtime hours worked if they are considered non-exempt employees under the Fair Labor Standards Act.

Depending on the employer, some paralegals are paid a salary and others are paid hourly wages. What happens regarding overtime pay is different depending on the manner in which the paralegal is paid.

If paid a salary, the paralegal receives a specified amount of compensation each year, such as $62,500 per year, and is not entitled by law to overtime compensation. However, if the legal employer gives annual bonuses based on overall performance and amount of work performed, a paralegal, like an attorney, may be eligible for an annual bonus based on strong performance. The awarding of annual bonuses is always within the employer's discretion and will depend both on the employer's performance that year (whether the law firm earned a significant profit from which it can pay bonuses) as well as the individual employee's performance.

On the other hand, if a paralegal is paid wages on an hourly basis, such as $25 per hour, rather than a salary, she may not be in the pool of employees eligible for annual bonuses, depending on the employer's policy. However, she may receive overtime compensation for overtime hours actually worked.

Paralegals who are paid hourly wages are often paid overtime compensation of at least one and one-half times the regular hourly wage rate, for hours worked in excess of 40 hours per week. The Fair Labor Standards Act (the FLSA), a federal labor

> *Some firms pay hourly wages to their paralegals, while also giving an annual bonus. Overtime may not be required. There might not be a specific billable hour requirement even though timekeeping may be regularly recorded in six-minute intervals.*
> **Kristina Winter**

law, requires that overtime compensation be paid in an amount of at least one and one-half times the regular wage rate for non-exempt employees. Under FLSA, exempt employees, such as executives, professionals, and administrative employees, are not entitled to overtime pay; they are exempt from FLSA's overtime pay requirement. There is some debate about whether a paralegal is an exempt or non-exempt employee under FLSA, as there is debate about whether a paralegal position is a "professional" one. Clearly, attorneys are exempt, professional employees, not entitled to overtime compensation under FLSA. Many legal employers pay their full-time paralegals on a salary basis. However, where employers pay their paralegals an hourly wage, many also pay overtime compensation. When interviewing for a paralegal position, it is important for the candidate to ask the amount and method of compensation. Clearly, this is relevant, particularly regarding the overtime pay issue.

The paralegals interviewed for the Paralegal Viewpoints answered questions about their compensation structure. Here is what they said:

- Hourly or salary:
  Of 14 respondents, nine are paid hourly wages and five are paid salaries.
- Hours worked:
  Of 14 respondents, one works 30 hours per week (she is a law school student), two work 35 hours per week,

U.S. Department of Labor

As recently as January 7, 2005, the U.S. Department of Labor's Wage and Hour Division formally opined that a paralegal position is a non-exempt one under the Fair Labor Standards Act. This opinion can be found at http://www.dol.gov/whd/opinion/FLSA/2005/2005_01_07_9_FLSA_Paralegal.htm.

one works 37.5 hours per week, and 10 work 40 or more hours per week.

- Billable hours requirement:
  Of 13 respondents, 10 have no billable hours requirement, one has a requirement of 1,000 hours per year, one has a requirement of 1,250 hours per year, and one has a requirement of 1,400 hours per year.
- Timekeeping requirement:
  Of 13 respondents, all keep timekeeping records, whether they have a billable hours requirement or not.

- Eligible for overtime pay:
  Of 13 respondents, six are eligible for overtime pay, while seven are not.
- Eligible for annual bonuses:
  Of 13 respondents, 10 are eligible for annual bonuses, and three are not.

On the subject of interviewing for a paralegal position, how does a person obtain employment in this profession? We will examine the employment search process next.

FINDING PARALEGAL EMPLOYMENT

We will begin our discussion of how a person locates, then "lands," a paralegal position with the process of locating opportunities for paralegal employment.

A person seeking a paralegal job can look for opportunities in many ways. First, she can monitor classified advertisements for employment in local newspapers as well as trade journals, particularly those in the field of law. In doing this, she should review not only the print advertisements, but the online advertisements for those publications as well. Many more opportunities may be posted online than appear in the print advertisements for the same publication.

Besides monitoring classified advertisements for employment, a paralegal job seeker can utilize the services of an employment search firm. There are some very prominent employment search firms that specialize in recruiting for the legal field. They recruit for all positions in legal employment, including legal secretaries, paralegals, and attorneys. They post opportunities for full- and part-time employment, temporary and permanent placement, as well as employee and contract hiring. Employers pay the cost of using the placement firms, so their use is of no cost to the job applicant. Recruiters' services are available not only to experienced paralegals, but also to paralegals entering the field.

If a paralegal is a graduate of some type of paralegal education program, the school from which she graduated will likely have a career placement office. If the student is a graduate from an ABA (American Bar Association)-approved paralegal education program, that program is required to offer ongoing job placement services for its students. Schools' career offices normally serve both current students and alumni. Many today provide online databases for prospective employers to post positions, including paralegal positions. A school's career placement office is a great resource for locating employment opportunities.

In addition, networking is a very valuable tool to use in finding paralegal employment opportunities. **Networking** is the process of making personal connections and establishing professional relationships with others in the profession. For paralegals, that means networking with other paralegals, attorneys, other legal professionals (such as law office managers), and paralegal educators. One great place for paralegals and paralegal students

Start the job search early, maybe sophomore year of your paralegal studies program. A paralegal student can start by looking at assistant or proofreader positions, jobs that allow for growth and advancement.
Tenae Smith

to network is at professional paralegal association meetings and events, such as local NALA (National Association of Legal Assistants) and NFPA (National Federation of Paralegal Associations) chapters. Some state bar associations have paralegal subcommittees. These subcommittees hold meetings and events that offer valuable networking opportunities. In addition, continuing

Networking is the process of making personal connections and establishing professional relationships with others in a profession, such as the paralegal profession.

education events are good networking resources as well. Meeting other paralegals and paralegal employers is a wonderful and effective way to discover specific job opportunities.

Another important tool for finding paralegal employment is performance of an internship. Many paralegal education programs build internships into their curriculums. An **internship** is where a student performs supervised training in her field of study. So a paralegal internship involves a paralegal student working as a paralegal for a legal employer. While many internships are unpaid, performed by students to gain practical employment experience, some legal employers will pay paralegal interns for work performed during the internship. Internships are useful in two ways. First, an intern who performs very well may be offered permanent employment by the legal employer. Second, internship experience counts as professional paralegal experience on a résumé and employment application.

Accordingly, reviewing classified advertisements, using legal recruiters, using career placement offices, effective networking, and internships are all valuable tools that can be used to locate paralegal employment opportunities.

Next we will review tips for landing the opportunity located. Now that you have learned of an opportunity, how can you increase your chances of being the candidate selected?

To apply for an employment opportunity, an applicant must first submit a cover letter and résumé, including a list of professional references. A **cover letter** is correspondence that introduces the applicant and briefly and effectively states why she is interested in, and qualified for, the position. The cover letter references the applicant's résumé, which is attached. A **résumé** is a clear and concise summary of the applicant's employment and educational background. A résumé may include a list of professional references, or that list may be provided separately. Today, employers routinely contact the references listed—so before listing a professional reference on any job application, be

sure to get permission from the reference listed! It reflects badly on an applicant when a prospective employer contacts an applicant's reference only to be told by the "reference" that he had no idea the applicant had listed his name.

It is important that the cover letter, résumé, and list of professional references be well written because they are the first impression a prospective employer has of the applicant. These documents will be judged against other candidates' cover letters, résumés, and lists of professional references.

For help in improving one's drafting of these documents, self-help books in this area are widely available. Schools' career placement offices offer instruction in cover letter and résumé writing, interviewing, and other job search tools. Have a friend or family member proofread these documents for you before you send them out, so they have the benefit of a fresh set of eyes to look for errors and to make recommendations for improvements.

In addition to submitting these documents, applicants are asked to complete an application form. This may be part of the initial submission of documents or occur later, perhaps after a successful interview. Always be truthful and accurate in the information you report in all employment-related application documents. Employers do check!

Today, paralegal education programs, as well as programs in other disciplines, often have students prepare professional

Seek out a paralegal internship during college to gain experience and make connections with attorneys in the area. Recognize that paralegals have roles in many different settings—law firms, corporations, government, etc.—and keep an open mind during your job search.
Anatoly Smolkin

An **internship** is where a student performs supervised training in her field of study.

A **cover letter** is correspondence that introduces a job applicant and briefly and effectively states why she is interested in, and qualified for, the position.

A **résumé** is a clear and concise summary of a job applicant's employment and educational background.

> *First, I would suggest using all the resources available to search for a job, such as the Internet, newspapers, instructors at your school, and other work placement organizations. Also, it is important to work hard in preparing your résumé to make sure it has no spelling or grammar mistakes, as this is the first thing a prospective employer will see and use to decide whether to call you for an interview.*
> Tatyana Bronzova

Truthfulness in Job Applications

Make sure the information you report on a job application is truthful and accurate. Employers will check it.

KEY Point

Professional Portfolios
Professional portfolios are valuable tools for students seeking employment early in their careers, including paralegal students.

portfolios as they progress through their education programs. These portfolios contain documents such as an additional copy of the student's résumé, a list of professional references, letters of recommendation, employer performance appraisals, samples of legal writing, samples of nonlegal writing, and other documents relevant to a job search. Portfolios can be maintained in print form or online. They should be made available at a job interview to help demonstrate the applicant's qualifications beyond what appears in the cover letter and résumé. The portfolio should contain a selection of the student's best work and effectively demonstrate why that student should be selected for a position over the other applicants for it.

Using Professional References on Job Applications

Always be sure to get current permission before listing a reference on a job application. Employers increasingly contact the persons listed. It is embarrassing for someone to be contacted as a reference if he did not agree in advance to serve as a reference—this happens to the author, as a paralegal program director, with surprising frequency. It is a good idea to contact a person you want to use as a reference and ask his permission, also telling the prospective reference the position being applied for, so that the reference is expecting to be contacted and knows who, specifically (by name, if available), will be contacting him and regarding what position.

A candidate submitting a promising cover letter and résumé (and, perhaps, job application) will be asked to interview with the employer. Before attending a job interview, a candidate should prepare for it. An interviewee should prepare for a job interview by researching the employer—for example, the law firm—to know its "vital statistics." The candidate should not only research the employer, however. In addition, the candidate should research the person who will be conducting the interview, such as the potential supervising attorney, if that person's name is known. She should anticipate questions the interviewer will likely ask and work out suitable answers in advance—especially for tricky questions, such as why she was terminated from her previous employment or why she received a "D" in her civil litigation course. In addition, the interviewee should prepare thoughtful questions in advance to ask the interviewer, because most interviews include the interviewer asking, "What questions do you have for me?" Importantly, the interviewee should represent herself as a legal professional, coming to the interview well groomed and professionally attired, demonstrating good manners and appropriate social skills. Plan to arrive early to the interview to be sure you are not late. Nothing can end an applicant's chances like missing, or being late for, an interview.

After the interview, send the interviewer follow-up correspondence. Thank the interviewer for his time and remind him of your keen interest in the position. While many interviewees today use e-mail correspondence for this purpose, e-mail is less formal and may appear less professional than a traditional thank-you letter. To make the best impression, a formal and well-written thank-you letter is recommended.

> *Be prepared at all times. You never know when an employment opportunity will come your way, and it may come from an unexpected situation.*
> Kristina Winter

KEY `Point`

Preparing for a Job Interview

- Research the employer and its business.
- Anticipate questions the interviewer may ask and prepare suitable answers in advance.
- Prepare relevant, thoughtful questions to ask the interviewer about the position and/or the employer.
- Arrive on time for the interview.
- Arrive well groomed and professionally dressed.

In most job searches, including paralegal position searches, a person applies for multiple positions. A job searcher should keep separate files for each position to which she applies. In each file, maintain contact information for employer representatives, copies of all documents submitted, and correspondence with the prospective employer. This filing system can be used to keep track of job search activities by application, for the job search process can take weeks or months.

One word of caution for applicants who maintain profiles on social networking Internet sites such as Facebook. Employers today access these profiles to learn more about job applicants. When creating a social networking profile, a person often is working from a personal point of view rather than a professional one. Consider how you would feel if you knew prospective employers were accessing and reviewing your social networking profiles. A job seeker may wish to edit her profile's content, or take down the profile entirely, at least during the job search process.

Social Networking Profiles

Today, employers access and review the social networking profiles, such as Facebook profiles, of their applicants. If you have such a profile, will its contents help you, hurt you, or neither in the process of searching for a paralegal position?

> *Experience listed on my résumé assisted me in attaining my job. Network, and list all experience and skills on your résumé. Even if it is internship or volunteer work, it still counts as experience that you can expand on.*
> Christine Rentz

CHAPTER SUMMARY

- Paralegals can perform many of the legal tasks that attorneys perform so long as the tasks are performed under the direct supervision of an attorney and are not forbidden by law from being performed by a non-attorney. Paralegals perform both legal and administrative tasks.

- Paralegals, like lawyers, can work in a variety of legal specialty areas. These areas include, among others, litigation, corporate law, criminal law, estate planning and probate administration, family law, real estate law, securities law, bankruptcy law, environmental law, administrative law, labor and employment law, immigration law, banking law, elder law, and intellectual property law.

- Employers who employ paralegals include law firms, corporate law departments, governments, legal aid offices, and other businesses where knowledge of the law and strong professional skills are valued, such as insurance companies, banks, and title companies. The vast majority of paralegals work for law firms.

- Law firms may be organized as sole proprietorships, partnerships, professional corporations, and limited liability corporations.

- A paralegal may be paid an annual salary or hourly wages. If she is paid an annual salary, she may earn year-end bonuses. If she is paid hourly wages, she may earn at least one and one-half times her regular hourly wage for overtime hours worked. Employment benefits are a part of paralegal compensation.

- Factors affecting the amount of compensation a paralegal receives include the type of employer, the size of the employer, the education of the paralegal, the experience of the paralegal, the geographic location of the employer, and the paralegal's legal specialty practice area.

- Paralegal employment opportunities can be located through the use of online and print classified advertisements, use of legal recruiting firms, paralegal education programs' career placement services offices, use of professional networking, and internships.

- To apply for a paralegal position, an applicant first must submit a cover letter, résumé, and list of professional references. She will complete and file an application for employment with the prospective employer. Background checks will be conducted about the applicant. One or more interviews will be conducted between the applicant and representatives of the employer.

- An applicant for a paralegal position can prepare for a job interview by researching the employer and its business, by anticipating questions that will be asked during the interview and preparing suitable answers in advance, by preparing relevant questions to ask the interviewer about the position and/or the company, by arriving on time, and by arriving well groomed and professionally attired.

- Professional portfolios are tools students (and graduates) can use when seeking employment. These demonstrate the skills learned through the students' paralegal education programs as well as through prior work experiences.

CONCEPT REVIEW AND REINFORCEMENT

Key Terms and Concepts

Legal specialty area
Litigation
Corporate law
Criminal law
Estate planning and probate administration
Family law
Domestic relations law
Real estate law
Securities law
Bankruptcy law
Boutique firm
Environmental law
Administrative law
Labor and employment law
Immigration law
Banking law
Elder law
Intellectual property law
Law firm
Sole proprietorship
Sole proprietor
Solo practitioner
Partnership
Partner
Managing partner
Associate attorneys
Staff attorneys
Contract attorneys
Summer associates
Law clerks
Professional corporation
Limited liability corporation
Networking
Internship
Cover letter
Résumé

Questions for Review

1. What tasks do paralegals perform?
2. What are the major legal specialty areas in which paralegals work?
3. Where do paralegals work?
4. How are paralegals compensated?
5. How does a person locate and get a job as a paralegal?

DEVELOPING YOUR PARALEGAL SKILLS

Critical Thinking Exercises

Pretend that you have asked your favorite professor for a letter of recommendation to use in an application for a paralegal scholarship or a paralegal internship. The professor willingly agrees to recommend you; but given that she gets numerous such requests each term, she asks each student to submit a first draft of the recommendation letter, along with a résumé. The professor will build on your draft in writing her recommendation letter (a common university practice). What are the skills, talents, and experiences that qualify you for this scholarship or internship? List the attributes and accomplishments that you would include about yourself. Think about what your audience will want to know to evaluate you, including attributes that set you apart from other candidates for the scholarship or internship. Now:

1. Draft the letter of recommendation that you will submit to your professor.
2. Draft your résumé so you can submit it, along with the letter of recommendation draft, to your professor.

Assignments and Practical Applications

Draft your résumé. Research sample forms at your library or online. As needed, seek guidance at your school's career placement office, for résumé writing assistance is likely available there. Have your résumé reviewed and critiqued by a friend or family member before submitting it to the instructor for grading; feedback from others is a valuable tool for improving a résumé.

Research the local newspapers in your area to see what employment opportunities are available. See the classified advertisements section for paralegal positions. In particular, if your area has a legal newspaper or journal, review its classified advertisements for employment opportunities. Note that often the online classified advertisements for these publications contain substantially more advertisements than the hard-copy versions do. Can you find any advertisements for paralegal positions? If so, what are the positions? Where are they (law firms, companies, governments)? Share your research results with the class.

In the state of Maryland, limited liability corporations became authorized by law in 1993. Research to find your state's limited liability corporation statute and review the requirements for organizing and operating a limited liability corporation in your state.

The author of this text was employed as a lawyer in the corporate law department of The Coca-Cola Company. Research that company for information about its law department. How many lawyers work in-house for Coca-Cola? Are paralegals employed in Coca-Cola's corporate law department? What specialty areas of law are practiced within this department? At the time of the author's employment, Coca-Cola called its in-house law department the "Legal Division." It had further subdivisions within the Legal Division, calling them "Departments." These were subdivided by legal specialty area and included the Food Law Department, the Intellectual Property Law Department, and the Litigation Department, as examples. What legal departments exist today within the Legal Division at The Coca-Cola Company?

The author of this text was also employed as an assistant city solicitor for the city of Baltimore. Research either the Baltimore City Law Department or a state or local government's law department in your jurisdiction. What legal professionals does it employ? Lawyers? Paralegals? How many? What types of legal work are handled by that government's law department?

Perform research to determine if there are any legal placement companies, often referred to as "recruiters" or "recruiting firms," located in your area. These companies can be located through the Internet, state bar associations, local professional paralegal associations, and paralegal education programs. What companies are present? Do they place applicants in fields other than the legal field? What job opportunities in the legal field are they posting today? What does an applicant have to do to be considered for placement by the recruiting firm?

Portfolio Development Assignment

Purpose

A portfolio is a collection of work that reflects your learning, achievement, and development. It allows for self-assessment and self-reflection. A portfolio takes time to prepare and organize. The process will take place during your entire academic career at this school.

General Objective

To determine that, upon completion of the program, you possess the requisite skills to effectively perform responsibilities as a paralegal.

Specific Objectives

The portfolio contents should demonstrate, at a minimum, your ability to:

- conduct factual and legal research
- apply recognized legal authority to factual situations
- prepare documents, forms, and other materials based upon an accumulation of legal knowledge
- communicate effectively, both in writing and orally
- organize materials

Contents

1. Cover sheet—must include your name. A border is optional. The cover sheet must have a professional appearance. White paper is recommended.
2. Title page—should contain your name, address, telephone number, the date you started in your school's paralegal program, and your anticipated graduation date (include the statement "Started ____ University's Paralegal Studies Program on [date] and anticipate graduation on [date] with a ____ Degree").
3. Personal essay—should contain a statement of your career goals, your professional and educational background, the unique experiences you bring to your career, unique jobs,

service experiences or volunteer experiences you bring to your career, your values and how they have influenced you over the years, and the like. This essay should be 2–3 pages in length, word-processed and double-spaced, with 1-inch margins and 12-point type (Times New Roman is the font recommended).

4. Your résumé.
5. A cover letter.
6. Employer performance evaluations.
7. Sample work product from each of your law courses.
8. A list of all courses completed each semester and a statement of the knowledge, skills, and so on that you acquired from each course.
9. A reflective essay, to be written during your taking of the paralegal capstone course your last year in the program.
10. Optional inclusion (highly recommended) of sample work product from liberal arts courses (such as English, history, philosophy, religion, and so on) demonstrating critical thinking skills, analytical skills, and written communication skills.
11. If you maintain your portfolio after graduation, you should include college transcripts for all degrees awarded.

Grading Criteria

Your portfolio will be graded several times during your program of study. It will make up part of your grade in this Introduction course. You should prepare and submit for grading the following portfolio parts: cover sheet, title page, personal essay, and résumé. Also prepare a list of potential personal references that you may wish to use, upon getting their permission, when you apply for summer paralegal employment or a paralegal internship.

Use

It is your responsibility to maintain your portfolio, whether a graded component of each law class or not, so that by the time the student takes the capstone course, he has included work product from most law courses and other relevant courses where work product demonstrates effective oral and written communication skills, critical thinking skills, and other relevant legal employment skills. The portfolio may be maintained in print, using a binder of some sort, or online. If the portfolio is maintained online, the student should be prepared to provide prospective employers with access to it, which information is typically exchanged at an interview. If the portfolio is maintained in print, the student should bring his binder to interviews to show to the interviewer (the student will keep the portfolio, not give it away). If the employer requires a writing sample, the student may provide copies of his best written work, the originals of which are kept in the portfolio.

Technology Resources and Internet Exercises

Using the website http://freedomlaw.com/PracticeAreas.html, review information about the various legal specialty areas discussed in this chapter.

Using the Internet, review the U.S. Department of Labor's Bureau of Labor Statistics' website regarding the percentage of paralegals that work for law firms. Also review information about other types of employers who are employing paralegals in today's job market. What other types of employers are employing paralegals?

Using the U.S. Department of Labor's Bureau of Labor Statistics' website, review the compensation data for paralegals, as broken down by industry. Note the factors affecting the amount of paralegal compensation.

The U.S. Department of Labor considers paralegals to be non-exempt employees under the Fair Labor Standards Act. Review the U.S. Department of Labor's website at http://www.dol.gov/whd/opinion/FLSA/2005/2005_01_07_9_FLSA_Paralegal.htm for its official opinion in this regard.

Review the Delaware Professional Service Corporations statute found at http://delcode.delaware.gov/title8/c006/index.shtml. What is required to form one of these corporations? How must the name be designated?

Using the Cornell University Law School website for its Legal Information Institute, found at http://www.law.cornell.edu/, find your state's legal ethics code. Use it to answer the following Ethical Applications.

Ethical Applications

At the law firm of Bodie, Smith & Kellogg, P.C., Rodney E. Wilhelm, a paralegal, drafts a confirmation letter to the firm's client, Fidelity Insurance Company of Rockland, to remind its chief financial officer to attend his scheduled deposition on Thursday, May 17, starting at 10:00 a.m., and to remind him of certain "tips" for giving a deposition—for example, to ask for clarification of any question he does not understand or to answer only the question asked and not volunteer additional information. Rodney is newly employed by this firm and has never met a representative of this client. While Rodney's supervising attorney, Cheryl Jenkins, will review the letter before it is sent, the letter is drafted in Rodney's name as its author and typed by Rodney's secretary, Wilma S. Greene. Rodney ends the letter with salutation and signature, as follows:

Very truly yours,

Rodney E. Wilhelm
REW/wsg

Has Rodney appropriately drafted the salutation/signature portion of the letter? Is there something missing? If so, what? Can Cheryl Jenkins get in trouble for how Rodney signed this letter? If so, with whom and why?

VIDEO CASE STUDIES

Video Interview of Shanae Golder

Paralegal case study videos to accompany this textbook are accessible from within both the New MyLegalStudiesLab Virtual Law Office Experience course and the Resources Website for Paralegal Studies.

ENDNOTES

1From the U.S. Department of Labor's Bureau of Labor Statistics' website, http://www.bls.gov/oco/ocos114.htm.

3

Sources of American Law and the Civil and Criminal Law Systems

Julianne Ennis

Criminal Prosecution Paralegal at the Office of the State's Attorney for Baltimore County, Maryland

Julianne is a paralegal in the Citizen Complaint Bureau Unit of the Office of the State's Attorney in Baltimore County, Maryland. Through her paralegal studies program internship and networking, Julianne obtained her employment. She works in the area of criminal law, on the side of the prosecution, and uses state criminal law in her practice. The types of cases she handles include misdemeanor drug cases, criminal citation cases (such as minors in possession of alcohol), certain bad check cases (both misdemeanors and felonies), and assorted other misdemeanor cases, including malicious destruction and second degree assault. Describing her role supporting an assistant state's attorney, Julianne says she works directly for the citizens of Baltimore County in public service.

In her position, Julianne regularly performs factual research, often conducting background checks on defendants, searching court records for prior cases, gathering rap sheets, and locating motor vehicle records. She also drafts legal documents, including petitions, orders, and correspondence; communicates with victims, witnesses, defense attorneys, and criminal defendants; and maintains hundreds of case files at a time.

Use of technology is critical to Julianne's practice, for she is "on the computer all day long." She uses word processing software, e-mail, the Internet, electronic calendaring, databases, and electronic forms.

Julianne states that organizational and communication skills are critical to her success. Julianne says that, as a paralegal, "you will be required to handle a very large case load in whichever area of law you choose to work. Without organization you will lose track of files and deadlines." Also, as a paralegal, "you will be required to work with others. You will also have contact with clients. You must keep communication open and flowing smoothly in order to adequately perform a paralegal's job."

The full video interview is accessible from within both the New MyLegalStudiesLab Virtual Law Office Experience course and the Resources Website for Paralegal Studies.

The chapter will answer the following questions:

- What are the main sources of American law?
- How are the civil and criminal law systems distinguished?

- What is civil procedural law?
- What is criminal procedural law?

This chapter examines the main sources of law in the United States. It reviews the civil law system and the criminal law system; then it describes the features that distinguish those two systems of law. The chapter concludes with an examination of civil procedure and criminal procedure. Our study begins with an examination of the main sources of American law.

SOURCES OF AMERICAN LAW

The early legal system in the United States, a former British colony, was based on English law. In fact, the colonists who first came to America were governed by English law. When America fought for and then won its independence from England in 1776, its founding fathers used the familiar English law as the basis of, or model for, the new country's law. Over time, U.S. law has evolved and changed to meet the needs of American society today. Now U.S. law is its own unique body of law, similar to that of some countries in certain ways and different in other ways.

© Frank Jr/Shutterstock

In identifying the main sources of American law, it is important to first clarify the meaning of the term "law". **Law** is the body of rules of conduct and procedure that are established, recognized, and enforced to govern a society. Law is binding. It is recognized as authority by the community bound by it. In regulating conduct, law defines right and wrong.

There are two different types of law. These two types are substantive law and procedural law. **Substantive law** includes both the civil and criminal laws that define acceptable conduct and consequences when that conduct is unacceptable. It defines the rights and duties of persons. In setting methods of procedure, **procedural law** specifies the steps that must be followed to proceed through the civil or criminal law systems. Procedural law, then, sets forth the procedures, methods, or process used to enforce a legal right via a civil or criminal action. The civil and criminal law systems are defined and distinguished later in this chapter.

Law is not permanent. Rather, it is ever changing and evolving. As society evolves—whether in attitudes toward marriage, improvements in technology, needs in education or taxation, or desire to protect the environment or workers, as examples—law must adapt to meet changes in attitudes, improvements,

needs, and desires. Take abortion law, for example. Decades ago, abortion was illegal in the United States. In 1973, as a product of the women's rights movement and a changed view toward abortion, the landmark U.S. Supreme Court case of *Roe v. Wade* made abortion legal in the United States, subject to certain restrictions; the Court allowed states to regulate or restrict abortion procedure when a woman was in her second

Law is the body of rules of conduct and procedure that are established, recognized, and enforced to govern a society.

Substantive law is law that defines the rights and duties of persons.

Procedural law is law that sets forth the procedures, methods, or process used to enforce a legal right via a civil or criminal action.

or third trimester of pregnancy. A woman's right to an abortion versus a fetus's right to be born continues to be a very hotly debated political topic in America. As American society's view changes regarding the balancing of these interests, law in this area adapts as well. It is as easy to further restrict abortion procedure, or to further free it from restrictions, as it was for the Supreme Court to substantially legalize it in the *Roe v. Wade* decision. That is true of all law. It can, and is, modified and adapted to meet the needs and desires of a society at a given time. Law reflects a society's value system and beliefs at a point in time.

KEY Point

Law Is Flexible and Changing

U.S. law reflects American society's value system and beliefs at a point in time. It adapts to meet the needs and desires of society, which change over time.

The governing body that makes law is usually a branch of government. It could be the executive, legislative, or judicial branch. Further, in the United States, law can be made at the federal, state, and local levels. Besides governments, others may create law as well. For example, Indian tribes have authority to self-govern, subject to overriding federal government authority. Accordingly, Indian tribes are protected from state government authority. That said, most American law comes from four sources: constitutions, court cases, statutes, and administrative regulations.

What Would Happen without Law?

By setting enforceable rules that citizens must follow, law provides predictability because people know what the law is, as it has been written down since the time of Moses and the Ten Commandments. Law also provides stability, for people know they must abide by it because the law is enforced and there are consequences for breaking it.

Law provides a framework that defines acceptable and unacceptable conduct and its consequences. It specifically defines right and wrong. This is substantive law, discussed earlier. Law also provides a framework of process for the enforcement of substantive law, called procedural law.

Without this framework called law, society would be much more chaotic and probably not very civil. It would be like a classroom with no rules, but on a much grander scale.

KEY Point

Four Main Sources of American Law

- Constitutional law
- Common law
- Statutory law
- Administrative law

CONSTITUTIONAL LAW

A fundamental source of American law is constitutional law. We will discuss this source of law first. **Constitutional law** is law found in the federal constitution and each of the 50 state constitutions.

The federal constitution, called the United States Constitution, is often referred to as the "supreme law of the land." It is supreme because any other law that contradicts it is invalid and is deemed "unconstitutional." Adopted at the Constitutional Convention in Philadelphia in 1787, the U.S. Constitution includes not only the original document signed by George Washington and others but also all amendments to it. To date, the U.S. Constitution has been amended 27 times. The first 10 amendments to the U.S. Constitution are called the "**Bill of Rights**."

KEY Point

The Supreme Law of the Land

The U.S. Constitution is often called the "supreme law of the land" because it trumps any law inconsistent with it. Many U.S. Supreme Court cases involve the determination of whether another law is unconstitutional.

Constitutional law is law found in the federal and state constitutions.

The **Bill of Rights** is comprised of the first 10 amendments to the U.S. Constitution.

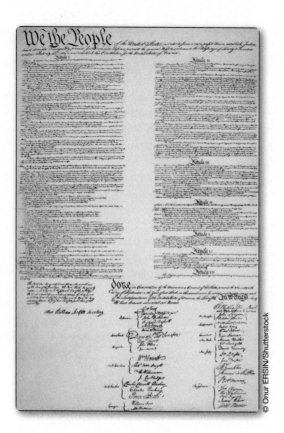

© Onur ERSIN/Shutterstock

An important job of the U.S. Supreme Court is to interpret the U.S. Constitution and its provisions and amendments.

The U.S. Constitution provides the framework of organization for the federal government. It defines the relationship between the federal government and each state's government, as well as the relationship between the federal government and the country's citizens. The U.S. Constitution also establishes the three branches of government: the executive, legislative, and judicial branches. The President of the United States heads the executive branch of the federal government (per Article II of the Constitution). The federal government's legislature is called the Congress, and it is comprised of two houses: the House of Representatives and the Senate (per Article I of the Constitution). The U.S. Supreme Court heads the judicial branch of the federal government (per Article III of the Constitution). The Constitution specifies the powers and duties of each of these branches and their relationship to one another.

KEY Point

Three Branches of Government

The U.S. Constitution establishes three branches of federal government—executive, legislative, and judicial.

The Bill of Rights

The First Amendment guarantees the freedoms of religion, speech, and the press. It also grants the right to assemble peaceably and the right to petition the government for redress of grievances.

The Second Amendment guarantees the right of people to keep and bear arms.

The Third Amendment prohibits, during peacetime, the quartering, meaning lodging, of soldiers in a private home without the owner's consent (this Amendment had more relevance in the late 1700s than now, based on what was happening during that time in U.S. history).

The Fourth Amendment guards against unreasonable searches and seizures by the government of people and property.

The Fifth Amendment protects against government abuses in legal proceedings. It guarantees the right to indictment by a grand jury in a criminal case. It prohibits double jeopardy and self-incrimination. It guarantees the right to due process of law. Finally, it guarantees the right to just compensation in eminent domain cases.

The Sixth Amendment sets forth rights relating to criminal prosecutions. It guarantees the accused the rights to a speedy public trial and to an impartial jury. It also guarantees the accused the right to be informed of the charge against him, the right to compel testimony from favorable witnesses, the right to confront the prosecution's witnesses (through cross-examination), and the right to defense counsel.

The Seventh Amendment guarantees a right to trial by jury in a civil case involving more than $20.

The Eighth Amendment prohibits excessive bail and fines. It also prohibits cruel and unusual punishment.

The Ninth Amendment gives people rights in addition to those specifically enumerated in the Constitution.

The Tenth Amendment reserves to the states and the people those powers not granted to the federal government nor prohibited to the states or the people by the Constitution.

The Constitution also expressly reserves to the states and the people all unenumerated powers. This means that powers not delegated to the federal government in the Constitution are reserved for the states and for citizens.

Besides the federal constitution, each state has its own constitution. Since there are 50 states today, there are 50 state constitutions. State constitutions are often modeled after the federal constitution in terms of organization and overall content, setting forth the state government's organization, its powers, and its limitations. However, many state constitutions are longer than the U.S. Constitution (which is approximately 7,500

How Many Constitutions Are There?

There are 51 constitutions.

There is one federal constitution, and a state constitution for each of the 50 states in the United States.

words), setting forth in greater detail the relationship between the state's government and its people. More specifically, state constitutions outline the structure of the state's government, establish a bill of rights for its citizens, and set forth the branches of the state's government, including an executive branch, headed by a governor, and a state legislature and state courts. State constitutions include law that the states consider of greater importance than law found in statutes. Remember that the Tenth Amendment to the U.S. Constitution—a part of the Bill of Rights—reserves to the states or the people the powers not delegated to the federal government in the Constitution. State constitutions, like the U.S. Constitution and the federal government, are fundamental sources of law for each state.

COMMON LAW

Now that we have discussed constitutional law, we will examine another major source of U.S. law, common law. **Common law** is law established by judges in the courts. It is also called **case law**.

In Chapter 9, we will study how to perform legal research, including how to research case law. We will learn that a case includes the following components: case title, citation, and docket number; the date decided (and perhaps the date of appellate arguments); a syllabus; headnotes (sometimes); names of counsel representing the parties; names of the judges or justices writing the opinion; the opinion (body) of the case; the court's conclusion; and any concurring or dissenting opinions. We will also study how to brief a case. We will learn that a case brief consists of the following components: case name and citation, a summary of the key facts, the issue(s) presented in the case, the court's holding(s) on the issue(s), and a summary of the court's reasoning. These holdings of the court are case law, meaning the rules of law established by judges in court cases.

Judges try to be consistent in their decisions where possible and appropriate by basing their rulings on those from earlier cases. **Precedent** is an earlier court ruling that decided a

History of the Term "Common Law"

The term "common law" originated in England in the 1150s and 1160s, during the reign of King Henry II. This was the term given to the law that emerged as "common" throughout the king's realm, where the king's judges followed each other's decisions in rending their own. Thanks to the work of these judges, this created the basis for a unified common law throughout England.

Common law is law established by judges in the courts; it is also called **case law**.

Precedent is an earlier court ruling that decided a case involving a similar legal issue and based on similar facts.

case involving a similar legal issue and based on similar facts. Precedent can be used to decide current cases that are similar, where judges refer to these earlier cases to help decide the present ones. Under the **doctrine of *stare decisis***, Latin for "to stand by that which is decided," a court must follow precedent established by a higher court within that jurisdiction. You can see how use of this doctrine makes case law somewhat predictable and stable.

KEY Point

The Doctrine of *Stare Decisis*

The doctrine of *stare decisis* helps make case law stable and predictable by requiring lower courts to follow the decisions of higher courts within their jurisdiction where cases have similar legal issues and similar facts.

Not all precedent is binding upon a court, as noted above. Only precedent from a higher court in that jurisdiction is binding. A decision made by a higher court in the jurisdiction, which is thereby a binding precedent, is a type of **binding authority** or **mandatory authority**.

That said, an inferior court, meaning a lower court (rather than a court of lower quality), can overturn binding precedent if there is a strong reason to do so. A lower court does so by overruling precedent, even binding precedent. A strong reason to overrule binding precedent is to change the law—for example, if the society's views on a subject have changed (remember the discussion about abortion law and the *Roe v. Wade* Supreme Court decision). Another reason is if the precedent is clearly erroneous, such as because of an obviously wrong application of the law. Note that in a case where a court overturns binding precedent, that decision is subject to review on appeal. In many cases where an inferior court wants to rule in a way different from a higher court in that jurisdiction, the lower court will try to distinguish the earlier case rather than overturn it. To distinguish an earlier case, the court will show how the current case is different, so that the current ruling can be different without overturning precedent. The court thereby limits the scope of the binding precedent without overruling it.

What if a court is ruling on a case that has different legal issues and facts than ever heard before in that jurisdiction? In other words, what if there is no precedent in that jurisdiction to help this court decide the present case? Such a case is called a case of first impression. A **case of first impression** is a court case on which there is no binding precedent to base a decision. In such a situation, a court can look to the decisions of courts in other jurisdictions, or lower courts in its jurisdiction.

Wisconsin Rules of Appellate Procedure on the Precedential Value of Court Opinions

Under the Wisconsin Rules of Appellate Procedure, Rule 809.23, selected opinions of the Court of Appeals are published in the official reports, namely *Callaghan's Wisconsin Reports* and West's *North Western Reporter*. The rule says that published opinions have precedential value and may be cited as controlling authority in Wisconsin. However, unpublished opinions do not have precedential value and may not be cited as authority in any Wisconsin court.

Cases that are not legally binding precedent on a court but that can be used as guidance by the court in making its decision are a type of **persuasive authority**, also called **persuasive precedent**. While a court need not follow these cases that are merely persuasive authority, it can. Other types of persuasive authority include legal encyclopedias, law reviews, and other scholarly legal periodicals. Note that in cases of first impression, besides looking at persuasive authority for guidance in deciding the cases, courts can also consider public policy, societal values, customs, and nonlaw principles underlying other court decisions.

Court decisions may or may not be published. Those that are published have precedential value; unpublished opinions generally do not have precedential value (see the Rule on Point). Regarding state court decisions, most state trial court decisions are not published but are merely filed in the clerk of court's office, where they are available for public inspection.

The **doctrine of *stare decisis*** is a legal doctrine that requires a court to follow precedent established by a higher court within that jurisdiction.

Binding authority is legal authority that must be followed by a court in deciding a case. It consists of decisions made by higher courts in the jurisdiction as well as statutes from the jurisdiction. It is also called **mandatory authority**.

A **case of first impression** is a court case on which there is no binding precedent to base a decision.

Persuasive authority is legal authority that is not binding on a court, but may be used as guidance by the court in making its decision. Besides court opinions, persuasive authority includes legal encyclopedias, law reviews, and other scholarly legal periodicals. It is also called **persuasive precedent**.

Today, though, with the advent of computerized databases, more unpublished opinions can be found in online databases, such as those maintained by Westlaw and Lexis. State appellate court decisions are routinely published in state reporters—in both official and unofficial reporters. States are grouped geographically and their decisions reported in West's unofficial regional reporter system as well. Federal court decisions are also published. District court (trial court) cases are published in West's *Federal Supplement*, an unofficial reporter. U.S. courts of appeals decisions are published in West's *Federal Reporter*, another unofficial reporter. U.S. Supreme Court cases are published in the *United States Reports*, the official reporter, and two unofficial reporters.

Also remember from our discussion of constitutional law earlier in this chapter that the judiciary is one of three branches of government, whether at the federal or state level. A major function of the judicial system is to interpret other sources of law, such as federal and state constitutions and statutes. In effect, courts can make law—case law—as they interpret other laws.

STATUTORY LAW

Besides constitutional law and common law, statutory law is another main source of American law. **Statutory law** is law enacted by legislatures at any level of government. At the state and federal levels of government, these laws are called **statutes**. At the local level of government statutory law still exists, but these laws are typically called **ordinances** rather than statutes. So statutory law is law found in statutes.

KEY Point

Examples of Statutory Law

- An example of a federal statute is the Copyright Act of 1976.
- An example of a state statute is the Maryland Tort Claims Act.
- An example of a local ordinance is the Council of the District of Columbia's Anti-Graffiti Amendment Act of 2000–2001.

Federal statutes are enacted by the U.S. Congress. Remember from our earlier discussion of constitutional law that the legislative branch is one of three branches of the federal government, in addition to the executive and judicial branches. The federal legislature is the Congress, and it is comprised of two bodies, the House of Representatives and the Senate. Also remember from our constitutional law discussion that any statute that conflicts with the U.S. Constitution is considered invalid, or unconstitutional.

KEY Point

Who Enacts Statutes?
- Federal statutes are enacted by the U.S. Congress.
- State statutes are enacted by state legislatures, such as general assemblies.
- Local ordinances are enacted by local governments, such as city councils.

Federal statutes are codified and published in the official reporter, the *United States Code* (U.S.C.). The *United States Code* contains 50 titles based on subject matter and is further broken down into chapters or sections. It is published every six years by the Office of the Law Revision Counsel of the House of Representatives. Unofficial versions of the federal statutes can also be found in the *United States Code Annotated* and the *United States Code Service*.

KEY Point

Codes for Federal Statutes
Federal statutes officially are codified and published in the *United States Code*.

There are unofficial versions of federal statutes as well, very useful in research because of their annotations. A particularly helpful unofficial code of the federal statutes is the *United States Code Annotated*. This code, published by West, is extremely useful in conducting research because of its annotations.

There are a vast number of federal statutes. A few examples include the Clean Air Act and the Clean Water Act in the area of environmental law, the Securities Act and the Securities Exchange Act in the area of securities law, the Copyright Act in the area of copyright law, the Civil Rights Act in the area of employment discrimination, and the Fair Labor Standards Act in the area of labor law.

Statutory law is law enacted by legislatures at any level of government.

Statutes are laws enacted by legislatures, at the state and federal levels of government.

Ordinances are laws enacted by local governments.

Each state also has statutes and codifies and publishes them in codes. Every state has a legislature that enacts statutory law. State codes may be called codes, or they may be called something else—like general statutes, compilations, consolidations, or revisions.

State statutes may cover subject matter also covered in federal statutes, such as employment discrimination statutes, environmental protection statutes, trademark statutes, and securities law statutes. Other state statutes cover subject matter not addressed (at least not yet) in federal statutes. Examples of these include statutes governing real property law, estates and trusts law, domestic relations law, corporate and other business entity formation and operation law, and commercial codes. Note that most criminal law is set forth in state statutes, although there are some federal criminal statutes, such as the Racketeer Influenced and Corrupt Organizations Act (RICO).

Local statutes are called ordinances, as noted above. They are enacted by the legislatures of local governments, such as cities or counties. For example, in Baltimore, the city's legislature is the City Council of Baltimore. It typically deals with matters not covered by federal or state statutes, handling more local issues. Examples of matters typically covered in local ordinances are land use and zoning laws, building and safety codes, housing and historic property laws, and some traffic laws.

Federal statutes apply to all states. State statutes apply only to that state. Because of this, state statutes vary from state

to state. For example, while most states have patterned their commercial statutes after the Uniform Commercial Code, a model act that is not law but rather an expert recommendation to legislatures, in enacting their own specific commercial codes, variations will be present from state to state. Different state legislatures enact their own customized versions of that uniform code by rejecting part (or even all) of the model act and rewriting it to fit the needs or desires of their states.

State statutes and local ordinances may not violate the U.S. Constitution or the relevant state constitution. Further, they may not violate federal statutes. For example, while states may—and do—enact statutes to address employment discrimination, these statutes may not conflict with the federal employment discrimination statutes. In following that hierarchy down, local ordinances may not violate state statutes either.

ADMINISTRATIVE LAW

Another main source of American law is administrative law. **Administrative law** is law made by administrative agencies of the government.

As we just discussed, federal and state legislatures enact statutes. To help implement the statutes they enact, these legislatures sometimes delegate this duty to administrative agencies. In addition, sometimes governments' chief executives

create administrative agencies. There are administrative agencies at all levels of government, including federal, state, and local levels.

Administrative agencies often are created by these legislatures. The Congress and state legislatures enact enabling legislation. **Enabling legislation** creates many administrative agencies, names them, and defines their purpose, duties, powers, and organization. Examples of administrative agencies at the federal level include, as a few examples, the Environmental

---

KEY Point

Examples of Administrative Law

- Federal elections regulations found in Title 11 of the Code of Federal Regulations.
- New Jersey's wage and hour regulations.
- Baltimore City's food control regulations.

Administrative law is law made by administrative agencies of the government.

Enabling legislation is legislation, meaning statutes, that create administrative agencies.

© Jerric Ramos/Shutterstock

implementing the relevant statutes in their areas. They may also conduct hearings to resolve legal disputes. Some administrative agencies permit nonlawyers, such as paralegals, to represent parties before them in resolving legal disputes. Administrative agencies may also levy fines to enforce their regulations. These rules, regulations, orders, opinions, and such constitute the body of administrative law.

In researching administrative law, a person can find federal agency regulations published in the *Code of Federal Regulations*. States have codes of regulations as well. For example, Maryland has the Code of Maryland Regulations, or COMAR; New Jersey has the New Jersey Administrative Code, or NJAC.

Now that we have thoroughly examined the four main sources of American law, we will discuss the two different law systems in the United States—the civil law system and the criminal law system.

Protection Agency, the Securities and Exchange Commission, the Food and Drug Administration, the Patent and Trademark Office, the Immigration and Naturalization Service, the Internal Revenue Service, and the Equal Employment Opportunity Commission. As you can see from this list of examples, administrative agencies are often created in very technical areas of the law, such as securities law, intellectual property law, and environmental protection. Each state also has administrative agencies. Because many federal and state statutes both deal with the same technical legal specialty areas, such as trademarks, environmental protection, and securities laws, many of these state agencies parallel federal agencies. On the other hand, some areas of law are reserved in the Constitution for the federal government, such as bankruptcy law, patent law, and copyright law. Only federal agencies may be created in these areas of law because only federal statutes, not state statutes, are involved. Remember that local governments create administrative agencies as well, to deal with the implementation of local ordinances.

The role of administrative agencies covers rulemaking, adjudication, and enforcement, all specific to the legal specialty area involved (such as patent law or environmental protection). Administrative agencies, whether at the federal, state, or local levels, are empowered to enact rules and regulations in their respective areas of law. In addition, they can issue orders and opinions about questions that arise in

Source of Administrative Agencies

Legislatures, at the federal, state, and local levels of government, create administrative agencies to help them implement statutory law through rulemaking, adjudication, and enforcement. These are called independent regulatory agencies.

Executive agencies are administrative agencies created under the authority of the government's chief executive (the president for federal executive agencies and the governor for state executive agencies) either as a cabinet department or as a subagency within a cabinet department.

Administrative agencies are discussed in more depth in Chapter 13.

DISTINGUISHING THE CIVIL AND CRIMINAL LAW SYSTEMS

Civil law is the system of law dealing with the definition and enforcement of all private or public rights. It can be distinguished from **criminal law**, which is the system of law defining and governing actions that constitute crimes as defined by statutes. Criminal law deals with wrongful actions perpetrated against society, although these actions may affect an individual's rights. These are wrongful acts for which society demands redress.

For a detailed comparison of these two systems of law, see Table 3-1. Civil law is concerned with rights and duties between private persons, or between private persons and the government, concerning noncriminal matters. The process of carrying on a civil action is called **litigation**. The parties to a civil action, called a **lawsuit**, are the **plaintiff**, who brings the action, and the **defendant**, who is being sued. The **burden of proof** in a civil case, meaning a party's duty to prove a disputed assertion, typically is a "**preponderance of the evidence**," meaning that the allegations are "more likely than not" true. Where liability is found, remedies may be awarded.

Liability means legal responsibility. **Remedies** are judicial awards by which legal rights are enforced and the violations of rights are compensated.

Clear and Convincing Evidence

The typical standard of proof in a civil case is "preponderance of the evidence." The normal standard of proof in a criminal case is "beyond a reasonable doubt." However, sometimes in a civil case a standard of proof higher than "preponderance of the evidence" but lower than "beyond a reasonable doubt" is applied. This standard of proof is "clear and convincing evidence." This standard is typically applied in cases where the loss of an important legal interest—such as potential termination of parental rights—is at issue.

Clear and convincing evidence means the party must demonstrate that it is *substantially* more likely than not that the allegations are true. In other words, the evidence establishes the truth of a disputed fact by a high probability.

Civil law is the system of law dealing with the definition and enforcement of all private or public rights.

Criminal law is the system of law defining and governing actions that constitute crimes as defined by statutes.

Litigation is the process of carrying on a civil action.

A **lawsuit** is a civil legal action brought by a party against another.

A **plaintiff** is the party bringing suit in a civil case.

A **defendant** is the party being sued in a civil case, or the party being prosecuted in a criminal case.

Burden of proof is a party's duty to prove a disputed assertion in a lawsuit or prosecution.

"Preponderance of the evidence" is the standard of proof typically applied in a civil case, by which the party must demonstrate that it is more likely than not that the allegations are true.

Liability means legal responsibility.

Remedies are judicial awards by which legal rights are enforced and the violations of rights are compensated.

© John Foxx/iStockphoto

TABLE 3-1 The Civil/Criminal Law Distinction

Area of Distinction	Civil Law System	Criminal Law System
Who brings the action?	A private person* who suffers harm (called a plaintiff)	The government, either state or federal
What is the wrongful act being addressed?	Injury or harm to a person* or to his property	A criminal statute prohibiting certain conduct has been violated
Who is concerned?	Rights and duties between private persons* and other persons* and/or their government	Society, because crimes are offenses against society as a whole
What is the legal action called?	Lawsuit or litigation	Prosecution
What is the standard of proof?	Preponderance of the evidence (typically)	Beyond a reasonable doubt
What is the issue?	Liability	Guilt
What is the result?	Remedy, at law or in equity, usually in the form of money damages	Punishment, through penalties, in the form of fines, imprisonment, probation, or even death

*Person(s), in the legal sense, includes not only humans but also businesses and other legal entities.

CASES on POINT

Civil Law

To demonstrate the use of the civil law system, consider these two examples. First, today civil lawsuits are being filed in various states challenging bans on gay marriage. This is because some states by law, such as constitutional amendment or statute, either prohibit gay marriage or define marriage as a union between a man and a woman. Proponents of gay marriage are challenging these laws as unconstitutional. However, to date, they have met only limited although growing success. Such legal challenges are brought within the civil law system.

Another example of use of the civil law system is certain products liability lawsuits pending against Toyota for injuries caused by the unintended acceleration and braking system problems of some of its vehicles. Persons injured in accidents caused by these problems are suing Toyota, in tort, for products liability, alleging defective manufacture and/or design of these vehicles (or their parts). Products liability lawsuits are civil lawsuits brought in the civil law system.

CASE on POINT

Criminal Law

The following example demonstrates the use of the criminal law system in a highly publicized case. On December 2, 2010, Steven Hayes was sentenced to death for the sexual assault, torture, and murder of the wife and minor daughters of Dr. William Petit, of Chesire, Connecticut. Dr. Petit was severely beaten and then restrained in the basement. He survived the ordeal in which Steven Hayes and Joshua Komisarjevsky entered his home in a gruesome home invasion that began on July 22, 2007, and ended in the murders noted and the burning of the Petit home on July 23, 2007. The Petit family was targeted by the killers for this home invasion after Mrs. Petit and her youngest daughter were spotted by Hayes and Komisarjevsky in a local grocery store in the late afternoon of July 22 and they were followed. The family was tormented by their attackers for seven hours before Mrs. Petit and her daughters were killed. The severely injured Dr. Petit escaped the house and called for help to a neighbor, who did not recognize Dr. Petit because of the severity of his injuries. Police responding to the 911 call spent more than a half hour assessing the situation and setting up a vehicle perimeter to secure the area while the killers committed the murders and the arson. The killers fled the house driving the Petit family car but were arrested by police only one block away. Jurors in the Hayes triple-murder trial, for the first time in Connecticut's judicial history, were offered posttraumatic stress assistance because of the disturbing images and grisly testimony they had to see and hear during the trial.

CASE *on* POINT

Orenthal James (O. J.) Simpson

A single action can give rise to both a civil action and a criminal prosecution. Consider the case of O. J. Simpson.

On June 12, 1994, Nicole Brown Simpson, ex-wife of O. J. Simpson, the former professional football player and Heisman Trophy winner, and her friend Ronald Goldman were found stabbed to death outside Brown's home in Brentwood, California. Days afterward, following an infamous televised, slow-speed chase of O. J. Simpson in his white Ford Bronco driving down Interstate 405 in the Los Angeles area, Simpson was arrested and criminally prosecuted for the murders of both Brown and Goldman. The criminal trial, conducted in 1995, included 134 days of televised testimony. In his closing argument, Johnny Cochran, one of Simpson's defense lawyers, famously quipped, "If it doesn't fit, you must acquit," in reference to a glove, covered in the victims' blood and produced as evidence during the trial, which appeared to be too small for the defendant to wear. After only three hours of deliberation concluding a trial lasting from January 25 until October 3, 1995, Simpson was acquitted of both murders by a jury of his peers (and, some allege, his fans).

Unsatisfied with the outcome of the criminal trial, the families of the victims brought a civil (tort) action against O. J. Simpson for the wrongful deaths of Brown and Goldman. In 1997, a civil jury found Simpson liable for the wrongful deaths of both victims and rendered a judgment against O. J. Simpson in the amount of $33.5 million. To date, that judgment remains largely unpaid.

Why the different results? The reason for the difference in results reached in the two cases, beyond a difference in jurors, is the difference in burden of proof. The burden of proof in a criminal case is very high, and the defense need only establish a reasonable doubt in the mind of one juror for the verdict to be "not guilty." However, the burden of proof in a civil case is much lower, with the plaintiff usually needing only to establish his claim for liability by a preponderance of the evidence, meaning it is more likely than not the plaintiff's allegations are true.

Criminal law concerns wrongs committed against society as a whole and prosecuted by the government. The parties to a criminal action are the government (normally the state, but sometimes the federal government) and the criminal defendant. The burden of proof in a criminal case, called a **prosecution**, is "**beyond a reasonable doubt**," meaning the prosecution must prove its case by leaving no reasonable doubt as to the guilt of the defendant in the minds of the jurors. A criminal defendant is found **guilty** when he is convicted of committing a crime. **Penalties** may be imposed on the guilty party, including fines, imprisonment, probation, and even death.

Now that we have reviewed the distinction between the civil and criminal law systems, let us review the procedures used by each system in adjudicating matters, for these procedures differ. We begin with an examination of civil procedure.

> *There is never a dull moment [working in criminal defense].*
> Lindsay Ann Thomas

A **prosecution** is a legal action brought against a criminal defendant alleging the commission of a crime.

"Beyond a reasonable doubt" is the standard of proof applied in a criminal case, by which the prosecution must prove the case sufficiently so that there is no reasonable doubt in the mind of any juror that the defendant committed the crime.

Guilty is a verdict that means the criminal defendant is convicted of committing the crime.

Penalties are what are imposed on a defendant found guilty in a criminal prosecution.

CIVIL PROCEDURE

Remember that substantive law is the body of civil and criminal laws that define acceptable conduct and the consequences when that conduct is unacceptable. Contrast substantive law and procedural law. Procedural law specifies the steps that must be followed to proceed through the civil or criminal law system.

Civil procedure is the body of procedural law that governs the process of civil litigation. From where does this procedural law come?

The Federal Rules of Civil Procedure (FRCP) are the procedural rules that apply to federal courts in civil litigation matters. The Federal Rules of Civil Procedure are promulgated by the U.S. Supreme Court pursuant to the Rules Enabling Act, a federal statute. Then they are approved by the U.S. Congress. Modifications to the rules, which occur from time to time, normally are based on recommendations from the federal judiciary's internal policy-making body, the Judicial Conference of the United States. In addition to the federal rules, each state has its own rules of civil procedure, codified in its state statutes. State rules are used in state courts. While these rules differ from jurisdiction to jurisdiction, we can discuss the general rules of procedure that most jurisdictions apply. What are those procedures when the case is a civil one?

In civil litigation, a paralegal and attorney's work begins long before trial. It even begins before the first pleading is filed. When a client seeks legal representation to resolve a legal dispute, the first tasks the attorney and/or paralegal perform are to conduct an initial interview with the client, perform a preliminary investigation to determine the facts of the matter, and open a litigation file. If the decision is made by the client, with the attorney's support, to sue, litigation is commenced by the filing of a complaint, the first of several pleadings that are possible.

> *I use civil procedure [rules] every day. You must know the proper procedure and requirements for filing pleadings, motions and other court filings such as what the format and content is for a specific filing or what the time restrictions for filing are.*
> Sherry Myers

A **complaint** is a document that initiates a lawsuit by setting forth the plaintiff's claim, the basis for the court's jurisdiction over the matter, and a demand for a remedy. The complaint is filed with the relevant court (today, often electronically), and the court's filing fee is paid. This is the time when the case is assigned a docket number and, in some states, a judge.

The court then issues a **summons** directing the defendant to appear in court and answer the complaint. Together the complaint and summons are delivered to the defendant, called **service of process**. Under changes to the Federal Rules of Civil Procedure (FRCP 4(d)) in 1993, a defendant may be notified of the lawsuit via the mail and be requested to waive personal service of a summons.

The defendant has a time period specified under the rules in which to respond, such as 60 days. If the defendant fails to respond, a **default judgment** is entered against him. In that case, the plaintiff is awarded the damages requested. Usually, however, the defendant responds to the complaint and defends against it. He does so by filing with the court, and serving on the plaintiff, a pleading called an answer.

Rules of Civil Procedure

The Federal Rules of Civil Procedure (FRCP) are rules of procedure required to be used in civil cases tried in the federal courts.

State rules of civil procedure are the rules of procedure each state requires to be used in civil cases in the state's courts; they vary from state to state.

Civil procedure is the body of procedural law that governs the process of civil litigation.

A **complaint** is a document that initiates a lawsuit by setting forth the plaintiff's claim, the basis for the court's jurisdiction over the matter, and a demand for a remedy.

A **summons** is a court order directing a defendant to appear in court and answer the complaint.

Service of process is the act of delivering to the defendant the plaintiff's complaint and the court's summons.

A **default judgment** is a judgment entered by a court against a party who fails to respond to a claim brought against him.

An **answer** is the defendant's response to the allegations made in the plaintiff's complaint. In his answer, the defendant admits or denies the truth of each allegation, or says that he lacks sufficient knowledge to admit or deny an allegation. Importantly, the defendant may also assert one or more **affirmative defenses**, stating why he should not be held liable even if the plaintiff's allegations are true. The defendant may also assert one or more **counterclaims**, which are claims back against the plaintiff—in effect they are countersuits. In addition or in the alternative, where there are multiple defendants in a lawsuit, a defendant may assert one or more **cross-claims**, which are claims against other defendants (note that cross-claims may also be brought by one plaintiff against another plaintiff in the same case). Subject to court rules and restrictions, pleadings may be amended as the discovery process unfolds, new facts are learned, and evidence is gathered.

After a complaint is filed, the defendant may file a motion to dismiss the complaint, called a motion to dismiss. A **motion to dismiss** is a request made to the court by the defendant to dismiss the case. Several reasons can be the basis for a motion to dismiss, including the failure of the plaintiff to state a claim for which relief can be granted, lack of jurisdiction over the defendant, improper service of process, and the expiration of a statute of limitations.

Besides motions to dismiss, other pretrial motions may be made. One is a motion for judgment on the pleadings. A **motion for judgment on the pleadings** is a motion filed by either the plaintiff or the defendant in an action asking the court to enter a judgment in her favor based on the information contained in all the pleadings. Only if there are no facts in dispute and the only issue is how the law applies to the undisputed facts will a motion for judgment on the pleadings be granted.

Another pretrial motion is a motion for summary judgment. A **motion for summary judgment** can be made by either the plaintiff or the defendant in an action. It asks the court to enter a judgment in her favor based not only on the pleadings but also on other supporting evidence, such as answers to interrogatories, witness affidavits, and other evidence gathered so far in the discovery process. This other evidence is referred to as evidence "outside the pleadings."

The most time-consuming and also an expensive part of litigation is the discovery process. **Discovery** is the process of searching for and obtaining information and evidence relevant to the case. The rule of what information can be discovered is fairly broad. Information can be discovered, meaning it is "discoverable," if it is relevant and not privileged. "Relevant" means

logically related to the matter. "Not privileged" means not considered confidential between persons, such as between a lawyer and her client. Therefore, it does not have to be *evidence* that is sought in discovery; it is enough that it is information that is relevant and not privileged. Discovery is sought both from the opposing party and from witnesses.

KEY Point

What Information Is Discoverable?
Information is discoverable if it is relevant and not privileged.

Several tools are used in the discovery process. One very popular discovery tool is depositions. A **deposition** is the sworn testimony of a party or witness, given during a question and answer proceeding conducted before trial. Only attorneys may take and defend depositions because taking and defending them—in which sworn testimony is given—is considered the practice of law. That said, it is fine for a paralegal (as well as an

An **answer** is the defendant's response to the allegations made in the plaintiff's complaint.

An **affirmative defense** is a response to a plaintiff's claim that asserts why the defendant should not be held liable to the plaintiff.

A **counterclaim** is a claim made by the defendant against a plaintiff.

A **cross-claim** is a claim made by a defendant against another defendant in the same case or a claim made by a plaintiff against another plaintiff in the same case.

A **motion to dismiss** is a request made to the court by the defendant after the filing of the complaint asking the court to dismiss the action.

A **motion for judgment on the pleadings** is a motion filed by either the plaintiff or the defendant in an action asking the court to enter a judgment in her favor based on the information contained in all the pleadings.

A **motion for summary judgment** is a motion filed by either the plaintiff or the defendant in an action asking the court to enter a judgment in her favor based not only on the information contained in the pleadings but also on other supporting evidence from outside the pleadings.

Discovery is the process of searching for and obtaining information and evidence relevant to the case.

A **deposition** is the sworn testimony of a party or witness, given during a question and answer proceeding conducted before trial.

attorney) to prepare a party or witness to give a deposition, just as it is to prepare a party or witness to give testimony at trial. Preparing a party or witness to give testimony at a deposition is not coaching the party or witness on what testimony to give. Rather, it helps the deponent (the party or witness who gives deposition testimony) know what to expect when she arrives, what to wear, how to feel as comfortable as possible in the situation, and how to respond truthfully and appropriately to questions asked. Depositions normally are recorded by a court reporter, and a transcript of the deposition is made. This transcript can be used as evidence during trial as well as to impeach a party or witness at trial.

Another very popular discovery tool is interrogatories. **Interrogatories** are written questions prepared by a party, submitted to the other party, to be answered under oath. Court rules may limit the number of interrogatories that may be asked. Further, the rules set a deadline within which the answers must be submitted. Under the Federal Rules of Civil Procedure (FRCP 33) today, that deadline is 30 days after the receipt of the interrogatories.

Requests for production, physical examination, and admission are other discovery tools. **Requests for production** are requests by a party to another party for documents or other tangible things, such as a written contract, or for permission to enter on the land or other property of the party for the purpose of conducting an inspection. Similarly, **requests for examination** are requests by a party to the court asking the court to order the other party to submit to a physical or mental examination. **Requests for admission** are requests by a party to the other party asking for admission to the truth of certain matters relating to the lawsuit. Why would the other party admit to anything? The answer is simple. The value of admissions is that they save time; parties need not waste time proving facts that they agree on. For example, in a breach of lease contract case, if both parties agree that they entered into a lease agreement on September 20, 2011, there is no value in the defendant denying this fact (the date the lease agreement was entered into by the parties) if it is alleged in the plaintiff's complaint. Admissions are considered conclusively established at trial (unless they are appropriately withdrawn or amended). If a party fails to admit something he should have in a request for admission, a court can impose discovery sanctions on him.

With advances in technology today, information to be discovered may be maintained in electronic form. When that is the case, electronic discovery methods are used to gather and authenticate this information. Whole college courses today are devoted to the process of electronic discovery.

After discovery has been completed, if the case has not been otherwise dismissed by the court or settled between the parties, the case will go to trial. By far the vast majority of civil litigation is settled by the parties, meaning it is resolved out of court. When litigation is settled by the parties, the parties enter into a settlement agreement and often sign releases. A **settlement agreement** is a contract entered into by the parties to a lawsuit that sets forth the terms and conditions of the resolution and settlement of the dispute. A **release** is a document that formally relinquishes a legal claim. In addition, if a lawsuit has been filed, the parties will agree to dismiss the lawsuit. A legal dispute can settle at any time before, during, or even after trial while the appeals process continues. Most litigation, however, settles before trial.

If the parties fail to settle in time, a pretrial conference is conducted prior to the start of the trial. A **pretrial conference** is a conference, or meeting, held prior to trial. At a pretrial conference the attorneys for both parties meet with the judge to discuss matters including possible settlement of the dispute, the evidence that will be presented at trial, and how the trial will be conducted.

When a trial begins, the first order of business is jury selection if there is a right to jury trial that has not been waived (remember our discussion earlier in this chapter on constitutional

Interrogatories are written questions prepared by a party, submitted to the other party, to be answered under oath.

Requests for production are requests by a party to another party for documents or other tangible things.

Requests for examination are requests by a party to the court asking the court to order the other party to submit to a physical or mental examination.

Requests for admission are requests by a party to the other party asking for admission to the truth of certain matters relating to the lawsuit.

A **settlement agreement** is a contract entered into by the parties to a lawsuit that sets forth the terms and conditions of the resolution and settlement of the dispute.

A **release** is a document that formally relinquishes a legal claim.

A **pretrial conference** is a meeting between the attorneys and the judge, held prior to trial, to discuss possible settlement as well as trial matters.

FIGURE 3-1   **Sample Settlement Agreement**

Settlement Agreement

THIS SETTLEMENT AGREEMENT (the "Agreement") is made and entered into this 15th day of July, 20__, by and between John M. Douglas, an individual residing at 84 Westbury Court, Syracuse, New York 13201 (the "Claimant"), and Robert F. Jones, an individual residing at 16 Simsbury Circle, Brookfield, Wisconsin 53005 (the "Opponent").

WHEREAS, the parties have been involved in a legal dispute resulting in the litigation noted below, where the Claimant filed a legal action and the Opponent denied any liability and asserted certain counterclaims related thereto;

WHEREAS, this Agreement is made as a compromise between the parties for the complete and final settlement of their claims, differences, and causes of action with respect to the dispute now pending in Circuit Court in Onondaga County, New York entitled Douglas v. Jones, and identified as case number CV-9384756 (the "Action"); and

WHEREAS, the parties desire to reach a full and final compromise and settlement of all matters and all causes of action arising out of the facts and claims as set forth, pursuant to the terms and conditions hereof.

NOW, THEREFORE, in consideration of the foregoing and other good and valuable consideration, the receipt and sufficiency of which is hereby acknowledged, the parties hereto agree as follows:

1.   The Opponent agrees to pay the Claimant eighty-five thousand dollars ($85,000), to be paid in a lump sum cash payment (the "Payment") on or before July 30, 20__.

2.   Both parties hereto agree that all claims, demands, rights, and causes of action that either has or may have against the other with respect to the above-described dispute are satisfied, discharged, and settled.

3.   The Claimant shall seek, obtain, and be bound by a dismissal with prejudice of the Action, with dismissal shall be obtained on or before August 1, 20__.

4.   Each party hereto releases and discharges the other, and their heirs and legal representatives, from any and all claims, damages, causes of action of any kind, for personal injuries or property damage suffered by either in connection with the above-described dispute and the Action, whether now known or to become known, and whether existing or subsequently arising.

5.   This Agreement shall be binding on and inure to the benefit of the parties and their respective legal representatives, successors, and assigns.

IN WITNESS WHEREOF, the parties hereby execute this Settlement Agreement on the day and year first above-written.

_____
John. M. Douglas

_____
Robert F. Jones

I, Lucy Stewart, Esq., attorney for the Claimant, have explained to my client all the terms and conditions of this Agreement, and my client has represented to me that all the terms and their significance are understood, and my client has signed this Agreement on my advice.

Dated:_____

_____
Lucy Stewart, Esq.

I, Marcy Abrams, attorney for the Opponent, have explained to my client all the terms and conditions of this Agreement, and my client has represented to me that all the terms and their significance are understood, and my client has signed this Agreement on my advice.

Dated:_____

_____
Marcy Abrams, Esq.

Sworn and subscribed before me this ___ day of July, 20__.

_____
Jordan Michaels
Notary Public
State of New York

law and the right to a jury trial in certain civil cases). **Jury selection** is the process of assembling a panel of jurors to hear a case. To empanel a jury, first the court creates a jury pool by choosing random prospective jurors, usually from motor vehicle records or voter registration records. The number of jurors on a jury varies; but for civil trials, the number normally is between six and twelve jurors. Attorneys for the parties have the opportunity to help select specific jurors from the jury pool. They do this through a process called *voir dire*. **Voir dire** is the juror selection process where attorneys or judges question individual or groups of prospective jurors in the case to determine who among them might be favorable to a party, or biased against, a particular party. During *voir dire*, attorneys may exercise challenges to strike (remove) certain persons from the jury. Alternate jurors normally are selected as well, so that if any juror is prevented from serving through the whole trial, for instance if a juror becomes ill, then another can be substituted and the trial can continue. The number of alternate jurors varies from jurisdiction to jurisdiction, but normally one to three alternates are present throughout the whole trial until deliberations.

Once the jury is selected and seated, then the actual trial of the case begins. **Opening statements** by counsel are made first. In their opening statements, attorneys for the parties provide a brief summary of their clients' positions, setting forth their version of the facts and providing a preview of the evidence they plan to offer. Normally, the plaintiff's attorney goes first and the defendant's attorney goes last.

After the opening statements, the parties begin their presentation of evidence. Again, the plaintiff's side goes first—the plaintiff will present her case. Counsel for the plaintiff will call witnesses favorable to the plaintiff and perhaps the plaintiff herself. Counsel will ask questions of the witnesses she calls, known as **direct examination**, and the witnesses will answer the questions under oath. After the direct examination of each witness for the plaintiff, counsel for the defendant may then cross-examine each witness. **Cross-examination** is the

Jury selection is the process of assembling a panel of jurors to hear a case.

Voir dire is the juror selection process where attorneys or judges question prospective jurors in the case to determine who among them might be favorable to, or biased against, a particular party.

An **opening statement** is a brief summary by an attorney of the client's position and evidence, offered at the start of a trial.

Direct examination is the questioning of a party or witness by the side that calls her to testify.

Cross-examination is the questioning of a party or witness by the opposing side.

questioning of a witness by the opposing side's counsel in an attempt to demonstrate to the jury that the witness is not credible (assuming the witness has offered damaging testimony). Note that, during presentation of the defendant's case later in the trial, direct examination is the defense counsel's questioning of witnesses he calls, and cross-examination is the plaintiff's counsel's questioning of these witnesses. The scope of cross examination questions is limited to matters covered in the direct examination as well as matters relating to the witness's credibility. **Redirect examination** of a witness is the re-questioning of a witness, done after the other side's cross-examination. Redirect examination is usually limited to the subjects that were covered during cross-examination. **Recross-examination** is the re-questioning of an opposing witness after the other side's redirect examination. Recross-examination is usually limited to subjects that were covered during redirect examination.

After the plaintiff's side has called all of her witnesses and introduced all of her evidence, counsel for the defendant can make a motion for directed verdict. A **motion for directed verdict** is a motion made to the court by the defendant's counsel asking for judgment in the defendant's favor, meaning judgment made as a matter of law. A court will grant this motion when the plaintiff's side has offered insufficient evidence to meet its burden of proof, for the plaintiff bears that burden. In essence, no reasonable jury could rule in favor of the plaintiff when a motion for directed verdict is successful. While these motions are regularly made to preserve certain rights on appeal, they are rarely granted by the courts.

If a motion for directed verdict is not made, or in the likely event it does not succeed, then the defendant's side will call his witnesses and introduce his evidence—in other words, the defendant will present his case. The goal of the defendant's presentation of evidence is to refute the plaintiff's claims and perhaps establish his own (in the event counterclaims are present in the lawsuit at the time of trial). The same procedures regarding direct examination, cross-examination, redirect examination, and recross-examination apply.

After the conclusion of the defendant's case, attorneys for each side make closing arguments, also called closing statements or summations. **Closing arguments** are summarizations by the attorneys of their clients' cases, emphasizing their side's strengths as well as pointing out the weaknesses in the other side's case.

Before sending the jury to the deliberation room, the judge will instruct the jury on the rules of law that apply to the case.

Jury instructions, written on a jury charge, are the rules of law given by the judge that the jury must apply to the facts of the case in order to render a verdict. Note that jurors do not make law. Rather, they are told the law by the presiding judge, then decide the facts and apply those facts to the law provided. Once given their instructions, the jury retires to the jury deliberation room to **deliberate**, meaning they discuss the case and work toward a verdict.

Upon successful deliberations, a jury will reach and render a verdict. A **verdict** is the jury's decision, reached upon completion of a jury trial. The verdict will be in favor of one of the parties. If it is in favor of the plaintiff, a remedy, such as a specific amount of money damages, may be awarded. If the verdict is in favor of the defendant, then the defendant will be found not liable and no remedy will be awarded. Upon rendering the verdict, the jury is discharged by the court. Note that in bench trials, where there is no right to jury trial or the right to jury trial has been waived, the judge renders the verdict.

A litigant who wins a jury award of damages must, to collect that money, enforce the judgment. To **enforce a judgment** means to collect the money or other property owed to the winning party by the losing party to civil litigation. It is not enough to be awarded a judgment; it is important also to collect that

---

Redirect examination is the re-questioning of a witness after the other side's cross-examination.

Recross-examination is the re-questioning of an opposing witness after the other side's redirect examination.

A **motion for directed verdict** is a motion made to the court by the defendant's counsel asking for judgment in the defendant's favor, when the plaintiff has offered such insufficient evidence that no reasonable jury could rule in the plaintiff's favor.

Closing arguments are summarizations by the attorneys of their clients' cases emphasizing their sides' strengths and the other side's weaknesses; they are also called closing statements or summations.

Jury instructions are the rules of law given by the judge to the jury that the jury must apply to the facts of the case in order to render a verdict in the case.

To **deliberate** means the jury retires to the jury room to discuss the evidence and work toward a verdict.

A **verdict** is the jury's decision, reached upon completion of a jury trial, or a judge's decision, reached upon the conclusion of a bench trial.

To **enforce a judgment** means to collect the money or other property owed to the winning party by the losing party to civil litigation.

FIGURE
3-2
Flowchart of the Civil Procedure Process

Accident or Other Event Giving Rise to a Legal Dispute

Injured Person Retains Legal Counsel

Counsel Performs Initial Investigation

Plaintiff's Attorney Files the Complaint

Defendant Is Notified of the Lawsuit through
Service of Process

Defendant's Attorney Files the Answer

Motion for Judgment on the Pleadings May Be Made

Discovery

Motion for Summary Judgment May Be Made

Pretrial Conference with the Judge

Jury Selection for a Jury Trial

Opening Statements

Presentation of the Plaintiff's Case

Motion for Directed Verdict May Be Made

Presentation of the Defendant's Defense

Closing Statements

Jury Instructions If a Jury Trial

Jury Deliberations If a Jury Trial

Verdict

Posttrial Motions May Be Made

Appeal(s) May Be Made

Enforce Judgment

Usually litigants voluntarily pay the verdicts rendered against them. In such cases execution is not necessary. However, sometimes a litigant refuses to voluntarily pay an adverse judgment. Such a litigant is called a **judgment debtor** because a money judgment was rendered against him and he has failed to pay it. The person owed the judgment is called the **judgment creditor**.

Judgment creditors, to reach the assets of their judgment debtors, can obtain a writ of execution from the court. A **writ of execution** is a court order granting the judgment creditor the right to pursue the judgment debtor's assets to satisfy the monetary judgment owed. A writ of execution authorizes an official, typically a sheriff, to take possession of the judgment debtor's property. The property then is sold in a sheriff's sale. Proceeds from the sale are given to the judgment creditor to satisfy part or all of the judgment (and excess funds, if any, are returned to the former judgment debtor). If possible, the asset taken is simply money from the judgment debtor's bank accounts. Note that some property is exempt from such execution, such as social security income or unemployment income in a bank account, tools of one's trade, and the judgment debtor's home—but the amount of the exempted property may be limited.

After the trial, the losing party may file a posttrial motion, either a motion for judgment notwithstanding the verdict (abbreviated JNOV, and in the federal courts, called a motion for judgment as a matter of law) or a motion for a new trial. A **motion for judgment notwithstanding the verdict** is a motion brought by the losing party asking the court to enter judgment in its favor on the basis that the verdict was clearly unsupported by the evidence at trial. While this motion is rarely granted, it allows the court the discretion to overturn an extremely unreasonable jury verdict.

> **Execution** is the legal process where assets of the losing party to litigation are taken and/or sold to pay an adverse judgment.
>
> A **judgment debtor** is a litigant who owes a money judgment and has failed to pay it.
>
> A **judgment creditor** is a litigant who has been awarded a money judgment that has not been paid.
>
> A **writ of execution** is a court order granting the judgment creditor the right to pursue the judgment debtor's assets to satisfy the monetary judgment owed.
>
> A **motion for judgment notwithstanding the verdict (JNOV)** is a motion brought by the losing party asking the court to enter judgment in its favor on the basis that the verdict was clearly unsupported by the evidence at trial.

judgment. Some judgments are paid by insurance proceeds, thus paid by insurance companies, where the losing party was insured for this type of loss. Other judgments are personally paid by the losing party, out of bank accounts, stock portfolios, real estate, cars, and other personal assets. These assets can be taken and/or sold to pay an adverse judgment in a legal process called **execution**.

A **motion for a new trial** is a motion made by the losing party that asks the court to order a new trial because there were significant legal errors in the conduct of the first one. In essence, the losing party argues that this trial was fundamentally flawed, with vital errors in the court's handling of the case. Examples of fundamental flaws include the admission or exclusion of important evidence, newly discovered material evidence, and incorrect jury instruction. Motions for a new trial are sometimes granted. A motion for a new trial can accompany a motion for judgment notwithstanding the verdict, or it can be filed separately.

If posttrial motions are not filed by the losing party, or if they are filed but unsuccessful, the losing party may appeal the verdict. An **appeal** is a legal proceeding undertaken to have a court's decision reviewed by a higher court. Note that either party can appeal a verdict; for example, the winning party could appeal if she thinks she did not win enough. However, it is usually the losing party who appeals a verdict.

Under the common law, civil litigants are guaranteed at least one appeal after a final judgment in a trial court. However, by statute in 47 states, appeal is merely a privilege and is not a guaranteed right. Accordingly, state statute has superseded the common law principle in those states. Further, the U.S. Supreme Court has regularly ruled that there is no federal constitutional right to an appeal, making appeal a privilege, not a right.

Appeals are heard by panels of judges, as opposed to one judge who hears a trial court case. Appellate reviews are concerned primarily with errors of law committed at the trial court level. Findings of fact are not made at the appellate level nor are they typically reviewed at the appellate level. Findings of fact are determined at the trial court level and normally are not reviewed at the appellate level *unless* the findings of fact were clearly erroneous. In that situation, the appellate court may remand the case to the trial court for further proceedings.

An appellate review is based on the trial transcript from the lower court, the pleadings, and exhibits—together called the **record on appeal**. In addition to the record on appeal, the appellate court reviews appellate briefs written and submitted by the attorneys for the parties, arguing their positions on appeal. After reading the record and the appellate briefs, the appellate court hears oral arguments from the attorneys in support of their briefs. At oral arguments, the appellate judges ask the attorneys questions about their arguments and solicit answers on which they will base their decision. An appellate court reviews the lower court's decision and can **affirm** (uphold), **modify** (change), or **reverse** (overrule) it. Further, the appellate court can **remand** the case, sending it back to the trial court for further proceedings at that level.

Depending on whether the case is in the federal court system or one of the state court systems, there may be two levels of appeal, an intermediate (middle) one and a higher one. For instance, the federal court system has two levels of appellate review, the U.S. courts of appeals and the U.S. Supreme Court. Note that not all state court systems include an intermediate level of appeal, as some states have only one level of appeal—to the state's highest court. The decisions of intermediate appellate courts, where they exist, *may* be further appealed by the parties to a higher level appellate court. However, most of the highest level appellate courts in the states, and the highest court in the federal system (the U.S. Supreme Court), have discretion in deciding whether or not they will accept an appeal to review a case. Appeal to these courts is not automatic, then, but rather discretionary. These courts are said to have discretionary review authority. However, these courts may be mandated, meaning required, to review certain types of cases, such as death penalty cases or cases involving the interpretation of the state's constitution. Note, however, that some of the state court systems that have no intermediate level of appeal allow automatic, rather than discretionary, appeal of trial court decisions to them. Nevada, for example, operates with no intermediate level of appeal, and its highest court automatically reviews all appeals from the trial courts.

When appeals are permitted or required for state court cases, this means the case may be heard by the highest court in the state, often (but not always) called the state supreme court. Certain cases may be appealed to the U.S. Supreme Court as well. What cases the Supreme Court can hear are discussed in the next chapter.

Now that we have discussed civil procedural law, we will review the other type of procedural law—criminal procedure.

A **motion for a new trial** is a motion made by the losing party that asks the court to order a new trial because there were significant legal errors in the conduct of the first one.

An **appeal** is a legal proceeding undertaken to have a court's decision reviewed by a higher court.

Record on appeal consists of the trial court transcript, the pleadings, and exhibits and is used during appellate review of a case.

To **affirm** means to uphold the lower court's decision.

To **modify** means to change the lower court's decision.

To **reverse** means to overrule, or rule against, the lower court's decision.

To **remand** means to send a case back to the trial court for further proceedings.

CRIMINAL PROCEDURE

Criminal procedure is the body of procedural law that governs the process of criminal prosecutions. Like civil procedure, it varies from jurisdiction to jurisdiction. That said, there are many procedures that most jurisdictions follow. Those are reviewed now, starting with criminal procedure before prosecution.

The criminal law system is triggered when a person is taken into custody. In other words, the system begins with a person's arrest. An **arrest** is the taking into custody of a person in response to a criminal investigation. It involves the exercise of legal authority over a person to restrict his liberty. That person is a suspect in a crime.

After arrest, a suspect is booked. **Booking** is the recording of the suspect's name, offense, and time of arrival in the police blotter. A **police blotter** is a log, or record book. It records the daily arrests at a police station. At this time, the suspect is told of the reasons for his arrest. He is fingerprinted and photographed. He is allowed to make a phone call as well.

After booking, the police may conduct further investigation and determine if there is insufficient evidence to prosecute the suspect for a crime. In that situation the suspect is released and the case is closed. On further investigation the police may find the evidence supports a different, or lesser, charge. In that situation the police may modify the charge. If the evidence is sufficient and the charge is correct, but the arrest was for an offense that is not very serious, the suspect may be released for the time being. Later, he will be required to appear in court to defend the charge.

Unless the suspect is released from custody and the case is dropped, the case then moves from the police station to the prosecutor's office. This is when the prosecution begins. To initiate a prosecution, the prosecutor must demonstrate **probable cause**, meaning reasonable suspicion that a crime was committed and that the suspect committed it.

A prosecution may begin with the filing of a complaint by the prosecutor. This is a different document than a complaint in a civil case, as discussed above. A **criminal complaint** is a legal document containing a statement of the charges that are being brought by the government against the suspect and the basis for them. At this point, the suspect becomes a criminal defendant, often just referred to as a defendant. Again, note that the use of the term "defendant" can apply to a person defending either a civil or a criminal case.

In many jurisdictions soon after arrest, a defendant is taken before a **magistrate**, who is a judicial officer with limited law enforcement and administration authority, to make an initial appearance. An **initial appearance** is when the defendant appears before a magistrate soon after arrest (often within hours of it) to determine whether or not there is probable cause for his arrest. The magistrate confirms that the person charged is the person identified in the criminal complaint. The magistrate informs the defendant of the charges against him and explains to the defendant his constitutional rights as a criminal defendant. The defendant is informed of his right to counsel, and counsel may be appointed for him by the magistrate.

Then the magistrate may release the defendant until he is next due in court. If the defendant is charged with a misdemeanor, he may be released on his own recognizance, meaning

Who Is a Defendant?

Remember that the person defending a case, whether it is a civil case or a criminal case, is called a defendant.

- The defendant in a civil case is being sued by one or more plaintiffs.
- The defendant in a criminal case is being prosecuted by the government.

Criminal procedure is the body of procedural law that governs the process of criminal prosecutions.

An **arrest** is the taking into custody of a person in response to a criminal investigation.

Booking is the recording of the suspect's name, offense, and time of arrival in the police blotter.

A **police blotter** is a log, or record book, of daily arrests at a police station.

Probable cause means a reasonable suspicion that a crime was committed by the suspect.

A **criminal complaint** is a legal document containing a statement of the charges that are being brought by the government against the suspect and the basis for them.

A **magistrate** is a judicial officer with limited law enforcement and administration authority.

An **initial appearance** is when the defendant appears before a magistrate soon after arrest to determine whether or not there is probable cause for his arrest.

on condition that he promise to appear in court when scheduled to answer the criminal charge. If the defendant is charged with a more serious crime, he may be released on posting bail. **Bail** is an amount of money that a defendant can post, the amount of which is set by the court. The court sets bail at a sufficiently high amount to ensure that the defendant will appear in court to answer the criminal charge. Normally, the defendant's attorney arranges bail with a bail bondsman. A **bail bondsman** is a person who pledges money or property as bail for a criminal defendant. Why would a bail bondsman make this pledge? For a fee is the answer. Bail bondsmen charge nonrefundable fees for their services, normally about 10 to 12 percent of the amount of bail. For the most serious crimes, the defendant may be denied bail, or the court may set bail so high that the defendant is unable to meet it. In such a case, the defendant is not released from custody.

Next, in some jurisdictions, a criminal defendant appears before a magistrate or judge at a preliminary hearing. A **preliminary hearing** is an evidentiary and adversarial hearing to determine whether there is enough evidence to bring the defendant to trial. The defendant may be, and in some jurisdictions has the right to be, represented by counsel at this hearing. The judge must find that there is probable cause that a crime was committed and that this defendant committed it. If probable cause is not found, then the case usually is dropped (though some jurisdictions allow the prosecution to seek a new preliminary hearing, perhaps for a reduced charge). If the judge finds probable cause, then the prosecutor issues an information. An **information** is a formal accusation that takes the place of the criminal complaint, and it initiates the criminal prosecution.

In some jurisdictions, instead of the process involving preliminary hearings and informations, grand juries are called to review the prosecutor's evidence to determine if it is sufficient to bring a defendant to trial. A **grand jury** is a group of people who are selected, convened, and sworn in by the court to determine whether the prosecutor has sufficient evidence to support the finding that there is probable cause to prosecute a defendant. A grand jury proceeding is not an adversarial process. Rather, only the prosecution presents evidence; the defense does not.

If the grand jury does not find probable cause, the case is dropped by the prosecution. However, if the grand jury finds probable cause exists, then it issues an indictment, also called a true bill, against the defendant. An **indictment**, or **true bill**, is a formal accusation by a grand jury that a defendant has

committed a crime. The indictment is filed with the court and becomes the formal charge against the defendant, initiating the criminal prosecution.

Based on an information or an indictment, depending on the jurisdiction, the defendant is then arraigned. **Arraignment** is the court's formal reading of a criminal complaint in the presence of the defendant. It informs the defendant of the charges against him. The defendant then enters a plea. While the kinds of acceptable pleas differ from jurisdiction to jurisdiction, they normally include "guilty," "not guilty," and peremptory pleas (peremptory pleas are pleas that set reasons why a trial cannot proceed, and have nothing to do with the issue of guilt). A plea of "*nolo contendere*" (meaning "no contest") is allowed under certain circumstances. The plea of "*nolo contendere*" has the effect of a guilty plea, but the defendant does not admit or deny guilt; rather, he is not contesting, meaning not fighting, the charge.

Often at arraignment, the defendant pleads guilty to a lesser charge as part of a plea bargain. A **plea bargain**, also called a plea agreement, a plea deal, or the result of copping a plea,

---

Bail is an amount of money that a defendant can post, the amount of which is set by the court, sufficiently high enough to ensure that the defendant will appear in court to answer the criminal charge.

A **bail bondsman** is a person who pledges money or property as bail for a criminal defendant.

A **preliminary hearing** is an evidentiary and adversarial hearing to determine whether there is enough evidence to bring the criminal defendant to trial.

An **information** is a formal accusation that takes the place of the criminal complaint and that initiates the criminal prosecution.

A **grand jury** is a group of people who are selected, convened, and sworn in by a court to determine whether the prosecutor has sufficient evidence to support the finding that there is probable cause to prosecute a defendant.

An **indictment** is a formal accusation by a grand jury that a defendant has committed a crime; it is also called a **true bill**.

Arraignment is the court's formal reading of a criminal complaint in the presence of the defendant.

A **plea bargain** is an agreement between the prosecution and the criminal defendant that the defendant plead guilty to a lesser charge or to the original charge but with the prosecution's recommendation of a sentence of less than the maximum allowed by law, and that is subject to court approval; it is also called a plea agreement, plea deal, or the result of copping a plea.

Examples of Pretrial Motions in Criminal Prosecutions

- Motion to suppress evidence that was illegally obtained
- Motion to dismiss the prosecution because of a violation of the defendant's constitutional rights
- Motion in *limine* to limit the use of prejudicial or objectionable evidence
- Motion for a continuance to delay the start of the trial
- Motion for a change in venue to find a more impartial and unbiased jury in another geographic location
- Motion to recuse a biased judge from the case
- Motion to sever the joint trying of multiple defendants

is an agreement between the prosecution and the criminal defendant that the defendant plead guilty to a lesser charge or to the original charge but with the prosecution's recommendation of a sentence of less than the maximum allowed by law. Plea bargains are reached through negotiation between the prosecution and the defense. They are subject to court approval.

A variety of pretrial motions can be made by criminal defendants. These are usually based on alleged violations of the defendant's constitutional rights (remember our earlier study in this chapter of constitutional law and the Bill of Rights, where numerous defendants' rights are found). These motions include motions to suppress evidence, or keep the evidence out at trial, because it was illegally obtained; motions to dismiss the prosecution because one of the defendant's constitutional rights was violated; motions in *limine* to limit the use of certain prejudicial or objectionable evidence; motions for a continuance to delay the start of the trial; motions for a change in venue in an effort to find a more impartial and unbiased jury in another geographic location; motions to recuse, or remove, a biased judge from a case; and motions to sever the joint trying of multiple defendants so that a defendant is tried separately.

Before trial begins, discovery is conducted. During discovery, the criminal defendant is entitled to view the evidence that the prosecution intends to introduce at trial, such as physical evidence like a weapon, stolen property or DNA, statements previously made by the defendant to the authorities, the names and statements of witnesses the government plans to call, reports from tests on evidence, and reports from examinations of the defendant or a victim. Remember from our earlier discussions that criminal defendants have many constitutional

protections, such as the right against self-incrimination, the right to compel testimony from favorable witnesses, the right to confront the prosecution's witnesses, and the right to defense counsel. Because of these constitutional safeguards, discovery in criminal cases is more limited in scope than discovery in civil cases. Further, in criminal cases compared to civil cases, more restrictive time limits on discovery often are imposed.

As discussed earlier in this chapter, the trial of a criminal case is called a prosecution. If the prosecution involves a misdemeanor crime, then the case may be heard and decided by a judge—called a **bench trial**—rather than a jury. A **misdemeanor** is a "lesser" crime, meaning it is a crime less serious than a felony. A misdemeanor typically is punishable by fine and/or incarceration for one year or less. If the prosecution involves a felony, then the case is likely heard and decided by a jury—called a **jury trial**. A **felony** is a more serious crime than a misdemeanor and usually can be punished by incarceration for more than one year (fines and capital punishment may also be available punishments for felonies). While the definitions of misdemeanor and felony differ from jurisdiction to jurisdiction, the federal government, and most states, use these definitions.

The conduct of a criminal prosecution is similar to a civil trial. Both sides, meaning the prosecution and the defense, make opening statements. Then both sides present their evidence, with the prosecution going first and the defense going last. This presentation of evidence includes the direct examination, cross-

Infractions

Violations of administrative regulations are called regulatory offenses, or infractions. An example is a parking ticket. Infractions are even less serious than misdemeanor crimes. They usually are punished less severely than both felonies and misdemeanors.

A **bench trial** is a trial where a judge hears and decides the case.

A **misdemeanor** is a "lesser" crime, meaning a crime less serious than a felony and usually punishable by a fine and/or incarceration for one year or less.

A **jury trial** is a trial where a jury hears and decides the case.

A **felony** is a more serious crime than a misdemeanor, usually punishable by a fine, incarceration for more than one year, and/or death.

examination, redirect examination, and recross-examination of witnesses. Both sides may make closing statements as well.

However, despite the similarities, many constitutional safeguards differentiate a criminal prosecution from a civil trial. For example, the defendant in a criminal prosecution has the right to counsel. That means that if the defendant cannot afford to pay for a lawyer, the government will provide a lawyer, free of charge to the defendant (paid for by the taxpayers, who pay the salaries and other expenses of public defenders).

Defendants in criminal cases also have the constitutional right to a speedy and public trial. In addition, juries in criminal cases usually must unanimously agree on the verdict in the case, meaning that everyone on the jury must vote "guilty" for a criminal defendant to be convicted. In civil litigation, less-than-unanimous vote is the rule so that depending on the jurisdiction, two-thirds or three-fourths of the jury must vote in favor of the verdict.

In criminal prosecutions, the defendant's innocence is presumed. There is no such assumption that a civil defendant is not liable.

The standard of proof in a criminal prosecution is higher than it is for civil litigation. As mentioned earlier, the standard of proof in a criminal case is "beyond a reasonable doubt." This means the prosecution has a heavy burden to meet; if it fails to meet this burden, the defendant should be found "not guilty." On the other hand, in most civil cases, the standard of proof that the plaintiff must meet is a "preponderance of the evidence," meaning that the plaintiff must show that the allegations are more likely than not true. In other words, the greater weight of the evidence (at least slightly more than 50 percent) supports one side—the plaintiff or the defendant.

Another constitutional protection is the privilege against self-incrimination. This protection extends to criminal defendants as well as to witnesses. It prohibits the government from compelling a person to give testimony that is likely to incriminate him.

"Plead the Fifth"

The constitutional protection against self-incrimination is found in the Fifth Amendment to the U.S. Constitution. When a criminal defendant or witness "pleads the Fifth," it means he refuses to answer the question when giving testimony in a criminal trial because the answer could provide incriminating evidence against him, and subject him to criminal prosecution. Further, a prosecutor may not comment to the jury on a criminal defendant's invoking of this Fifth Amendment right.

KEY Point

Constitutional Safeguards in Criminal Prosecutions

- Right to legal counsel
- Right to a speedy and public trial
- Unanimous verdict usually required
- Innocence is presumed
- The prosecution bears a higher burden of proof—that of "beyond a reasonable doubt"
- Privilege against self-incrimination

After jury deliberations (assuming a jury trial was conducted), the jury renders a verdict. The jurors normally are dismissed after the rendering of the verdict. If a defendant is found not guilty, he is released from custody and the case is ended. A "not guilty" verdict is also called an **acquittal**.

If, however, the defendant is found guilty at trial, he must then be sentenced. **Sentencing** is the process of a court imposing penalties on a defendant found guilty of committing a crime. The sentence may be pronounced after the jury's rendering of the guilty verdict, or it may be pronounced in a separate legal proceeding devoted to sentencing. Such a later proceeding is called a sentencing hearing. A **sentencing hearing** is a hearing held sometime after the guilty verdict is rendered when the court hears arguments and evidence from both sides of a prosecution regarding aggravating and mitigating factors the court should consider in sentencing the defendant.

A sentence usually is issued by a judge, and the jury is not involved. However, juries may recommend sentences to the court, especially in death penalty cases. Certain states permit judges to override jury recommendations on sentencing.

Criminal statutes may set forth the range of maximum and minimum penalties that should be imposed by a court for their violation. Some jurisdictions use sentencing guidelines, providing judges with recommended (not mandatory) ranges of sentences for various crimes.

An **acquittal** is a "not guilty" verdict rendered at the end of a criminal prosecution.

Sentencing is the process of a court imposing penalties on a defendant found guilty of committing a crime.

A **sentencing hearing** is a hearing held sometime after the guilty verdict is rendered when the court hears arguments and evidence from both sides of a prosecution regarding aggravating and mitigating factors the court should consider in sentencing the defendant.

FIGURE
3-3

Flowchart of the Criminal Procedure Process

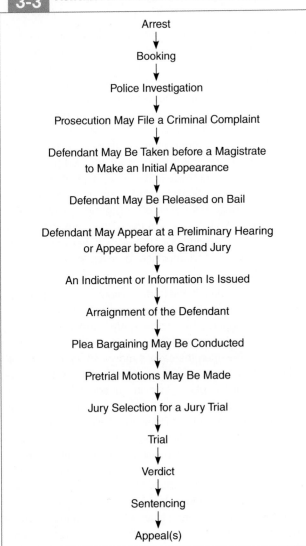

Arrest

↓

Booking

↓

Police Investigation

↓

Prosecution May File a Criminal Complaint

↓

Defendant May Be Taken before a Magistrate
to Make an Initial Appearance

↓

Defendant May Be Released on Bail

↓

Defendant May Appear at a Preliminary Hearing
or Appear before a Grand Jury

↓

An Indictment or Information Is Issued

↓

Arraignment of the Defendant

↓

Plea Bargaining May Be Conducted

↓

Pretrial Motions May Be Made

↓

Jury Selection for a Jury Trial

↓

Trial

↓

Verdict

↓

Sentencing

↓

Appeal(s)

Depending on the severity of the crime, various types of punishments can be used in sentencing criminal defendants. A common punishment is incarceration in jail (for shorter terms, typically up to one year) or prison (for longer "stays"). House arrest may be used as an alternative to imprisonment. Probation is another common sentence. Probation is a form of supervised release. It can be formal or informal, with the difference basically being the extent of supervision of the parolee, accomplished by the parolee's regularly reporting to a probation officer. Fines and other types of financial penalties, such as orders to make restitution to a victim, are another common type of sentence. Community service is another type of punishment that can be imposed for less serious offenses. For the most serious offenses, namely, capital offenses like first degree murder, some jurisdictions authorize the death penalty. Remember that the Constitution, in the Eight Amendment, prohibits cruel and unusual punishment. That is why no U.S. jurisdiction puts to death a petty thief or cuts off his hands—feeling the punishment far outweighs the crime. Rather, the death penalty, in states where it is permitted, is allowed only in cases involving the intentional killing of a human being.

Note that two or more types of punishment can be combined in a sentence. For example, a criminal defendant found guilty of robbery may be sentenced to a period of time in prison and required to make restitution to the victim. After his prison release, he may be put on probation and have to meet regularly with a probation officer for a period of time.

A criminal defendant found guilty of committing a crime may appeal that conviction—as a matter of right. As with civil cases, if the jurisdiction has an intermediate court of appeal, the appeal is heard in that court. If the jurisdiction has no intermediate court of appeal, the appeal is heard at the state's highest court. While many convictions that result in incarceration, and nearly all that result in a death sentence, are appealed, most convictions are not reversed on appeal.

What if a conviction is reversed on appeal? Can the government retry the defendant for that crime? The answer depends on whether the conviction was reversed "with prejudice" or "without prejudice." Only a conviction reversed "without prejudice" may be retried by the government.

CHAPTER SUMMARY

- Law is the body of rules of conduct and procedure that are established, recognized, and enforced to govern a society. Substantive law is law that defines the rights and duties of persons. Procedural law is law that sets forth the process used to enforce a legal right via a civil or criminal action.

- The four main sources of American law are constitutional law, common law, statutory law, and administrative law. Constitutional law is law found in the federal and state constitutions. Common law is judge-made law, found in court opinions; it is also called case law. Statutory law is law enacted by legislatures. Administrative law is law made by administrative agencies of the government.

- Civil law is the system of law dealing with the definition and enforcement of all private or public rights. Parties to civil actions, called lawsuits, are plaintiffs and defendants. The usual burden of proof in a civil case is "preponderance of the evidence," and remedies may be awarded where liability is found.

- Criminal law is the system of law defining and governing actions that constitute crimes as defined by statutes. Parties to criminal actions, called prosecutions, are governments and defendants. The burden of proof in a criminal case is "beyond a reasonable doubt," meaning that the prosecution must prove its case sufficiently so that there is no reasonable doubt in the mind of any juror that the defendant committed the crime. Punishments may be imposed where guilt is found.

- Civil procedure is the body of procedural law that governs the process of civil litigation. A civil lawsuit is initiated with the filing of a complaint by the plaintiff. The complaint and the court's summons are served on the defendant, called service of process. The defendant must respond to the complaint in an answer, filed with the court, or else a default judgment will be entered against him. A defendant may make counterclaims against the plaintiff. The defendant may make cross-claims against other defendants; the plaintiff may make cross-claims against other plaintiffs. The defendant may file with the court a variety of motions to dismiss the complaint. Also before trial, either party may file a motion for judgment on the pleadings or a motion for summary judgment. Then discovery is conducted. Discovery is the process of searching for and obtaining information and evidence relevant to the case. Popular discovery tools include depositions, interrogatories, requests for production, requests for examination, and requests for admission. A pretrial conference is conducted between the attorneys for both sides and the judge to try and resolve the dispute in advance of trial, and to prepare for the trial if settlement is not reached. At trial, the first order of business is to empanel a jury through the jury selection process if it is a jury, rather than a bench, trial. Then the parties make opening statements. After opening statements, the

parties present their evidence, including testimony from witnesses. After the presentation of the plaintiff's case, the defendant's attorney may make a motion for directed verdict. If that motion is unsuccessful, then the defendant will present his evidence in the case. After the presentation of evidence, the parties make closing arguments. Then the judge gives the jury instructions, for use in their deliberations. The jurors render a verdict, then are released from service. If the plaintiff is successful, she will have to enforce any judgment made in her favor—typically collect the monetary award. The losing party may file a postjudgment motion for judgment notwithstanding the verdict. He may also make a motion for a new trial. Either party may appeal the trial court's ruling. On appeal, a lower court's decision may be affirmed, modified, or reversed, and the case remanded.

- Criminal procedure is the body of procedural law that governs the process of criminal prosecutions. The criminal law system is triggered by an arrest. After arrest, a suspect is booked. If further investigation does not result in the suspect's release, then the case is moved to the prosecutor's office. The prosecution of a suspect begins with the filing of a criminal complaint. In many jurisdictions, soon after arrest, the suspect, now a criminal defendant, is brought before a magistrate to make an initial appearance in court. The magistrate may release the defendant on his own recognizance, or upon the posting of bail—or the magistrate may not release the defendant at all, when a very serious crime has been committed. Next, a criminal defendant faces either a preliminary hearing or a grand jury proceeding. A preliminary hearing is an evidentiary and adversarial hearing to determine whether there is enough evidence to bring the defendant to trial. If so, an information is issued by the prosecutor, formally accusing the defendant of the crime. In jurisdictions using grand juries, a group of people are asked by the court to determine whether the prosecutor has sufficient evidence to support the finding that there is probable cause to prosecute a defendant. A grand jury proceeding is a non-adversarial proceeding where only the prosecutor presents evidence. If the grand jury finds probable cause exists, it issues an indictment, formally accusing the defendant of the crime. Then the defendant is arraigned, where the court formally reads the charges against the defendant and asks the defendant to enter a plea—typically "guilty," "not guilty," a peremptory plea, or "*nolo contendere.*" The prosecution and defendant may agree to a plea bargain, and submit that to the court for approval. Otherwise, the case proceeds toward trial. Discovery is conducted, though discovery in a criminal case is of lesser scope than in a civil case. Then the case goes to trial. The conduct of a criminal prosecution is similar to a civil trial. Both sides make opening statements, present evidence, and make closing arguments. However, numerous constitutional safeguards provide protections to criminal defendants during their prosecutions that are not available to defendants in civil lawsuits. After deliberations, the jury in a jury trial renders a verdict, then usually is dismissed. Either directly after the verdict or in a later sentencing hearing, the judge issues a sentence, punishing the criminal defendant for the crime for which he was found guilty. The main types of punishments that can be issued in sentencing include incarceration, house arrest, probation, fines and other financial penalties like restitution, community service, and death. The defendant may appeal his conviction. If a conviction is reversed on appeal, the prosecution may retry the defendant only if the reversal was made "without prejudice."

CONCEPT REVIEW AND REINFORCEMENT

Key Terms and Concepts

Law
Substantive law
Procedural law
Constitutional law
Bill of Rights
Common law
Case law
Precedent
Doctrine of *stare decisis*
Binding authority
Mandatory authority
Case of first impression
Persuasive authority
Statutory law
Statutes
Ordinances
Administrative law
Enabling legislation
Civil law
Criminal law
Litigation
Lawsuit
Plaintiff
Defendant
Burden of proof
Preponderance of the evidence
Liability
Remedies
Prosecution
Beyond a reasonable doubt
Guilty
Penalties
Civil procedure
Complaint
Summons
Service of process

Default judgment
Answer
Affirmative defense
Counterclaim
Cross-claim
Motion to dismiss
Motion for judgment on the pleadings
Motion for summary judgment
Discovery
Deposition
Interrogatories
Request for production
Request for examination
Request for admission
Settlement agreement
Release
Pretrial conference
Jury selection
Voir dire
Opening statements
Direct examination
Cross examination
Redirect examination
Recross-examination
Motion for directed verdict
Closing arguments
Jury instructions
Deliberate
Verdict
Enforce a judgment
Execution
Judgment debtor
Judgment creditor
Writ of execution
Motion for judgment notwithstanding the verdict
Motion for new trial
Appeal
Record on appeal
Affirm
Modify
Reverse
Remand
Criminal procedure
Arrest
Booking
Police blotter
Probable cause
Criminal complaint
Magistrate
Initial appearance
Bail
Bail bondsman
Preliminary hearing
Information
Grand jury
Indictment

True bill
Arraignment
Plea bargain
Bench trial
Misdemeanor
Jury trial
Felony
Acquittal
Sentencing
Sentencing hearing

Questions for Review

1. What are the main sources of American law?
2. What is constitutional law?
3. What is common law?
4. How is common law different from case law, if at all?
5. What is statutory law?
6. What is administrative law?
7. What is the civil law system?
8. What is the criminal law system?
9. How are the civil and criminal law systems distinguished?
10. What is civil procedural law?
11. What is criminal procedural law?

DEVELOPING YOUR PARALEGAL SKILLS

Critical Thinking Exercises

1. Refer to the O. J. Simpson Case on Point. How could O. J. Simpson be found not guilty of the murders of his ex-wife and her friend, yet be held liable for their wrongful deaths?
2. The standard of proof in a criminal case is "beyond a reasonable doubt." The standard of proof in a civil case usually is "preponderance of the evidence." Which standard is higher, meaning that it requires a greater amount of proof? Does this make sense? Why or why not?
3. Does being found "not guilty" in a criminal prosecution mean the defendant is innocent? Why or why not?

Assignments and Practical Applications

Review the U.S. Constitution, including all of its amendments. To view it online, go to http://www.usconstitution.net/const.html.

Find and review at least one of the federal statutes referenced in this chapter. You can use the Library of Congress website to help locate the statutes, or simply visit your law library and peruse its copies of the official or unofficial federal code.

What is the name of the legislature in your state? What is the name of your state's code? Go to your law library and locate your state's code. Find its commercial code title and review its table of contents.

Can you locate your city or county's ordinances? See if they are available online or if they are in print form in your law library.

This chapter provides examples of well-known federal administrative agencies. Find and name two state governmental agencies in your state and two local agencies in your local government. Share yours with the class.

Using your law library, locate your state's rules of civil procedure.

Technology Resources and Internet Exercises

Using the Cornell Law School website at http://topics.law.cornell.edu/wex/american_indian_law, review American Indian law and how it relates to and co-exists with other U.S. laws.

Review the discussion of the *Roe v. Wade* Supreme Court decision regarding abortion found on the Wikipedia website at http://en.wikipedia.org/wiki/Roe_v._Wade.

Access the Library of Congress website at http://www.loc.gov/index.html and locate an electronic copy of the constitution for your state.

Using the website for the Office of the Law Revision Counsel of the U.S. House of Representatives, located at http://uscode.house.gov/, you can search the *United States Code*. Remember from the chapter that the Office of Law Revision Counsel writes federal statutes.

A list of federal government agencies is included on the government website found at http://www.usa.gov/Agencies/Federal/All_Agencies/index.shtml. See if you can find a federal agency not mentioned as an example in the chapter but that you have heard of and know about.

The murder and wrongful death trials of O. J. Simpson were not the last of his legal entanglements. More recently, O. J. Simpson was arrested, charged with, and, in 2008, convicted of criminal actions relating to entering another's hotel room in Las Vegas and taking property. Simpson currently is serving a multiyear prison sentence. Using the Internet, locate and read Associated Press releases on this prosecution and conviction.

Using the Cornell University Law School website for its Legal Information Institute, found at http://www.law.cornell.edu/, find your state's legal ethics code. Use it to answer the following Ethical Applications.

Ethical Applications

Ralph Widener is a paralegal working for the personal injury law firm Benson, Brauman & Rogers, LLC. Around 4:30 p.m. one Friday afternoon, Ralph is in a hurry to finish a research project for his supervising attorney, Michelle Brauman. Ralph has been researching the law of contributory negligence in his state, which is Maryland. He believes he heard that contributory negligence continues to be a defense to negligence in Maryland, though almost all other states have adopted comparative negligence as a defense and abandoned the defense of contributory negligence.

Ralph cannot quickly pinpoint recent case law on point. Wanting to beat the rush-hour traffic, he "embellishes" his research results. Then he reports to his supervisor that he has confirmed (though he has not) the law on this issue, and that contributory negligence is a valid defense to negligence in Maryland at this time. Ralph is *correct*. Michelle thinks this sounds reasonable, and she does not review or follow up on Ralph's work.

Under your state's legal ethics rules, has Ralph Widener violated an ethical duty? Can he be sanctioned by his state bar's disciplinary board? Has Michelle Brauman violated an ethical rule or duty? Can she be sanctioned by the state bar that licenses her? Can either, or both, be held liable for malpractice because of their actions or inactions?

VIDEO CASE STUDIES

Video Interview of Julianne Ennis

Paralegal case study videos to accompany this textbook are accessible from within both the New MyLegalStudiesLab Virtual Law Office Experience course and the Resources Website for Paralegal Studies.

4

The Court Systems, Litigation, and Alternative Dispute Resolution

Anatoly Smolkin

Paralegal at Gallagher Evelius & Jones, LLP

Anatoly worked full-time as a paralegal for the law firm of Gallagher Evelius & Jones LLP while earning a degree in paralegal studies and before attending law school. This employment opportunity came from his internship experience, coordinated through his paralegal education program. His practice area was the civil litigation group, and his cases involved construction, medical malpractice, and general commercial litigation at both the trial and appellate court levels. Occasionally, Anatoly worked on bankruptcy matters and employment discrimination cases. In his practice, Anatoly used state and federal laws, including statutes, case law, and administrative regulations.

Anatoly believes that paralegals play an important role in civil litigation. He notes that it is cost-saving for clients and time-saving for attorneys to utilize paralegals for performing legal tasks. "Clients do not want to pay higher fees for attorneys performing work that [paralegals] can do," says Anatoly.

Attributes useful for paralegals, highlights Anatoly, are being hard-working, self-motivated, smart, diligent, and attentive. These attributes helped him in his litigation practice, where he often conducted factual investigations by researching persons' backgrounds, performed document collection and review, drafted legal documents (including pleadings), performed legal research, and helped attorneys prepare for depositions and trials. As a paralegal for a medium-sized law firm, Anatoly also performed some administrative tasks, such as photo-copying and preparing exhibits for depositions. In his practice, Anatoly communicated directly with clients, typically by e-mail and telephone. He often relayed to clients updates on cases given by the attorneys.

Technology was important to Anatoly in his paralegal work. He used various technology applications, including word processing, e-mail, electronic spreadsheets, electronic timekeeping, electronic calendaring, and electronic databases. Anatoly regularly performed computerized legal research as well.

The full video interview is accessible from within both the New MyLegalStudiesLab Virtual Law Office Experience course and the Resources Website for Paralegal Studies.

The chapter will answer the following questions:

- What are the court systems in the United States?
- How are the courts organized?
- What types of cases do the different courts adjudicate?

- How are legal disputes resolved through litigation?
- What alternative dispute resolution methods exist, and how do they work?

CHAPTER **INTRODUCTION**

This chapter identifies and examines the different court systems in the United States. It reviews their organization and the types of cases different courts adjudicate. The use of litigation to resolve legal disputes is discussed. Alternative methods of dispute resolution are examined in the last part of this chapter. We begin with a discussion of the court systems existing in the United States.

THE COURT SYSTEMS

Remember the discussion in the previous chapter concerning constitutional law. Federal and state constitutions establish the three branches of government for their jurisdictions, including the judicial branch. The judicial branch of a jurisdiction's government is the court system. The **court systems** are the judicial branches of the federal and state governments that are charged with the application, interpretation, and enforcement of the law. The law that courts are applying, interpreting, and enforcing is that derived from the three other sources of law discussed in the previous chapter: constitutional, statutory, and administrative.

The courts in the United States are divided into two separate systems, the federal system and the state system. The state court system is further subdivided by jurisdiction. Each state, and the District of Columbia, has its own court system. These court systems are administered separately. Therefore, there are 52 court systems in the United States—the federal court system, a court system for each of the 50 states, and a court system for the District of Columbia. The court systems are independent of each other and of the other branches of government in their jurisdictions.

Consider the federal court system and the state court system. Are federal courts superior to state courts? Not at all. The court systems are merely independent. They have different authority derived from different sources. That authority and its impact on the organization of the court systems are examined next.

Judicial Review

Examination by the courts of the actions of the other branches of government, namely the executive and legislative branches, to ensure that those branches of government conform to the provisions of the U.S. Constitution, is called judicial review. Judicial review is a doctrine pursuant to which the actions of the executive and legislative branches of government are subject to review by the judicial branch (the courts).

ORGANIZATION OF THE COURTS

The federal court system derives its authority from Article III of the U.S. Constitution, where the judicial power of the United States was vested in one supreme court and such inferior courts as the Congress established. Pursuant to that mandate, the Congress has established three levels within the federal court system by adding two levels of inferior courts (lower courts) below the U.S. Supreme Court, which Supreme Court was authorized by Article III of the U.S. Constitution.

The federal court system is organized into three levels, or tiers. One level is a trial court level and the other two are appellate court levels. The trial court level consists of the U.S. district courts. **U.S. district courts** are federal trial courts. There are 94 judicial districts today. Every state has at least one district court, and some states have more than one. In addition, the District of Columbia and U.S. territories such as Puerto Rico and the U.S. Virgin Islands have district courts. According to the Constitution, district court judges are appointed via nomination by the president and confirmation by the Senate. They are appointed for life, meaning until they die, retire, or are removed from office.

The federal court system has an intermediate appellate court level. The intermediate level of appeal in this system consists of the **U.S. courts of appeals**. The U.S. courts of appeals are organized into 13 circuits. Twelve of the 13 circuits hear appeals from the U.S. district courts that are located within their geographically defined circuits. The 13th circuit is called the Federal Circuit Court of Appeals. It handles (has jurisdiction over) certain types of federal cases, as discussed in the next section on the types of cases courts adjudicate (hear). Because the U.S. courts of appeals are divided by circuit, they are also referred to as **circuit courts** or **U.S. circuit courts of appeals**.

A party may appeal a U.S. district court decision to a U.S. court of appeals. At this level of intermediate appeal, a panel of three or more judges reviews the decision of the trial court, looking for errors of law committed at that level. According to the Constitution and like district court judges, courts of appeals judges are appointed via nomination by the president and confirmation by the Senate. They are appointed for life.

The district courts and courts of appeals hear a variety of cases (more fully discussed in the next section). The federal court system also has certain special courts that hear either trial or appellate matters on special topics, called subject matter. For example, the federal court system has special bankruptcy, tax, and federal claims courts of original (trial) jurisdiction. It has special appellate courts for veterans' claims and armed forces cases.

The highest level of appeal in the federal court system is the U.S. Supreme Court. The **U.S. Supreme Court** is the highest federal court in the United States. The U.S. Supreme Court is composed of nine justices. According to the Constitution, each justice is appointed via nomination by the president and confirmation by the Senate. Supreme Court justices are appointed

for life. One of the nine justices is appointed the head of the court, or the **chief justice**. As chief justice, he is the highest federal judicial officer in the United States. The other Supreme Court justices are called associate justices.

As discussed in the next section, the U.S. Supreme Court mainly has appellate jurisdiction, meaning that it adjudicates cases on appeal from lower courts. However, in a few types of

FIGURE
4-1   **The Federal Court System**

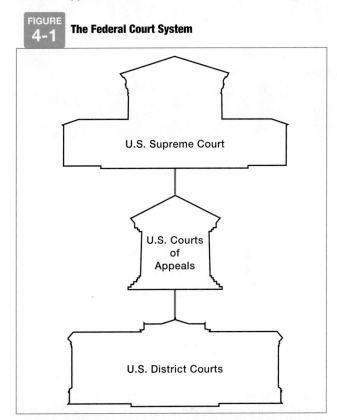

Federal Judges and Justices

Federal judges and justices are appointed via nomination by the president and confirmation by the Senate. They are appointed for life.

Judges presiding over appellate courts are sometimes called "justices," including those presiding over the U.S. Supreme Court.

U.S. district courts are federal trial courts.

U.S. courts of appeals are the 13 circuit courts of intermediate appeal within the federal court system; they are also called **circuit courts** or **U.S. circuit courts of appeals**.

The **U.S. Supreme Court** is the highest federal court in the United States.

The **chief justice** is the head of the U.S. Supreme Court and the highest federal judicial officer in the United States.

KEY **Point**

Levels of the Federal Court System

The federal court system has trial courts, called U.S. district courts; intermediate appellate courts, called U.S. courts of appeals (also known as circuit courts); and the U.S. Supreme Court.

© Konstantin L/Shutterstock

cases the Supreme Court has original (trial court) jurisdiction, as discussed in the next section.

How does a case reach the Supreme Court? If a person wants to bring a case before the U.S. Supreme Court, she has to petition the Court, asking it to review her case. There is no automatic right to present one's case to the Supreme Court.

In asking permission, a party files a petition for *certiorari*. A **petition for *certiorari*** is a petition brought by a party asking the U.S. Supreme Court to hear a case. At least four of the nine justices must approve any petition for the Court to agree to hear the case—this requirement is called the "**rule of four**." If fewer than four justices approve a petition, then the petition is denied, and the case will not be heard by the Supreme Court. Most petitions meet this fate. However, if four or more justices approve a petition, then the Court will issue a writ of *certiorari*. A **writ of *certiorari*** is an order by the Supreme Court formally accepting a party's petition to hear a case. In effect, the writ asks the lower court to send over the record of the case, for the Supreme Court's review and ultimate adjudication.

As mentioned in the previous section, each state and the District of Columbia have their own court systems, and these systems vary from state to state. In fact, no two state court systems are identical. However, like the federal court system, the state court systems use a tiered model of organization. Also like the federal courts, they have courts that hear a variety of types of cases and certain special courts that hear particular types of cases.

The lowest level of state court is sometimes called an inferior court. Juvenile court, divorce court, probate court, traffic court, police court, magistrate court, municipal court, justice of the peace court, small claims court, and county court are examples. These courts handle minor civil and/or criminal matters. The

Is There a Right to Be Heard by the U.S. Supreme Court?

There is no automatic right to bring one's case to the U.S. Supreme Court. The Court exercises discretion in choosing the cases it will adjudicate (hear).

proceedings in these courts often are quite informal. Legal representation (attorneys) may, or may not, be used by the parties.

More serious civil and criminal cases in the state court system are heard in higher level trial courts called a variety of names, such as district courts, circuit courts, or superior courts. These courts are presided over by one judge, who may be appointed or elected. Normally these courts are organized by county. While they may hear appeals from the inferior courts, the primary function of these courts is to exercise original jurisdiction (discussed thoroughly in the next section) over civil and criminal cases. It is at this court level where trials are conducted, juries are used, and attorneys make opening statements, introduce evidence, and make closing arguments.

As just noted, the trial court level is the level in the state court system where juries are used. The judge, with the assistance of a jury in a jury trial, renders a decision on each case before the court. In a jury trial, the jury decides questions of fact and applies facts to the law provided by the judge in the jury instructions. Judges decide questions of law. However, in bench trials, judges decide all questions—of fact and of law. Remember from the study of constitutional law that there is a constitutional right to trial by jury that applies to most cases—to criminal cases and to civil cases where more than $20 in money damages is requested. However, the right to jury trial can be waived by the parties.

Every state has at least one level of appellate court review. Remember that appellate courts review the decisions of lower courts. Appellate courts do not retry cases—so they do not make findings of fact, nor do they review findings of fact unless such findings were clearly erroneous, meaning wholly unsupported by

A **petition for *certiorari*** is a petition brought by a party asking the U.S. Supreme Court to hear a case.

The **rule of four** is the requirement that at least four of the nine Supreme Court justices must approve any petition for *certiorari* for the Court to agree to hear the case.

A **writ of *certiorari*** is an order by the Supreme Court formally accepting a party's petition to hear a case.

Use of Juries

Remember that juries are used in both the federal and state court systems, but only in the trial court level, where findings of fact are made.

the evidence presented at the trial. In appellate review, appellate courts mainly are looking for errors of law committed at the trial court level.

For states with an intermediate level of appeal, there also is a higher appellate court. About 75 percent of the states have intermediate courts of appeal. For states with only one level of appeal (the other 25 percent or so) that appellate level is the state's highest court. The highest court in a state often is called the supreme court. However, some states call their highest court something else—in Maryland, the highest court is called the Court of Appeals, for example.

As discussed earlier, on appeal, a panel of three or more judges reviews the record of the case from the lower court.

The record will include such materials as the trial transcript, pleadings, and exhibits. In addition, the judges will review appellate briefs submitted by the parties, arguing their positions on appeal. The judges will hear oral arguments from the parties' counsel regarding their briefs as well as pose questions to counsel, asking them, for example, to clarify or further support their positions. Keep in mind that appellate court judges mainly are looking for errors of law committed by the lower courts. In their rulings, appellate courts can affirm, modify, or reverse trial court rulings, and may remand cases for further proceedings in the trial court. For a few types of cases, such as cases involving elections, appellate courts may exercise original jurisdiction and hear cases for the first time.

Can parties appeal to the U.S. Supreme Court from a state supreme court? Only in certain situations. A decision from the highest appellate court in a state is a final one. It cannot be appealed to the U.S. Supreme Court unless it involves an issue of federal law, for the federal courts hear different types of cases than do the state courts. What kinds of cases the different courts can hear is examined next.

FIGURE 4-2 **The State Court Systems**

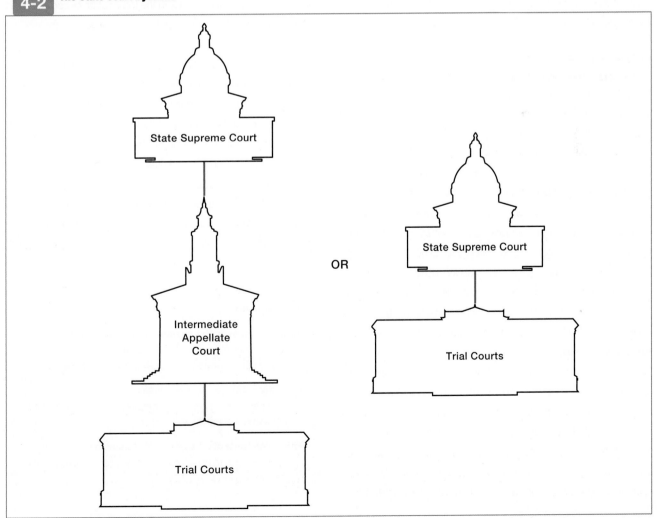

State Supreme Court

Intermediate Appellate Court

Trial Courts

OR

State Supreme Court

Trial Courts

TYPES OF CASES DIFFERENT COURTS ADJUDICATE

For a specific court to hear a case, it must have jurisdiction. **Jurisdiction** means the power of a court to hear a case. The term "jurisdiction" comes from two Latin words—"*juris*", meaning "the law" and "*dicere*", meaning "to speak." Combined, then, jurisdiction is Latin for "to speak the law."

There are three types of jurisdiction: jurisdiction over the person, jurisdiction over the property, and jurisdiction over the subject matter of the case. Each of these is discussed in turn.

Jurisdiction over the person means the court has the power to adjudicate a matter involving this person. It is also called **personal jurisdiction** or *in personam* **jurisdiction**. The general rule on jurisdiction over the person is that a court can exercise personal jurisdiction over residents of a certain geographic area. For a U.S. district court, it means persons within that geographic district. For a state trial court, it usually means residents of that county. More specifically, personal jurisdiction is found where the people involved in the litigation are present in the state or are legal residents of the state in which the lawsuit has been filed, or if the transaction at issue has a substantial connection to the state.

KEY Point

General Rule on Personal Jurisdiction

A court can exercise personal jurisdiction over residents of a certain geographic area.

Consider this example regarding personal jurisdiction. What if, while driving to work in Baltimore County, you are injured in a car accident caused by the negligence of another driver who is visiting Baltimore from Dade County, Florida. Do you have to go to Dade County, Florida, to sue for the injuries you sustained because the defendant is from that county? Fortunately, you do not, for that would be inconvenient for you, a person who works in Baltimore County.

Though the general rule on personal jurisdiction is that a court has jurisdiction over *residents* of its geographic area, states have expanded this to reach certain nonresidents. States have enacted **long arm statutes** to allow their courts to exercise personal jurisdiction over nonresident defendants who have "minimum contacts" with the state. **Minimum contacts** is a test applied under the states' long arm statutes to determine if it is fair for a court to exercise jurisdiction over a nonresident defendant. Note that nonresident defendants can be people, but they can also be legal entities, such as corporations. Minimum contacts must arise from some act by which the defendant

CASE *on* POINT

Gomez v. Aragon, 705 F. Supp. 2d 21 (D.D.C. 2010).

The U.S. District Court, District of Columbia, quoting the famous U.S. Supreme Court case of *Int'l Shoe Co. v. Washington*, said that in establishing personal jurisdiction over a nonresident defendant, the issue is whether a defendant's minimum contacts with the forum state establish that maintaining the action "does not offend traditional notions of fair play and substantial justice."

purposefully avails himself of the privilege of conducting activities within the forum state (the state in which the court sits), thereby invoking the benefits and protections of the forum state's law. For example, he may own property in the forum state or commit a tort in the forum state. The test has been interpreted by the courts, including the U.S. Supreme Court, to be whether it is fair for a court to exercise jurisdiction over a defendant because the defendant's contacts with the forum state are such that the defendant could reasonably expect to be brought into court in that state. Further, courts require that the exercise of jurisdiction over nonresident defendants not offend traditional notions of fair play and substantial justice (see the Case on Point).

Reconsider the earlier example of the traffic accident. According to a state's long arm statute, you could sue the defendant for negligence in Baltimore County, where the accident occurred. This is true even though the defendant is a resident of

Jurisdiction is the power of a court to hear a case.

Jurisdiction over the person means the court has the power to adjudicate a matter involving this person; it is also called **personal jurisdiction** or *in personam* **jurisdiction**.

Long arm statutes are state statutes that allow courts to exercise personal jurisdiction over nonresident defendants who have "minimum contacts" with the state.

Minimum contacts is a test applied under the states' long arm statutes to determine if it is fair for a court to exercise jurisdiction over a nonresident defendant.

Minimum Contacts

Minimum contacts must arise from some act through which the defendant purposefully avails himself of the privilege of conducting activities with the forum state. This invokes the protections and benefits of that forum state's law. Accordingly, the defendant's conduct and his connection with the forum state are sufficient that he should reasonably anticipate being "haled" into court there.

Dade County, Florida. So the defendant would have to come to Baltimore County to defend the suit—perhaps giving him incentive to settle the dispute because of the inconvenience and cost involved in defending a lawsuit in another state. Remember that the minimum contacts test is used by a court in one state to exercise personal jurisdiction over a defendant who is a resident of another state (a nonresident defendant).

What if a civil dispute is about the ownership of a parcel of real estate or a car? When does a court have jurisdiction over real or personal property?

Jurisdiction over the property means the court has the power to adjudicate a matter involving certain property. It is also called *in rem* **jurisdiction**. A court has jurisdiction over property when the property that is the subject matter of the dispute is located within the court's boundaries. Note that the property can be real or personal property (real property is land and anything permanently attached to it, such as a building; personal property is all property that is not real property). For example, if a resident of Maryland and a resident of Florida dispute title to a farm located in Lancaster County, Pennsylvania, a state trial court in Lancaster County would have jurisdiction over that property and could adjudicate that case.

Can all courts hear property title disputes or negligence cases? Can they all adjudicate criminal prosecutions or patent litigation? No, they cannot. What types of cases specific courts can hear is a matter of subject matter jurisdiction.

Jurisdiction over the subject matter of a case, also called **subject matter jurisdiction**, is the power of a court to hear a certain type of case—such as a criminal prosecution, a negligence lawsuit, a small claims matter, or a patent infringement lawsuit. It is authority over the subject matter of the legal issues involved in the case. Jurisdiction over the subject matter deals with the nature of the claim or controversy involved.

Many courts are courts of general jurisdiction. A court having **general jurisdiction** can adjudicate a wide variety of types of cases, including both civil and criminal cases. Some courts are courts of limited jurisdiction. A court having **limited jurisdiction**

can adjudicate only certain types of cases, such as traffic violations, bankruptcy matters, tax matters, small claims, family matters, misdemeanor crimes, or probate matters. Who determines what types of cases a court is authorized to hear?

Courts are created either by constitution or statute. The constitution or statute that creates the court also defines the court's subject matter jurisdiction. Subject matter jurisdiction can be limited in a variety of ways. For example, the constitution or statute creating a court can limit its subject matter jurisdiction based on the subject matter of the lawsuit, such as probate matters or tax claims. It may limit the court's subject matter jurisdiction based on whether a prosecution is of a misdemeanor or a felony charge. It may limit the court's subject matter jurisdiction based on the amount of money in controversy (meaning the amount of damages asked for) in the lawsuit. It may limit the court's subject matter jurisdiction based on whether the legal proceeding is a trial or an appeal.

It is important to distinguish the jurisdiction of trial courts and the jurisdiction of appellate courts. Trial courts hear cases for the first time. Where a right to jury trial exists and has not been waived, these proceedings are the ones that use juries. Trial courts have original jurisdiction. **Original jurisdiction** is the power of a court to hear a case for the first time. Remember our discussions in the previous chapter regarding civil and

Types of Limitations on a Court's Subject Matter Jurisdiction

- The subject matter of the lawsuit.
- The nature of the criminal charge—misdemeanor or felony.
- The amount in controversy in the lawsuit.
- Whether the legal proceeding is a trial or an appeal.

Jurisdiction over the property means the court has the power to adjudicate a matter involving property located within its boundaries; it is also called *in rem* **jurisdiction**.

Jurisdiction over the subject matter of a case means the court has the power to adjudicate a legal matter of this type; it is also called **subject matter jurisdiction**.

General jurisdiction means the power of a court to adjudicate a wide variety of types of cases, including both civil and criminal cases.

Limited jurisdiction means the power of a court to adjudicate only certain types of cases, such as tax matters or probate matters.

Original jurisdiction is the power of a court to hear a case for the first time.

© s44/ZUMA Press/Newscom

criminal procedure and the process of appeal. Verdicts made by trial courts may be appealed to appellate courts.

Appellate courts have appellate jurisdiction. **Appellate jurisdiction** is the power of a court to review a decision from a lower court. Appellate courts are comprised of a panel of judges, rather than one judge presiding over a trial court proceeding. Further, juries are not used in appellate courts.

Earlier in the chapter, we explained the federal and state court systems. Let us look at each of those systems and consider what types of cases can be heard at each level of each system. We will begin with an examination of the jurisdiction of the federal courts.

Remember that the trial courts in the federal court system, the courts of original jurisdiction in the federal court system, are the U.S. district courts. Within limits set by the U.S. Constitution and the Congress, U.S. district courts have jurisdiction to hear nearly all categories of federal cases, both civil and criminal in nature. U.S. district courts adjudicate two main types of cases: federal questions and diversity cases. **Federal questions** are cases that involve, at least in part, an alleged violation of the U.S. Constitution or other law of the United States (such as a federal statute), or a treaty to which the United States is a party. Examples of federal questions include patent, copyright, and bankruptcy matters. **Diversity cases**, also called **diversity of citizenship cases**, are cases that involve lawsuits between citizens of different states, between citizens and foreign countries, and between citizens and non-U.S. citizens. The most common type of diversity case is that involving citizens from different states. Note that, similar to the use of the term "persons" in the law, the term "citizens" means both humans and legal entities. In terms of its residence, a corporation is considered a citizen of the state in which it is incorporated as well as the state in which its principal place of business (its headquarters) is located. For example, The Coca-Cola Company was incorporated in Delaware, but its world headquarters is located in Georgia; Coca-Cola, then, is a citizen of Delaware and Georgia.

In addition to the diverse citizenship requirement, for diversity jurisdiction to exist, there must be an amount in controversy and that amount in controversy must be at least $75,000 (which amount changes by law from time to time, but not often). Note that in cases where an equitable remedy, not a legal one, is sought, such as an injunction rather than damages, there is no amount in controversy. Accordingly, diversity of citizenship would not apply.

Consider the negligence case mentioned above (the one between you and the resident of Dade County, Florida). Assume you were not alone in the car, but were with your family as well. All of you were injured and your expensive, luxury car was destroyed. You seek damages in the amount of $600,000. Can you bring your case to federal court? Yes, you can. You are a resident of Maryland and the defendant is a resident of Florida—so you are citizens from different states. Since the amount in controversy exceeds $75,000, you may bring your case in federal court. Do you have to bring your case in federal court, or could you choose state court?

Courts may have jurisdiction that is exclusive or concurrent. **Exclusive jurisdiction** exists where a court has exclusive authority over a subject matter or territory, meaning it is the only court authorized to adjudicate the matter. **Concurrent jurisdiction** exists where a court has shared jurisdiction with another court or

KEY Point

Two Types of Federal Subject Matter Jurisdiction
- Federal questions
- Diversity of citizenship

Appellate jurisdiction is the power of a court to review a decision from a lower court.

Federal questions are cases involving, at least in part, an alleged violation of the U.S. Constitution or other law of the United States (such as a federal statute), or a treaty to which the United States is a party.

Diversity cases are cases that involve lawsuits between citizens of different states, between citizens and foreign countries, and between citizens and non-U.S. citizens where there is an amount in controversy of at least $75,000; they are also called **diversity of citizenship cases**.

Exclusive jurisdiction exists where a court has exclusive authority over a subject matter or territory, meaning it is the only court authorized to adjudicate the matter.

Concurrent jurisdiction exists where a court has shared jurisdiction with another court or other courts; more than one court has authority to adjudicate the matter.

Schrock v. Learning Curve Int'l Inc., 586 F.3d 513 (7th Cir. 2009).

Discussed in Chapter 3 as an example of case law, this is also an example of a case involving a federal question and the subject matter jurisdiction of the federal courts. The case involved a professional photographer who sued the owner of a copyright in characters upon which some children's toys were based as well as the licensee that produced the toys. The legal claim asserted by the photographer alleged copyright infringement—the infringement of the photographer's claimed copyright in the photographs the licensee hired the photographer to take. This is because the photographer's photographs of the copyrighted works (the toys) may constitute a derivative work, which may also be copyrightable (by the photographer, in this case).

Copyright law originates in Article 1, Section 8, Clause 8, of the U.S. Constitution. This is known as the Copyright Clause. The Copyright Clause permits Congress to enact legislation regarding copyrights. Congress did this via federal statute, in the Copyright Act. Case law helps to interpret this statute.

This case is an example of a case involving copyright law, which is exclusively federal law. Therefore, the case involves a federal question. Accordingly, federal courts have jurisdiction to hear this case (and only federal courts, not state courts, for federal courts have exclusive jurisdiction in cases involving copyright infringement).

---

other courts. In other words, more than one court has authority to adjudicate the matter.

Federal questions fall within the subject matter jurisdiction of the federal court system. Unless the subject matter falls within the exclusive jurisdiction of the federal courts according to the law establishing the court (copyright cases and bankruptcy cases are two examples of exclusive subject matter jurisdiction in the federal courts), state courts may hear federal question cases as well. Federal questions may be brought in federal court. Diversity cases fall within the concurrent jurisdiction of the federal and state courts. When jurisdiction is shared between federal and state courts, the plaintiff can choose the forum in which to bring a case. This is called **forum shopping**, where a plaintiff in a case involving concurrent jurisdiction has the option to file suit in state or federal court, depending on which forum she feels is more beneficial to her. Factors a plaintiff may consider in selecting a court, when facing that choice, include which forum will more likely be sympathetic to the claim, which court will get the dispute to trial faster, how the law is applied in each court, how familiar the lawyer is with that court and its procedures, whether a procedure used in only one of the courts provides an advantage over the other party, and what results have been reached in similar cases in that court.

Reconsider the negligence case example. If juries in the state courts in Baltimore County, Maryland, are known to be very compassionate toward injured plaintiffs and known to award large personal injury judgments, you may opt to sue in state court rather than federal court when you bring your

KEY Point

Questions to Consider in Forum Shopping

- Which forum is more likely to be sympathetic to your claim?
- Which court will get you to trial more quickly (assuming you do not want delay)?
- How is the law applied in each court?
- Is your lawyer familiar with each court and its procedures?
- Does a procedure available in only one of the courts offer you an advantage over the other party?
- What have the results been in each court in similar cases?

negligence claim. That is forum shopping, arising out of the existence of concurrent jurisdiction.

Taking into consideration both federal questions and diversity cases, then, U.S. district courts adjudicate cases alleging violations of the U.S. Constitution or other federal laws, maritime law disputes, cases directly involving a state or the federal government, and cases in which foreign governments, non-U.S. citizens, or citizens from different states are involved.

> **Forum shopping** is where the plaintiff in a case involving concurrent jurisdiction has the option to file suit in state or federal court, depending on which forum she feels is more beneficial to her.

Harper v. Maverick Recording Co, 131 S. Ct. 590 (2010).

The U.S. Supreme Court heard this petition for *certiorari* out of the U.S. Court of Appeals for the Fifth Circuit. The case involved a 16-year-old girl who was found to have infringed the Maverick Recording Company's copyrights by downloading digital music files.

The main issue in the case was whether and how a particular section of the Copyright Act (§402(d)) applied to the case in terms of whether the infringer was an "innocent" infringer because these were digital files, which, unlike phonorecord technology, do not physically bear a copyright notice. The Fifth Circuit ruled that the innocent infringer defense did not apply because the recording company provided proper copyright notice on each of its works (the phonorecords from which the digital files were taken and made available through file-sharing), and the girl had access to the phonorecords. Further, the Fifth Circuit ruled that the infringer need not actually see a material object with a copyright notice on it, but rather it is enough that the infringer could have ascertained that the work was copyrighted.

The petition for *certiorari* was denied by the Supreme Court. The most important reason given by the Court for the denial of the petition for *certiorari* was that there was no present conflict among the Circuits on the interpretation of §402(d) of the Copyright Act.

The intermediate level of appeal in the federal court system, as discussed earlier in this chapter, is the U.S. courts of appeals. These courts hear appeals from their respective districts. In addition, U.S. courts of appeals have original jurisdiction in cases involving a challenge to an order of a federal administrative agency, such as the Environmental Protection Agency or the Securities and Exchange Commission.

The U.S. Supreme Court may review decisions made by the U.S. courts of appeals. It may also hear appeals from the highest appellate courts in the state system (usually called the state supreme courts) if a constitutional or other federal issue is involved. Remember that the U.S. Supreme Court has discretion to pick and choose which cases it wishes to hear on appeal. It tends to choose cases that involve important constitutional issues and cases on which other courts are divided (see the Case on Point).

Also, in a very few types of cases, the Supreme Court has original jurisdiction to hear cases for the first time. For example, a case between two U.S. states can be heard for the first time by the Supreme Court. These suits may involve disputes regarding boundary lines, water claims, and other property issues. As another example, a case involving a high-ranking diplomat from another nation can be heard for the first time by the Supreme Court.

In addition to these federal courts, the federal court system has certain other courts that handle only particular types of disputes. There are U.S. Bankruptcy Courts that have exclusive jurisdiction over all bankruptcy cases, as bankruptcy is federal law only (there is no state bankruptcy law). The U.S. Court of International Trade adjudicates cases involving U.S. trade with foreign countries as well as customs issues. The U.S. Court of Federal Claims adjudicates claims for money damages made against the U.S. government, federal contract disputes, and disputes regarding the "taking" of land by the federal government under its power of eminent domain. There is a U.S. Tax Court handling federal taxation cases. On the appellate level, the Court of Appeals for Veterans' Claims and the U.S. Court of Appeals for the Armed Forces are other examples of specialized federal courts with limited subject matter jurisdiction. Note that special judges serve on these special courts; but unlike other federal judges, they do not serve for life terms.

Terms of Appointment for Federal Judges

Judges on the U.S. district courts, the U.S. courts of appeals, and the U.S. Supreme Court are appointed for life terms. They are appointed by the president and confirmed by the Senate.

Judges on the special federal courts do not serve for life terms. For example, judges on the U.S. Bankruptcy Courts are appointed by a majority of judges on the U.S. courts of appeals and for 14-year terms. How many are appointed is determined by Congress.

Snyder v. Phelps, 131 S. Ct. 1207 (2011).

In this case, attorneys for the fundamentalist Westboro Baptist Church in Topeka, Kansas, argued that the church members' carrying of offensive signs and demonstrating outside of military funerals was protected speech under the First Amendment to the U.S. Constitution. Church members picketed military funerals, carrying signs with messages reading "Thank God for Dead Soldiers," "God Hates the U.S.A.," "You're Going to Hell," and "God Hates Fags," as examples.

Albert Snyder sued the church for the tort of intentional infliction of emotional distress, among other claims, after its members picketed the funeral of his 20-year-old son, Lance Corporal Matthew Snyder, who died in a Humvee accident in 2006 while serving military duty in Iraq. In addition to picketing the funeral, the protestors posted a poem on the church's website entitled "The Burden of Marine Lance Cpl. Matthew Snyder." The poem was addressed to Lance Corporal Snyder's parents and said, among other things, "They taught him to support the largest pedophile machine in the history of the entire world, the Roman Catholic monstrosity." At trial, Snyder won an $11 million judgment against the church, which was later reduced by a judge to $5 million. The case was eventually appealed to the U.S. Supreme Court.

The underlying issue presented by this case was how much protection private figures should have against hurtful, outrageous, and insulting speech. The case required the Court to balance the interests of the father, who suffered additional emotional pain because of the protestors' actions, against the protestors' right of free speech. Such a legal issue, one involving the First Amendment to the U.S. Constitution, is a type of case the Supreme Court may hear at its discretion.

Ultimately, in this case the Court ruled that the actions of the church were entitled to First Amendment protection, so the church was shielded from tort liability for its picketing actions. The Court reasoned, in part, that "speech is powerful. It can stir people to action, move them to tears of both joy and sorrow, and—as it did here—inflict great pain." The Court further reasoned that it could not react to the pain by punishing the speaker. "As a Nation we have chosen a different course—to protect even hurtful speech on public issues to ensure that we do not stifle public debate," the Court stated.

Now we will review subject matter jurisdiction in the state courts. State trial courts have either general or limited subject matter jurisdiction. Whether a specific court is one of general or limited subject matter jurisdiction is determined by what is authorized in the state statute creating each court. Many state trial courts have general jurisdiction and can adjudicate a wide variety of both civil and criminal matters. Some of the inferior state trial courts are special courts with limited subject matter jurisdiction. They have authority to adjudicate in certain specialty areas of law. Examples include juvenile courts, divorce courts, probate courts, traffic courts, justice of the peace courts, misdemeanor crimes courts, police courts, magistrate courts, and municipal courts. In addition, they may be authorized to hear certain types of cases, such as small claims, where the amount in controversy is less than a statutorily set maximum, such as $5,000. At least one state court has subject matter jurisdiction to adjudicate any type of controversy that can be heard in state court. Additionally, state courts are presumed to have the power to hear virtually any claim arising under federal or state law except those claims that fall under the exclusive jurisdiction of the federal courts (such as copyright and bankruptcy cases).

Now that we have examined the types of cases that different courts can hear, we will review the process of resolving a legal dispute through the court system via litigation.

Small Claims Court

Small claims courts are state courts that, by statute, have authority to hear claims involving small amounts of money, ranging from $1,000 to $5,000, depending on state law.

RESOLVING LEGAL DISPUTES THROUGH LITIGATION

Litigation is the process of carrying on a civil lawsuit. In the previous chapter we examined the civil law system and civil procedure. We will summarize that process again now.

First, a client often seeks legal representation for help adjudicating her claim. Once represented, her attorney initiates the lawsuit by filing a complaint and having it, along with the court's summons, served on the defendant. The defendant usually files an answer to the plaintiff's complaint and perhaps makes counterclaims and/or cross-claims. The defendant may make a motion to dismiss the complaint; both parties may make a motion for judgment on the pleadings or a motion for summary judgment. If the case is not resolved through motions or settlement, discovery is conducted. One of the most time-consuming and expensive processes in civil litigation is the discovery process. Before trial, a pretrial conference is conducted by the judge assigned to the case and attended by each party's attorney. If the case does not settle, it proceeds to trial.

At trial, a jury is selected if a right to jury trial exists and has not been waived by the parties. Attorneys for the parties make opening statements. Then they present their evidence. The defendant's counsel may make a motion for directed verdict after the close of the plaintiff's case—meaning after all of the plaintiff's evidence has been presented. If the motion for directed verdict is not granted, the defendant presents his evidence. After the presentation of all evidence, attorneys for the parties make closing arguments. The judge then instructs the jury on the relevant law. The jury retires to deliberate and to reach a verdict. Once the verdict is rendered, the jury is dismissed. The losing party may file a motion for judgment notwithstanding the verdict and/or a motion for a new trial. If a party wins a judgment, it must enforce that judgment to collect it. Either party may appeal the verdict.

© Stockbyte/Getty Images

To bring a lawsuit, from beginning to end, takes months, if not years. It is not a quick process. In addition, litigation is a very expensive process. Not only is it customary and advisable to engage legal counsel, for which legal fees normally must be paid, but costs associated with the litigation process, especially discovery, can be enormous. Further, the process of litigation is public, not private. Litigation is an adversarial process. It pits two opposing sides against one another. The goal is winning rather than the pursuit of justice. Whether a jury or bench trial is conducted, the outcome of litigation is never predictable or controllable. Though the outcome is not predictable or controllable, however, litigation will resolve the dispute—one way or the other.

Given the disadvantages of litigation as a means of resolving legal disputes, what alternatives are there? Alternative dispute resolution is examined next.

KEY Point

Advantages and Disadvantages of Litigation as a Means of Resolving Legal Disputes

\+ will resolve the dispute

– time-consuming

– expensive

– public, not private, proceeding

– adversarial process

– outcome not predictable or controllable

Litigation is the process of carrying on a civil lawsuit.

ALTERNATIVE DISPUTE RESOLUTION (ADR)

Alternative dispute resolution (ADR) is the resolution of legal disputes in ways other than the traditional judicial process—litigation. The vast majority of legal disputes are resolved through settlement. While the congestion of court dockets makes it seem like there is way too much litigation—and maybe there is—the vast majority of cases never go to trial. Settlement of cases is achieved through a method of alternative dispute resolution.

There are many forms of alternative dispute resolution. The three most common are negotiation, mediation, and arbitration. Each method has advantages and disadvantages, just as litigation as a form of legal dispute resolution does. We will now examine each of these methods, define them, and discuss their respective advantages and disadvantages.

Negotiation is a process where the parties to a legal dispute informally communicate, themselves or via their attorneys, to discuss possible settlement of their legal dispute. Negotiation can be conducted in person, over the telephone, or through correspondence (using letters or electronic technology—e-mail).

The skill of negotiation will be discussed in Chapter 11. Note that while the parties may negotiate with each other directly, they often negotiate through their attorneys. That task typically is not delegated to paralegals. Remember that legal ethics rules prohibit one party's attorney from directly negotiating with the other party if that other party is represented by counsel. Either the parties should negotiate directly or their lawyers should negotiate with each other on behalf of the parties.

© Image Source/Alamy

If the parties reach settlement through negotiation, they enter into a settlement agreement to evidence the terms and conditions of their resolution. A **settlement agreement** is a contract that evidences the terms and conditions of the resolution of a legal dispute. A sample settlement agreement was provided in Chapter 3.

There are many advantages to using negotiation to resolve a legal dispute. One is that the process is very quick. Negotiation can be performed at any time. It can also be performed over and over again.

Negotiation is inexpensive. Lawyers are not necessary for it, though they can be useful. Many lawyers are skilled and experienced negotiators, used to working in an adversarial system.

Unlike litigation, negotiation is a private process. It is not subject to public scrutiny. It takes place in the presence of the parties and perhaps their attorneys.

Parties to the dispute can predict and control the outcome when negotiation is used. They know the outcome because they, or their attorneys, negotiate it. They do not agree to a

KEY **Point**

Three Main Types of ADR

- negotiation
- mediation
- arbitration

proposed resolution or term of settlement if it is not favorable enough. This is unlike litigation, where the judge and jury, not the parties, control the outcome.

The major disadvantage to negotiation as a form of alternative dispute resolution is that it may not resolve the legal dispute. Some parties simply cannot agree on how to settle a legal dispute. No degree of negotiation will get them to agreement. Those parties must litigate their dispute in order to resolve it; they will not resolve it themselves. Accordingly, they must let someone else, namely a jury or judge, render the decision on how their dispute is resolved.

KEY Point

Advantages and Disadvantages of Negotiation
+ quick
+ inexpensive
+ private, not public
+ can predict and control the outcome
− may not resolve the dispute

Another major form of alternative dispute resolution is mediation. **Mediation** is a nonadversarial process where a neutral third party, called a **mediator**, facilitates communications between parties to a legal dispute to help them resolve it. It is sometimes called "assisted negotiation" because it is very similar to the ADR method of negotiation. However, with mediation, a neutral third person assists the parties, who may or may not be represented by counsel at the mediation, to communicate in an attempt to reach an agreement. Because of its effectiveness in resolving disputes, some courts require parties to submit to mediation before their cases can be tried in court.

Mediation has several advantages. Because mediation is a nonadversarial process, it is a dispute resolution method that may be more pleasant for parties to participate in compared to litigation.

> *Mediation is usually the preferred method [of ADR], and finding a good and fair mediator is crucial to the outcome. The result you seek is one favorable to all parties and avoids the high cost of trial.*
> Christine Rentz

KEY Point

Advantages and Disadvantages of Mediation
+ quick
+ inexpensive
+ nonadversarial
+ private, not public
+ can predict and control the outcome
− may not resolve the dispute

In addition, mediation is inexpensive and quick compared to litigation. While mediation may be more expensive than negotiation if attorneys are present or because the mediator is paid a fee, it is less expensive than litigation. The mediation process normally takes hours, not the months or years that litigation takes. That said, scheduling the mediation and going through the process, while quick, takes more time than simple negotiation between the parties or their attorneys.

Like negotiation, mediation is a private process. With the exception of the mediator's presence, the process involves only the parties, and their attorneys if their representation at mediation is requested.

Also like negotiation, the outcome of the process is predictable and controllable. The parties agree to the terms and conditions of the settlement of their dispute. No one else decides the outcome for them, including the mediator.

The disadvantage of mediation as a form of ADR is the same as it is for negotiation. Mediation may not resolve the dispute. There is no guarantee that even with the help of a mediator the parties will be able to reach settlement terms. Rather, the dispute must be put in the hands of someone else, namely a jury or judge, to render a decision that resolves the dispute.

The final major form of alternative dispute resolution is arbitration. **Arbitration** is an out-of-court process where parties submit their legal dispute to a neutral third party or parties for

Mediation is a nonadversarial process where a neutral third party facilitates communications between parties to a legal dispute to help them resolve it.

A **mediator** is a neutral third party who conducts a mediation session.

Arbitration is an out-of-court process where parties submit their legal dispute to a neutral third party or parties, called an arbitrator or arbitration panel, who hears evidence and renders an award.

resolution. Either one arbitrator or an arbitration panel presides over the arbitration proceedings. The parties, who may or may not be represented by counsel, submit evidence in a more informal process than a trial in court. The process is an adversarial one, similar in that way to a trial. The evidence is considered by the arbitrator or arbitration panel in rendering a decision. The decision of the arbitrator or arbitration panel is called an **award**. Arbitration awards usually are enforced by the courts. However, an arbitration award can be set aside by a court where, for instance, the arbitrator exceeded his authority, where he acted in bad faith, or where he was biased against one party.

An arbitration award may or may not be legally binding. Whether an arbitration award is binding depends on the parties' agreement as to whether or not they want to be bound by it. Parties can agree on whether or not to accept nonbinding arbitration awards. Binding arbitration awards can be appealed to the appropriate court system for review, but on very limited grounds, such as for arbitrator misconduct or when the arbitrator acted beyond the scope of his authority.

Arbitration may be voluntary or compelled. More and more, parties include arbitration provisions in their contracts in terms of voluntary submission to arbitration, agreeing to submit to arbitration any dispute that arises under the contract. In an arbitration provision, the parties can also set forth the forum for arbitration, identify the arbitrator(s), and agree to the rules and procedures to be followed in conducting the arbitration. Some courts compel arbitration in certain cases, requiring the parties to submit their dispute to arbitration. Usually when arbitration is compelled by a court, however, the arbitration award is nonbinding. A party dissatisfied with the arbitration award can then have the dispute litigated at trial. Some laws compel arbitration as well. For example, federal statute requires binding arbitration in federal labor management agreements, though parties to the agreements may negotiate the terms and conditions pursuant to which the arbitration is conducted. Further, many consumer contracts today compel arbitration, though it may not be binding on a consumer who does not like the outcome.

Arbitration is a commonly used ADR method for commercial disputes. It is especially popular outside the United States. Arbitration is often used to resolve legal disputes in other countries as well as disputes involving international commercial transactions.

As with negotiation and mediation, there are advantages and disadvantages to arbitration as a form of ADR. Though informal compared to litigation, arbitration is a more formal method of ADR compared to negotiation and mediation.

The American Arbitration Association

The American Arbitration Association (AAA) is a nonprofit organization that is a major provider of ADR services. It has offices throughout the United States.

Other nonprofit and many for-profit organizations also provide ADR services, including the popular for-profit provider JAMS/Endispute.

Arbitration is cheaper and quicker than litigation. However, it is neither as cheap nor as quick as either negotiation or mediation.

Like negotiation and mediation, arbitration is private. While witnesses and arbitrators are present at arbitration proceedings, the public is not. Only the parties and their attorneys, along with the arbitrators and any witnesses, are present.

In terms of disadvantages, unlike the ADR methods of negotiation and mediation, a party cannot predict or control the outcome in arbitration. Similar to a trial with a jury and/or judge, a neutral third party or parties (the arbitrator or arbitration panel) renders an award. The rendering of that award is out of the parties' control.

Further, like the other main forms of ADR, arbitration may not resolve the dispute. If the award is nonbinding, the parties are not bound by the decision and may resort to litigation to resolve the dispute. Even if the award is binding, the parties may appeal it to the courts for review, but the basis for appeal is limited.

While we have discussed the three major forms of alternative dispute resolution—the ones often used in the United States today—there are other forms of ADR. Some of these include conciliation (where a third party conciliator is used by

KEY Point

Advantages and Disadvantages of Arbitration

+ quick
+ inexpensive
+ private, not public
+ informal process
− cannot predict or control the outcome
− may not resolve the dispute

An **award** is the decision made by the arbitrator or arbitration panel.

the parties to a dispute to help them build a positive relationship); cooperative problem-solving (where the parties work together to resolve an issue of mutual concern); dispute panels (where an impartial panel helps to clarify misperceptions, gathers missing information, and reviews conflicting facts to suggest to the parties ways to resolve their dispute); early neutral case evaluation (where an impartial third party provides a nonbinding evaluation of the strengths and weaknesses of each side's case—this process is used in many U.S. district courts); facilitation (where a facilitator, similar to a mediator, assists the parties in communication, but remains less involved in the substantive issues of the dispute than does a mediator); fact-finding (where an impartial expert selected by the parties is used to determine what facts are in dispute); mediated arbitration (also

KEY Point

Other Methods of ADR

- Conciliation
- Cooperative problem-solving
- Dispute panels
- Early neutral case evaluation
- Facilitation
- Fact-finding
- Mediated arbitration
- Mini-trials
- Negotiated rulemaking
- Settlement conferences
- Ombudsmen
- Peer review

When ADR Is Recommended or Required

Remember that many courts encourage, and even require, parties to litigation to participate in alternative dispute resolution practice—in particular, in mediation or arbitration—before they may bring their disputes to trial in court. Some laws compel parties to utilize ADR methods, such as nonbinding arbitration.

called "med-arb," where the parties authorize a neutral third person to mediate their dispute until an impasse is reached, at which point the third person issues a binding opinion on the cause of the impasse or the remaining issues disputed); mini-trials (where each party, through counsel, presents a summary of its case before a representative, such as a former judge or expert in the relevant field of law, who has authority to settle the dispute); negotiated rulemaking (also called "reg-neg," where representatives from various interest groups and a federal agency negotiate the text of a proposed rule); settlement conferences (where the judge in the case meets with attorneys for the parties in a pretrial conference designed to attempt settlement of the dispute and to prepare for trial if settlement is not reached); ombudsmen (where a person uses techniques such as counseling, mediating, conciliating, and fact-finding to review the dispute and make recommendations to the party regarding resolution); and peer review (where an employee takes a dispute before a panel of her peers for review and a binding or nonbinding decision).

CHAPTER SUMMARY

- The court systems are the judicial branches of the federal and state governments that are charged with the application, interpretation, and enforcement of the law. In the United States, the courts are divided into two separate systems, the federal system and the state system. The state system is further subdivided, by jurisdiction.

- The federal court system is divided into three levels: the trial court level (U.S. district courts), the intermediate appellate level (U.S. courts of appeals), and the highest appellate level (the U.S. Supreme Court). The U.S. Supreme Court has discretion to hear cases and, when granting a request to hear a case, issues a writ of *certiorari*.

- Each state and the District of Columbia has its own court system, and the systems vary from state to state. State court systems use a tiered model of organization, having lower level specialized trial courts, higher level trial courts of general jurisdiction, and one or two levels of appellate courts.

- Whether in federal or state court, the trial court level is where juries are used (where there exists a right to jury trial that has not been waived by the parties). One judge presides over trial courts. Appellate courts, presided over by panels of three or more judges, review for errors of law committed at trial or findings of fact at trial that were clearly erroneous. They may affirm, modify, or reverse lower court judgments as well as remand cases back to the trial court for further proceedings.

- Jurisdiction is the power of a court to hear a case. There are three types of jurisdiction: jurisdiction over the person, jurisdiction over the property, and jurisdiction over the subject matter of the case.

- Jurisdiction over the person, also called personal jurisdiction or *in personam* jurisdiction, means the court has the power to adjudicate a matter involving this person. The general rule is that a court can exercise personal jurisdiction over residents of its geographic area. Where a defendant is a nonresident of the jurisdiction, state long arm statutes allow courts to exercise personal jurisdiction when a nonresident defendant has "minimum contacts" with the state. "Minimum contacts" is a test applied under the states' long arm statutes to determine if it is fair for a court to exercise jurisdiction over the nonresident defendant. To meet this test, the defendant must have minimum contacts with the forum state, and these contacts must arise from some act of the defendant in which he purposefully avails himself of the privilege of conducting activities with the forum state, thus invoking the benefits and protections of that state's law. In other words, the defendant's conduct and connection with the forum state are such that he should reasonably anticipate being brought into court there.

- Jurisdiction over the property, also called *in rem* jurisdiction, means the court has the power to adjudicate a matter involving certain property. A court has jurisdiction over real or personal property when the property that is the subject matter of the dispute is located within the court's boundaries.

- Jurisdiction over the subject matter of a case, also called subject matter jurisdiction, means the court has the power to adjudicate a legal matter of this type. It deals with the nature of the claim or controversy involved. General jurisdiction is the power of a court to adjudicate a wide variety of types of cases, including both civil and criminal cases. Limited jurisdiction is the power of a court to adjudicate only certain types of cases, such as tax or probate cases, or small claims matters. What types of cases a court can hear is defined in the constitution or statute that created the court. Original jurisdiction is the power of a court to hear a case for the first time. Appellate jurisdiction is the power of a court to review a decision from a lower court.

- Federal trial courts (U.S. district courts) can hear two types of cases: federal questions and diversity cases. Federal questions are cases involving, at least in part, an alleged violation of the U.S. Constitution, other law of the United States (such as a federal statute), or a treaty to which the United States is a party. Diversity cases are lawsuits between citizens of different states, between citizens and foreign countries, and between citizens and non-U.S. citizens, where there is an amount in controversy of at least $75,000.

- Exclusive jurisdiction exists where a court has exclusive authority over a subject matter or territory, meaning it is the only court authorized to adjudicate the matter. Concurrent jurisdiction exists where a court has shared jurisdiction with another court or other courts; more than one court has authority to adjudicate the matter. In situations where concurrent jurisdiction exists, the plaintiff can forum shop to find the forum likely to be more beneficial to her.

- In the federal court system the U.S. courts of appeals hear appeals from their respective circuits. They also have original jurisdiction in cases involving a challenge to an order of a federal administrative agency. The U.S. Supreme Court may review decisions made by the U.S. courts of appeals and from the highest appellate courts in the state system if a constitutional or other federal issue is involved. In a very few cases the Supreme Court has original jurisdiction to hear cases for the first time, such as cases involving boundary disputes between states. The federal court system also has certain other courts that handle only particular types of cases, such as U.S. Bankruptcy Courts and the U.S. Court of International Trade.

- State trial courts have either general or limited subject matter jurisdiction as set by the state statutes creating each court. Many have general jurisdiction to adjudicate a wide variety of civil and criminal matters. Some of the inferior state trial courts are special courts with limited subject matter jurisdiction. They have authority to adjudicate in certain specialty areas of law, such as probate or divorce, or to adjudicate claims where the amount in controversy is less than some threshold amount—small claims court.

- Litigation is the process of carrying on a civil lawsuit. Its disadvantages are that it is time consuming, expensive, public, adversarial, and its outcome unpredictable and uncontrollable. Its advantage is that it will definitively resolve the dispute.

- Alternative dispute resolution (ADR) is the resolution of a legal dispute in a way other than litigation. The three major forms of ADR are negotiation, mediation, and arbitration. Negotiation is a process where the parties to a legal dispute communicate, themselves or via their attorneys, to discuss possible settlement of a legal dispute. If the dispute is settled via negotiation, the parties enter into a settlement agreement, which is a contract that evidences the terms and conditions of the resolution of a legal dispute. Mediation is a nonadversarial process where a neutral third party, called a mediator, facilitates communications between parties to a legal dispute to help them resolve it. Arbitration is an out-of-court process where parties submit their legal dispute to a neutral third party or parties, called an arbitrator or arbitration panel, who hears evidence and renders an award. The advantages of ADR methods over litigation include that they are quicker and less expensive processes; they are conducted privately rather than publicly; and for some (negotiation and mediation), their outcomes are predictable and controllable. However, a major disadvantage of all three of these forms of ADR is that the legal dispute may not be resolved, and litigation may be necessary to resolve it.

CONCEPT REVIEW AND REINFORCEMENT

Key Terms and Concepts

Court systems
U.S. district courts
U.S. courts of appeals
Circuit courts
U.S. circuit courts of appeals
U.S. Supreme Court
Chief justice
Petition of *certiorari*
Rule of four
Writ of *certiorari*
Jurisdiction
Jurisdiction over the person
Personal jurisdiction
In personam jurisdiction
Long arm statutes
Minimum contacts
Jurisdiction over the property
In rem jurisdiction
Jurisdiction over the subject matter
Subject matter jurisdiction

General jurisdiction
Limited jurisdiction
Original jurisdiction
Appellate jurisdiction
Federal questions
Diversity cases
Diversity of citizenship cases
Exclusive jurisdiction
Concurrent jurisdiction
Forum shopping
Litigation
Alternative dispute resolution
Negotiation
Settlement agreement
Mediation
Mediator
Arbitration
Award

Questions for Review

1. What are the court systems in the United States?
2. How many court systems are there in the United States?
3. Are federal courts superior to state courts?
4. How are the courts organized?
5. What types of cases do the different courts adjudicate?
6. How are legal disputes resolved through litigation?
7. What alternative dispute resolution mechanisms are there?
8. How do the alternative dispute resolution mechanisms work?

DEVELOPING YOUR PARALEGAL SKILLS

Critical Thinking Exercises

Christine Nelson traveled from her home in Gwinnett County, Georgia, to Baltimore City, Maryland, for surgery at the Johns Hopkins Hospital, a world-renowned medical center. During surgery a distracted surgeon made a careless mistake, leaving a clamp inside Christine before sewing her up. Ill for months after surgery, Christine's physician back home performed an x-ray to try to determine the cause of his patient's continued sickness. The doctor discovered the surgical clamp sewn up inside Christine. Christine underwent a second surgery to remove the clamp. Complications from that surgery caused Christine serious ongoing medical problems. She plans to sue the Johns Hopkins Hospital and her surgeon there for medical malpractice, claiming damages of $450,000.

a. What state court has personal jurisdiction over the Johns Hopkins Hospital?
b. Is in rem jurisdiction relevant in this case?
c. What court or courts have subject matter jurisdiction in this case?
d. In your answer to c., is that subject matter jurisdiction exclusive or concurrent? Why?

Assignments and Practical Applications

Research how many petitions for *certiorari* are granted each term by the U.S. Supreme Court. What are the chances that a petition you file will be granted? Are such petitions frequently granted, rarely granted, or somewhere in between?

Research to find out the names and levels of the courts in your state's court system. What are your state's trial courts of general jurisdiction called? Does your state have an intermediate level of appeal? What is the highest court in your state called?

Research a state or federal trial court near where you live or go to school. Check the court's docket to find an upcoming trial that you can observe for a few hours. A civil trial is recommended, as most paralegals work in the civil law system. Note in performing your background research that some courts post their calendars online while other courts provide information over the telephone about upcoming cases or direct you to judges for that information. Go to that court and attend several hours of a trial. Write a one-page summary of what you observed (case name and number, part of the litigation or prosecution process, nature of the claim or charge, and so on) and what you learned from the experience. Share your summary with the class.

State courts in Baltimore City, Maryland, automatically assign mediators in all divorce cases involving children. Research to see if your jurisdiction has compulsory mediation in divorce or child custody matters.

Technology Resources and Internet Exercises

Review the government website http://www.uscourts.gov/outreach/resources/fedstate_lessonplan.htm for help in understanding the federal and state court systems.

For a further review of the federal court system, see http://usgovinfo.about.com/od/uscourtsystem/a/fedcourts.htm.

Using the Federal Judicial Center's website, review how cases move through the federal courts as well as the federal court systems' approach to settlement and ADR at http://www.fjc.gov/federal/courts.nsf/autoframe!openform&nav=menu1&page=/federal/courts.nsf/page/207.

Review the U.S. Office of Personnel Management's website, located at http://www.opm.gov/er/adrguide/Section1-a.asp, for a useful guide on ADR.

See the website for the nonprofit ADR provider, the American Arbitration Association, at http://www.adr.org/. Also see the website for the for-profit ADR provider JAMS/Endispute at http://www.jamsadr.com/.

Using the Cornell University Law School website for its Legal Information Institute, found at http://www.law.cornell.edu/, find your state's legal ethics code. Use it to answer the following Ethical Applications.

Ethical Applications

Roma Novak was seriously injured some time ago when a hair dryer she was using caught fire and burned her. Roma has come to the law firm of Fritz, Kramer & Wilkens, P.C., for legal representation in bringing suit against the hair dryer's manufacturer. Harold Potler is a litigator at the firm, with years of products liability experience. Harold instructs his paralegal, Janice Murphy, to prepare the complaint and file it with the court within the next three days. Harold tells Janice that the injury occurred and cause of action accrued nearly four years ago, and the statute of limitations is about to run. In fact, it will run in 10 days. Janice, busy with other work and preoccupied with thoughts of her upcoming wedding, forgets to draft and file the complaint. After 14 days have passed, Harold asks Janice why she did not give him the complaint to review before she filed it. Quickly, Janice drafts the complaint and gives it to Harold to review.

a. Has Janice violated any legal ethics rule? What rule? Has Harold? Can the complaint be filed now, since its lateness was not the client's fault? What happens to the client's products liability claim after the running of the statute of limitations? What course of action could the client take against the law firm, attorney, and/or paralegal because of this occurrence?

Now assume that Janice drafted and filed the complaint (after showing it to Harold for his review and approval) two days after being giving the assignment, so the complaint was filed in a timely manner. When the client came to the firm seeking legal representation, in establishing the fee arrangement, Harold told the client that she would be charged the standard hourly rates that Harold and Janice charge. However, for the drafting and filing of the complaint, twice the regular hourly rate would be charged because the attorney and paralegal have to postpone work on their existing matters and focus all attention on this one to draft and file this complaint before the statute of limitations runs out and the time to file a claim expires.

b. Can Harold charge the client such a fee premium? Is it ethical? Why or why not?

VIDEO CASE STUDIES

Video Interview of Anatoly Smolkin

Paralegal case study videos to accompany this textbook are accessible from within both the New MyLegalStudiesLab Virtual Law Office Experience course and the Resources Website for Paralegal Studies.

5

The Regulation of Paralegals and an Introduction to Legal Ethics

Lois Shaw

Corporate Paralegal at Erickson Living Management, LLC

Lois first became interested in the legal profession when she worked as a legal secretary. Exposed to paralegals who performed substantive legal work, Lois decided to enroll in a paralegal education program. During her paralegal studies, Lois focused on litigation coursework but also took some courses in corporate law, wanting to have employment options for working as a paralegal at places in addition to law firms. Also during her studies, Lois began working in the Corporate Legal Department of Erickson Living Management, LLC, a company that manages large-scale continuing care retirement communities.

Lois's specialty areas of practice are corporate law and contract law. In her practice, Lois primarily drafts legal documents, including corporate organizational documents, partnership agreements, corporate resolutions and consents, subleases, professional services and consultant contracts, and construction and renovation contracts. She also maintains corporate minute books, manages departmental projects for counsel, and provides comprehensive administrative support.

Lois decided to sit for NFPA's PACE exam, feeling the exam would challenge her and that passing it would be a great accomplishment. Her RP/PACE Registered Paralegal certification requires Lois to stay current in her profession. To maintain this certification, Lois completes at least 12 hours of continuing legal education every two years, with at least one hour in legal ethics. In addition, as a RP/PACE Registered Paralegal, Lois must comply with the legal ethics rule of NFPA.

The legal ethics rules that impact Lois the most are those relating to the unauthorized practice of law and confidentiality. Lois says she works independently a great deal of the time; so to avoid the unauthorized practice of law, she includes her supervising attorneys in matters that require their attention. Also, in dealing with various corporate departments in her company, she does not give legal advice; rather, she relays legal advice given by the attorneys to constituents asking for it. Further, Lois acknowledges that paralegals must keep client information confidential. To do this, she does not discuss client information in public places, she locks her computer when she steps away from her desk, and she shreds all papers that contain client information rather than place them in the trash.

The full video interview is accessible from within both the New MyLegalStudiesLab Virtual Law Office Experience course and the Resources Website for Paralegal Studies.

The chapter will answer the following questions:

- How are paralegals regulated?
- How is the regulation of paralegals different from the regulation of attorneys?

- What are legal ethics?
- What are legal ethics codes and paralegal utilization guidelines, and where are they found?

CHAPTER **INTRODUCTION**

This chapter examines regulation of the legal profession and regulation of legal professionals. Included in this discussion is a comparison of the ways paralegals and attorneys are regulated, and reasons for the differences in that regulation. The topic of legal ethics is introduced as a part of regulation of the legal profession. The chapter discusses various legal ethics codes and paralegal utilization guidelines. It reviews where these are found, as each state has its own legal ethics code and many states have paralegal utilization guidelines. Our discussion begins with an examination of paralegal regulation. Are paralegals regulated?

THE REGULATION OF PARALEGALS

Regulation means the process of controlling something by rule or restriction. Regulating paralegals involves the process of controlling the paralegal profession by rule or restriction. Specifically, **paralegal regulation** means the direct regulation of paralegals by the states in which they work, through licensing requirements and legal ethics rules. Is there paralegal regulation today?

Regulation of the legal profession and legal professionals takes two forms. First, regulation involves licensing requirements set by the states. Second, regulation includes legal ethics rules to which certain legal professionals are bound. In this and the following section, we focus on the first part of regulation—licensing. In the last two parts of this chapter, we focus on regulation through legal ethics rules adopted by each state. Remember the two parts to regulation: licensing requirements and ethical rules of conduct.

The regulation of paralegals and the paralegal profession has been the subject of debate in recent years. In all jurisdictions, there is no regulation of paralegals as there is for attorneys. Rather, most states permit anyone to work as a paralegal, without restricting entry into the profession. However, many states are reviewing the concept of paralegal regulation, and several are trying out different forms of regulation—mostly voluntary

so far. One state, California, has regulation "by definition." This state enacted a "title" statute that defines certain minimum requirements a person must meet to use the title "paralegal" or a synonym for that term, such as "legal assistant" or "lawyer's assistant." In other words, the statute makes it

> **Regulation** means the process of controlling something by rule or restriction.
>
> **Paralegal regulation** means the direct regulation of paralegals by the states in which they work, through licensing requirements and legal ethics rules.

KEY Point

Two Parts to Regulation

The two parts to regulation are licensing requirements and ethical rules of conduct.

unlawful for a person to hold herself out as a paralegal unless she has met certain statutory requirements, discussed below. However, these requirements fall far short of the requirements to be an attorney. For paralegals to be regulated in a manner similar to attorneys, they would have to obtain licenses from their states after meeting educational requirements, qualifying to take an examination, taking and passing the examination, demonstrating good moral character, completing continuing legal education and ethics education requirements, and paying annual dues, at a minimum.

That said, other states have been considering paralegal regulation in various, inconsistent ways. Some states, such as Florida, have implemented voluntary registration programs for paralegals. **Registration** is the act of recording a person's identifying information in certain records. **Paralegal registration** specifically means the identification of a person as a participant in a voluntary registration program for paralegals. Other states are waiting and watching to see what develops in terms of the regulation of paralegals in other jurisdictions.[1] Professional paralegal associations such as the National Federation of Paralegal Associations (NFPA) and the National Association of Legal Assistants (NALA) offer voluntary certification as a way of regulating the profession. They offer PACE, CLA, CLAS, and CP designations for paralegals who meet their qualification requirements, as discussed in Chapter 1. At this time, however, there is no consistent movement among the states to regulate the paralegal profession, especially through licensing programs. Further, developments in this area of paralegal profession regulation are not numerous and not uniform—at least not yet.

Why regulate the paralegal profession? Why not regulate it? The legal profession is split on whether or not regulating paralegals is a good idea. Many legal professionals support voluntary regulation, but there is a real lack of consensus on whether mandatory paralegal regulation, achieved through licensing, is beneficial to the legal profession or the paralegal profession.

Certification

Remember that certification is the process by which an organization grants recognition to a person who meets defined qualification requirements. Normally, certification permits a person to use a certain title. NFPA, with its PACE certification, and NALA, with its CLA, CLAS, and CP certifications, are examples.

Paralegals Who Offer Services Directly to the Public

While most paralegals work under the direct supervision of their employing attorneys, some paralegals provide services directly to the public. Besides presenting an "unauthorized practice of law" issue, a few jurisdictions mandate that the nonlawyer legal service provider register with the government, after meeting minimum requirements such as education requirements, good character requirements, and bonding requirements. For example, by statute in California, registration with the government is required for legal document assistants, who are people who provide certain self-help legal services directly to the public.

Here are the most recognized arguments in support of paralegal regulation through licensing. Licensing of paralegals ensures minimum standards of quality of performance by controlling who can be a paralegal and what a paralegal can do through requirements in education, training, experience, attorney supervision, and continuing education. Licensing of paralegals means public recognition of the paralegal as a professional and part of the legal services delivery team. In effect, it raises the professional status and profile of the profession. With minimum qualification requirements, licensing assures clients and employers of a paralegal's qualifications and protects the public from unqualified practitioners. Further, licensing requirements help standardize paralegal education, as education programs would be geared toward helping program graduates meet licensing requirements.

> *I think that paralegal regulation is very important . . . I would get a license to practice as a paralegal.*
> Tatyana Bronzova

Registration is the act of recording a person's identifying information in certain records.

Paralegal registration means the identification of a person as a participant in a voluntary registration program for paralegals.

On the other side of the debate, a main argument against the licensing of paralegals is that licensing simply is not needed. Many legal professionals believe that attorney supervision provides sufficient oversight of the paralegal profession. Another main argument against licensure is that licensing requirements create a barrier to entry into the profession, raising the cost of legal services. Only those people meeting the licensing requirements can become paralegals. Not all people interested in working as paralegals will meet these requirements, so they would be prevented from working in this profession. Fewer paralegals, created by the barrier to entry into the profession, would increase paralegal salaries. This is good for paralegals, but contrary to the purpose of the profession, which is to provide lower cost legal services. In addition, the licensing of paralegals restricts their geographic movement because, like attorneys, they would need a license to be a paralegal in every jurisdiction in which they work. Also, there is a monetary cost to paralegals to pay for licensing. Finally, while also a "pro" argument, the standardization in paralegal education that would result from mandatory paralegal licensing could make paralegal education unnecessarily uniform.

> *I think paralegals are somewhat regulated because the attorney can be held responsible for the paralegal's acts.*
> **Sherry Myers**

Barrier to Entry

Remember that the paralegal profession evolved from a societal need for the provision of lower cost legal services. Creating a barrier to entry into the paralegal profession through licensing requirements, thus increasing paralegal salaries, defeats this purpose.

Adding to the paralegal regulation debate is the issue of who would be responsible for the regulation. There are many opinions as to who should regulate paralegals. As discussed in the next section, attorneys are self-regulating, mainly through the state bar associations, which are delegated regulation responsibilities from their states' highest courts. In the event of paralegal licensure, state bar associations would be the most likely candidates to regulate the paralegal profession, given their involvement in the self-regulation of attorneys.

What do professional paralegal associations favor in terms of paralegal regulation? NALA favors voluntary certification, such as CLA, CLAS, and CP certifications, but opposes mandatory licensing. NALA's position is that paralegals already work under attorney supervision, and attorneys are bound by state ethical codes; indirectly, then, paralegals already are regulated by state ethical codes. Further, NALA believes the paralegal profession should not be subject to occupational licensing by state government–imposed regulation. Rather, it is the responsibility of the paralegal profession to regulate itself. NFPA has a different view. NFPA favors regulation of the paralegal profession in the form of licensing requirements on the state level, so requirements are set on a state-by-state basis. Supporting this position, NFPA publishes a Model Act for Paralegal Licensure, hoping to guide states in developing requirements in occupational licensing for paralegals. ABA has taken the position that regulation of paralegals is a responsibility that is best left to individual states. Further, to date ABA has not proposed a model for paralegal regulation. AAfPE has not yet taken a position on paralegal regulation through licensing, but rather focuses its attention on educational standards for paralegals.

If public opinion grows to support the regulation of the paralegal profession, what form should that regulation take? Several states have considered general licensing programs for paralegals (including Hawaii, New York, and Texas).

KEY Point

Pros and Cons of Paralegal Licensing

Pros:

- Ensures minimum standards of performance quality
- Provides public recognition of paralegals as professionals
- Raises the professional status and profile of the paralegal profession
- Assures clients and employers of paralegal qualifications
- Protects the public from unqualified practitioners
- Helps to standardize paralegal education

Cons:

- Unnecessary because attorney supervision provides sufficient oversight
- Creates a barrier to entry into the profession
- Increases the cost of legal services
- Restricts the geographic movement of paralegals
- Cost of licensing
- Unnecessarily standardizes paralegal education

California is an early state to act on paralegal regulation, as discussed above. California has a mandatory definition statute for paralegals, regulating in the form of a title scheme. The California state statute requires any person who holds herself out as a paralegal to meet certain educational, training, and/or work experience requirements; to work under the direction and supervision of an attorney; and to meet continuing legal and ethics education requirements. Further, tasks that paralegals perform are enumerated in that statute. These criteria must be met in order for someone to work as a paralegal and perform those tasks. In fact, the statute makes it unlawful for a person not meeting the requirements to identify herself using the term "paralegal" or the like (for the statute includes synonymous terms such as "legal assistant" or "lawyer's assistant"), and it authorizes a penalty for the law's violation. That said, there is no requirement that a prospective paralegal apply to take and pass an examination, such as the bar examination required for attorneys.

Florida has a voluntary registration system within a program instituted by the Florida Bar Association. Pursuant to this program, if a paralegal wishes to become a Florida Registered Paralegal, she must meet the program requirements. These requirements are substantially similar to the California requirements involving education, training, and work experience; working under the direction and supervision of an attorney; and meeting continuing legal and ethics education requirements for maintenance of that registration. The main distinction between California's definition statute and Florida's registration program is that California's program is mandatory for a person wanting to hold herself out as a paralegal, while Florida's program offers voluntary registration—only those paralegals who want the distinction of being registered with the Florida Bar Association need comply with the requirements.[2] In Florida, anyone can hold herself out as a paralegal. That is not true in California.

Because the legal profession is split on whether or not regulation of the paralegal profession is useful or warranted, regulation of the profession by state is not yet common. States supporting no regulation of the paralegal profession believe

STATUTE *on* POINT

Cal. Bus. & Prof. Code §§ 6450-6456 (2010).

- The California statute states that a "paralegal" means a person who holds herself out to be a paralegal; who is qualified by education, training, or work experience; who contracts with or is employed by an attorney, law firm, corporation, governmental agency, or other organization; who performs substantial legal work specifically delegated to her by an active member of the State Bar of California or an attorney practicing in the federal courts in California; and whose work is performed under the direction and supervision of that attorney.

- The term "paralegal" includes the synonymous terms "legal assistant", "attorney assistant", "freelance paralegal", "independent paralegal", and "contract paralegal".

- Tasks the paralegal may perform include (as an illustrative, but not exclusive, list) case planning, development and management; legal research; interviewing clients; fact gathering and retrieving information; drafting and analyzing legal documents; collecting, compiling, and utilizing technical information to make an independent decision and recommendation to the supervising attorney; and representing clients before a state or federal administrative agency if that representation is permitted by law.

- A paralegal shall not give legal advice; represent a client in court; select, explain, draft, or recommend the use of any legal document to or for any person other than the attorney who supervises the paralegal; act as a "runner or capper"; contract with or be employed by a person other than an attorney to perform legal services; induce a person to make an investment in connection with providing paralegal services; or establish the fees to charge a client for the paralegal services.

- Every two years, a paralegal must complete four hours of continuing education in legal ethics and four hours of continuing legal education in general law or a specialized area of law.

- It is unlawful for a person to identify herself as a paralegal unless she has met the qualifications set forth in the statute and performs all her paralegal services under the direction and supervision of an attorney who is an active member of the State Bar of California or an attorney practicing law in the federal courts in California.

- An attorney who uses the services of a paralegal is liable for any harm caused as a result of the paralegal's misconduct or negligence.

that sufficient oversight of the profession is achieved through attorney supervision. Because of this, licensing of paralegals is not required. Of the states interested in regulation of the profession, more appear interested in a voluntary program than a mandatory one, at least at this time. Perhaps a voluntary program is the best of both worlds in that it creates no barriers to entry into the profession, because such a program is merely optional. At the same time, a voluntary program establishes a degree of quality for those who meet the program requirements. Voluntary regulation can be achieved through registration or certification programs. Remember that registra-tion is the identification of a person as a participant in a voluntary registration program. Certification is recognition that a person has met the requirements of the granting organization. Such voluntary registration or certification enhances a paralegal's qualifications in the marketplace, probably enhancing her salary as well. Voluntary registration or certification, however, creates no barrier to entry into the profession as mandatory licensing does.

How is paralegal regulation (or lack thereof) different from the regulation of attorneys? How the regulation of these professions is distinguished is examined next.

DISTINGUISHING THE REGULATION OF PARALEGALS FROM THE REGULATION OF ATTORNEYS

In Chapter 1 the qualifications to become an attorney were examined. These are a type of regulation for lawyers. Regulation of lawyers is achieved through state courts and state bar associations. The highest court in each state is responsible for making rules relating to law practice admission in that jurisdiction, as well as rules regarding lawyers' ethical conduct (discussed in the following sections)—both of which, combined, constitute the regulation of lawyers. The courts delegate to the state bar associations the duty to enforce certain of these regulations.

To review, an attorney must have a license to practice law in every jurisdiction in which she practices. **Licensing** is a government's official act granting permission to a person to perform some service or use a particular title, such as practice law or hold oneself out as an attorney, which is prohibited without such permission. A license gives a lawyer the right to practice law in a jurisdiction. That right is also a privilege that can be lost if abused, as discussed in the next section. The licensing of attorneys is handled at the state level of government. Each state has its own licensing requirements for attorneys. While requirements vary from state to state, most states require the following.

First, a person typically must earn a bachelor's degree from a college or university and must graduate from law school with a doctorate in jurisprudence. Most states require that the law school be accredited by the American Bar Association. Note that graduating from law school earns a person a doctoral degree in jurisprudence. It does not give a person the right to practice law—law school graduation is merely a big step in the licensing process.

Next, the prospective attorney typically applies to take the state's bar examination. If her application is accepted, she must then take the state's bar examination. Her grade on the bar examination must be passing, based upon

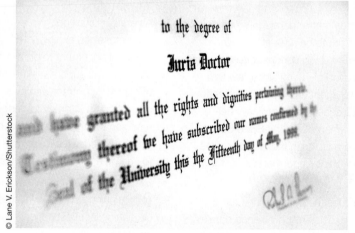

© Lane V. Erickson/Shutterstock

to the degree of

Juris Doctor

... have granted all the rights and dignities pertaining thereto. ... thereof we have subscribed our names confirmed by the ... of the University this the Fifteenth day of May, 1999.

Licensing is a government's official act granting permission to a person to perform some service or use a particular title, such as practice law or hold oneself out as an attorney, which is prohibited without such permission.

Admission into Federal Courts

Admission to a state bar does not entitle an admitted attorney to practice before a United States federal court. Admission to a federal district court or federal court of appeals is granted on paying a fee and taking an oath of admission (the requirements may be different, such as no fee required, when the attorney is to appear in federal court on behalf of the United States, such as an assistant U.S. attorney). The attorney must apply to each district separately, as well as to each federal court of appeals. Some federal district courts have extra admission requirements as well, such as requiring the attendance at a class on practice and procedure in that district or passing an entrance examination. Some federal district courts require that attorneys be members of the state bar where the court sits as well. To appear before the U.S. Supreme Court, an attorney must apply for admission. Minimum requirements for appearing before the Supreme Court are admission to a state bar for at least three years prior, sponsorship of the applicant by two attorneys already admitted to the Supreme Court bar, payment of a fee, and taking a written oath.

the grading criteria established by that state. Also, she must pass a personal background investigation to verify that she is qualified to engage in the legal profession and able to abide by its ethical rules for the conduct of lawyers—in effect, she must demonstrate good moral character. Some states require additional steps be taken prior to bar admission, such as passing a legal training or ethics course, paying dues, and/or making an oath in court at a swearing in ceremony.

If an attorney moves to another geographic location (another state), she must meet the licensing requirements in that new state in order to obtain a license to practice law there. That likely means she must take and pass another bar examination for starters.[3] After being granted a license to practice law in a state, the attorney must continue to meet the state's license maintenance requirements, such as by completing periodic continuing legal and ethics education requirements and paying annual dues. Note that it is not until a person has received a license to practice law in a state that she has the right to hold herself out as an attorney or lawyer (remember, the terms "attorney" and "lawyer" are synonymous, just as are "paralegal" and "legal assistant").

Attorneys are considered self-regulating. They are self-regulating because they establish the rules that govern their profession. These rules are enforced by state authorities, namely state bar associations, courts, and legislatures. Typically, each state's highest court mandates the licensing requirements for attorneys, defining who may exercise the privilege of practicing law in that state. Even the U.S. Supreme Court occasionally gets involved in attorney regulation issues. Consider the Case on Point. State legislatures enact statutes affecting attorneys as well, such as criminal statutes regarding the unauthorized practice of law. The regulation of attorneys, through licensing, protects the public by establishing educational and other requirements that ensure lawyer competence. Such regulation also defines ethical rules of conduct to guide attorneys in the ethical practice of law and to prohibit and punish their unethical conduct.

Attorneys, then, are subject to direct regulation by the state that licenses them. They must meet and maintain compliance with the state's licensing requirements in order to be able to practice law in that jurisdiction.

As discussed above, paralegals are not directly regulated by their states—at least not the way attorneys are with

CASE *on* POINT

Bates v. State Bar of Arizona, 433 U.S. 350 (1977).

At that time in history (the 1970s), lawyers did not advertise their legal services, as advertising of legal services was thought to demean the profession. In this case, two Arizona lawyers had advertised low-cost legal services at their law clinic via an advertisement in a local newspaper. They were disciplined by the State Bar of Arizona for conducting that advertising because, at that time, the State Bar of Arizona prohibited attorneys in that state from advertising their legal services. On appeal to the U.S. Supreme Court, the Court held that lawyer advertising was a form of commercial speech that was protected by the First Amendment of the U.S. Constitution. The Court went on to say that states could prohibit advertising only in limited circumstances, such as if the advertising is false, misleading, or deceptive. The Court allowed states to impose reasonable time, place, and manner restrictions on lawyer advertising; however, states could not totally prohibit it. This Arizona statute was held to be unconstitutional as a violation of the First Amendment.

regard to mandatory licensing. Paralegals are not licensed by the states where they work. That may change as time passes, however, depending on the outcome of the paralegal licensing debate and views of those in the legal profession. For now, however, stringent licensing requirements do not need to be met by paralegals for them to work in the profession, as opposed to lawyers who must obtain licenses to practice law in their jurisdictions. Paralegals, then, are regulated indirectly through the regulation of their supervising lawyers and the requirement that lawyers supervise, and are responsible for, their paralegals' work. This "indirect regulation" concept is fully analyzed in the legal ethics discussion that follows.

Not only are attorneys regulated by licensing requirements of the state, they are also regulated by legal ethics codes and rules adopted by each state. Paralegals, too, are indirectly regulated by rules of legal ethics. Legal ethics are examined next.

LEGAL ETHICS

Each state has its own rules of legal ethics that govern the legal profession. **Legal ethics** are the minimum standards of conduct prescribed in a jurisdiction's code of ethical conduct that govern those engaged in the practice of law. In most jurisdictions, the highest court in the state issues an order adopting the state's legal ethics rules governing the professional conduct of lawyers. In other states, courts delegate to their states' bar associations the responsibility to adopt the legal ethics rules for their jurisdictions. States' highest courts are ultimately in charge of lawyer discipline for ethics violations.

© RubberBall/SuperStock

Further, many of the states' highest courts delegate to their states' bar associations the responsibility for carrying out the regulation of the practice of law, including bar admissions and bar disciplinary actions. Many state legislatures have passed statutes to supplement the legal ethics rules adopted by the courts and state bar associations as well. For example, most states have enacted criminal statutes making the unauthorized practice of law, meaning the practice of law without a license, a crime. It is most often classified as a misdemeanor, such as in Minnesota. However, some states, such as South Carolina, classify the unauthorized practice of law as a felony. In that state the unauthorized practice of law is punishable by up to five years in prison and/or a $5,000 fine. State legislatures may also adopt legal ethics rules, as well as enact statutes defining the ethical conduct of lawyers and setting bar admissions requirements. Case law also regulates lawyer conduct. Case law includes court decisions involving lawyer malpractice and decisions involving disqualification from the practice of law due to ethical violations. Further defining ethical conduct for lawyers, the American Bar Association, as well as state and local bar associations and state ethics commissions of some states' highest courts, through ethics committees created by them, issue nonbinding ethics advisory opinions to help guide attorney conduct. Ethics advisory opinions often are responses to questions posed by attorneys. They may be formal or informal. For example, on August 5, 2010, the American Bar Association's Standing Committee on Ethics and Professional Responsibility issued Formal Opinion 10-457 on the

KEY Point

Legal Ethics Rules Apply Directly to Lawyers

In the United States, legal ethics rules are understood to apply directly to lawyers. This is because lawyers are regulated directly by the states that license them. Failure to abide by the legal ethics rules in one's state can subject an attorney to disciplinary action.

Legal ethics are the minimum standards of conduct prescribed in a jurisdiction's code of ethical conduct that govern those engaged in the practice of law.

TABLE 5-1	Sources of Legal Ethics Regulation	

State Judicial Systems	State Bar Associations
• the highest court in the state has ultimate authority to regulate the ethical conduct of attorneys licensed in that jurisdiction	• often are delegated by the state's highest court the authority to enforce the state's code of legal ethics (especially if the bar association is an integrated one)
• may adopt the jurisdiction's code of legal ethics governing the conduct of attorneys licensed in that jurisdiction	• may adopt the jurisdiction's code of legal ethics governing the conduct of attorneys licensed in the jurisdiction (especially if the bar association is an integrated one)
• may oversee attorney admissions to practice law in the jurisdiction	• may oversee attorney admissions to practice law in the jurisdiction
• may be responsible for disciplining attorneys for violations of the code of legal ethics, or may delegate disciplinary authority to the state's bar association (subject to approval authority over more serious disciplinary sanctions, especially disbarment)	• may be responsible for disciplining attorneys for violations of the code of legal ethics
• may appoint a committee to issue ethics advisory opinions	• may appoint a committee to issue ethics advisory opinions
• may interpret, amend, or overrule provisions of the legal ethics code adopted in the jurisdiction	

Note that violations of the legal ethics rules are disciplinary in nature rather than civil or criminal violations. It is the disciplinary authority of the state, which body differs from state to state, that handles issues involving the violation of ethical rules by attorneys. That said, the process of bringing a disciplinary action against an attorney is similar to a criminal prosecution. First, either the wrongdoing is discovered by the disciplinary authority or a client files a complaint with that authority. Next, the wrongdoing or complaint is investigated by the disciplinary authority. Upon investigation, if sufficient evidence is found to charge the attorney with a violation, a formal complaint is filed against the attorney by the disciplinary authority. The attorney may settle the matter by agreeing to a deal with the disciplinary authority, such as to make restitution to an injured client or to not practice law for a certain period of time. In the alternative, the attorney may defend himself. In that situation, a hearing is conducted giving

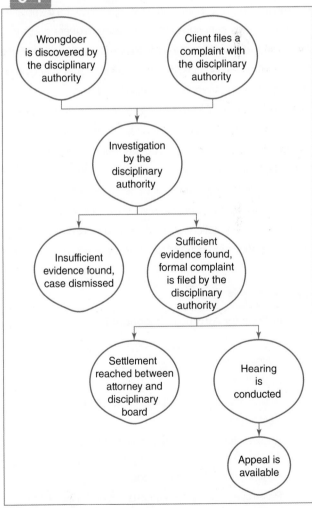

FIGURE 5-1 The Disciplinary Process

Sanctions are punishments a court or state bar association may levy against an attorney for violating a legal ethics rule.

topic of lawyer websites. Ethics advisory opinions may be published for the benefit of all attorneys in that jurisdiction; or, where a response letter is sent only to the requesting attorney, they may not be published. While opinions do not have the force of law like case law, statutes, and ethics rules do, they do provide guidance to lawyers in their practices, as well as to judges who are adjudicating issues regarding attorney ethical violations.

As noted above, either codes of legal ethics are promulgated by each state's highest court or responsibility is delegated to the state bar association to adopt such code. The legal ethics code is enforced by the court and, where delegated the responsibility, the state's bar association. Legal ethics codes set forth the rules of ethical conduct that must be followed by lawyers in their practices in that jurisdiction. These codes have methods for disciplining lawyers for their violation, in the form of sanctions. **Sanctions** are punishments a court or state bar association may levy against an attorney for violating a legal ethics rule.

the attorney the opportunity to present his defense. There is an appeal process as well, if either party (usually the attorney accused of wrongdoing) wishes to appeal the result of the hearing. If the attorney is ultimately found to have violated a legal ethics rule, then one or more sanctions may be imposed against him.

In states with integrated bar associations, where membership in the state bar association is required, the state bar association often is responsible for the disciplinary process for attorneys. In states where membership in the bar association is voluntary, also called a nonintegrated bar association, the state's highest court may appoint a body to oversee attorney discipline, calling that body a committee or commission. While the structure of the disciplinary body differs from state to state, most disciplinary bodies include the following: an office of disciplinary counsel to investigate and evaluate ethical complaints brought against lawyers, a hearing officer or panel that conducts disciplinary hearings (which hearings are public in most states, but private in a few states) and issues reports, a state disciplinary board that reviews the hearing reports and either dismisses the complaints or recommends sanctions, and the state's highest court that makes final decisions on attorney discipline issues and imposes the more severe sanctions, including revoking or suspending an attorney's license to practice law, discussed below.

Remember that sanctions are the consequences of disciplinary actions against lawyers. There are several different sanctions for attorney misconduct under the legal ethics rules, depending on the severity of the violation. The sanctions disciplinary bodies can impose include disbarment, suspension, probation, reprimand/reproval, restitution, assessment of costs of the disciplinary action, completion of a legal ethics or other continuing education course, taking and passing a professional

ethics exam or the bar exam, and imposing limitations on a lawyer's law practice. Each of these sanctions is discussed in turn.

Disbarment is the revocation of a lawyer's license to practice law in the state. This is the most severe sanction that can be imposed on a lawyer for a legal ethics violation. While severe, most states will readmit to practice a disbarred lawyer who can demonstrate rehabilitation. So disbarment is not necessarily permanent. **Suspension** is the temporary revocation of a lawyer's license to practice law. Suspension is for a period of time. The American Bar Association, in its Standards for Imposing Lawyer Sanctions (discussed below), recommends not less than six months, or more than three years, as a suspension period. Suspension is the second most severe type of disciplinary sanction imposed against lawyers. Probation is another form of sanction. **Probation** is when an attorney is permitted to practice law, subject to certain conditions, such as making restitution to an injured client, passing an ethics exam, attending an ethics course, or obtaining counseling. **Reprimand**, also called **reproval**, is a form of scolding that declares a lawyer's conduct to be ethically improper. It is a less severe form of lawyer discipline than revocation or suspension of a license. Reprimand can be public or private. **Public reprimand** occurs when a notice about the ethics violation and admonishment of the attorney is published in a bar journal or legal newspaper, so the public is made aware of it. **Private reprimand**, also called **admonition**, occurs when an unpublished communication is sent to the attorney by the disciplinary body, admonishing the attorney for his conduct, or the reprimand is published to educate other

---

KEY Point

Sanctions for Attorney Misconduct

- Disbarment
- Suspension
- Probation
- Reprimand or reproval (public or private)
- Restitution
- Assessment of the costs of the disciplinary action
- Completion of a professional ethics course or other continuing legal education course
- Passing a professional ethics exam or the bar exam
- Being subject to limitations placed on the lawyer's practice

---

Disbarment is the revocation of a lawyer's license to practice law in the state.

Suspension is the temporary revocation of a lawyer's license to practice law.

Probation is when an attorney is permitted to practice law, subject to certain conditions.

Reprimand is a form of scolding that declares the lawyer's conduct to be ethically improper; it is also called **reproval**.

Public reprimand occurs when a notice about the ethics violation and admonishment of the attorney is published in a bar journal or legal newspaper, so that the public is made aware of it.

Private reprimand occurs when an unpublished communication is sent to the attorney by the disciplinary body, admonishing the attorney for his conduct, or is published to educate other attorneys, but without the lawyer's name to identify him; it is also called **admonition**.

The American Bar Association on Re-admittance after Disbarment

In its Standards for Imposing Lawyer Sanctions, the ABA *recommends* that an attorney who has been disbarred not be permitted to apply for readmittance until at least five years after his disbarment. After the five-year period, a disbarred attorney may apply for readmittance. To succeed, he must establish by clear and convincing evidence both (1) successful completion of the bar examination and (2) rehabilitation and fitness to practice law.

What Can a Disbarred Lawyer Do for a Living?

He cannot practice law. Many states also prohibit disbarred lawyers from working as paralegals. Upon disbarment, a former lawyer needs to find a new occupation, in a different profession—one outside the practice of law.

attorneys, but without the lawyer's name to identify him. A reprimand becomes a part of the attorney's record with the licensing authority. An order of **restitution** can be made against the lawyer, requiring him to monetarily reimburse a person he financially harmed through his misconduct. Additionally, the lawyer can be assessed the costs of the disciplinary action, can be required to complete a professional ethics course or other continuing legal education course, can be required to take and pass a professional ethics exam or the bar exam, and can have limitations placed on his law practice as other forms of sanction.

Disciplinary bodies consider several factors in determining which sanction is appropriate for a given violation. These factors include the nature of the ethical violation, the severity of the violation, the attorney's mental state, the potential or actual injury caused by the lawyer's misconduct, the extent to which the attorney cooperated in the investigation, the attorney's reputation and contributions to the community through public service and professional activities, the circumstances surrounding the violation, whether the violation was a single occurrence or one that was repeated, and the extent of the attorney's remorse for his conduct and his willingness to make amends. Also, the American Bar Association issues Standards for Imposing Lawyer Sanctions, which, among other things, set forth four factors that courts should consider in imposing sanctions on attorneys for ethical violations (see the end-of-chapter exercise identifying and using these standards).

Lawyers also may be disciplined under the ethics rules for wrongful behavior that is outside their practice of law. This behavior may be criminal, such as theft, illegal drug use or drug dealing, driving under the influence, filing fraudulent income tax returns, and other crimes that demonstrate lack of good moral character, a prerequisite for a license to practice law, as discussed earlier. For example, a lawyer who commits theft, even if unrelated to his law practice, may be both prosecuted in the criminal law system and sanctioned under the disciplinary system for lawyers (for instance, he could be disbarred).

In addition to sanctions that can be imposed by the disciplinary body of the state, attorneys may face consequences in the legal system. They may be sued for malpractice by their clients—where claims of professional negligence are made. The goal of these lawsuits, which are tort lawsuits, is to recover damages from the attorneys. For violations of certain ethics rules, like comingling of funds, attorneys may also be prosecuted under criminal statutes, such as for theft or fraud. Attorneys may be held in contempt of court when they engage in unethical conduct in court proceedings, which conduct adversely impacts the court's administration of justice.

As mentioned above, attorneys are directly bound by the ethics codes of their states. Is the same true for paralegals? No, it is not.

Restitution is an order requiring the attorney monetarily reimburse a person he financially harmed through his misconduct.

Paralegal Consequences

Note that paralegals may be sued for malpractice and/or prosecuted for violations of criminal statutes. However, they may not be disciplined under a state's legal ethics code.

Paralegals often face adverse employment consequences, such as termination, for engaging in unethical conduct.

Paralegals Are Indirectly Bound by States' Legal Ethics Codes

Because paralegals are not licensed by the states in which they work, they are not directly bound by the legal ethics codes adopted by their states. However, because the attorneys who supervise them are responsible for their paralegals' ethical conduct, paralegals are indirectly bound by the legal ethics rules.

Paralegals are not directly bound by their states' ethics codes. This is so because paralegals do not possess licenses issued by their states. In other words, they are not regulated like lawyers are. Accordingly, they cannot be sanctioned by a court or a state bar association for violation of an ethical rule. Attorneys, however, are bound by the ethics rules in such a way as to ensure that the paralegals they supervise comply with these rules.

Paralegals, as employees and agents of the attorneys who employ them, then, are indirectly bound by the ethics rules of conduct binding lawyers in their states. This is true for a couple of reasons. First, attorneys can be disciplined for their paralegals' ethical violations, thereby indirectly binding paralegals to the rules. Because of the supervising attorney's responsibility for the ethical conduct of his paralegals, the attorney will require that the paralegals' conduct always be ethical. Second, paralegals who violate the legal ethics rules, subjecting their employers to discipline for

these actions, will likely face adverse employment consequences, such as termination or demotion. Accordingly, ethical rules imposed by state law on lawyers also affect paralegals.

To summarize, attorneys become subject to the legal ethics rules of their states when they obtain licenses to practice law in their jurisdictions. Further, legal ethics rules for lawyers expressly make them responsible for the conduct of the paralegals they supervise, thus making paralegals also responsible for obeying the ethical codes of conduct for lawyers. Accordingly, the rules of legal ethics that directly apply to lawyers also indirectly apply to paralegals. In addition, paralegal conduct can be guided by the ethical codes issued by national, state, and local paralegal associations as well as by the guidelines for the utilization of paralegal services adopted by paralegal associations, both of which are binding on paralegals who are members of those associations. These codes and guidelines are examined next.

LEGAL ETHICS CODES AND PARALEGAL UTILIZATION GUIDELINES

Whether a lawyer or a paralegal, it is essential to know the legal ethics rules for the jurisdiction to understand one's responsibilities as a legal practitioner. As already discussed, attorneys are directly bound by legal ethics rules in their states because they exercise the privilege to practice law there and obtain licenses. Also, because attorneys are directly responsible for the unethical conduct of all of their nonlawyer employees, including paralegals, paralegals must know and follow the states' legal ethics rules, too. To know the rules, one has to locate and read them. Where, then, are the legal ethics codes found?

© age fotostock/supterstock

As already discussed, each state has its own legal ethics code dictating rules of professional conduct for lawyers. Today all are based, at least in part, on the American Bar Association's Model Rules of Profession Conduct.

Since the early 1900s, the American Bar Association has utilized committees and commissions to develop model rules of ethics for lawyers. These model rules provide a national framework for states in promulgating rules of professional conduct for lawyers. Like the Uniform Commercial Code in the area of commercial law, these model codes are not laws themselves. Rather, they are models, meaning collections of sample rules, for states to consider when they draft, then adopt, their legal ethics codes—which state codes are laws. Model rules are drafted by legal scholars and other experts in the field. They can be, and often are, used by the states as a starting point in drafting their jurisdictions' rules. Keep in mind that ABA model rules and codes do not become law until they are adopted by a state.

KEY Point

Application of Model Codes of Ethics

Remember that ABA model codes of conduct are not laws themselves. They must be adopted by a state as the professional rules of lawyer conduct in order to become legally enforceable in that jurisdiction. Rules adopted by a particular state are legally enforceable against the lawyers of that state, and lawyers subject themselves to those rules by obtaining licenses to practice law in that jurisdiction. They are enforceable against lawyers via disciplinary proceedings and sanctions. However, they are not legally enforceable against nonlawyers, such as paralegals.

The ABA promulgated its first code of legal ethics in 1908. This code was called the Canons of Professional Ethics. Later, in 1969, the ABA promulgated the Model Code of Professional Responsibility—called the Model Code. Back when it was issued, this Model Code was adopted, in whole or in part, by every state. However, now all states have adopted a new code based upon the Model Rules of Professional Conduct promulgated by

KEY Point

History of ABA Model Ethics Codes and Rules

- 1908 Canons of Professional Ethics
- 1969 Model Code of Professional Responsibility (the Model Code)
- 1983 Model Rules of Professional Conduct (the Model Rules)

ABA in 1983 and revised in 2002—called the Model Rules. Today, all 50 states have adopted the Model Rules, either in whole or in part. When the Model Rules were revised in 2002, some states adopted those changes at that time while others did not. Legal ethics rules and their revisions are for each state to determine and update through revision on a state-by-state basis.

Besides ABA, the paralegal associations NFPA, NALA, and NALS have developed their own paralegal codes of ethics. Originally adopted in 1993 and revised in 1997 to add enforcement provisions, NFPA's most recent code is called the Model Code of Ethics and Professional Responsibility and Guidelines for Enforcement. NFPA's Code covers paralegal competence and integrity, standards of professional conduct, the duty of confidentiality, conflicts of interest, the unauthorized practice of law, and title disclosure. Adopted in 1975 and revised from time to time, NALA's code is the Code of Ethics and Professional Responsibility for paralegals. The focus of NALA's Code, found in its 10 canons, is the unauthorized practice of law, working under the close supervision of an attorney, competence, integrity, confidentiality, and conflicts of interest. NALS issues the Code of Ethics and Professional Responsibility governing the conduct of members of its association too. NALS's Code contains ten canons that include a focus on the unauthorized practice of law, working under the direct supervision of an attorney, competence, integrity, and confidentiality. While useful guidance, compliance with any of these paralegal association codes is voluntary, not mandatory.

NFPA's Model Code of Ethics and Professional Responsibility and Guidelines for Enforcement

NFPA, in its Code, includes guidelines for enforcement, authorizing disciplinary sanctions against paralegals. In 1997, NFPA added enforcement to its model to recognize that compliance with ethics codes is more than aspirational; it is a true obligation of paralegals. In doing so, NFPA offers a framework for professional discipline of paralegals, including imposition of a variety of sanctions against paralegals for ethical violations. These sanctions include such disciplinary measures as a letter of reprimand, completion of an ethics course, imposition of a fine, reporting of criminal activity to relevant authorities, and assessment of costs. However, this framework is not law. Accordingly, compliance with it is voluntary, though it could be adopted as part of a paralegal regulation scheme in a jurisdiction to become mandatory.

Remember that members of professional paralegal associations like NFPA and NALA, or local affiliates of either, are bound by their association's ethics codes. Violations of such codes can result in loss of membership.

State codes are based on models, such as the ABA Model Rules of Professional Conduct, and then usually adopted by the states' highest courts. As law, they typically are called Rules of Professional Responsibility or Rules of Professional Conduct. For example, in Maryland the legal ethics code is called The Maryland Lawyers' Rules of Professional Conduct. These codes function similar to statutes, but they are adopted by states' highest courts rather than by legislatures. Publishers of states' statutes usually also publish court rules, including legal ethics rules adopted by the courts. For example, in Maryland, the publishers of the Annotated Code of Maryland also publish the Maryland Lawyers' Rules of Professional Conduct (the Maryland Rules)—and provide the publication to the Maryland State Bar Association (MSBA) for distribution to attorneys newly admitted to MSBA. The Maryland Rules are also available for sale by the publisher. Many of the states' legal ethics codes are available online as well.

As discussed already, every state has a regulatory body, usually the state bar association or an ethics committee or commission, which enforces the legal ethics rules for lawyers. When lawyers are licensed to practice law in a state, they subject themselves to this disciplinary authority. Ultimate responsibility for the enforcement of the legal ethics rules in a state, however, lies with the state's highest court.

In addition to these ethics codes, ABA and NALA offer model guidelines, and about two-thirds of the state bar associations have adopted state guidelines to assist attorneys in ethically and efficiently utilizing paralegals services. These guidelines, among other things, emphasize that attorneys are responsible for the ethical conduct of the paralegals they supervise. ABA's guidelines are called the Model Guidelines for the Utilization of Paralegal Services. NALA's guidelines are called Model Standards and Guidelines for Utilization of Legal Assistants. These various guidelines often define what tasks paralegals may perform (and today paralegals may perform nearly any legal task so long as the work is supervised by an attorney and does not constitute the unauthorized practice of law), what their professional responsibilities should be, how attorneys can best use paralegal services, and what attorneys' responsibilities should be with regard to paralegals' work.

For a specific example, NALA's Standards and Guidelines set forth minimum qualifications for legal assistants in its "Standards" section. That section sets forth standards that may be used to determine a person's qualifications to be a legal assistant, including successful completion of NALA's CLA or CP certification examination; graduation from an ABA-approved legal assistants educational program; graduation from an institutionally accredited legal assistants educational program with not less than 60 hours of classroom study; graduation from a course of study for legal assistants that is not ABA-approved or institutionally accredited plus not less than six months of in-house legal assistants training; a bachelor's degree in any field plus not less than six months of in-house legal assistants training; at least three years of law-related experience under the supervision of an attorney with at least six months of in-house legal assistants training; or two years of in-house legal assistants training.

In the "Guidelines" section of NALA's Standards and Guidelines, NALA issues five guidelines pertaining to paralegal utilization. Guideline 1 deals with what legal assistants should do: disclose their status, preserve client confidences, and understand the legal ethics codes for their jurisdictions. Guideline 2 covers what legal assistants should not do: establish attorney-client relationships, set legal fees, give legal advice, represent clients in court unless authorized by the court to do so, or engage in the unauthorized practice of law. Guideline 3 delineates services legal assistants may perform, emphasizing the role of attorneys in the direct supervision of legal assistants and the ultimate responsibility of attorneys for their legal assistants' work. Guideline 4 details what attorneys should consider when supervising legal assistants, such as assigning work that corresponds to the legal assistants' abilities, knowledge, training, and experience; educating and training legal assistants regarding professional responsibility, local rules and practices, and firm policies; monitoring the work and professional conduct of legal assistants; providing legal assistants with continuing legal education; and encouraging legal assistants to join professional organizations. Guideline 5 delineates specific tasks legal assistants may perform: conduct client interviews and maintain client contact after establishment of the attorney-client relationship; locate and interview witnesses; conduct investigations; conduct legal research; draft legal documents; draft correspondence and pleadings; attend closings, depositions, court hearings, and trials; and write and sign letters so long as the legal assistants' status is disclosed and legal advice is not given. Guideline 5 reiterates that most of these tasks should be performed for the responsible attorneys' review.

CHAPTER SUMMARY

- Regulation is the process of controlling something by rule or restriction. Paralegal regulation means the direct regulation of paralegals by licensing requirements and legal ethics rules of the states. At this time, there are no licensing requirements for paralegals as there are for attorneys. However, some states have considered or are considering regulating the paralegal profession through general licensing, title regulation, and voluntary registration and certification programs.

- Each state sets its own licensing requirements for attorneys. A person must meet these requirements and obtain a license to practice law in that jurisdiction. Licensing is a government's official act granting permission to a person to perform some service or use a particular title, such as practice law or hold oneself out as a lawyer. A license to practice law is a privilege that can be lost.

- Legal ethics are the minimum standards of conduct prescribed in a jurisdiction's code of ethical conduct that govern those engaged in the practice of law. Lawyers are directly regulated by the legal ethics rules in the states that license them. Lawyers can be disciplined for violations of their states' ethical rules, and sanctions can be imposed on them. Sanctions can include disbarment, suspension, probation, reprimand/reproval (public or private), restitution, assessment of the costs of the disciplinary action, completion of a professional ethics course or other continuing legal education course, passing a professional ethics exam or the bar exam, or being subject to limitations on the lawyer's practice. Disciplinary bodies, typically the state bar association or a committee or commission appointed by the state's highest court, consider several factors in determining which sanction is appropriate for a given violation.

- In addition to facing disciplinary actions pursuant to legal ethics code, attorneys who engage in unethical conduct may be sued for malpractice by their clients, prosecuted by the government under criminal statutes, and held in contempt of court.

- Paralegals who are not licensed by their states are indirectly bound by legal ethics rules. This is so because the lawyers for whom the paralegals work are responsible for the paralegals' ethical conduct and can be disciplined for their paralegals' violations of the ethics rules. While paralegals may not be disciplined under state ethics codes, they may be sued for malpractice by their clients, prosecuted by the government under criminal statutes, and face adverse employment consequences.

- Each state has its own legal ethics code setting forth the rules of professional conduct that apply to all lawyers licensed in that jurisdiction. All are based, at least in part, on the American Bar Association's Model Rules of Professional Conduct. Rules of ethics become enforceable once adopted by a state's highest court or bar association. Responsibilities regarding lawyer discipline under legal ethics code, as well as regarding bar admission, may be delegated by the states' highest courts to state bar associations.

- The ABA, NALA, and about two-thirds of the state bar associations have adopted guidelines to assist attorneys in the ethical and efficient utilization of paralegal services. These guidelines define what tasks paralegals may perform, what their professional responsibilities should be, how attorneys can best use paralegal services, and what attorneys' responsibilities should be with regard to paralegals' work.

CONCEPT REVIEW AND REINFORCEMENT

Key Terms and Concepts

Regulation
Paralegal regulation
Registration
Paralegal registration
Licensing
Legal ethics
Sanctions
Disbarment
Suspension
Probation
Reprimand
Reproval
Public reprimand
Private reprimand
Admonition
Restitution

Questions for Review

1. What is regulation?
2. How are paralegals regulated?
3. How is the regulation of paralegals different from the regulation of attorneys?
4. What are legal ethics?
5. What are legal ethics codes and paralegal utilization guidelines?
6. Where are legal ethics codes and paralegal utilization guidelines found?
7. Are paralegals *directly* bound by legal ethics codes? Are attorneys? Why or why not?

DEVELOPING YOUR PARALEGAL SKILLS

Critical Thinking Exercises

1. Identify three other professionals and their professions, besides lawyers in the legal profession, that are regulated through licensing.
2. Using the ABA's Model Guidelines for the Utilization of Paralegal Services, which you can find on ABA's website

(http://www.abanet.org/legalservices/paralegals/downloads/modelguidelines.pdf), answer the following questions. Reference the relevant guideline in your answer.

    a. May a lawyer bill a client for a paralegal's time?

    b. Is it the supervising lawyer's responsibility to take every possible measure to make sure that his paralegal preserves client confidences?

    c. May a lawyer put his paralegal's name on the firm's letterhead and/or business cards?

    d. May a lawyer delegate to a paralegal the task of establishing the amount of fee to be charged a client for a legal service?

    e. Is a lawyer responsible for all of the professional actions of a paralegal working under his direction?

    f. Can a lawyer split his legal fee with a paralegal?

3. Using ABA's Standards for Imposing Lawyer Sanctions (found on ABA's website, as well as in print sources), list four factors that a court should consider in imposing sanctions on a lawyer for ethical misconduct. Considering the fourth factor, give an example of an aggravating factor and an example of a mitigating factor.

4. Pat is a paralegal. He works for Ethyl, an attorney, at a law firm. One Friday afternoon, Pat was finishing a legal research and writing assignment for Client Z. At 5:00 p.m., Pat had completed everything he needed to do except cite check a few of his important cases. Not wanting to stay at work late on a Friday, Pat decided to submit the assignment to Ethyl without doing the cite check. "How often is a case overturned anyway?" Pat asked himself.

    That weekend, Ethyl prepared an opinion letter for Client Z based on Pat's research and legal memorandum, then sent it to the client. Unfortunately, an important case included in the memo was overturned in this jurisdiction. As a result, the opinion given by Ethyl to the client was based on law that was no longer good.

    Client Z follows the advice given by Ethyl, sues its competitor, and after expending about $50,000 on lawyer fees, loses the lawsuit, as case law in this jurisdiction does not support Client Z's position.

    a. What can Client Z do about the mistakes made by its law firm, lawyer, and paralegal?

    b. What can happen to Ethyl as a result of this?

    c. What can happen to Pat?

5. Locate the American Bar Association's ethics advisory Formal Opinion 10-457 either on the ABA website or other Internet site and answer the following questions:

    a. What content may be on lawyer websites?

    b. What information may be in lawyer websites about the lawyers themselves?

    c. What information may be in lawyer websites about their law firm?

    d. How should lawyer websites avoid misleading readers regarding information about the law?

    e. For what purpose(s) would lawyer websites include warnings or cautionary statements to limit, condition, or disclaim a lawyer's obligations to website visitors?

ASSIGNMENTS AND PRACTICAL APPLICATIONS

California is the first state to directly regulate the paralegal profession via a title scheme found in its Business and Professions Code (Sections 6450-6456). In that statute, the state of California defines the term "paralegal" and enumerates the tasks a paralegal may perform. The statute also imposes continuing education requirements, both in law and legal ethics, on paralegals. Locate and review this statute. Who may hold herself out as a "paralegal" according to that statute? What tasks may a paralegal perform?

Florida has a voluntary registration program for paralegals called the Florida Registered Paralegal Program. Research that program, its requirements, and benefits. Do you like the program? If available in your state, would you take advantage of such a program and become a registered paralegal? See the Florida Bar Association's website (http://www.floridabar.org) for more information.

North Carolina has a voluntary paralegal certification program, approved by its highest court in 2004. Research to locate information about this program. What are the program's requirements?

Does your state regulate paralegals with a title, registration or certification scheme? If so, how? Prepare an outline of your state's requirements.

Research to see if your state has a criminal statute regarding the unauthorized practice of law, in other words practicing law without a license. If so, what does the statute say? Is the crime classified as a misdemeanor or a felony?

Locate the Minnesota and South Carolina statutes on the unauthorized practice of law, discussed in the chapter. One of these statutes classifies the unauthorized practice of law as a misdemeanor crime while the other classifies it as a felony. Compare and contrast those statutes.

Research to locate your state's legal ethics code for lawyers. Review that code and use it to answer the Ethical Applications questions near the end of this chapter.

Does your state have guidelines for the utilization of paralegals? If so, what do the guidelines cover?

Technology Resources and Internet Exercises

On its website, the National Federation of Paralegal Associations (NFPA) includes a summary of different states' regulation of paralegals. See http://www.paralegals.org/displaycommon.cfm?an=1&subarticlenbr=795.

See NFPA's Model Act for Paralegal Licensure at http://www.paralegals.org/displaycommon.cfm?an=1&subarticlenbr=341.

See http://www.nala.org/LicIssues.htm for a position statement by the National Association of Legal Assistants (NALA) on why paralegals should not be subject to regulation by license.

For more information about the *Bates* Case on Point, see http://en.wikipedia.org/wiki/Bates_v._State_Bar_of_Arizona.

Using Duke Law School's website, review a discussion of legal ethics and how to research issues in professional responsibility. http://www.law.duke.edu/lib/researchguides/legale.

Use the Cornell University Law School website to review ABA's Model Rules of Professional Conduct. See http://law.cornell.edu/ethics/aba/current/ABA_CODE.HTM.

Using the Internet, locate and review NFPA's Model Code of Ethics and Professional Responsibility and Guidelines for Enforcement.

Using the Internet, locate and review NALA's Code of Ethics and Professional Responsibility.

See http://www.abanet.org/legalservices/paralegals/downloads/modelguidelines.pdf for the ABA's Model Guidelines for the Utilization of Paralegal Services.

Using the Cornell University Law School website for its Legal Information Institute, found at http://www.law.cornell.edu/, find your state's legal ethics code. Use it to answer the following Ethical Applications.

Ethical Applications

Statutes of limitations limit the time period during which a plaintiff may bring a legal action. Consider the implication of a paralegal asked by her supervising attorney to file a client's breach of contract complaint before the statute of limitations runs out (meaning that the time to file suit runs out). Unfortunately, the paralegal misses the deadline.

What are the implications of the paralegal missing the court's filing deadline? What consequences can the paralegal face, if any? What consequences can the supervising attorney face, if any? What can a law firm do to protect itself in situations like this one?

VIDEO CASE STUDIES

Video Interview of Lois Shaw

Paralegal case study videos to accompany this textbook are accessible from within both the New MyLegalStudiesLab Virtual Law Office Experience course and the Resources Website for Paralegal Studies.

ENDNOTES

[1] In the state of Maryland, the Maryland State Bar Association's Special Committee on Paralegals continues to monitor other states' paralegal regulation efforts, watching for uniform developments in this area and for successful regulation schemes in other jurisdictions that it might wish to propose in Maryland. The author of this text is a member of that committee.

[2] The state of Florida was considering two bills proposed in the Florida Senate and House regarding adoption of mandatory paralegal regulation via a licensing requirement, which bills failed in May 2011.

[3] Unless the state permits the attorney to "waive" into that state's bar association without the taking of the state's bar examination, as discussed in Chapter 1.

6

The "Big Three"
Legal Ethics Areas

Christine Rentz

Corporate Paralegal at RTKL Associates, Inc.

Christine had been working in the legal field for many years when she realized that she wanted to enhance her skills and become a paralegal. So she enrolled in a paralegal education program. Having responded to an advertisement in a local newspaper, Christine is now an in-house corporate paralegal for RTKL Associations, Inc., an architecture, engineering, and design firm.

Christine finds that communication, technology use, and organizational and time management skills are useful to her practice as a paralegal. She also recommends that a paralegal demonstrate a willingness to learn, work hard, and complete tasks in a timely manner.

In her practice, Christine drafts many types of legal documents, including promissory notes, affidavits, contracts (such as vendor agreements, nondisclosure agreements, and subcontractor agreements), corporate documents, powers of attorney, and pleadings. She also performs factual investigations, assists with subpoena filings, performs legal research, drafts corporate resolutions, helps establish joint ventures and partnerships, reviews contracts and proposals, assists in litigation preparation, and performs many other varied tasks. Performing administrative tasks, such as answering telephones, paying invoices, and setting up meetings, is another part of Christine's job.

Technology is used extensively in Christine's practice, where she uses applications for word processing, e-mail, the Internet, electronic spreadsheets, electronic timekeeping, electronic calendaring, and PowerPoint. She performs online legal research, as well as uses specialty software relating to her employer's industry, such as architecture business–related software.

The legal ethics rules that impact Christine's practice the most are those relating to confidentiality— in particular, confidential and privileged documents. In her job, Christine reviews and analyzes documents to determine if they are confidential and privileged. If they are, she marks them "Confidential or Legally Privileged." She is always careful about what documents she sends to third parties; if she is unsure of how to treat a document, she checks with her supervising attorney.

The full video interview is accessible from within both the New MyLegalStudiesLab Virtual Law Office Experience course and the Resources Website for Paralegal Studies.

The chapter will answer the following questions:

- What are the "big three" legal ethics areas affecting paralegals?
- What is the unauthorized practice of law and what legal ethics rules and other laws prohibit it?

- What are the legal ethics rules regarding confidentiality?
- What are conflicts of interest and what are the legal ethics rules pertaining to them?

CHAPTER **INTRODUCTION**

This chapter examines the three main areas of legal ethics that apply to paralegals. It defines the unauthorized practice of law and examines the legal ethics rules and other laws prohibiting the unauthorized practice of law. The chapter also provides students with a basic understanding of the rules of legal ethics pertaining to the duty of confidentiality. Finally, conflicts of interest are defined, and the legal ethics rules involving them are examined. Our study begins by identifying the "big three" legal ethics areas affecting paralegals.

All of the ethics rules impact a paralegal and all are of the utmost importance because violation of any of the rules can, depending on what occurs as a result of the violation, lead to serious consequences for the paralegal and the attorney. The attorney [can] be sanctioned or sued for malpractice. As a paralegal, you could also lose your job, which could make it hard for you to get another job as a paralegal.
Sherry Myers

THE "BIG THREE" LEGAL ETHICS AREAS AFFECTING PARALEGALS

Each jurisdiction has legal ethics rules that directly bind all lawyers licensed to practice there. As discussed in the previous chapter, paralegals are indirectly bound by their states' legal ethics rules. These legal ethics rules are discussed in this chapter and in Chapter 7.

In this chapter we focus on three major areas of legal ethics. These three areas receive special treatment because they are especially critical not only to attorneys but also to paralegals. Because of their particular importance to paralegals, we will examine them separately in greater depth. These "big three" legal ethics areas affecting paralegals are the unauthorized practice of law, confidentiality, and conflicts of interest. Now we will discuss each of these, in turn, beginning with the unauthorized practice of law.

THE UNAUTHORIZED PRACTICE OF LAW

To practice law, a person must have a license to do so in that jurisdiction, meaning that state or the District of Columbia. Earlier in the text, we discussed the requirements to obtain a license to practice law. Nonlawyers are prohibited from practicing law, just as nonsurgeons are prohibited from performing surgery. This prohibition exists to protect the public from the harm that can result when a person who lacks the necessary knowledge and skill to adequately perform a task performs it anyway. Laws and rules prohibiting the unauthorized practice of law, specifically, are meant to protect the public from harm that can result from unqualified persons representing others in legal matters. Legal ethics rules regarding the unauthorized practice of law help to protect the legal profession as well, by keeping the quality of service high through licensing requirements for attorneys. Keep in mind, though, that only attorneys are directly bound by legal ethics rules, and nonlawyers are not bound by those rules. Because only lawyers may engage in the practice of law, what does the "practice of law" mean?

There is no universal definition of what constitutes the practice of law. Nor is there a defined list of tasks that constitute the practice of law. The definition of "practice of law" has no fixed boundaries—rather, it is flexible. The definition varies from state to state as well. As you will see, legal ethics rules and criminal statutes help define the practice of law in jurisdictions. The highest court in a jurisdiction has the final authority to interpret that definition.

Legal ethics rules, criminal statutes, and court cases all provide guidance in defining the practice of law. First, regarding legal ethics rules, many states have adopted an "unauthorized practice of law" rule, such as Maryland's Rule 5.5, which restricts the practice of law by lawyers admitted in jurisdictions other than Maryland. Remember that licenses to practice law are issued on a state-by-state basis. Admission to the bar in one state does not authorize a lawyer to practice law in another state unless she has special permission or authorization to do so. That is why it is common for attorneys to have licenses to practice law in more than one jurisdiction.[i] It is the unauthorized practice of law for an attorney (rather than a nonlawyer) to practice law in a state where she is not licensed or otherwise does not have the court's permission to practice law in some limited or temporary capacity. An attorney may receive a court's permission to handle a specific matter in a jurisdiction where the attorney is not licensed, but only under special and limited circumstances, as noted in Maryland Rules 5.5(c) and (d). In addition, attorneys who practice in the federal court system must get admitted to practice before the relevant federal courts for their cases. A federal court usually admits attorneys who are licensed to practice law in the state in which the court sits.

The Maryland Rules on the unauthorized practice of law also prohibit a Maryland-licensed lawyer from practicing law in a jurisdiction in violation of that jurisdiction's regulation of the legal profession. They also prohibit a lawyer from assisting another in doing so. Accordingly, attorneys may not assist unauthorized persons, including paralegals, in practicing law without a license. This prohibition can apply to disbarred or suspended attorneys, who may work as paralegals if the law and legal ethics rules in the jurisdiction permit. Disbarred and suspended attorneys cannot legally practice law, and those supervising them if they are working as paralegals may not assist the disbarred or suspended attorneys in the unauthorized practice of law. Remember that legal ethics rules apply directly to lawyers, and not paralegals, so these rules address lawyer conduct only.

In addition to the legal ethics rules expressly governing the unauthorized practice of law and multijurisdictional practice such as the Maryland Rules just noted, states' legal ethics rules also delineate attorneys' responsibility for the supervision of their employees. Attorneys who supervise nonlawyers are responsible for the nonlawyers' conduct and may be held accountable for it. Among the supervision duties of attorneys is the requirement that attorneys ensure that the

> *Anytime someone asks me for legal advice, I explain that I am a paralegal and not an attorney and cannot give legal advice. If I even think that certain information could be interpreted as legal advice, I explain that I cannot give out that information and that the person should contact an attorney.*
> Julianne Ennis

Summary of Certain Unauthorized Practice of Law and Multijurisdictional Practice of Law Rules in Maryland

Rule 5.5(a) prohibits a Maryland-licensed lawyer from practicing law in a jurisdiction in violation of that jurisdiction's regulation of the legal profession, and from assisting another in doing so.

Rule 5.5(b) prohibits a lawyer who is not licensed in Maryland from establishing a law office in Maryland or holding herself out as a lawyer licensed to practice in Maryland.

Rule 5.5(c) allows a lawyer admitted in another jurisdiction and not disbarred or suspended in any jurisdiction to provide legal services on a temporary basis in Maryland if certain conditions are met, including that she associates herself with a lawyer who is admitted in Maryland.

Rule 5.5(d) allows a lawyer admitted in another jurisdiction and not disbarred or suspended in any jurisdiction to provide legal services in Maryland if the lawyer's services are provided to the lawyer's employer or its organizational affiliates and they are not services for which the court requires *pro hac vice* admission (where a court grants permission for a lawyer who is licensed in another jurisdiction to participate in a particular matter that is within the court's jurisdiction) or the legal services are ones that the lawyer is authorized, by federal law or some other law in Maryland, to provide.

education, training, and experience of the paralegal and the degree of difficulty of the task being performed. Attorneys, then, are responsible for preventing the unauthorized practice of law by the nonlawyers they supervise. Under both legal ethics rules and criminal statutes, attorneys may not allow a nonlawyer to engage in, or assist a nonlawyer in engaging in, the practice of law.

In addition to legal ethics rules defining the "practice of law," tests have been created by the courts to determine whether or not an activity constitutes the practice of law. These tests include whether the service performed required the knowledge and skills of an attorney rather than a layperson; whether the service performed was one that is usually rendered by an attorney; whether the service performed was essentially legal in nature or was incidental to some nonlegal transaction; and

> *Nothing goes out of this office without a stamp of approval from one of the attorneys.*
> Lindsay Ann Thomas

Summary of Part of the Massachusetts Rules of Professional Conduct about Supervising Nonlawyer Assistants

Rule 5.3(b) requires a lawyer who has direct supervisory authority over a nonlawyer to make reasonable efforts to ensure that the nonlawyer's conduct is compatible with the professional obligations of the lawyer.

Rule 5.3(c) makes a lawyer responsible for the conduct of a nonlawyer where the nonlawyer's conduct would be a violation of Massachusetts' legal ethics rules if engaged in by the lawyer and (1) the lawyer orders or ratifies the nonlawyer's conduct or (2) the lawyer is a partner in a law firm in which the nonlawyer is employed, or has direct supervisory authority over the nonlawyer, and knows of the conduct at a time when its consequences can be avoided or mitigated and fails to take reasonable remedial action.

nonlawyers they employ do not engage in the unauthorized practice of law (see the Rules on Point from Massachusetts for an example). If attorneys fail to adequately provide this supervision, they may be found to have assisted nonlawyers in the unauthorized practice of law, which is both an ethical violation for which attorneys can be disciplined and criminal misconduct. As a general rule, the degree of supervision required makes it necessary for attorneys to have direct contact with those they supervise, including their paralegals. The extent of that contact depends on such factors as the

Court Tests for Determining Whether an Activity Constitutes the Practice of Law

- Whether the service performed required the knowledge and skills of an attorney
- Whether the service performed was one that is usually rendered by an attorney
- Whether the service performed was essentially legal in nature or was incidental to some nonlegal transaction
- Whether harm was caused to a third person as a result of the service rendered

STATUTE *on* POINT

Tex. Gov't Code Ann. § 81.101 (2010).

Section 81.101(a) defines "practice of law" as the preparation of a pleading or other document incident to an action or special proceeding or the management of the action or proceeding on behalf of a client before a judge in court as well as a service rendered out of court, including the giving of advice or the rendering of any service requiring the use of legal skill or knowledge, such as preparing a will, contract, or other instrument, the legal effect of which under the facts and conclusions involved must be carefully determined.

Section 81.101(b) states that the definition is not exclusive, and that the judiciary retains the power and authority under the statute and case law to determine whether other services not enumerated in the definition also constitute the practice of law.

Section 81.101(c) expressly excludes from the definition of the "practice of law" the design, creation, publication, distribution, display, or sale, including publication, distribution, display, or sale by means of an Internet website, of written materials, books, forms, computer software, or similar products if the products clearly and conspicuously state that the products are not a substitute for the advice of an attorney.

whether harm was caused to a third person as a result of the service rendered.

Finally, criminal statutes prohibiting the unauthorized practice of law sometimes (but not always) attempt to define the practice of law. For example, Texas enacted an unauthorized practice of law statute that includes a definition of the practice of law. The Texas statute defines "practice of law" as the preparation of a pleading or other document incident to an action on behalf of a client before a judge in court as well as a service rendered out of court, including the giving of advice or the rendering of any service requiring the use of legal skill or knowledge, such as preparing a will, contract, or other instrument, the legal effect of which under the facts and conclusions involved must be carefully determined. That statute goes on to say that the definition is not exclusive, and the judiciary can determine whether other services also constitute the practice of law. The statute also expressly excludes from the definition of the "practice of law" the design, creation, publication, distribution, display, or sale, including publication, distribution, display, or sale by means of an Internet website, of written materials, books, forms, computer software, or similar products if the products clearly and conspicuously state that they are not a substitute for an attorney's advice.

Now we have defined, as best definable, the "practice of law." Through that definition the *unauthorized* practice of law is determined. The **unauthorized practice of law** is the practice of law by a person who is not authorized. A person without a license to practice law in the jurisdiction is not authorized. Certain activities have come to be known as falling clearly within the definition of the practice of law, so these activities are reserved for authorized person's to perform. These activities

include establishing the attorney-client relationship and setting legal fees, giving legal opinions or advice, and representing a client before a court or other tribunal unless nonlawyer representation is authorized by the court or tribunal.[2] No person should engage in, encourage, or contribute to any act that could constitute the unauthorized practice of law. Accordingly, these tasks enumerated above may not be delegated by an attorney to a nonlawyer, such as a paralegal. Note, however, this is not an exhaustive list. Other tasks may constitute the practice of law and thus be reserved for licensed attorneys to perform. These tasks may be, or become, defined by ethics

The **unauthorized practice of law** is the practice of law by a person who is not authorized, meaning a person who does not have a license to practice law in the jurisdiction.

The Practice of Law

These tasks are generally considered to constitute the practice of law:

- Establishing the attorney-client relationship and setting the fee to be charged for a legal service

- Giving a legal opinion or legal advice

- Representing a client in a court or other tribunal proceeding (unless authorized by the court or tribunal)

- Engaging in, encouraging, or contributing to any act that could constitute the unauthorized practice of law

rules and other laws, such as case law. Each of these activities is discussed in turn.

Only a lawyer can enter into a relationship with a client to represent the client in a legal matter. In other words, only a lawyer can agree to represent a client and agree to the scope of that representation. Establishing the attorney-client relationship constitutes the practice of law. Therefore, it is the unauthorized practice of law for a nonlawyer, including a paralegal, to attempt to establish a relationship between a client and a lawyer. Accordingly, a supervising lawyer cannot delegate this duty to her paralegal. Therefore, a paralegal should never sign a retainer agreement on behalf of his supervising lawyer.

Similarly, setting the fee to be charged for a legal service also constitutes the practice of law. It is the unauthorized practice of law for a nonlawyer to attempt to set a fee to be charged a client for a legal matter. Accordingly, a supervising lawyer cannot delegate this duty to her paralegal.

However, it is fine for a nonlawyer, such as a paralegal, to meet with a prospective client to gather information before the client meets with the attorney (subject to confidentiality obligations and conflict of interest requirements, discussed in the following sections). It is common for both paralegals and attorneys to perform initial interviews of prospective clients. However, the paralegal must be careful not to agree to represent the client in the matter and not to make an arrangement regarding the fee to be charged for handling the legal matter. It is also fine for a paralegal to attend a meeting between the client and the attorney where the attorney agrees to representation and sets the fee to be charged for handling the legal matter. A distinction is made between being present when the attorney establishes the attorney-client relationship and sets a fee and actually performing those functions on behalf of the attorney.

Rendering legal opinions and giving legal advice are also considered the practice of law. Rendering legal opinions and giving legal advice require the exercise of independent professional judgment by an attorney. Rendering legal opinions and giving legal advice includes such activities as explaining to a client his legal rights and responsibilities, recommending a course of action to a client regarding how to proceed in a legal matter, evaluating the probable outcome of a legal matter, and interpreting laws (constitutions, statutes, court cases, and administrative rules and regulations) and legal documents for clients. Tests that courts use in determining whether a person gave legal advice differ from jurisdiction to jurisdiction. However, many jurisdictions consider whether the knowledge of the information imparted (the "advice") generally requires advanced legal knowledge and skill, whether the communication is intended to advise a person about her legal rights, and whether the advice is advice that is not normally given by a nonlawyer as part of a business or other transaction.

Keep in mind that a paralegal may not give legal advice. A paralegal may, however, relay the supervising attorney's legal advice to the client. It is the giving of legal advice by a nonlawyer that is prohibited, not the communicating of the attorney's legal advice. If the attorney renders the legal opinion or gives the legal advice, while it can come directly from the attorney to the client, it can also be communicated through the paralegal to the client. Because paralegals may be more readily available and easier to reach in their offices than attorneys, who attend many meetings and, perhaps, go to court, paralegals can be useful resources in conveying information from attorneys to clients.

Know what you are and are not allowed to do as a paralegal and don't be tempted to cross the line. Clients may try to get you to give them legal advice . . . Stick to your guns no matter how tempting, for giving legal advice is a big NO-NO.
Sherry Myers

When Is Advice "Legal Advice"?

A person gives legal advice if:

- The knowledge of the information imparted (the "advice") generally requires advanced legal knowledge and skill;

- The communication is intended to advise a person about her legal rights; or

- The advice is advice that is not normally given by a nonlawyer as part of a business or other transaction.

A nonlawyer, such as a paralegal, may not represent a client before a court, administrative agency, or other tribunal unless authorized by the court, agency, or other tribunal to do so. To represent a client before a court, administrative agency, or other tribunal without authorization constitutes the unauthorized practice of law. The representation of a client in court is called making a court appearance. Making a court appearance requires specialized knowledge and skills that only attorneys possess, gained through their special legal education, training, and experience.

This restriction on representing clients in court is broad enough to encompass all appearances made on behalf of a client—including depositions, which are a form of discovery where sworn testimony is obtained from parties and witnesses before trial. Because deposition testimony can be introduced at trial, it is as important as testimony given under oath at trial, so taking a deposition falls within this rule. Accordingly, paralegals should not take depositions of parties or witnesses. The restriction is also broad enough to encompass not only proceedings in court but proceedings in front of administrative agencies and other types of tribunals. That said, paralegals often accompany attorneys while the attorneys are making court appearances—including being present at depositions, hearings, and trials. Paralegals can assist attorneys at these times, such as by attending proceedings and taking notes, or being available to conduct last-minute legal research. Paralegals, however, may not represent clients during court appearances.

There are some exceptions to this rule. The most important exception is where the tribunal, typically an administrative

> *I avoid the unauthorized practice of law by always stating to the client that the attorney asked me to relay [the] information.*
> **Kristina Winter**

agency, authorizes a nonlawyer, often a paralegal, to represent persons before it. Many federal administrative agencies authorize paralegals and other nonlawyers to represent people appearing before them. For a few familiar examples, the following administrative agencies are among the federal governmental agencies permitting representation by paralegals: the Internal Revenue Service, the Department of Labor, the Department of Justice, the General Accounting Office, the Small Business Administration, the Social Security Administration, the Immigration and Naturalization Service, the Food and Drug Administration, and the Department of Health and Human Services. State and local administrative agencies, such as workers' compensation boards and unemployment compensation committees, may authorize paralegal and other nonlawyer representation as well, though many do not.

Other exceptions to this requirement that only attorneys may represent clients in court is where the appearance is simply to ask the court for a continuance—meaning an extension of time. Some jurisdictions permit a nonlawyer to appear in court on behalf of the nonlawyer's employing attorney if the purpose is to request a continuance of a matter on the attorney's behalf. Also, some jurisdictions allow law students to represent clients in certain courts if they are doing so under the supervision of attorneys (remember Elle Woods in the first *Legally Blonde* movie). Further, in many cases, persons may represent themselves in legal matters; they are said to appear *pro se*, meaning they are representing themselves and have no lawyer representation in the matter. In certain jurisdictions, corporations can represent themselves as well. Finally, some court rules permit specific nonlawyers to appear in court on behalf of another person for a specific reason—such as to relay information from the attorney to the court by way of a paralegal "messenger."

Finally, paralegals should not engage in, encourage, or contribute to any act that could constitute the unauthorized practice of law. This last category is a catch-all, designed to "catch" other misconduct that goes beyond the four clearly enumerated categories just discussed. It also prohibits paralegals from encouraging or contributing to another's violation of the unauthorized practice of law rules.

ABA's Model Guidelines for the Utilization of Legal Assistant Services, adopted in whole or part in many states, offer guidance for attorneys regarding the unauthorized practice of law. Guideline 1 holds attorneys responsible for the conduct of paralegals working under their supervision. Guideline 2 permits attorneys to delegate to paralegals any tasks normally performed by attorneys unless a statute, court rule, administrative rule or regulation, other controlling authority, the jurisdiction's legal ethics rule, or ABA's Model Guidelines prevents the delegation of that specific task. The Model Guidelines, in Guideline 3, expressly prohibit attorneys from delegating to paralegals responsibility for establishing the attorney-client relationship, for setting the legal fee to be charged, and for rendering a legal opinion to a client. That said, performing legal services, including drafting legal documents, if done by a paralegal under the supervision of an attorney who is ultimately responsible for the work, presents no issue of the unauthorized practice of law. Rather, this is exactly how paralegals are supposed to assist in the provision of legal services at an effective cost. Supporting this, NALA's Model Standards and Guidelines for Utilization of Legal Assistants allow paralegals to perform any task delegated by an attorney unless that specific task delegation to a nonlawyer is prohibited by law.

In addition to ABA's Model Guidelines, national, state, and local professional paralegal associations also establish ethics rules concerning the unauthorized practice of law—specifically addressing that issue as it relates to the paralegal profession. NFPA's Model Code of Ethics and Professional Responsibility and NALA's Code of Ethics and Professional Responsibility both contain provisions expressly prohibiting the unauthorized practice of law by their members, who typically are paralegals. For example, NFPA's Model Code expressly requires that a paralegal not engage in the unauthorized practice of law, and requires him to comply with the applicable legal authority governing the unauthorized practice of law in the jurisdiction in which he practices. NALA, in its Code of Ethics (Canon 3), expressly requires that a paralegal not engage in, encourage, or contribute to any act that could constitute the unauthorized practice of law and that he must not establish attorney-client relationships, set fees, give legal opinions or advice, or represent a client before a court or agency unless the court or agency authorizes that representation. However, these rules are not legal authority, so they are not legally binding. Loss of membership in the organization is the only way for these associations to enforce their rules.

Does the employment status of the paralegal impact the unauthorized practice of law determination? Yes and no. A paralegal usually is employed by a law firm, corporation, or government agency. As an employee, he is working under the direct supervision of one or more lawyers also employed by that employer.

Giving Legal Advice and the Internet

Many law firms today advertise using websites accessible on the Internet. Users from all over the world can access these websites. These sites typically provide information about the firm and its practice, its lawyers and perhaps its paralegals, and its news and upcoming events (such as seminars the firm is offering for clients), among other things.

Unauthorized practice of law issues can arise when attorneys answer questions posed by Internet users because, unless access is restricted, users may be from outside the jurisdiction(s) where the attorney giving the legal advice is licensed. To prevent these problems, as well as problems relating to the confidentiality of information, establishment of the attorney-client relationship, and conflicts of interest (confidentiality and conflicts of interest are discussed in the next sections), firms commonly include disclaimers on their websites, informing site users that the information provided on the website does not constitute the giving of legal advice and, further, that information exchanged is not confidential and communications made over the Internet do not establish the attorney-client relationship.

However, some paralegals are freelance paralegals. **Freelance paralegals** are self-employed paralegals who are contractually engaged by attorneys to perform legal work, but they work for themselves, typically out of a home office. Because they are self-employed, freelance paralegals are not working in an employment situation for an attorney. Rather, they have a contract to perform services for an attorney. Freelance paralegals must abide by the unauthorized practice of law requirements of all paralegals and nonlawyers. This means that they must ensure that they receive adequate supervision from the attorneys who engage them. Otherwise, they may commit the unauthorized practice of law. While the "unauthorized practice of law" rules and laws do not distinguish between employee-paralegals and self-employed paralegals, there must be adequate attorney supervision of all paralegals who are performing legal work. This may be more difficult when the paralegal works from home rather than in a law office alongside the supervising attorney. That it

A **freelance paralegal** is a self-employed paralegal who is contractually engaged by attorneys to perform legal work, but who works for herself, typically out of a home office.

may be more difficult is no excuse, and sufficient supervision is a "must" to avoid committing the unauthorized practice of law.

A greater "unauthorized practice of law" issue arises in the case of independent paralegals. **Independent paralegals** are paralegals who offer their services directly to the public, without attorney supervision. They also identify themselves as legal document preparers, legal document assistants, and other names. Note that independent paralegals are providing services directly to the public and not working for an attorney and under an attorney's supervision. Independent paralegals often assist persons who are using self-help services. As nonlawyers who are assisting others in self-representation, independent paralegal services raise an unauthorized practice of law issue. Some jurisdictions regulate the conduct of independent paralegals. Refer back to the Texas statute noted earlier, which excludes from the definition of the "practice of law" the design, creation, publication, distribution, display, or sale, including publication, distribution, dis-

play, or sale by means of an Internet website, of written materials, books, forms, computer software, or similar products if the products clearly and conspicuously state that the products are not a substitute for the advice of an attorney. The key with respect to the work of independent paralegals is that they can assist in a person's self-representation but they can never render a legal opinion or give legal advice. So they may market, distribute, and sell legal forms to the public, including providing instructions on their use such as by providing printed material drafted by attorneys explaining how to fill out the forms. But an independent paralegal must never render a legal opinion or give legal advice, for he has no license to practice law. Independent paralegals must be careful not to give legal advice when they assist those using self-help materials.

Jurisdictions may also regulate the work of independent paralegals by requiring them to register to prepare certain legal documents. California, for example, regulates the legal document preparation profession via a Legal Document Assistant (LDA) program. Under the statute in California, a Legal Document

Self-Representation

Out of necessity or desire, some people represent themselves in their legal matters rather than hire attorneys. Self-representation is fairly common today in certain types of matters, such

© Annette Shaff/Shutterstock

as domestic relations matters (often divorce cases), traffic court cases (defending against traffic tickets), and the drafting of estate planning documents (simple wills, typically). Self-help materials, such as books, forms, and software programs, are available to purchase both in print and online to help those who are representing themselves in legal matters—particularly in the drafting of legal documents like simple wills, leases, and buy/sell agreements. An unauthorized practice of law issue arises if a paralegal assists a person who is representing herself in the filling out of the self-help forms because there is no attorney supervising the paralegal's work.

Some jurisdictions regulate self-help legal software and its use. Remember the Texas "unauthorized practice of law" statute summarized earlier. Section 81.101(c) of the Texas statute expressly excludes from the definition of the "practice of law" the design, creation, publication, distribution, display, or sale, including publication, distribution, display, or sale by means of an Internet website of written materials, books, forms, computer software, or similar products if the products clearly and conspicuously state that the products are not a substitute for the advice of an attorney.

Independent paralegals are paralegals who offer their services directly to the public, without attorney supervision; they are also called legal document preparers or legal document assistants.

Assistant is authorized to provide legal document preparation services directly to the public, after complying with the statute's registration and bonding requirements. Because they are not lawyers, LDAs may not give legal advice, discuss legal strategies, answer questions of a legal nature, select forms for consumers to use, or appear in court on a consumer's behalf. However, LDAs may assist consumers who are representing themselves in legal matters by preparing and processing legal documents. Many of California's LDAs have paralegal education, training, and experience. However, paralegals in California may not provide services directly to the public. Paralegals in California must be employed by an attorney, law firm, corporation, governmental agency, or other entity, and work under the direct supervision of a licensed attorney. In California, neither paralegals nor LDAs may engage in the practice of law.

The paralegal profession is the obvious profession most concerned with the unauthorized practice of law. Paralegals, by definition, perform certain substantive legal work for and delegated by a lawyer, under the lawyer's supervision and for which the lawyer is responsible. Other professions also face some risks regarding the unauthorized practice of law, though. For example, accountants, realtors, and bankers often use legal documents, including contracts, in their professional work. Many jurisdictions enact statutes and other rules to permit certain practices and activities by professionals who often deal with certain legal documents—such as realtors who routinely draft contracts for their clients to purchase and sell real estate. These special rules often provide for training of the nonlawyer in the performance of the permitted task and limit the activity to drafting the legal document. The nonlawyer professional must still refrain from giving legal advice or representing the client before a legal tribunal, as those practices are reserved for lawyers.

Several tools are available to the government to enforce the unauthorized practice of law rules and laws. These tools can result in negative consequences both to attorneys and to nonlawyers, including paralegals.

Against nonlawyers who commit the unauthorized practice of law, courts can issue injunctions ordering nonlawyers to stop engaging in activities that constitute the practice of law. Courts can bring civil contempt proceedings against nonlawyers who engage in the unauthorized practice of law. Governments can bring criminal prosecutions against nonlawyers who violate the jurisdiction's unauthorized practice of law criminal statutes. Paralegals may also be sued for malpractice, a tort action for professional negligence, when their misconduct, such as the unauthorized practice of law, causes harm to a client.

In such circumstances, however, clients choose to sue the deeper pockets—the law firm and the supervising lawyer. A paralegal who engages in the unauthorized practice of law, particularly one who gets his firm and/or supervising attorney in trouble for it—such as gets them sued for malpractice by the client—will likely face adverse employment consequences, such as termination.

I always get the attorney involved in what I am doing early and often. I do not finalize any nonstandard legal document without first running it by the attorney for approval. Susan Campbell

Attorneys who engage in the unauthorized practice of law (typically by practicing outside the jurisdictions in which they are licensed) or who assist a nonlawyer, such as their paralegal, in the unauthorized practice of law, including by failing to properly supervise the nonlawyer, may face the same consequences as nonlawyers who engage in this conduct, as just noted. Courts may issue injunctions ordering a lawyer to stop engaging in the unauthorized practice of law or in assisting a nonlawyer in engaging in the unauthorized practice of law. Attorneys may be cited for civil contempt as well. They can be prosecuted by the government if they violate the jurisdiction's criminal statutes on the unauthorized practice of law. Where a paralegal's unauthorized practice of law causes harm to a client, a realistic consequence is a malpractice lawsuit filed by the client against the law firm and the supervising attorney. In addition, because they are licensed to practice law in their jurisdictions, attorneys can be disciplined by their state bar associations and/or their states' highest courts for these violations. The sanctions may

TABLE 6-1	Consequences for the Unauthorized Practice of Law	
Attorney Consequences	**Paralegal Consequences**
Injunctions	Injunctions
Civil contempt	Civil contempt
Criminal prosecution	Criminal prosecution
Malpractice lawsuit	Malpractice lawsuit (though clients typically choose to sue the law firm or supervising attorney instead)
Discipline, including sanctions, under the legal ethics rules of the jurisdiction	Adverse employment action, including termination

be imposed on attorneys found to have violated their states' legal ethics rules regarding the unauthorized practice of law.

What can paralegals do to reduce their risk of committing the unauthorized practice of law? Well, there are several things. First, they can be diligent in never appearing to render a legal opinion or give legal advice. They must never attempt to establish an attorney-client relationship or set the fee to be charged for legal services. In addition, they must never represent a person in court unless the court authorizes such nonlawyer representation. Remember that the rule regarding representation in court is broad enough to encompass all court appearances, including depositions. It also includes administrative proceedings and proceedings of other tribunals. To avoid problems, paralegals should always disclose their status as paralegals to third parties, whether communications with the third parties are made in person, over the telephone, via e-mail, on legal correspondence, or on business cards. Third parties, especially clients, who deal with paralegals need to know that they are dealing with a paralegal and not a lawyer. Presenting oneself as an attorney when one is not may constitute the unauthorized practice of law. In fact, in many states, misrepresenting oneself as an attorney is a misdemeanor crime. All legal correspondence and any legal document prepared by paralegals should be reviewed and approved by their supervising attorneys before being distributed. The preparation of legal documents usually requires a superior knowledge of the law that nonlawyers do not possess, and these documents can affect clients' legal rights. In preparing legal documents, exercising independent professional legal judgment and giving legal advice is often required. Because of this, attorney supervision is crucial. If a paralegal feels his supervising attorney has not sufficiently reviewed the work, the paralegal should urge the attorney's further review of it—in other words, the paralegal

KEY Point

Tips for Paralegals to Avoid the Unauthorized Practice of Law

- Never render a legal opinion or give legal advice.
- Never attempt to establish the attorney-client relationship.
- Never attempt to set the fee to be charged for legal services.
- Never represent a client in court or before another tribunal, unless authorized to do so by the court or tribunal.
- Always disclose one's paralegal status.
- Obtain supervising attorney review and approval of all legal correspondence and documents one drafts before they are distributed.
- Obtain the supervising attorney's signature on any legal document (after review of the document by the attorney) when an attorney's signature is required.
- Never discuss the merits of a case with opposing counsel or attempt to negotiate settlement of the client's matter.

should take responsibility to make sure adequate supervision is provided. While some documents can be prepared for the paralegal's signature, such as legal correspondence from the paralegal, many legal documents should be, or may be required by law (such as pleadings) to be, signed by the supervising attorney. Paralegals cannot sign pleadings and other documents filed with the court on behalf of a client, because the document filed with the court constitutes a court appearance that only a licensed attorney can make. However, paralegals may prepare pleadings and other documents to be filed with a court so long as they are reviewed by the supervising attorney, who will adopt the paralegal's work as her own when the attorney signs the document. Also, a paralegal should never discuss the merits of a client's case with opposing counsel. Certainly a paralegal should never attempt to negotiate a settlement with the opposing counsel on behalf of the client or supervising attorney. That is the lawyer's job, and only the lawyer is qualified to perform it. It can be considered the unauthorized practice of law for a paralegal to do it—whether he discloses his status or not.

Now that we have reviewed the very important laws and rules regarding the unauthorized practice of law, we will examine the second major legal ethics area applicable to paralegals. That critical area is confidentiality.

CONFIDENTIALITY

There are two aspects to confidentiality. One is the ethical duty of confidentiality. Another is the attorney-client privilege. The ethical duty of confidentiality is very broad and covers most information learned in the course of legal representation of a client in a matter. The attorney-client privilege is a rule of evidence and is related to, but much more narrow than, the ethical duty of confidentiality. We will examine both of these aspects to confidentiality, starting with the ethical duty of confidentiality.

To provide the best possible legal representation, attorneys must know all the relevant information their clients possess regarding the legal matter. Full disclosure by a client is essential to effective legal representation. This means that clients must divulge all information they possess regarding the legal matter for which they obtained legal representation—even if that information is damaging or embarrassing to them. How does the legal profession encourage clients to divulge all relevant information? It does this by imposing a duty of confidentiality on attorneys and those who work for them with respect to client confidences. When a client knows the attorney cannot disclose the information she provides, the client will more freely divulge information.

The duty of confidentiality is paramount to the legal profession. The general rule on the duty of confidentiality is that all information relating to the representation of a client must be kept confidential by the lawyer and her employees and other agents. In other words, attorneys and those who work for attorneys have an ethical duty to maintain client confidences.

What information is protected under this duty of confidentiality? All information relating to the legal representation of the client in a matter, regardless of its source, normally is protected. Accordingly, most information learned by an attorney during the course of and relating to the representation of a client on a matter, whether the information is learned from the client or from another source, is covered. There are some exceptions, which are discussed below. Despite these exceptions, the ethical duty of confidentiality is very broad.

KEY Point

Information Protected by the Ethical Duty of Confidentiality

The ethical duty of confidentiality normally protects all information relating to the legal representation of the client in a matter, regardless of its source.

When does this duty of confidentiality begin, and when does it end? The ethical duty of confidentiality begins at a very early stage. It applies even before the establishment of the attorney-client relationship—to a prospective client who consults with an attorney in seeking legal representation, whether or not that attorney is ultimately retained by the client or whether the attorney agrees to accept that representation. The duty lasts beyond the termination of work on the legal matter for which the attorney was retained by the client as well. Even after the termination of the attorney-client relationship, the duty continues. Even after the death of the client, the duty continues.

The duty of confidentiality obviously applies to clients who are people—meaning humans. It also applies to clients who are organizations, such as corporations or limited liability companies. Keep in mind that when lawyers represent a corporate client, it is the corporation, not its directors, officers, stockholders, and employees, that is the client. The duty of confidentiality applies to the client but not necessarily to its representatives and employees—for they are not the attorney's client.

What does it mean to keep the client's information "confidential"? It means the attorney must not disclose the client's information to anyone other than her nonlawyer team members, such as paralegals, who are assisting with work on the matter for the client. It is a duty not to disclose. Accordingly, attorneys and their agents should not disclose client confidences to the media. It also means they should not disclose such confidences to any third parties—including family and friends, even when the confidential information makes for interesting conversation.

KEY Point

The General Rule on the Duty of Confidentiality

All information relating to the representation of a client must be kept confidential by the lawyer and her employees and other agents.

> *The duty of confidentiality means that you can't share the information from a client's case with anyone other than the persons in the firm who are working with the attorney on the case, such as paralegals, legal secretaries, and associate attorneys.*
>
> Sherry Myers

> *Remember to not discuss cases outside the [legal] team is my advice to any new paralegal.*
> Peg Hartley

KEY Point

Duty Not to Disclose

The duty of confidentiality is a duty not to disclose the client's information to others.

We have noted that there are some exceptions to the duty of confidentiality. What are these exceptions? Exceptions to the duty of confidentiality vary a bit from state to state. Common exceptions to the duty of confidentiality include when the client gives informed consent to disclosure; when disclosure is needed to carry out the representation; when disclosure is required to prevent death or substantial bodily harm to a third party; when disclosure is necessary to prevent, mitigate, or rectify a financial loss to a third party caused by the client's misconduct where the attorney's services are used to further the crime or fraud; when disclosure is necessary to obtain legal advice concerning the lawyer's legal ethics responsibilities; when disclosure is needed for the attorney to defend a legal claim or disciplinary action arising out of the representation of the client; and when disclosure is required to comply with the law or a court order. Each of these exceptions is discussed in turn.

KEY Point

Common Exceptions to the Duty of Confidentiality

- When the client gives informed consent to disclosure
- When disclosure is needed to carry out the representation
- When disclosure is required to prevent death or substantial bodily harm to a third party
- When disclosure is necessary to prevent, mitigate, or rectify a financial loss to a third party caused by the client's misconduct where the attorney's services are used to further the crime or fraud
- When disclosure is necessary to obtain legal advice concerning the lawyer's legal ethics responsibilities
- When disclosure is needed for the attorney to defend a legal claim or disciplinary action arising out of the representation of the client
- When disclosure is required to comply with the law or a court order

Clients may give attorneys their express permission to disclose client confidences. However, to be effective, the client's permission, called consent, must be given *after* the attorney has fully explained the alternatives to and risks of such disclosure to the client. It is *informed* consent that is required. To protect herself against claims of violation of the duty of confidentiality, it is a very good idea for an attorney to obtain the client's consent in writing rather than just orally. By reducing the consent to writing, signed by the client, good evidence of the client's consent exists. The written consent should include an acknowledgment by the client that the attorney first explained the alternatives to and risks of disclosure to him, evidencing *informed* consent was given.

KEY Point

Informed Consent

It is a good idea for an attorney to get the client's informed consent in writing to provide good evidence of that consent.

Another exception relates to the conduct of the representation itself. To represent a client in a matter, the attorney must have the client's implicit authorization to discuss the client's matter with others when necessary, such as opposing counsel in trying to negotiate the settlement of a tort claim. An attorney is implicitly authorized to disclose client confidences when doing so is necessary to perform the legal representation—in other words, to handle the client's matter. For example, the extent of the client's injuries are important to a damage claim asserted by the client in a tort action, so disclosure of their extent may be necessary to successfully negotiate a settlement of the claim with the opponent. For another example, disclosures made to an expert witness retained by the lawyer are permitted because they are necessary to the representation. Clients may limit this implied authority, however, such as by giving instructions restricting the use of confidential information.

Note that these two exceptions to the duty of confidentiality, namely, informed consent and disclosure implicitly authorized to adequately represent the client, both benefit the client. They advance the client's interests or goals. The remaining exceptions to the duty of confidentiality advance the interests of those other than the client, namely, third persons, the general public, or the attorney herself. Disclosure in these cases may be adverse to the client's interests but allowed nonetheless.

A very important exception to the ethical duty of confidentiality is the "future crimes" exception. In many jurisdictions, as a further exception to the duty of confidentiality, an attorney may, or may be required to (in other words "must"), disclose confidential client information if the attorney is reasonably certain that disclosure is necessary to prevent death or substantial bodily harm to a third party. For example, a client may make threats of physical harm against a third party to his attorney, such as by warning, "I'm going to make her pay for calling the cops on me. I'll put her lights out when I see her at work next Monday." At the time the client reveals his intention to commit a future crime, the attorney should try to talk her client out of committing it. Further, in making the disclosure to others, the attorney should reveal only that information needed to prevent the future crime and not additional information. Note that this exception applies only with respect to future actions of the client. If the client confesses that he has already murdered someone, or has beaten someone up, because the act is a past one, this "future crimes" exception does not apply, and a duty to keep the information confidential exists. But note that, where a client confesses to a past crime, the attorney is not required to accept, and where acceptance has already occurred is often not required to continue, that representation. Also note that jurisdictions differ as to the language of this exception. Some states *permit* disclosure of confidential information to prevent future crimes. Other states *require* disclosure by attorneys to prevent future crimes. Some jurisdictions apply this exception to many types of future crimes (states that permit, but do not require, disclosure), while others apply it to only certain crimes—typically more serious ones like those resulting in death or substantial bodily harm (in states that require disclosure). Always remember that this exception applies only to future crimes, not past ones.

In many jurisdictions, an attorney may disclose certain confidential client information if disclosure is necessary to prevent a substantial financial or property loss to a third party. This exception is designed to *prevent* the client's *commission* of the crime or fraud. The crime or fraud must relate to the matter for which the attorney is representing the client. For example, if a client tells his corporate attorney that he plans to falsify the company's financial statements to obtain a needed bank loan, where the attorney is the client's corporate counsel representing the client in financial and other corporate matters, the attorney may disclose this confidential client information to the extent necessary to protect the bank from loss. Remember that the injury faced by the third party must be substantial, rather than simply some injury. Also note that the attorney's services must be being used by the client to further the crime or fraud for disclosure to be permitted.

A related exception is recognized in many jurisdictions. This exception permits an attorney to disclose client confidences to the extent the attorney is reasonably certain disclosure is needed to prevent, mitigate, or rectify substantial injury to the financial or property interests of a third party. Note that this exception applies when the client *has already committed* the crime or fraud, but the attorney, through disclosure of the client confidences, may prevent, mitigate, or rectify substantial losses being or already incurred by the third party. Remember that the injury faced by the third party must be substantial and that the attorney's services must be being used by the client to further the crime or fraud for disclosure to be permitted.

Another exception recognized in many jurisdictions permits an attorney to disclose confidential client information when the attorney is seeking legal advice concerning her responsibilities under legal ethics rules. All lawyers are bound by the legal ethics rules of the states that license them to practice law. If a lawyer has a question about how to comply with any of these ethics rules, she may disclose client confidences to the extent necessary to obtain legal advice pertaining to such compliance to meet her ethical obligations.

Yet another exception to the duty of confidentiality permits an attorney to disclose client confidences to the extent necessary to defend herself against a legal claim made against her by a client—often a malpractice claim. This is sometimes called the "attorney defense" exception. When a civil claim or criminal charge is brought against an attorney based on her representation of a client, client confidences may be disclosed by the attorney to the extent necessary to defend against such a claim or charge. An attorney may also disclose confidential client information to the extent necessary to defend herself against a disciplinary charge for ethical misconduct. An attorney may even divulge confidential client information to establish a claim against a client—such as a claim for nonpayment of legal fees, where the attorney would have to reveal sufficient information

> *Confidentiality is the legal ethics rule that impacts me the most. We must get authorization from the client to give out information to family members, financial institutions, etc.*
> Kristina Winter

Summary of ABA Model Rules on Confidentiality

Rule 1.6(a) requires that an attorney not reveal information relating to a client's representation unless the client gives informed consent, if the disclosure is implicitly authorized for the attorney to carry out the representation, or if one of the exceptions in 1.6(b) applies.

Rule 1.6(b) allows an attorney to reveal information relating to a client's representation to the extent the lawyer reasonably believes it is necessary to:

1. prevent reasonably certain death or substantial bodily harm to a third party;

2. prevent the client from committing a crime or fraud that is reasonably certain to result in substantial injury to a third party's financial interests or property where the client has or is using the attorney's services to perpetrate that crime or fraud;

3. prevent, mitigate, or rectify substantial injury to the financial interests or property of a third party that is reasonably certain to result from, or has resulted from, the client's commission of a crime or fraud where the client has used the attorney's services to perpetrate it;

4. obtain legal advice regarding the attorney's compliance with legal ethics rules;

5. establish a claim or defense when the attorney is involved in a legal controversy with the client, establish a defense to a criminal charge or a civil lawsuit against the lawyer based on the client's conduct, or respond to allegations relating to the attorney's representation of the client; or

6. comply with a law or an order of a court.

to support the fee charged for the particular legal services rendered. Keep in mind that the scope of the disclosure is limited to what the attorney reasonably believes is necessary to establish her defense.

Another exception to the duty of confidentiality recognized in many jurisdictions permits an attorney to disclose confidential client information if some law requires it. Further, she may disclose confidential information when a court orders it. Compliance with a law or order of a court trumps the duty of confidentiality in these jurisdictions that permit disclosure.

How does the ethical duty of confidentiality apply to paralegals? The ethical duty of confidentiality extends to an attorney's nonlawyer employees and other agents, such as paralegals, receptionists, messengers, and other law office personnel assisting with the client's matter at the attorney's request. The legal ethics rules make attorneys responsible for the safeguarding of confidential client information against unauthorized disclosure by those whom they supervise. In other words, an attorney's duty to supervise her paralegals extends to require her to ensure the confidentiality of client information from disclosure by his paralegals. Remember that NALA and NFPA both have codes of ethics that guide

> *The best way to avoid breaching my duty of confidentiality is to not talk about work with friends.*
> **Michael Weiland**

and bind their members. Both of these professional associations' codes expressly impose on paralegals a duty of confidentiality. In addition to legal ethics rules requirements, in the approximate two-thirds of the states that have enacted guidelines for the utilization of paralegal services, these guidelines often require attorneys to ensure that paralegals preserve client confidences. Because the ethical rules of confidentiality, including the exceptions to the duty of confidentiality, vary from state to state, it is important to know your state's rules.

The second aspect of confidentiality, discussed at the beginning of this section, is the attorney-client privilege. The **attorney-client privilege** is a rule of evidence that protects certain communications made between a client and his attorney. Note that it is a rule of evidence, rather than a rule of legal ethics, that governs the use of certain information in judicial proceedings. The rule states

The **attorney-client privilege** is a rule of evidence that protects certain communications made between a client and his attorney.

> *I am always careful not to disclose a client's confidential information to friends and family. I can discuss the work that I do in general terms, but I do not tell anyone outside the law firm about the clients and specific work that I do.*
> Anatoly Smolkin

that a client who seeks an attorney's advice or assistance may invoke an unqualified privilege not to testify and to prevent the attorney from testifying about communications made by the client in confidence to the attorney. In other words, a lawyer who is called on to provide evidence or testify concerning the representation of a client should assert the attorney-client privilege and refuse to provide that evidence or testimony. As you will see, the attorney-client privilege is narrower than the ethical duty of confidentiality.

KEY Point

The Attorney-Client Privilege Rule

A client who seeks an attorney's advice or assistance may invoke an unqualified privilege not to testify and to prevent the attorney from testifying about communications made by the client in confidence to the attorney.

What constitutes privileged information under the attorney-client privilege is defined both in state statutes and in case law. Usually privileged information under the attorney-client privilege encompasses any confidential communications made between the attorney and the client, whether oral or written, concerning the client's legal rights or the legal matter. The attorney-client privilege arises when a client communicates with an attorney regarding a legal matter—whether that matter is possible litigation, a future transaction, or seeking legal advice and assistance. However, the communication must be confidential, so it must be made in a confidential setting to merit attorney-client privilege protection, such as by being made to an attorney in a private office as opposed to in a crowded elevator.

KEY Point

Information Protected by the Attorney-Client Privilege

Information protected by the attorney-client privilege includes any confidential communications made between the attorney and the client, whether oral or written, concerning the client's legal rights or the legal matter.

It does not matter if the communication is made by a prospective client during an initial consultation and the client decides not to retain the attorney or the attorney decides not to accept the representation. The communication is still protected. The client must be seeking the attorney's assistance on a legal matter, however, rather than on a business or personal matter, for the privilege to apply. It is irrelevant whether the attorney charges the client a fee, or performs the work *pro bono* (meaning that it is free of charge). Further, the attorney-client privilege continues even after the termination of the attorney-client relationship—that is, after the representation ends. Usually, it continues even after the client's death.

Some matters are not covered by the attorney-client privilege. Such matters include a criminally accused person's identity, his whereabouts, physical evidence pertaining to a crime, and the fee arrangement. Also, inadvertent or accidental disclosures of confidential communications may defeat the privilege, such as where the attorney mistakenly faxes confidential information meant for the client to opposing counsel. (Oops! Malpractice.)

Note that the client is the holder of the privilege. Accordingly, the client can waive the privilege. Waiver of the attorney-client privilege is, in effect, giving the attorney permission to disclose the client's confidential information. By waiving the privilege, the client consents to the attorney's disclosure of the privileged communication. A client's waiver may be expressly made, orally or in writing, or implied, through conduct—such as by the client's telling a third party the privileged information. Remember that an attorney cannot waive the privilege because she does not hold it. But if the client waives the privilege, the attorney may disclose confidential information.

KEY Point

Waiver of the Attorney-Client Privilege

Waiver of the attorney-client privilege occurs when the client gives the attorney permission to disclose confidential information. Waiver by the client may be made expressly (orally or in writing) or by implication (through the client's conduct).

An important exception exists when the attorney is permitted to divulge information protected by the attorney-client privilege. This exception arises when the client makes a claim against the attorney for criminal misconduct, civil malpractice, or ethical misconduct. In such a case, the attorney may defend herself by disclosing otherwise privileged communications, similar to the "attorney defense" exception to the ethical duty of confidentiality.

In an exception similar to the ethical duty of confidentiality, an attorney may disclose confidential communications about future crimes or fraud that a client is planning to commit. This is called the "crime-fraud" exception to the attorney-client privilege. This exception is essential to the welfare of the public because it protects third parties from certain harms.

Are paralegals impacted by the attorney-client privilege? Yes, they are. The attorney-client privilege extends to attorneys' agents, including paralegals and other persons on an attorney's legal services delivery team, when the client communicates either directly to the agent or in the presence of the agent. Communications between the client and a paralegal are covered by this privilege. A paralegal who is told confidential information directly by a client should share that information with her supervising attorney—such disclosure is permitted, as the paralegal and the attorney working together on the legal matter are considered "one." There is no disclosure to a third party in that situation. The paralegal must not disclose that information to a third party, however, because that disclosure is prohibited under the attorney-client privilege.

Certain materials relating to a lawyer's preparation of a client's case for trial are also considered privileged under another rule of evidence, the work product doctrine. The **work product doctrine** is a rule of evidence that protects from discovery by opposing counsel materials prepared by an attorney (or his agents) in anticipation of litigation.

CASE *on* POINT

In the Matter of R. L. Sutton, 77 F.3d 464 (3d Cir. 1996).

In this unpublished opinion, the Third Circuit Court of Appeals permitted not only attorneys, but also a paralegal, to invoke the attorney-client privilege and the work product doctrine. In doing so, it denied the opposing counsel's motion to compel production pursuant to certain subpoenaed testimony and documents.

The work product doctrine originated in a U.S. Supreme Court case entitled *Hickman v. Taylor* (see the Case on Point). In that case, the Supreme Court excluded from discovery by opposing counsel some statements made by witnesses to an attorney

CASE *on* POINT

Hickman v. Taylor, 329 U.S. 495 (1947).

In this case, Hickman was a representative of one of five employees who died in an accident involving the defendant's tugboat. The tugboat sank in the Delaware River, near Philadelphia, for unknown reasons while towing a train car float. Five of the nine crew members onboard drowned.

The issue before the Court was whether the district court that tried the case erred in requiring the defendant's production of documents that were obtained or prepared by its legal counsel in anticipation of litigation. The defendant refused to produce the documents, arguing they were privileged and that sharing them would reveal the defense counsel's litigation strategy. On appeal, the Third Circuit Court of Appeals reversed the district court's decision, holding that the information sought to be discovered was the work product of the lawyer and was privileged from discovery under the Federal Rules of Civil Procedure.

The U.S. Supreme Court agreed with the Third Circuit Court of Appeals, affirming its judgment. The Supreme Court recognized the work product doctrine, holding that written information obtained or prepared by or for attorneys in anticipation of litigation is protected from discovery under the Federal Rules of Civil Procedure. The Court said it was "dealing with an attempt to secure the production of written statements and mental impressions contained in the files and the mind of the [defense] attorney . . . without any showing of necessity or any indication or claim that denial of such production would unduly prejudice the preparation of the [plaintiff's] case or cause him any hardship or injustice." Accordingly, the Supreme Court agreed with the Third Circuit Court of Appeals in holding that the information sought was protected from discovery as the "work product of the lawyer."

The **work product doctrine** is a rule of evidence that protects from discovery by opposing counsel materials prepared by an attorney (or her agents) in anticipation of litigation.

involving a legal dispute the attorney anticipated would result in litigation. The work product doctrine has since been incorporated into modern Federal Rules of Civil Procedure, in Rule 26(b)(3), as well as in states' rules of civil procedure.

The work product doctrine's goal is to limit the discovery of an attorney's trial preparation materials in order to allow each party to fully and privately prepare for litigation. Remember that this doctrine only protects material prepared in anticipation of litigation. This doctrine protects two types of trial preparation materials. It protects the informational materials gathered by an attorney or by her agent, including her paralegal, such as witness statements and other factual research results. It also protects the attorney's mental impressions, meaning her ideas on how to conduct the case, whether she is bringing or defending it. This includes her legal theories or defenses, her case strategies, her legal opinions, her conclusions, and her legal research results.

KEY Point

What the Work Product Doctrine Protects

The work product doctrine protects material prepared by attorneys in anticipation of litigation. It protects two types of trial preparation materials: (1) informational materials and (2) the attorney's mental impressions.

In comparing the attorney-client privilege and the work product doctrine, remember that the work product doctrine protects materials prepared by attorneys in anticipation of litigation. This is narrower than the attorney-client privilege, which protects confidential communications between lawyers and clients generally.

In comparing the ethical duty of confidentiality and the two rules of evidence just discussed, remember that the ethical duty of confidentiality covers virtually all information relating to the legal representation, regardless of its source and regardless of when it was learned by the attorney. There is no private setting requirement as there is for the attorney-client privilege. Also, the information subject to the duty of confidentiality need not have been communicated directly by the client to the attorney, as is required for the attorney-client privilege to apply. The information covered by the duty of confidentiality may be learned before, during, or after the legal representation. The client need not request that the attorney maintain confidentiality—confidentiality is automatically required. That the information becomes public through no fault of the attorney does not relieve the attorney of her obligation under the ethical duty of confidentiality, though it does under the attorney-client privilege.

Why are there these differences between the ethical duty of confidentiality and the rules of evidence pertaining to confidential client information? The scope of the attorney-client privilege

is defined more narrowly because its effect, while encouraging clients to fully disclose information to their attorneys, keeps information from the legal system. Therefore, the privilege applies only to judicial proceedings where attorneys may be called to provide evidence or give testimony regarding the representation of clients. Also, the privilege applies only to communications made by a client directly to the attorney or the attorney's agent (such as his paralegal) and to those communications made in a confidential setting in order to secure legal advice or assistance. So information received from outside sources is not protected. Further, disclosures of confidential client information outside of judicial proceedings are not prohibited.

> *A lot of times we have family members that have . . . separate [related] cases and they ask questions about [my clients'] cases, so I simply tell them that I cannot disclose any information to anyone but my client.*
> **Tatyana Bronzova**

What are some things attorneys and paralegals can do to preserve client confidences? They can do many things. Attorneys and paralegals can restrict their cell phone use and use cell phone technology only for nonconfidential communications. They can protect, restrict access to, and secure client files and documents. When not using client files and documents, they should be secured in a locked, preferably fireproof, location. When using client files and documents, they should be protected and not left open on a desk overnight, or when their user is out of the room, or when someone not associated with the matter has joined the user in her office—such as for a meeting. Attorneys and paralegals should properly dispose of confidential materials by shredding them before throwing them away or sending them for recycling. They can label confidential documents and records as "confidential," and keep them separate from nonconfidential materials. Attorneys and paralegals should secure all computer records and data involving their clients. They should keep their computer screens private and protected when working with confidential client information, such as by turning computer screens away from doors and windows and removing confidential information from screens before leaving the room. They should use discretion in communicating with others about client matters and not disclose client confidences to third parties (without client consent). Attorneys and paralegals should communicate in private, rather than public, areas when confidential information is being discussed, such as behind closed doors in private offices and conference rooms rather than in reception areas and other public places. If communicating about a client matter in a public area, attorneys and paralegals should use care to be sure they are not overheard by any third party. They should use discretion in utilizing facsimile technology and not use that technology for sending or receiving confidential communications. If they use fax technology to send confidential communications, it is critical that they correctly input the fax number for the intended recipient to ensure that the information is sent to the correct place; it is advisable to call the recipient before sending the fax to announce it is coming so that the recipient can be situated to retrieve it as soon as it is received. Fax cover sheets noting the confidential nature of the faxed material and providing instructions on what to do if a person receives the fax in error should be utilized when fax technology is used by attorneys and paralegals to convey confidential client information. Attorneys and paralegals should restrict their use of e-mail technology to nonconfidential information unless the e-mail is encrypted or password protected. Law offices often invest in technology to help protect the confidentiality of e-mail, perhaps making office e-mail more secure than personal e-mail sent from the attorney or paralegal's home computer—so an office computer should be used, rather than a home computer, to send confidential client information via e-mail technology. They can use care regarding the content of messages they leave on voicemail and answering machines. Finally, attorneys and paralegals can execute confidentiality agreements to bind third parties to their promises not to disclose information, such as when using outside services for law office photocopying, billing, or file storage.

> *I don't discuss my cases with others outside the office.*
> Julianne Ennis

Now that we have finished reviewing the second of the "big three" legal ethics areas that apply to paralegals, we will examine the third—conflicts of interest. What are conflicts of interest, and how do legal ethics rules deal with them?

CONFLICTS OF INTEREST

What are conflicts of interest, and how do legal ethics rules deal with them? The attorney-client relationship is a fiduciary one. A **fiduciary relationship** is a relationship between two persons that is based on trust and confidence. In a fiduciary relationship, one party to it relies on and is influenced by the other party, which other party owes a fiduciary duty to act for the first party's benefit. Because of the fiduciary nature of the relationship between an attorney and her client, the attorney owes a duty of loyalty to her client, meaning she must act in her client's best interest.

However, sometimes the interests of the client and the attorney differ. For example, a client and an attorney who have entered into a business transaction together have distinct interests—they both want to benefit, individually, from the business transaction. Sometimes the interests of the client and

A **fiduciary relationship** is a relationship between two persons that is based on trust and confidence and that gives rise to a duty to act with loyalty toward the other party to the relationship.

© age fotostock/SuperStock

another client of the attorney differ. For example, if an attorney represents both the husband and the wife in a divorce case, her clients' interests not only differ but are completely adverse. Where the attorney cannot act with undivided loyalty to a client in the carrying out of the legal representation, there exists a conflict of interest. A **conflict of interest** exists when the interests of a client conflict with the interests of the attorney or other clients who are or were represented by the attorney. Conflicts of interest can arise from an attorney's relationship with another client, from her responsibilities to a former client, and from her own personal or business interests that conflict with a client's interests.

Now we will review the different ways that conflicts of interest can arise. In summary, they can arise in several ways. They can arise when the interests of two of the attorney's clients are adverse. Similarly, they can arise when the attorney's representation of a client could be materially limited by the attorney's representation of another client. They can arise when the attorney's representation of a client could be materially limited by the attorney's representation of a former client. They can arise when the attorney's representation of a client could be materially limited by a personal or business interest of the attorney. ABA Model Rules deal with each of these situations, and we will discuss each of them in order.

ABA Model Rules (Rule 1.7) prohibit a lawyer from representing a client if the representation involves a "concurrent conflict of interest." The Model Rules stipulate that a "concurrent conflict of interest" exists when the representation of one client is directly adverse to the interests of another client or if there is a significant risk that the representation of one or more clients

is materially limited by the lawyer's responsibilities to another client, to a former client or a third party, or by a personal interest of the lawyer.

Nonetheless, when a concurrent conflict of interest exists, ABA Model Rules allow representation of the client by the lawyer if (1) the lawyer reasonably believes that she will be able to provide competent and diligent representation to each impacted client, (2) the law does not prohibit such representation, (3) the representation does not involve the assertion of a legal claim by one client against another client in the same litigation or other court proceeding, and (4) each impacted client

RULES *on* POINT

Summary of ABA Model Rules on Concurrent Conflict of Interest and Waiver

Rule 1.7(a) prohibits a lawyer from representing a client if the representation involves a "concurrent conflict of interest." This rule stipulates that a "concurrent conflict of interest" exists when the representation of one client is directly adverse to the interests of another client, or when there is a significant risk that the representation of one or more clients is materially limited by the lawyer's responsibilities to another client, to a former client or a third party, or by a personal interest of the lawyer.

Rule 1.7(b) allows representation even when a concurrent conflict of interest exists if (1) the lawyer reasonably believes that she will be able to provide competent and diligent representation to each impacted client, (2) the law does not prohibit such representation, (3) the representation does not involve the assertion of a legal claim by one client against another client in the same litigation or other court proceeding, and (4) each impacted client gives written, informed consent to the attorney, thereby waiving the conflict of interest.

A **conflict of interest** exists when the interests of a client conflict with the interests of the attorney or other clients who are or were represented by the attorney.

Courts consider several factors in determining whether a client's consent is effective to constitute a waiver of a conflict of interest, including:

- the extent of the disclosure the attorney made to the client regarding the conflict of interest situation;
- whether the client's consent was given voluntarily, or was pressured by the attorney or a third person;
- when during the process the attorney raised the conflict of interest issue with the client;
- whether the client possessed the capacity to understand the implications of the consent and its consequences in the representation;
- whether the client consulted with and relied on independent legal counsel in reaching the decision to consent; and
- whether the consent is in writing and signed by the client, or whether it is oral or implied.

gives written, informed consent to the attorney, thereby waiving the conflict of interest. In the case of a waiver of a concurrent conflict of interest, the attorney should fully advise her clients regarding the existence of the conflict of interest and its potential consequences if concurrent representation is to be effectively consented to by them. In other words, the attorney must see to it that the clients' consent is informed and knowing by explaining alternative courses of action and the risks involved for the clients.

Because an attorney owes a duty of loyalty to each of her clients, states' legal ethics rules on conflicts of interest generally do not permit an attorney to represent multiple parties where their interests are directly adverse. This is sometimes referred to as **simultaneous representation**—when an attorney represents two clients whose interests are directly adverse. As noted, an attorney should not represent both the husband and the wife in a divorce case, even if the use of one attorney is less expensive than hiring two. This is because the interests of the clients, the husband and the wife, are directly adverse. There is no way the attorney can represent both the husband and the wife with undivided loyalty in their divorce action against each other. The lawyer cannot zealously represent the husband in protecting his legal interests while, at the same time, zealously representing the wife in protecting her interests. Even in a nonlitigation setting, such as

in the purchase and sale of a business, a negotiated transaction, an attorney should not represent both the buyer and the seller of a business because their interests are directly adverse. The buyer wants, among other things, to purchase the business for a lower purchase price, while the seller wants, among other things, to sell his business for a higher purchase price. Each party to the transaction, just as each party to litigation, should have his own attorney to zealously represent his interests.

In situations involving an attorney's representation of a client that is not *directly adverse* to her responsibilities to another client, or to a former client or third party, that representation may still give rise to a conflict of interest. When there exists a significant risk that the representation of a client would be *materially limited* by the attorney's responsibilities to another client, to a former client, or to a third party, a concurrent conflict of interest exists and the attorney should decline representation. What does it mean that the client's representation would be "materially limited" by the attorney's responsibilities to another? It means that the attorney's loyalties may be divided and her ability to exercise independent professional judgment for the benefit of the client may be impacted. For example, what if the attorney's client is a closely held corporation? The corporation wishes to admit a new stockholder as an owner and operator of the business. Should the attorney represent the new stockholder in negotiating and drafting the shareholders' agreement with the corporation? No, she should not. The attorney represents the corporation. While the interests of the new shareholder are not directly adverse to the interests of the corporation, the lawyer's concurrent representation of the new shareholder would create a conflict of interest. The new shareholder should have independent legal counsel negotiating this contract for him because the attorney's representation of the new shareholder would be materially limited by her responsibilities related to her representation of the corporation.

Not only may another client's or third person's interest conflict with those of a current client, but so may the attorney's. For example, what if the attorney loaned her client money and the attorney needed the client's case to settle so that she could be repaid? In that situation, the lawyer's personal interest impacts her ability to exercise independent professional judgment in the handling of the client's litigation. ABA Model Rules, in Rule 1.8, address several types of situations where an attorney's personal

Simultaneous representation is when an attorney represents two clients whose interests are directly adverse.

or business interests may impact her ability to exercise independent professional judgment on behalf of a client. These rules are reviewed next.

Model Rule 1.8(a) prohibits an attorney from entering into a business transaction with a client or acquiring an interest adverse to a client unless (1) the terms of the transaction are fair and reasonable and are fully disclosed, in an understandable writing, to the client; (2) the client is encouraged to seek independent legal counsel; and (3) the client gives written, informed consent. This rule does not prohibit commercial transactions between attorneys and clients where the attorney uses the commercial products or services of the client that the client provides to the public generally—so an attorney for The Coca-Cola Company may purchase a Coke to drink, a lawyer for Bank of America may have a checking account with that bank, and a lawyer for the Johns Hopkins Hospital may obtain medical services at Johns Hopkins.

Model Rule 1.8(b) generally prohibits an attorney from using information related to the representation to the client's disadvantage, unless the client gives informed consent. Model Rule 1.8(c) prohibits an attorney from soliciting a substantial (valuable) gift from a client or from preparing a legal instrument in which the attorney or a close member of her family is given a substantial gift, unless the attorney or family member is also related to the client. For example, an attorney should not draft a will pursuant to which she will receive a bequest. The rule does not prohibit clients and attorneys from sending each other inexpensive, simple gifts, such as holiday presents or tokens of appreciation.

Model Rule 1.8(d) prohibits an attorney from executing or negotiating an agreement giving the lawyer literary or media rights relating to representation of the client until after the representation ends. Model Rule 1.8(e) prohibits an attorney from providing financial assistance to a client in connection with contemplated or pending litigation, except for advancing court costs and litigation expenses (even if the repayment of these costs and expenses is contingent on the outcome of the litigation) and representing an indigent client for whom the attorney is permitted to pay the court costs and litigation expenses. So an attorney may not pay a client's living expenses, for example.

Model Rule 1.8(f) prohibits an attorney from accepting compensation for representing a client from someone other than that client unless the client gives informed consent, unless there exists no interference with the lawyer's exercise of independent professional judgment or with the attorney-client relationship, and unless the information relating to the representation is protected in terms of the ethical duty of confidentiality.

Typical applications of this rule are when parents agree to pay the legal fees for their children's representation, corporations agree to pay the legal fees for corporate officers or directors, or a spouse agrees to pay the legal fees of the other spouse. So while a third party may pay the legal fees of a client if the requirements of this rule are met, it is critical that the attorney maintain confidentiality with respect to the client and not disclose confidential information to the person paying his legal fees, at least not without the client's informed consent.

Model Rule 1.8(g) prohibits an attorney who represents multiple clients from making an aggregate settlement of civil claims, or an aggregated agreement regarding guilty or *nolo contendere* pleas, without the written informed consent of each client. Model Rule 1.8(h) prohibits an attorney from making an agreement limiting her malpractice liability to a client unless the client has independent legal representation in making that agreement. It also prohibits a settlement of a claim or potential claim for malpractice liability with either an unrepresented client or a former client unless the client is provided a written recommendation from the attorney to seek independent legal counsel.

Model Rule 1.8(i) prohibits an attorney from obtaining a proprietary interest in litigation in which the attorney is representing a client, with the exception that the attorney may obtain a lien to secure her legal fee or expenses and may charge a reasonable contingency fee in a civil action. Model Rule 1.8(j) prohibits an attorney from having sexual relations with a client unless a consensual sexual relationship between the two existed prior to the commencement of the representation. Model Rule 1.8(k) states that when an attorney works for a firm and any of these conflicts of interest from Rule 1.8(a) through (i) (but not (j)) exist, then such conflicts of interest are imputed, meaning extended, to all attorneys in that firm.

Remember from our discussion in the preceding section that the ethical duty of confidentiality lasts beyond the end of the representation of the client by the attorney on a matter. Similarly, the attorney's duty of loyalty to a client extends beyond the termination of the representation. Because of this, conflicts of interest can arise between attorneys' current clients and former clients. This is called **successive representation**. Most states prohibit an attorney from

> **Successive representation** is when an attorney represents a current client whose interests conflict with the interests of a former client.

RULES on POINT

Summary of ABA Model Rules Regarding Current Clients

Rule 1.8(a) prohibits an attorney from entering into a business transaction with a client or acquiring an interest adverse to a client unless:

1. the terms of the transaction are fair and reasonable and are fully disclosed in an understandable writing to the client,
2. the client is encouraged to seek independent legal counsel, and
3. the client gives written, informed consent.

Rule 1.8(b) generally prohibits an attorney from using information related to the representation to the client's disadvantage, unless the client gives informed consent.

Rule 1.8(c) prohibits an attorney from soliciting a substantial, meaning valuable, gift from a client, or from preparing a legal instrument in which the attorney or a close member of her family is given a substantial gift, unless the attorney or family member is also related to the client.

Rule 1.8(d) prohibits an attorney from executing or negotiating an agreement giving the lawyer literary or media rights relating to the representation of the client until after the representation ends.

Rule 1.8(e) prohibits an attorney from providing financial assistance to a client in connection with contemplated or pending litigation except for:

1. advancing court costs and litigation expenses (even if the repayment of these costs and expenses is contingent on the outcome of the litigation), and
2. representing an indigent client for whom the attorney is permitted to pay court costs and litigation expenses

Rule 1.8(f) prohibits an attorney from accepting compensation for representing a client from someone other than that client unless the client gives informed consent, there exists no interference with the lawyer's exercise of independent professional judgment or with the attorney-client relationship, and the information relating to the representation is protected in terms of the ethical duty of confidentiality.

Rule 1.8(g) prohibits an attorney who represents multiple clients from making an aggregate settlement of civil claims, or an aggregated agreement regarding guilty or *nolo contendere* pleas, without the written informed consent of each client.

Rule 1.8(h) prohibits an attorney from making an agreement limiting her malpractice liability to a client unless the client has independent legal representation in making that agreement, as well as prohibits a settlement of a claim or potential claim for malpractice liability with either an unrepresented client or a former client unless the client is provided a written recommendation from the attorney to seek independent legal counsel.

Rule 1.8(i) prohibits an attorney from obtaining a proprietary interest in litigation in which the attorney is representing a client, except that the attorney may obtain a lien to secure her legal fee or expenses and may charge a reasonable contingency fee in a civil action.

Rule 1.8(j) prohibits an attorney from having sexual relations with a client unless a consensual sexual relationship between the two existed prior to the commencement of the representation.

Rule 1.8(k) imputes the conflicts of interest indentified in Rule 1.8(a) through (i) (but not (j)) to all attorneys in a firm where one attorney in that firm has such a conflict of interest.

representing a new client if the new client has interests that are materially adverse to a former client and the matter is the same or is substantially related.

ABA Model Rules (Rule 1.9) deal with duties of loyalty owed by attorneys to their former clients. Rule 1.9(a) prohibits an attorney who has formerly represented a client in a matter from representing another person in the same or a substantially related matter where that person's interests are materially adverse to the interests of the former client, unless the former client gives written, informed consent to the representation. To be required to decline representation, then, the subject matter of the new representation must be the same or substantially related, rather than unrelated, to the attorney's representation of the former client. For example, if the attorney represented the husband in a divorce from his wife, then the attorney represented the wife, years later, in negotiating an employment agreement with her new employer, though the husband is a former client, the wife's matter is not the same or substantially related to the divorce matter and their interests are not materially adverse. What if the

Summary of ABA Model Rule on Duties to Former Clients

Rule 1.9(a) prohibits an attorney who has formerly represented a client in a matter from representing another person in the same or a substantially related matter where that person's interests are materially adverse to the interests of the former client, unless the former client gives written, informed consent to the representation.

Summary of ABA Model Rule on an Attorney Called as a Witness in a Matter

Rule 3.7 prohibits an attorney from acting as an advocate at a trial in which the attorney is likely to be called as a witness unless the testimony the attorney would give relates to an uncontested issue or relates to the nature and value of legal services rendered in the case, or if disqualification of the attorney would create a substantial hardship for the client.

---

husband's employer sought to retain the lawyer to represent it in a breach of contract action against the husband? In that case, the questions to consider are whether the representation of the husband's employer now, in a breach of employment contract action, is the same or a substantially related matter to the divorce case and whether the representation of the husband's employer is materially adverse to the interests of the former client, the husband. Could any confidential information obtained in the representation of the husband in the divorce matter be used to his detriment in representing the employer now suing the husband for breach of contract? The key in considering these types of conflicts of interest is whether the new representation in any real way disadvantages, or is detrimental to, the former client. If so, declining representation is best. So, in summarizing this "former client" rule, attorneys should not oppose a former client in the same or a substantially related matter where the new representation is materially adverse to the former client's interests. However, if the matters are unrelated or the new representation is not materially adverse to the former client's interests, the new representation is permissible.

A conflict of interest may also arise when an attorney who is representing a client as an advocate at trial is also called to be a witness in that proceeding. ABA Model Rules (Rule 3.7) prohibit an attorney from acting as an advocate at a trial in which the attorney is likely to be called as a witness. The rule makes exceptions when the testimony the attorney would give relates to an uncontested issue or relates to the nature and value of legal services rendered in the case, or when disqualification of the attorney would create a substantial hardship for

the client. A lawyer should withdraw from the representation as soon as she learns that she is likely to be called as a witness. Note that client consent to this conflict of interest generally is not permitted.

Many attorneys work in law offices with other attorneys. Does a conflict of interest involving one attorney affect the other attorneys in that law office? Yes, it does. How does it affect the other attorneys? In the practice of law, it is assumed that an attorney may share confidential client information with others in that firm, particularly others providing assistance on the matter. Because of this, rules of ethics impute to the other lawyers in the firm the conflicts of interest of any one of them. Accordingly, the general rule on imputation of conflicts of interest is that all attorneys in the law office are disqualified from representing a client if one of the attorneys in the office has a conflict of interest regarding this representation. States' legal ethics rules may model ABA Model Rules on this point. ABA Model Rules (Rule 1.10) deal with imputation of conflicts of interest. Rule 1.10 states that while attorneys are associated in a firm, all the attorneys in that firm are prohibited from representing a client when any one of them practicing law alone would be prohibited from representing the client under conflicts rules relating to current and former clients. However, representation is permitted if: (1) the prohibition is based on a personal interest of the disqualified attorney that does not create a significant risk of materially limiting the representation of the client by the other attorneys in the firm or (2) the prohibition is based on a duty to a former client that arises out of the disqualified attorney's association with a prior law firm and the disqualified lawyer is screened from participation in the matter and receives no part of the fee from it, written notice is given to the former client, and certifications of compliance with the legal ethics rules and with screening procedures are given to the former client on his reasonable request and on termination of the screening procedures.

When an attorney first consults with a prospective client, before allowing the client to reveal confidential information, the attorney should first check to see if any conflicts of interest exist. If the attorney discovers that a conflict of interest would result from representation of the client in the matter, the attorney should decline that representation. Further, if a conflict of interest develops during the course of representation of a client, the attorney should withdraw from that representation. Even if the attorney with the conflict of interest does not voluntarily withdraw from the representation, opposing counsel can make a motion to the court to disqualify an attorney with a conflict of interest from such representation. When an attorney represents a client in a matter where there is a conflict of

RULES *on* POINT

Summary of ABA Model Rules on Imputation of Conflicts of Interest

Rule 1.10 states that while attorneys are associated in a firm, all the attorneys in that firm are prohibited from representing a client when any one of them practicing law alone would be prohibited from representing the client under conflicts rules relating to current and former clients.

However, representation is permitted if:

1. the prohibition is based on a personal interest of the disqualified attorney that does not create a significant risk of materially limiting the representation of the client by the other attorneys in the firm, or

2. the prohibition is based on a duty to a former client that arises out of the disqualified attorney's association with a prior law firm and the disqualified lawyer is screened from participation in the matter and receives no part of the fee from it, written notice is given to the former client, and certifications of compliance with the legal ethics rules and with screening procedures are given to the former client upon his reasonable request and upon termination of the screening procedures.

Special Rules for Former and Current Government Officers and Employees

In addition to the general conflict of interest rules applied to all lawyers, lawyers who formerly worked as government officers and employees must abide by special conflicts of interest rules. For example, as governmental officers or employees, such former government workers may have had access to confidential information about other people acquired through work in those offices. Once in private practice as a lawyer, a former government officer or employee should not accept representation of a client whose interests are adverse to a person in a matter in which confidential information, obtained from the government employment, could be used to that person's material disadvantage. In other words, the lawyer should not use confidential information learned during previous public service employment to the unfair advantage of his new private client. ABA Model Rule 1.11 addresses special conflict of interest rules for former government officers and employees currently working as lawyers in private practice.

interest, there exists the possibility that adverse consequences may result. These consequences can include a civil malpractice claim brought by the client seeking an award of damages against the attorney or a disciplinary action brought against the attorney for violation of the state's legal ethics rules pertaining to conflicts of interest. Where an attorney works with other attorneys in a firm, one attorney's conflict of interest is imputed to disqualify the other attorneys from accepting that representation. Imputed disqualification is based on the notion that all attorneys in a firm know everything about all the clients and matters being handled by the firm. However, under certain circumstances, through effective screening of the disqualified lawyer from the representation and by avoiding any sharing of the fee, other lawyers in the firm may be able to accept that representation—creating an exception to the imputed disqualification rule. This screening process is also known as creating a Chinese Wall or erecting an Ethical Wall. Screening isolates the disqualified person (who can be an attorney or nonlawyer employee of the firm, such as a paralegal, discussed below) by setting up law office procedures to prevent the disqualified person from participating in the matter or giving or receiving any communications regarding the matter.

Kanawha County, West Virginia, Personal Injury Action

Reported in the news in April 2011, Kanawha County Commissioners asked that a complaint be filed against an attorney, Mike Clifford, for representing a woman in a personal injury action. The legal claim made in the personal injury case was that the woman's property was ruined when the police conducted a search of her property. The search was conducted over a nine-day period when investigators used heavy machinery to excavate and search for evidence on the woman's property relating to a sniper murder case.

The basis of the conflict of interest complaint was that Clifford, the woman's attorney, was Kanawha County's prosecuting attorney during the sniper investigation. Therefore, the Commissioner's attorney filed a complaint to have Clifford dismissed as the plaintiff's counsel in the personal injury action on the basis of West Virginia's Rules of Professional Conduct that state that a lawyer cannot represent both sides in a case. One Commissioner said, "To be privy to this investigation . . . and then turn around and file a claim is repugnant." Clifford defended his representation of the woman by arguing that the sniper case never fell within the confines of his prosecutor's office. (The dispute was pending when this text went to print.)

Special Rules for Former Judges, Arbitrators, and Mediators

Special conflicts of interest rules also apply to lawyers who have formerly worked as judges, arbitrators, mediators, and the like. For example, an attorney should not represent a client in connection with a matter in which the attorney participated as a judge, arbitrator, or mediator, unless all parties to the matter give their written, informed consent to the representation. ABA Model Rule 1.12 addresses special duties for former judges, arbitrators, mediators, and the like.

How are conflicts of interest detected? Hopefully, they are detected early, before representation is agreed to by the attorney. To detect conflicts of interest, before receiving any confidential communications from a prospective client, the attorney

When Organizations Are Clients

Remember that an attorney whose client is an organization, such as a corporation or partnership, represents that organization. Since an organization is not human, it must act through its agents and other representatives who are human. That said, the humans themselves are not the attorney's clients—the organization is. Sometimes the interests of an organization and its agents and other representatives are adverse. For example, if in representing a corporation the lawyer learns that the company's chief financial officer intentionally misstated the company's financial statements, the attorney represents the company and his duty is to act in its best interests—not the interest of the chief financial officer. The attorney should not represent directors, officers, employees, or other agents of the organization if they have interests adverse to the organization's interests. ABA Model Rule 1.13 sets forth ethics rules regarding organizations as clients.

should perform a conflicts check by asking basic background questions to the prospective client about himself and about the matter to see if there is any potential conflict that would disqualify the lawyer from this representation. A **conflicts check**, or **conflicts of interest check**, is the process of evaluating a prospective client to determine if representation of the prospective client on a matter would create any conflicts of interest for the lawyer. Note that it is important to check for conflicts of interest before the client starts revealing confidential information to the attorney regarding the matter for which he is seeking representation. Use of a new client form, asking questions designed to solicit answers to conflict of interest questions—such as the names of all potential plaintiffs and defendants involved in a legal dispute or the name of the other side in a transaction—is common. In addition, when new employees such as attorneys and paralegals are hired by a law firm, conflicts checks should be performed to identify any potential conflicts of interest arising out of the new employee's former employment. The larger the firm, the more sophisticated the conflicts check process may be. For example, some firms maintain databases where searches of clients and adverse parties can be performed to check for conflicts of interest. Memorandums listing new clients

A **conflicts check** is the process of evaluating a prospective client to determine if representation of the prospective client on a matter would create any conflicts of interest for the lawyer; it is also called a **conflicts of interest check**.

and matters, or reports generated from databases, may be circulated to the lawyers for review of conflicts of interest.

Do conflicts of interest rules apply to paralegals? They certainly do. Paralegals must know and abide by the conflicts of interest rules just like attorneys. Their personal and business interests should not conflict with a client's interests. Of particular concern is when paralegals change employers. What happens when the interests of the clients of the current employer conflict with the interests of the clients of the former employer? In such a case, the new employer may be disqualified from that representation. However, both the courts and ABA work to avoid restricting the employment and movement of paralegals. They do this by focusing on protecting the confidentiality of client information through encouraging the use of effective screening procedures. These screening procedures must keep the paralegal from participating in a matter involving a conflict of interest arising out of former employment. In addition, they should keep the paralegal from learning information pertaining to that matter and keep her from revealing information she possesses regarding her former employer's client. While NALA's Code of Ethics and Professional Responsibility is silent on the issue of conflicts of interest and paralegals, NFPA's Model Code of Ethics and Professional Responsibility expressly addresses a paralegal's role in avoiding conflicts of interest and disclosing possible conflicts of interest to employers or clients. Having said that the conflicts of interest rules apply to paralegals, however, it is important to note that it is up to attorneys to accept or decline representation of a client on a matter—and it is a violation of the legal ethics rules for anyone other than an attorney to accept representation and set a fee. The paralegal should focus on detecting possible conflicts of interest involving her and reporting those to her supervising attorney. Because of the nature of their work, it is most often litigation paralegals who more regularly face conflicts of interest issues. Accordingly, they should pay particular attention to their role in detecting and reporting potential conflicts of interest.

I believe legal ethics rules impact every paralegal regardless of what area of law she practices.
Lois Shaw

CHAPTER SUMMARY

- Three legal ethics areas especially critical to paralegals are the unauthorized practice of law, confidentiality, and conflicts of interest.

- The unauthorized practice of law is the practice of law by a person who is not authorized, meaning who does not have a license to practice law in that jurisdiction. Both attorneys and nonlawyers can engage in the unauthorized practice of law.

- Establishing the attorney-client relationship, setting the fee to be charged for a legal service, giving a legal opinion or legal advice, and representing a client in a court or other tribunal proceeding (unless authorized by the court or tribunal) are tasks clearly within the definition of "practice of law" and for which a person needs a license to practice law in the jurisdiction in order to perform them. Further, a person should not engage in, encourage, or contribute to any act that could constitute the unauthorized practice of law.

- Freelance paralegals and, even more so, independent paralegals face "unauthorized practice of law" issues if they perform legal services other than while under the direct supervision of attorneys.

- Consequences for attorneys who violate the unauthorized practice of law rules include having injunctions issued against them by a court, being held in civil contempt, being criminally prosecuted, being sued for malpractice, and facing disciplinary actions under the legal ethics rules of their states.

- Consequences for paralegals who violate the unauthorized practice of law rules include having injunctions issued against them by a court, being held in civil contempt, being criminally prosecuted, being sued for malpractice, and facing adverse employment actions such as termination.

- The general rule on the ethical duty of confidentiality is that all information relating to the representation of a client must be kept confidential by the lawyer and his employees and other agents. It is a duty not to disclose confidential client information.

- Common exceptions to the ethical duty of confidentiality include when the client gives informed consent to disclosure; when disclosure is needed to carry out the representation; when disclosure is required to prevent death or substantial bodily harm to a third party; when disclosure is necessary to prevent, mitigate, or rectify a financial loss to a third party caused by the client's misconduct where the attorney's services are used to further the crime or fraud; when necessary to obtain legal advice concerning the lawyer's legal ethics responsibilities; when needed for the attorney to defend a legal claim or disciplinary action arising out of the representation of the client; and when required in order to comply with the law or a court order.

- The attorney-client privilege is a rule of evidence (not legal ethics) that protects certain communications made between clients and their attorneys. The privilege provides that a client who seeks an attorney's advice or assistance may invoke an unqualified privilege not to testify and to prevent the attorney from testifying about communications made by the client, in confidence, to the lawyer.

- The work product doctrine is a rule of evidence (not legal ethics) that protects from discovery by opposing counsel materials prepared by an attorney in anticipation of litigation.

- Conflicts of interest exist when the interests of a client conflict with the interests of the attorney or other clients who are or were represented by the attorney.

- Conflicts of interest arise in the attorney-client relationship because that relationship is a fiduciary one, based on trust and confidence, giving rise to a duty of loyalty owed by the attorney to his client, meaning the attorney must act in her client's best interest.

- Attorneys should perform conflicts checks before receiving any confidential communications from prospective clients to detect any potential conflicts of interest for which representation of the client in the matter should be declined.

- Simultaneous representation is when an attorney represents two clients whose interests are directly adverse.

- Successive representation is when an attorney represents a client whose interests conflict with the interests of a former client.

- Where a conflict of interest exists, the best practice is for the lawyer to decline the representation (if she learns of it before she has accepted the representation) or to promptly withdraw from representation (when she learns of it after she has accepted representation). In some cases, the conflict of interest may be waived upon the written, informed consent of the client.

- A conflict of interest involving one lawyer can be imputed to other lawyers in the same law office, disqualifying them from accepting the representation. However, through the effective use of screening procedures, the disqualified lawyer may be "screened" from working on the client's matter, giving or receiving any confidential information regarding the matter, and sharing the legal fee, thereby permitting other lawyers from the law office to represent the client in the matter. The same is true with respect to paralegals who have conflicts of interest, particularly conflicts created when a paralegal changes employment and the interests of a client of the new employer conflict with the interests of a client of the former employer. The paralegal may be effectively screened in such as way as to permit the firm to represent the client in the matter.

CONCEPT REVIEW AND REINFORCEMENT

Key Terms and Concepts

Unauthorized practice of law
Freelance paralegals
Independent paralegals
Attorney-client privilege
Work product doctrine
Fiduciary relationship
Conflict of interest
Simultaneous representation
Successive representation
Conflicts check

Questions for Review

1. What are the "big three" legal ethics areas affecting paralegals?
2. What is the practice of law?
3. What is the unauthorized practice of law?
4. What are the possible consequences for a lawyer who engages in the unauthorized practice of law?
5. What are the possible consequences for a paralegal who engages in the unauthorized practice of law?
6. What is the ethical duty of confidentiality?
7. How is the ethical duty of confidentiality distinguished from the attorney-client privilege?
8. What is the work product doctrine?
9. How do the legal ethics rules regarding confidentiality apply to paralegals?
10. What are conflicts of interest?
11. What are the legal ethics rules pertaining to conflicts of interest?

DEVELOPING YOUR PARALEGAL SKILLS

Critical Thinking Exercises

Answer the following questions using ABA's Model Rules of Professional Conduct. The Model Rules can be found on the American Bar Association's website at http://www.abanet.org/cpr/mrpc/mrpc_toc.html. In your answer, reference the specific rule you use to answer the question.

1. May a lawyer who is not admitted to practice law in this jurisdiction but who is admitted in another jurisdiction hold himself out to the public as a lawyer admitted in this jurisdiction?
2. May a lawyer who is admitted to practice law in another U.S. jurisdiction and who is suspended from the practice of law for six months in that jurisdiction practice law on a temporary basis in this jurisdiction if the representation is undertaken in association with a lawyer who is admitted to practice in this jurisdiction and who is an active participant in the matter?
3. When is a lawyer responsible for the conduct of a paralegal (called a "nonlawyer assistant" in the relevant Model Rule)?
4. May a lawyer reveal the information relating to the representation of a client if the client gives informed consent?
5. Must a lawyer reveal information relating to the representation of a client if the lawyer reasonably believes it is necessary to prevent the reasonably certain death of another?
6. May a lawyer reveal information relating to the representation of a client if the lawyer reasonably believes that disclosure is necessary to comply with a court order?
7. When does a concurrent conflict of interest exist?
8. What is necessary for a lawyer to represent multiple clients where there exists a concurrent conflict of interest?
9. Should a lawyer draft a will for his cousin if, in that will, the lawyer will inherit a valuable antique car?
10. When, if ever, can a lawyer execute an agreement with his client giving the lawyer media rights relating to the representation?
11. Is charging a reasonable contingency fee in a civil case considered acquiring "a proprietary interest" in a cause of action, something that is prohibited under the Model Rules?
12. When, if ever, can a lawyer who has formerly represented a client in a matter represent another client in the same or a substantially related matter when the new client's interests are materially adverse to the former client's interests?
13. Will a conflict of interest be imputed to all the lawyers in a law firm where a conflict of interest is based on a personal interest of one lawyer (the disqualified lawyer) and it does not present a significant risk of materially limiting the representation of the client by the remaining lawyers in the firm?
14. Does a lawyer employed or retained by a corporation represent the organization and its representatives, such as its directors, officers, and employees?
15. May a lawyer act as an advocate at a trial in which he is likely to be called as a witness if the testimony relates to the nature and the value of the legal services rendered in the case?

Assignments and Practical Applications

Using print or online sources, locate the legal ethics rules in your state regarding the unauthorized practice of law, confidentiality, and conflicts of interest. What do these rules require of attorneys and of paralegals?

Find your state's legal ethics rule on the unauthorized practice of law. Compare your state's requirements to those in Rule 5.5 of ABA's Model Rules.

Locate NALA's Model Standards and Guidelines for Utilization of Legal Assistants. Review Guideline 5. Using this Guideline, list the tasks that NALA believes may be delegated to paralegals. Is this list illustrative or exhaustive—meaning, is it the total and complete list or can it be supplemented by other tasks?

Research your state's statute on the unauthorized practice of law. Is the practice of law without a license a crime in your state? If so, is it classified as a misdemeanor or a felony? How can it be punished?

Locate and review the California statute authorizing Legal Document Assistants (LDAs). What are the requirements to become an LDA in that state? What does this government recognition permit a person to do?

Using your state's legal ethics rules, list the exceptions to the duty of confidentiality that apply in your state.

Using your state's legal ethics rules, summarize your state's conflict of interest rules and waiver requirements.

If you have not seen the movie *Legally Blonde* with Reese Witherspoon, you should! That very entertaining movie about Harvard Law School depicts one of the exceptions to the rule that nonlawyers cannot represent clients in court. What exception is depicted?

Technology Resources and Internet Exercises

For a discussion of ways a *lawyer* can engage in the unauthorized practice of law, see this article from the Utah State Bar Association's website at http://www.utahbar.org/sites/litigation/html/avoid_the_unauthorized_practic.html.

Using the Internet, research and locate a website for a large law firm in your area. See what type of marketing and other information is available on that website. Does the website include a disclaimer saying that no legal advice is given through use of the firm's website? What else is included in the website's disclaimer? Does the website require a user to register, restricting access to certain information, so that jurisdictional boundaries are protected relating to attorney licensing?

Review the disclaimer on the King & Spalding website—King & Spalding is a major law firm originally based in Atlanta, now with offices throughout the United States and abroad. See http://www.kslaw.com. Make a list of what is disclaimed by the firm on its website.

Using the Internet, locate and read NALA's and NFPA's codes of ethics rules, discussed in the chapter, regarding the unauthorized practice of law. Provide the citation for where these rules are found in each of these codes.

Using NFPA's website, review the list of federal and state agencies permitting representation of parties by paralegals. See http://www.paralegals.org/displaycommon.cfm?an=1&subarticlenbr=334.

Using the Cornell University Law School website for its Legal Information Institute, found at http://www.law.cornell.edu/, find your state's legal ethics code. Use it to answer the following Ethical Applications.

Ethical Applications

1. Jerry Winfrey is a paralegal working for a large law firm. He works in the corporate law department of that firm. The lawyer for whom Jerry often works, Sally Williams, routinely introduces Jerry to clients and encourages clients to call Jerry for updates on their matters. You see, Jerry is more easily accessible in the office than the attorney, who is often in court and at meetings.

   One day, a client, Montel Raphael, telephones Jerry to check on the status of a matter the firm is handling. The law firm has been asked to organize a subsidiary for the client. The client asks Jerry, "Should we organize the new business as a limited liability company in order to reap the benefits of both the corporate and partnership forms of business organization?" Further, the client asks, "In what state should we organize the business?"

   Jerry has been working in the area of corporate law for a long time. In fact, he has been working in this area for about 20 years. Sally was admitted to the bar about 18 months ago, and she is just "learning the ropes." Jerry believes that the limited liability company form of business organization is the recommended one for the client, and forming it in the parent company's home state of Maryland is preferable. He is certain Sally would agree with him. In fact, Sally would probably ask him to tell her the answer to the client's questions anyway.

   Jerry, in his own effort to provide legal services at a lower cost, as any good paralegal would, informs Montel that the subsidiary should be organized as a limited liability company in Maryland. The client is most pleased with this prompt service and happy to receive immediate answers to his questions. Later that day, Montel telephones Sally to compliment the fine work of her paralegal, Jerry.

   Should Sally be concerned? Should Jerry? Should Montel? Why or why not?

   Suppose that when the client posed the questions about how and where to organize, Jerry responded, "Let me get back to you as soon as I speak with Sally about this." In fact, Jerry speaks to Sally about this the very next morning. Shortly thereafter, Jerry calls the client to relay that Sally recommended the subsidiary be formed as a limited liability company in the state of Maryland. Jerry said he would begin the paperwork the next day.

   Should anyone be concerned about this conduct?

2. George Jetson is an attorney who practices tax law. Firmly believing in a person's responsibility to those of less fortunate means, George volunteers about 20 hours of his valuable time every year to provide *pro bono* legal services in his community. He volunteers to prepare tax returns, for free, as part of a community project, volunteering every other Saturday in the month of February.

George, in making conversation with his wife at the dinner table, discusses a client's tax return that he prepared, as a volunteer, earlier that day. George tells his wife that his client is single and has four children, ranging in age from 14 months to 22 years. She is 40 years old and works as a medical office technician. She earns about $30,000 per year. She has investment income of about $200 per year. With various refundable tax credits, the client pays no income tax on her earnings, and she receives over $5,000 from the federal government as an income tax refund. He explains to his wife the tax laws and how they apply so that a wage and investment income earner pays no income taxes and receives a refundable tax credit from the federal government to help support her family.

Did George breach his duty of confidentiality by disclosing this information to his wife? Does it matter whether or not George identifies his client by name? Does the fact that the client was not charged a fee by George impact his duty?

Now assume that George is not an attorney but rather is a paralegal student preparing tax returns on a *pro bono* basis as part of his paralegal education program's tax law clinic. Note that the program's director, an attorney, supervises the students during the law clinic.

May George disclose the client's information because he is not an attorney? Why or why not?

3. Mary O'Reily is madly in love. Her beloved, Jack White, recently proposed and she accepted. She is thrilled to be engaged and so excited to get married! Mary and Jack are planning a simple ceremony with a few friends and family present. It is in five weeks.

Yesterday, Jack asked Mary if she would sign on the "dotted line" of a little agreement his lawyer drew up. Mary did not sleep a wink last night. She believes marriage and family are about love and not a contract. However, she is afraid that Jack will "postpone" the impending wedding if she does not sign.

Today, Mary asked Jack what the document said. He offered not only to let her read it, but recommended she speak with his lawyer, Sean Smart, who drafted it. Jack offers Mary the lawyer's telephone number and suggests she contact him for an appointment, which Mary does.

Should Mary and Jack use the same attorney when entering into a prenuptial agreement? Should Sean Smart, the attorney, allow Jack and Mary to both use him as their attorney regarding the prenuptial agreement? If so, is there anything Sean Smart can or should do, in this dual representation, to protect himself?

VIDEO CASE STUDIES

Video Interview of Christine Rentz

Paralegal case study videos to accompany this textbook are accessible from within both the New MyLegalStudiesLab Virtual Law Office Experience course and the Resources Website for Paralegal Studies.

ENDNOTES

[1] The author of this text maintains licenses to practice law in two jurisdictions, Georgia and Maryland.
[2] From NALA's Model Standards and Guidelines for Utilization of Paralegals, Guideline 2.

7 Other Legal Ethics Rules for Paralegals

Tenae Smith

Elder Law Paralegal at Hodes, Pessin & Katz, P.A.

Tenae works as an elder law paralegal at a law firm. Tenae was placed in an internship with this firm by her paralegal education program. In her internship, Tenae acted as a proofreader of legal documents. Asked to continue working at the firm after completing her internship, Tenae was promoted to performing part-time paralegal work while she completed her degree. She now works full-time for that firm.

Drafting legal documents and correspondence is an extremely important part of Tenae's practice. Tenae depends on her supervising attorneys to review her work and make appropriate comments and suggestions. When drafting, Tenae recommends that the drafter keep in mind who the intended reader is because a drafter's approach may differ depending on whether the reader is a client or someone else. Correct use of grammar and punctuation in drafting is key, emphasizes Tenae. Besides performing legal tasks while working at a smaller firm, Tenae also performs many administrative, nonlegal tasks, such as making copies, assembling packages for clients, opening new client matters, maintaining client files, and assisting with client billing and collection.

Tenae recognizes that legal ethics rules have a major impact on her firm's practice. The firm holds meetings on such matters as how to protect client confidentiality when attaching documents to e-mails. The two areas of legal ethics that Tenae says impact her practice most are confidentiality and conflicts of interest. In terms of confidentiality, Tenae describes the duty of confidentiality as "the responsibility not to reveal the client's identity and personal information." Tenae notes the importance of not discussing client matters with friends or family members. Regarding conflicts of interest, Tenae's firm searches its database for potential conflicts of interest before opening any new client matter.

Tenae's firm is active in advertising its services. Attorneys from the firm appear on a radio talk show to discuss elder law issues and related matters. The firm also holds estate planning and elder law seminars and similar marketing events. In an effort to generate business for her firm, Tenae has business cards that she distributes, as appropriate, to prospective new clients.

The full video interview is accessible from within both the New MyLegalStudiesLab Virtual Law Office Experience course and the Resources Website for Paralegal Studies.

The chapter will answer the following questions:

- What are the legal ethics rules regarding lawyer advertising and client solicitation?
- What are the legal ethics rules pertaining to legal fees and protecting client funds and other property?

- What legal ethics rules and other laws address competency in the performance of legal services?
- What legal ethics rules deal with advocacy, since lawyers act as advocates for their clients?

CHAPTER **INTRODUCTION**

This chapter examines other legal ethics rules that affect paralegals beyond the "big three" discussed in Chapter 6. We review the legal ethics rules regarding lawyer advertising and the solicitation of clients. Legal ethics rules regulating legal fees and protecting client funds and other property are discussed. Laws and legal ethics rules addressing competency in the performance of legal services are examined. The chapter ends with a review of legal ethics rules pertaining to a lawyer's role as an advocate. Our discussion begins with a study of legal ethics rules pertaining to lawyer advertising and the solicitation of clients.

ADVERTISING AND SOLICITATION

Advertising

Advertising is communication designed to persuade a person to purchase a product or service. Specifically regarding legal services, **lawyer advertising** is communication by a lawyer designed to persuade a person to engage the lawyer's services. Historically, ethics rules prohibited lawyer advertising. It was thought to demean the legal profession. Lawyer advertising was considered unprofessional and undignified. Today those views have changed. Lawyers now advertise their services in a variety of ways, through a variety of mediums.

For example, many law firms today maintain websites offering an abundance of information about their practices and their attorneys. Many law firms, especially larger ones, use brochures to market their various legal practice areas and their attorneys, including information such as in what legal specialties their attorneys practice and where their attorneys are licensed to practice. Some firms publish newsletters for their clients to announce significant events in the firm, such as introducing new personnel and updating clients on changes in the law and current events occurring in the firm. Law firms may hold seminars for clients and prospective clients, updating them on changing laws in areas relevant to their clients' businesses. They may hold social events where their lawyers can network with clients and prospective clients. They may issue press releases to announce important firm events, such as the hiring of a prestigious lawyer, former judge, or politician, or announce the opening of a new office. Law firms and lawyers may participate in community events and perform community service to enhance and maintain their stature within their communities. Law firms sometimes conduct surveys of their clients to evaluate their clients' satisfaction with their services, to improve relationships with clients, and to assess client needs. Lawyers and law firms in certain types of practice areas, such as family law, bankruptcy law, workers' compensation, Social Security, immigration law, and especially personal injury law are known for advertising their services on television; in print advertisements, such as in telephone directories, newspapers, and other periodicals; over the radio; and on billboards.

Advertising is communication designed to persuade a person to purchase a product or service.

Lawyer advertising is communication by a lawyer designed to persuade a person to engage the lawyer's services.

Methods of Lawyer Advertising

- Maintaining websites
- Publishing and distributing law firm brochures
- Publishing and distributing newsletters
- Conducting seminars
- Holding social and networking events
- Issuing press releases
- Participating in community events and performing community service
- Surveying client satisfaction and needs
- Placing television, print, radio, and billboard advertisements

Remember the *Bates* Case on Point from Chapter 5. In that case, two Arizona lawyers had advertised low-cost legal services at their law clinic via an advertisement in a local newspaper. They were disciplined by the State Bar of Arizona for conducting that advertising because, at that time, the State Bar of Arizona prohibited attorneys in that state from advertising their legal services. The U.S. Supreme Court held that lawyer advertising was a form of commercial speech that was protected by the First Amendment of the U.S. Constitution. The Court said that states could prohibit advertising only in limited circumstances, such as if the advertising is false, misleading, or deceptive. The Court allowed states to impose reasonable time, place, and manner restrictions on lawyer advertising; however, it did not allow states to totally prohibit it. According

to the U.S. Supreme Court, advertising of lawyer services is permissible, subject to some limitations. Legal ethics codes must not conflict with Supreme Court rulings, and as Supreme Court rulings on the subject of lawyer advertising are made, ethics rules adapt to reflect current law. What are the legal ethics rules pertaining to lawyer advertising, then, since lawyer advertising today is both legal and widely conducted?

ABAs Model Rules provide that a lawyer must not make a false or misleading communication about the lawyer or the lawyer's services. The rules define a "false or misleading communication" as a communication that contains a material misrepresentation of fact or law or that omits a fact necessary to make the statement considered as a whole not materially misleading. This, then, is a broad permissive grant supporting attorney advertising—the rule only prohibits false and misleading advertisements.

The Model Rules also permit a lawyer to advertise her services through written, recorded, or electronic communication, including the public media. Further, they require that any advertising communication include the name and office address of at least one lawyer or the law firm responsible for the communication's content.

These Model Rules also address the payment of referral fees by lawyers, a topic related to advertising of legal services. Restricting the payment of referral fees by a lawyer, under the Model Rules, a lawyer is not allowed to give anything of value to a person for recommending the lawyer's services other than paying the reasonable costs of permitted advertisements and communications, paying the usual charges of a legal service

RULES *on* POINT

Summary of ABA's Model Rules on Lawyer Advertising

Rule 7.1 prohibits lawyers from making false or misleading communications about themselves or their services. It defines "false or misleading communication" as a communication that contains a material misrepresentation of fact or law or that omits a fact necessary to make the statement considered as a whole not materially misleading.

Rule 7.2(a) permits a lawyer to advertise her services through written, recorded, or electronic communication, including the public media.

Rule 7.2(c) requires that any communication made pursuant to the Model Rules on lawyer advertising include the

name and office address of at least one lawyer or the law firm responsible for the communication's content.

Rule 7.2(b) prohibits a lawyer from giving anything of value to a person for recommending the lawyer's services other than paying the reasonable costs of permitted advertisements and communications, paying the usual charges of a legal service plan or a not-for-profit or qualified lawyer referral service, paying for a law practice pursuant to its purchase, and referring a client to another lawyer or other nonlawyer professional pursuant to a permitted agreement if the agreement is not exclusive and the client is informed of it.

plan or a not-for-profit or qualified lawyer referral service (qualified means one approved by an appropriate regulatory authority), paying for a law practice pursuant to its purchase, and referring a client to another lawyer or other nonlawyer professional pursuant to a permitted agreement if the agreement is not exclusive and the client is informed of it. In other words, an attorney generally may not pay a referral fee to another for referring her to a prospective client.

In advertising her services, may a lawyer communicate her fields of practice? Legal ethics rules speak to this question. According to ABA's Model Rules, an attorney may communicate that she does (or does not) practice in a particular field of law. Also, an attorney specially admitted to practice before the United States Patent and Trademark Office as a patent attorney may communicate the earned designation "Patent Attorney." However, an attorney may not state or imply that she is certified as a specialist in a particular field of law unless the lawyer has been certified as a specialist by an organization that was approved by the appropriate state authority or accredited by the ABA, and unless the name of the certifying organization is clearly identified in the communication.

What about communications using firm names and letterhead as another form of advertising? There are some restrictions on these communications that are imposed by legal ethics rules. ABA's Model Rules prohibit a lawyer from using a firm name, letterhead, or other professional designation that violates the ethics rules prohibiting false and misleading communications concerning a lawyer's services. The general rule regarding law firm names is that they may include the name of any practicing attorneys in the firm as well as the names of any deceased partners (or other former owners of the firm, such as members in a limited liability company).

Law firms with offices in multiple jurisdictions can use the same name in each jurisdiction, but the identification of the lawyers in an office of the firm must indicate the jurisdictional limitations of those not licensed in the jurisdiction where the office is located. This rule matters when a law firm has offices in multiple jurisdictions and uses letterhead listing attorneys with the firm but who are licensed and working in other jurisdictions. Note that if nonlawyers' names appear on firm letterhead (where permitted by law), their titles should be used to disclose their status to prevent unauthorized practice of law problems.

Further, the name of a lawyer holding a public office may not be used in the name of a law firm or in communications on the firm's behalf during any substantial period when the lawyer is not actively and regularly practicing with the firm. Also, lawyers

RULES *on* POINT

Summary of ABA's Model Rules on Communication of Fields of Practice and Legal Specialization

Rule 7.4(a) permits an attorney to communicate that she does (or does not) practice in a particular field of law.

Rule 7.4(b) permits an attorney specially admitted to practice before the United States Patent and Trademark Office as a patent attorney to communicate the earned designation "Patent Attorney."

Rule 7.4(d) prohibits an attorney from stating or implying that she is certified as a specialist in a particular field of law unless the lawyer has been certified as a specialist by an organization that was approved by the appropriate state authority or accredited by the American Bar Association, and unless the name of the certifying organization is clearly identified in the communication.

RULES *on* POINT

Summary of ABA's Model Rules on Firm Names and Letterhead

Rule 7.5(a) prohibits a lawyer from using a firm name, letterhead, or other professional designation that violates the ethics rules prohibiting false and misleading communications concerning a lawyer's services.

Rule 7.5(b) permits law firms with offices in multiple jurisdictions to use the same name in each jurisdiction, but the identification of the lawyers in an office of the firm must indicate the jurisdictional limitations of those not licensed in the jurisdiction where the office is located.

Rule 7.5(c) prohibits the name of a lawyer holding a public office from being used in the name of a law firm or in communications on the firm's behalf during any substantial period when the lawyer is not actively and regularly practicing with the firm.

Rule 7.5(d) allows lawyers to state or imply that they practice in a partnership or other organization only if the statement or implication is true.

may state or imply that they practice in a partnership or other organization only when they do so—therefore only when that statement or implication is true.

To summarize the legal ethics rules regarding lawyer advertising and their impact, then, advertising lawyer services obviously helps the lawyer in that it can generate more business. It helps the public as well. Through lawyer advertising, people are made aware of attorneys who are available in their areas to assist them, what services the attorneys can perform, and even their fees and if a fee must be paid up front or before work begins. So long as the advertising is informative and truthful, these benefits are achieved. The legal ethics rules help to prevent false and misleading advertisement by lawyers.

Generating business is a big part of my daily work. I personally generate a list of the people arrested the previous day in all of [my geographic area]. Then we send them letters explaining that [our firm] handles criminal cases and invite them to come in for a free consultation. The attorneys advertise by doing jail visits . . . and we receive referrals by word of mouth.
Lindsay Ann Thomas

We have determined that attorneys may advertise their services. Can paralegals advertise their services? As discussed in Chapter 2, most paralegals are employed by law firms. In this setting, paralegals often have business cards that they use in performing their work and in networking. The paralegal's status should be clearly disclosed on the business cards to avoid unauthorized practice of law issues. In jurisdictions permitting it, law firms sometimes use paralegals' names on their letterhead. This is an effective form of advertising the paralegals' services so long as the paralegals' status is clearly disclosed. Of course, paralegals should use this letterhead only for business purposes, not personal purposes. This is because, by use of the letterhead, there is an implication the correspondence is authorized by the firm. Further, in the case of a paralegal, there is an implication that the correspondence was reviewed and approved by a supervising attorney. Keep in mind that paralegals who bring business to their firms or supervising attorneys may not be paid referral fees or receive other valuable compensation for doing so. While a paralegal may bring business to the firm or supervising lawyer, the legal ethics rules prohibit the attorney from paying a referral fee or giving anything of value to a nonlawyer for bringing them business. Paralegals who obtain professional paralegal association certification, such as PACE, CLA, CP, and CLAS certification, may use these designations as a form of advertising. Both NFPA and NALA have guidelines and standards for how their designations should be used. Freelance paralegals, who are self-employed and hired by attorneys to help them with matters, are permitted to advertise their services. NFPA, in an ethics opinion, issued guidelines for such advertising including, among other conditions, that attorneys, rather than the public, be the target of the advertising and that the paralegal's status be clearly disclosed. Independent paralegals, meaning those paralegals who perform legal services directly to the public, generally may advertise their services too. However, independent paralegals should be sure to clearly disclose their status as paralegals and not attorneys in their advertising. In addition, independent paralegals should clearly indicate that they cannot give legal advice or perform other services that constitute the practice of law. Now that we have reviewed legal ethics rules on lawyer advertising, we will consider a related topic—solicitation of clients.

Solicitation

Solicitation is an attempt to gain business. Legal ethics rules place certain restrictions on a lawyer's direct solicitation of prospective clients. These restrictions are put in place to prevent any use of intimidation, undue influence, or unfair bargaining position that an attorney might assert when making direct contact with prospective clients.

Direct contact by an attorney may put undue pressure on a layperson during a time of trauma or tragedy in the layperson's life, which trauma or tragedy gave rise to a legal claim for which he may need legal representation. The legal ethics rules attempt to balance the interests of the prospective client, who may be well served by engaging legal counsel but who also may have very recently suffered harm or loss and not be thinking clearly enough to properly evaluate his alternatives, and the attorney, who has a financial self-interest in obtaining new business.

Solicitation is an attempt to gain business.

Under ABA's Model Rules an attorney is prohibited from using in-person, live telephone, or real-time electronic contact to solicit professional employment for his services from prospective clients when a significant motive for the lawyer's conduct is his pecuniary gain, unless the person contacted is an attorney or has a family, close personal, or prior professional relationship with the attorney. Even if the contact is permitted under this rule, an attorney may not solicit professional employment from a prospective client by written, recorded, or electronic communication or by in-person, telephone, or real-time electronic contact if the prospective client has made known to the attorney a desire not to be solicited, or the solicitation involves coercion, duress, or harassment.

Note that the legal ethics rules restrict direct, rather than indirect, solicitation of prospective clients. Use of indirect means of communication, as opposed to direct contact, is permitted—such as lawyer advertising. Where solicitation is permitted, the Model Rules require the permitted solicitation materials to include the words "advertising material" if the recipient is not a lawyer or does not have a family, close personal, or prior professional relationship with the lawyer making the solicitation.

Also note that an exception is made under the Model Rules to allow an attorney to participate in a prepaid or group legal service plan that is operated by an organization that is not owned or directed by the attorney where the plan uses in-person or telephone contact to solicit memberships or subscription for the plan from people who are not known to need legal services in a particular matter covered by the plan. Such prepaid or group legal services plans are normally offered as employment benefits, and member employees pay premiums to cover certain legal services that may be needed in the future, much like medical insurance plans.

These legal ethics rules prohibit "ambulance chasers," also called "runners and cappers." "Ambulance chaser" is a term that refers to a lawyer or agent of a lawyer who preys on recent accident or other victims by soliciting them directly, either at the accident scene or at the hospital where they are being treated for their injuries. Listening to communications over a police scanner to learn of accidents and then to contact and solicit the victims is another example.

Note that an exception is made to the direct solicitation prohibitions, however, for political action organizations such as the National Association for the Advancement of Colored People (NAACP) and the American Civil Liberties Union (ACLU). These organizations may directly solicit plaintiffs in legal cases

RULES on POINT

Summary of ABA's Model Rules on Solicitation of Clients

Rule 7.3(a) prohibits an attorney from using in-person, live telephone, or real-time electronic contact to solicit professional employment for his services from prospective clients when a significant motive for the lawyer's conduct is his pecuniary gain, unless the person contacted is an attorney, or has a family, close personal, or prior professional relationship with the attorney.

Rule 7.3(b) provides that even if the contact is permitted under Rule 7.3(a), an attorney may not solicit professional employment from a prospective client by written, recorded, or electronic communication or by in-person, telephone, or real-time electronic contact if the prospective client has made known to the attorney a desire not to be solicited, or the solicitation involves coercion, duress, or harassment.

Rule 7.3(c) requires that permitted solicitation materials include the words "advertising material" if the recipient is not a lawyer or does not have a family, close personal, or prior professional relationship with the lawyer making the solicitation.

Rule 7.3(d) makes an exception to the solicitation restrictions when an attorney participates in a prepaid or group legal service plan that is operated by an organization that is not owned or directed by the attorney where the plan uses in-person or telephone contact to solicit memberships or subscription for the plan from people who are not known to need legal services in a particular matter covered by the plan.

that further a specific political or social principle sought to be advanced by the organization, such as civil rights or freedom of speech or religion. Since the legal representation these organizations provide is not offered for the organization's own pecuniary benefit (in fact, the representation likely will use the organization's resources), but rather to advance a political or social cause, the direct solicitation rules do not prohibit such solicitation. Another exception is made for attorneys who directly solicit potential members of a class in a federal class action lawsuit. The Federal Rules of Civil Procedure permit an attorney's direct contact with people who are potential plaintiffs in a class action lawsuit.

Can a lawyer use an employee or other agent, such as a paralegal, to perform direct solicitation, that she is prohibited from making herself? The answer is no. Solicitation by proxy is not allowed. An attorney may not use a paralegal or other agent to circumvent the direct solicitation restrictions. The conduct of the agent is attributed to be the conduct of the attorney, for which the attorney is responsible under the legal ethics rules of the jurisdiction licensing her. So an attorney cannot use an agent to perform an act of direct solicitation that the ethics rules prohibit her from personally performing.

KEY Point

Direct Solicitation of Clients by Paralegals

Solicitation by proxy is not allowed. An attorney cannot use an agent to perform an act of direct solicitation that the ethics rules prohibit her from personally performing.

Another area of legal ethics also impacts paralegals to some degree. That area is legal fees and protecting client funds and other property. Rules regarding legal fees and the duty to protect client funds and other property are discussed next.

LEGAL FEES AND PROTECTING CLIENT FUNDS AND OTHER PROPERTY

Legal Fees

While there are many types of fee arrangements that lawyers can enter into with their clients, the three most common types of fee arrangements are fixed fees, hourly fees, and contingency fees. **Fixed fees**, also called **flat fees**, are fees for legal services of a set amount for the performance of a routine legal service. For example, a lawyer may charge $750 for incorporating an organization or $500 for preparing a simple will. Lawyers charge fixed fees when the legal matter is fairly simple and the lawyers know about how much time it will take for them to perform the work.

Hourly fees are fees for legal services that are based on hourly rates and the amount of time actually spent performing the work. Hourly fees are the most common method of billing in legal matters other than in plaintiff civil litigation (discussed next). Lawyers and paralegals may bill clients for their services using hourly fee arrangements. Hourly fees can range from under $100 an hour for paralegals and inexperienced attorneys working outside big cities to $1,000 an hour or more for experienced lawyers working in major metropolitan areas and handling complex legal matters. The hourly rate charged a client will vary depending on such factors as the experience of the person performing the work, the nature and complexity of the work itself, the geographic location where the work is being performed (for instance, legal work tends to be more expensive in New York City than in a smaller community such as Lancaster, Pennsylvania), and whether the client receives a discounted rate (important clients sometimes do).

KEY Point

Factors Impacting Hourly Rates

The hourly rate charged a client will vary depending on such factors as:

- the experience of the person performing the work,
- the nature and complexity of the work itself,
- the geographic location where the work is being performed, and
- whether the client receives a discounted rate.

In hourly fee-based structures, clients are normally sent monthly bills when their matters are actively being worked on and the attorney's and paralegal's time is being spent on them. In order to bill clients for time actually spent on matters, lawyers and paralegals must keep accurate timekeeping records to know who to bill and for how much. Lawyers and paralegals usually record their time in either six or ten minute intervals—all day, every business day. Fractions of hours may be billed, not just full hours. Attorneys and paralegals responsible for recording their time (timekeepers) record the name of the client, the

Fixed fees are fees for legal services of a set amount for the performance of a routine legal service; they are also called **flat fees**.

Hourly fees are fees for legal services that are based on hourly rates and the amount of time actually spent performing the work.

matter being worked on, and the nature of the work being performed. Timekeeping often is entered using timekeeping software—this function has become computerized in the past few decades. It is recommended that timekeeping be entered daily, since it can be very difficult to reconstruct an 8-, 10-, or even 12-hour work day once it has passed. As you will see when we review the legal ethics rules on client fees, it is critical that lawyers and paralegals keep truthful, accurate records of the time they spend working on client matters.

Contingency fees, also called **contingent fees**, are fees for legal services that are based on a percentage of recovery in a civil case. Payment of them is contingent on there being a successful outcome for the client, hence the fees' name. Typical contingency fees range from about 25 percent to 40 percent of the plaintiff's recovery. They can be set on a sliding scale, where the percentage increases based on the time and effort expended by the attorney and the degree of risk accepted by the attorney in agreeing to this type of fee arrangement (the "risk" factor is discussed below). So in a contingency fee arrangement where the attorney is to be paid 30 percent of the plaintiff's recovery and the plaintiff recovers $100,000 via judgment at trial or settlement of the case, the attorney gets paid $30,000 in legal fees and the plaintiff keeps the remainder (subject, perhaps, to repayment of the lawyer for the costs and expenses of that litigation). In a sliding scale scenario, if the fee arrangement is to pay the attorney 25 percent if the case settles before trial, 30 percent if the case goes to trial, and 35 percent if the case is appealed, when a judgment is rendered after trial in favor of the plaintiff for $100,000, the attorney's fee is $30,000.

If you think these fees are too high, consider this example. An attorney works diligently on a plaintiff's case for two years, declining other work to have more time to devote to the plaintiff's case. She has a contingency fee arrangement with the client to be paid 40 percent of the plaintiff's recovery. This may seem like a lot. However, at trial, the plaintiff loses—and recovers nothing. What is the lawyer paid in legal fees for her two years' of work? Nothing. According to the math, 40 percent of $0 is $0. There is a risk, then, when using contingency fees as the legal fee arrangement. The risk is that the lawyer will receive no fee at all for the work performed. Although the percentage

of the fee may seem high, this is misleading—for the attorney bears a risk in charging this type of fee that she will not be paid for her services at all. Only when there is a successful outcome for the plaintiff, her client, will the lawyer be paid her fee. Also note that with contingency fees it is not until the conclusion of the matter that the lawyer gets paid. The lawyer could wait months or even years to collect her legal fees, as opposed to hourly fees that are billed and paid on a monthly basis.

Why use contingency fees, then, if they are risky to the lawyer and may end up being expensive to the client? Some people who need legal representation, such as to bring a tort claim for serious injuries sustained in a car accident caused by another's negligence, cannot afford the hourly fees that attorneys charge or the costs of civil litigation. Because of this, these people would be denied access to the legal system to pursue their claims if they could not obtain representation using a contingency fee arrangement. Contingency fees, then, provide access to legal services to people who have a legal claim but cannot afford to hire a lawyer to represent them on an hourly fee basis.

Contingency fees are allowed only in certain types of cases, however. They normally are used by plaintiff's attorneys in civil litigation—especially personal injury litigation. As you will see, the legal ethics rules limit their use, for they cannot be used in criminal matters and in certain family law matters. Further, they would not be used in civil litigation defense because, in defending claims, defendants recover nothing. A party must make a claim against another for there to be a chance of recovery. In all cases where the lawyer is defending a client against a legal claim, contingency fees are not used—because any percent of $0 recovery is $0, and there is no recovery when no claim is asserted. Also, the percentage that may be charged in a contingency fee arrangement may be limited by law. See the Statute on Point for an example.

Where used, it is a very good idea for attorneys to get contingency fee agreements in writing and signed by the client. The writing provides good evidence of the attorney and client's agreement, especially when there is a large recovery for the plaintiff and the attorney stands to make a significant fee. In fact, as we will discuss, many states require use of a writing for contingency fee arrangements in their legal ethics rules.

As you will soon see when the legal ethics rules regarding legal fees are examined, contingency fees are subject to court scrutiny for reasonableness. Where the percentage of fee charged

KEY Point

Contingency fees are typically used by plaintiff's attorneys in civil litigation, especially personal injury cases. They cannot be used in criminal cases or in certain family law matters.

Contingency fees are fees for legal services that are based on a percentage of recovery in a civil case; they are also called **contingent fees**.

The Federal Tort Claims Act

The Federal Tort Claims Act (FTCA) is a federal statute that permits private parties to sue the U.S. government in federal court for most torts committed by persons acting on behalf of the United States, in effect limiting the governmental immunity of the federal government. This statute expressly limits the amount of contingency fees that can be charged in cases brought under the FTCA to a maximum fee of 25 percent of the plaintiff's recovery.

General Rule of Legal Fees and Expenses

Legal ethics rules prohibit lawyers from agreeing to, charging, or collecting an unreasonable fee or an unreasonable amount for expenses.

is considered by the court to be excessive, or where the fee is significantly out of proportion to the work actually performed or the risk accepted by the lawyer, a court can disallow or modify a contingency fee, reducing it to a more reasonable amount.

Most states' legal ethics rules prohibit lawyers from agreeing to, charging, or collecting an unreasonable fee. Some states call such unreasonable fees "excessive" fees or "unconscionable" fees. For example, in the Maryland Lawyers' Rules of Professional Conduct, Rule 1.5, an attorney is prohibited from making an agreement for, charging, or collecting an unreasonable fee or an unreasonable amount for expenses. The rule sets forth several factors that should be considered in determining whether a fee is reasonable, including the time and labor required, the novelty and difficulty of the issues involved, and the skill needed to properly perform the legal services; the likelihood, if apparent to the client, that the acceptance of the employment will preclude other employment for the lawyer (meaning that, by taking the client's matter, the lawyer will have to forgo other matters for other clients); the fee customarily charged in the locality for similar legal services; the amount involved and the results obtained by the lawyer; the time limitations imposed by the client or by the circumstances (such as if the client brought the matter to the attorney only days before the statute of limitations on the claim ran out and the attorney had to put aside other matters to get the complaint quickly filed in this case); the nature and length

Summary of ABA's Model Rule on Legal Fees

Rule 1.5(a) prohibits an attorney from making an agreement for, charging, or collecting an unreasonable fee or an unreasonable amount for expenses. Factors that should be considered in determining whether a fee is reasonable include:

- the time and labor required, the novelty and difficulty of the issues involved, and the skill needed to properly perform the legal services;
- the likelihood, if apparent to the client, that the acceptance of the employment will preclude other employment for the lawyer;
- the fee customarily charged in the locality for similar legal services;
- the amount involved and the results obtained;
- the time limitations imposed by the client or the circumstances;
- the nature and length of the professional relationship between the attorney and the client;
- the experience, reputation, and ability of the lawyer(s) performing the work; and
- whether the fee is fixed or contingent.

of the professional relationship between the attorney and the client; the experience, reputation, and ability of the lawyer(s) performing the work; and whether the fee is fixed or contingent.

For a simple example of an unreasonable fee, think back to our earlier discussion of the Federal Tort Claims Act. That act limits the amount of contingency fees in tort cases brought against the federal government to 25 percent of the plaintiff's recovery. If an attorney set or collected a fee of 30 percent in an FTCA case that fee would be unreasonable because it exceeds the statutory limit of 25 percent. In such a situation, a court could reduce the fee to the prescribed amount under FTCA.

Attorneys and paralegals who are charging fees based on an hourly fee arrangement must be diligent, accurate, and honest in their timekeeping, as discussed earlier. It is unethical to inflate time spent on a client matter in order to increase the legal fee. This is true despite the enormous pressure put on attorneys (especially associate attorneys), and sometimes paralegals, to bill a significant number of hours per year to be eligible for a bonus or even to remain employed by the law firm.

Consider this example. An associate attorney employed by a hypothetical large firm is required to bill 2,000 hours per year. How much time must he spend at work to accomplish this? Not all lawyers' work is billable. Only time spent actually handling a client's matter is. So time spent reading legal journals or researching to stay abreast of changing law, networking to obtain new business, meeting continuing legal education requirements, attending firm meetings, performing administrative tasks like timekeeping, attending computer training, supervising paralegals and other employees, and the like, are not billable tasks. That said, they are important tasks and may be performed daily. So part of each day is spent by the lawyer doing billable work and part of it is spent doing nonbillable work, probably averaging a ratio of between 2:1 and 3:1 of billable to nonbillable hours. This may easily require an attorney to work a minimum of 60 hours each week, with a couple of weeks vacation (if he can get away from the office to take them) and firm holidays. Given that pressure to work very, very hard to bill the required minimum number of hours each year, attorneys (and paralegals) must not succumb to pressure to inflate the time they spend on client matters.

> *Paralegals who do have a time requirement must be prudent in their billing so as not to violate the ethics rules by, for example, overbilling or double billing in an attempt to meet a billable hour requirement.*
> **Sherry Myers**

If an attorney has to fly to another city to take a deposition for a matter he is working on for Client X, may he charge the client for the time he spends traveling? Of course, so long as that is permitted in the fee agreement—and it is reasonable to charge for travel time because it is time the attorney is working for the client and is not free to do as he pleases, such as be with his family. What if, on the four-hour flight, the attorney writes a legal brief for Client Y? May the attorney bill Client Y for the four hours spent drafting the legal brief? Sure! That is legal work performed for the client. It does not matter that it was performed out of the office, on an airplane. Here is the tougher question. May the attorney bill Client X for four hours of travel time *and* bill Client Y for four hours of drafting the legal brief? Absolutely not! This is called double-billing, and it is unethical. An attorney (or paralegal) may not bill eight hours of work for four hours of time. A better way to handle this situation is for the client to split his time between the two, perhaps billing Client X two hours for travel and Client Y two hours for legal document drafting—for a total of four billable hours, which is the actual time the attorney spent working.

What if an inexperienced attorney, or a paralegal working on a task she has never performed before, spends several hours "spinning her wheels" trying to figure out what she is doing before she can actually perform the assigned task? The task takes her six hours to complete, but it should have taken her three hours. What amount of time should she bill? Well, that is a bit of a trick question. The attorney or paralegal should record the full six hours on her timekeeping, including recording the client matter, and work performed. She can then communicate to her supervising attorney why the work took as long as it did—that it was a task new to her and it took her a while to figure out how to do it. (Note that, before spinning her wheels for too long, the inexperienced attorney or paralegal should ask the supervising attorney who assigned the task for assistance, for the supervising attorney would rather provide some guidance than have the subordinate waste hours figuring out what to do.) The supervising attorney will review the subordinate's timekeeping while performing the review of draft client bills, because client bills are reviewed by supervising attorneys before they are sent. Bills are edited so that the client is charged a reasonable amount for time spent on matters, such as when the actual time spent on a task is in excess of what was reasonable. Keep in mind that just because an attorney or paralegal records accurate billable time on their timekeeping does not mean the client will necessarily be charged for all that time—supervising attorneys review, revise, and approve timekeeping when they review drafts of bills before they are sent to clients. Time spent on matters is routinely adjusted if it is not reasonable. Remember that legal fees charged must be reasonable; the legal ethics rules require it.

What about costs and expenses incurred in conducting the representation? May lawyers and law firms bill these to the clients as well as legal fees? Certainly, as long as the costs and expenses are reasonable and, at the start of the representation, the client agrees (preferably in writing) to pay them. Refer back to ABA's Model Rule 1.5(b), which requires that expenses charged and collected by attorneys must be reasonable, just like fees.

What costs and expenses may be charged back to clients? Lawyers can charge clients the reasonable costs of things like messenger services, copy costs, delivery services, depositions transcripts, telephone and fax charges, court filing fees, travel expenses, postage, and other costs and expenses directly related to the client's representation. Costs and expenses are itemized on the client's bill so the client can see what each charge represents. Included in flat fees and hourly fees, so already built into these fee structures, is a charge for firm overhead, where clients help pay the costs for things like the firm's receptionist's salary, office space, office equipment, and other expenses necessary to maintain a law office. For the firm must operate at a profit, meaning it must cover its expenses and have money left over to stay in business.

Legal ethics rules also regulate the communication of fee arrangements with clients, including agreements regarding the client's repayment of the attorney's costs and expenses. A lawyer should fully explain to her client the terms of their fee arrangement as soon as practicable after she agrees to the representation. Communicating this in writing is recommended (if not required) by states' legal ethics rules. ABA's Model Rules require that the scope of the representation and the basis or rate of the legal fee and expenses to be charged to the client be communicated to the client, preferably in writing. This communication should be made before or within a reasonable time after agreeing to the representation, except when the attorney regularly represents the client, in which case the attorney may use the same basis or rate as is normally charged without having to meet this communication obligation. However, any changes in the basis or rate of the legal fee or expenses must be communicated to the client.

RULE *on* POINT

Summary of ABA's Model Rule on Communication of Legal Fees

Rule 1.5(b) requires that the scope of the representation and the basis or rate of the legal fee and expenses to be charged to the client must be communicated to the client, preferably in writing, before or within a reasonable time after agreeing to the representation. An exception is made when the attorney regularly represents the client, in which case the attorney may use the same basis or rate as is normally charged without having to meet this communication obligation. However, any changes in the basis or rate of the legal fee or expenses must be communicated to the client.

Remember from the material regarding the unauthorized practice of law that paralegals cannot set the legal fee to be charged a client on a matter. Only attorneys may agree to accept representation of a client in a legal matter and set the fee to be charged for that representation.

> *I am impacted by the ethics rules pertaining to legal fees because I cannot set or discuss legal fees with clients. That is a job handled by the attorney.*
> Sherry Myers

In accepting representation of a client in a matter, attorneys may charge advanced fees. **Advanced fees** are legal fees paid by the client at the beginning of the representation and which are usually refundable if the fees are not later earned by the attorney through the performance of legal services. On the other hand, **retainer fees** are legal fees the client agrees to pay in advance to secure the lawyer's services and that are not normally refundable. They compensate the attorney for foregoing other matters to work on the matter for this client, as well as guarantee that the attorney will be available to handle the matter as needed for the client. Retainer fees normally are considered earned when paid.

Consider this example. Maria consults with an attorney and considers having the attorney represent her in her divorce. After meeting the attorney and speaking with him, Maria would like to hire him to represent her in this matter. The attorney agrees to the representation, and Maria becomes the attorney's client. They discuss the fee arrangement, and Maria agrees to pay the attorney's hourly rate, as well as the hourly rate of his paralegal, for time spent working on the matter. She also agrees to pay for reasonable expenses, and the specific expenses she agrees to reimburse the lawyer for are defined in a written fee agreement, which she signs. At this time, Maria is required to pay $5,000 to the attorney. After the attorney works on the matter for a

Advanced fees are legal fees paid by the client at the beginning of the representation and which are usually refundable if the fees are not later earned by the attorney through the performance of legal service.

Retainer fees are legal fees the client agrees to pay in advance to secure the lawyer's services and that are not normally refundable.

few weeks and spends about 10 hours of attorney time on the matter so far (and the attorney charges $350 per hour), Maria reconciles with her husband. What money can she get back, if any? That depends on whether the fee was an advanced fee or a retainer fee—and which type it was should have been expressed in the written fee agreement at the time the fee was collected. If it was a retainer fee, it is nonrefundable, and Maria is entitled to none of it back. The reasoning behind this is that the attorney, at least in theory, had to forgo representation of other clients on other matters when he agreed to take Maria's case. The retainer fee compensates him for that, as well as his guarantee to be available to Maria to handle her matter. However, if the fee was an advanced fee, Maria would be entitled to a refund of the amount not earned by the attorney. Since the attorney worked for 10 hours on the case and charges $350 per hour, he earned $3,500 of the fee (plus reimbursement for any expenses incurred, per their agreement). Maria would be entitled to a refund of the difference—$1,500 (if no expenses were incurred).

Are there special legal ethics rules pertaining to contingent fees? Yes, there are. According to ABA's Model Rules, an attorney may not enter into an arrangement to charge or collect any fee in a domestic relations (family law) matter where the payment or amount is contingent on securing a divorce or is contingent upon the amount of alimony, support, or property settlement. In addition, an attorney may not enter into an agreement to charge or collect a contingent fee for representing a defendant in a criminal matter. Unless prohibited by the above or some other law, a legal fee may be contingent on the outcome of the matter for which the service is rendered. There must be a contingency fee agreement in effect, in writing and signed by the client, which states the method for determining the fee and the expenses to be deducted from any recovery, including when the expenses are to be deducted (either before or after the contingency fee calculation).

May lawyers who are not with the same firm divide, or split, a legal fee? Under the legal ethics rules, that depends. Under ABA's Model Rules, they may split the fee if the division is in proportion to the work each lawyer performs on the matter or each lawyer assumes joint responsibility for the representation, if the client agrees in writing, and if the total fee is reasonable.

What about fee splitting with nonlawyers? May a lawyer share a legal fee with a nonlawyer? No, generally attorneys are prohibited, under the legal ethics rules, from sharing fees with nonlawyers (though there are some exceptions). This

RULES *on* POINT

Summary of ABA's Model Rules on Contingency Fees

Rule 1.5(d) prohibits an attorney from entering into an arrangement to charge or collect any fee in a domestic relations (family law) matter where the payment or amount is contingent on securing a divorce or is contingent on the amount of alimony, support, or property settlement. In addition, an attorney may not enter into an agreement to charge or collect a contingent fee for representing a defendant in a criminal matter.

Rule 1.5(c) states that unless it is prohibited by Rule 1.5(d) or some other law, a legal fee may be contingent on the outcome of the matter for which the service is rendered. There must be a contingency fee agreement in effect, in writing and signed by the client, which states the method for determining the fee and the expenses to be deducted from any recovery, including when the expenses are to be deducted (either before or after the contingency fee calculation).

RULE *on* POINT

Summary of ABA's Model Rule on Fee Splitting by Lawyers

Rule 1.5(e) permits lawyers from different firms to split a legal fee if the split is in proportion to the work each lawyer performs on the matter or each lawyer assumes joint responsibility for the representation, if the client agrees in writing, and if the total fee is reasonable.

prohibition applies to fee sharing with paralegals—attorneys may not share their legal fees with paralegals. Sharing a legal fee with a nonlawyer raises many legal ethics issues, including the unauthorized practice of law, direct solicitation, and, most importantly, interference with the attorney's exercise of independent professional judgment. Accordingly, legal ethics rules generally prohibit attorneys from establishing partnerships with nonlawyers if any of the activities of the partnership constitute the practice of law. This prohibition exists to avoid the same problems created by fee splitting with nonlawyers—issues with the unauthorized practice of law, direct solicitation, and interference with the attorneys' exercise of independent professional judgment. Of greatest concern with regard to fee sharing with nonlawyers is the possibility that the lawyer's independent professional judgment would be impaired by conflicting interests of the nonlawyers involved.

KEY Point

Fee Splitting

- Attorneys may split legal fees if the division is in proportion to the work each lawyer performs on the matter or each lawyer assumes joint responsibility for the representation, if the client agrees in writing, and if the total fee is reasonable.
- Attorneys, generally, are prohibited from sharing legal fees with nonlawyers.

RULES *on* POINT

Summary of ABA's Model Rules on Professional Independence of a Lawyer

Rule 5.4(a) prohibits a lawyer or law firm from sharing legal fees with a nonlawyer, except that:

- an agreement by a lawyer with the lawyer's firm, partner, or association may provide for the payment of money over a reasonable period of time after the lawyer's death to the lawyer's estate or other specific person(s);
- a lawyer who purchases the practice of a deceased, disabled, or disappeared lawyer may pay the purchase price to the estate or other representative of the lawyer;
- a lawyer or law firm may include nonlawyer employees in a compensation or retirement plan even if the plan is based on a profit-sharing arrangement; and
- a lawyer may share court-awarded legal fees with a nonprofit organization that employed, retained, or recommended the lawyer's representation in the matter.

Rule 5.4(b) prohibits an attorney from forming a partnership with a nonlawyer if any activities of the partnership constitute the practice of law.

Protecting Client Funds and Other Property

Now that we have examined legal fees, we will review the ethical obligations of attorneys and paralegals with regard to protecting client funds and other property, for these topics are related in that they both deal with money or other property that belongs to the client. Legal ethics rules require attorneys to maintain client funds separately from their own, or their law firm's, funds. They do this by establishing client trust accounts. **Client trust accounts** are bank accounts that are set up by lawyers to maintain funds that belong to one or more clients. Note that there can be one account, for all client funds, or multiple accounts, by client. Money owed to clients, such as recoveries received from the opponent in settlement of a client's claims, and advanced fees not yet earned by the attorney, must be maintained as separate from the lawyer's or firm's funds.

ABA's Model Rules address the safekeeping of client property, including client funds, by lawyers. They require lawyers to hold the property of clients or third persons that is in the lawyers' possession in connection with a representation separate from the lawyer's own property. Funds (money) must be kept in a separate account maintained in the state where the lawyer's office is located, or elsewhere with the client or third person's consent. Maintaining client funds together with the lawyer's or law firm's funds is called "commingling" of funds and is prohibited by the legal ethics rules. The client or third person's property must be appropriately safeguarded. Complete records of fund accounts and other property must be kept by the lawyer and preserved for five years after the termination of the representation. Note that a leading cause of disciplinary actions against attorneys arises out of mishandling of client funds—so this is an important legal ethics rule. Regarding advanced fees, a lawyer must deposit into a client trust account legal fees and expenses that have been paid in advance but not yet earned (they can be withdrawn by the lawyers as fees when they are earned and as expenses when they are incurred and the client is billed for them).

KEY Point

How Important Is It for Attorneys to Properly Handle Client Funds?

A leading cause of disciplinary actions against attorneys arises out of mishandling of client funds. So it is very important.

Client trust accounts are bank accounts that are set up by lawyers to maintain funds that belong to one or more clients.

Under ABA's Model Rules, when a lawyer receives funds or property in which a client or third person has an interest (such as funds from the opposing side in settlement of the client's claim), the lawyer must promptly notify the client or third person, and generally must promptly deliver to the client or third person the funds or property to which the client or third person is entitled. She must provide a full accounting regarding the property, such as an accounting of the contingency fee and expenses being subtracted from the settlement amount before it is turned over to the client.

If, during the course of legal representation, a lawyer in possession of property in which two or more persons (one of whom may be the lawyer) claim interests, the property must be kept separate by the lawyer until the dispute is resolved. Any portion of the property not disputed should be promptly distributed to its owner.

Note that these rules cover not only client funds but also funds of third persons, such as a lien holder (a lien holder is a person with a legal claim to the property of another as security for a debt). It may be that a lawyer has received funds relating to a client's representation that belong to a third party. These funds must be kept separate from the attorney's funds, just as client funds must be.

Further, the rules cover more than just funds, but also other property belonging to clients or third persons, such as jewelry or stock certificates and bonds. What are a lawyer's duties with regard to property? According to the legal ethics rules noted above, the lawyer must safeguard property held for clients or third persons. This means she should keep the property in a safety deposit box or other secured environment where it is both locked up securely and protected from fire and other hazards.

Lawyers must also keep accurate and complete records of their holding of client and third person's funds and property. Lawyers must do so for five years after the termination of representation of the client under the Model Rules. On termination of representation, lawyers should return all client and third person's funds and property (such as legal documents, legal titles, jewelry, securities, and the like) because those funds and that property belong to the clients or third persons.

Discussed earlier, client funds are maintained by lawyers in separate bank accounts called client trust accounts. These accounts may be interest-bearing, meaning their deposits should earn interest. For example, when an attorney holds substantial funds in a client trust account for a significant period of time, the attorney may be required to maintain those funds in an interest-bearing account. Interest on these accounts may be payable to the client. However, when small amounts of funds are maintained by attorneys for short periods of time, what happens to any interest earned on these deposits? Does it go to the clients? Many states require attorneys to hold this money in an Interest on Lawyers Trust Accounts (IOLTA).

RULES *on* POINT

Summary of ABA's Model Rules on Safekeeping Property of Clients and Third Persons

Rule 1.15(a) requires a lawyer to hold the property of clients or third persons that is in the lawyer's possession in connection with a representation separate from the lawyer's own property. Funds (money) must be kept in a separate account maintained in the state where the lawyer's office is located or elsewhere with the client or third person's consent. The property must be appropriately safeguarded. Complete records of fund accounts and other property must be kept by the lawyer and preserved for five years after the termination of the representation.

Rule 1.15(c) requires a lawyer to deposit into a client trust account legal fees and expenses that have been paid in advance but not yet earned.

Rule 1.15(d) requires that when a lawyer receives funds or property in which a client or third person has an interest, the lawyer must promptly notify the client or third person, and generally must promptly deliver to the client or third person the funds or property to which they are entitled, including a full accounting regarding the property.

Rule 1.15(e) states that if during the course of legal representation, a lawyer in possession of property in which two or more persons (one of whom may be the lawyer) claim interests, the property must be kept separate by the lawyer until the dispute is resolved. Any portion of the property not disputed should be promptly distributed to its owner.

account. IOLTA accounts are special client trust accounts where deposits are "pooled" from several clients when the funds, on their own, are too small to generate meaningful interest income sufficient to offset the administrative costs of maintaining separate accounts for each client. In most jurisdictions today, interest earned from the deposits in these accounts does not go to the clients. Instead, it typically goes to fund some nonprofit organization, such as an organization providing legal services to the poor, or to the state bar association's disciplinary program for lawyers, or to a client security fund that holds money to reimburse clients who have been harmed by attorney misconduct. Some jurisdictions have mandatory programs requiring attorneys to participate in this funding program, while other jurisdictions' participation in such a funding program is voluntary and attorneys can choose whether or not to participate. In some jurisdictions the programs are set up so that attorneys automatically participate in them, but they can take affirmative steps to opt-out of program participation. Keep in mind that the principle of these accounts always belongs to the clients. What happens to the interest earned on these accounts varies from state to state, with states' IOLTA programs using some of these funds to finance social and legal services programs.

As mentioned above, mishandling of client funds is a major cause of disciplinary actions against attorneys for legal ethics rule violations. Client funds must be kept separate from the attorney's funds. Client funds must not be taken for the attorney's personal use or for use by the firm. They cannot be taken permanently, and they cannot be taken temporarily (or "borrowed"). Defenses asserted by attorneys—such as that they planned to or did return the client funds, that they paid interest on the funds "borrowed," that their firms were being mismanaged, or that they needed the client funds to handle personal financial problems—are not successful and do not save attorneys from disciplinary

sanctions. Mishandling client funds is a very serious violation of the legal ethics rules. Accordingly, disbarment is the usual sanction imposed on attorneys who mishandle client funds.

Further, actually taking a client's funds and using them, without permission, can constitute a civil wrong called a tort—namely, the tort of conversion. **Conversion** is the intentional exercise of dominion and control over another's personal property that seriously interferes with the owner's right to possession. When an attorney is found liable for committing the tort of conversion by taking a client's funds (or other property), the client is awarded a remedy, typically money damages. Because conversion is an intentional tort, both compensatory and punitive damages may be recoverable from the attorney. Taking a client's funds without permission can also constitute a crime (such as theft) under a jurisdiction's criminal statutes. Attorneys can be prosecuted for committing theft of client funds or related crimes.

How do the legal ethics rules regarding legal fees and protecting client funds affect paralegals? They affect paralegals in many ways. First, regarding hourly fee arrangements, clients can be billed for the amount of time paralegals spend working on their matters. Paralegals, then, must keep accurate, honest, and complete timekeeping records. Also, attorneys must not share legal fees with paralegals. A paralegal should never accept any portion of a legal fee. Where paralegals are responsible for administration and recordkeeping relating to maintaining client funds and safeguarding client property, they must abide by the rules that govern attorneys in these areas to ensure that client funds are not commingled with the supervising attorney's or law firms funds and that other property is appropriately safeguarded from harm or loss.

Next, we will review another area of legal ethics that affects both paralegals and attorneys. This area is competence.

COMPETENCE

Competence means the ability to successfully perform a task. A good synonym for competence is proficiency. A lawyer must provide to his client competent representation. That means the lawyer must be able to successfully perform the legal service. It does not mean that the lawyer must successfully win a negotiation or a lawsuit. It does mean that the lawyer must use his education, training, and experience to best serve his client. **Competent representation** means that

Conversion is the intentional exercise of dominion and control over another's personal property that seriously interferes with the owner's right to possession.

Competence means the ability to successfully perform a task.

Competent representation means the lawyer possesses the legal knowledge, skill, thoroughness, and preparation reasonably necessary for the client's representation in a matter.

I provide competent representation by working closely with the attorneys, being accurate and diligent with the matter I am handling, keeping aware of time management, and maintaining excellent communication and writing skills.
Christine Rentz

the lawyer possesses the legal knowledge, skill, thoroughness, and preparation reasonably necessary for the client's representation in a matter.

Failure to perform legal services competently can give rise to both legal claims against attorneys and paralegals, as well as disciplinary actions against attorneys. This duty to perform competently also makes attorneys responsible for the work of paralegals and other nonlawyers they supervise. In other words, the lawyer is ultimately responsible for the competent handling of a legal matter for a client, even when paralegals and other nonlawyers assist on that matter. First, we will discuss disciplinary actions that can be brought against attorneys for violations of the legal ethics rule on competency. Then we will consider legal claims that can be made against incompetent lawyers and paralegals.

ABA's Model Rules require that an attorney provide competent representation to a client. The Model Rules define competent representation as the exercise of legal knowledge, skill, thoroughness, and preparation that is reasonably necessary to represent the client in the matter.

This legal ethics rule on competency creates an ethical standard that attorneys must meet. Failure to meet this ethical standard regarding competency can subject an attorney to discipline in any jurisdiction where he is licensed and the breach, or failure to meet the standard, occurs. Sanctions may be imposed against an attorney for violation of the ethics rules on competency. Remember that only lawyers are directly bound by the legal ethics rules of the jurisdictions that license them, so only lawyers can be disciplined under states' legal ethics

RULE *on* POINT

Summary of ABA Model Rule on Competence

Rule 1.1 requires an attorney to provide competent representation to a client. Competent representation means an attorney must exercise the legal knowledge, skill, thoroughness, and preparation that is reasonably necessary to represent his client in the matter.

codes. Paralegals who violate legal ethics rules, however, likely face adverse employment consequences, such as termination, for their misconduct.

How does an attorney meet his ethical duty of competence? The ethical duty of competence owed by attorneys is generally held to require the following: legal knowledge, skill, thoroughness, and preparation. It can also be thought of more expansively to also require reasonable diligence and promptness, and communication with clients to keep them reasonably informed about the status of their matters. Under ABA's Model Rules, legal knowledge, skill, thoroughness, and preparation are included in the competence rule, in Rule 1.1. Diligence is covered in Rule 1.3. Communication with clients is covered in Rule 1.4. Together these rules create a broader duty of competence than the Rule 1.1 obligations alone.

To begin, what are the competence elements of legal knowledge, skill, thoroughness, and preparation? Legal knowledge is

KEY Point

Four Parts to Competence under ABA Model Rule 1.1

- legal knowledge
- skill
- thoroughness
- preparation

KEY Point

Competence, a Broader View

Attorneys' duty of competence more broadly includes:

- Legal knowledge, skill, thoroughness, and preparation;
- Reasonable diligence and promptness; and
- Communication with clients to keep them reasonably informed about the status of their matters.

knowledge of the law and legal system gained through formal education. Not only is an understanding of substantive legal principles expected but so is an understanding of court rules and procedures that apply to legal matters on which an attorney works. Being able to perform legal research necessary for client representation is also part of legal knowledge. It also includes education in general subject areas, such as in oral and written communication and in critical thinking and analysis. Remember that the knowledge required by attorneys is different and beyond the knowledge required by paralegals because only lawyers exercise independent, professional legal judgment in the performance of legal services. While a paralegal may assist in steps leading up to the decision on how to proceed in a legal matter and the steps taken after that decision is made, it is for the attorney to exercise independent, professional judgment in rendering legal opinions and giving legal advice to clients, which clients then consider in deciding their own courses of action.

With the current complexity and enormity of the entire body of U.S. law, there is a trend toward specialization in the legal profession. In other words, there is a trend away from the generalized practice of law to a more specialized practice. Today many attorneys practice in only one or a few areas of law, such as intellectual property law, immigration law, real estate transactions, personal injury litigation, environmental law, or securities law.

In terms of legal knowledge, in particular, most states require lawyers to complete minimum continuing legal and ethics education requirements each year to maintain their licenses. Other states that do not require continuing education for lawyers still encourage it, and a variety of continuing legal education programs are offered in every state—even states without mandatory continuing legal education requirements for lawyers. Courses are offered in nearly every legal specialty area and are normally taught by attorneys with expertise in that field of law. In addition, paralegals who have achieved PACE, CLA, CP, or CLAS designations must meet continuing legal and ethics education requirements to maintain their certifications. Paralegals may attend continuing education programs designed specifically for paralegals and are often invited to attend programs offered for attorneys as well.

Another aspect of competence is the possession of an appropriate level of skill. Skill is the learned capacity of a person to do something, like perform a particular legal task. Skills are gained through formal education, training, and work experience. The skills needed by lawyers differ from the skills needed by paralegals. Paralegals can possess skills in conducting legal and factual research, drafting legal correspondence and documents, conducting interviews and investigations, administration and organization, and so on. In addition to these skills, attorneys must also possess skills in advocacy and negotiation, as they are the only people authorized, by law to "practice" law. In addition, attorneys often manage and supervise nonlawyer personnel, such as paralegals, so management and supervision skills are essential as well.

Attorneys who lack the legal knowledge or skill to handle a particular type of matter have a few options. They may educate themselves in the area of law involved to gain the requisite legal knowledge. Further, they may associate themselves with another lawyer who has expertise in such matters, and both of them may work together in representing the client if the client consents. A third option is to refer the matter to a lawyer with the requisite expertise. Attorneys have a duty to refer complex, specialized cases in which they are not knowledgeable (or cannot become knowledgeable through self-education or association with another lawyer) to attorneys with the appropriate knowledge and expertise to perform that legal task. In other words, they should not accept representation in a matter where they lack the legal knowledge and skill to competently perform the legal services.

Lawyers and paralegals need to be both thorough and prepared in their work. In being thorough, they must perform their work carefully and completely. In being prepared, they must be ready to handle their clients' matters and "do their homework" before representing a client in a matter. Thoroughness and preparation include the performance of relevant factual investigation and legal research to understand and evaluate a client's claim or matter in order to successfully provide representation and to give legal advice and counsel. Legal practitioners must be careful, complete, detailed, and meticulous in their work. They must be well-prepared to handle a client's matter, such as by carefully gathering and reviewing background materials and then understanding the relevant law before negotiating or drafting a contract for a client, or by diligently preparing a case for trial.

I am always very conscientious about the work that I do. I always double-check my work. That helps me to be sure that I am not making mistakes. I advise always double-checking your work.
Julianne Ennis

I make sure that every minute spent working on tasks for a client is done to the best of my ability. I work extremely hard to keep the client's matter progressing.
Shanae Golder

The level of competence expected under the legal ethics rule addressing legal knowledge, skill, thoroughness, and preparation is that level normally possessed by attorneys in good standing working on similar legal matters. For legal ethics rules purposes, attorneys may be held to the competency standard of a general practitioner unless expertise in a specialized area of law is required for handling the legal matter, at which point they can be held to the standard of proficiency of a similar specialist practicing in that area of law.

Lawyers and paralegals must pay persistent attention to each of their pending legal matters. They must pursue legal matters for clients without unreasonable or unnecessary delay. This constitutes another element of the attorneys' broader duty of competence, the ethical requirement of diligence. **Diligence** means acting with steady and persistent effort. ABA's Model Rules require an attorney to act with reasonable diligence and promptness when representing a client in a legal matter. In doing so, attorneys must demonstrate commitment to their clients and dedication to their clients' matters. Lawyers should not procrastinate in their representation of clients, and they should not neglect their clients' matters. They should work efficiently and handle matters within a reasonable period of time—and certainly never miss a legal deadline, such as a statute of limitations, which could defeat a client's legal claim (and likely give rise to a malpractice lawsuit and a complaint to the jurisdiction's legal ethics disciplinary authority).

Another element of the attorneys' broader duty of competence is a "reasonable communication" requirement. Attorneys must engage in understandable, complete, and prompt communications with their clients. They should do this at each important stage of representation in their clients' legal matters. As indicated in ABA's Model Rules, attorneys must promptly inform clients of any decision or circumstance for which the clients' informed consent is required. They must reasonably consult with clients about how to accomplish the clients' objectives through the representation. Attorneys must keep their clients reasonably informed about the status of their matters and must comply with and respond to clients' reasonable requests for information about their matters. Also, attorneys must explain matters to clients in an understandable way so that the clients can make informed decisions regarding their matters.

Communication with clients is particularly important in civil litigation and criminal prosecutions when settlement offers or plea bargain offers are made. Attorneys should communicate all serious settlement offers or plea bargain offers made by

RULES on POINT

Summary of ABA's Model Rules on Communications

Rule 1.4 requires an attorney to:

- promptly inform the client of any decision or circumstance with respect to which the client's informed consent is required by the Model Rules;
- reasonably consult with the client about the means pursuant to which the client's objectives will be accomplished by the representation;
- keep the client reasonably informed about the status of the matter;
- promptly comply with reasonable requests for information made by the client; and
- consult with the client about any relevant limitation on the attorney's conduct when the attorney knows the client expects assistance not permitted by the Model Rules or the law.

The rule also requires a lawyer to explain a matter to a client to the extent reasonably necessary to allow the client to make informed decisions regarding the legal representation.

RULE on POINT

Summary of ABA's Model Rule on Diligence

Rule 1.3 requires an attorney to act with reasonable diligence and promptness when representing a client in a legal matter.

Diligence means acting with steady and persistent effort.

opposing counsel (in civil cases) or the prosecution (in criminal cases). It is the client's decision, for example, whether or not to accept a settlement offer in litigation—even a bad offer. It is never the attorney's decision (though he may recommend against accepting an offer he, in his exercise of independent professional judgment, considers to be unfavorable). A client cannot accept or decline an offer that has not been communicated to him. So communication from attorneys regarding important developments in the matter is critical.

As noted, paralegals may be in their offices and available more than attorneys because attorneys tend to be out of the office or unavailable a greater amount of time due to meetings, conferences, court appearances, and the like. Therefore, a good use for paralegals is to help maintain regular communications with clients to keep clients informed of the status of their matters and to answer questions or to relay questions to the attorney. In other words, paralegals make effective communication conduits and can be very useful in meeting this element of the duty of competence. Remember, however, that if an attorney delegates some of the communication tasks to a paralegal, the paralegal must never give legal advice to a client (though she may relay the lawyer's legal advice). That said, a lawyer should never delegate to a paralegal all or most of the communication with a client. That is because the client expects, and wants, to hear from the lawyer handling the matter at important stages in the representation.

> *Keep a log on a calendar to call each client once a month or once every two weeks, depending on the case. Always keep your clients updated on their cases.*
> Tatyana Bronzova

Besides state legal ethics rules, some professional paralegal associations have established ethical standards for paralegal competence that apply to their members. For example, NFPA's Model Disciplinary Rules and Ethical Considerations (in Ethical Consideration 1.1) address competence by stating that a paralegal should achieve competence through education, training, and work experience. Further, a paralegal should try to complete a minimum of 12 hours of continuing legal education every two years, including at least one hour of ethics education. Finally, a paralegal should perform all assignments in a prompt and efficient manner. NALA's Code of Ethics and Professional Responsibility (in Canon 6) also addresses paralegal competency. That canon requires a paralegal to strive to maintain a high degree of competence through education and training in professional responsibility, through local

rules and practice, and through continuing education in substantive areas of law. In addition, AAfPE (remember that AAfPE is the American Association for Paralegal Education) publishes core competencies that paralegals should possess and that paralegal education programs should develop in their students. These competencies include a common core of legal knowledge, critical thinking skills, organizational skills, general communication skills, legal research skills, legal writing skills, computer skills, interviewing and investigation skills, knowledge of professional and ethical obligations, and law office management skills.

In addition to the ethical duty of competence, there is a legal duty of competence owed by attorneys to clients as well. Tort law recognizes professional negligence claims. These claims are called malpractice claims, and they are brought in the civil law system. **Malpractice** is professional negligence. Malpractice is committed by a professional who breaches a duty of care owed to another, which breach causes the other person harm. It occurs when a professional, such as a lawyer, doctor, accountant, architect, engineer, or the like, breaches a duty of care in the performance of professional services, injuring another.

Note that professionals are not legally liable for every mistake they make that causes injury to others; the injury must

AAfPE's Paralegal Core Competencies

The American Association for Paralegal Education (AAfPE) publishes the following core competencies that paralegals should possess:

- Legal knowledge
- Critical thinking skills
- Organizational skills
- General communication skills
- Legal research skills
- Legal writing skills
- Computer skills
- Interviewing and investigation skills
- Knowledge of professional and ethical obligations
- Law office management skills

Malpractice is professional negligence; it is committed by a professional who breaches a duty of care owed to another, which breach causes the other person harm.

TABLE 7-1	Consequences for Violations of Competency Rules and Laws	
Attorney Consequences	**Paralegal Consequences**	
Malpractice lawsuits	Malpractice lawsuits	
Discipline under the jurisdiction's legal ethics rules	Adverse employment consequences, such as termination	

be caused by the professional's wrongful conduct for the tort of negligence to be committed. Also, the standard of care against which a particular professional's conduct is measured is a higher standard of care than applied to laypersons. This is because professionals possess special knowledge, skill, training, education, and expertise in their profession. Accordingly, they are held to the standard of a reasonable professional in similar circumstances. In other words, the professional must exercise the degree of skill and expertise commonly possessed by members of the profession in good standing. A breach of the duty of care by a professional, measured using a higher standard of care than that of a layperson, is malpractice where the other essential elements of the tort of negligence are met.[1]

Malpractice lawsuits brought in the legal setting (for they can be brought against other types of professionals, such as doctors and accountants) are typically brought against attorneys and the firms employing them. While they can be brought against paralegals personally, for paralegals can also breach their duty of professional care owed in the performance of paralegal services, they usually are not. This is because plaintiffs prefer to sue defendants with deeper pockets, meaning a greater ability to pay an adverse judgment. In these situations that means attorneys and the firms employing them.

Are there things that lawyers and paralegals can do to reduce the risk of malpractice claims being brought against them? Yes, there are. While malpractice claims are a cost of doing business today in any profession, there are many things lawyers and paralegals can do to reduce their risks in this area.

The Practice of Law and Malpractice Insurance

Lawyers and their law firms routinely carry malpractice and errors and omissions insurance to insure themselves against claims of professional negligence and other errors that may be committed in the performance of legal services. These insurance policies often cover the actions of subordinate employees, such as paralegals, too.

For example, attorneys should handle only those legal matters within their expertise and abilities, and refer other matters to attorneys competent to handle them. They should never promise clients a certain result in a matter, for the result is not within the attorney's control. Attorneys should charge reasonable fees, and use well-written fee agreements to specify the scope of the legal representation and the fee arrangement agreed to by the attorneys and their clients. Attorneys should select their clients carefully! Some people are simply more prone to blame others for their problems—including their attorneys. Attorneys must adequately supervise their paralegals, provide them with sufficient instructions to perform their work, and satisfactorily review their work. Attorneys must keep clients regularly informed about the status of their legal matters, and return the clients' telephone calls and other attempts to communicate with the attorney. Attorneys should listen carefully to their clients, and respect their clients' decisions. They should use great care with

KEY Point

Avoiding Malpractice Claims—Attorneys

Here are some things attorneys can do to minimize their exposure to legal malpractice claims being brought against them (or their firms) by their clients:

- Only handle legal matters in which you feel competent, and refer those you feel are beyond your expertise and abilities.
- Do not promise the client a certain result.
- Charge a reasonable fee.
- Use written, complete fee agreements to clarify the scope of the legal representation and the legal fees to be charged.
- Select your clients carefully.
- Be sure to adequately supervise your paralegals and their work, for you are responsible for both the paralegals' conduct and the paralegals' work.
- Provide adequate instructions when assigning work to paralegals and be available to answer a paralegal's questions about the work.
- Keep the client regularly informed about the status of their matter and return the client's telephone calls and other communications (such as e-mail, but be careful regarding e-mail technology and confidentiality).
- Listen carefully to the client and respect the client's decisions.
- Handle client funds appropriately and carefully.
- Know your capabilities and your limitations.
- Perform to the best of your ability.

client funds and handle them appropriately. They should know their capabilities and limitations in accepting representation and in performing legal work. For junior attorneys, they should not misrepresent their level of experience and expertise to a supervising attorney. Attorneys should always perform to the best of their ability to help minimize exposure to malpractice claims.

Paralegals, too, can minimize their malpractice exposure. Paralegals can make sure that their supervising attorneys provide adequate supervision and review of their work. In addition, they should ask their supervising attorneys questions when they do not understand a task. Paralegals can educate themselves when the situation calls for it. They should ask for assistance when they need it.

Both attorneys and paralegals should know their capabilities and their limitations. They should perform to the best of their abilities on a consistent basis and not undertake matters

KEY Point

Avoiding Malpractice Claims—Paralegals

Here are some things paralegals can do to minimize their exposure to legal malpractice claims being brought against them by their clients:

- Ensure that the supervising attorney provides adequate supervision and review of their work
- Ask your supervising attorney questions when they do not understand a task, educate themselves where appropriate, and ask for assistance when they need it
- Know their capabilities and your limitations, and do not misrepresent their level of expertise to their supervising attorney
- Perform to the best of their ability

I double- and triple-check my work and make sure the attorney does as well.
Michele Shipley

(in the case of attorneys) or assignments (in the case of junior attorneys and paralegals) for which they are unable to perform proficiently.

Additionally, both attorneys and paralegals must remember that providing legal services to clients involves customer service. The client is the lawyer's and the paralegal's customer. The client should be treated accordingly well. Every client wants personal attention and prompt, effective legal service. Consider this scenario. What if a lawyer represents a client in a litigation matter and the client loses his case? If the lawyer represented the client well, worked very hard on the case and had expertise in the subject matter, promised the client no particular outcome at the outset of the representation, kept the client informed about the matter on a regular basis, and listened to the client's perspective and respected the client's decisions (such as not to settle the matter), the client may be pleased with the lawyer's service despite the fact that they lost the case. On the other hand, if the lawyer did not return the client's phone calls, came to court less than fully prepared, and failed to explain to the client the litigation process and settlement offers, the client is much more likely to be displeased with the lawyer's service. An unhappy client is more likely a litigious one—more willing to file a malpractice lawsuit against his attorney.

Now that we have discussed the legal ethics rules on competency, we will review one final, important area of legal ethics. That area is advocacy.

ADVOCACY

Many lawyers today never go to court; they do not work in civil litigation or criminal prosecution. Rather, many lawyers practice in legal specialty areas such as corporate law, tax law, business transactions, real estate transactions, and estate planning and probate administration. On the other hand, most paralegals work in the legal specialty area of litigation. Those legal professionals who work in civil litigation or criminal prosecutions should know, and abide by, the legal ethics rules regarding advocacy. What, then, is advocacy?

Advocacy, in the legal setting, is the act of arguing on behalf of another in a legal action. A person who engages in advocacy is called an **advocate**. Attorneys who represent clients in civil litigation (advocating for plaintiffs or defendants) and in

Advocacy is the act of arguing on behalf of another in a legal action.

An **advocate** is a person who engages in advocacy.

© Chris Ryan/Alamy

requirement, which is also part of the competence duty. The Comment to Model Rule 1.3 explains this duty as follows: an attorney should pursue a client's matter despite opposition, obstruction, or personal inconvenience of the attorney, and can take whatever lawful and ethical measures that are necessary to vindicate a client. An attorney must also act with commitment and dedication to the interests of the client and with *zeal* in advocating on the client's behalf.

In representing a client zealously, however, the lawyer is restricted to engaging in conduct that is both legal and ethical. Obviously, this means a lawyer must not violate any law when diligently advocating on a client's behalf. Even where the conduct of the attorney is not defined as a violation of a civil or criminal law, an attorney should not engage in unethical conduct in advocating for a client. Ethical conduct is defined by the legal ethics codes of each state. Some legal ethics rules specifically define such unethical conduct. These rules are discussed next.

The legal ethics rules, along with statutes, case law, and court rules, prohibit attorneys from bringing unmeritorious claims and defenses. An **unmeritorious claim or defense**

criminal prosecutions (as prosecutors, advocating for the government, or as criminal defense attorneys or public defenders, advocating for criminal defendants), as advocates for their clients, must abide by the legal ethics rules on advocacy.

An important legal ethics rule regarding advocacy is found in Canon 7 of ABA's earlier Model Code of Professional Responsibility, and in the Comment to Model Rule 1.3 (the "diligence" rule) of ABA's more recent Model Rules of Professional Conduct. An attorney has the ethical duty to represent her clients zealously, within the boundaries of the law. This means that a lawyer should use her best efforts on the client's behalf when acting as an advocate. To do so, she must demonstrate commitment and dedication to her client's interests. This is part of the diligence

RULE *on* POINT

Summary of Canon 7 of ABA's Model Code of Professional Responsibility on Zealous Representation

An attorney should represent a client zealously, within the bounds of the law.

RULE *on* POINT

Summary of ABA's Model Rules of Professional Conduct on the "Zeal" Requirement

The Comment to ABA's Model Rule 1.3 requires, among other things, that an attorney act with commitment and dedication to the interests of the client and with *zeal* in advocating on the client's behalf.

An **unmeritorious claim or defense** is a legal claim or defense that is frivolous and lacks merit.

RULE on POINT

Summary of ABA's Model Rule on Meritorious Claims and Contentions

Rule 3.1 prohibits an attorney from bringing or defending a proceeding, or asserting or controverting an issue in a proceeding, unless there is a basis in law and fact for doing so that is not frivolous. Nonetheless, an attorney may assert a claim or defense that constitutes a good faith argument for an extension, modification, or reversal of existing law.

is a legal claim or defense that is frivolous and lacks merit. ABA's Model Rules prohibit an attorney from bringing or defending a proceeding, or asserting or controverting an issue in a proceeding, unless there is a basis in law and fact for doing so that is not frivolous. That said, a lawyer may assert a claim or defense that constitutes a good faith argument for an extension, modification, or reversal of existing law.

Accordingly, claims and defenses that are not warranted under existing law may not be brought by an attorney unless the attorney has a good faith argument to change the law. This exception is allowed because, where there is a good faith argument to change existing law, such a claim or defense is not frivolous.

Where the use of litigation or criminal prosecution is improper, a tort action for malicious prosecution may be asserted by the person against whom a claim or prosecution is wrongfully brought. **Malicious prosecution** is the initiation of a criminal prosecution or a civil lawsuit against another party with malice and without probable cause. A plaintiff, when her malicious prosecution lawsuit is successful, can recover a legal remedy. The typical remedy in a malicious prosecution case is damages. Further, when a person uses the legal system for an improper purpose, such as to harass or embarrass another, a tort action for abuse of process may be asserted by the person

against whom the action is brought. **Abuse of process** is the use of civil or criminal proceedings for an improper purpose or an ulterior motive. Note that the proper purpose for bringing a legal action is to pursue justice. Any other purpose is improper. The typical remedy for a successful abuse of process tort lawsuit is damages.

Besides legal ethics rules and tort actions prohibiting misuse of the legal system, Rule 11 of the Federal Rules of Civil Procedure provides for sanctions against attorneys and unrepresented parties who file unwarranted or objectionable pleadings and other papers with the court. See the following Rule on Point for an examination of Rule 11.

RULE on POINT

Rule 11 of the Federal Rules of Civil Procedure

Rule 11 of the Federal Rules of Civil Procedure requires that all papers filed with the court be signed by the attorney if a party is represented by counsel, or by the party if she is unrepresented. By presenting a paper to the court, the attorney or party certifies that, to the best of the presenter's knowledge, information, and belief, formed after a reasonable inquiry, the paper is not being presented for any improper purpose, such as to harass, cause unnecessary delay, or needlessly increase the cost of litigation; the claims, defenses, and other legal contentions are warranted by existing law or by a nonfrivolous argument for extending, modifying, or reversing existing law or for establishing new law; the factual contentions have evidentiary support; and the denials of factual contentions are warranted.

The rule provides for sanctions against both attorneys and parties for its violation. These sanctions are meant to deter, rather than punish, misconduct. Sanctions may include nonmonetary directives, an order to pay a penalty into court, and an order directing payment to the moving party of that party's attorney's fees and other expenses resulting from the violation.

KEY Point

Tort Actions Involving Unmeritorious Claims

Two tort actions are available to victims of unmeritorious claims. They are malicious prosecution and abuse of process.

Malicious prosecution is the initiation of a criminal prosecution or a civil lawsuit against another party with malice and without probable cause.

Abuse of process is the use of civil or criminal proceedings for an improper purpose or an ulterior motive.

Summary of ABA's Model Rule on Expediting Litigation

Rule 3.2 requires an attorney to make reasonable efforts to expedite litigation in a way consistent with the interests of the client.

Summary of ABA's Model Rules on Candor Toward the Tribunal

Rule 3.3(a)(1) prohibits a lawyer from making a false statement of fact or law to a tribunal, or failing to correct a false statement of material fact or law previously made to the tribunal by the lawyer.

Rule 3.3(a)(2) prohibits a lawyer from failing to disclose to the tribunal legal authority in the controlling jurisdiction known to the lawyer to be directly adverse to the client's position and that is not disclosed by opposing counsel.

Rule 3.3(a)(3) prohibits a lawyer from offering evidence the lawyer knows is false. If a lawyer discovers that she has offered material evidence that is false, she must take reasonable remedial measures, which may include disclosure of the falsity to the tribunal. A lawyer may refuse to offer evidence, other than the testimony of a criminal defendant, which the lawyer reasonably believes is false.

Another legal ethics rule regarding advocacy requires an attorney to make reasonable efforts to expedite litigation in a way consistent with the interests of the client. In other words, attorneys must not delay litigation, such as for the attorney's personal convenience, for financial gain, or to frustrate her opponents. A part of the litigation process particularly prone to abuse in this way is the discovery process. Excessive discovery or unnecessary discovery should not be conducted. Both excessive and unnecessary discovery increase the cost of litigation, cause delays, and burden the opponent.

Yet another legal ethics rule pertaining to advocacy requires attorneys to act with candor toward the tribunal. Lawyers have a duty to be honest in their representation of clients. This duty of honesty does not require attorneys to disclose everything they know. Rather, the duty requires that attorneys not make false statements of law or fact, offer false evidence, or fail to disclose adverse controlling authority when their opponents fail to do so. Under ABA's Model Rules, an attorney may not make a false statement of fact or law to a tribunal or fail to correct a false statement of material fact or law previously made to the tribunal by the attorney. An attorney may not fail to disclose to the tribunal legal authority in the controlling jurisdiction known to her to be directly adverse to the client's position and not disclosed by opposing counsel. Finally, an attorney must not offer evidence that she knows is false. If an attorney discovers that she has offered material evidence that is false, she must take reasonable remedial measures, which may include disclosure of the falsity to the tribunal. In addition, a lawyer may refuse to offer evidence, other than the testimony of a criminal defendant, which the lawyer reasonably believes is false.

The legal ethics rules on advocacy also require certain fairness to both opposing parties and their counsel. The Model Rules prohibit a lawyer from unlawfully obstructing another party's access to evidence or from unlawfully altering, destroying, or concealing a document or other material with potential evidentiary value. Further, a lawyer must not counsel or assist another person (such as her paralegal) in doing this. In addition, a lawyer must not falsify evidence, counsel or assist a witness to testify falsely, or offer an inducement to a witness that is prohibited by law (such as by paying a lay witness to testify). She also must not knowingly disobey an obligation under the rules of a tribunal except for an open refusal based on an assertion that no valid obligation exists. In addition, a lawyer must not make a frivolous discovery request or fail to make reasonably diligent effort to comply with a legally proper discovery request from the opponent. At trial, a lawyer must not allude to any matter that the lawyer does not reasonably believe is relevant or that will not be supported by admissible evidence; assert personal knowledge about facts in issue except when providing testimony as a witness; or state a personal opinion regarding the rightness of a cause, the credibility of a witness, the culpability of a party to civil litigation, or the guilt or innocence of a criminal defendant. Further, a lawyer must not request a person other than a client refrain from voluntarily giving relevant information to another party unless the person is a relative or employee or other agent of the client and the lawyer reasonably believes the person's interests will not be adversely affected by not giving the information.

Summary of ABA's Model Rules on Fairness to the Opposing Party and to Opposing Counsel

Rule 3.4(a) prohibits a lawyer from unlawfully obstructing another party's access to evidence, or from unlawfully altering, destroying, or concealing a document or other material with potential evidentiary value. Further, a lawyer must not counsel or assist another person (such as a paralegal) in doing this.

Rule 3.4(b) prohibits a lawyer from falsifying evidence, counseling or assisting a witness to testify falsely, or offering an inducement to a witness that is prohibited by law.

Rule 3.4(c) prohibits a lawyer from knowingly disobeying an obligation under the rules of a tribunal except for an open refusal based on an assertion that no valid obligation exists.

Rule 3.4(d) prohibits a lawyer from making a frivolous discovery request, or failing to make reasonably diligent effort to comply with a legally proper discovery request from the opponent.

Rule 3.4(e) prohibits a lawyer from alluding, during trial, to any matter that the lawyer does not reasonably believe is relevant or that will not be supported by admissible evidence; asserting personal knowledge about facts in issue except when providing testimony as a witness; or stating a personal opinion regarding the rightness of a cause, the credibility of a witness, the culpability of a party to civil litigation, or the guilt or innocence of a criminal defendant.

Rule 3.4(f) prohibits a lawyer from requesting a person other than a client refrain from voluntarily giving relevant information to another party unless the person is a relative or employee or other agent of the client and the lawyer reasonably believes the person's interests will not be adversely affected by not giving the information.

Other legal ethics rules on advocacy govern lawyer conduct relevant to impartiality and decorum of the tribunal. ABA's Model Rules prohibit a lawyer from seeking to influence a judge, juror, prospective juror, or other official by any means that is prohibited by law. In other words, no bribing court personnel! The Model Rules also prohibit a lawyer from communicating *ex parte* (meaning that only one party to the lawsuit is present) with a judge, juror, prospective juror, or other official during the tribunal proceedings unless the lawyer is authorized by law or court order to do so. No jury tampering! Further, a lawyer is prohibited from communicating with a juror or prospective juror after discharge of the jury (after the completion of the jury's service) if the communication is prohibited by law or court order, if the juror has made known to the lawyer her desire not to communicate, or if the communication involves misrepresentation, coercion, duress, or harassment. Finally, a lawyer is prohibited from engaging in any conduct that is intended to disrupt a tribunal. Accordingly, attorneys have a duty to conduct themselves in a dignified and courteous manner in court and should not behave in a disrespectful, rude, or otherwise inappropriate manner.

Attorney conduct with regard to trial publicity is also covered by states' legal ethics rules on advocacy. ABA's Model Rules

Summary of ABA's Model Rules on Impartiality and Decorum of the Tribunal

Rule 3.5(a) prohibits a lawyer from seeking to influence a judge, juror, prospective juror, or other official by any means that is prohibited by law.

Rule 3.5(b) prohibits a lawyer from communicating *ex parte* with a judge, juror, prospective juror, or other official during the tribunal proceedings unless the lawyer is authorized by law or court order to do so.

Rule 3.5(c) prohibits a lawyer from communicating with a juror or prospective juror after discharge of the jury if the communication is prohibited by law or court order, if the juror has made known to the lawyer a desire not to communicate, or if the communication involves misrepresentation, coercion, duress, or harassment.

Rule 3.5(d) prohibits a lawyer from engaging in any conduct that is intended to disrupt a tribunal.

prohibit a lawyer who is participating or has participated in the investigation or litigation of a matter from making any extrajudicial (outside of judicial proceedings) statement that the lawyer knows or reasonably should know will be publicly communicated and that will have a substantial likelihood of materially prejudicing an adjudicative proceeding of the matter. The rules make several exceptions, however. They permit a lawyer to state the claim, offense or defense involved, and (except when prohibited by law, such as when the person involved is a minor) the identity of the person involved; any information within the public record; that an investigation of the matter is in progress; the scheduling or result of any step in the litigation; a request for assistance in obtaining evidence and information; a warning of danger concerning the behavior of the person involved when there is reason to believe that there is a likelihood of substantial harm to a personal or public interest; and, in a criminal case, the identity, residence, occupation, and family status of the accused, if the accused has not been apprehended, as well as information to aid in his apprehension, the fact, time, and place of an arrest, the identity of investigating and arresting officers or agencies, and the length of the investigation. In addition, a lawyer is permitted to make a statement that a reasonable lawyer believes is necessary to protect a client from the substantial undue prejudicial effect of recent

publicity that was not initiated by the lawyer or the client (but this statement is limited to such information as is necessary to mitigate the recent adverse publicity).

Already discussed in Chapter 6 on conflicts of interest but also relevant to advocacy, a conflict of interest may arise when an attorney who is representing a client as an advocate at trial is also called to be a witness in that proceeding. ABA's Model Rules prohibit an attorney from acting as an advocate at a trial in which the attorney is likely to be called as a witness. The

RULE *on* POINT

Summary of ABA's Model Rule on an Attorney Called as a Witness in a Matter

Rule 3.7 prohibits an attorney from acting as an advocate at a trial in which the attorney is likely to be called as a witness unless the testimony the attorney would give relates to an uncontested issue or relates to the nature and value of legal services rendered in the case, or when disqualification of the attorney would create a substantial hardship for the client.

RULES *on* POINT

Summary of ABA's Model Rules on Trial Publicity

Rule 3.6(a) prohibits a lawyer who is participating or has participated in the investigation or litigation of a matter from making any extrajudicial statement that the lawyer knows or reasonably should know will be publicly communicated and that will have a substantial likelihood of materially prejudicing an adjudicative proceeding of the matter.

Rule 3.6(b) permits a lawyer to state:

- the claim, offense or defense involved, and (except when prohibited by law) the identity of the person involved;

- any information within the public record;

- that an investigation of the matter is in progress;

- the scheduling or result of any step in the litigation;

- a request for assistance in obtaining evidence and information;

- a warning of danger concerning the behavior of the person involved when there is reason to believe that there is a likelihood of substantial harm to a personal or public interest; and

- in a criminal case, the identity, residence, occupation and family status of the accused, if the accused has not been apprehended, information to aid in his apprehension, the fact, time and place of an arrest, the identity of investigating and arresting officers or agencies, and the length of the investigation.

Rule 3.6(c) permits a lawyer to make a statement that a reasonable lawyer believes is necessary to protect a client from the substantial undue prejudicial effect of recent publicity that was not initiated by the lawyer or the client (but this statement is limited to such information as is necessary to mitigate the recent adverse publicity).

rules make exceptions when the testimony the attorney would give relates to an uncontested issue or relates to the nature and value of legal services rendered in the case, or when disqualification of the attorney would create a substantial hardship for the client. A lawyer should withdraw from the representation as soon as she learns that she is likely to be called as a witness.

Finally, the legal ethics rules regarding advocacy restrict certain attorney communications with opponents. In representing a client, a lawyer is not permitted to communicate about the subject matter of the representation with a person the lawyer knows is represented by counsel in the matter, unless the lawyer has the consent of the other lawyer or is authorized by law or court order to do so. In other words, when the opponent in a legal matter is represented by counsel, the lawyer must communicate with the other party's counsel—not with the other party directly. Subject to the exceptions noted, lawyers are prohibited from communicating with parties who are represented by counsel.

What about people who are not represented by legal counsel? Unlike the prohibition on communications with parties who are represented by counsel, lawyers are restricted (not prohibited) in their communications with unrepresented

Special Advocacy Responsibilities for Prosecutors

States' legal ethics rules include special advocacy responsibilities that apply to prosecutors. Remember that prosecutors represent the government in bringing criminal actions against those accused of committing crimes. Because of their special role in bringing criminal prosecutions, prosecutors must abide by additional legal ethics rules. Prosecutors should not bring unsupported criminal charges or continue to pursue unsupported prosecutions. Further, they must disclose information they learn that reasonably indicates a defendant was wrongfully convicted of a charge, and try to remedy the conviction. These rules are articulated in ABA's Model Rule 3.8. That rule requires prosecutors in criminal trials, among other things:

- to refrain from prosecuting a charge that they know is not supported by probable cause;

- to make reasonable efforts to assure that the accused person has been advised of his right to counsel and has been given reasonable opportunity to obtain counsel;

- to not seek to obtain from an unrepresented accused person a waiver of important pretrial rights;

- to make timely disclosure to the defense of all evidence or information known to the prosecutor that tends to negate the guilt of the accused or mitigates the offense against him;

- to refrain from making extrajudicial comments that have a substantial likelihood of heightening public condemnation of the accused person (except for statements needed to inform the public of the nature and extent of the prosecutor's action and that serve a legitimate law enforcement purpose);

- when there is a reasonable likelihood that a convicted defendant did not commit an offense for which he was convicted, to promptly disclose the evidence to an appropriate court or authority, and if the conviction is from the prosecutor's jurisdiction, to promptly disclose the evidence to the defendant unless the court authorizes delay and to undertake further investigation to determine whether the defendant was wrongfully convicted; and

- when a prosecutor knows of clear and convincing evidence establishing that a defendant in the prosecutor's jurisdiction was convicted of an offense that the defendant did not commit, to seek to remedy the conviction.

RULES on POINT

Summary of ABA's Model Rules on Communication with Represented Persons and Dealing with Unrepresented Persons

Rule 4.2 prohibits a lawyer in representing a client from communicating about the subject matter of the representation with a person the lawyer knows is represented by counsel in the matter, unless the lawyer has the consent of the other lawyer or is authorized by law or court order to do so.

Rule 4.3 states that when representing a client and dealing with a person who is not represented by counsel, a lawyer must not state or imply that the lawyer is disinterested. When the lawyer knows or reasonably should know that the unrepresented person misunderstands the lawyer's role in the matter, the lawyer must make reasonable efforts to correct the misunderstanding. The lawyer must not give legal advice to an unrepresented person, other than the advice to obtain legal counsel, if the lawyer knows or reasonably should know that the interests of the person are or have a reasonable possibility of being in conflict with his client's interests.

persons. When representing a client and dealing with a person who is not represented by counsel (meaning the opponent in a matter did not hire a lawyer to represent him), under the legal ethics rules a lawyer must not state or imply that he is disinterested. When the lawyer knows or reasonably should know that the unrepresented person misunderstands the lawyer's role in the matter, the lawyer must make reasonable efforts to correct the misunderstanding. The lawyer must not give legal advice to an unrepresented person, other than the advice to obtain legal counsel, if the lawyer knows or reasonably should know that the interests of the person are or have a reasonable possibility of being in conflict with his client's interests.

Remember that attorneys cannot circumvent the legal ethics rules regarding advocacy by delegating unethical tasks to their paralegals. Conduct that is unethical if the attorney performs it is adopted by the attorney, as his own conduct, if he asks his paralegal to perform it instead. For example, a lawyer is restricted in his communications with unrepresented persons. A lawyer cannot circumvent this restriction by sending his paralegal to communicate with the unrepresented. Rather, the paralegal's acts are attributed to the supervising attorney. Accordingly, paralegals working in litigation and criminal prosecutions must know the legal ethics rules on advocacy and must abide by them.

CHAPTER SUMMARY

- Advertising is communication designed to persuade a person to purchase a product or service. Lawyer advertising is communication by a lawyer designed to persuade a person to engage the lawyer's services. Today, lawyers and paralegals advertise their services in many ways.

- Legal ethics rules generally prohibit lawyers from making false or misleading communications about themselves of their services. They also generally prohibit lawyers from giving anything of value to a person for recommending the lawyer's services.

- Solicitation is an attempt to gain business. Legal ethics rules generally restrict lawyers' direct solicitation of clients, in most states prohibiting them from using in-person, live telephone or real-time electronic contact to solicit professional employment for services from prospective clients when a significant motive for the lawyer's conduct is pecuniary gain.

- The most common types of legal fee arrangements are fixed fees, hourly fees, and contingency fees. Fixed fees, also called flat fees, are fees for legal services of a set amount for the performance of a routine legal service. Hourly fees are fees for legal services that are based on hourly rates and the amount of time actually spent performing the work. Hourly fees are the most common type of fee arrangement other than in plaintiff civil litigation, and hourly fee arrangements can be used to bill both attorney and paralegal time. Contingency fees, also called contingent fees, are fees for legal services that are based on a percentage of recovery in a civil case. Contingency fees are typically used by plaintiff's attorneys in civil litigation, especially personal injury cases, and are not allowed in all cases.

- Legal ethics rules generally prohibit an attorney from making an agreement for, charging, or collecting an unreasonable fee or an unreasonable amount for expenses. The ethics rules themselves set forth factors that should be considered in determining whether a fee is reasonable. Only attorneys may agree to representation of a client in a matter and set the fee to be charged for that matter.

- Legal ethics rules generally also require that the scope of the attorney's representation and the basis or rate of the legal fee and expenses to be charged to the client be communicated to the client, preferably in writing, before or within a reasonable time after agreeing to the representation.

- Advanced fees are legal fees paid at the beginning of the representation and which are usually refundable if the fees are not later earned by the attorney through the performance of legal services. Retainer fees are legal fees paid at the beginning of the representation, but which are not refundable.

- Attorneys generally may split legal fees with other lawyers if certain conditions are met, but they generally may not share legal fees with nonlawyers.

- Client trust accounts are bank accounts that are set up by lawyers to maintain funds that belong to one or more clients.

- Legal ethics rules require lawyers to hold the property of clients or third persons that is in the lawyers' possession in connection with a representation separate from the lawyers' own property. Further, the client's or third person's property must be appropriately safeguarded and certain records must be kept. Mishandling of client funds is a major cause of disciplinary actions against attorneys.

- Competence means the ability to successfully perform a task. Competent representation means the lawyer possesses the legal knowledge, skill, thoroughness, and preparation reasonably necessary for the client's representation in a legal matter.

- Attorneys' broader duty of competence includes legal knowledge, skill, thoroughness, and preparation; reasonable diligence and promptness; and communication with clients to keep them reasonably informed about the status of their matters. Diligence means acting with steady and persistent effort. Attorneys can be disciplined under the legal ethics rules for violating their ethical duty of competence.

- Besides owing an ethical duty of competence to their clients, attorneys and paralegals also owe a legal duty of competence. Failure to meet this legal duty of competence can give rise to a claim of malpractice by the client. Malpractice is professional negligence. It is a tort cause of action that can be brought when a professional, such as a lawyer or paralegal, breaches a duty of care owed to another, such as the client, which breach causes the other person (the client) damages.

- Advocacy is the act of arguing on behalf of another in a legal action. An advocate is a person who engages in advocacy. Legal ethics rules on advocacy apply to those who practice as advocates, representing clients or the government in litigation or prosecutions.

- Attorneys have an ethical duty to represent their clients zealously, within the boundaries of the law and ethics. Accordingly, an attorney should not assert an unmeritorious claim or defense, meaning a legal claim or defense that is frivolous and lacks merit, unless the attorney is making a good faith argument to extend, modify, or reverse existing law.

- The advocacy rules also require attorneys to make reasonable efforts to expedite litigation in a way consistent with the client's interests. They must also be honest and truthful to tribunals, such as courts. In addition, lawyers acting as advocates must act with fairness to the opposing party and to opposing counsel and act appropriately in court and in dealings with judges, jurors, prospective jurors, and other court officials. They are restricted in their communications to the public about their litigation or prosecution matters, in their ability to appear as witnesses in cases where they act as advocates for clients, and in their communications with opposing parties who may or may not be represented by counsel.

CONCEPT REVIEW AND REINFORCEMENT

Key Terms and Concepts

Advertising
Lawyer advertising
Solicitation
Fixed fees
Flat fees
Hourly fees
Contingency fees
Advanced fees
Retainer fees
Client trust accounts
Conversion
Competence
Competent representation
Diligence
Malpractice
Advocacy
Advocate
Unmeritorious claim or defense
Malicious prosecution
Abuse of process

Questions for Review

1. What is lawyer advertising?
2. Is lawyer advertising permitted by the legal ethics rules? If so, when?
3. What is client solicitation?
4. How is solicitation of clients restricted by the legal ethics rules?
5. What are the three most common types of legal fees?
6. What are the legal ethics rules pertaining to legal fees?
7. What are the legal ethics rules regarding protecting client funds and other property?
8. What is the duty of competence?
9. What rules of legal ethics address competency in the performance of legal services?
10. What other laws address competence in the performance of legal services?
11. What is advocacy?
12. What are the legal ethics rules pertaining to advocacy and when do they apply?

DEVELOPING YOUR PARALEGAL SKILLS

Critical Thinking Exercises

Answer the following questions using ABA's Model Rules of Professional Conduct found on the American Bar Association's website. See http://www.abanet.org/cpr/mrpc/mrpc_toc.html. In your answer, reference the specific rule you use to answer the question.

1. May a lawyer pay a referral fee to a person who recommends the lawyer's service to a client, generating new business for the lawyer?
2. May a lawyer solicit, both directly and in-person, professional employment from a person with whom the lawyer has a prior professional relationship if the purpose of the solicitation is the lawyer's pecuniary gain?
3. May a lawyer communicate the fact that she practices in a particular field of law?
4. Ruby Wednesday, Esq., a solo practitioner, practices law using the law firm name "Wednesday, Robbins & Bell, Professional Corporation." Ruby is the only person in the firm. She uses the name of a fictitious organization because she thinks that making prospective clients believe she is part of a bigger firm is good for obtaining new business. Is Ruby's use of this firm name appropriate?
5. Must the scope of legal representation and the basis for an hourly fee charged be communicated to the client in writing?
6. Must a contingent fee agreement, where permitted, be reduced to writing and signed by the client?
7. May a lawyer share a legal fee with a nonlawyer?
8. May a lawyer form a partnership with a nonlawyer if none of the activities of the partnership constitute the practice of law?
9. Where must a lawyer hold funds in his possession that belong to his clients?
10. Where should a lawyer deposit advance fees?
11. Must a lawyer comply with a client's request for information?
12. May a lawyer intentionally delay the discovery process in order to burden the opposing party?
13. A lawyer inadvertently makes a false statement to a court of law, then discovers his mistake later, while the matter is still pending. What should the lawyer do, if anything?
14. May a lawyer conceal evidence that is detrimental to his client's interests?
15. Is it permissible for a lawyer to chat with a juror while on a short afternoon break during a trial?
16. May a lawyer who is participating in a legal matter make a public warning that a person involved is dangerous?
17. When, if ever, may a lawyer communicate about a legal matter directly with a person the lawyer knows is represented by counsel in a matter in which the lawyer is representing a client?
18. May a lawyer give legal advice to a person who is not represented by counsel?

Assignments and Practical Applications

Locate your jurisdiction's legal ethics rules on advertising and solicitation. Do your state's rules differ from ABA's Model Rules? If so, how?

Research how your jurisdiction handles interest on client trust accounts. Does your state require that the interest be used to fund a social program; if so, what is that program? Does your program allow attorneys to opt-out of the program or to choose not to participate?

Research to locate your jurisdiction's legal ethics rule on competence. What does your rule require? Is your rule the same as ABA's, Model Rule, or is it different? If it is different, how does it differ?

Research to locate your jurisdiction's legal ethics rule on diligence, which relates to the competence rule. What does your rule require? Does it differ in any way from ABA's Model Rules? If so, how?

Using your state's legal ethics code, list the rules on advocacy that apply in your jurisdiction. Do your state's rules differ from ABA's Model Rules? If so, how do they differ?

Technology Resources and Internet Exercises

Florida's legal ethics rules go beyond ABA's Model Rules to expressly address Internet advertising by lawyers (typically done through the use of websites) and the unique problems presented by use of the World Wide Web. Using the Internet, locate these Florida legal ethics rules. What special disclosures do these rules require?

Using the website IOLTA.org (http://www.iolta.org/grants/item. IOLTA_History), review the IOLTA requirements for your state. Remember from the chapter that IOLTA means "Interest on Lawyers' Trust Accounts" and refers to the interest earned on certain attorney-maintained client trust accounts.

Using Internet resources, research specific actions that a legal practitioner, such as a lawyer or paralegal, can take to minimize her exposure to malpractice claims when engaged in the practice of law or in performing paralegal services. The first step is to insure against this risk, by purchasing malpractice and errors and omissions insurance. Who offers this type of insurance, and how much does it cost? What other things can a law practitioner do to minimize malpractice liability exposure? As a class, create a list of "good practices" a law practitioner can follow to minimize her malpractice exposure.

Review the paralegal core competencies recommended by the American Association for Paralegal Education (AAfPE). They can be found, online, at http://www.aafpe.org/p_about/core_comp.pdf.

Using the Cornell University Law School website for its Legal Information Institute, found at http://www.law.cornell.edu/, find your state's legal ethics code. Use it to answer the following Ethical Applications.

Ethical Applications

1. Rhonda Fuller, a paralegal with the law firm of Wright, Serio & Stringer, P.A., is asked by her supervising attorney, Charles Wilhelm, to draft an employment contract for a client. Rhonda, new to the firm but with several years' experience as a paralegal, has no idea how to draft a contract, for she worked primarily in litigation at her old firm. Not wanting to embarrass herself, Rhonda does not mention this to Charles. Instead, she drafts an employment contract that is of very poor quality and does not adequately protect the client's interests. Very busy trying a big case, Charles approves Rhonda's draft without thoroughly

reviewing it. Assuming the contract is a good one, the client and the employee execute it. Months later, a dispute arises under the contract. In reviewing the contract to determine the client's rights under it, Charles finally realizes what a poor job was done—but it is too late.

   a. Does Rhonda, a paralegal, owe the client an ethical duty of competence? Does she owe the client a legal duty of competence? What recourse does the client have against Rhonda? What recourse does the firm have against Rhonda?

   b. Does Charles, an attorney, owe the client an ethical duty of competence? Does he owe the client a legal duty of competence? Is Charles responsible for the poor quality of Rhonda's work? Is Charles responsible for his insufficient supervision of Rhonda and her work?

   c. What recourse does the client have against Charles? What recourse does the client have against the law firm? What can the lawyer and the firm do to protect themselves in this type of situation?

2. In an effort to gain new business, Murphy Lucas, Esq., advertises his services in television, radio, and billboard advertising. Murphy is an experienced and rather successful plaintiff's attorney, specializing in personal injury and medical malpractice cases. In his advertisements, Murphy markets his use of contingency fees, saying, "I charge no fee until you recover." He also says, "If you have a phone or a computer, you have a lawyer," indicating that all it takes to gain his legal representation is a telephone call or e-mail to him about the prospective client's case.

   Under the legal ethics rules discussed in the chapter (or those adopted in your state, if they differ), is Murphy's advertising permissible? Why or why not?

3. Ruth Christopher consulted with Mark Mulligan, an attorney, seeking legal representation. Ruth, a middle-aged adult, wants to sue the local school system because the school system will not permit Ruth to "redo" her four years of high school. Ruth, having money to spare, does not mind paying the attorney's $450 per hour legal fee to handle her case.

   Should Mark represent Ruth in this matter? Why or why not? Mark knows that Ruth has no valid legal claim—in fact, her request to retake high school is ridiculous. Ruth can pay the fee, though, and Mark would like additional work.

VIDEO CASE STUDIES

Video Interview of Tenae Smith

Paralegal case study videos to accompany this textbook are accessible from within both the New MyLegalStudiesLab Virtual Law Office Experience course and the Resources Website for Paralegal Studies.

ENDNOTES

[1] The essential elements of the tort of negligence are (1) duty of care, (2) breach of the duty of care, (3) causation, and (4) damages.

8 Skills for Workplace Success

Kristina Winter

Estates and Trusts Paralegal at Jensen, Hassani & Focas, P.A.

Kristina says that her role in her estates and trusts practice is to act as an assistant to the attorney and to perform a variety of tasks to carry out legal objectives. Under the supervision of an attorney, Kristina provides a wide range of legal services to clients at a less costly rate than if the attorney performed the tasks, allowing the client to save money while still receiving accurate and complete legal services.

Kristina considers the following skills to be the most important in the estates and trusts practice. She says that organizational skills are vital because it is the paralegal's job to keep track of important deadlines, to maintain files, and to work efficiently. Communication skills are important because a paralegal must effectively and clearly speak to clients, both in written correspondence and in person. Technology skills are critical because many of the tasks delegated by attorneys to paralegals today must be completed on a computer or through the Internet.

Drafting legal documents is an integral part of Kristina's estates and trusts practice. Kristina often drafts multiple legal documents in a workday, including such documents as correspondence, pleadings, wills, trusts, powers of attorney, advance health care directives, and deeds. Kristina also prepares fiduciary income tax returns. Another part of her job is to research and appropriately apply state and federal statutory law to her clients' legal situations.

Technology is integral to the estates and trusts practice. Kristina uses the computer for "everything." She uses word processing, e-mail, electronic spreadsheets, calendaring, tax, Internet research, and timekeeping programs.

How did Kristina prepare for her career as an estates and trusts paralegal? Kristina completed a degree program in paralegal studies. During her course of study, she took courses in estates and trusts, as well as tax law. Taking these courses prepared Kristina for employment with this estates and trust firm.

The chapter will answer the following questions:

- What are some of the most useful skills for successful paralegals?
- How does a paralegal demonstrate the skill of professionalism?
- How are technology skills important to paralegals?

CHAPTER **INTRODUCTION**

This chapter begins a series of four chapters on the topic of paralegal skills. While Chapters 9 through 11 discuss skills directly associated with the practice of law, such as conducting legal research, drafting legal documents, and conducting interviews, this chapter focuses on more generalized skills that contribute to paralegal success. The first part of the chapter reviews several of the most important paralegal skills that apply beyond the practice-of-law setting, such as organizational and time-management skills. Then the chapter examines in greater detail the critical skill of professionalism. The chapter concludes with a study of technology skills, which are very important to modern paralegals.

Given today's marketplace, an introduction to legal studies is not complete until students understand the practical application of the substantive and procedural laws they will study as they relate to employment. Accordingly, here and in the following three chapters, we will discuss and develop practical employment skills useful to paralegals working in the legal field.

Note that the focus of these four chapters is the skills needed to perform legal tasks. Legal tasks include tasks such as drafting legal documents, performing legal research, and answering discovery responses. Paralegals perform administrative tasks as well as legal tasks. Examples of such administrative tasks include calendaring and tracking deadlines, and organizing and maintaining client files. The smaller the law practice, the more involved a paralegal may be in performing administrative tasks. This is because smaller legal employers tend to have fewer administrative resources, including secretarial assistance, so paralegals may perform some or all of the tasks normally delegated to an administrative assistant where an administrative assistant is not available.

We begin our discussion of paralegal skills with an overall review of useful skills for paralegals. These are skills that, if possessed, contribute to paralegal success in the workplace. These skills help paralegals accomplish their varied employment tasks but are not limited in application to the legal profession.

Note Regarding Paralegal Skills and Other Coursework

Some of these paralegal skills, such as conducting legal research and drafting legal documents, are covered in depth and in a broader context in an introduction to legal studies course in legal research and writing as well as in civil litigation courses. They are included in this text to introduce these skills, allowing them to be utilized in exercises and assignments included in this text. Students should refer to texts and materials in those other courses for more detailed study of these skills.

USEFUL SKILLS FOR PARALEGALS

There are many skills useful to paralegals. The most important of these skills help paralegals perform the legal and administrative tasks required of them from employers. That said, these skills may be practiced in any business setting and are also useful in one's personal life. These important skills include analytical skills, communication skills, organizational skills, time-management skills, teamwork skills, professionalism skills, and technology skills. We will address each of these skills now.

KEY Point

Useful Skills for Paralegals

- Analytical skills
- Communication skills
- Organizational skills
- Time-management skills
- Teamwork skills
- Professionalism skills
- Technology skills

Important skills include being able to manage many tasks simultaneously, to switch from one task to the next with ease, to establish rapport with clients, to effectively prioritize, to be well-organized, to effectively manage time, to be able to take direction and constructive criticism, to communicate effectively with people, and to be cooperative.
Sherry Myers

Analytical Skills

First, successful paralegals have strong analytical skills. Analytical skills include the ability to visualize, articulate, and solve complex problems and to think critically. These skills allow a person to make sensible decisions based on available information. They allow a paralegal to make deductions using logical thinking. In the practice of law, paralegals are often called on to break down complex factual situations into their component parts and apply complicated laws to them to represent their clients' interests. Analytical skills also are critical to conducting legal research and factual investigations.

KEY Point

Analytical Skills

Analytical skills encompass the ability to visualize, articulate, and solve complex problems and to think critically.

Communication Skills

Communication skills, both oral and written, are critical to success for paralegals. These skills encompass the ability to speak appropriately and clearly, to listen and reflect, and to write effectively. Paralegals must be able to express themselves well, orally and in writing. The practice of law depends on communication, either advocating for a client in litigation or prosecution, or representing a client in a negotiated transaction. Recognizing its importance, paralegal education programs typically require one or two legal writing courses as part of their curriculum. Further, many paralegal education programs, especially ABA-approved programs, focus on the development of practical paralegal employment skills, including oral and written communication skills. These are practiced using assignments such as drafting legal documents and developing interviewing skills.

KEY Point

Communication Skills

Communication skills encompass the ability to speak appropriately and clearly, to listen and reflect, and to write effectively.

Organizational Skills

Good organizational skills are also very useful to paralegals. Organizational skills help people arrange what surrounds them, systematically creating or improving order. Tracking deadlines, maintaining files, and making and using interview checklists are examples of ways to use organizational skills in the law office. Paying attention to and managing details is important to good organization. Further, as professional support for an attorney, a paralegal is often expected not only to organize her own work, but to help keep her supervising attorney organized as well.

© Amy Dunn/Shutterstock

KEY Point

Organizational Skills

Organizational skills help people arrange what surrounds them, systematically creating or improving order.

Time-Management Skills

Successful paralegals are good time managers. Working as part of a legal services delivery team, paralegals work for multiple clients on a variety of matters at any given time. They must balance each matter so that all legal services are provided in a timely manner and all deadlines are met. Some deadlines, particularly those imposed by courts and laws such as statutes of limitations, must be met—period. Paralegals must set priorities within their assortment of matters, and start and complete matters within a reasonable time. In addition, paralegals, like lawyers, normally track and record their time, usually in six or ten minute intervals throughout every work day. If the paralegal works for a law firm, a client is billed for much of that time. Being a good time manager makes a paralegal an effective practitioner and keeps the clients' bills reasonable. It is critical to client and supervising attorney satisfaction that paralegals deliver quality work product on time.

> *Critical thinking, organization and time management . . . [are] crucial [skills] in order to work at a high level of efficiency.*
> Michele Shipley

KEY Point

Time-Management Skills

Time-management skills encompass the ability to balance assignments so that work is completed on time and performed efficiently.

Statutes of Limitations

Remember that statutes of limitations are laws enacted by legislatures that set time limits during which plaintiffs may bring certain types of actions and that begin to run when the cause of action accrues. Failure to file a lawsuit within the statute of limitations period forever bars the bringing of that claim—so the claim is lost. So statutes of limitations are inflexible deadlines that *must* be met by paralegals and attorneys in bringing actions on behalf of clients.

Time-Management Practice

Paralegal students can develop time-management skills useful for employment by treating class assignments as if they are real, on-the-job assignments from their legal employers. This way, students will develop a commitment to high-quality work that must be completed when due—without exception or excuse.

Teamwork Skills

Because paralegals work as part of a legal services delivery team, by definition working under the supervision of a lawyer, teamwork is another critical skill for paralegals. Working as a team means having the ability to compromise and to communicate tactfully. It also means a paralegal must step in and perform if another team member has "dropped the ball." Teamwork is about interpersonal relationships and the ability to interact well with others—including supervising attorneys, administrative assistants, and clients.

KEY Point

Teamwork Skills

Teamwork skills encompass the ability to work well with others.

Professionalism Skills

Paralegals must act professionally. Remember that paralegalism is a profession. To act professionally includes the ability to be responsible, reliable, ethical, and organized. Professionalism also includes the use of appropriate communication skills, such as being courteous and respectful in demeanor no matter the circumstances. Dressing in appropriate business attire and being well groomed are also part of the role of being a professional.

KEY Point

Professionalism Skills

Professionalism skills encompass the ability to act as a legal professional, in a businesslike manner, conforming to the standards of skill, competence, character, and presentation normally expected of a properly qualified and experienced person in a work environment.

In summary, to be professional is to act in a businesslike manner. Businesslike behavior means behavior that conforms to the standards of skill, competence, character, and presentation normally expected of a properly qualified and experienced person in a work environment. Professionalism, because of how critical it is to employment success, is discussed more fully in the following section of this chapter.

Technology Skills

A successful paralegal must be able to effectively use technology in her work. In fact, she may be asked to use technology not only for her own work but also for her supervising attorney. Particularly with reference to the mature generation of attorneys still practicing today, some attorneys rely on their paralegals and administrative assistants to handle law office technology for them. Paralegal use of technology in the workplace is examined in greater detail later in this chapter.

Successful paralegals possess all, or most, of the skills noted above. Skills are not traits people are born with. Rather, skills are developed, through practice and experience. As a student studying to be a paralegal, you can practice time management as well as professional dress and grooming. In your courses, you will practice oral and written communication skills, use of analytical skills, and technology use. You can practice teamwork skills when you work in groups on course assignments, and you will have the opportunity to join teams in participating in extracurricular activities—such as student government, student clubs, and mock trial competition teams. It is never too early or too late to develop your skills in these areas.

Now that we have reviewed several useful skills for paralegals, we will concentrate on one critical skill mentioned above, namely, professionalism. Professionalism is more thoroughly examined next.

KEY Point
Technology Skills
Technology skills encompass the ability to effectively use computers and other forms of technology in the workplace.

KEY Point
Skill Development
Skills are not traits people are born with. Rather, skills are developed through practice and experience.

Technology is very important in my work. We use the computer for everything. I use word processing systems, e-mail, Internet, electronic spreadsheets calendaring, and tax programs. We regularly check the Register of Wills website for updates on the forms for pleadings. We also use the tax forms on the IRS and Comptroller of Maryland websites for our preparation of estate tax returns and fiduciary tax returns.
Kristina Winter

PROFESSIONALISM

Professionalism means the ability to act like a professional. A **professional** is a person who engages in an occupation that requires advanced education, training, and/or skill. As noted earlier in this chapter, paralegalism is a profession, and paralegals are professionals.

Professionalism means the ability to act like a professional.

A **professional** is a person who engages in an occupation that requires advanced education, training, and/or skill.

Professionalism encompasses the use of appropriate communication skills, being appropriately dressed and groomed, and behaving in a businesslike manner with an appropriate display of business etiquette skills. We will discuss each of these aspects of professionalism.

Oral and Written Communication

Professionalism is demonstrated, among other ways, by skillful communication, both oral and in writing. Communication is critical to the practice of law, as discussed earlier in this chapter. Remember we said that communication skills, both oral and written, encompass the ability to speak appropriately and clearly, to listen and reflect, and to write effectively. Like attorneys, paralegals must express themselves well, whether orally or in writing.

Oral communication is regularly used by paralegals in the workplace. Paralegals must know how to converse with supervising attorneys, other co-workers, clients, and court personnel, among others. Paralegal professionals should talk to others in a dignified, courteous, and respectful manner—no matter who the others are or how the speaker feels about them. Conversation is a two-way street, where participants should both speak and listen. Paralegals must know how to speak well to a variety of people in different roles, as noted above, as well as listen effectively to what others are saying. In addition to conversation, paralegals may make presentations in the workplace. For example, a paralegal may perform training to teach new associate attorneys how to use the law office's evidence preparation software. The ability to speak before a group is another important oral communication skill for paralegals.

In oral communication, avoid the use of profanity. Use of profanity is considered vulgar and unprofessional by many. It has no place in the law office. More on this topic appears later in the chapter, on business etiquette and behavior. Similarly, paralegals should avoid using slang or other informal language. Orally express yourself in language that demonstrates you are an educated, experienced, and trained professional.

Paralegals use the telephone regularly in their practices. Over the telephone, paralegals should speak clearly and slowly and must demonstrate proper choice of words, tone, voice pitch, and rate of speech to be effective communicators. Telephone etiquette is also important. Do not multitask while on a professional telephone call—do not type on your computer keyboard, eat, read, and so on, for the person on the other end of the telephone conversation will likely know you are not focused on him. Save use of speakerphone to conference calls or otherwise have the need for using this hands-free device. Go to a private area before using speakerphone to ensure your privacy and to not distract others. Before using speakerphone, you should ask permission of the person with whom you are speaking and then introduce all parties to the conversation. Try to answer telephone calls by the second ring. Avoid answering telephone calls when others are in your presence, for doing so implies a caller is more important than the person(s) present. Instead, let the telephone call go to voice mail and check the message when you are alone. Get permission from the person to put him on hold. Also, do not leave a person on hold for more than about a minute; instead, ask the person if you can return his call so that he no longer needs to remain on hold. When a person, particularly a client, leaves you a telephone message, be sure to return the telephone call no later than the next business day—and the sooner, the better.

KEY Point

Telephone Tips

Here are some tips for telephone usage in the law office:

- Carefully choose your words, tone, voice pitch, and rate of speech.
- Speak clearly and slowly.
- Do not multitask while on a telephone call.
- Use speakerphone only when you are on a conference call or need to use this hands-free device; ask for permission from the person to whom you are speaking before putting him on speakerphone.
- Introduce all parties to a speakerphone conversation.
- Try to answer telephone calls by the second ring.
- Avoid answering telephone calls when others are in your presence and let the calls go to voice mail.
- Get permission before putting a person on hold and do not leave him on hold for more than about a minute.
- Return telephone calls no later than the next business day.

KEY Point

Profanity

Avoid the use of profanity in the law office, for it has no place in professional communications.

Voice mail is a common communication tool. Know these rules of etiquette pertaining to voice mail use. When leaving a voice mail message, make it brief and clear. No one likes to listen to voice mail messages that go on for minutes and meander to their point. In your voice message, simply state your name, the purpose of your call and your telephone number. It is good practice to repeat your name and telephone number a second time because this assists the listener in writing down the message. Regarding voice mail messages you receive, check your voice mail regularly, respond to your messages, and clear out your voice mailbox. Also, be sure your voice mail greeting is professional and businesslike, rather than personal in nature.

KEY Point

Voice Mail Tips

Here are some tips for voice mail usage in the law office:

- When leaving voice mail messages, keep your messages brief and clear.
- In messages, state your name, the purpose of your call, and your telephone number, then repeat your name and telephone number a second time.
- Check your voice mail regularly.
- Promptly respond to voice mail messages you receive.
- Clear out your voice mailbox regularly.
- Regarding your voice mailbox greeting, make it businesslike and professional, not personal, in nature.

Written communication is regularly used by paralegals in the workplace. **Legal writing** is a type of technical writing used by lawyers, judges, and legislators to communicate legal analysis and legal rights and duties. Legal writing is examined in detail in Chapter 10. In this chapter, we examine writing more generally in the business context. Here we consider office memorandums, e-mails, and other forms of business writing used by paralegal professionals.

What if in your role as a paralegal your supervisor asks you to let the professional staff know about the year's upcoming in-house seminars. To communicate this information, you prepare an office memorandum, also called an office or interoffice memo. How do you write an office memorandum? See the sample office memorandum (Figure 8-1).

An office memorandum often is written on letterhead. When letterhead is used, write "MEMORANDUM" in bold just under the letterhead (often it is centered, but some prefer it left-justified on the page). If not using letterhead, write the word

FIGURE 8-1 **Sample Office Memorandum**

MEMORANDUM

TO: Associate Attorneys

FROM: Patricia Smith, Corporate Dept. Paralegal

DATE: January 5, 2012

RE: In-House Seminars

The following seminars will be offered by the firm this year:

- February 20, Recent Developments in Bankruptcy Law
- May 15, Marketing Your Legal Services
- July 24, Advanced Estate Planning
- October 5, Electronic Discovery Techniques
- December 12, Meeting Your Clients' Legal Needs

Each seminar begins at 12:00 noon and ends at 4:30 p.m. Seminars take place in the 4th floor conference room. Lunch is provided. Please make reservations in advance for each seminar you plan to attend by calling extension 4629.

"MEMORANDUM" in bold about two or three inches from the top of the page. An office memorandum should contain the following information. First, it should contain heading information including the name(s) of the recipient(s), the name of the sender, the date, and the subject matter of the memorandum.

In a memorandum heading, the "TO" line names the recipient(s) (for there may be one or many). You must identify those who should receive the memorandum (its recipients or addressees). If there are a small number of recipients, you can name them individually. In doing so, use their names and titles (and departments if that is part of your law office's protocol). If they are part of a large group, you can just name the group using a collective title, such as "Associate Attorneys." Next you identify yourself by name and title (and department if you want) as the author of the memorandum. This information goes in the "FROM" line. Then provide the date of the memorandum in the

Legal writing is a type of technical writing used by lawyers, judges, and legislators to communicate legal analysis and legal rights and duties.

"DATE" line. Finally, identify the purpose of the memorandum, such as to announce upcoming in-house seminars, in the subject line, called the "RE" line (for "regarding").

After the heading information in a memorandum, it is common to see a line across the page, separating the heading from the body of the memorandum—its message. Your message goes in the body of the memorandum. Use bullet points if your memorandum contains checklist-type information, for checklists can be easier to read than a narrative paragraph.

Note that the heading of the memorandum is double-spaced, while the body of the memorandum is single-spaced. Use one-inch left, right, and bottom margins, 12-point font size, Times New Roman or Courier font, which is standard business writing practice. *Proofread* your memorandum thoroughly before distributing it; an error in an office memorandum looks unprofessional and reflects badly on its author. If your secretary types the memorandum for you, carefully review his draft before he finalizes, prints, and distributes it.

An important topic when discussing professionalism in written communication is electronic messaging. First, remember that office computers belong to the office, not to the users. Accordingly, office computers should be used for business purposes only. Personal use of office computers is a misuse of company resources and is unprofessional. Do not send personal messages using business e-mail accounts. It is a great idea to refrain from personal Internet use and electronic messaging using office equipment and during work hours, for doing otherwise could lead to adverse employment consequences (it is fine to catch up on personal messaging and such on a lunch break, in private, using your own equipment like a personal smart phone or iPad).

Also, when setting up an e-mail account that you will use for business purposes (even if it is a personal e-mail address that you will use to apply for paralegal employment), choose an appropriate and dignified user name. Do not use one that *should* be embarrassing. For example, using your name or parts of it, such as hmsmith@gmail.com, is far preferable to using redhotstuff@gmail.com or wholelottalovemarty@yahoo.com.[i] Choosing and using improper user names is a common mistake in professionalism made especially by young adults.

Remember that electronic messaging, whether in e-mail or texting, *is* written communication. It should be as thoughtfully and carefully drafted as an office memorandum or legal letter. When writing e-mails, include the business subject in the subject line of the e-mail so your recipient can identify it and know it is not junk mail. Do not use messaging "shorthand"

(such as "lol") in business e-mails and texts. E-mail shorthand, slang, acronyms, and codes should never be used in electronic messaging for business purposes. Instead, use proper writing style, just as you would with a written letter. Use an appropriate salutation as well, such as "Dear Mr. Brown" or "Dear Carol."

Carefully check all outgoing messages for correct grammar and spelling before sending. Electronic messaging should be proofread as carefully as any other type of written communication.

Do not send e-mail messages with oversized letters or letters that are all capitalized. Such emphasis in lettering is generally interpreted as electronic yelling, and it is discourteous. Similarly, exclamation points should not be overused in e-mail messages. Only use exclamation points if they are essential to what you are writing.

Because of the instantaneous nature of e-mail communications and texting, especially in an emotional situation, think about the message you are sending before you send it. Just because it is electronic messaging does not make it any less permanent than if the message was sent in a business letter. Further, e-mails are easily forwarded to others—many others—and you cannot control that forward distribution. So think before you "send."

KEY Point

Electronic Messaging Tips

Here are some tips for proper business use of electronic messaging:

- Do not send personal electronic messages using company resources (company equipment or company time).
- Choose appropriate and dignified user names for e-mail accounts that you will use for business or for personal accounts that you may use in searching for paralegal employment.
- Use proper writing style, not messaging "shorthand."
- Carefully check your grammar and spelling.
- Do not use "all caps" or oversized letters that could be interpreted as electronic "yelling."
- Do not overuse exclamation points.
- Think before you "send."

One final topic on communication deals with social networking websites. Many young adults (and other people, too) participate on a personal and nonprofessional basis in one or more social networking websites such as Facebook. They post all kinds of information about themselves on these sites.

Many employers and prospective employers ask employees to consent to allowing them access to review the sites of employees and prospective employees. Imagine how far denying consent will get you in a job application—not far at all. Because of how accessible the information posted is, and the extensiveness of some people's postings, a paralegal professional should think long and hard about (a) what to post before posting it and/or (b) whether to participate at all on a social networking site. Perhaps consider a business-oriented social networking site instead, such as LinkedIn, for your social networking experience.

Another important aspect of professionalism is dress and grooming. A person's appearance at work is a reflection on her and her employer. Dress and grooming are discussed next.

Dress and Grooming

Visual appearance is an important factor in making a first impression. Co-workers and clients form attitudes about a person based, in part, on her appearance. Also, a person's appearance at work reflects both her level of maturity and the importance she places on her job.

How a paralegal dresses and is groomed influences how colleagues and clients perceive her. Her physical presence impacts how others in the work environment respond to her. Further, the way a paralegal looks reflects on the law office for which she works. That is why proper dress and grooming are so important. Appropriate dress and good grooming habits are the foundation for exhibiting a professional appearance.

Because a law office is a business, a business that sells legal services, law office professionals should dress for business success. What is appropriate dress for a legal professional? Dress in such a way as to make the best impression possible both for yourself and for your employer—in other words, dress to impress.

One Paralegal's Experience

This is a true story of what happened to one recent paralegal program graduate. During a job interview for a paralegal position, the recent graduate was asked to pull up his Facebook page for the interviewer to review! The graduate did so, and—thankfully—maintained a very professional Facebook page. The graduate ultimately was hired for the paralegal position.

After the interviewer reviewed the graduate's Facebook page, the graduate asked what would have happened if he had not agreed to show it. The interviewer replied that the employer would have tried diligently to access the page so it could be reviewed as part of the decision-making process. Also, the interviewer said that if an applicant does not consent to pull up his or her Facebook page (assuming he or she has one, for not everyone does), the employer becomes suspicious of the applicant—probably taking the applicant out of consideration for the position.

It was a trend a few years ago for business attire to be worn Monday through Thursday, and then for "casual" Friday to be observed. Today, casual dress in the law office environment just has not "stuck." Most lawyers want their appearance to reflect their level of training, education, and skill—they like to "look the part" as the prominent members of the business community that they are. That means they typically wear business suits. Business suits for men and business suits for women are very different; in the many years since women entered the workforce in professional positions, their business wardrobes have evolved to become much more feminine in style—women need not dress like men to look professional. Further, business attire follows fashion trends, as does casual attire and formalwear. Just because attire is meant for the workplace does not mean it is not flattering to wear. Also, varieties of styles are available in business attire, just as in casual attire and formalwear, and a professional can pick styles that fit individual taste and body type.

If lawyers typically dress in business suits, how should paralegals dress? A good rule of thumb for presenting the best appearance at work is to dress one employment position above your current position. For a paralegal in a law office that may mean dressing similar to the supervising attorney(s) in terms of formality—so wear business suits, too. Do not underdress by wearing clothes that are too casual, for you may be perceived as being immature and/or not caring enough about your job.

A paralegal should assemble a work wardrobe consisting of clothing worn primarily to work and work-related functions. This wardrobe need not be expensive or extensive if good quality basic pieces are chosen. It is important to be conservative

KEY Point

Dressing "Rule of Thumb"

A good rule of thumb for presenting the best appearance at work is to dress one employment position above your current position. For a paralegal that means dressing similar to your supervising attorney(s) in terms of formality.

in dress, whether you are a man or a woman, in most law office settings. For example, men should wear business suits or dark slacks with a matching dress shirt, jacket, and tie. Women should wear business suits or dark skirts or pants with a matching blazer. Remember that pants for business, whether for men or women, should be dress pants and not jeans or other casual pants. Business attire may be purchased inexpensively at discount and secondhand stores, so paralegal students can start assembling their work wardrobes before they begin interviewing for internships and permanent employment. A person can buy a fine business suit at a thrift store for a price less than the cost to have the suit dry cleaned and pressed.

The clothes you wear are only part of your appearance. Grooming is as important to appearance as is attire. Here are some things a legal professional should do to demonstrate good grooming habits.

KEY Point

Work Wardrobe

A work wardrobe should consist of clothing worn primarily to work and work-related functions.

A legal professional should be clean. She should shower every day and use antiperspirant. If a scented perfume, cologne, or lotion is used, it should be used sparingly and tastefully. She should brush her teeth regularly and use mouthwash if needed to freshen her breath. Hair should be kept clean, so it should be washed regularly. It should be cut in a dignified style and cut regularly so as to not get shaggy. If hair is colored, the color should be natural in tone, so blonde or brunette rather

Hats

Hats should not be worn inside buildings unless they are worn for religious purposes.

than pink or blue, as examples. Men's faces should be clean-shaven or their facial hair neatly trimmed; nose and ear hairs should be trimmed as well. Fingernails should be kept at a reasonable length and neatly trimmed. For women, if nail polish is worn, it should be a conservative color and maintained without chips and peeling. Jewelry should complement a person's attire and not be distracting. Jewelry definitely should not be noisy. It is a good idea to keep jewelry to a "classy" minimum. Women who wear makeup should apply it for "day" wear. Save the dark eyeliner, dark eye shadow, and bright lipstick for nonwork functions. Clothing should be clean, pressed, in good shape (not worn, stained, tattered, or torn), and should not smell of perspiration, smoke, or other unpleasant odors. It should fit properly. Clothing should never fit too tight, for besides being uncomfortable to work in, too-tight clothing sends entirely the wrong message about professionalism. Wear a neutral, plain belt if your pants or skirt has belt hoops (unless you are a man with a style for suspenders). Shoes should be in good condition, cleaned, polished, and free of scuff marks. Men should wear socks that match their shoes and their pants. Women should wear shoes with heels of low to medium height (not high heels, especially if they look sexy) and in good condition. For women, sandals may not be acceptable in your law office environment. While many women today no longer

© Andrey Arkusha/Shutterstock

Dressing and Grooming "Dos"

When dressing and grooming for law office success, you should:

- dress conservatively;
- put together a work wardrobe consisting of clothing worn primarily to work and work-related functions;
- be clean;
- wear antiperspirant;
- use perfume and other scents sparingly and tastefully;
- brush your teeth and use mouthwash;
- wash your hair, cut it in an appropriate style, keep it trimmed, and use a natural color tone if you color your hair;

- be clean-shaven;
- maintain neat fingernails;
- wear minimal jewelry;
- wear "day" makeup, if makeup is worn;
- wear clean and pressed clothes that are in good shape, as well as smell and fit well;
- wear a belt (or suspenders) when needed;
- wear shoes that are in good condition and are cleaned and polished (women's heels should not be too high or sexy);
- if a man, wear socks that match your shoes and pants; and
- if wearing pantyhose, make sure they are run-free.

wear pantyhose, if pantyhose are worn they should be run-free. Women in skirts without pantyhose should have clean-shaven legs.

Hair and clothes should never be messy and unkempt. Nor should a paralegal professional, or her clothing, be dirty. Shirttails should be tucked in. Attire should be age appropriate and never sexually suggestive. Women should save "sexy" looks for nonwork functions. They should show no cleavage, no bare midriffs, and no bare thighs (keep skirts around the knee or longer) at the workplace. Underwear should be worn and should not be visible. A paralegal professional should want to be known for her work product. Do not dress or groom yourself in a way that will distract people from your work capabilities.

Body art is an issue today when it comes to young workers and professionalism. Although piercings and tattoo body art may be trendy today, body piercings and tattoos are generally not considered acceptable in the law profession (and in

many other professional occupations). It is fine to have pierced ears, and *one* earring per ear is preferable; any more than two earrings per ear appears unprofessional to many. Also, it is best not to wear nose, eye, lip, and tongue rings in a law office. Body piercing jewelry on body parts other than those mentioned should not be visible; otherwise, it sends a distracting and undignified message. Similarly, body tattoos should not be visible at work in a law office. Cover them with clothing or makeup, or have them removed. Remember that you will get farther in your career if the way you look does not distract people from your work capabilities. Further, you can use your appearance to advance your career by always looking well dressed and groomed in the law office.

Appearance

You can use your appearance to advance your career by always looking well dressed and groomed in the law office.

Dressing and Grooming "Don'ts"

In dressing and grooming for law office success, you should not:

- have messy or unkempt hair or clothes,
- be dirty or wear dirty clothes,
- wear sexy clothing or clothing that is too tight,
- show cleavage, bare midriffs, or bare thighs,
- "forget" to wear underwear,
- have visible underwear,
- be unshaven, or
- display body art in the form of body piercings or tattoos.

Body Art

Body piercings and tattoos, while growing in popularity, seriously detract from a person's professional appearance. They are generally not accepted by today's professional community.

Think long and hard about the impact of body art on your career before getting a body piercing beyond traditional ear piercing or before getting a tattoo. You could consider removing the body art by letting a piercing close or getting a tattoo removed. At the very least, do not wear body piercing jewelry (beyond one pair of earrings) to work in a law office. Also, do not go to work with a visible tattoo.

Another important aspect of professionalism is behavior in the workplace. Business etiquette and behavior are examined next.

Business Etiquette and Behavior

As with dress and grooming, the way a paralegal behaves at work is a reflection on herself and her employer. Proper business etiquette is critical in defining appropriate behavior for legal professionals, including paralegals, who work in law offices. Remember that law offices are businesses—businesses providing legal services.

Etiquette is our society's accepted standard of social behavior. When applied to the business environment, that is **business etiquette**. In other words, it is appropriate behavior, or manners, that must be utilized by business persons. To succeed in business, a person must demonstrate appropriate business etiquette. In a law office setting, paralegals are among the law practitioners who must demonstrate appropriate business etiquette. They do this by showing appropriate business behavior; in other words, act as a paralegal professional should.

How do you define the acceptable standard of conduct required of a paralegal professional? What behavior is required? It is that conduct displayed by mature, dignified, respectful adults—in other words, ladies and gentlemen. Here are some important attributes of conduct displayed by ladies and gentlemen. First, they exercise good manners. They say "please" and "thank you," for example. Also, they are courteous, polite, and pleasant. Ladies and gentlemen demonstrate civility in interactions with others. They firmly shake hands when greeting a person. They make appropriate introductions of people. They address people using appropriate titles and surnames. Ladies and gentlemen are tactful in conversation regardless of the circumstances. They are also punctual. Ladies and gentlemen show consideration for others. They let a person walk ahead, they open a door and hold it for a person, and they offer a helping hand. Ladies and gentlemen also treat others with respect, meaning they behave toward others in such a way as to show they hold the others in high regard and esteem. Paralegals, as professionals, should demonstrate the standard of conduct of ladies and gentlemen in order to exhibit professional behavior.

Professional Standard of Conduct

What is the acceptable standard of conduct required of a paralegal professional? It is that conduct displayed by mature, dignified, respectful adults—in other words, ladies and gentlemen.

Here are some other basic behavior tips for exhibiting appropriate workplace behavior. Do not dominate a conversation. To converse means to share information. Be sure to share talking and listening time. If the person with whom you are speaking is sharing very little, try asking him questions to get him more involved in the conversation rather than dominating it yourself. Do not interrupt others while conversing. Wait your turn before speaking. Interrupting another person implies that what that person is saying is not important. If you accidentally interrupt another person during conversation, immediately apologize and ask that person to continue what he was saying. As just indicated, when you make a mistake, sincerely apologize for it. Then move on. On the flip side, be careful to avoid the bad habit of continually and unnecessarily apologizing. But if you made a mistake, it shows maturity to sincerely apologize for it, especially where your mistake caused another person harm. Also, avoid the use of profane language. It is not ladylike or gentlemanly. Knock before entering another's office, and wait to be invited inside. Similarly, when entering another's office, wait to be invited to sit rather than take a seat wherever you want. Finally, put others first. Let a colleague go ahead of you in line. Open the door for your client. Let your

© NotarYES/Shutterstock

Office Gossip

Professionals prefer to avoid participating in office gossip and stick to "business."

Etiquette is our society's accepted standard of social behavior.

Business etiquette is our society's accepted standard of social behavior in the business environment.

colleague order lunch first. Showing deference to others in business situations shows good manners.

Other helpful behavior traits for paralegals include the use of direct eye contact, firm handshakes, and smiles. These traits demonstrate self-confidence. These actions are interpersonal skills that are valuable in exhibiting professionalism in the workplace.

Technology etiquette is a growing problem in professionalism. Decades ago, no one carried a cell phone, iPod, iPad, or other similar electronic device. Now almost everyone carries one or more of these devices. When to use these devices in the presence of others is an important part of business etiquette. Here is the golden rule on use of electronic devices—they should not be seen or heard in public. When in the presence of one or more people, especially in a business setting, silence or turn off, and put away, the electronic device. If you must use it, excuse yourself from the presence

of others beforehand and use the device in private. Remember that it is impolite to answer telephone calls or conduct electronic messaging in front of others; doing so sends the message that the person you are with is less important than the person on the telephone or other electronic device. During meetings, either do not take your cell phone or silence it and put it away.

Today's work environment requires paralegals to be adept in working with technology. Next we will examine how paralegals use technology in their employment, for technology use by paralegals is a critical employment skill.

TECHNOLOGY USE BY PARALEGALS

Use of technology has grown significantly in law offices as it has in other types of businesses over the last several decades. Technology use has been integrated into the court systems and courtrooms as well. While technology once played a minor role in the practice of law, now it permeates that practice. Beyond that, technology continues to be constantly changing, for it evolves as new technologies are developed. Law offices today employ technology professionals to assist legal professionals in incorporating technology use in their practices. It has become essential for modern legal professionals to be effective in using computers and computer applications.

Paralegals are expected to be proficient in their use of technology within the law office environment. Being exceptional in the use of technology can be an employment advantage for a paralegal, and provide that paralegal with additional opportunities for advancement. Incompetence in this area makes a paralegal nearly unemployable.

Every document that comes in [to the law office] is scanned into each of the client's [respective] electronic files and stored on the firm's network.
Sherry Myers

KEY **Point**

How Important Is It for Paralegals to Use Technology Effectively?
It is critical. Legal employers expect paralegals to be proficient users of technology within the law office environment. Being strong in this area is an employment advantage; being weak in this area is a significant employment disadvantage.

Computer technology and applications software are used in many ways within the law office environment. Effectively utilizing word processing software is a critical skill for paralegals, as is the ability to use e-mail technology. The ability to use the Internet and Internet search engines is a requirement of today's paralegals. The capability to prepare electronic spreadsheets is important as well. Being able to use electronic timekeeping/billing software is required in most law offices. Law office accounting systems are computerized today. Electronic calendaring systems are available and also commonly used. Law firms maintain databases, which paralegals must be able to access and search. Being able to scan documents into electronic format and to search documents electronically are other valuable technology skills for paralegals. Many law are easy to share electronically with others. Microsoft Word has a "track changes" tool that permits users to highlight changes in documents as they are made, which is very useful for those paralegals and attorneys who regularly negotiate and draft contracts. Microsoft Word is the major word processing application used by law offices today.

E-mail technology is used regularly, often constantly, by modern legal professionals. E-mail, or electronic mail, is a quick, easy way to communicate with co-workers, clients, opposing counsel, and the courts. Keep in mind, however, that e-mail technology is not necessarily secure, so confidential client information should not be sent using this method of communication unless that communication is secured, such as through password protection or encryption.

firms also maintain online forms files for documents drafted by their lawyers and paralegals. Paralegals working in litigation should be proficient in using case management software. They should also be able to use graphics presentation software for courtroom and law office uses, as well as trial presentation/evidence preparation software for the production and display of evidence in court. All paralegals should be proficient in the use of computerized legal research applications, such as Westlaw and Lexis—preferably, both.

Word processing applications permit users to electronically prepare documents, such as contracts, legal memorandums, and legal correspondence. Word processing is the most commonly used technology application in law offices today. Word processing files are easy to modify, can be spell- and grammar-checked, and

The Internet is an enormous web of computers that are linked together in such a way as to allow users to search all the connections in the Web for information. The Internet is a very useful tool for legal practitioners. As we will discuss in Chapter 11, it can be used to conduct factual investigations. It can also be used to access Westlaw and Lexis subscription databases to conduct online legal research. The Internet can be used to

[I use] Microsoft Outlook (e-mail and calendar), Internet (to access LexisNexis and other sources of law, legal information such as Maryland Judiciary Case Search and miscellaneous information such as contact information), Word (documents), Excel (spreadsheets), Quickbooks (client billing and time tracking), CaseMap (discovery management/trial prep), Adobe Acrobat, DPA (family law financial statements, child support guidelines), and the firm network (where all client file information found in paper form is stored electronically).
Sherry Myers

access court forms and records as another example. It can be used to research federal trademark and copyright registrations. As you can see, the Internet can be used in many ways by a law practitioner. To conduct research using the Internet, a researcher uses a search engine such as the popular Google, Yahoo!, or Bing. By typing in a key word or words—for example, "Westlaw" if you are trying to access the Westlaw website—search results will be displayed on your computer screen and you can choose the result that best meets your search objective. The search providers use highly sophisticated algorithms to search for relevant information, then they generate a list of research results ordered according to their relevancy based on the search term(s) used.

> ## KEY Point
>
> ### Internet Use
> Paralegals can use the Internet to perform online legal research and to conduct factual investigations, among other uses.

Electronic spreadsheet applications are also regularly used in law offices. Spreadsheets may be used to present numerical, especially financial, information and perform calculations. They may also be used to track deadlines, such as trademark registration renewal dates. Microsoft Excel is a very popular electronic spreadsheet program.

Electronic timekeeping and billing systems are frequently used in law offices today. Because most paralegals and attorney record their time in six or ten minute increments daily, their time records must be kept. While these records used to be maintained on paper, today most legal practitioners input their time electronically into an electronic timekeeping system such as Timeslips or Abacuslaw. These programs can sort the timekeeping data that is input, apply billing rates for attorneys and paralegals, and electronically generate bills for clients. (These bills should be reviewed for reasonableness and accuracy by the supervising attorney before they are sent to clients, per the legal ethics rules.) Similarly, accounting systems have become computerized so that accounting records can be kept and

I use Microsoft Excel heavily, Outlook for e-mail, Internet for land record research, and computerized timekeeping.
Michael Weiland

reports generated electronically. With computerized accounting systems, accountants enter financial data into the system. Then the system, using mathematical algorithms, computes the information necessary to generate accounting ledgers (records) and financial statements, as well as create reports and analyses.

> ## KEY Point
>
> ### Electronic Timekeeping
> Most attorneys and paralegals record their time in six or ten minute intervals every workday. Electronic timekeeping applications streamline this process.

Some legal professionals use electronic calendars. These calendars can be used to track appointments and generate appointment reminders. They can be set up to be accessed and maintained by the legal professional's administrative assistant. Microsoft's Outlook e-mail application contains a popular electronic calendaring function.

Law offices also use database programs to deposit and store electronic information. For example, detailed information about clients and matters can be stored, searched, sorted, and retrieved using a database program. Microsoft Access is an example of a popular database program.

Most law offices convert hard copies of legal documents and records to electronic format by scanning the documents and records onto the computer. This is easily done by using an office printer that also acts as a scanner. Once converted to electronic format, these documents and records can be searched electronically. This is electronic document searching, and it is quick and easy to perform.

Most law offices maintain online forms files. In these files attorneys and paralegals can keep legal documents, such as contracts they draft, as well as research results in the form of case briefs and legal memorandums. Online forms files are typically maintained on document management systems.

In litigation practice, case management software is widely used. Case management software, also called litigation management/support software, is used to electronically track and manage the handling of cases through electronic document management. In a case management system, case files are maintained electronically and can include such documentation as records of interviews of clients and witnesses, expert witness reports, factual investigation reports, pleadings, legal research results, and trial preparation materials. Summation, Concordance, and CaseMap are examples of popular case management and litigation support programs.

Graphics presentation programs, such as the popular Microsoft PowerPoint, are used by law offices to prepare presentations. Presentations may be used in training employees, in seminars offered to clients, and in court, for example. For modern paralegals and attorneys who practice litigation, trial presentation/evidence preparation software is widely used as well. This type of software helps legal professionals prepare charts, tables, video clips, and the like, as well as present evidence, such as blow-ups of documents or diagrams of intersections, to fact-finders (often juries) in court. As a further example, such software programs can generate simulations of accidents in personal injury cases or display relevant portions of larger documents.

To be discussed in Chapter 9, it is critical for paralegals and attorneys to know how to conduct online legal research. Two popular and reliable fee-based subscription databases used by legal professionals for conducting online legal research are West-law and Lexis. Free online databases that are also reliable but not nearly as comprehensive as Westlaw and Lexis are FindLaw and the Legal Information Institute at Cornell University Law School. Government websites are also reliable sources of online statutory materials for their jurisdictions.

Other ways that technology is being used in the legal profession today include electronic filing of legal documents with the courts; use of videoconferencing technology to allow for conferencing/meetings in multiple, different geographic locations; and remote access to law office servers to allow long-distance retrieval of documents and records. As technology that aids in the practice of law is developed, it becomes incorporated into law offices where attorneys and paralegals can take advantage of it.

Note that employers often do not expect prospective employees to be knowledgeable in using specific brands of technology software. It is usually enough that the prospective employee knows how to use that *type* of software. For example, an employer may have a Lexis subscription for performing

> *[I used the] Concordance database for document organization and review. During production of documents, I reviewed the client's documents for relevance and privilege to determine what documents must be produced (an attorney reviewed my selections for accuracy). Also, after the opposing party produced its documents, I used Concordance to review those documents to see if they were helpful.*
> **Anatoly Smolkin**

online legal research. A paralegal job applicant many be experienced in using Westlaw to perform online legal research but be inexperienced with Lexis. This should not hurt the applicant's chances, however, because the employer really is interested in an employee being able to conduct online legal research. Having experience with one of the major database providers is likely just fine, for that employee can easily be trained on using the Lexis brand database if she already knows how to conduct online legal research using Westlaw. The key is that the applicant already knows how to conduct online legal research. So keep in mind that employers are more interested in a prospective employee's ability to effectively use technology adopted by the firm in the relevant practice area for that paralegal. So long as the prospective employee has experience in types of technology used by the firm, such as word processing, e-mail, electronic spreadsheet, and timekeeping applications, using any particular brand of application (such as Lexis) can be taught fairly easily. That said, because of the widespread use of Microsoft software products, especially for word processing and electronic spreadsheet generation, any paralegal without experience in these popular Microsoft products should learn how to use them to be most "employable."

Many paralegal education programs today incorporate technology skill development into their curriculums. ABA-approved programs are required to incorporate the use of law office technology into their curriculums. Many paralegal education programs now offer courses in this area, including courses such as law office technology and electronic discovery.

For paralegals who entered the profession before the use of technology became commonplace or who are less proficient than they want or need to be, training programs are available from many sources. A person can take one or more courses, as a non-degree-seeking student, at an institution offering the relevant technology curriculum. Many law firms conduct their own training, specific to the hardware and the software programs they use. Law firms also are willing to invest in their paralegals by supporting their attendance at outside-sponsored technology

I keep my e-mails marked as 'unread' until I am ready to address them thoroughly so that nothing slips through the cracks.
Susan Campbell

training programs to increase their employees' proficiency and effectiveness. Continuing legal education providers often offer courses in the area of technology and the law as well. Training is readily available to paralegals who seek it.

Not only do law offices use technology today, but so do court systems and courtrooms, as discussed previously. Therefore, to practice litigation today, it is important to know how to utilize the technology for each court in which a person is practicing. Interestingly, attorneys often rely on their paralegals to understand this technology usage and to be responsible for it. Because of the paralegal's role in supporting the attorney, the paralegal should know the relevant court technology, not only for herself, but for her supervising attorney. Being proficient in the use of technology is a great employment advantage for today's modern paralegal.

CHAPTER SUMMARY

- Useful skills for paralegals include analytical skills, communication skills, organizational skills, time-management skills, teamwork skills, professionalism skills, and technology skills. These skills can be developed through practice and experience.

- Professionalism means the ability to act like a professional person. A professional person is a person who engages in an occupation that requires advanced education, training, and/or skill.

- A paralegal is a professional, and professionalism is an important employment skill for paralegals. It encompasses effective oral and written communication, appropriate dress and grooming, and proper business etiquette and behavior.

- Effective use of technology is critical for modern paralegals. Technology skills can be learned through paralegal education programs, workplace training, outside-sponsored training, and continuing legal education.

- Types of technology that paralegals are expected to use in their employment include word processing, e-mail, the Internet and Internet search engines, electronic spreadsheets, electronic timekeeping and billing, computerized accounting systems, electronic calendaring, databases, document scanning, electronic document searching, online forms files, graphics presentation software, trial presentation and evidence preparation software, and computerized legal research.

CONCEPT REVIEW AND REINFORCEMENT

Key Terms and Concepts

Professionalism
Professional
Legal writing
Etiquette
Business etiquette

Questions for Review

1. What are some of the most useful skills for paralegals to possess?
2. What are analytical skills?
3. What are communication skills?
4. What are organizational skills?
5. What are time-management skills?
6. What are teamwork skills?
7. What are professionalism skills?
8. What are technology skills?
9. What is professionalism?
10. What is a professional?
11. Explain the key aspects of professionalism discussed in the chapter.
12. What kinds of technology do paralegals use in their employment?

DEVELOPING YOUR PARALEGAL SKILLS

Critical Thinking Exercises

Review the useful skills for paralegals examined in the first part of this chapter. Remember that skills are developed through practice and experience. For each skill discussed in the chapter (analytical, communication, organization, time management, teamwork, professionalism, and technology), perform a self-evaluation to assess your level of development in each skill area. Write a list of several examples of your use of each skill. Consider ways you can improve your performance in each skill area. Then draft a skill development plan by identifying three specific things you can do to improve your performance in each skill area.

Assignments and Practical Applications

Practice oral communication skills through this "presentation" exercise. Prepare a short (three to five minute) speech on why you want to be a paralegal (or lawyer, as the case may be). Present your speech to the class. Make sure you wear professional attire and are appropriately groomed for this classroom presentation using the guidelines discussed in this chapter.

Write an office memorandum to your classmates explaining to them how to dress like a paralegal professional. Turn your memorandum in for grading.

Practice time management through this timekeeping exercise. For the equivalent of one paralegal work week (assume 8:00 a.m. to 5:00 p.m., Monday through Friday), keep a record of everything you do during the day, in 10-minute increments. Remember that in law practice, most paralegals (and attorneys) keep timekeeping records of their workdays, recording time based on either six or ten minute increments. Make sure that every time entry you make sufficiently details not only your time spent but also the matter on which you spent it—similar to the way a paralegal records time spent, client names, matters, and task descriptions on paralegal timekeeping records. Turn in your "timesheets" for grading.

Evaluate your work wardrobe based on the material presented in this chapter. If you think you may need some good quality basic pieces but do not want to invest a lot of money in them, shop a discount store or a thrift store to acquire them (clean and press pieces, as necessary, if bought secondhand).

Evaluate your technology skills. Make a list of types of software applications that you have used before and are familiar with. Using the information provided in the chapter, make another list of the technology applications commonly used by legal practitioners today that you are not familiar with. Research your school's course catalog to see what course offerings are available to teach you technology applications that would make you more marketable to legal employers. Consider enrolling in one or more of these courses.

Technology Resources and Internet Exercises

Take the results of the self-evaluation from the Critical Thinking Exercise, on page 90, and prepare an electronic spreadsheet. You might want to list each skill down a left-hand column, the noted instances of use of that skill in a middle column, and ways to improve that skill in a right-hand column. Remember to label each column. Turn your spreadsheet in for grading.

Review how to write an office memorandum using the following website: http://www.ehow.com/how_4810398_write-office-memo.html.

Practice using professionalism in electronic messaging. Whenever you use e-mail or text messaging, write your messages as if they are workplace messages, written by you, a paralegal professional.

Practice using Internet search engines to locate the website for Westlaw, a leading online legal research subscription database.

Using the Cornell University Law School website for its Legal Information Institute, found at http://www.law.cornell.edu/, find your state's legal ethics code. Use it to answer the following Ethical Applications.

Ethical Applications

At the law firm of Sweeney & Barry, LLC, the civil litigation specialist, Brian Ludwig, is busy preparing for a hearing he will be attending later in the day. A prospective client comes to the office, wishing to discuss a legal issue involving tort law and wanting to know if Brian will represent him and handle the matter. Although Brian appreciates the opportunity for new business, he is just too busy to meet with the prospective client at this time. Not wanting to lose the new business, he sends his very capable paralegal, Brenda Todd, to meet with the visitor and gather information about the legal issue.

Is it okay for Brenda to meet with the prospective client to gather information about the matter?

What if, in addition to gathering information about the matter, Brenda, under Brian's direction and with his authority, agrees that Brian and the firm will represent the client in that matter, and also sets the fee arrangement pursuant to which the client will pay the standard hourly fees charged by both her and Brian for work on the case.

Is it okay for Brenda's interview with the prospective client to cover these issues (accepting the representation and setting the fees)? Why or why not?

ENDNOTES

[1] One reviewer of this text reported having had a student who listed on her résumé the e-mail address of dabitchuluvtohate@yahoo.com. Having such an e-mail address cannot have been helpful to the student in finding paralegal employment.

9

Conducting
Legal Research
and Briefing Cases

Michael Weiland

Corporate Paralegal at Lockheed Martin

Michael is an in-house, corporate paralegal for a wholly owned subsidiary of Lockheed Martin, one of the world's largest defense contractors. Michael obtained this in-house position through networking.

At Lockheed Martin, Michael works as a records management coordinator. He reviews and manages property contracts and related records. He also reviews property sale and lease agreements, as well as deeds. In his practice, Michael uses mainly federal and state statutory laws in the areas of contracts, property, zoning, and environmental law. Technology use is also a part of Michael's practice. He regularly uses the Internet, as well as spreadsheet, e-mail, timekeeping, and document scanning technology.

Working in-house for a large defense contractor, confidentiality is highly critical to Michael and his practice, where he routinely handles highly sensitive information. Michael describes the duty of confidentiality as "the ability to keep your mouth shut." To meet his duty of confidentiality, Michael is careful to discuss work only with co-workers and only in the office.

Prior to working for Lockheed Martin, Michael performed an internship with a medical malpractice firm. He gained interviewing experience in that position, where he interviewed prospective clients. In conducting those interviews, Michael found that the best way to begin an interview was to ask as few questions as was necessary and let the client say what he wanted to say. Then, after the client had freely expressed what he wanted, Michael would ask not only more detailed questions about the case, but also questions about clients to make the client feel more comfortable. Michael found the practice of making client feels comfortable made it easier work cooperatively and productively with them in the future.

Today, Michael works part-time in his paralegal position at Lockheed Martin while pursuing his law degree.

The full video interview is accessible from within both the New MyLegalStudiesLab Virtual Law Office Experience course and the Resources Website for Paralegal Studies.

The chapter will answer the following questions:

- What does "conducting legal research" mean?
- What preliminary steps precede the conduct of legal research?
- How is common law researched?
- How is statutory law researched?
- How is administrative law researched?
- How is constitutional law researched?
- What is the difference between researching using print materials and researching using online resources?
- How do you read, analyze, and brief court cases?

CHAPTER **INTRODUCTION**

This chapter examines two important practical employment skills for paralegals: conducting legal research and briefing cases. The chapter begins with an introduction to the skill of conducting legal research. Preliminary matters in conducting legal research, namely defining the legal issue(s) and identifying the source of law to be researched, are discussed. How to research common law is examined. Then how to research statutory law is studied. Researching administrative law is reviewed. How to research constitutional law is discussed. We conclude our review of conducting legal research by comparing the two methods of conducting legal research, using print materials and online resources. The chapter ends with a discussion of how to read, analyze, and brief court cases. Our discussion begins with an introduction to conducting legal research. What is legal research and why is it important?

AN INTRODUCTION TO CONDUCTING LEGAL RESEARCH

Legal research is the process of locating an answer to a legal question. Legal research is a critical part of the job, both for attorneys and for paralegals. It is important to know how to research the law to (1) know what it is and (2) determine how it affects your client. Most law and paralegal students take one to two courses devoted specifically to the conduct of legal research and writing.

Legal research may be conducted manually, using print materials (law books) or using technology, specifically, computerized legal research (using proprietary software or the Internet). Because the most reliable and widely used computerized legal research database services, available through Westlaw and Lexis, are very expensive, not all employers use them or allow

© Sean Nel/Shutterstock

unrestricted use of them by their employees. Therefore, all lawyers and paralegals need to know how to conduct both manual and computerized legal research, though computerized legal research is conducted frequently and increasingly today. Whether legal research is conducted using print materials or online technology, the goal is to find relevant, useful, and current law on a legal issue.

> *Legal research can seem like a daunting task. It is best to ask the attorney's advice on where to begin researching. Also, check in with the [supervising attorney] periodically to make sure that you are on the right track.* **Anatoly Smolkin**

Legal research is the process of locating an answer to a legal question.

PRELIMINARY MATTERS IN CONDUCTING LEGAL RESEARCH

Defining the Legal Issue(s) to be Researched

To conduct legal research, the researcher must first define the legal issue or issues to be researched. In other words, the researcher must preplan what she is looking for in conducting the research—what question(s) she seeks to answer by performing this legal research. Brainstorming words that describe the issue is a typical first step in defining the issue(s). The researcher may define one issue, or multiple issues, that need to be researched for a client matter. Knowing the goal, the researcher may begin searching for law on point, meaning dealing with the legal issue being researched and involving similar facts.

For example, if the client was injured in a car accident caused by a "texting" driver, what impact does the client's failure to wear a seatbelt while driving have, if any, on her recovery? This fact pattern raises the legal issue of whether the plaintiff's own negligence impacts her recovery from the defendant.

Identifying the Source of Law to Be Researched

After defining the legal issue(s) involved, the researcher must know where to look to find the answer(s). In researching law, a researcher must know the different sources of law that are her options. Remember from Chapter 3 the four main sources of law: (1) common law, (2) statutory law, (3) administrative law, and (4) constitutional law.

Common law is law established by judges in the courts. More specifically, it is made by appellate court judges in published appellate court opinions. It is also called **case law**. **Statutory law** is law enacted by legislatures at the state or federal level of government. At the local level of government, statutory law still exists, but those laws are typically called **ordinances** rather than statutes. **Administrative law** is law made by administrative agencies of the government at the federal, state, and local levels, such as the following two federal administrative agencies: the Environmental Protection Agency or the Securities and Exchange Commission. **Constitutional law** is law found in the federal and state constitutions.

If the researcher is not sure what source of law applies, she may begin her research using a secondary source of law, such as a legal encyclopedia, to learn what source of law applies. Secondary sources of law are discussed further in the following section. For example, what if a legal researcher needs to know whether her jurisdiction recognizes contributory negligence as a defense to a negligence claim? If she does not know what "type" of law contributory negligence is, such as whether it is common law or statutory law, the researcher could review the topic in a

Common law is law established by judges in the courts; it is also called **case law**.

Statutory law is law enacted by legislatures.

Ordinances are statutory laws enacted by local governments.

Administrative law is law made by administrative agencies of the government.

Constitutional law is law found in the federal and state constitutions.

Where to Look for Different Sources of Law

A researcher must determine what source(s) of law she will use–whether common law, statutory law, administrative law, or constitutional law—to find the answer to her legal research question. Different sources of law are found in different places. Common law of precedential value is reported in case reporters. Statutory law is found in codes. Administrative law is found in administrative rules and regulations. Constitutional law is found in the federal and state constitutions. A researcher must know where to look to find the answer to her research question based on the issue she has defined.

legal encyclopedia to learn that contributory negligence is a *common law* defense to the tort of negligence. Now the researcher has identified the relevant source of law for her research—common law. How does a person research common law? That question is answered next.

> *You can never learn enough or get too much experience [when it comes to performing legal research].*
> Michael Weiland

RESEARCHING COMMON LAW

In researching common law a researcher ultimately is searching for reported court cases that are on point, meaning dealing with the legal issue being researched and involving similar facts. A **case on point** is a previous court case involving similar facts and legal issues to those being researched. The researcher is especially looking for binding authority. **Binding authority**, also called **mandatory authority**, is legal authority that a court must follow in deciding the issue, such as a prior case that is precedent in the jurisdiction. Note that for a case to be binding authority on an issue, it must be both on point and from a higher court within the jurisdiction. When researching case law, the best binding case law authority is a decision made by the highest court in the jurisdiction or by the U.S. Supreme Court, as those cases have greatest precedential value. How, then, does a researcher find these cases?

A researcher often begins her research for cases by searching secondary sources of law. **Secondary sources of law** are resources that summarize or interpret the law; they are not law themselves. They are research tools, sometimes called "finding tools," used to get the researcher headed in the right direction in finding the relevant law. Many contain indexes or tables of contents to help a researcher locate relevant material. Secondary sources of law that a researcher might use in researching cases include case digests, legal encyclopedias, treatises, *Restatements of Law*, *American Law Reports*, and law reviews. By reviewing secondary sources of law, the researcher can gain an understanding of the issue and its context, as well as obtain citations to primary sources of law.

Binding Authority

Remember from Chapter 4 that the court systems are "tiered" systems, with a trial court typically on the lowest level and one or two levels of appellate courts above. A lower court (such as a trial court that is below one or more levels of appellate courts, or an intermediate level of appeals court that is below the state's supreme court) is bound to follow the decisions of any higher courts within that jurisdiction. However, a higher court is not bound to follow the decisions of lower courts within the jurisdiction, though it can look to them for guidance. Nor is a court bound to follow the decisions of courts in other jurisdictions, though those decisions, too, may be used as guidance. Nor are courts of equal authority (such as U.S. circuit courts, as an example) bound to follow each other's decisions, though they may look to them for guidance.

Accordingly, decisions of the highest court in the jurisdiction carry the greatest weight. In conducting case law research, look for these cases first because they are the most persuasive.

A **case on point** is a previous court case involving similar facts and legal issues to those being researched.

Binding authority is legal authority that a court must follow in deciding an issue; it is also called **mandatory authority**.

Secondary sources of law are resources that summarize or interpret the law and can be used to locate primary sources of law; they are not law themselves.

TABLE
9-1   **Examples of Secondary Sources of Law**

Case digests	Series of books that summarize specific points of law that have been discussed in cases and that are alphabetized, by topic
Legal encyclopedias	Such as *American Jurisprudence*, Second Edition (Am. Jur. 2d) and *Corpus Juris Secundum* (CJS), alphabetically cover a broad range of legal topics, including cross-references to other primary and secondary sources of law
Treatises	Scholarly publications containing all the law relating to a particular area, such as torts or contracts
Restatements of Law	Detailed explanations on a variety of subjects of U.S. common law, such as contracts and torts, written by legal scholars and published by the American Law Institute
American Law Reports (ALR)	Multivolume sets of selected court cases and related annotations that collect, organize, and evaluate specific points of case law
Law Reviews	Scholarly journals that focus on legal issues and are usually published by law schools using editors who are top law students—for example, the *North Carolina Law Review*, which is the law journal published by the University of North Carolina School of Law

Primary sources of law establish the law on an issue and include such sources of law as court decisions, statutes, administrative regulations, and constitutions. Ultimately, it is the primary sources of law the researcher is searching for in conducting legal research. The relevant primary source of law when researching common law is court cases. Case law can be either federal or state, depending on which court system heard the case. The two court systems, federal and state, were examined fully in Chapter 4.

State court decisions are found separately from federal court decisions. Regarding state court decisions, most state *trial* court decisions are not published but are merely filed in the clerk of court's office, where they are available for public inspection. Today, however, with the advent of computerized databases, more and more unpublished opinions can be found

Using Primary versus Secondary Sources of Law

Primary sources of law do not always contain indexes or tables of contents. So using secondary sources of law may be necessary to lead a researcher to the appropriate primary source of law.

in these databases—such as Westlaw and Lexis—using electronic resources. *Appellate* cases are routinely published in state reporters. **Reporters** are books of reported cases published in numbered, multivolume sets arranged chronologically by date of decision. Most states have their own official reporters (sometimes more than one), as designated by the state's legislature, and/or unofficial reporters, which are often published by West's National Reporter System. In addition, state court opinions are also published in seven regional reporters, published by West's National Reporter System. These regional reporters group states by geographic region in publishing regional court decisions, which can be useful for researchers who need to know case law in their own and in neighboring states. For example, the *Atlantic Reporter* contains published opinions of appellate courts from Connecticut, Delaware, the District of Columbia, Maine, Maryland, New Hampshire, New Jersey, Pennsylvania, Rhode Island, and Vermont.

KEY Point

Reporters

Court decisions, where published, are found in various reporters, including state, regional, and federal reporters. Reporters are books of reported cases published in numbered, multivolume sets arranged chronologically by date of decision.

Published vs. Unpublished Opinions

Remember from Chapter 3 that some court decisions are published and others are not. Not all opinions are approved for publication. For example, if an opinion is merely repetitive of opinions already published, if an opinion has obvious mistakes that would be reversed on appeal, or if an opinion is poorly written, it normally is not approved for publication. Accordingly, it is not published in a reporter. Opinions that are published have precedential value. Unpublished opinions generally do not have precedential value.

Primary sources of law establish the law on an issue and include such sources of law as court decisions, statutes, administrative regulations, and constitutions.

Reporters are books of reported cases published in numbered, multivolume sets arranged chronologically by date of decision.

Federal court decisions are also published, including some trial court (district court) opinions. U.S. district court cases are published in West's *Federal Supplement*, an unofficial reporter. U.S. courts of appeals decisions are published in West's *Federal Reporter*, another unofficial reporter. U.S. Supreme Court decisions are published in several different reporters, including the *United States Reports*, the official reporter, and West's *Supreme Court Reporter* and West's *Lawyers' Edition of the Supreme Court Reports*, two unofficial reporters.

Once identified, a case can be located using the case's name and citation. A **case name** identifies the parties to the action. A **case citation** is its locator reference and typically includes the following information: the volume number of the reporter in which the case is published, the name of the reporter, the page number on which the case begins in that volume of that reporter, identification of the court rendering the decision, and the year of the decision. Note that sometimes the term "case citation" is used to reference both the case name and its locator reference. Case citations provide information about how to find cases in the state or federal reporter systems. When an opinion is published in more than one reporter (such as is published in the state reporter and again in the relevant regional reporter), parallel citations are used. A **parallel citation** is a second (or even third) citation for a case when the case is published in more than one reporter. Note that when citing a case published in two or more reporters using parallel citations, the official reporter's citation is listed first.

It may be that the researcher cannot find binding authority on an issue in the relevant jurisdiction. In that case, the researcher may turn to sources of persuasive authority to gain insight in answering the legal question. **Persuasive authority** is legal authority that is not binding on a court but may be used as guidance by a court in making its decision. Examples of persuasive authority in case law research include previous court opinions from other jurisdictions or from lower courts in the jurisdiction, legal encyclopedias, or law reviews and similar scholarly legal periodicals.

When using a case, it is important to check to make sure the case is still good law and has not been reversed or modified by an appellate court. A prudent attorney or paralegal always checks to make sure a case he wishes to cite is still good law by performing a search of its subsequent history, meaning what happened to it in later court proceedings, such as appeals, if any occurred. Citation services, such as Shepard's Citations and KeyCite, are useful print and computerized means for verifying that a case is still good law. Online citators are more up-to-date than printed ones, and many attorneys and paralegals find technology particularly useful when it comes to checking citations, including case citations.

Case Names and Citations

Case citations follow case names and include the reporter volume number, reporter name, page number on which the case begins, identification of the court rendering the decision, and the year of the decision. For example, "*Palsgraf v. Long Island R.R. Co.*, 162 N.E. 99 (N.Y. 1928)" is the case name and citation for the famous *Palsgraf* negligence case. Sometimes the term "case citation" is used to reference both the case name and its locator reference.

Form of Citation: How to Cite Cases and Other Legal Authority

The Bluebook: A Uniform System of Citation

The Bluebook (as it is called) is widely regarded as the authority for proper legal citation form, including case citation. It is accurately marketed as the leading legal citation guide used in the United States, and it is widely used by lawyers, judges, legal scholars, law students, and other legal professionals such as paralegals. *The Bluebook* is published by the Harvard Law Review Association. It is typically a required text in law schools and paralegal education programs.

ALWD Citation Manual: A Professional System of Citation is another legal citation guide, compiled by the Association of Legal Writing Directors, as an alternative professional system of citation for legal materials. It has been adopted by some law schools, paralegal programs, law reviews, moot-court competitions, and courts.

Some states use their own legal style manuals providing proper form of citation. For example, California uses the California Style Manual, which was adopted by the California Supreme Court as the state's official guide for formatting citations.

Case names identify the parties to legal actions.

Case citations are the locator references that provide information about how to find cases in the state or federal reporter systems.

A **parallel citation** is a second (or even third) citation for a case when the case is published in more than one reporter.

Persuasive authority is legal authority that is not binding on a court but may be used as guidance by a court in making its decision.

Understand all of the legal resources available to you and what each of them will do for you. Also, don't forget to use the annotations and comments because they often have cites to other sources that may be very helpful. [When conducting online research,] try using a variety of search terms and be ready to either narrow or broaden your search terms depending on the result of each search you perform.
Sherry Myers

Another source of law regularly researched by attorneys and paralegals is statutory law. Next we will review the process for researching statutory law.

RESEARCHING STATUTORY LAW

Statutory law is law enacted by legislatures like the U.S. Congress and state legislatures as discussed above. Remember that statutes enacted by local governments, as opposed to the federal or state governments, are referred to as ordinances. Ordinances fall within the body of statutory law.

To locate statutory law, a researcher must begin by finding where the statute has been published. First we will review some of these publications for federal statutes, then for state statutes.

The official version of federal statutes is published in the *United States Code*. This publication organizes statutes into 50 different titles based on their subject matter. These topical titles are further subdivided into chapters or sections, and then subchapters. Unofficial versions of the federal code can be found in the *United States Code Annotated* and the *United States Code Service*.

Each state has its own code containing its statutes. State codes may be called codes or they may be called something else—such as general statutes, compilations, consolidations, or revisions. Parts of a statute are called **statutory provisions**.

Annotated Statutes

Annotated statutes are unofficial versions of both federal and state codes. They provide useful information about court cases that have interpreted the statutes in comments following the statutory provisions, called annotations. Because of these comments on how courts have interpreted the meaning, constitutionality, and limitations on enforceability of statutory provisions, annotated statutes are valuable legal research tools.

The Process of Enacting Statutes

At both the federal and state levels of government the process of enacting statutes is similar. First, a bill is introduced to the legislature for consideration and debated. The bill, once tweaked and revised, is voted on by the legislature. If the bill is passed, it is sent to the executive officer (the U.S. President for federal legislation and the state's governor for state legislation) to be signed into law—or vetoed. Once the legislation is signed by the relevant executive officer of the government, it is published and becomes statutory law.

Statutory provisions are parts of a statute.

Statutes are amended, even repealed, from time to time by the legislatures that enacted them. Codes are updated via the publisher's issuance of supplemental pocket parts (which slip into a "pocket" in the back of a volume of the code) or by loose-leaf services. That is how published codes are kept current.

When researching statutory law, a researcher should begin by examining the code's index. Looking through the index, the researcher should be able to find reference to the relevant statutory provisions. Using these references, the researcher can locate the statutory provisions themselves, by citation. An example of a statutory citation is Neb. Rev. Stat. § 28-304 (2011). This citation references Nebraska's second degree murder statute, discussed in the criminal law section in Chapter 13. Through this citation, a researcher learns that this statutory provision is found in Chapter 28, Article 3 of Nebraska's Revised Statutes.

As with briefing a case, as discussed later in the chapter, the process of researching statutory law involves locating the relevant statute or statutory provision, then reading and analyzing it. Statutes often contain definitions relating to terms contained in them. Drafters of legislation seem to love run-on sentences, which is clear to the legal researcher who reads statutes. Therefore, in analyzing statutes, it is important to break down long sentences, many with numerous conjunctions (like "and" and "or") and subparts. Researchers may find it useful to diagram the statute's sections and subsections and their relationship(s) to analyze and understand the meaning of complex provisions.

Remember that one function of the courts is to interpret statutes. To further help analyze and understand statutory provisions, **statutory rules of construction** exist. These are rules that courts follow in interpreting statutory provisions. These rules control the judicial (court) interpretation of statutes and include rules like the following: specific provisions are given greater weight than general provisions, more recent provisions are given greater weight than older provisions, and singular nouns include their plurals. Another statutory interpretation tool is the plain meaning rule. This rule of construction states that statutes should be interpreted using the ordinary meaning of the language of the statute unless the statute explicitly defines certain terms differently. In other words, if the meaning of a statute is clear on its face, then the court should interpret that statute according to its plain meaning. Legislative intent, meaning the purpose and intent of the legislature in writing the statute, is often considered by a court in interpreting a statute that is not clear on its face—as many are not. Legislative intent

behind a statute can be found in legislative committee reports, transcripts from legislative hearings regarding the drafting of the statute, and the wording of the statute as published in session law form, such as in the *United States Statutes at Large* for federal statutes. Finally, to understand the meaning of a statute, previous judicial interpretations of that statute in case law can help decipher its meaning, for courts are the ultimate interpreters of the meaning of the language set forth in statutes.

To summarize, once a researcher finds the relevant statute by finding the proper code and identifying the applicable statutory provision using the code's index, she must then read (often reread) and analyze the statute to understand how it applies to her situation. As noted above, statutes are not necessarily easy to read. Breaking statutory provisions down into their

Publication of a Federal Statute

The first official publication of a federal statute is called a slip law. Each slip law has a public law number, called a P.L. number, assigned to it.

Federal statutes passed during a legislative session are batched and compiled in session laws, published in the *United States Statutes at Large*.

Codes are compilations of the final publication of statutes. Statutes within the codes are arranged by topic. While codes are the "final" publication of statutes, statutes can be amended and repealed over time. Therefore, codes are updated regularly, using pocket part supplements or loose-leaf services.

Relationship between Statutory Law and Common Law

Some statutes replace the common law. For example, commercial codes based on the Uniform Commercial Code (UCC) replace the common law of contracts for certain aspects of sales of goods transactions. Some statutes supplement the common law. For example, a state statute may make employment discrimination based on sexual orientation illegal.

Statutory rules of construction are rules that courts follow in interpreting statutory provisions.

component parts and reviewing them in relation to other related provisions may be helpful in understanding the meaning of a particular statute. It is important for a researcher, to carefully and methodically read a statute to understand and apply it.

Administrative law is another main source of law. Researchers often research administrative law, though probably not as often as they research common law and statutory law. How to research administrative law is examined next.

RESEARCHING ADMINISTRATIVE LAW

Administrative law is law made by administrative agencies of the government. It largely consists of regulations issued by federal and state administrative agencies, and is another primary source of law because regulations, rules, orders, and decisions of administrative agencies are legally binding.

Federal administrative agency regulations are published in the *Code of Federal Regulations* (C.F.R.). The C.F.R. is organized by topic. It uses the same titles as the *United States Code*, with each title further divided into chapters, subchapters, parts, and sections. However, while both the *Code of Federal Regulations* and the *United States Code* use the same total number of titles (50 of them), the subject matter covered in similarly numbered titles is not necessarily the same in both.

States have codes of regulations as well. For example, Maryland has the Code of Maryland Regulations, or COMAR. As they do when conducting statutory research, researchers of administrative laws should use indexes associated with these codes of regulations to find relevant administrative laws.

Next we will review the last of the four primary sources of law, constitutional law, and discuss where it is found and how it is researched.

RESEARCHING CONSTITUTIONAL LAW

Constitutional law is law found in the federal constitution and the constitutions of each of the 50 states. Constitutions are amended from time to time, and these amendments are part of the constitutions and constitutional law. Each constitution sets forth the powers, responsibilities, and limitations of the various branches of that jurisdiction's government.

The U.S. Constitution is easy to find, both online and in print sources, including textbooks. Annotated versions of the U.S. Constitution and each of the state constitutions can be found through the Library of Congress. In addition, the *United States Code Annotated,* as well as the *United States Code Service,* publishes the U.S. Constitution and its amendments. Because courts interpret constitutional provisions, these publications also contain useful citations to cases interpreting specific constitutional provisions. State constitutions typically are reprinted in publications of state statutes as well.

Many courts help to interpret constitutional provisions, but a major function of the U.S. Supreme

© Exactostock/SuperStock

Local Government "Constitutions"

Local governments have "constitutions" called charters, such as city or county charters. These charters set forth the local governments' organization and powers.

Court is to interpret the U.S. Constitution. So common law is a source of law that helps to interpret the body of constitutional law.

Now that we have studied how a person researches each of the four main areas of law, we will consider the option of conducting legal research either in print or online. There are advantages and disadvantages to both methods of conducting legal research, as we will discuss.

RESEARCH USING PRINT MATERIALS AND ONLINE

As mentioned earlier, legal researchers have the choice of using print materials found in a law library or computerized services to perform their research. Which legal research method is better? Both methods have advantages and disadvantages. For reasons we will note, attorneys and paralegals should be skilled in conducting legal research using both methods.

Obviously, when conducting legal research using print materials, the researcher must visit a law library where the necessary resources can be found. Larger law firms typically have their own law libraries containing most print materials their lawyers and paralegals need to use in conducting legal research for client matters. Many lawyers and paralegals today use computers to perform legal research, rendering a trip to the law library unnecessary. Another advantage to conducting computerized research is that online materials, including sources of case law, are updated more frequently and more quickly, making online research results more timely and up-to-date. A major disadvantage of the use of computerized legal resource technology, whether through a proprietary software license or online via the Internet, is its cost. The cost of subscriptions to the two main legal research service databases, Westlaw and Lexis, are notable. As a result, not all employers subscribe to these services or allow unrestricted use of these services by their employees. Accordingly, all legal researchers must know how to research using both computer technology and print materials.

Note that many primary sources of law can be found online, including state and federal statutes, administrative regulations, and court opinions. Secondary sources, such as legal encyclopedias, are less readily available online. Accordingly, print materials may be the only source of certain secondary sources of law.

Although most computer users are accustomed to performing Google searches and finding what they need online, legal research using Westlaw or Lexis requires something more than a generalized search using a search engine of that type. The reason is that, in searching for law, particularly primary sources of law, it is imperative that the computerized database used contain *reliable and accurate* information. For example, a court case available online should be the verbatim case published in print form or released to the clerk of court for public filing. The researcher should trust the reliability of the data on the site before using primary sources of law from it. That is why Westlaw and Lexis are the main sites used by legal professionals to perform computerized legal research. Westlaw and Lexis are well-established and well-known providers of computerized legal research services, with by far the most accurate and comprehensive databases available. Subscribers to Westlaw and Lexis, who as noted pay a substantial fee for use of the services, have online access to extensive collections of legal and business databases maintained by the sites, through which legal researchers can access specific documents, such as cases, and check citations.

Most law firms and legal departments are moving away from print materials because of the cost and it is quite time-consuming to update them. It is more convenient to research electronically if you become proficient at it, especially when time is of the essence and a trip to the law library is not convenient.
Lois Shaw

Computer-Assisted Legal Research

Computer-assisted legal research (CALR) means use of technology by attorneys, paralegals, and judges to perform legal research through the Internet or other research software. The two largest CALR services today are Westlaw and Lexis.

Some reliable and accurate legal information is accessible, free of charge, over the Internet. Government sites are often reliable sources for obtaining statutory materials from their jurisdictions. Also, two free Internet sites providing reliable and accurate general legal resources are FindLaw and the Legal Information Institute at Cornell University Law School.

Caveat: Consider the Source

When performing computerized legal research, know that the site you are using contains reliable and accurate information before you use primary sources of law from it.

Performing legal research, using print materials or online services, is a critical skill for legal professionals. Looking back at researching case law in particular—for case law probably is the most researched source of law—once an attorney or paralegal finds a case she needs through legal research, she must read and analyze the case in order to understand the law for which it stands. The next section discusses how to read, analyze, and brief cases.

HOW TO READ, ANALYZE, AND BRIEF COURT CASES

Both paralegals and attorneys must understand how to read, analyze, and understand court cases. A court case, or **case**, is a written judgment of a court. This process is called briefing a case, or **case briefing**. To brief a case is, in essence, to read, analyze, and summarize it. The resulting document is called a **case brief**.

What Is a Court Case?

As just noted, a case is a written judgment of a court. Case law is comprised of the body of reported cases. Court cases vary in size and complexity, from one or two pages to hundreds of pages of complicated facts, complex legal rulings, and supporting reasoning. As with any form of writing, some court cases are written more clearly than others. Some cases discuss more complicated subject matter than others. Accordingly, some cases are easier to read and understand than others. To understand any case you read, however, it is likely you will have to re-read at least portions of it, perhaps several times, to understand fully the court's ruling and its reasoning. No matter the complexity of the case or how well or poorly it is written, understanding the components of a case will help the reader understand the case itself. Here are the usual components of a case.

First, a case has a title indicating the names of the parties to the litigation, separated by a "*v.*" which means "versus." Normally, the plaintiff's name appears first, followed by the defendant's

name. On appeal, however, the order may change. For instance, when the defendant is the appellant, the appellate court may list the appellant's name first. The facts of the case will clarify who the parties are if the order of the appearance of their names in the title leaves this unclear.

KEY Point

Components of a Case

- Case title, case citation, and docket number
- Date decided (and perhaps the date of appellate arguments)
- Syllabus and headnotes (sometimes)
- Names of counsel representing the parties, and the judges or justices writing the opinion
- Opinion (or body) of the case
- Conclusion
- Concurring and/or dissenting opinions (if present)

A **case** is a written judgment of a court.

Case briefing is the process of reading, analyzing, and summarizing a court case.

A **case brief** is the written summary of a court case.

© Alina Solovyova-Vincent/Alina555

(and headnotes, if there are any). The name of the judge or justice authoring the opinion, or a notation that the decision was authored *per curium,* meaning by the entire court, immediately precedes the opinion.

Although the term "opinion" is commonly used to refer to an entire court decision, the precise meaning of the term is more restricted. In fact, an **opinion** is the formal—usually lengthy—analysis, decision, and reasoning of the court in ruling on a case. The opinion normally includes a statement of the facts of the case, a summary of the legal issues raised, the remedies sought by the parties, errors of law (if any) in the lower court if the case is on appeal, and application of the law to the facts of the case. Courts normally cite other laws, such as statutes, administrative regulations, or case precedents, or relate public or social policies or other nonlaw considerations in support of their rulings in their reasoning. An appellate opinion is called a **unanimous opinion** when all the judges agree to it, or a **majority opinion** when more than half of the judges agree to it.

The opinion of the court is normally followed by the court's conclusion. The court's conclusion states the decision the court reached in the case on each of the legal issues presented. If the decision of the court was set forth earlier, in the opinion itself, then it is normally reiterated, clearly and concisely, in the court's conclusion. If the case is an appellate one, the conclusion also states whether the lower court's decision is being affirmed (upheld), reversed (overturned), or remanded (returned to the trial court) for further proceedings. Whether the case is affirmed, reversed, or remanded is called the **disposition of the case**, referencing how the case was "disposed of" by the reviewing court.

When an appellate judge agrees with the court's decision, but for different reasons, or disagrees with the court's decision

A case citation is found near the case title, usually just above or below it. The case citation indicates the volume number, reporter, and beginning page number where the case is reported, identification of the court rendering the decision, and the date of the decision. It sometimes includes the date of the oral arguments when the case is an appellate one. In addition, a docket number assigned by the clerk of court follows the case title. Although the docket number is not part of the official case citation, it is a useful tool in researching the case for previous or subsequent cases and/or related legal briefs.

A case syllabus typically follows the docket number. The case syllabus is normally a paragraph containing a condensed statement of the facts of the case, the issues facing the court, and the court's ruling. For official reporters the courts may prepare the syllabi, but for unofficial reporters they are usually prepared by the reporter's publisher. Keep in mind that when briefing a case, the court's opinion itself reflects the law, not the publisher's summary of what it thinks the opinion is saying, found either in syllabi or in headnotes, discussed next.

Unofficial reporters, which are very widely used because they are very helpful to researchers, often contain headnotes. Headnotes are paragraph breakdowns of the case in summary form. Like syllabi from unofficial reporters, headnotes are written by publishers, not the courts, and they are not part of the court's opinion. Thus they are not the law set forth in the case, no matter how well the publisher summarizes the law in them. Nonetheless, headnotes are useful tools for legal researchers, helping them to locate and understand cases.

The names of counsel representing the parties, if the parties are represented by counsel, normally appear after the syllabi

---

An **opinion** is the formal analysis, decision, and reasoning of the court in ruling on a case.

A **unanimous opinion** is an opinion in which all the judges agree to it.

A **majority opinion** is an opinion in which more than half of the judges agree to it.

Disposition of the case means whether the appellate court affirmed, reversed, or remanded the case.

altogether, that judge (or judges) may write a **concurring opinion** (in which she agrees with the decision but for different reasons) or a **dissenting opinion** (in which she disagrees with the ruling of the court). Concurring and dissenting opinions, where they exist, follow the majority opinion of the court.

In reading a case, only certain statements within it are legally binding. The legally binding principle(s) established by the case are called the court's holding(s). Other statements made by the court that do not directly address the specific facts and issues of the case, but are the judge's "editorializing" about the case or that merely explain or provide additional information and are not essential to the case, are called *dicta*. **Dicta**, the nonlaw statements made by judges in their opinions, have no precedential value and are not binding in later court decisions. Only the court's holding is considered precedent in subsequent cases, and a case reader must be able to distinguish between the court's holding and *dicta*.

Dicta

Dicta, plural for *dictum*, comes from the Latin phrase *obiter dictum*, meaning "a remark by the way."

A **concurring opinion** is an opinion in which a judge (or judges) agrees with the court's decision but for different reasons.

A **dissenting opinion** is an opinion in which a judge (or judges) disagrees with the ruling of the court.

Dicta are the nonlaw statements made by judges in their opinions.

FIGURE 9-1   **Sample Court Case**

[Reporter citation]
457 F. Supp. 2d 590, 34 Media L. Rep. 2574

[Court hearing the case]
United States District Court,
D. Maryland.

[Case title – names the parties to the case, docket number, and date of decision]
Tonya BARNHART
v.
Paisano Publications, Llc.
Civil No. JFM-06-318.
Oct. 17, 2006.

[Case syllabus – a brief summary of the case, prepared by the courts for official reporters and by the publishers for unofficial reporters; *this summary was prepared by the text author as an example*]
Plaintiff brought suit against defendant publisher for the tort of invasion of privacy. Defendant publisher moved for summary judgment.

The District Court held that plaintiff's conduct in baring her chest at a public event could not reasonably constitute a private act, the photograph taken at the event did not constitute false light, and publication of plaintiff's photograph did not constitute appropriation of plaintiff's likeness.

Defendant's motion for summary judgment was granted and judgment entered against plaintiff.

[Headnotes – paragraph summaries regarding points of law of the case, prepared by the publisher; *using on-line legal research technology (such as Westlaw or Lexis) or a law library containing the F. Supp. Reporter, locate and review the numerous headnotes prepared by the publisher, West, for this case*]

[Counsel for the parties]
David Ellin, Melissa A. Proctor, Law Office of David Ellin PC, Baltimore, MD, for Tonya Barnhart.
Michael D. Sullivan, Thomas Curley, Levine Sullivan and Koch LLP, Washington, DC, for Paisano Publications, LLC.

(continued)

MEMORANDUM

[Judge authoring the opinion]
MOTZ, District Judge.

[Opinion of the court]
This action arises from the publication of a photograph of the Plaintiff, Tonya Barnhart, in the March 2005 issue of *Easyriders*, a magazine published by Defendant Paisano Publications. Ms. Barnhart appears partially nude in the photograph. As a result of its publication, she asserts several claims for invasion of privacy against the Defendant. Paisano Publications has filed a motion for summary judgment. For the following reasons, the motion will be granted.

I.

The undisputed facts are as follows. Tonya Barnhart is a 29 year-old woman employed as a retail clerk; she is not a celebrity, and she has never been paid to perform or to make any other public appearance. On August 28, 2004, Ms. Barnhart attended the Toop's Troops Second Annual Pig Roast.FN1 The Pig Roast was a fund-raising event attended by motorcycle enthusiasts, and included music, food, games, and vendors selling motorcycling paraphernalia. At least 200 people were present. The party was "bring your own" alcohol, and continued all day and into the early hours of the next morning. At some point during the day women began removing their shirts in return for being given beads. Ms. Barnhart, swept up by the Mardi Gras type atmosphere, was hoisted onto the shoulders of two men and voluntarily lifted up her shirt. At that moment, Bill Cromwell, a photographer who often submitted his pictures to *Easyriders* magazine for publication, snapped a photograph of Ms. Barnhart in her exposed state. He later submitted that picture to *Easyriders*, and it was published in the magazine's March 2005 edition.

FN1. *The record is unclear as to whether the name of the organization is "Toop's Troops" or "Tube's Troops." "Toop's Troops" is the name used in the Declaration of a member of the organization. (Dec. of Ralph Stambaugh 1).*

II.
A.

Motions for summary judgment should be granted when the record establishes that there is no genuine issue of material fact, and the moving party is entitled to judgment as a matter of law. Fed.R.Civ.P. 56(c); Celotex Corp. v. Catrett, 477 U.S. 317, 322, 106 S.Ct. 2548, 91 L.Ed.2d 265, (1986). The substantive law of the cause of action determines which facts are material. Anderson v. Liberty Lobby, Inc., 477 U.S. 242, 248, 106 S.Ct. 2505, 91 L.Ed.2d 202 (1986). The existence of other factual disputes between the litigants does not defeat an otherwise proper motion for summary judgment if none of the material facts are in dispute. Id. A dispute about a material fact is genuine and summary judgment is inappropriate if the evidence is such that a reasonable jury could return a verdict for the nonmoving party. Id. at 248, 106 S.Ct. 2505. In analyzing whether a genuine issue of material fact exists, the evidence and reasonable inferences from that evidence must be viewed in the light most favorable to the nonmoving party. Id. at 255, 106 S.Ct. 2505.

B.

This is a diversity action, and Maryland's choice of law provisions apply. "In tort actions, Maryland applies the doctrine of lex loci delicti, which provides that *593 the substantive law of the state where the wrong occurs governs." Rockstroh v. A.H. Robins Co., 602 F.Supp. 1259, 1262 (D.Md.1985). In this case, the event at which plaintiff was photographed was held in Maryland, and plaintiff and defendant both assume that Maryland law applies. The fact that *Easyriders* magazine is distributed nationally does not provide a basis for overturning this assumption, and I will apply Maryland law.

The Restatement of Torts defines four different types of the tort of invasion of privacy: (1) unreasonable intrusion upon the seclusion of another, (2) unreasonable publicity given to another's private life, (3) publicity that unreasonably places another in a false light before the public, and (4) appropriation of another's name or likeness. Under Maryland law a plaintiff may assert a claim for any of these types of invasion of privacy, see Lawrence v. A.S. Abell Co., 299 Md. 697, 475 A.2d 448, 450-51 (2001), and Maryland cases look to the definitions and comments contained in the Restatement in applying invasion of privacy law. See Hollander v. Lubow, 277 Md. 47, 351 A.2d 421, 424-26 (1976); see also Bagwell v. Peninsula Regional Medical Center, 106 Md.App. 470, 665 A.2d 297, 318-19 (1995).

III.

An intrusion upon seclusion claim requires that the matter into which there was an intrusion is entitled to be private and is kept private by the plaintiff. Hollander, 351 A.2d at 424 (citing W. Prosser, The Law of Torts, 808 (4th ed.1971)); Restatement Second of Torts § 652B (1977). Likewise, an unreasonable publicity claim requires that the matter that is publicized is private in nature. In that regard the Maryland Court of Appeals has ruled that "anything visible in a public place can be recorded and given circulation by means of a photograph, to the same extent as by a written description, since this amounts to nothing more than giving publicity to what is already public and what anyone would be free to see." Hollander at 426 (quoting W. Prosser, The Law of Torts, 810 (4th ed.1971)). The court went on to say that "facts disclosed to the public must be private facts, and not public ones. Certainly no one can complain when publicity is given to information about him which he himself leaves open to the public eye." Id. at 427 (quoting Prosser, Privacy, 48 Cal. L.Rev. 383 (1960)).

Here, plaintiff's lifting up of her shirt cannot reasonably be said to have constituted a private act. She exposed herself at an outdoor fund-raising event open to any member of the public who purchased a ticket. According to plaintiff's own estimate, about 200 people were present at the event. Although she alleges that at the moment she removed her shirt she was in the company of only about 10 people, all of whom she knew and trusted, the fact remains that she exposed herself in a public place where anyone could have seen her.

Furman v. Sheppard, 130 Md.App. 67, 744 A.2d 583 (2000), is very much on point. There, the defendant had trespassed onto the property of a private club and filmed plaintiffs on their yacht without their consent. The court held that plaintiff's intrusion claim had been properly dismissed because they were seen participating in activities that could have been observed by nontrespassing members of the public as well. Id. at 587. Likewise, in Solomon v. National Enquirer, 1996 WL 635384 (D.Md.1996), the court held that a photograph taken of a woman as she stood inside her house by the window could not give rise to an invasion of privacy because any passerby on the street could have viewed her through the window. Furman *594 and Solomon both mandate the entry of summary judgment for defendant on plaintiff's seclusion and unreasonable publicity claims.FN2

FN2. Plaintiff relies heavily upon Capdeboscq v. Francis, 2004 WL 463316, 2004 U.S. Dist. LEXIS 3790 (E.D.La.2004), in which the court denied a motion for summary judgment filed by defendants where plaintiffs had been photographed lifting their tee shirts and exposing their breasts. Capdeboscq, of course, was decided under Louisiana, not Maryland law. Moreover, in denying defendants' motion, the court noted that plaintiffs alleged that they had been photographed only after having been asked to do so several times and after being told that they would not appear on any "Girls Gone Wild" video. In fact, their photographs ultimately appeared on the cover of a video/dvd entitled "Girls Gone Wild Doggie Style." Even under those circumstances, the court found that it was "a close call" as to whether defendants' summary judgment motion should be denied.

IV.

To establish a successful claim for false light invasion of privacy, a plaintiff must prove (1) that the defendant gave "publicity to a matter concerning another that places the other before the public in a false light," (2) that "the false light in which the other person was placed would be highly offensive to a reasonable person," and (3) that "the actor had knowledge of or acted in reckless disregard as to the falsity of the publicized matter and the false light in which the other would be placed." Bagwell v. Peninsula Regional Medical Center, 106 Md.App. 470, 513-14, 665 A.2d 297 (Md.App.1995). A defendant is entitled to judgment as a matter of law if the facts disseminated regarding the plaintiff are true. Id.

(continued)

In Furman v. Sheppard, supra, the Maryland Court of Special Appeals found that because the videotape there at issue recorded the plaintiff's activities accurately, it was not actionable under a false light theory. 130 Md.App. 67, 744 A.2d 583, 587-88 (2000). Similarly, in AIDS Counseling and Testing Centers v. Group W Television, 903 F.2d 1000 (4th Cir.1990), the Fourth Circuit held that summary judgment had properly been entered for defendant on a false light claim because any inaccuracies in a television station's reporting were minor and did not cause the story to produce a different effect on the audience than would have been produced had the truth been reported. Id. at 1004.

Here, however, plaintiff's claim is not that the published photograph somehow distorts her true appearance, but that the photograph's publication gives the impression that she is the type of person who consents to having a topless photograph of herself published in *Easyriders* magazine. There does not appear to be a Maryland case directly on point, in which plaintiffs claimed not that the information contained in the picture or article itself was false, but that the publication gave the false impression that the plaintiff consented to the dissemination of the information. Cases in other jurisdictions, however, have addressed the issue.

Braun v. Flynt, 726 F.2d 245, 247 (5th Cir.1984), involved an accurate picture of the plaintiff published in a hard core men's magazine called *Chic*. The picture depicted the plaintiff performing her routine as an entertainer at an amusement park, in which a pig dove into a pool and swam to the plaintiff, who was waiting with a bottle of milk for him. The picture was accompanied by a caption written in a tongue in cheek manner.FN3 The court upheld the *595 jury's finding of liability, finding the fact that the plaintiff's picture had been placed without her consent in a "magazine devoted exclusively to sexual exploitation and disparagement of women" was sufficient for the jury to find that she had been placed in a false light. Id. at 255.

FN3. The caption read: "SWINE DIVE-A pig that swims? Why not? This plucky porker performs every day at Aquarena Springs Amusement Park in bustling San Marcos, Texas. Aquarena staff members say the pig was incredibly easy to train. They told him to learn quick, or grow up to be a juicy ham sandwich." Id. at 248 n. 2.

The same result was reached in Douglass v. Hustler Magazine, 769 F.2d 1128 (7th Cir.1985). There, Robyn Douglass, a model and actress, consented to being portrayed in the nude in *Playboy* magazine. Id. at 1131. Her picture, however, was published in *Hustler* magazine instead. Id. The court delineated the differences between *Hustler* and *Playboy* as shown by the record and found that the evidence was such that a reasonable jury could find that it was degrading for a woman to be portrayed as the type of person who would consent to be published in *Hustler* even if she had consented to be published in *Playboy*. Id. at 1137. In addition, the court found that the accompanying text in *Hustler* could have been understood to insinuate that Ms. Douglass was a lesbian, which she is not. Id. at 1135. Thus, although the court reversed a jury verdict in plaintiff's favor on other grounds, it concluded that plaintiff had a viable false light claim.

In Braun and Douglass the plaintiffs presented voluminous evidence demonstrating in detail the degrading and lewd content of *Chic* and *Hustler*. Plaintiff has presented no such evidence here. Unquestionably, the record discloses that a few of the pictures in *Easyriders* are a bit racy, including bikini-clad women and two women (one of whom is plaintiff) lifting up their shirts. However, the only direct evidence concerning the nature of *Easyriders* is contained in the deposition of Kimberly James Peterson, the editor of the "In The Wind" section of the magazine in which plaintiff's picture was published. According to Peterson, the purpose of that portion of the magazine is to illustrate the "exhilaration" of the motorcycling lifestyle. (Dep. of Kimberly James Peterson 12). Likewise, the caption accompanying plaintiff's photograph says only "Pegging the fun meter." This caption is not itself offensive, and did not imply, as did some of the text in the *Hustler* magazine involved in Douglass, that plaintiff is a lesbian.

Most importantly, there is nothing in the record to suggest that *Easyriders* is more sexually explicit than *Playboy*, and in Douglass the very premise of the court's holding was that plaintiff's consent to have her photograph appear in *Playboy* did not give rise to a false light claim. It was only because the court found that a consent to be photographed for *Playboy* was qualitatively different from a consent to be photographed for *Hustler* that the court held that plaintiff's false light claim was viable.

V.

The final claim asserted by plaintiff is for appropriation of her likeness. The Restatement of Torts provides that "[o]ne who appropriates to his own use or benefit the name or likeness of another is subject to liability to the other for invasion of his privacy." Restatement (Second) of Torts § 652C (1977). The tort is intended to protect against a person using the identity of another to advertise his business or for other commercial purposes. Thus, an appropriation claim does not arise from incidental uses of a person's identity or likeness. Id. As set forth in the Restatement the value of a person's image is not appropriated when it is published for purposes other than taking advantage of his reputation, prestige, or other value associated with *596 him, for purposes of publicity. No one has the right to object merely because his name or his appearance is brought before the public, since neither is in any way a private matter and both are open to public observation. It is only when the publicity is given for the purpose of appropriating to the defendant's benefit the commercial or other values associated with the name or likeness that the right of privacy is invaded. The fact that the defendant is engaged in the business of publication, for example of a newspaper, out of which he makes or seeks to make a profit, is not enough to make the incidental publication a commercial use of the name or likeness. Thus a newspaper, although it is not a philanthropic institution, does not become liable under the rule stated in this Section to every person whose name or likeness it publishes. Id.

Applying the rules of the Restatement, in Lawrence v. The A.S. Abell Company, supra, the Maryland Court of Appeals held that because the plaintiffs picture was taken while they were in a public place at a newsworthy event, an action for appropriation could not lie. 475 A.2d at 453. Furthermore, the court stated that even if the use of the plaintiffs' photograph in an advertising campaign was not merely "incidental," a person's likeness must also have some commercial or other value before an action for appropriation can succeed. Id. Because the plaintiffs in Lawrence were neither famous nor professional models, they could not show that the newspaper had taken advantage of any special value associated with their pictures. Id.

Lawrence is controlling here. The record does not establish that plaintiff is famous or a professional model or that there is any special value associated with her likeness. Moreover, as in Lawrence, plaintiff's photograph was taken at a public, outdoor event. Accordingly, her appropriation claim fails as a matter of law.FN4

FN4. In her opposition papers, plaintiff argues that she did not consent to the publication of her photograph. That is immaterial. The issue of whether a plaintiff consented is relevant only in determining whether a defendant has a defense to the plaintiff's invasion of privacy claim. See Bagwell v. Peninsula Regional Medical Center, 106 Md.App. 470, 665 A.2d 297, 319 (Md.1995). Here, for the reasons I have stated, plaintiff cannot meet the threshold requirements for any invasion of privacy claim.

A separate order effecting the rulings made in this memorandum is being entered herewith.

[Conclusion and order of the court]
ORDER
For the reasons stated in the accompanying memorandum, it is, this 17th day of October 2006
ORDERED
1. Defendant's motion for summary judgment is granted; and
2. Judgment is entered in favor of defendant against plaintiff.

Review the sample case set forth in this section to help you understand a case's component parts. Remember that the process of reading, analyzing, and summarizing a court case is case briefing. Now that we have reviewed the parts of a case, we will review case briefing.

What Is a Case Brief?

As noted, a case brief is a mechanism for summarizing a court case in written form as read and analyzed by the brief's author. The form of a case brief can vary, depending on the author and/or the requestor of the brief. For instance, a paralegal's supervising attorney may request that the paralegal brief a case in a certain format. However, case briefs generally contain the following parts, numbered and labeled: (1) case name and citation, (2) a summary of the material facts of the case, (3) a statement of the issue(s) presented by the case, (4) the court's holding(s), and (5) a summary of the court's reasoning for its decision.

The first part of a case brief is the case name and citation. Abbreviations may be used. The names of multiple plaintiffs or defendants may be omitted in the case title. *The Bluebook* style of legal citation, discussed earlier, is used by most lawyers and judges in uniformly citing legal authority, including case citations.

The second part of a case brief is a summary of the key facts of the case. Key facts are those that are material (important) to understanding the decision rendered by the court. For instance, that the plaintiff is a female might not be important in a breach of contract case, but it is likely material to a Title VII gender discrimination case. Extraneous facts should be omitted, and material facts should be presented succinctly—this is a case "brief," after all. In reading a case to find the important facts, remember that while facts often appear at the beginning of the case, they can appear anywhere in the case.

In this second section of a case brief, the brief writer may wish to include a short procedural history of the case in one or two sentences, indicating how the case got to the present court. This is especially true if the procedure is relevant to the court's decision in the case. If the procedural history of the case

is not relevant to the court's decision or useful to the briefer, it may be omitted from the case brief.

The third part of a case brief is the issue or issues presented by the case. Cases often present many legal issues. Each issue should be phrased concisely and should set forth the essential question to be decided by the court. In addition, each issue should be stated separately, normally in the form of a question that can be answered yes or no if that makes sense in the situation. Also, each issue should be stated in sufficient detail that the answer to the yes/no question will reflect the court's holding in the case. A sufficiently detailed issue also will allow a person reading the case brief to more completely understand what issue is being decided by the court. The statement of an issue should be specific and should join the facts and the law together. The following is an example of how to phrase an issue: "Did the plaintiff's unreasonable conduct of not wearing her seatbelt while driving contribute to the injury she suffered due to the defendant's negligence, barring her recovery?"

The fourth part of a case brief is the court's holding or holdings. A court's holding is the decision it renders on an issue in the case. The holding constitutes the law of the case. There may be one, or multiple, holdings in a case correlating to the number of issues presented. The holding or holdings should state succinctly the rule(s) of law established in the case. Often a holding is phrased "yes, . . ." or "no, . . ." and answers the

KEY Point

Contents of a Case Brief

I. Case name and citation

II. Summary of the key facts

III. Issue(s)

IV. Holding(s)

V. Summary of the court's reasoning

question set forth in the issue. Based on the previous example, the holding might be: "Yes, the plaintiff's unreasonable conduct of not wearing her seatbelt while driving contributed to the injury she suffered due to the defendant's negligence, barring her recovery." You will learn when you study tort law that contributory negligence, a defense recognized in a handful of jurisdictions, is a defense to a negligence claim where the plaintiff contributes (at all) to the injury she suffered, completely barring her recovery. So in this example, the plaintiff's contributory negligence would act as a complete defense for the defendant, barring the plaintiff's recovery.[1] In other words, the defendant would be found not liable for the plaintiff's injuries. In the holding, some brief writers state who won the case, if that would be useful to them. For example, "The defendant was found not liable" (which means the defendant won the lawsuit). Remember, however, that the court's decision regarding who won the case (here, the defendant) is a different concept than the holding, which is the rule of law established by the case and may become legal precedent (here, that the plaintiff's contributory negligence barred her recovery).

The final part of a case brief is a summary of the court's reasoning. The court's reasoning may include specific facts about the case, law being relied on or interpreted by the court, public or social policy, and any other factors that affect the court's holding. The summary of the court's reasoning is often the longest part of a case brief. In this part, the brief writer summarizes the reasons why the court made the ruling that it did. Further developing the above example, the court's reasoning might be as follows: "By driving without wearing a seatbelt, which is against the law in this jurisdiction, the plaintiff contributed to the injury she suffered in the car collision caused by the defendant's negligence. The plaintiff's injuries were much more severe than they would have been if she had been wearing a seat belt." Just like with the summary of the key facts, this part of the brief should be a summary, preferably in the briefer's own words, and not simply a recitation of the court's reasoning—again, it should be "brief." Also, the case briefer summarizes the court's reasoning in his own words, which helps assure the reader that the case briefer has a genuine understanding of the court's analysis and is not merely copying words from the court's opinion.

FIGURE
9-2   **Sample Case Brief (using the Sample Case from Figure 9-1)**

I. *Barnhart v. Paisano Publ'ns, LLC*, 457 F. Supp. 2d 590 (D. Md. 2006).

II. The plaintiff, an adult woman who is not a celebrity, attended an outdoor fundraising event for motorcycle enthusiasts. The event was open to the general public. At the event, there was music, food, games, motorcycle vendors, and drinking alcohol was allowed. Women began removing their shirts in exchange for being given beads, Mardi Gras style. The plaintiff, upon being lifted onto the shoulders of two men, voluntarily lifted her shirt and exposed her breasts. A photographer at the event took a photograph of the plaintiff's exposure and submitted it, for publication, to "Easyriders" magazine, published by the defendant. The magazine published the photograph. The plaintiff sued the defendant for invasion of privacy as a result of this publication.

Procedure: On defendant's motion for summary judgment. Motion granted.

III.
(a) Has the plaintiff stated a claim for the invasion of privacy tort of intrusion on seclusion?

(b) Has the plaintiff stated a claim for the invasion of privacy tort of false light?

(c) Has the plaintiff stated a claim for the invasion of privacy tort of appropriation?

IV.
(a) No, the plaintiff has not stated a claim for the invasion of privacy tort of intrusion on seclusion.

(b) No, the plaintiff has not stated a claim for the invasion of privacy tort of false light.

(c) No, the plaintiff has not stated a claim for the invasion of privacy tort of appropriation.

(continued)

211

V. The plaintiff chose to lift up her shirt at an outdoor fund-raising event which was open to the public and where about 200 people were present, according to the plaintiff's own estimate. Her actions in exposing her breasts in public could not reasonably have constituted a private act giving rise to a claim of intrusion upon seclusion. Rather, it was a public act. For an intrusion on seclusion claim to exist, that matter into which there was an intrusion must be a private one, not a public one.

There was no actionable claim of false light because the photograph's publication did not give the false impression that the plaintiff consented to the dissemination of the information contained in the photograph. Further, the photograph did not distort the plaintiff's appearance in any way, its caption was not offensive ("Pegging the fun meter"), and there was no evidence that the magazine published degrading and lewd content.

In regards to her appropriation claim, there was no appropriation of the plaintiff's likeness where there was mere incidental use, and not commercial use, of the likeness. Further, the plaintiff was not famous or a professional model, and there was no other special value associated with her likeness. Without commercial or other value to one's name or likeness, an appropriation claim does not lie under Maryland law.

The "IRAC" Method

Another common format for briefing cases is the IRAC method. IRAC means I-issue, R-rule, A-application, C-conclusion.

"Issue" means the legal issue(s) presented in the case.

"Rule" means the law to be applied to the facts of the case.

"Application" means application of the law to the facts of the case.

"Conclusion" means the decision of the court after applying the law to the facts of the case.

To use IRAC, do the following for *each* legal issue presented in the case:

1. State a legal issue presented. For example, "The issue is whether Bob committed the tort of battery when he kissed Pam without her consent."
2. State the law involved. Articulate the rule of law to be applied by the court to the facts of the case in order to make its determination. For example, case law in the jurisdiction defines the essential elements of the intentional tort of battery as (a) an act, (b) harmful or offensive contact with the plaintiff's person, (c) intent, and (d) causation.
3. Apply the law to the facts of the case. Here is where the case briefer analyzes the facts of the case in conjunction with the law that applies. In this example, the act of committing the unconsented-to kiss is evaluated based on the essential elements defined in part 2.
4. Make a conclusion about each issue using logical analysis that relates the rule of law to the facts of the case. For example, the conclusion may be that Bob committed the tort of battery when he kissed Pam without her consent.

Case briefs have many uses. One is that they are used in law school and paralegal education programs to teach case law as well as critical thinking and analysis. Case briefs often constitute the daily discussion in law school classes. Case briefs are also used in performing legal research as a basis for preparing court documents, such as legal briefs. They are also noted in legal memoranda prepared for supervising attorneys (legal writing, including legal memoranda, is examined in the next chapter).

Remember, in briefing cases different people may brief in different formats. Nonetheless, those who are reading, analyzing, and summarizing cases, for whatever use (to discuss in a law school class, to use in a court document, or to note in a research memorandum for a supervisor), are synthesizing the same information and, ultimately, also finding the rule of law established by the case as well as the reasons for it.

Becoming a proficient case briefer takes time and practice. Students learning to read and brief cases should be patient as they develop this skill, for court cases can be very difficult to read and understand. No one is born with the immediate ability to effectively brief a case. It is through practice that this skill, specific to the practice of law, is developed.

CHAPTER SUMMARY

- Legal research is the process of locating an answer to a legal question. Its goal is to find relevant, useful, and current law on a legal issue.

- Before conducting legal research, a legal researcher must define the legal issue(s) to be researched and must identify the source of law to be researched.

- Attorneys and paralegals perform legal research. In doing so, they search for law in one of four primary sources: common law, statutory law, administrative law, and constitutional law. Common law, also called case law, is law established by judges in the courts. Statutory law is law enacted by legislatures. Administrative law is law made by administrative agencies of the government. Constitutional law is law found in the federal and state constitutions.

- In researching common law, a researcher is looking for reported court cases that are on point, meaning previous court cases involving similar facts and legal issues. A court case is binding authority, also called mandatory authority, meaning authority that must be followed, if it is precedent in the court's jurisdiction. A case is precedent in a jurisdiction if it is on point and comes from a higher court in the jurisdiction. Authority that is not binding on a court but that may be used as guidance by the court in making its decision is called persuasive authority. A case from a lower court in the jurisdiction or from another jurisdiction is persuasive authority.

- Legal researchers may use secondary sources of law to locate primary sources of law. Secondary sources of law are resources that summarize or interpret the law and include resources such as case digests, legal encyclopedias, treatises, *Restatements of Law*, *American Law Reports* (ALRs), and law reviews.

- A case can be located using its name, which identifies the parties to the action, and its citation, which is a locator reference that includes the volume number of the reporter in which the case is published, the name of the reporter, the page number on which the case begins in that volume of that reporter, identification of the court rendering the decision, and the year of the decision.

- It is critical for a researcher to cite check cases before using them to make sure they are still good law and have not been reverse or modified on appeal.

- To research statutory law, a researcher must first determine where the relevant statute has been published. Each state, and the federal government, have statutes for their jurisdiction, published in codes. Statutes within codes are arranged by topic. Codes have topical indexes that guide researchers to relevant statutes. After locating the relevant statute or statutory provision, a researcher must read and analyze it. Annotated versions of codes, though unofficial codes, are valuable research tools because they provide comments on how courts have interpreted statutes and statutory

provisions. Local governments enact statutory law, too, but call these laws ordinances.

- Administrative law is law made by administrative agencies of the government, mostly federal and state. Regulations issued by administrative agencies are another primary source of law, and jurisdictions, both federal and state, have codes of administrative regulations. These administrative codes are organized by topic, like statutory codes, with topical indexes that can be used in performing research.

- Constitutional law is the body of law found in the federal constitution and the constitutions of each of the 50 states. Constitutional law sets forth the powers, responsibilities, and limitations of the various branches of government in that jurisdiction. Constitutions can be found online and in print from many sources, including the Library of Congress and in federal and state statutory codes.

- Legal research may be conducted using print materials or online resources, and attorneys and paralegals should know both methods.

- A case is a written judgment of a court. Case briefing is the process of reading, analyzing, and summarizing a court case. Case briefs are written summaries of a court case.

- The components of a case are case title, citation and docket number, date decided (perhaps the date of appellate arguments), syllabus and (sometimes) headnotes, names of counsel representing the parties (if present), names of the judges or justices writing the opinion, opinion (or body) of the case, conclusion, and concurring and/or dissenting opinions (if present).

- The components of a case brief are case name and citation, summary of the key facts, issue(s), holding(s), and summary of the court's reasoning. Cases should be cited in proper form, normally following *The Bluebook: A Uniform System of Citation*.

CONCEPT REVIEW AND REINFORCEMENT

Key Terms and Concepts

Legal research
Common law
Case law
Statutory law
Ordinances
Administrative law
Constitutional law
Case on point
Binding authority
Mandatory authority
Secondary sources of law

Primary sources of law
Reporters
Case name
Case citation
Parallel citation
Persuasive authority
Statutory provisions
Statutory rules of construction
Case
Case briefing
Case brief
Opinion
Unanimous opinion
Majority opinion
Disposition of the case
Concurring opinion
Dissenting opinion
Dicta

Questions for Review

1. What is legal research?
2. What steps should be taken preliminary to conducting legal research?
3. What are the four main sources of law a paralegal or lawyer uses in legal research?
4. What are primary and secondary sources of law?
5. What is binding authority and what is persuasive authority?
6. What steps do you take to research common law?
7. How do you cite court cases?
8. What steps do you take to research statutory law?
9. What steps do you take to research administrative law?
10. What steps do you take to research constitutional law?
11. What are the advantages and disadvantages of the two methods of conducting legal research, namely using print materials and using online resources?
12. What is a court case?
13. What is a case brief?
14. How do you brief a court case?

DEVELOPING YOUR PARALEGAL SKILLS

Critical Thinking Exercises

1. You are a paralegal at a law firm that specializes in personal injury cases, representing plaintiffs. Your supervising attorney asks you to research the law on the standard of care used to measure whether or not a surgeon was negligent in the performance of a sterilization procedure on a patient (your firm's client, a female, became pregnant two years after the performance of the sterilization procedure).

   Where will you begin your legal research? Will you go straight to a primary source of law or will you begin with a secondary source of law? If you begin with a secondary source of law, what source might you use?

2. Refer to question 1, above. Your initial research of the *Restatement (Second) of Torts* leads you to case law in your jurisdiction on the standard of care required of a medical professional (a surgeon). You find a case defining the standard of care required to be used by physicians (this legal issue is relevant to a claim of medical malpractice, a type of negligence action).
   a. Is there anything you should do before you provide your supervisor with this case?
   b. If you said "cite check" in response to a., above, why is it important to perform a cite check of this case?

3. Below is a sample statute of frauds. Use this statute to answer the questions that follow it.

Statute of Frauds

Section XX-X-XX. Agreements required to be in writing and signed.

   No action shall be brought whereby:

1. To charge any executor or administrator on any special promise to answer damages out of his own estate;
2. To charge the defendant upon any special promise to answer for the debt, default or miscarriage of another person;
3. To charge any person under any agreement made on consideration of marriage;
4. To charge any person on any contract or sale of lands or tenements or any interest in or concerning them; or
5. To charge any person on any agreement that is not performed within the space of one year from the making thereof; Unless the agreement on which such action shall be brought or some memorandum or note thereof shall be in writing and signed by the party to be charged therewith or some person thereunto by himself lawfully authorized.

   a. Under this statute, what must a person do besides reduce the agreement to writing?
   b. Do contracts for the sale of goods priced at $500 or more fall under this statute of frauds, which provision is a common statute of frauds requirement among the state codes? If so, what subsection?
   c. Do contracts where one party guarantees to pay the debt of another fall under this statute of frauds? If so, what subsection?
   d. Do prenuptial agreements fall under this statute of frauds? If so, what subsection?

Assignments and Practical Applications

Working with one other student from the class, use a case digest to help locate a case in your state that identifies the essential elements of the tort of negligence. From the material provided in the case digest, find the case in the relevant reporter. Copy the case and then label its parts using the case parts identified in the chapter. Then read and brief the case.

Using your school's law library or online resources, find your state's code—the primary source of statutory law in your state. What is the name of the official version of that code? Is there an unofficial code published in your state? What is its name? What is the main difference between the official and unofficial versions of the code?

Using your state's code, find the criminal law statute on second degree murder. What conduct constitutes second degree murder in your jurisdiction?

Using your state's commercial code, research what types of contracts fall within your state's statute of frauds. Make a list of those types of contracts to discuss in class.

Review the parts of a case brief as well as the sample case brief. You may use these samples when performing assignments involving case briefing.

Go to your school or a local law library and find and review the secondary sources of law that may be useful to legal researchers, including legal encyclopedias (*American Jurisprudence* and *Corpus Juris Secondum* are the two main legal encyclopedias), case digests for your state, *Restatements of the Law*, law treatises, and *American Law Reports*. Look through each one and see if you can determine the answer to the question, "What are the essential elements of the tort of negligence?"

Using your law library or online resources, locate the case *MacPherson v. Buick Motor Co.*, 111 N.E. 1050 (N.Y. 1916). This is an early, landmark products liability case. Read and brief this case using the format set forth in this chapter.

Technology Resources and Internet Exercises

Using the Internet, research to determine which of the regional reporters in West's National Reporter System publishes appellate court opinions for your state.

Using the Internet, identify your state's code of administrative regulations. Is it available online on a government website?

Access the Library of Congress website and find the constitution for your state. Read your state's constitution and think about how it compares with what you know about the U.S. Constitution.

Using the Internet, see what computerized legal research resources are available by typing in searches such as for "legal research," using a search engine such as Google, AOL Search, or Yahoo!. In your search, find the following: Cornell Law School's informative site at www.law.cornell.edu, the popular free legal site Find Law at www.findlaw.com, and the two leading computerized legal research databases, Westlaw (http://web2.westlaw.com) and Lexis (www.lexis.com). See also the Duke Law website (www.law.duke.edu/lib/researchguides/formbks) for useful information on form books and how to locate legal forms online, such as through Westlaw, Lexis, and Findlaw.

Using the Cornell University Law School website for its Legal Information Institute, found at http://www.law.cornell.edu/, find your state's legal ethics code. Use it to answer the following Ethical Applications.

Ethical Applications

Jonathan Quintano is a paralegal in the boutique law firm of Jones, Masters, and Serio, P.C., a plaintiff's firm. Jonathan is an experienced paralegal who is excellent at what he does. One day, one of the firm's clients, Tax-Made-EZ Software, Inc., calls the firm to speak to Jonathan's supervising attorney, Gloria Milford. Gloria is in a meeting and will be unavailable all day, as the receptionist tells the client. The client's vice president for development, who has placed the call on behalf of his company, asks to speak to Jonathan, who is available, in lieu of Gloria. In speaking with Jonathan, the client's representative asks Jonathan whether the earned income credit will be repealed by federal legislators for the upcoming tax year so that the company may finalize the updating of its federal tax return software for copying, distribution, and sale. Jonathan, who is up to date and very knowledgeable about federal tax law, responds, "I'm sure that it's safe to finalize your software; the earned income credit will not be repealed by Congress this year." In fact, although there were some discussions during recent legislative sessions about repealing the earned income credit, the credit was not repealed, and Jonathan is correct (and confident that he is).

Was Jonathan's conduct appropriate? If so, why? If not, what was wrong with it? What can happen to Jonathan because of this conduct? What, if anything, can happen to Gloria because of Jonathan's conduct?

VIDEO CASE STUDIES

Video Interview of Michael Weiland

Paralegal case study videos to accompany this textbook are accessible from within both the New MyLegalStudiesLab Virtual Law Office Experience course and the Resources Website for Paralegal Studies.

ENDNOTES

[1]Most jurisdictions have abandoned the defense of contributory negligence and replaced it with some form of comparative negligence. There are different forms of comparative negligence but generally speaking, the defense of comparative negligence allows for apportionment of the damages between the plaintiff and the defendant when a plaintiff's negligence contributes to the harm she suffers as a result of the defendant's negligence.

10 Legal Writing

Tatyana Bronzova

**Litigation Paralegal at the Law Office
of Alex Poberesky, P.A.**

Tatyana first became interested in the paralegal profession when she realized that paralegals have the ability to help people experiencing legal problems. Before becoming a paralegal, Tatyana worked as a legal secretary. An advertisement in a newspaper led Tatyana to her paralegal position, where she works mostly in civil litigation, primarily representing plaintiffs in personal injury and workers' compensation cases, along with performing some criminal defense work.

In her position, Tatyana regularly drafts legal documents and conducts interviews. Tatyana believes that drafting legal documents is a primary responsibility for paralegals, and that knowing and applying the local rules and requirements for pleadings is crucial to litigation practice. She emphasizes the need for paralegals to use careful wording and correct grammar in all legal document drafting because these documents reflect on the supervising attorney's professionalism, as well as the paralegal's professionalism. In conducting interviews of clients, Tatyana obtains information needed to handle their cases, including information to respond to discovery requests. She also helps prepare clients for depositions, mediation, and trial.

Tasks Tatyana regularly performs in her practice include conducting legal and factual research, preparing and filing pleadings and motions, preparing exhibits, performing negotiations, drafting correspondence and agreements, interviewing clients, reviewing records, performing discovery, and organizing files. She regularly communicates with her clients by telephone, written correspondence, and e-mail. She is particularly diligent in regularly contacting her clients to keep them updated on the status of their matters.

The full video interview is accessible from within both the New MyLegalStudiesLab Virtual Law Office Experience course and the Resources Website for Paralegal Studies.

The chapter will answer the following questions:

- What is legal writing?
- What are important good writing skills?
- How do you draft legal correspondence?
- How do you draft legal memoranda?

- How do you draft contracts?
- How do you draft pleadings and other litigation-related documents?

The chapter examines legal writing, another important task performed by paralegals. We begin by defining legal writing, and good writing skills are identified. Drafting different types of legal correspondence is reviewed. The chapter provides instruction on how to draft legal memoranda. It also discusses the process of drafting contracts. At the end of the chapter, drafting important litigation-related documents, including pleadings, discovery requests and responses, and legal briefs is examined. Our discussion begins with an introduction to legal writing.

INTRODUCTION TO LEGAL WRITING

Paralegals, like lawyers, spend much of their professional time using their communication skills, both oral and written. Legal writing, then, is a critical paralegal skill.

What is legal writing? As discussed in Chapter 8, **legal writing** is a type of technical writing used by lawyers, judges, and legislators to communicate legal analysis and legal rights and duties. Legal writing may be related to the legal research process discussed in Chapter 9. For example, you may write a case brief summarizing a court case or a legal memorandum summarizing a particular area of law. Legal writing may be unrelated to the legal research process. For example, you may write legal correspondence (letters), discovery requests and responses, and pleadings for filing with courts.

Legal writing can be objective or persuasive. **Objective legal writing** is legal writing that is neutral and unbiased. Objective legal writing presents a balanced analysis of all sides of a legal issue. A legal memorandum is an example of objective legal writing. Legal memoranda are discussed more fully later in this chapter. **Persuasive legal writing** is legal writing that advocates your client's position. This type of writing presents the facts and legal issues in a way that favors the client and disfavors the opponent. In other words, it is biased writing—biased in favor of the position of the client you represent. An example of persuasive legal writing is a legal brief. Legal briefs are discussed more fully later in this chapter.

Supervising attorneys assign legal writing projects to paralegals. When you receive a writing assignment from a supervisor, be sure you understand the nature of the assignment and the type of document expected by the supervisor. If you are unclear about what you are supposed to do, or what the writing assignment should look like when it is completed, be sure to ask the supervising attorney questions to clarify the assignment so you can perform it well. Know what kind of document you are expected to produce. See if your supervising attorney has a preferred format for you to use. For example, if the document requested is a legal memorandum, ask the supervising attorney what format she would like you to use, if she has a preference.

> *Use examples and forms . . . for guidance in your drafting. If you do not have a form or example to use, first gather your thoughts and organize your objectives before beginning to draft.*
> Kristina Winter

KEY Point

Understand the Writing Assignment

Before beginning a legal writing assignment, be sure you understand what kind of document you are expected to produce. See if the supervising attorney who requested the document has a preferred format that you should use.

Legal writing is a type of technical writing used by lawyers, judges, and legislators to communicate legal analysis and legal rights and duties.

Objective legal writing is legal writing that is neutral and unbiased.

Persuasive legal writing is legal writing that advocates your client's position.

© ImageFonds/Alamy

Time Management

When receiving a legal writing assignment, be sure to find out from the supervising attorney when it must be completed. Allow time to have the document reviewed by the supervising attorney before it must be sent out (for example, to the court for filing, to the client, or to opposing counsel). Always meet drafting deadlines.

Also, it is important when receiving a legal writing assignment to know when it is due and to complete it on time. Some legal documents have court-imposed deadlines, such as for filing pleadings. These usually are not flexible deadlines. Other legal documents have client-imposed deadlines, such as if the client wants to execute the contract for a deal by a certain date. Other legal documents have supervisor-imposed deadlines, such as if the supervising attorney wants a case brief by the end of the day so she can incorporate the case into a legal brief to be filed with the court. Considering the legal ethics rules, remember that paralegals must have their legal writing reviewed by their supervising attorneys. Allow a reasonable time before the due date of a writing assignment to present a draft to the supervising attorney for her review. In summary, know when legal writing results are due, allow time for the supervising attorney to review them before they are sent out (to a client, court, opposing counsel, etc.), and manage your time so that drafting deadlines are met.

Now that we have introduced the topic of legal writing, we will discuss ways to be a good legal writer. Specifically, we will review good writing skills.

GOOD WRITING SKILLS

Communication, both oral and written, is paramount in the legal profession and to legal professionals. Now we will examine written communication skills and how to exhibit good ones. Good writing skills are critical to success for paralegals. No matter what type of legal document you are drafting, the following suggestions will help to improve your written work.

First and foremost, write for your audience. It is important to remember that the document you are drafting is being created to communicate some information to a specific reader, and you should keep your target audience in mind. For example, the document could be drafted for the supervising attorney, the client, the opposing counsel, or the court. Accordingly, remember to tailor your document for your intended audience.

In addition, what you draft should follow (exactly!) the directions of the person requesting it. Normally for a paralegal this means following the instructions of the supervising attorney.

If the reader is not a lawyer or paralegal, use plain English that a layperson can understand rather than legalese. **Legalese** is the body of terms used by legal professionals, also called **legal jargon**. An example of legalese is *locus standi*, which means a person's "standing" to sue—in other words, the right of a person to bring a legal action. Avoid the use of legalese if your target audience is not a legal professional.

Draft well-written sentences with appropriate use of grammar and sound sentence structure. Draft well-organized paragraphs including topic sentences with supporting detail sentences. Include appropriate introductions, transitions, and conclusions in your writing.

Legalese is the body of terms used by legal professionals; it is also called **legal jargon**.

Regarding sentence structure, use the active voice (subject/verb/object order), rather than the passive voice (object/verb/subject order), unless your use of the passive voice is purposeful. "The Buyer shall pay the Seller One Million Dollars ($1,000,000) upon execution of this Agreement" is a contract provision using the active voice. "One Million Dollars ($1,000,000) shall be paid by the Buyer to the Seller upon execution of this Agreement" is a contract provision using the passive voice. Note how much more clear use of the active voice makes the contract provision.

Your written work should make sense and be clear. Write efficiently. To do this, be concise and to the point in your writing. Concise statements can be more powerful and/or persuasive than rambling ones, so avoid unnecessary verbiage. Also, in being an efficient writer, avoid redundancy (repetition) unless redundancy is needed for emphasis. For example, instead of using the phrase "null and void" to describe a document that no longer has legal effect, it is enough to say it is "void" or "has no force and effect."

Format your document so that it is easy to read and attractive. Give it headings, subheadings, and the like, to improve its organization and readability. Headings and subheadings provide a roadmap for readers and are commonly used in contract drafting, as one example. Organize and structure your written work. Thoughtful organization and structure of a document can greatly improve its readability.

Law firms typically have styles and formats they require for documents prepared by their employees, such as the use of Times New Roman font in 12-point size. If you are drafting a document for filing with a court, remember that the court will have established rules for filed documents, to which your document must conform. Today these court rules are often published online. Keep your writing style and formatting consistent within a document. Do not change your writing style within a document. Do not alter your formatting within a document either. Make sure you do not change font or letter size within the document unless there is a logical reason for it.

Be gender-neutral in your writing. For example, use "workers' compensation" instead of "workmen's compensation" or "police officers" instead of "policemen." For another example, avoid exclusive use of the masculine form for indefinite pronouns; instead, alternate between masculine and feminine pronouns, as is done in this textbook—that is, vary "he" and "she"; make the noun plural so you can use "they" or "them," which are gender-neutral pronouns; or do not use a pronoun and instead repeat the noun itself (so instead of "she" say "the client").

Avoid using contractions or abbreviations in formal writing. Instead of writing "doesn't," write "does not." That is how you avoid use of contractions. Rather than use abbreviations, use the long form of the word or phrase. For example, rather than write "bar," write "state bar association" to refer to the state bar association. For another example, rather than write "MSBA," write the "Maryland State Bar Association" to specifically talk about that state bar association.

Most important, proofread your work very, very carefully. Using spell check and grammar check on word processing software is only the start of proofreading, for these tools catch only limited spelling and grammar errors. Nothing speaks more about your professionalism than your ability to produce written documents that are free from errors—especially grammatical and typographical ones.

Before drafting a legal document, it may be helpful to prepare an outline, which allows you to generate, record, and organize ideas. Outlines can be written the old-fashioned way, with a pen and paper or word processed. If an outline is word processed, it is very easy to use the word processing application's tools to edit and reorganize the outline.

Additionally, to write the best you can, have reference tools available including a dictionary, a thesaurus, and a style manual such as the popular The Elements of Style by William

" *In most instances there are form letters and documents within the files on the firm's server that you can use to get you started drafting. Do not get discouraged when drafting legal documents such as correspondence, contracts, deposition abstracts, and pleadings, when the attorney gives [them] back to you with revision requests and notes all over your work. Remember that the attorney is trying to get you to conform to his/her writing style.* "
Shanae Golder

Tips for Legal Writing

- Write for your audience.
- Follow directions.
- Use plain language; avoid legalese.
- Use good grammar.
- Pay attention to sentence, paragraph, and overall structure.
- Use active voice.
- Be organized, structured, clear, and concise.
- Avoid redundancy.
- Use appropriate formatting and style.
- Be consistent in your writing and formatting.
- Be gender-neutral.
- Avoid using contractions and abbreviations.
- Proofread.

Strunk Jr. and E.B. White, *The Elements of Style*. Another good writing tool is a grammar textbook, such as your high school or middle school grammar textbook—it contains the important basics of good grammar.

What types of documents are drafted when performing legal writing? Several different types of legal documents are commonly drafted by lawyers and paralegals. These include documents such as legal correspondence, legal memoranda, contracts, pleadings, discovery requests and responses, and legal briefs. Successful paralegals possess strong writing skills and are able to draft effective legal documents. How to draft each of these documents is the subject of detailed study and practice in legal research and writing, civil procedure, and contract law courses for law and paralegal students. An introduction to each of these types of legal documents, and how to draft them, is covered next, starting with legal correspondence.

LEGAL CORRESPONDENCE

Paralegals engaged in the performance of legal services regularly draft and send letters to clients, opposing counsel, witnesses, and others. These letters are called **legal correspondence**. Such correspondence may be informative, such as to inform the client of a deadline or a settlement offer. It may be an opinion letter, providing a legal opinion about the client's matter. However, as discussed in Part III of this text, legal opinions may be given only by attorneys, so paralegals should not draft or sign opinion letters. Frequently, legal correspondence is used to confirm information that was already conveyed orally, either in person or over the telephone. These are called confirmation letters. Attorneys and paralegals may draft demand letters, in which the sender of the letter demands a third party to cease and desist from some action based on a legal claim the sender is threatening to assert. Demand letters, also known as cease-and-desist letters, are adversarial in nature. They are used to advance the clients' interests, often by trying to resolve legal disputes without litigation. As an example of a demand letter used in a tort matter, an attorney may send a cease-and-desist letter to a third party who continues to trespass across his client's land. This letter, with the goal of resolving the dispute without the need for litigation, would inform the third party of the client's legal position and both firmly and professionally request the third party to stop performing the activity the client believes is infringing on his rights, such as repeatedly

entering on his land. Demand letters are regularly used to try to resolve intellectual property infringement disputes and avoid expensive infringement litigation, if possible. Because they may involve statements opining the current law in a jurisdiction, demand letters are typically written and signed by attorneys rather than paralegals.

KEY Point

Types of Legal Correspondence

- Informative letters convey information to a person (such as a client, opposing counsel, a witness, or a court) and include cover letters accompanying documents.
- Opinion letters are written by attorneys to clients to convey legal opinions about the clients' matters.
- Confirmation letters repeat (confirm) to their recipients information previously conveyed in person or over the telephone.
- Demand letters are used by parties to explain their legal positions in legal disputes and to firmly request the recipients to cease and desist from taking some action, such as trespassing on property or infringing a copyright.

Legal correspondence means legal letters.

© Ben Molyneux/Alamy

is used for later pages of a multipage legal letter. Letterhead should always be used when writing a letter as a representative of the firm or company. It should never be used for personal correspondence.

The basic components of a legal letter include the following. The first item below the letterhead is the date of the letter. This is followed by the method of delivery of the letter, which may be first-class mail, hand delivery, Federal Express, and/or facsimile, as examples (some letters are sent by two methods, such as by facsimile and by first-class mail). Then the name, title, and address of the recipient of the letter appear. The recipient information is followed by a reference line identifying the legal matter or other subject matter of the letter. Next, a salutation or greeting, such as "Dear Mrs. Smyth" (followed by a colon or a comma) appears. After the salutation, the body of the letter is written; this is the meat of the letter. A closing, normally "Sincerely" or "Very truly yours," follows the body of the letter. The signature and title of the sender of the letter follows the closing. Remember that a paralegal should always disclose his status here unless the paralegal is writing the letter for the attorney's signature. Following the signature, the initials of the author and the typist are written; these are set forth as "ABC/def," where the author's initials are capitalized and the typist's are lowercase. If one or more documents are included with the letter, "Enclosure" or "Enclosures" is written following

Written correspondence is better evidence of what was said between the parties than is oral communication; so legal professionals, perhaps even more than other professionals, often write their communications to preserve them. Also, if the oral communication was vague or ambiguous, use of written correspondence can clarify the understanding of those involved. It can also be used to fill in any gaps in fact or understanding.

Legal correspondence is written on the letterhead and stationary of the firm or corporate law department from which it is sent. Letterhead usually contains the firm or company's name, its address, its telephone and facsimile numbers, and its e-mail address. Letterhead may contain the names of attorneys, and even paralegals (along with their titles) associated with the office. Letterhead is used only for the first page of a legal letter. Plain stationery

Use of Law Office Letterhead

Anything written on law office letterhead is considered to be signed by the law office. So even if the document appearing on the letterhead is not signed by its author, it can be deemed to be a legally signed document of the law office. Because of this, some law firms keep their letterhead under lock and key, to be used only with the knowledge of one of the partners.

KEY Point

Components of a Legal Letter

- The date
- The method of delivery
- The name, title, and address of the recipient
- A reference line
- A salutation or greeting
- The body of the letter
- A closing
- The signature and title of the sender
- The initials of the author and the typist
- Enclosure(s), if any
- Copy recipients, if any

the author/typist information. Under the "Enclosure" reference, the name of the enclosed document may be listed; for multiple enclosures, the number of enclosures may be noted (with or without parentheses). Finally, recipients of copies, if any, are listed. Two sample legal letters are provided in Figures 10-1 and 10-2.

Another type of legal document that paralegals typically draft is legal memoranda. How to draft legal memoranda is discussed next.

FIGURE 10-1 Sample Legal Correspondence #1

Murphy, Smith & Payne, P.C.
9385 South Charles Street, Suite 100
Baltimore, Maryland 21210
Telephone: 410-372-6600
Facsimile: 410-372-6601
E-mail: MSPlaw@laol.com

July 17, 20___

<u>Via Facsimile and First Class Mail</u>
Sylvia Russell
265 Schwann Valley Road
Hunt Valley, Maryland 21110

Re: Deposition Scheduled for July 20, 20___ (Case No. CV-649684)

Dear Ms. Russell:

This letter is to confirm your attendance at your deposition, scheduled for 9:30 a.m. on Wednesday, July 20, at our offices. Please arrive at least one half hour early so that I may answer any final questions you may have before the deposition begins. The deposition is expected to take most of the day, as we discussed during our preparation meeting last week.

I have enclosed our firm's deposition preparation tip sheet for your review prior to the taking of your deposition. It summarizes what we discussed last week.

If you have any questions or concerns prior to your arrival for the deposition, please let me or Linda know so that we may address them. I look forward to seeing you on July 20.

Very truly yours,

Lucas R. Payne, Paralegal

LRP/nrt

Enclosure

cc: Linda M. Duncan, Esq.

FIGURE
10-2 Sample Legal Correspondence #2

Sharpe and Michaels, LLC
94 Palm Way
Indialantic, Florida 32904
Telephone: 528-453-6200
Facsimile: 528-453-6201
E-mail: SharpeandMichaels@hmail.com

March 6, 20__

<u>Via Facsimile and Certified Mail</u>
Robert Johns, President
Rob Johns Surfing Shop
100 Longbeach Road
Daytona Beach, Florida 32416

Re: Infringement of Trademark "Ron Jon" U.S./Reg. No. 1,234,567

Dear Mr. Johns:

I represent Ron Jon's, Inc. in its intellectual property matters. Ron Jon's, Inc., is the owner of the U.S. Trademark Registration No. 1,234,567 for the well-known trademark "Ron Jon" used consistently in interstate commerce by Ron Jon's, Inc. for more than 30 years in connection with its surf and beach supply business. A copy of Ron Jon's trademark registration is enclosed. This trademark is a valuable asset of Ron Jon's, Inc. and the company has expended significant resources to develop the goodwill of this mark in association with its products in the minds of consumers.

Recently the company became aware of your use of the mark "Rob Johns" in connection with a surf shop. Your use of this substantially similar mark on similar goods is likely to cause confusion, mistake, or deception in the minds of consumers as to the origin and source of your products. This infringing use is a violation of federal copyright laws pursuant to the U.S. Trademark Act. Further, the infringing use is causing my client ongoing and significant damages as well as diminishing the value of the goodwill associated with my client's famous trademark.

Ron Jon's, Inc. hereby demands that Rob John's Surfing Shop immediately cease and desist use of the trademark "Rob Johns" or any other mark confusingly similar to Ron Jon's mark. Further, my client demands that you immediately cease and desist from marketing, distributing, or selling any products bearing the infringing mark or any confusingly similar mark.

Because of the critical nature of this violation of my client's legal rights, I request that you respond within seven (7) business days of the date of this letter to confirm your intention to immediately cease and desist from any further infringing use of the mark "Rob Johns" or any confusingly similar mark. If I do not receive a satisfactory response from you within the designated time, my client plans to take legal action to obtain injunctive relief and to recover damages for trademark infringement, which damages may be trebled by a court of law, as well as to recover attorneys' fees and costs associated with the legal action necessary to protect the trademark "Ron Jon."

I look forward to hearing back from you or your legal counsel in the next few days. Thank you for your prompt attention to this important matter.

Very truly yours,

Harry J. Michaels, Esq.

HJM/ccb

Enclosure

cc: Cynthia Turner, Esq.

LEGAL MEMORANDA

Paralegals engaged in the delivery of legal services also draft legal memoranda. **Legal memoranda** are documents that thoroughly analyze and summarize the law in a particular area, on the basis of legal research, and inform the requestor of the strengths and weaknesses of the client's legal position. They are prepared for internal use by a law firm or corporate law department. Attorneys, and paralegals at the request of their supervising attorneys, often prepare these documents to better understand a client's matter and to formulate a realistic legal opinion on the merits of the client's legal position. A well-written legal memorandum is an objective analysis of the law on a particular matter. It includes both the strengths and the weaknesses of the client's position, and whether that position is a legal claim or a defense. Thus, it is an evaluation tool used by the preparer or requester to formulate a realistic opinion on the strength of the client's position.

How a legal memorandum is organized and formatted depends on office protocol or the directions of the supervisor requesting the memorandum. There is no universally accepted way to structure a legal memorandum, but legal memoranda are typically divided into the following distinct parts: heading, statement of the facts involved, questions presented (and perhaps a brief conclusion answering the questions presented), analysis or discussion, and conclusion.

The heading identifies the person for whom the memorandum is prepared as well as identifies the person who prepared it. Then the heading sets forth the date of the memorandum (the date submitted to the recipient). Last, the heading includes a reference line briefly describing the memorandum's nature.

The statement of the facts sets forth the material (important and relevant) facts regarding the legal issue involved. These material facts include both those favorable to the client's

---

KEY Point

Parts of a Legal Memorandum

I. Heading

II. Statement of the facts

III. Questions presented (and perhaps a brief conclusion answering the questions presented)

IV. Analysis/discussion

V. Conclusion

KEY Point

Purpose of Legal Memoranda

Legal memoranda are written for internal use by a law office. They provide an objective analysis of the law on a particular matter. They are often used to objectively analyze a client's legal position.

Legal memoranda are documents that thoroughly analyze and summarize the law in a particular area, on the basis of legal research, and inform the requestor of the strengths and weaknesses of the client's legal position.

position and those detrimental to it. Remember that a legal memorandum is a form of objective legal writing, rather than persuasive legal writing. Because of this, the reader needs to know what facts not only support the client's position, but also what facts do not support it. The facts should be organized in a logical manner. Chronological order often works well in organizing facts in a statement of the facts.

The section on questions presented should clearly set forth the legal issues being addressed by the memorandum. To clearly set forth the issues, the legal issues should be stated with specificity and in detail. Note that one, or multiple, questions may be presented in a legal memorandum, depending on its nature. Some legal memorandum preparers include brief answers to the questions presented in this part of the legal memorandum, whereas others only provide answers later, in the conclusion. If brief conclusions are presented, they should be organized to correspond with the questions presented.

The fourth part of the memorandum is the analysis, or discussion, section. In this part, the writer provides a legal analysis and discussion of each issue presented for resolution. When multiple questions are presented, it is a good idea to organize the analysis section into parts, each examining a particular legal issue. Legal research is performed by the writer, who then applies the research results to the facts of the client's matter. This application of the law to the facts is what is embodied in the analysis and discussion section of a legal memorandum. The IRAC method of analysis (issue, rule, application, conclusion) discussed in Chapter 9 may be used to analyze each legal issue by applying the relevant laws to the facts of the case. This section of a legal memorandum contains appropriate citations to legal authority and sets forth the relevant law being applied by using appropriate citation style, such as *Bluebook* style discussed in Chapter 9. The analysis section is the longest, most detailed, and comprehensive part of a legal memorandum.

The final part of a legal memorandum is the conclusion. After the legal issues have been fully analyzed, the writer gives an opinion on the relative strength of the client's legal position, and may make recommendations regarding a course of action to take—such as to make a settlement offer if the client's position does not appear to be strong as a result of the research and analysis performed in drafting the legal memorandum.

An example of a legal memorandum being used in tort law (the substantive law of torts is discussed in greater detail in Chapter 13) is to evaluate whether the client/plaintiff was contributorily negligent by speeding at the time of a collision, and whether the defendant had the last clear chance to avoid the accident. See the sample legal memorandum in Figure 10-3.

Many legal writers also draft contracts. How to draft contracts is examined next.

FIGURE 10-3 **Sample Legal Memorandum**

MEMORANDUM

To: Martin I. Boone, Partner

From: Jennifer Clayton, Paralegal

Date: September 6, 20__

Re: Application of Contributory Negligence Defense and Last Clear Chance Doctrine in Maryland

STATEMENT OF FACTS

Jane Smith, the firm's client, was involved in a car collision caused by the alleged negligence of the defendant, Jackson Doe, another driver. At the time of the collision, Mrs. Smith was driving north on the Jones Falls Expressway, near the Druid Hills Parkway entrance ramp. In her complaint, Mrs. Smith alleged that Mr. Doe failed to yield the right-of-way to her as he attempted to merge onto the Jones Falls Expressway from the Druid Hills Parkway entrance ramp. In his answer to the client's complaint, Mr. Doe asserted that the client was speeding at the time of the collision, contributing to its cause, and asserting the client's contributory negligence as a defense.

In an interview, Mrs. Smith stated that the defendant had the opportunity to avoid the accident by yielding the right-of-way or by driving on the shoulder of the road when the collision seemed imminent. Mr. Doe failed to do so, and the collision occurred.

You asked me to research the law in the state of Maryland on the defense of contributory negligence and the last clear chance doctrine as they relate to this case.

QUESTIONS PRESENTED

1.   Does Maryland recognize the defense of contributory negligence and if so, how would it apply to these facts?

2.   Does Maryland recognize the last clear chance doctrine, and if so, how would it apply to these facts?

BRIEF CONCLUSION

1.   Yes, Maryland is one of few remaining jurisdictions recognizing contributory, rather than comparative, negligence, and the client's alleged speeding may constitute contributory negligence, barring her recovery. However, another law in Maryland, the boulevard rule, may change this result.

2.   Yes, Maryland recognizes the last clear chance doctrine, and if the defendant had the last clear chance to avoid the collision by driving onto the shoulder of the road, the client may recover for the harm she suffered despite her contributory negligence.

DISCUSSION

I.   CONTRIBUTORY NEGLIGENCE DEFENSE

Maryland recognizes the defense of contributory, rather than comparative, negligence. Under Maryland law, the plaintiff's contributory negligence completely bars recovery against a negligent defendant. Wooldridge v. Price, 2009 966 A.2d 955 (Md. App. 2009). Accordingly, if the defendant can "adduce some evidence of negligence on the part of the [plaintiff], her claims against [him] would be barred." Id. at 961.

In applying that law to our client's case, if the defendant can produce evidence that our client was speeding at the time of the collision, and that speeding contributed to its cause, then the defense of contributory negligence could bar her recovery. However, this bar is subject to both the last clear chance doctrine (see II., below) and the boulevard rule.

The boulevard rule is a law in Maryland that imposes a duty upon drivers entering or crossing a highway from another highway or private roadway to stop and yield the right-of-way to through traffic on the highway. If the driver of a vehicle approaches a through highway, the driver shall: (1) stop at the entrance to the through highway; and (2) yield the right-of-way to any other vehicle approaching on the through highway. Md. Code Ann., Transp. § 21-403 (b) (2011). Accordingly, the boulevard rule imposed a duty upon the defendant to yield to our client's automobile when merging onto the Jones Falls Expressway. The boulevard rule has been held inapplicable where the favored driver (the one traveling on the highway) fails to exercise due care. However, speeding alone is not ordinarily considered sufficient to strip a driver on a through highway of his favored status. Palenchar v. Jarrett, 507 F.Supp.2d 502 (D. Md. 2007). Accordingly, even if the client was speeding at the time of the collision, that alone should not strip her of her favored status under the boulevard rule.

(continued)

II. LAST CLEAR CHANCE DOCTRINE

In some contributory negligence situations, the last clear chance doctrine can apply to allow recovery. Wooldridge at 961. Under Maryland law, for the last clear chance doctrine to apply, these requirements must be met: (1) the defendant must be negligent; (2) the plaintiff must be contributorily negligent; and (3) the plaintiff must make "a showing of something new or sequential, which affords the defendant a fresh opportunity (of which he fails to avail himself) to avert the consequences of his original negligence." Id.

The third requirement has been interpreted to mean that the doctrine will apply only if the acts of the parties were sequential rather than concurrent; in other words, the defendant must have had the opportunity to avoid the injury after the plaintiff's negligent action was put in motion. Id. The last clear chance doctrine assumes that, after the primary negligence of the plaintiff and the defendant, "the defendant could, and the plaintiff could not, by the use of the means available avert the accident." Id. The defendant should recognize and respond to the plaintiff's position of "helpless peril." Id.

To apply the last clear chance doctrine, courts require a showing that the plaintiff be in a position of helpless peril and the defendant have a fresh opportunity to exercise due care to avoid the injury. If driving off the shoulder of the road to avoid the collision was considered a fresh opportunity for Mr. Doe to avoid the collision, then his failure to so act could trigger the application of the last clear chance doctrine in our case, permitting our client's recovery.

CONCLUSION

Under current Maryland law, if Mr. Doe can prove that the client was speeding at the time the collision occurred, and that her speeding contributed to the personal injury and property damage she suffered, that contributory negligence could bar her recovery from the defendant for his negligence. However, the application of the boulevard rule in Maryland, where the plaintiff's speeding is all that is alleged to constitute her contributory negligence, would likely change this result, permitting her recovery.

Even if the client's contributory negligence can be established by the defendant, if the client can prove that the defendant had the last clear chance to avoid the collision, such as by driving onto the shoulder of the road, then the effect of her contributory negligence is negated and she can recover, fully, from the defendant for her injuries and other harm suffered. To establish the application of the last clear chance doctrine, the client must demonstrate that the defendant had a fresh opportunity to avoid the collision.

CONTRACTS

Paralegals commonly draft contracts as part of their practices. **Contracts** are legal documents used to evidence the terms and conditions of agreements between two or more parties; they are also called **agreements**. In some cases contracts are required to be in writing; while in other cases they can be oral (see Chapter 12 for a more thorough discussion of the substantive law of contracts). Parties to an agreement may choose to evidence their agreement in writing—via drafting and executing a contract—even where the agreement is not required to be in writing.

When parties wish to enter into a transaction, such as for the purchase of a car, they begin by negotiating the terms of their deal. (The skill of negotiation is discussed in Chapter 11.) After the parties have negotiated the deal terms, they may be required to, or may wish to, evidence their agreement in the form of a written contract. Both attorneys and paralegals routinely draft contracts.

> **Contracts** are legal documents that are used to evidence the terms and conditions of agreements between two or more parties; they are also called **agreements**.

To draft a contract, a drafter typically begins by locating a form contract for a similar transaction to use as the starting point. Form contracts are normally found either in the law firm or corporate law department's law library, in form books, or in form files maintained by the law practice. Using a form document and the deal terms, a drafter can construct an agreement to commemorate and evidence the parties' agreement.

After a contract is drafted by the legal representation of one party to it, the draft is then submitted to the other side for review and comment. This submission is often followed by contract revisions—perhaps several rounds of them—before a final draft is approved by all sides to the transaction. At that point, the parties will sign the contract, called contract execution. When a paralegal drafts a contract, the attorney from whom the assignment was delegated should review the draft before it is sent to the other side for consideration.

A contract has several parts. These may include a title, preamble, recitals, words of agreement, definitions section, action sections, other substantive business provisions, termination provisions, boilerplate/general provisions, signatures, and exhibits/schedules. Not all contracts have a separate definitions section, other substantive business provisions, and

Legal Ethics Note

Contract Drafting by Paralegals

When paralegals draft contracts, they should submit their drafts to their supervising attorneys for review before sending them out to the other side of the transaction.

KEY Point

Parts of a Contract

- Title
- Preamble
- Recitals
- Words of agreement
- Definitions section
- Action sections
- Other substantive business provisions
- Termination provisions
- Boilerplate/general provisions
- Signatures
- Exhibits/schedules

exhibits/schedules (see the sample contract in Figure 10-4), but most contracts contain all the other contract parts.

Contracts typically begin with a title. The title is centered on the top of the first page of the contract. Contract titles should reflect the nature of the contract, such as Settlement Agreement, Employment Agreement, or Asset Purchase Agreement.

The next part of a contract is the preamble. The preamble to a contract sets forth the name of the contract (exactly as it appears in the title), its date, and identifies the parties to it.

The next part of a contract is the recitals. The recitals provide background information about the parties, their relationship, and the purpose of the contract. In the traditional form, each recital begins with "WHEREAS" followed by a comma.

Words of agreement follow the recitals. These show that the parties agree to be bound by the terms and conditions of the contract; the traditional form of words of agreement includes a statement of consideration (see the words of agreement in Figure 10-4).

Some contracts have a separate definitions sections. Other contracts define contract terms whenever the commonly used terms appear for the first time in the contract. When a contract has a separate definitions section, it often appears immediately after the words of agreement (but does not have to).

The action sections of a contract appear next. These are the meat of the contract just like the body is the meat of a legal letter. Here is where the subject matter of the contract is discussed. For example, action sections may state that the parties are settling a legal dispute by one party paying the other some consideration, and that the lawsuit will be dismissed by the party who filed it.

Other substantive business provisions may follow the action sections. Other substantive business provisions include representations and warranties (for example, that the seller has good title to the property being sold under the contract) and conditions (for example, that the buyer's obligation to purchase the residence is conditioned upon him obtaining a mortgage in the amount of $450,000 at an interest rate not to exceed 6.5 percent).

Termination provisions typically come next. In termination provisions, parties can provide for what will happen when the contract ends, either under friendly terms (the consummation of the transaction to sell the vehicle) or unfriendly terms (when one party breaches the contract, entitling the other to a legal remedy).

General provisions, often called boilerplate provisions, are the last contract provisions before signatures. These are miscellaneous provisions that govern the administration of the contract, such as whether or not the contract can be assigned, and what law will apply to any dispute that arises under the contract.

Signatures follow the general provisions. This is where parties execute contracts, giving them legal effect.

Some contracts have exhibits or schedules. Exhibits and schedules come after the signature page. For example, in an employment agreement the action sections may reference that a employee will provide the employer certain services, and a list of those services, especially if lengthy, can be set forth in an exhibit or schedule.

The settlement agreement provided in Chapter 3 is repeated here for review of the parts of a contract.

Some legal documents are specifically related to civil lawsuits. The last type of legal writing we will discuss is pleadings and other litigation-related documents. These are examined next.

FIGURE 10-4 **Sample Contract**

[Title:]   Settlement Agreement

[Preamble:] THIS SETTLEMENT AGREEMENT (the "Agreement") is made and entered into this 15th day of July, 20__, by and between John M. Douglas, an individual residing at 84 Westbury Court, Syracuse, New York 13201 (the "Claimant"), and Robert F. Jones, an individual residing at 16 Simsbury Circle, Brookfield, Wisconsin 53005 (the "Opponent").

[Recitals:] WHEREAS, the parties have been involved in a legal dispute resulting in the litigation noted below, where the Claimant filed a legal action and the Opponent denied any liability and asserted certain counterclaims related thereto;

WHEREAS, this Agreement is made as a compromise between the parties for the complete and final settlement of their claims, differences, and causes of action with respect to the dispute now pending in Circuit Court in Onondaga County, New York entitled *Douglas v. Jones*, and identified as case number CV-9384756 (the "Action"); and

WHEREAS, the parties desire to reach a full and final compromise and settlement of all matters and all causes of action arising out of the facts and claims as set forth, pursuant to the terms and conditions hereof.

[Words of Agreement:]
NOW, THEREFORE, in consideration of the foregoing and other good and valuable consideration, the receipt and sufficiency of which is hereby acknowledged, the parties hereto agree as follows:

[Action Sections:]
1. The Opponent agrees to pay the Claimant eighty-five thousand dollars ($85,000), to be paid in a lump sum cash payment (the "Payment") on or before July 30, 20__.

2. Both parties hereto agree that all claims, demands, rights, and causes of action that either has or may have against the other with respect to the above-described dispute are satisfied, discharged, and settled.

3. The Claimant shall seek, obtain, and be bound by a dismissal with prejudice of the Action, with dismissal shall be obtained on or before August 1, 20__.

4. Each party hereto releases and discharges the other, and their heirs and legal representatives, from any and all claims, damages, causes of action of any kind, for personal injuries or property damage suffered by either in connection with the above-described dispute and the Action, whether now known or to become known, and whether existing or subsequently arising.

[General/Boilerplate Provisions:]
5. This Agreement shall be binding on and inure to the benefit of the parties and their respective legal representatives, successors, and assigns.

6.   Any dispute arising under the Agreement shall be resolved in accordance with the laws of the State of New York.

[Signatures:]

IN WITNESS WHEREOF, the parties hereby execute this Settlement Agreement on the day and year first above-written.

_____

John. M. Douglas

_____

Robert F. Jones

I, Lucy Stewart, Esq., attorney for the Claimant, have explained to my client all the terms and conditions of this Agreement, and my client has represented to me that all the terms and their significance are understood, and my client has signed this Agreement on my advice.
Dated:_____

_____

Lucy Stewart, Esq.

I, Marcy Abrams, attorney for the Opponent, have explained to my client all the terms and conditions of this Agreement, and my client has represented to me that all the terms and their significance are understood, and my client has signed this Agreement on my advice.
Dated:_____

_____

Marcy Abrams, Esq.

Sworn and subscribed before me this ___ day of July, 20__.

_____

Jordan Michaels
Notary Public
State of New York

PLEADINGS AND OTHER LITIGATION-RELATED DOCUMENTS

Pleadings

Paralegals engaged in litigation practice also draft pleadings, discovery requests and responses, and legal briefs, which are part of the process of civil litigation discussed in Chapter 3. These documents, written for the court in advocating a particular legal position on behalf of the client, are written persuasively. In other words, they are types of persuasive legal writing, written from the perspective of an advocate for a client's position, unlike legal memoranda, which are written objectively from a neutral position. We will examine pleadings first.

Both attorneys and paralegals typically prepare pleadings for civil cases. **Pleadings** are the initial documents prepared by the parties in either bringing a lawsuit or in responding to the filing of a lawsuit. A pleading is called the **complaint** when it is filed by the plaintiff and initiates the lawsuit. The defendant's response

> **Pleadings** are the initial documents prepared by the parties in either bringing a lawsuit or in responding to the filing of a lawsuit.
>
> A **complaint** is the initial document prepared by a party to bring a lawsuit.

to the plaintiff's complaint is called the **answer**. A **counter-claim** is a claim initiated by the defendant against the plaintiff. A **cross-claim** is a claim initiated by one plaintiff against another, or by one defendant against another. Whether a complaint, answer, counterclaim, or cross-claim, the pleadings inform the other side of the claims or defenses asserted against him and the facts alleged in support of those claims or defenses.

To initiate a civil lawsuit, the plaintiff files a complaint with the appropriate court, be it federal or state. In addition, the complaint is served on the defendant, called service of process, to notify the defendant of the action filed against him so that he can defend himself to the court. The complaint must be filed within the period of time prescribed by law, for statutes of limitations and statutes of repose define time limits for bringing particular kinds of lawsuits.

A complaint typically contains the following information. It begins with a caption. The caption is like the heading of a legal memorandum. It names the parties to the action, the court in which the complaint is filed, the case number (called a docket number by some courts) assigned by the court, and identifies the document as a complaint. Because the case or docket number is assigned by the court after it receives the complaint,

Parts of a Complaint
- Caption
- Jurisdictional allegations
- General allegations
- Prayer for relief
- Signature
- Demand for jury trial, if there is a right to jury trial and it is not waived

the drafter of the complaint leaves a blank line after "Case Number" for the court to fill in once a number is assigned.

Next, allegations supporting the jurisdiction of the court over the persons and subject matter of the dispute are set forth. The court set to hear the case must have the authority to hear a case involving these parties. It must also have the authority to adjudicate this type of action. Each jurisdictional allegation is numbered, and they are logically arranged to support both personal and subject matter jurisdiction, as discussed in Chapter 4.

The general allegations follow the jurisdictional allegations in a complaint. The general allegations constitute the body, or meat, of the complaint. The general allegations set forth the claims being made by the plaintiff. They do so by presenting the facts supporting each element of each cause of action alleged, as well as outlining the injury suffered by the plaintiff and the relief sought. Each allegation is set forth separately and numbered. Allegations are then arranged in a logical order, which may be chronological. The numbers of the general allegations sequentially follow the numbers of the jurisdictional allegations. So, if there are three jurisdictional allegations, the first general allegation is numbered "4," the next general allegation is numbered "5," and so on. Remember that a pleading, such as a complaint, is persuasive legal writing. In the general allegations, the drafter should advocate the client's position, presenting the facts both truthfully and in a light most favorable to the client.

Next, a request for the court to grant a remedy is made by the plaintiff. This is called a "prayer for relief."

STATUTE *on* POINT

Ind. Code § 34-20-3-1 (2011).

Indiana Statutes of Limitations and Repose for Products Liability Actions

In Indiana, products liability actions must be brought within two years after the cause of action accrues (statute of limitations) or ten years after delivery of the product to the initial user or consumer (statute of repose).

Effect of Missing a Statute of Limitations or Repose

The effect of not filing a lawsuit within the time prescribed by a governing statute of limitations or statute of repose is that the lawsuit is barred, meaning it can never be brought.

What if a client comes to an attorney before the running (expiration) of a statute of limitations or statute of repose but the attorney misses the filing deadline? Not only is the lawsuit barred, but the attorney can be subject to malpractice liability and/or discipline for violation of the legal ethics rules on competency.

An **answer** is the initial document prepared by a party responding to a lawsuit being filed against her.

A **counterclaim** is a claim initiated by the defendant in a case against the plaintiff.

A **cross-claim** is a claim initiated by one plaintiff against another, or by one defendant against another.

Signature follows the prayer for relief. If the plaintiff is not represented by counsel, she signs the complaint. Often, a plaintiff has legal counsel. If the plaintiff is represented by counsel, then counsel filing the pleading signs the complaint. By signing the complaint, the attorney certifies that he has read the complaint and is familiar with the facts and claims presented in it, that there exists a basis in law for the claims asserted, that there is no improper purpose (such as to harass) for filing the pleading, that an investigation of the facts was conducted, and that to the best of his knowledge the information contained in the complaint is true and accurate. In some courts, a similar statement is prepared for the plaintiff to sign. This statement, called a verification, is a certification by the client that the information contained in the complaint is true.

Finally, if there is a right to jury trial and it has not been waived, a demand for jury trial is made. In federal courts and most states where there is a right to jury trial, one of the parties must request a jury trial, or the right to jury trial is presumed to be waived. A sample negligence complaint is provided in Figure 10-5.

The Right to Jury Trial

The Sixth Amendment to the U.S. Constitution guarantees a right to jury trial in criminal prosecutions.

The Seventh Amendment to the U.S. Constitution provides a right to jury trial in certain civil cases. This Amendment guarantees the right to a jury trial in federal courts in all civil actions when the amount in controversy exceeds $20. Most state constitutions have a similar guarantee, but some states have raised the minimum dollar restriction.[1] Note that this guarantee requires there be an amount in controversy—so an action where damages are sought. Remember that sometimes damages are not the remedy sought, but rather an equitable remedy, such as an injunction, is sought. For example, if a person regularly trespasses on the client's land but does not harm the land, the remedy sought is an injunction to stop the trespass, not damages. There is no right to jury trial in such cases.

FIGURE 10-5 **Sample Negligence Complaint**

JANE SMITH,	)	IN THE CIRCUIT COURT
Plaintiff	)	FOR
	)	BALTIMORE CITY,
v.	)	MARYLAND
	)	
JACKSON DOE,	)	Civil Action No. 01-C-01-12345
Defendant	)	

COMPLAINT FOR NEGLIGENCE AND DEMAND FOR JURY TRIAL

Plaintiff, Jane Smith, by her undersigned counsel, sues Defendant, Jackson Doe, and in support, alleges as follows:

1.

Plaintiff Jane Smith is a resident of Baltimore City, Maryland.

2.

Defendant Jackson Doe is a resident of Baltimore City, Maryland.

3.

This action arises out of an automobile collision which occurred on July 6, 2011, on the Jones Falls Expressway, near the ramp for Druid Hills Parkway, both public roads in Maryland.

4.

At approximately 9:50 a.m., while driving north on the Jones Falls Expressway, Plaintiff's vehicle was violently struck on the passenger's side by Defendant's vehicle while Defendant was merging onto the Jones Falls Expressway from the Druid Hills Parkway ramp.

(continued)

Plaintiff was driving in a careful and prudent manner in the moments before and at the time of the collision.

6.

It was the duty of Defendant to use reasonable care to watch where he was driving, to maintain a proper lookout for other automobiles, to drive at an appropriate speed, to yield the right of way to oncoming traffic while performing a merge onto the expressway, and to operate and control his automobile in a reasonable manner when performing a merge onto the expressway in order to avoid a collision.

7.

Defendant breached his duty of care to Plaintiff by failing to use reasonable care when performing a merge onto the expressway, by failing to watch where he was driving, by failing to maintain a proper lookout for other automobiles, by failing to drive at an appropriate speed on the merge lane, by not yielding the right of way to oncoming traffic while performing a merge onto the expressway, and by failing to operate and control his automobile in a reasonable manner when performing a merge onto the expressway in order to avoid a collision.

8.

Plaintiff suffered severe physical injuries and mental anguish, and her automobile extensive damage, as a direct and proximate result of Defendant's negligence in causing the collision. Plaintiff has incurred expenses for medical care and treatment, medicines, nursing services, physical therapy, and other medical services. Plaintiff has lost wages and will continue to lose wages in the future due to the injuries she sustained. Plaintiff continues to suffer physical pain and discomfort due to injuries sustained. Plaintiff's automobile was towed to an auto body shop, where it underwent extensive repairs. All the above damages were directly and proximately caused by the aforementioned negligence of Defendant and were incurred without contributory negligence or assumption of the risk on the part of Plaintiff, and Plaintiff also did not have the opportunity to avoid this accident.

WHEREFORE, Plaintiff demands judgment against Defendant for ONE MILLION DOLLARS ($1,000,000.00) in damages, plus interests and costs of the action, and any further relief the court considers proper.

DEMAND FOR JURY TRIAL

Plaintiff demands a trial by jury.

This 27th day of October, 2011.

Respectfully submitted,

LOWELL, ROWE & TURNBILL, P.A.

By:_____
Sylvia G. Rowe, Esq.
Maryland State Bar No. 5397045
3000 N. Charles Street, Suite 100
Baltimore, Maryland 21210
(410) 372-6500
Attorney for Plaintiff

To avoid a default judgment being entered against her, the defendant must respond to the plaintiff's complaint in a pleading called an answer. In the defendant's answer, the defendant responds to the allegations made by the plaintiff in the complaint by admitting or denying each of them, or stating that she has insufficient knowledge at the time to admit or deny them. She also asserts affirmative defense in her answer, such as the plaintiff's contributory or comparative negligence, which tell the court the reasons why she believes she is not liable to the plaintiff. She may also assert counterclaims against the plaintiff relating to the same incident, such as that the plaintiff's negligence caused the collision. She may assert cross-claims against other defendants named in the complaint; for example, that the defendant was the passenger, not the driver, of the car that caused the collision that injured not only the plaintiff but also this defendant. Like other pleadings, answers are signed by the defendant (her attorney, if she is represented by counsel), include a prayer for judgment, and can include a demand for jury trial.

Both attorneys and paralegals routinely draft pleadings in civil cases; styles, formatting, and the like for use in drafting pleadings can often be obtained from the law firm's or corporate law department's forms files. In preparing litigation documents, requirements of the particular court must be followed, both in content and in formatting.

There are general form books, such as *American Jurisprudence Legal Forms* and *West's Legal Forms*, that alphabetically

Form Books

Form books are secondary sources of law that can be useful for attorneys and paralegals who regularly represent clients in litigation or who routinely draft legal documents such as contracts and wills. Form books contain sample forms that drafters can use in preparing legal documents, including litigation-related documents such as pleadings and motions.

Legal writers may use form books as a beginning point for drafting legal documents, especially when their law offices have no relevant forms in their forms files. Forms found in form books can also be useful checklists for legal writers to ensure they have not overlooked any important language in their documents. When using forms found in form books, a legal writer should carefully review a form to make certain that all provisions contained in the form are relevant for her document and omit provisions that do not apply.

State-Specific Form Books

Form books are published for each state, among other types of form books. These state-specific form books include forms tailored using the jurisdiction's law. An example is *California Forms of Pleading and Practice*, published by Matthew Bender.

arrange subjects by topic in a manner similar to encyclopedias. Many contain a topical index. General form books provide forms on substantive legal matters such as wills, leases, and other types of contracts, called legal forms. They also provide litigation-related forms such as forms of pleadings and motions, called pleading and practice forms.

Some publishers publish form books that are limited in subject matter to a particular area of law. Typical areas of law with specialty form books include corporate law, real estate law, bankruptcy, taxation, contracts, and pleading and practice.

Further, most states have legal form books for their jurisdictions. These form books may be published by the state's courts, the state's bar association, or a private publisher. If a legal writer is drafting a document that must comply with state law, such as a will, it is critical for the drafter to use a form that incorporates the current state law requirements.

Some of the better form books also include annotations on the law relating to particular forms. *American Jurisprudence Pleading and Practice Forms Annotated* is an example of a form book set containing annotations that is found in most law libraries. This form book set can be especially useful to attorneys and paralegals who work in the area of litigation.

Forms also may be found online, though their reliability depends on their source. Reliable sources of online forms can be found on Westlaw, LexisNexis, and Findlaw Forms.

When using any form, whether from a form book or a law office's forms files, always adapt the form to fit your particular legal matter. All forms should be customized to properly address

Use examples and forms, or prior documents that you can use as guidance in drafting. It is very helpful to keep a library of forms from prior use.
Christine Rentz

FIGURE 10-6 Sample Answer to the Complaint from Figure 10-5

JANE SMITH,	)	IN THE CIRCUIT COURT
Plaintiff	)	FOR
	)	BALTIMORE CITY,
v.	)	MARYLAND
	)	
JACKSON DOE,	)	Civil Action No. 01-C-01-12345
Defendant	)	

ANSWER

Defendant, Jackson Doe, by his undersigned counsel, and in answer to the Complaint filed herein, states as follows:

1.   Defendant is without knowledge or information sufficient to form a belief as to the truth of the allegations contained in Paragraph 1 of Plaintiff's Complaint.

2.   Defendant admits the allegations of Paragraphs 2 and 3.

3.   Defendant denies the allegations of Paragraphs 4, 5, 6, and 7.

4.   Defendant is without knowledge or information sufficient to form a belief as to the truth of the allegations contained in Paragraph 8.

AFFIRMATIVE DEFENSE

If Plaintiff was injured as alleged, then those injuries were caused by the sole and/or contributory negligence of Plaintiff.

WHEREFORE, Defendant respectfully prays that the Complaint be dismissed, with costs to be adjudged against Plaintiff, or such other relief as the court considers proper.

Respectfully submitted,

HARDY & JAMES, P.A.

By:_____
Glenn S. Hardy, Esq.
Maryland State Bar No. 9548347
485 Pratt Street
Baltimore, Maryland 21202
(410) 546-7345
Attorney for Defendant

the client's situation. In other words, forms are the starting point in legal document drafting.

Paralegals who work in the area of litigation may draft discovery requests and responses. Discovery requests and responses are examined next.

Discovery Requests and Responses

Attorneys and paralegals also draft discovery requests and responses. Remember from Chapter 3 that **discovery** is the process of searching for and obtaining information and evidence relevant to a case. Paralegals play a particularly important role in drafting discovery requests and responses.

The purpose of drafting discovery documents is to facilitate factual investigations and gather evidence relating to the case. There are several important discovery devices, including interrogatories, depositions, requests for production, requests for examination, and requests for admission. All involve legal writing in some way, as discussed below.

Interrogatories are written questions prepared by a party, submitted to the other party, to be answered under oath. Note that interrogatories must be answered in writing, under oath, by the party asked. A paralegal for the party seeking the answers may draft the interrogatories. A paralegal for the party receiving interrogatories may draft her client's responses. Whether drafting the interrogatories or responding to interrogatories received, a paralegal should submit her work to the supervising attorney for review and approval.

In drafting interrogatories, begin with the case caption (similar to a caption in a pleading, illustrated earlier.) The caption should identify the party presenting the interrogatories and whether they are the first or a later set of interrogatories—for example, "Plaintiff's First Interrogatories to Defendant." Next, name the party who is to answer the interrogatories, provide instructions for that party, and define terms used in the interrogatories if definitions are appropriate. The body of the document contains the interrogatories themselves. These are the numbered questions to which the receiving party must respond. Some courts limit the number of interrogatories that can be asked, so the drafter of interrogatories must be aware of the relevant court rules. Write interrogatories clearly and arrange them logically. After the interrogatories, draft a signature line for the attorney to sign the document, followed by the attorney's name and address.

Interrogatories must be answered within the time period required by the rules of civil procedure (30 days under Federal Rules of Civil Procedure 33). In responding to interrogatories, it

is important that the answers be drafted both truthfully, as they are given under oath, and skillfully, to support the client's position (to the extent possible) and to not volunteer information not specifically requested in the interrogatories. Paralegals may work closely with clients, under attorney supervision, in drafting appropriate interrogatory responses. Figure 10-7 contains sample interrogatories for an auto accident personal injury case.

Depositions are the sworn testimony of a party or witness given during a question and answer proceeding conducted before trial. Depositions are conducted orally, so are not a form of written discovery. However, paralegals may be involved in drafting deposition questions ahead of time, for review by the

Discovery is the process of searching for and obtaining information and evidence relevant to a case.

Interrogatories are written questions prepared by a party, submitted to the other party, to be answered under oath.

Depositions are the sworn testimony of a party or witness given during a question and answer proceeding conducted before trial.

FIGURE
10-7 Interrogatories

IN THE CIRCUIT COURT FOR BALTIMORE CITY, MARYLAND

<table>
<tr><td>James Smith- Plaintiff</td><td>*</td><td></td></tr>
<tr><td></td><td>*</td><td></td></tr>
<tr><td>v.</td><td>*</td><td>CASE NO. 12-C-34-56789</td></tr>
<tr><td></td><td>*</td><td></td></tr>
<tr><td>Robert Jones- Defendant</td><td>*</td><td></td></tr>
<tr><td></td><td>*</td><td></td></tr>
</table>

PLAINTIFF'S INTERROGATORIES TO DEFENDANT

TO: Robert Jones, Defendant

FROM: James Smith, Plaintiff

The Plaintiff, James Smith, by his attorneys, Virginia George and George & Lyons, P.C., requests that the Defendant, Robert Jones, answer the following Interrogatories fully, under oath, and in accordance with the Maryland Rule of Civil Procedure, Rule 2-421, subject to the instructions set forth below:

INSTRUCTIONS

a.   These Interrogatories are continuing in character so as to require you to file supplementary answers if you obtain further or different information before trial.

b.   Unless otherwise stated, these Interrogatories refer to the time, place, and circumstances of the auto accident and personal injuries mentioned or complained of in the Complaint.

c.   Where name and identity of a person is required, please state full name, home address, and also business address, if known.

d.   Where knowledge or information in possession of a party is requested, such request includes knowledge of the party's agents, representatives, and unless privileged, his attorneys.

e.   The pronoun "you" refers to the party to whom the Interrogatories are addressed and the parties mentioned in clause (d).

f.   "Identify" when referring to an individual, corporation, or other entity shall mean to set forth the name and telephone number, and if a corporation or other entity, its principle place of business, or if an individual, the present or last known home address, his or her job title or titles, by whom employed and address of the place of employment.

g.   "Auto Accident" is defined as the car accident that occurred on January 5, 20011, as referenced in the Plaintiff's Complaint.

INTERROGATORIES

1.   Please state your full name, home address (and all home addresses for the last five (5) years), social security number, date of birth, and your marital status. Include in your answer the names of those who have lived with you in the five (5) year period before the accident.

2.   Please state the name and address of your employer, your position and duties, and your wages at the time of the auto accident and at the present time.

3.   If you contend that the personal injuries suffered by the Plaintiff were not caused by the Auto Accident, state with particularity the facts upon which you base your contention.

4.   Please state in detail your itinerary on the date of the Auto Accident, including each place at which you were present, your length of stay at each such place, and a detailed account of whom you saw and what you did at each such place.

5.   Please identify all persons known to you to have personal knowledge of the facts pertaining to the Auto Accident, indicate those who were eyewitnesses, and state the substance of their knowledge and articulate their expected testimony.

6.   Please identify all persons (excluding attorneys) who investigated the cause and circumstances of the Auto Accident for you.

7.   Please identify all persons who arrived at the scene of the Auto Accident within one (1) hour after its occurrence.

8.   Please identify the motor vehicle you were operating at the time of the Auto Accident, including its make, model, year, registration number, and registered owner.

9.   If you were not the owner of the vehicle mentioned in Interrogatory No. 8, please identify its owner, stating his, her, or its relationship to you, whether you had his, her, or its permission to operate the vehicle, the purpose for which you were operating the vehicle, and how you came to be operating the vehicle.

10.   Please identify all persons to whom you have given signed statements regarding the Auto Accident, the date thereof, and the name of the person in whose custody each is at this time.

11.   Please identify all persons who have given you signed statements regarding the Auto Accident or the personal injuries suffered by the Plaintiff in the Auto Accident.

12.   Please state whether you have within your possession or control photographs, plats, or diagrams of the scene of the Auto Accident or objects connected with the Auto Accident, stating what those objects are.

13.   Please give a concise statement of facts as to how you contend the Auto Accident took place.

14.   If you contend that the Plaintiff acted in such a manner as to cause or contribute to his personal injuries, state all facts upon which you rely in your contention.

15.   Please identify all expert witnesses who will be called at the trial of this case, the area of expertise of each, and a summary of the expected testimony of each.

16.   Please state whether you consumed any drugs, medicines, or alcoholic beverages within twenty-four (24) hours prior to the Auto Accident, the place where such drugs, medicines, or alcoholic beverages were obtained, the nature of the drugs, medicines, or alcoholic beverages, and the amount thereof.

17.   Please state whether you were under the care of a physician at the time of the Auto Accident. If so, please state the name and address of your physician, specify the illness or condition for which you were treated, and list any medications prescribed.

(continued)

18.	Please state when and where you obtained your learner's permit and your driver's license, including whether such permit or license is or was subject to any restriction, and the nature of such restriction, if any.

19.	Please list all insurance agreements you have made regarding the vehicle you were operating at the time of the Auto Accident, including the name of the owner, the name of the insurance carrier, the policy number, the type of coverage, the amount of coverage (specifying its upper and lower limits), and the effective dates of said policy for the past five (5) years.

20.	Please state whether you had any other insurance policies in effect at the time of the Auto Accident covering bodily injuries caused to other person. If so, please provide all pertinent information, including the name of the insurer, the policy number, the type of coverage, the amount of coverage (specifying its upper and lower limits), and the effective dates of said policy.

21.	Please list all prior motor vehicle accidents in which you have been involved, either with other persons or with property. Please include the name of any other driver or property owner involved, the location of the accident, the date and time of the accident, and the disposition of the matter.

22.	Please list all violations of the motor vehicle laws of the State of Maryland or any other jurisdiction with which you have been charged since you obtained your driver's license.

23.	Please state whether your automobile insurance has ever been cancelled, and if so, state the name of the insurer and the reason for cancellation.

24.	Please state whether the Plaintiff's vehicle was moving at the time of the auto accident, and if so, state the direction and speed of the vehicle to the best of your recollection.

25.	Please state in detail which part of your vehicle came into contact with which part of the Plaintiff's vehicle when the Auto Accident occurred.

26.	If you and the Plaintiff had any conversation after the Auto Accident, please state the substance of any such conversation.

27.	Please state in detail all actions you took or attempted to take in order to avoid the Auto Accident.

28.	Please identify all person(s) who drove with you during the day of the occurrence, including their full names and current addresses and telephone numbers.

29.	If any members of your family or anyone else had any conversation(s) with the Plaintiff, please state to the best of your knowledge the place of such conversation(s) and the nature of such conversation(s).

Respectfully submitted,

George & Lyons, P.C.

Virginia George
321 Charles Street, Suite 400
Baltimore, Maryland 21212
(410) 444-1000
(410) 444-1001(facsimile)

supervising attorney. Only attorneys may take depositions, according to the legal ethics rules, but paralegals may be involved in preparing deposition questions (and may attend depositions as well). After a deposition is taken, paralegals often prepare summaries of deposition transcripts.

Requests for production are written requests by a party to another party for documents or other tangible things, such as written contracts, or for permission to enter on the land or other property of a party for the purpose of conducting an inspection. **Requests for examination** are requests by a party to the court asking the court to order the other party to submit to a physical or mental examination. **Requests for admission** are requests by a party to the other party asking her to admit the truth of certain matters relating to the lawsuit. These requests are often drafted by paralegals, subject to review and approval by their supervising attorneys. Similarly, paralegals often are involved in working with their clients to respond to these requests. Figure 10-8 provides a form for requesting a physical examination in Superior Court in Delaware.

> **Requests for production** are written requests by a party to another party for documents or other tangible things, such as written contracts, or for permission to enter on the land or other property of a party for the purpose of conducting an inspection.
>
> **Requests for examination** are requests by a party to the court asking the court to order the other party to submit to a physical or mental examination.
>
> **Requests for admission** are requests by a party to the other party asking her to admit the truth of certain matters relating to the lawsuit.

FIGURE 10-8   Request for Physical Examination, Superior Court, Delaware

---

IN THE SUPERIOR COURT OF THE STATE OF DELAWARE

COUNTY: NEW CASTLE _____   KENT _____   SUSSEX _____

_____   :

Plaintiff(s)   :

     :   C. A. No.:

     :

v.   :

_____   :

Defendant(s)   :

REQUEST FOR PHYSICAL EXAM

Defendant, _____, hereby requests a medical examination of plaintiff, _____, regarding the injuries alleged. The examination is to be conducted by _____, at his/her office at _____, on _____, _____, 20__ at _____ o'clock.

_____

Attorney for Defendant

DATED: _____

Another litigation-related document that may be drafted by paralegals is a legal brief. Legal briefs are studied next.

Legal Briefs

Legal briefs are documents prepared by attorneys, advocacy organizations, or governments and submitted to the courts to present arguments in support of legal positions. They are sometimes just called briefs. Legal briefs are a form of persuasive legal writing, for they advocate the positions of clients. They are distinguishable from case briefs as discussed in Chapter 9.

The function of legal briefs is to set forth facts that are proven or to be proven at trial and present arguments applying those facts to applicable law to demonstrate why a party to litigation should prevail. Paralegals often help attorneys research to find the applicable law and draft legal briefs.

There are three main types of legal briefs. They are trial briefs, appellate briefs, and *amicus curiae* briefs. Trial briefs are submitted to trial courts before trial of cases setting forth arguments to be made during the upcoming trials. The purpose of a trial brief is to "convince" the trial judge prior to the start of trial that your interpretation of the case is the correct one. Appellate briefs are submitted to appellate courts stating their parties' positions on issues to be reviewed on appeal. Appellate briefs outline each party's view of the proper application of the law to the facts of the case. *Amicus curiae* briefs are submitted by nonparties in the lawsuit who are interested in the outcome of the litigation. *Amicus curiae* briefs are typically filed by advocacy groups, like the American Civil Liberties Union (ACLU) and government officials (such as the U.S. Attorney General).

KEY Point

Three Main Types of Legal Briefs

The three main types of legal briefs are trial briefs, appellate briefs, and *amicus curiae* briefs.

Legal briefs may contain the following parts: a title page, a table of contents, a table of authorities alphabetically listing laws referred to within the brief, a statement of the legal issues involved in the case, a statement of relevant facts that have been established, a statement indicating whether the party requests to make an oral argument, an argument section (the main part of the brief) that provides the parties' legal arguments, and a conclusion in which the party summarizes his position and states the relief requested. Exhibits, such as records and affidavits, may support a legal brief.

KEY Point

Components of a Legal Brief
- A title page
- A table of contents
- A table of authorities
- A statement of the legal issues
- A statement of the facts
- A statement requesting oral argument
- An argument section
- A conclusion
- Exhibits

Each court has its own rules for submitting legal briefs, with requirements including page limits, formatting rules, and filing deadlines. A party must file his legal brief with the court and submit a copy to the other party(ies) by a certain date. Then the other party(ies) have a certain number of days after receiving service of the brief to file a responsive brief. Judges review the briefs submitted, the record, and sometimes hear oral arguments in making their rulings.

Settlement agreements are another type of litigation-related document. Settlement agreements are discussed next.

Settlement Agreements

Settlement agreements are frequently drafted by attorneys and paralegals in litigation practice. As discussed in Chapter 3, **settlement agreements** are contracts entered into by parties to legal disputes that set forth the terms and conditions of the resolution and settlement of the disputes. So in litigation practice, when litigation is settled out of court, settlement agreements are drafted to evidence the terms and conditions of the parties' legal settlement. Because settlement agreements are types of contracts, they were addressed, and a sample provided, earlier in this chapter.

Legal briefs are documents prepared by attorneys, advocacy organizations, or governments and submitted to the courts to present arguments in support of legal positions; they are also called briefs.

Settlement agreements are contracts entered into by parties to legal disputes that set forth the terms and conditions of the resolution and settlement of the disputes.

CHAPTER SUMMARY

- Legal writing skills are critical to paralegal success. Legal writing is a type of technical writing used by lawyers, judges, and legislators to communicate legal analysis and legal rights and duties. Legal writing may be objective, meaning neutral and unbiased, or persuasive, meaning advocating a particular legal position.

- Good writing skills are useful to legal writing and include the ability to write for your audience; follow directions; use plain language and avoid legalese; use good grammar; pay attention to sentence, paragraph, and overall structure; use active voice; be organized, structured, clear, and concise; avoid redundancy; use appropriate formatting and style; be consistent in your writing and formatting; be gender-neutral in your writing; avoid the use of contractions and abbreviations; and proofread.

- Types of legal documents that paralegals commonly draft include legal correspondence, legal memoranda, contracts, and pleadings and other litigation-related documents.

- Legal correspondence means legal letters. The four types of legal correspondence include informative letters, opinion letters, confirmation letters, and demand letters. The basic components of a legal letter are the date; the method of delivery; the name, title, and address of the recipient; a reference line; a salutation or greeting; the body of the letter; a closing; the signature and title of the sender; the initials of the author and the typist; enclosures, if any; and copy recipients, if any.

- Legal memoranda are documents that thoroughly analyze and summarize the law in a particular area, on the basis of legal research, and inform the requestor of the strengths and weaknesses of the client's legal position. Legal memoranda are written for internal use by a law office and provide an objective analysis of the law on a particular matter. The parts of a legal memorandum typically include a heading, a statement of the facts, the questions presented, an analysis/discussion, and a conclusion.

- Contracts are legal documents used to evidence the terms and conditions of agreements between two or more parties; they are also called agreements. Parts of a contract may include a title, preamble, recitals, words of agreement, definitions section, action sections, other substantive business provisions, termination provisions, boilerplate/general provisions, signatures, and exhibits/schedules.

- Pleadings are the initial documents prepared by the parties in either bringing lawsuits or in responding to the filing of lawsuits. A complaint is the initial document prepared by a party to bring a lawsuit. An answer is the initial document prepared by a party responding to a lawsuit being filed against her. A counterclaim is a claim initiated by the defendant in a case against the plaintiff. A cross-claim is a claim initiated by one plaintiff against another, or by one defendant against another.

- The typical parts of a complaint are a caption, jurisdictional allegations, general allegations, a prayer for relief, a signature, and a demand for jury trial if jury trial is requested. A complaint must meet the content and format requirements of the court in which it is filed.

- Discovery is the process of searching for and obtaining information and evidence relevant to a case. Interrogatories are written questions prepared by a party, submitted to the other party, to be answered under oath. Depositions are the sworn testimony of a party or witness given during a question and answer proceeding conducted before trial. Requests for production are written requests by a party to another party for documents or other tangible things, such as written contracts, or for permission to enter onto the land or other property of a party for the purpose of conducting an inspection. Requests for examination are requests by a party to the court asking the court to order the other party to submit to a physical or mental examination. Requests for admission are requests by a party to the other party asking her to admit the truth of certain matters relating to the lawsuit. Paralegals often draft discovery requests and responses.

- Legal briefs are documents prepared by attorneys, advocacy organizations, or governments and submitted to the courts in order to present arguments in support of legal positions. The three main types of legal briefs are trial briefs, appellate briefs, and *amicus curiae* briefs. Components of a legal brief include a title page, a table of contents, a table of authorities, a statement of the legal issues, a statement of the facts, a statement requesting an oral argument, an argument section, a conclusion, and exhibits. Paralegals often assist attorneys in writing legal briefs.

- Settlement agreements are contracts entered into by parties to legal disputes that set forth the terms and conditions of the resolution and settlement of the disputes. They may be drafted by paralegals who practice litigation.

CONCEPT REVIEW AND REINFORCEMENT

Key Terms and Concepts

Legal writing
Objective legal writing
Persuasive legal writing
Legalese
Legal correspondence
Legal memoranda
Contracts
Agreements
Pleadings
Complaint

Questions for Review

1. What is legal writing?
2. What are some important good writing skills?
3. What is legal correspondence?
4. What are the four different types of legal letters?
5. What are the different parts of a legal letter?
6. What is a legal memorandum?
7. What is the purpose of a legal memorandum?
8. Is a legal memorandum objective or persuasive, legal writing?
9. What are the parts of a legal memorandum?
10. What is a contract?
11. What are the parts of a contract?
12. What is a complaint?
13. What are the parts of a complaint?
14. How do you draft an answer to a complaint?
15. What different types of documents may be drafted or responded to during the discovery process?
16. What is the purpose of legal briefs?
17. What are the three main types of legal briefs?
18. What are the components of a legal brief?

DEVELOPING YOUR PARALEGAL SKILLS

Critical Thinking Exercises

1. What type of legal letter is the sample letter found in Figure 10-1?
2. What type of legal letter is the sample letter found in Figure 10-2?
3. Using Duke University Law School's website information on legal forms found at http://www.law.duke.edu/lib/researchguides/formbks, answer the following questions:
   a. West's Legal Forms and American Jurisprudence Legal Forms are examples of what kinds of legal forms?
   b. Identify three good online sources of legal forms.
   c. Are legal forms available by area of law (subject)? If so, give three examples of legal forms by subject.
   d. Are legal forms available by jurisdiction? Explain your answer. Who publishes these form books?

Negotiation and Settlement Exercise

The Crestview Country Club pool has both a diving board and a slide at its deep end. Whenever swimmers are in the water, at least two lifeguards must be on duty, according to pool policy. A warning sign posted on the slide says, "Rider must ride feet first, on his/her back, with hands crossed over the chest, to avoid serious injury." Lifeguards are trained to monitor that swimmers use the pool slide properly. Timothy, a bit of a daredevil, rides down the slide head first, on his stomach. Unfortunately, he enters the water in a dive posture and slices to the bottom of the pool, where he hits his head and traumatizes his neck and spine, suffering serious injury, including permanent paralysis. At the time of the incident, the lifeguards were in the staff lounge, playing cards and having an afternoon snack. Timothy sues the Crestview Country Club for the tort of negligence (in Circuit Court of Norfolk County, case number CV-962547), seeking $1.25 million in compensatory damages, alleging that the country club failed to use reasonable care by not having lifeguards on duty who could have saved him or instructed him to ride the slide properly. The country club will defend the action by asserting that Timothy's own negligence, in riding the slide in the dangerous head-first position, contrary to pool policy and to the warning sign posted on the slide itself, caused or contributed to his injuries. The country club carries liability insurance in the amount of $750,000 and is in a state of financial difficulty. If the country club is ordered to pay an adverse judgment of more than $250,000, it will be bankrupted.

Partner with another student in class and each take a role as an attorney representing one of the parties. Negotiate a settlement of this legal dispute. Next, draft a settlement agreement reflecting your terms of settlement of this case. Share your settlement terms with the class.

Assignments and Practical Applications

You are an associate attorney with a plaintiff's firm that specializes in tort cases, especially personal injury matters. Draft a letter to your client, Sara Whitman, confirming your appointment with her, at your firm's offices (Franklin, Whiting & Sullivan, P.A., 145 Charles Avenue, Sparks, Maryland 21110) on November 15 of this year. You plan to meet at 10:00 a.m. to prepare her to testify at her upcoming trial. The meeting should last about two hours. Remind her to bring with her records of the physical therapy she is receiving, including the treatment plan prepared by her physician.

Your supervising attorney, Monica White, wants to know if the client's products liability claim is barred by the state's statute of limitations or statute of repose. Statutes of limitations and statutes of repose impose time limits on when particular types of legal actions can be brought, and once a statute has "run," the action is time-barred and can no longer be brought. The facts of your client's case are that she bought a clothes washer and dryer from Sears just over eleven years ago. Sears delivered and installed the washer and dryer the week after they were purchased. Almost three years ago, during a drying cycle, the clothes dryer overheated and caught on fire. The client was picking up her children from school when the fire started. By the time the client returned to the home, half of the first floor was aflame. The fire department eventually put out the fire, but extensive damage was caused to the home and its contents. In addition, the family dog suffered from the heat and smoke and required veterinary care. The type of action involved is a tort action, specifically, a products liability action. The client said she was so busy dealing with clean up and renovations after the fire that she did not seek legal advice until now. Your supervising attorney wants to know if it is too late to bring the client's products liability claim because almost three years have passed since the fire and more than eleven years have passed since the purchase of the clothes dryer. *Draft a legal memorandum to your supervising attorney analyzing the client's position on this issue using the law in your jurisdiction.*

Research in your school's or a local law library to find a form book specific for your state. Review the types of forms found in the book. If it has a form for a complaint, you can use that in the next exercise, which requires you to draft a negligence complaint.

Exactly 3 months ago today, Judy Miller went grocery shopping at Waul's Food Market in Lutherville, Maryland, located in Baltimore City. While strolling past the soda aisle, a display of soda bottles became unstable, toppling to the ground in a noisy crash. Unfortunately, several of the falling bottles struck Judy, causing her to be knocked to the floor, where she hit her head and suffered a mild concussion. Judy also broke her left arm and sprained her right ankle in the incident. Several other customers witnessed the occurrence, causing Judy embarrassment in addition to her physical injuries. One of these customers came to Judy's aid, calling 911 on her behalf, when no store employee came to render assistance. Pretend you are a lawyer and have agreed to represent Judy in her tort action, specifically, her negligence claim against the store. Draft the complaint you will file in Baltimore City Circuit Court to initiate the lawsuit. You may follow the format in Figure 10-5 for a negligence complaint or the format specific to your jurisdiction if you know or can find it.

Technology Resources and Internet Exercises

For additional resources, you can read an overview on legal writing found at http://topics.law.cornell.edu/wex/Legal_writing.

Pick a local trial court in your area. Look on the website for that court. Find the court's requirements for filing a complaint, including both content and format requirements. Be sure to find the amount of filing fee. Write an office memorandum summarizing those requirements (see Chapter 8 for the parts of an office memorandum).

For a comprehensive discussion of form books, see Duke University Law School's website at http://www.law.duke.edu/lib/researchguides/formbks.

Using the U.S. Supreme Court's website at http://www.supremecourt.gov/oral_arguments/briefsource.aspx, review the ways to locate legal briefs submitted to the Supreme Court.

Using the Cornell University Law School website for its Legal Information Institute, found at http://www.law.cornell.edu/, find your state's legal ethics code. Use it to answer the following Ethical Applications.

Ethical Applications

Rose Dawson, Esq., is a very successful and competent personal injury lawyer. Her reputation in her community (Denver, Colorado), which is well deserved, is as one of the best plaintiff's lawyers available. One day, just outside of Denver, there is a horrible commercial airliner crash, caused by mechanical failure of the plane, and there are no survivors. Rose is able to obtain a list of the names of the victims of the crash. She contacts the families of the victims, by visiting them in person or calling them on the telephone, and offers to represent them in a mass tort action against the airline that owned and operated the airplane. Rose is as competent as, if not more competent than, any lawyer to handle such claims, and the victims' families would be well represented by her and would do well to choose her as their lawyer.

Is there any problem with Rose contacting the families of the victims as she did and offering to represent them in a mass tort action? If so, what is the problem? Can it be overcome?

VIDEO CASE STUDIES

Video Interview of Tatyana Bronzova

Paralegal case study videos to accompany this textbook are accessible from within both the New MyLegalStudiesLab Virtual Law Office Experience course and the Resources Website for Paralegal Studies.

ENDNOTES

[1]In the state of Maryland, the minimum dollar restriction on the guarantee to a right to jury trial in civil cases is $10,000, not the $20 found in the Seventh Amendment to the U.S. Constitution.

11
Interviewing, Investigation, and Negotiation

Sherry Myers

Paralegal at Summerfield, Willen, Silverberg & Limsky, LLC

Sherry is a paralegal working in a law firm specializing in family law. Having earned a degree in paralegal studies, Sherry found her paralegal employment through an advertisement in a local business and law journal. Before applying for the position, Sherry researched the firm as well as the attorney to whom she would report. When applying, Sherry drafted her résumé and cover letter to be tailored to this specific position.

Drafting a variety of legal documents, including pleadings, motions, and agreements, is a daily part of Sherry's practice. She regularly conducts interviews of clients as well. Sherry often communicates with other paralegals, attorneys, and court personnel regarding her cases. Legal research is another task that Sherry regularly performs. Sherry also prepares and responds to discovery requests, schedules appointments for her supervising attorney, performs electronic timekeeping, sets up files, prepares client financial statements and child support worksheets, calendars important deadlines, and communicates with clients in person, on the telephone, and via e-mail. In addition to her paralegal practice, Sherry attends law school.

Previously, Sherry worked as a freelance paralegal, doing personal injury litigation work. As such, she provided paralegal services on a contractual and "as needed" basis to local law firms. She worked in a variety of areas of law and performed many legal research and writing projects. She called her business "Paralegal Services Plus."

The full video interview is accessible from within both the New MyLegalStudiesLab Virtual Law Office Experience course and the Resources Website for Paralegal Studies.

The chapter will answer the following questions:

- How do you conduct interviews of clients and witnesses?

- How do you conduct factual investigations?
- How do you conduct negotiations?

CHAPTER **INTRODUCTION**

This chapter examines certain other important legal skills for paralegals. The chapter begins with a discussion of conducting interviews of clients and witnesses. It then covers the skill of conducting factual investigations. Finally, the chapter ends with a review of negotiation, used more by attorneys but also relevant to paralegals depending on their law practices. We begin this last "paralegal skills" chapter with a discussion of how to conduct interviews of clients and witnesses.

CONDUCTING INTERVIEWS OF CLIENTS AND WITNESSES

Attorneys and paralegals may conduct client and witness interviews in the course of their legal work. An **interview** is a meeting held for the purpose of asking questions and eliciting responses. An attorney typically conducts the initial client interview, sometimes called the **intake interview**, when the decision is made whether to accept representation of the client in a particular matter and when the fee agreement is established. Legal ethics rules require that an attorney handle these issues

© Exactostock/SuperStock

directly, though paralegals may be, and sometimes are, present at these meetings. Afterward, the attorney or paralegal may conduct further client interviews to obtain more detailed information from the client. In addition, attorneys and paralegals may interview witnesses as part of the investigation of the client's claim(s) or defense(s). Both client and witness interviews are important parts of the evidence-gathering process.

To be an effective interviewer takes practice, advance planning, organization, and good communication skills. Certain preparation should be undertaken before the interview is

conducted. For example, a paralegal typically schedules the interview with the client or witness. He locates the witness (hopefully the location of the client is known), determines where the interview will be held, reserves the interview location, and

> An **interview** is a meeting held for the purpose of asking questions and eliciting responses.
>
> An **intake interview** is the initial client interview.

arranges transportation for any witness who is not local. As an important part of preparation for the interview, the attorney or paralegal conducting the interview should carefully review the file.

Planning the interview is as important as the interview itself to ensure that the right questions are asked and all of the necessary information is elicited from the client or witness. In advance of the interview, the attorney or paralegal should determine the information to obtain from the client or witness (if the interview is being conducted by a paralegal, this advance planning should be done with the assistance of the attorney), decide what questions to ask, and prepare an outline or checklist of these questions for use during the interview. If the purpose of the interview is to elicit information to enable the attorney or paralegal to fill out a legal form, such as a bankruptcy filing, then that legal form should be used as the basis, or outline, for the questioning. Some law offices have standardized interview forms for particular types of interviews, such as client intake interviews. These forms may be used in lieu of an outline or checklist.

Preparing for an Interview

A paralegal should prepare for a client or witness interview by:

- setting the appointment (date, time, location) for the interview with the client or witness;
- confirming the appointment with the client or witness (by letter is a good idea) and marking the appointment on his calendar;
- reviewing the file and organizing its contents;
- preparing the interview location so it is quiet, clean, and interruption and distraction-free;
- determining if the interview will be recorded and getting the interviewee's permission to record the interview;
- gathering a standardized interview form, gathering a legal form that needs to be filled out, or preparing an interview checklist; and
- discussing the interview plan with the supervising attorney.

Standardized Interview Forms

Some attorneys and firms have standardized interview forms they use. These forms may be generalized initial client intake forms or they may be more specific, relating to a particular type of legal claim, such as a personal injury action. Using standardized forms can help ensure that all essential information is gathered from the client or witness during the interview. An example of an initial client interview checklist is found in Figure 11-1.

FIGURE 11-1 Initial Client Interview Checklist

Date:

Interviewee information

Full name:

Address:

Home telephone number:

Work telephone number:

(continued)

Cell phone number:

Employer's name:

Employer's address:

Occupation:

Salary:

Birthdate:

Social security number:

Driver's license state/number:

Marital status:

Spouse's name (if any):

Children or other dependants (name, sex, age):

How did you learn about this firm/attorney?

Why are you seeking legal representation?

Nature of the legal problem (criminal, divorce/family law, business, bankruptcy, personal injury, employment/workers' compensation, immigration, other):

Are there other parties involved? If so, who are they? Do you have a relationship with them, such as family member, friend, or neighbor?

Are there any documents involved?

Have you seen any other attorney? If so, who? What was the result?

Have you seen a doctor? If so, what is the doctor's name, address and telephone number?

Briefly describe the facts of your case.

Provide the names of any witnesses and their contact information, if available.

What is the outcome you seek?

What other outcomes would you be satisfied with?

How urgent is your matter?

How will you pay your fee?

During the interview itself, the interviewer should refer to the interview checklist or outline as a *guide*. Using this guide, the interviewer can "stay on track" and succeed in eliciting all the information she planned to obtain. Of course, while the interviewer is questioning the interviewee, the interviewer should use the checklist or outline flexibly. The interviewer, using effective listening skills and modifying her questions accordingly, should adjust and adapt her questions based on the responses provided by the interviewee. The guide should not be used as a script. A good interviewer will know when to ask follow-up questions or modify her questions based on the responses she receives from the interviewee. That is, the interviewee's responses should direct the flow of the interview. Accordingly, during the interview it is important for the interviewer to be both flexible in departing from her pre-interview outline where appropriate, and interactive, responding to the interviewee's answers even when they lead to a departure from the interview outline. Before concluding the interview, however, the interviewer should refer back to and review her checklist or outline to be sure she has asked all the pertinent questions and obtained all the necessary information. Although it is important to pursue leads that arise during the course of the interview, it is also important for the interviewer to circle back and be sure she has obtained all the information she originally planned on eliciting, for the interviewer needs all of the "who, what, where, when, and how" of the matter.

Interviewers may wish to make recordings of their interviews so they can review them again later, or so another member of the legal team can review them. Before recording an interview, the interviewer should obtain the written consent of the interviewee. In addition, at the start of the interview, the inter-

viewer should state that the interview is being recorded on the interviewee's grant of consent and include on the recording the names of the interviewer, the interviewee, and anyone else present at the interview, as well as the date, time, and location of the interview. If an interviewer believes that recording an interview will stifle the responses of the interviewee, she may prefer to take notes during the interview rather than record it. If the interviewer is an attorney, she may request that her paralegal be present to take detailed notes of the interview while she is conducting it.

After the conclusion of the interview, it is a good idea for the interviewer to review and complete any notes she has taken before much time passes. It is easier to remember the details

KEY Point

Before Concluding an Interview

Before concluding an interview, the interviewer should refer back to and review her checklist or outline, or standardized or legal form if one is used, to be sure she has asked all the pertinent questions and obtained all the necessary information.

"Interviewer"/"Interviewee"

The *interviewer* is the person conducting the interview; the *interviewee* is the person being interviewed.

Tips for Conducting an Interview

- Greet the interviewee and introduce yourself.
- If you are a paralegal, inform the interviewee that you are a paralegal and not an attorney (in compliance with legal ethics rules on the unauthorized practice of law).
- Practice the art of conversation and be friendly, courteous, and polite to establish rapport and build trust with the interviewee.
- Act professionally in greeting and questioning the interviewee.
- Explain the purpose of the interview—that it is to gather and record information.
- Demonstrate confidence, for you control how the interview is conducted.
- Allow the interviewee to speak in his own words.
- Extract from the interviewee the pertinent information by asking the right questions.
- Follow up with additional questions based on the information the interviewee provides during the interview.
- Remember the importance of effective listening.
- Take good notes, even if the interview is being recorded.
- Obtain copies of all documents and records relating to the matter that the interviewee has in his possession or mentions during the interview.
- Arrange for the possibility of follow-up with the interviewee if you think that might become necessary.
- Thank the interviewee for participating and conclude the interview.

For the new paralegal, I would suggest never assuming anything when you interview a new client. Always ask a client specific questions that you prepare in advance. You might have to rephrase a question and ask a client several times to make sure the client understands you. Never use legalese when speaking with a client or the client may not understand you. It is always better to get extra information that you might not use later, rather than not have enough information.
Tatyana Bronzova

of the interviewee's responses immediately after the interview than at some later time. A written summary of the interview, prepared either by the interviewer or by a paralegal present to observe the interview, is a great way to preserve the information obtained during the interview. If a standardized interview form was used, the completed form itself serves as the interview summary.

Conducting interviews is a skill that a person develops through practice. In other words, it is a learned skill. Interviewing skills combine the use of communication, listening, and interpersonal skills. Just as a person becomes better at interviewing for a job through interview practice, a paralegal or attorney becomes better at interviewing clients and witnesses through interview practice. What are some things interviewers can do to improve their interview skills?

Effective interviewers do not go into interviews unprepared. Rather, they plan and prepare for their interviews in advance. Effective interviewers are active listeners. Active listeners focus not only on what the interviewee is saying, but they respond to the interviewee as well by providing feedback such as nodding their head, repeating what the interviewee said, asking the interviewee to "go on," and so forth. Importantly, active listeners provide feedback to the interviewee by summarizing what was said by the interviewee and repeating it back. This process demonstrates that the listener understood what the interviewee said. In other words, an active listener openly participates in the listening process. Effective interviewers also maintain direct eye contact with their interviewees. Effective interviewers are flexible in how they conduct their interviews, using a checklist or guide, but being willing to depart from that plan to adapt lines of questioning based upon the interviewee's answers. Effective interviewers ask clear and thoughtful questions to their interviewees, avoiding legalese and speaking to interviewees using language they understand. Effective interviewers are efficient, using the interview time wisely. Effective interviewers have the ability to ease the nervousness and discomfort of their interviewees by making them comfortable with the situation. Finally, effective interview-

ers develop a rapport with their interviewees and treat them with courtesy and respect.

KEY Point

Effective Interviewers . . .

- plan and prepare for interviews in advance;
- are active listeners;
- use direct eye contact;
- conduct interviews in a flexible manner, listening to interviewees and adapting their questions based on the interviewees' answers;
- ask clear and thoughtful questions;
- are efficient and use the interview time wisely;
- put their interviewees at ease;
- develop a rapport with their interviewees; and
- treat each interviewee with courtesy and respect.

Effective Listening

To be a successful interviewer, a paralegal must listen to what her clients and witnesses say. Here are some tips for becoming a more effective listener:

- Maintain eye contact with the interviewee to show that you have focused your attention on what he is saying.
- Pay attention to the interviewee and demonstrate your interest by showing signs of active listening such as nodding your head.
- Minimize interruptions and distractions by turning off electronic devices, forwarding telephone calls, closing doors and windows, not allowing visitors, and the like.
- "Read" the body language of the interviewee, because nonverbal communications (tone, expression, posture, and so on) can say as much as words.
- Repeat back to the interviewee what was said to ensure understanding of the communication.

As mentioned above, effective interviewers ask clear and thoughtful questions. Learning how to ask questions is another skill that interviewers develop through practice. There are different types of questions that interviewers can ask depending on the situation. These question types include open-ended questions, close-ended questions, and leading questions.

Open-ended questions are phrased to elicit a broad response. They give the interviewee much latitude in answering by allowing the client or witness to "tell his story." For example, "Why are you seeking legal representation?" from Figure 11-1 is an open-ended question. "What happened next?" is another example of an open-ended question used not only in interviews but in eliciting testimony at deposition or trial. This type of question works best when interviewing a client or a "friendly" witness, meaning a witness favorable to your client, for these interviewees are more likely to be forthcoming in their responses than a hostile witness, meaning a witness favorable to the opposing side, also called an adverse witness.

Close-ended questions, on the other hand, are phrased in a way to elicit a yes or no or other very narrow response. They are often used to clarify an interviewee's statement, to keep an interviewee on track, or to draw out information when interviewing an adverse or otherwise reluctant witness. For example, "Were you driving the truck?" is a close-ended question. So is "What color was the traffic light at the time you entered the intersection?"

Leading questions are questions that suggest to the interviewee the answer. Leading questions are typically used in interviews to get information from adverse or other reluctant witnesses. "Isn't it true that you were driving 65 miles per hour in a 45 mile per hour zone at the time the accident occurred?" is an example of a leading question. Another example is "As you approached the intersection, the signal light was red, wasn't it?" Knowing what types of questions to ask what types of interviewees, and when, is a component part of the skill of conducting interviews of clients and witnesses.

Friendly or Hostile Witness?

A friendly witness is a witness who is sympathetic toward a client, or biased against a client's adversary, in a legal matter.

A hostile witness, also called an adverse witness, is a witness who is sympathetic toward a client's adversary, or biased against a client, in a legal matter.

We have reviewed conducting interviews of both clients and witnesses. Interviewing skills that we have discussed apply to interviews of both types of interviewees, clients and witnesses. **Clients**, obviously, are the parties that you represent. Witnesses, on the other hand, establish facts relating to the client's case. A **witness** is a person who is not a party and who testifies under oath in a trial or in a deposition in a lawsuit. When interviewing witnesses, the types of questions you use depends on whether they are friendly or hostile witnesses — meaning whether they are favorable to your client or not. There are other different types of witnesses. One type is an eyewitness. An **eyewitness** is a person who observed an event and can testify about it. For example, someone who observes a car crash is an eyewitness to it. Another type of witness is a lay witness. A **lay witness** is a person who can testify about factual knowledge he possesses. The eyewitness noted in the previous example is also a lay witness. Another type of witness is an expert witness. A lay witness is any witness who is not an expert witness. What is an expert witness? An **expert witness** is a person possessing professional training or skill, advanced knowledge or education, and/or substantial experience

A **client** is a party who engages an attorney as counsel in a legal matter.

A **witness** is a person who is not a party and who testifies under oath in a trial or in a deposition in a lawsuit.

An **eyewitness** is a person who observed an event and can testify about it.

A **lay witness** is a person who can testify about factual knowledge he possesses.

An **expert witness** is a person possessing professional training or skill, advanced knowledge or education, and/or substantial experience in a specialized area, who is hired to testify in court or to render an opinion on a matter related to a client's case.

© Imagesource/PhotoLibrary

in a specialized area, such as forensics, medicine, or computer technology, who is hired to testify in court or to render an opinion on a matter related to a client's case. An example of an expert witness is a doctor hired by the plaintiff's lawyer to testify about the extent of harm suffered by the plaintiff.

When you interview a witness, you should consider how this person would appear to a court in the event she eventually will be called to testify at trial or to give testimony at a deposition. At the interview stage, you do not yet know whether the witness's testimony will be needed at trial or even if there will be a trial. However, because the witness could potentially be called to give testimony at trial or deposition, you should consider her qualifications as a witness. In doing so you evaluate her credibility. Credibility means a witness's believability—whether the witness appears truthful and reliable. You also evaluate a witness's competence. A lay witness is competent so long as she possesses personal knowledge of the matter on which she will testify. An expert witness, on the other hand, is considered competent only if she possesses special training, skill, knowledge, education, and/or experience relating to the subject matter for which she is called to testify. Finally, you evaluate a witness's potential bias. If a witness has an interest in the matter—for

example, is a family member or friend of one of the parties or is prejudiced against one of the parties—she is considered biased and her testimony may be discredited because she lacks impartiality.

In addition to conducting interviews, attorneys and paralegals conduct factual investigations in representing their clients. Factual investigations are discussed next.

Witness Statements

A witness statement is a written record of what the witness said during an interview. It is a formal summary of a witness interview. After being drafted, a witness statement is given to the witness to review for accuracy. Then the witness signs the statement to verify the accuracy of the statement's contents.

Court rules and statutes differ on how witness statements may be used. Depending on the relevant law or rule in the court or jurisdiction, the witness statement may be used as evidence (rarely), may be used to impeach (cast doubt on) the credibility of the witness, or may be used to refresh the witness's memory (if she forgot something about the matter on which she is testifying).

CONDUCTING FACTUAL INVESTIGATIONS

Paralegals and attorneys regularly conduct factual investigations in representing clients in legal matters. A **factual investigation** is an examination or inquiry into the facts of a legal matter. The outcome of a legal dispute depends largely on the facts of the case and the quality of the evidence obtained. This makes factual investigation a crucial part of a litigation practitioner's job.

Interviewing the client and witnesses, just discussed, is one form of factual investigation. Remember from our earlier discussion that before a witness can be interviewed, he must first be located. Locating a witness is another type of preliminary factual investigation. Other factual information a litigation practitioner may need, besides testimony from the client and witnesses, may include police reports, weather condition information, traffic condition information, medical records, employment records, business records, property ownership records, and insurance records, as a few examples.

Just as for conducting interviews, a preliminary investigation plan should be established before conducting a factual investigation. An **investigation plan** is a list of tasks an investigator plans to perform to obtain or verify factual information about a legal matter. In creating an investigation plan, the investigator should consider the factual information needed. An investigator may want to verify information, such as weather conditions testified to by a witness. He may also want to obtain new information or evidence, such as title documents to property involved in a dispute or photographs of an accident scene. It is important for an investigator to thoroughly review the information she already possesses about the matter in preparing an investigation plan gained from the file, from documents and records already obtained, and from any client or witness interviews already conducted. Before the investigation begins, attorneys should review the investigation plans of their paralegals, just as they would do for interview checklists, to ensure that the investigation plans are complete and meet all of the attorneys' objectives. Supervising attorneys may also

be able to suggest some investigative shortcuts that will save the paralegal time and the client money.

After the planning stage, the factual investigation is conducted. Computer searches and databases are often good starting points. Interviewing clients and witnesses is another

KEY Point

Planning a Factual Investigation

An investigator should plan her factual investigation before she begins it. When a paralegal drafts an investigation plan, it should be reviewed and approved by the supervising attorney.

A **factual investigation** is an examination or inquiry into the facts of a legal matter.

An **investigation plan** is a list of tasks an investigator plans to perform to obtain or verify factual information about a legal matter.

KEY Point

The Importance of Factual Investigations

The outcome of a legal dispute depends largely on the facts of the case and the quality of the evidence obtained.

Typical Parts of a Factual Investigation

Depending on the nature of the legal matter being investigated, here are some common searches paralegals perform in conducting factual investigations:

- Search records, such as employment records, medical records, and business records.
- Locate and interview witnesses who observed or have personal knowledge about the event.
- Contact police departments to get copies of incident reports, names of witnesses, names of investigating officers, and pictures of the scene and evidence found there.
- Contact the national weather service to obtain information about weather and daylight conditions at the date and time of the event.
- Search property records, such as land records or motor vehicle title and registration records.
- Contact insurance companies for information about policies and coverages.

Professional Investigators

Sometimes attorneys hire professional investigators to perform certain investigative tasks. For example, an attorney for an insurance company might hire a professional investigator to observe a person who is claiming disability to determine if the person is as disabled as he claims.

KEY Point

Value of Investigations in Resolving Legal Disputes

Knowledge gained through the investigative process is useful in trying to negotiate the resolution of legal disputes. The more that is known about the facts of a particular legal matter, in conjunction with the applicable law in the jurisdiction, the more able a party to litigation is to be able to evaluate the likely success of his claim or defense. This evaluation of possible success impacts settlement offers and acceptances.

good way to begin a factual investigation. Follow-up investigation, such as finding and reviewing records, visiting accident scenes, confirming weather conditions reported, and obtaining incident reports are all examples of factual investigation.

Although paralegals and attorneys regularly conduct factual investigations, some lawyers enlist the services of professional investigators, at least for certain investigative tasks. Engaging a professional investigator, though it incurs additional fees for which the client is ultimately responsible, relieves the attorney or paralegal of that responsibility and gives it to a professional who is trained, licensed, and experienced in the conduct of investigations, and who may have access to people and records that a nonprofessional investigator might not. At the request of the supervising attorney, paralegals may work with the professional investigator.

During and after the conduct of the investigation, the attorney or paralegal should document and record his results, preserving his findings for later review and use. On the conclusion of the investigation, the attorney or paralegal should document and summarize the findings and present recommendations based on the results of the investigation.

Factual investigations should be well planned and thoroughly executed. After they are completed, they should be thoroughly and carefully documented. That way, the best quality and quantity of evidence is obtained to help resolve the legal dispute, whether through negotiation and settlement or through trial.

In addition to conducting interviews and factual investigations, legal service providers, typically attorneys but sometimes paralegals, conduct negotiations. The skill of conducting negotiations is examined next.

CONDUCTING NEGOTIATIONS

Because most litigation is settled prior to trial, negotiation is a valuable skill. Attorneys can often resolve a legal dispute through negotiation rather than litigation. **Negotiation** is a process where the parties to a legal dispute communicate, themselves or through their attorneys, to try to resolve a legal dispute. It is an informal process. Negotiation can be conducted in person, over the telephone, or through correspondence (using letters

or electronic technology—e-mail). Negotiation is considered a form of alternative dispute resolution (ADR). In fact, it is the most

Negotiation is a process where the parties to a legal dispute communicate, themselves or through their attorneys, to try to resolve a legal dispute.

legal position to resolve the matter more efficiently than through a costly and time-consuming trial. Many courts require parties to a lawsuit to engage in settlement discussions before the start of trial, possibly at a settlement conference together with the judge assigned to the case.

If a settlement of the legal dispute is reached between the parties as a result of negotiation, a settlement agreement containing the terms of the resolution is executed by the parties. A **settlement agreement** is a contract entered into by the parties to a legal dispute that sets forth the terms and conditions of the resolution and settlement of the dispute. If a lawsuit has been filed, the settlement agreement typically is submitted to the court in which the litigation is pending and serves as the basis for dismissal of the legal action. A sample settlement agreement was provided in Chapter 3 and Chapter 10.

Another way that negotiation is used, besides as a form of ADR to resolve legal disputes, is to negotiate the terms of a transaction. For example, when a company wants to license the use of a patent from the patent's owner, the two parties, probably through their legal representation (attorneys), negotiate the terms and conditions of that license. Then, the parties will likely reduce that agreement to writing in the form of a written contract. For routine contracts that companies enter into, where there are standard terms and conditions, paralegals representing these companies may negotiate the terms and conditions of those routine transactions, as well as draft the related contracts so long as they do so under the direct supervision of an attorney to avoid engaging in the unauthorized practice of law.

In conducting both interviews and negotiations, attorneys and paralegals need to be skillful communicators. By using appropriate interpersonal skills, such as putting a nervous witness at ease by spending the early moments of an interview establishing a friendly rapport with him, an interviewer can be

commonly used form of ADR, as discussed in Chapter 4. The vast majority of cases are resolved this way before, or even during, trial.

Sometimes the parties themselves may negotiate to try to resolve their dispute, but often the negotiation is conducted via the parties' attorneys. Note that attorneys do not delegate this task of negotiating the resolution of legal disputes to their paralegals. During the negotiating process, both sides make offers and counteroffers, either in person, over the telephone, or in writing, to resolve the dispute. In presenting offers and counteroffers, usually through their attorneys, each side may provide additional information about their claim(s) or defense(s), sharing what they believe are the strengths of their

Negotiation and ADR

Negotiation is one commonly used form of alternative dispute resolution.

Other important forms of ADR include mediation and arbitration.

KEY Point
Legal Dispute Settlement
Remember that attorneys are the only legal representatives who can negotiate the settlement of a legal dispute and in doing so, they must abide by the clients' directions regarding settlement offers and/or acceptances. It is ultimately a decision for clients whether or not to make or accept settlement offers.

A **settlement agreement** is a contract entered into by the parties to a legal dispute that sets forth the terms and conditions of the resolution and settlement of the dispute.

I believe the best way to negotiate is to first listen to the other side and then present your case. If there is an impasse in the negotiations, you can say, 'I will need to do some further research on this and get back to you' and then seek guidance from the supervising attorney. I try to stay away from definitive declarations like 'we'll never do that' or 'it's not going to happen.'
Susan Campbell

KEY Point

Negotiation and the Paralegal

Negotiation is a skill used much more often by attorneys than by paralegals. Attorneys are the legal representatives who negotiate the settlement of a legal dispute. Further, attorneys often are the persons negotiating the terms of a transaction. That said, clients may negotiate the settlement of a legal dispute or the terms of a transactions.

Paralegals should not negotiate the settlement of a client's legal dispute, though they can assist attorneys in preparation for negotiation by conducting factual investigations and legal research to determine the likely success of a client's claim or defense. Also, paralegals must use caution in negotiating transaction terms, being careful not to engage in the unauthorized practice of law.

more effective. By asking appropriate open-ended questions to clients and friendly witnesses, close-ended questions to elicit specific responses, and leadings questions to draw out responses from witnesses who are reluctant to cooperate, an interviewer can be more successful in gaining useful information. In both interviews and negotiations, listening to the other side helps the interviewer or negotiator understand the statements or position of the other, advancing her cause of either eliciting useful information, reaching a settlement of a dispute, or reaching agreement on the terms of a transaction. Whether paralegals are conducting interviews, factual investigations, or negotiations, their skills and abilities improve with practice and experience.

CHAPTER SUMMARY

- An interview is a meeting held for the purpose of asking questions and eliciting responses. Attorneys and paralegals may conduct interviews of clients and witnesses.

- An interviewer should plan, in advance, for the interview. He may use a standardized interview form, a legal form, or prepare an interview checklist to use as a guide in conducting the interview. After the completion of an interview, the interviewer should complete a written summary of the interview, which may be the completion of the standardized interview form or legal form.

- Conducting interviews is a learned skill developed through practice. It involves the use of communication, listening, and interpersonal skills. Effective interviewers prepare, in advance, for the interview; are active listeners; use direct eye contact; conduct the interview in a flexible manner; ask clear and thoughtful questions; are efficient; put their interviewees at ease; develop a rapport with their interviewees; and treat each interviewee with courtesy and respect.

- Interviewers can ask open-ended, close-ended, or leading questions. Open-ended questions are used to elicit broad responses. Close-ended questions are used to elicit narrow responses. Leading questions are used to suggest responses to the interviewee. What type of question to use, and when, depends on whether the interviewee is a client or witness and, if she is a witness, whether she is a friendly or hostile witness. A friendly witness is a witness who is sympathetic toward a client or biased against a client's adversary in a legal matter. A hostile witness, or adverse witness, is a witness who is sympathetic toward a client's adversary or biased against a client in a legal matter.

- Interviews may be conducted of clients and witnesses. A client is a party who engages the attorney as counsel in a legal matter. A witness is a person who testifies under oath in a trial or in a deposition in a lawsuit. There are different types of witnesses. An eyewitness is a person who observed an event and can testify about it. A lay witness is a person who can testify about factual knowledge he possesses. An expert witness is a person who possesses professional training or skill, advanced knowledge or education, and/or substantial experience in a specialized area who is hired to testify in court or to render an opinion on a matter related to a client's case.

- A factual investigation is an examination or inquiry into the facts of a legal matter. Paralegals and attorneys regularly conduct factual investigations in their representation of clients on matters. Just as with interviews, factual investigations should be planned in advance, and an investigation plan should be drafted listing the tasks the investigator plans to perform to obtain or verify factual information about a legal matter. Professional investigators may be hired by attorneys to assist in factual investigation. Investigation results should be documented.

- Negotiation is the process where the parties to a legal dispute communicate, themselves or through their attorneys, to try to resolve a legal dispute. This type of negotiation is typically performed by attorneys. If the legal dispute is resolved through negotiation, then a settlement agreement is entered into by the parties setting forth the terms and conditions of the resolution and settlement of the dispute. Negotiation may also be used to negotiate the terms of a transaction; this type of negotiation is often performed by attorneys, but may be performed by paralegals when the transaction being negotiated is routine, with standard terms and conditions.

CONCEPT REVIEW AND REINFORCEMENT

Key Terms and Concepts

Interview
Intake interview
Client
Witness
Eyewitness
Lay witness
Expert witness
Factual investigation
Investigation plan
Negotiation
Settlement agreement

Questions for Review

1. What is an interview?
2. How do you prepare to conduct an interview?
3. How do you conduct interviews?
4. How is conducting an interview of a client different from conducting an interview of a witness, if at all?
5. What kinds of witnesses are there?
6. What different types of questions can interviewers use? When should each type be used?
7. What is a factual investigation?
8. How do you prepare to conduct a factual investigation?
9. How do you conduct factual investigations?
10. How is negotiation used as a form of ADR?
11. How else is the skill of negotiation used, other than to resolve a legal dispute?
12. Who can conduct negotiations?
13. How are negotiations conducted?

DEVELOPING YOUR PARALEGAL SKILLS

Critical Thinking Exercises

1. You are a paralegal specializing in tort law and products liability. Your firm is representing a client who is suing a hairdryer manufacturer, alleging strict product liability. As you will learn in the study of tort law in Chapter 13, a strict products liability claim can be brought when a defective product causes harm to a person and/or her property, and fault of the defendant need not be established. The claim arose out of an incident when the client was blow-drying her hair and the dryer exploded, causing her injury. Lauri, the client's best friend, was in the room when the incident occurred and witnessed the explosion. Your supervising attorney asks you to interview Lauri and obtain from her the information the firm will need to bolster the client's claim.

   Prepare an outline of the questions you plan to ask the witness during the interview, for submission to your supervising attorney for review prior to conducting the interview. Share your outline with the class.

2. You are conducting a factual investigation of your client's negligence matter. Your client was injured when he was struck by a car while walking across Jade Street in Pasadena, Texas. Your client said it was 6:45 p.m. on September 15, and light outside, when he walked into a pedestrian crossing while the pedestrian crossing light was lit, telling him to cross, and was struck by the defendant's car. The defendant has asserted that the plaintiff was not in the crosswalk but was jaywalking at the time of the incident, and that it was dusk and the plaintiff was wearing dark clothes, making him difficult to see. In conducting a factual investigation of the incident, where would you search for the following:

   a. To find any videotapes or cameras near that crossing that would show the incident?
   b. To find out if there were any other witnesses to the incident?
   c. To get a copy of the police report relating to the incident?
   d. To gain an understanding of the intersection involved, such as whether the intersection is in a busy area, and to see how the road and pedestrian crossing are configured? Remember that you want to preserve this scene for trial.
   e. To find the daylight conditions at that time on that day?
   f. To find out the weather conditions at the time of the incident?
   g. To get information about the extent and permanence of the plaintiff's injuries?
   h. To find out whether the defendant has a clean driving record or perhaps a history of DUIs (driving under the influence) or other driving infractions?

3. Your client is the plaintiff in a personal injury action. She was injured in a car accident when a car driven by the defendant crossed the center line and hit her car, head-on.

You think the driver of that car may have been texting at the time he crossed the center line. Jason, riding his bike down the road, saw the accident and stayed around to help the injured plaintiff. In the car with the defendant was Maurice, one of the defendant's co-workers.

   a. If you want to interview Jason to learn more about what he saw, what kind of questions would you ask him (open-ended, close-ended, or leading)? Why? Is Jason a friendly witness? A hostile witness? Is he neutral as a witness?
   b. If you want to interview Maurice, in particular to find out if he saw the defendant texting at the time he crossed the center line, what kinds of questions would you ask him (open-ended, close-ended, or leading)? Why? Is Maurice a friendly witness? A hostile witness? Is he a neutral witness?

Assignments and Practical Applications

Partner with one other student in your class. Prepare to interview that student to learn about the student, such as where the student is from, what she is studying, why she took this course, etc. Also, find out one special fact about the student. Prepare your interview checklist. Then conduct your interview. When you are finished, prepare an interview summary to turn in to your instructor.

Using the syllabus for the class for which you are reading this text, draft three open-ended questions, three close-ended questions, and three leading questions about the class based on the information found in the syllabus (in other words, the answers to the questions can be found in the syllabus). For example, an open-ended question may be "How will grades be calculated in the class?" Then interview a classmate using the questions you have prepared. Write an interview summary recording your classmate's answers.

Negotiation and Settlement Exercise

This exercise should be done in pairs.

Facts: The defendant is a company that owns and operates a chain of grocery stores. The defendant has established policies to clean up spills that occur on the premises of the stores to safeguard its customers and employees. Among these policies is a requirement that, upon notification that there has been a spill in a store, employees will promptly set up an orange cone to warn passersby of the spill, and thoroughly clean up the spill as soon as possible.

A customer, while removing a jar of maraschino cherries from the shelf, inadvertently dislodges the display, causing several jars to fall to the floor and break. The customer scoots quickly away, embarrassed. Another customer who comes down the aisle a few minutes later, on seeing the spill, reports it to customer service. An employee responds to customer service's request to clean the spill, and proceeds to the maraschino cherry aisle to check it out and see what cleaning supplies he will need, bringing an orange cone with him and placing it at the scene of the spill.

While the employee is off collecting the cleaning supplies, another store customer walks down the aisle toward the spill. This customer is throwing his child's birthday party that weekend, and is in the store to pick up party supplies, including ice cream sundae fixings. He needs hot fudge, butterscotch sauce, caramel sauce, and maraschino cherries from this aisle, all located in the same section of the shelves. The customer, in selecting these items, must walk on the spill, and does. Unfortunately, the customer slips on the wet floor and broken glass and falls to the floor, where he is cut by some of the broken glass, requiring many stitches. He also suffers a broken hip as a result of the fall.

The customer subsequently files a personal injury tort action against the defendant, alleging negligence (unreasonable conduct that causes harm to another). Recovery is sought in the amount of $75,000 in damages. This is a contributory negligence jurisdiction where, if the plaintiff's unreasonable conduct contributes to the harm suffered from the defendant's negligence, the plaintiff is completely barred from recovery.

Tasks: Neither party wants to go to trial. The parties hire you to represent them in this legal dispute, as their respective attorneys. Your first task is to settle this case. Each student represents one of the parties. Negotiate a settlement of all issues involved in this dispute. Once you have reached a settlement, your second task is to draft a settlement agreement to reflect your resolution (*one* agreement to resolve the dispute between two parties). Refer to form books and/or the sample settlement agreement given in Chapter 3 for a form agreement to use. (Remember that if one party pays money to the other, the party paying the money is going to want a release.)

Technology Resources and Internet Exercises

Review the article "How to Interview Clients" on the "Paralegal Today" website. "Paralegal Today" is a magazine published for the paralegal profession. The article is found at http://www.legalassistanttoday.com/issue_archive/features/feature2_ja08.htm.

Review the article on "Client Interview Techniques" for paralegals, found at http://paralegals.uslegalblogs.com/articles/client-interviewing-techniques/.

For a further review of client intake forms, review the sample form found on the Maryland State Bar Association's website at http://www.msba.org/departments/loma/articles/characteristics/intake.htm.

Using the Internet, conduct a factual investigation to answer the following questions:

    a. What is the location of the U.S. Copyright Office?
    b. In what regional reporter do you find appellate decisions from Colorado courts?
    c. What is the definition of mesothelioma?
    d. What is the name of the current U.S. Supreme Court Chief Justice, where and when was he born, and where did he earn his law degree?

Using the Cornell University Law School website for its Legal Information Institute, found at http://www.law.cornell.edu/, find your state's legal ethics code. Use it to answer the following Ethical Applications.

Ethical Applications

Jake Weber is a personal injury lawyer who specializes in complex litigation, handling many mass tort claims. Recently, he represented a class of victims harmed by the use of a formerly FDA-approved diet pill that was later found to cause heart problems and failure, and which was then banned by the FDA and recalled by the manufacturer. Under the terms of the fee arrangement, Jake will earn a contingency fee, as follows: 25 percent if the case settles prior to trial, 30 percent if the case settles during trial, and 40 percent if the case goes to verdict after trial. The case settles prior to trial after only one year in litigation, for $500 million. Typically, such a complex case takes many years in trial preparation alone. Jake's fee is 25 percent of the settlement, so he earns $125 million for a year's worth of work (and, presumably, he handled other cases for other clients during that year, as well).

Is Jake's fee ethical? Why or why not?

VIDEO CASE STUDIES

Video Interview of Sherry Myers

Paralegal case study videos to accompany this textbook are accessible from within both the New MyLegalStudiesLab Virtual Law Office Experience course and the Resources Website for Paralegal Studies.

12

Business-Related Legal Specialty Areas

Susan Campbell

Corporate Paralegal at AAI Corporation

Susan is an in-house, corporate paralegal for AAI Corporation, a defense contractor and a subsidiary of Textron. Susan began her career in law as a legal secretary for a corporate law firm. Later, she began working for AAI Corporation as a legal secretary after applying for a position advertised in the local legal news journal. Deciding she wanted to advance her legal career, Susan completed a degree program in paralegal studies by going to school part-time and continuing her full-time employment.

Susan thinks communication skills, organizational skills, and the ability to pay attention to detail are all important to paralegal success. She believes it is critical that a paralegal convey complex thoughts in "laymen's terms" to a variety of people. Susan says that written communication in the form of drafting is an important skill for her, for most of her practice involves legal document drafting. Susan's role as a contract drafter is a comprehensive one, for she obtains all information needed before beginning to draft a document, works with the supervising attorney to negotiate the terms of the contract, drafts the document itself, coordinates its execution by getting appropriate signatures, then distributes the executed agreement to all parties. Good drafting skills are "extremely important" to a corporate paralegal, says Susan. In addition, Susan believes organizational skills are critical because when an attorney "walks in and needs a document in a rush, you should be able to immediately get your hands on it." Finally, Susan thinks the ability to pay attention to detail "is a great quality to have as a successful paralegal."

In many law practices the attorneys, rather than the paralegals, perform negotiations; in Susan's unique job, under attorney supervision, Susan conducts negotiations for contracts in which she has much experience, such as in preparing nondisclosure agreements and teaming agreements.

Technology is important to Susan's practice, for most of her work is performed electronically. She uses word processing, e-mail, and electronic spreadsheet technology; performs computerized legal research; and regularly uses document storage databases.

The full video interview is accessible from within both the New MyLegalStudiesLab Virtual Law Office Experience course and the Resources Website for Paralegal Studies.

The chapter will answer the following questions:

- What is agency law, what is business organizations law, and how do they relate?
- What is bankruptcy law?
- What is contract law?

- What is employment law?
- What is environmental law?
- What is intellectual property, and how it is protected by law?

CHAPTER **INTRODUCTION**

In the next two chapters, we examine some of the most important legal specialty areas today, areas in which paralegals, as well as attorneys, may practice. In Part V, the legal specialty areas are divided because there is too much material to cover in only one chapter. The legal specialty areas are divided into those that are business-related, in Chapter 12, and those that are not directly related to business, in Chapter 13. The different areas are presented alphabetically within each chapter. This chapter covers agency law and business organizations, bankruptcy, contracts, employment, environmental, and intellectual property. The next chapter covers administrative law and government regulation; criminal law; domestic relations; estates, wills, and trusts; immigration; property; and torts.

In this chapter students review agency principles and relate agency principles to business organizations law. The major forms of business organization are examined. Bankruptcy and bankruptcy law are studied. Contracts and contract law are discussed and analyzed. Important employment laws are examined. Laws to protect the environment are reviewed. The chapter ends with a discussion of intellectual property and the laws that protect it. Our discussion begins with an examination of agency and business organizations.

AGENCY AND BUSINESS ORGANIZATIONS

How does a business organization "act" because it is not human? In other words, how does a business organization enter into contracts, hire new employees, develop new products or services, and the like when it is a legal entity and not a human being? A business organization, which is a legal entity, acts through its agents, who can be human (or other organizations). Agency law, then, is fundamental to understanding business organizations law.

An **agent** is a person or organization who agrees to act, and acts, on behalf of another person. The person or organization on whose behalf an agent agrees to act, and acts, is called a **principal**. Their relationship is an **agency relationship**—a relationship between a principal and an agent. Agency relationships are considered to be fiduciary relationships, meaning relationships based on trust and confidence, where the parties must act with loyalty and honesty toward each other, and in each other's best interest. In other words, the fiduciary nature of the agency relationship gives rise to duties that the principal and agent owe to each other. For example, a principal owes its agent a duty to cooperate with the agent, to reimburse the agent for expenses relating to the conduct of the agency relationship, and to provide safe working conditions. An agent

KEY Point

How Do Businesses "Act"?

Business organizations "act," meaning do things like hire employees and enter into contracts, through their agents, which may be human beings or other organizations (which other organizations act through their human agents).

An **agent** is a person who agrees to act, and acts, on behalf of another person.

A **principal** is a person on whose behalf an agent agrees to act, and acts.

An **agency relationship** is a relationship between a principal and an agent.

owes his principal the duty to perform competently, to act with loyalty toward the principal and its interests, to communicate with the principal about matters known to the agent regarding the agency relationship, and to make an accounting for how the principal's resources are used by the agent.

An agency relationship can be formed by express oral or written agreement between the agent and the principal. One can also be implied by the conduct of the parties, created if the principal ratifies (accepts) the unauthorized act of another after the fact (called agency by ratification), or formed if the principal creates the appearance of an agency by causing a third party to believe there is an agency relationship when none exists (called agency by estoppel).

© Yuri Arcurs/Shutterstock

Pursuant to agency law, a principal is bound by contracts entered into by the agent on the principal's behalf so long as the agent was acting within his express or implied authority. However, if the agent was acting outside of that authority and was engaging in unauthorized acts, the principal is not bound to such contracts unless it ratifies them (by accepting the agent's unauthorized conduct).

According to agency law, both a principal and an agent are individually and personally liable for their own tortious misconduct. In addition, a principal is vicariously liable for the tortious misconduct of its agent who is acting within the scope of his authority within the agency relationship. For example, under the legal **doctrine of *respondeat superior***, an employer (the principal in an employment relationship) is vicariously liable for the tortious misconduct of its employees (the agents in the employment relationship) committed within the course and scope of their employment. An agent, on the other hand, normally is not liable for the tortious misconduct of his principal unless the agent somehow participates in that misconduct.

An agency relationship can be terminated by an act of the parties, such as by selling the real estate that a real estate agent was contracted to sell by the owner/principal, which sales transaction achieves the purpose of the agency relationship. Other ways to terminate an agency relationship by acts of the parties include by their mutual agreement to terminate it, by lapse of time if the agency relationship was established to last for a particular period, or by the occurrence of an event specified at formation of the agency relationship to end the relationship. An agency relationship may also be terminated by operation of law, such as by the death or insanity of the principal or agent, or the bankruptcy of the principal. On termination of the agency relationship, the principal is no longer represented by the agent and is no longer bound by the agent's conduct.

KEY **Point** ⎯⎯⎯⎯⎯⎯⎯⎯⎯⎯⎯

Doctrine of *Respondeat Superior*

Under the doctrine of *respondeat superior*, an employer is vicariously liable for the tortious misconduct of its employees committed within the course and scope of their employment. An employee is an agent of the employer.

The **doctrine of *respondeat superior*** is a legal doctrine pursuant to which an employer may be held vicariously liable for certain wrongful acts of its employees.

KEY **Point** ⎯⎯⎯⎯⎯⎯⎯⎯⎯⎯⎯

Ways to Create an Agency Relationship

- Agency by express oral or written agreement
- Agency implied by the conduct of the parties
- Agency by ratification
- Agency by estoppel

Ways to Terminate an Agency Relationship

- By an act of the parties
- By mutual agreement of the parties
- By lapse of time
- By the occurrence of an event specified at the formation of the agency relationship to end it
- By operation of law

As discussed previously, business organizations act through their human agents. While there are many different possible forms of business organizations under the law, the four most common are sole proprietorships, partnerships, corporations, and limited liability companies (also called limited liability corporations). Each of these major forms of business organization is discussed next.

A **sole proprietorship** is the simplest form of business organization, in which the owner of the business actually is the business, and the business is not really a separate legal entity. Any person who does business without creating another form of business organization is a **sole proprietor** of a sole proprietorship. This means that the owner of the business is entitled to all the profits the business earns and is responsible for any losses it incurs. The owner also is responsible for the operations of the business, and income earned from the business is taxed on the owner's personal income tax return. The sole proprietor is personally liable for the debts and obligations of the business, meaning creditors of the business can go after the owner's personal assets (such as his home, car, boat, and so on) to satisfy those debts. When the sole proprietor dies or stops doing business, the sole proprietorship terminates.

Advantages of the sole proprietorship form of business are in its simplicity. A sole proprietorship is formed merely by one person operating a business. There are no statutory formalities

that must be met before the business is organized and legally exists, as is the case with many other forms of business organization (discussed subsequently). Further, the owner is the sole "chief" of the business and can make all decisions about the conduct of the business. The owner is entitled to all profits earned by the business. The owner is taxed on the profits of the business only once—on his personal income tax return.

The main disadvantage of the sole proprietorship form of business organization is the unlimited personal liability of the sole proprietor for the debts and obligations of the business. As noted, a sole proprietor's personal assets, such as his home and car, may be reached by creditors of the business to satisfy debts and obligations of the sole proprietorship. Sole proprietorships have other disadvantages. Sole proprietors may also have limited access to capital, having to rely on their own resources to invest in the business or in their ability to obtain loans from others. Also, a sole proprietorship lacks business continuity because, in the event of the death or incapacity of the sole proprietor, the business ends.

What happens when multiple people want to operate a business together? Sole proprietorships are a form of business organization involving only one owner/operator. In the case of more than one person as an owner/operator of the business, the partnership form of business organization is one option. A **partnership** is an association of two or more persons who carry on as co-owners of a business for profit. This does not mean that the partnership must earn a profit; it simply means that earning a profit must be the partners' intent. In other words, the organization's purpose must be to try to earn a profit. There are several different types of partnerships, including general partnerships, limited partnerships, limited liability partnerships, and limited liability limited partnerships. How a partnership is formed and what, if any, statutory formalities apply depend on the type of partnership created. The Uniform Partnership Act, which has been adopted in whole or in part by most states, codifies partnership law on issues relating to partnership formation, operation, and termination.

The Four Main Forms of Business Organizations

- sole proprietorship
- partnership (of which there are many different types)
- corporation (of which there are many different types)
- limited liability company

A **sole proprietorship** is the simplest form of business organization, in which the owner of the business is actually the business.

A **sole proprietor** is the owner of a sole proprietorship.

A **partnership** is an association of two or more persons who carry on as co-owners of a business for profit.

Different Types of Partnerships

There are several different types of partnership authorized by state law, and these may vary from state to state. Common partnership types include:

- General partnership
- Limited partnership
- Limited liability partnership
- Limited liability limited partnership

In a partnership, the partners share in the decision making relating to the business. However, in cases of limited partnerships, only the general partners are involved in the operations of the business. That said, even in general partnerships, one or more partners may be elected by the partnership to be managing partners, charged with the task of managing the business.

There are several advantages of a partnership as a form of business organization. First, partnerships, especially general partnerships, can be easy to form without statutory formalities having to be met (note that certain statutory formalities are required to be met for limited partnerships, limited liability partnerships, and limited liability limited partnerships). Any profit earned from the partnership flows through to the individual tax returns of the partners and is taxed only once—at that level. The same is true of losses. Losses flow through to the partners' individual income tax returns. Capital may be easier to raise in a partnership than a sole proprietorship because partnerships, by definition, have more than one owner, so more than one person can contribute assets or obtain a loan. Further, in terms of continuity of the business, while the death of a partner may terminate the partnership as a legal entity, the business can continue on the restructuring of it as a new partnership (one composed of slightly different partners).

In a general partnership, each partner assumes unlimited personal liability for the debts and obligations of the business. This means that the partners' personal assets may be used to satisfy debts of the partnership. That is the major disadvantage of the partnership form of business organization. However,

Taxation of Partnerships

Partnerships file informational tax returns only. Partnership income is distributed to the partners and taxed on their individual tax returns.

through forms of partnership other than a general partnership, unlimited personal liability of limited partners may be eliminated.

Agency principles, discussed previously, apply to partners and partnerships. Each partner in the partnership is an agent of both the partnership and all the other partners. Accordingly, each partner assumes fiduciary responsibilities toward the partnership and other partners, such as the duties of truthfulness and loyalty.

Another major form of business organization is the corporate form. Corporations are the most common form of business organization today. A **corporation** is a legal entity, separate and distinct from its owners, that is created according to state statute to carry on a business activity. There are many types of corporations, including public corporations, private corporations, publicly held corporations, not-for-profit corporations, professional corporations, closely held corporations, and Subchapter S corporations.

A corporation is formed upon meeting the statutory requirements established by the state of formation. These requirements vary from state to state. Corporations, then, are creatures of state statute. Typically, the main part of this organization process is drafting articles of incorporation and filing them with the secretary of state's office. Once accepted, a **certificate of incorporation**, also called a **corporate charter**, is issued by the state. Also part of corporate formation, **corporate bylaws** are adopted, either by the incorporators or the initial board of directors, setting forth the rules for managing the business and operations of the corporation.

After formation, different groups of players are involved in the operation of a corporation. These groups are stockholders, officers, and directors. First, the owners of a corporation are called its **stockholders**, or **shareholders**. The greatest advantage of the corporate form of business organization is that

A **corporation** is a legal entity, separate and distinct from its owners, that is created according to state statute to carry on a business activity.

A **certificate of incorporation** is the document issued by a state that incorporates a corporation; it is also called a **corporate charter**.

Corporate bylaws are rules adopted either by the incorporators or the initial board of directors that set forth how the business will be managed and operated.

Stockholders are the owners of a corporation; they are also called **shareholders**.

stockholders are not personally liable for the debts and obligations of the business. Rather, their liability is limited to the extent of their investment in the corporation. They are said to have limited liability or limited liability protection. Stockholders have many functions. For example, they elect the board of directors, have the right to vote on important corporate matters, and are entitled to share in the profits (and losses) of the corporation. However, shareholders do not operate the business or manage its affairs. Those tasks are for others—officers and directors.

Officers are employees of the corporation who are charged with the responsibility of running the day-to-day operations of the corporation. A corporation may authorize such officers as president, various vice presidents (such as for marketing, finance, development, and so on), treasurer, secretary, assistant treasurer, assistant secretary, and the like. They are fiduciaries of the corporation, owing it both a duty of trust and a duty of loyalty. Officers are appointed by the corporation's board of directors.

Boards of directors are groups of directors who are elected by the shareholders and are responsible for the management of the corporation. Directors are not involved in the daily operations of the corporation. Rather, they participate in decision making on a higher management level. Examples of tasks boards of directors perform include appointing and removing corporate officers, declaring and paying corporate dividends to shareholders, approving corporate budgets, and adopting important corporate policies such as corporate compliance policies. Like officers, directors are fiduciaries of the corporation, owing duties of trust and loyalty.

The main advantage of the corporate form of business organization is the limited personal liability of shareholders. Another advantage is the greater ability of a corporation to raise capital compared to a sole proprietorship or partnership. Also, decision making is controlled through use of officers and directors. In addition, this form of business organization allows for continuity in that the death or bankruptcy of a shareholder does not impact, much less terminate, the corporation itself as a separate legal entity.

The main disadvantage of the corporate form of business organization is double-taxation. Corporations, as separate legal entities, are taxed on the profits they earn. Then, when the profits are distributed to shareholders in the form of dividends, shareholders must report these dividends on their individual income tax returns, where they are likely taxed on them. Thus, corporate earnings typically are taxed twice. Another disadvantage of the corporate form of business organization is the

statutory formalities required to form a corporation. If these statutory formalities are not complied with, then a corporation probably is not formed—so the business's owners do not enjoy limited liability protection.

Because of the great disadvantage of double-taxation with the corporate form of business organization, in the 1990s many states enacted statutes permitting a new form of business organization—the limited liability company, also called the limited liability corporation. A **limited liability company**, or **limited liability corporation** (LLC), is a legal entity, separate and distinct from its owners, that is created according to state statute to carry on a business activity and that combines certain advantages of both the corporate form of business organization and the partnership form of business organization.

Like a corporation, a limited liability company is created according to statutory formalities established in a state. These formalities vary from state to state. Owners of limited liability companies are called **members**. **Articles of organization**, rather than articles of incorporation, are filed with the secretary of state's office as part of the limited liability company formation process, and the rules for the limited liability company's operation and management are set forth in an **operating agreement**.

As a hybrid form of business organization, members of limited liability companies enjoy limited liability protection, just as shareholders of corporations do. This is one major advantage. Limited liability protection means that members of limited liability

Officers are employees of the corporation who are charged with the responsibility of running the day-to-day operations of the corporation.

Boards of directors are groups of directors who are elected by the shareholders and are responsible for the management of the corporation.

A **limited liability company** is a legal entity, separate and distinct from its owners, that is created according to state statute to carry on a business activity and that combines certain advantages of both the corporate form of business organization and the partnership form of business organization; it is also called a **limited liability corporation.**

Members are owners of limited liability companies.

Articles of organization are filed with the secretary of state's office to form a limited liability company.

Operating agreements are contracts setting forth the rules of operation and management for limited liability companies.

companies are not personally liable for the debts and obligations of the business. Rather, members' liability is limited to their investment in the business. The second major advantage is a tax advantage. Limited liability companies may elect to be taxed like partnerships rather than corporations by filing such an election with the Internal Revenue Service. By doing so, they avoid double-taxation to which corporations are subject.

In addition to these important advantages, the ability of a limited liability company to raise capital is similar to that of a corporation, which is an advantage over a sole proprietorship or partnership. Decision making in limited liability companies is also similar to corporations, as managing members can be elected to oversee the operation of the business, and boards of directors and officers can be instated for the same purposes as with corporations. Like corporations, limited liability companies enjoy continuity of the business upon the death, incapacity, or departure of a member; such occurrences need not terminate the business entity.

As a disadvantage, limited liability companies must be formed in compliance with the state's statutory formalities. Note that this list of disadvantages is very short. The limited liability company form of business organization has become very popular because, in many ways, it offers the best of both worlds in that members can enjoy limited liability protection that shareholders cannot, while, at the same time, double-taxation of earnings can be avoided.

Another important legal specialty area is bankruptcy. There have been major changes to the bankruptcy laws in recent years. Bankruptcy and laws regulating bankruptcies are examined next.

BANKRUPTCY

Bankruptcy is the legally acknowledged inability of an individual or a business organization to pay the debts it owes to its creditors. **Bankruptcy law** is that body of federal law that legally acknowledges the inability of an individual or organization to pay its debts and that allows the debtor to pay certain creditors what it can while giving the debtor some relief from debts in order to make a "fresh start." As indicated, bankruptcy law is federal law, found in the U.S. Bankruptcy Code. Bankruptcy law, then, addresses federal questions, and, accordingly, federal courts have jurisdiction to hear bankruptcy cases. That said, there are some state laws in areas *related* to bankruptcy, such as state laws governing secured transactions, and laws relating to the filing of liens and the collection of judgments. Also note that there are two goals of bankruptcy law: (1) to treat creditors fairly in the collection of debts owed by debtors and paid out of debtors' remaining assets, and (2) to allow debtors "fresh starts," free from creditors' claims after the bankruptcy proceedings.

Bankruptcy law is found in Title 11 of the *United States Code* (U.S.C.) and is referred to as the U.S. Bankruptcy Code, as noted above. There are nine chapters in this code. Chapters 1, 3, and 5 of the code contain general information, such as definitions and administrative and procedural provisions. Generally speaking, these chapters apply to all types of bankruptcies. The remaining six chapters of the code (Chapters 7, 9, 11, 12, 13, and 15) set forth different types of bankruptcies available to certain debtors. These are Chapter 7 liquidation proceedings, Chapter 9 adjustment of debts for municipalities, Chapter 11 business reorganizations, Chapter 12 family farmer and family fisherman proceedings, Chapter 13 adjustment of debts for individuals with regular income, and Chapter 15 cross-border

KEY Point

Types of Bankruptcies

- Chapter 7 liquidation proceedings, also called ordinary bankruptcy or straight bankruptcy;
- Chapter 9 adjustment of debts for municipalities;
- Chapter 11 business reorganizations;
- Chapter 12 family farmer and family fisherman proceedings;
- Chapter 13 adjustment of debts for individuals with regular income; and
- Chapter 15 cross-border insolvency.

Bankruptcy is the legally acknowledged inability of an individual or a business organization to pay the debts it owes to its creditors.

Bankruptcy law is that body of federal law that legally acknowledges the inability of an individual or organization to pay its debts and that allows the debtor to pay certain creditors what it can while giving the debtor some relief from debts in order to make a "fresh start."

insolvency. Chapter 15 is a new chapter of the bankruptcy code, added as part of the extensive 2005 reforms, discussed below, dealing with foreign companies having U.S. debts. You may be familiar with "chapters" as a term relating to "bankruptcy." This is the origin for that terminology.

We will discuss further the three types of bankruptcy that are most commonly used and that apply to a wider variety of debtors. In other words, Chapter 9, which applies to municipalities, Chapter 12, which applies to family farmers and family fisherman, and Chapter 15, which applies to foreign companies with U.S. debts, are not reviewed in greater detail because their application is so limited. We will examine Chapter 7 liquidation, Chapter 11 business reorganization, and Chapter 13 adjustment of debts for individuals with regular income, as they are the most commonly used and widely applicable types of bankruptcy.

Chapter 7 is liquidation bankruptcy. In liquidation bankruptcy, a debtor turns his assets over to a trustee who sells ("liquidates") the non-exempt assets and distributes the sales proceeds to creditors of the debtor in a liquidation proceeding. Most of the debtor's remaining debts are discharged, meaning the debtor is legally relieved of the obligation to pay them. This type of bankruptcy is also called ordinary bankruptcy or straight bankruptcy. Individuals and certain types of businesses may be debtors under Chapter 7 bankruptcy. Further, debtors may voluntarily file for Chapter 7 bankruptcy, called voluntary bankruptcy. However, when certain requirements are met, creditors may file petitions to force debtors into Chapter 7 bankruptcy, called involuntary bankruptcy. So Chapter 7 bankruptcies can be both voluntary and involuntary.

Chapter 11 involves reorganizations, typically business reorganizations. This is the most commonly used type of bankruptcy for debtors that are corporations, though most types of debtors, including individuals, may file under Chapter 11. In this type of bankruptcy, the debtor and its creditors make a plan pursuant to which the debtor will pay part of its debts and the remaining debts will be discharged. What makes this form of bankruptcy often advantageous is that the debtor is allowed to continue in business throughout the proceedings and thereafter (assuming the debtor stays solvent). Just like with Chapter 7 proceedings, proceedings under Chapter 11 may be voluntarily brought by the debtor or involuntarily brought by creditors.

Chapter 13 is the individual repayment plan form of bankruptcy. It is available for individuals as well as for certain businesses. "Individuals" typically means people who are salaried employees, but the term also includes sole proprietors, earners of investment income, and recipients of welfare benefits, Social Security benefits, and fixed pension distributions. Further, Chapter 13 is for individuals who have regular income and who owe debts below a certain threshold (with a current threshold of fixed unsecured debts of less than $336,900 or fixed secured debts of less than $1,010,650). Unlike Chapter 7 and Chapter 11 bankruptcies, Chapter 13 bankruptcy may not be involuntarily brought—meaning it may not be

© Ken Durden/Shutterstock

Circuit City

Circuit City Stores, Inc., which opened its first store in 1949, was a U.S. retailer in brand name consumer electronics, personal computers, entertainment software, and large appliances. Very successful for decades, in the 1970s Circuit City pioneered the electronics superstore format. On November 10, 2008, Circuit City, at the time the second-leading electronics retailer in the U.S. after Best Buy, filed for Chapter 11 bankruptcy protection. This filing occurred one week after Circuit City announced it was closing 155 stores because of the economic downturn negatively impacting consumer spending. The decision to file under Chapter 11 demonstrates Circuit City's intent at the time to continue to do business and pay its workers while it restructured its debt and business operations.

However, Circuit City was unable to successfully rebound after the Chapter 11 bankruptcy filing. When the company announced it would liquidate all stores, 567 stores were in operation. The liquidation of these remaining stores began on January 16, 2009, and the last stores were closed by March 8, 2009. The Circuit City brand was sold at auction in May 2009 to Systemax, which company began to sell electronics online under the brand name. Circuit City's former corporate headquarters was sold in September 2010.

Chapter 11 bankruptcy cases to Chapter 13 on consent of the debtor.

Bankruptcy laws were significantly reformed and revised during 2005 in an effort to make it harder for debtors to file for bankruptcy protection and avoid paying their debts. Leading up to the 2005 bankruptcy law reforms, when debtors had the choice of which type of bankruptcy to file, many individuals filed for bankruptcy under Chapter 7, allowing them to liquidate their assets and have almost all of their debts discharged. This left many creditors at a great loss in terms of their debt collection. This bankruptcy practice was viewed as too easy on many debtors and too hard on many creditors. One of the new laws' major reform goals was to require more individuals to pay as much of their debt as possible, rather than have so much of their debt discharged in bankruptcy. With the enactment of the bankruptcy reform laws, debtors with higher incomes become prohibited from filing for bankruptcy under Chapter 7. In other words, eligibility for Chapter 7 filing now is restricted. Accordingly, today fewer debtors qualify for Chapter 7 filing, and most individuals must file for bankruptcy under Chapter 13. Under Chapter 13, debtors enter into individual repayment plans to pay as much of their debts as possible within a five-year period. Another reform enacted with these laws is the requirement that debtors receive credit counseling before they can file for bankruptcy under either Chapter 7 or Chapter 13.

Contracts are another very important legal specialty area. Contracts impact virtually all areas of law and business, from commercial transactions to real estate transactions to litigation settlements to consumer transactions. Contracts and contract law are reviewed next.

commenced by creditors of a debtor. Chapter 13 bankruptcy may only be commenced by a voluntary petition filed by the debtor or by the conversion of certain Chapter 7 or

CONTRACTS

A **contract** is a legally enforceable (binding) agreement between two or more parties. A contract consists of a promise or a set of promises made by one or more parties to the contract, for which the law provides a remedy in the event of breach of such promise(s). A **promise** is an assurance by a party to a contract that something will, or will not, happen in the future. For example, Harry may promise to mow Joshua's lawn if Joshua promises to pay Harry $75. This is a legally enforceable exchange of promises between two parties, with one party (Harry) promising to mow Joshua's lawn and the other party (Joshua) promising to pay Harry $75 for that service. As another example, this one of a promise *not* to do something,

Martha may promise not to sue Thomas for the damage he negligently caused her in a car accident if Thomas pays Martha $20,000.

Note that to be a contract more than one person must be involved, with "person" understood to mean a human or legal

> A **contract** is a legally enforceable agreement between two or more parties.
>
> A **promise** is an assurance by a party to a contract that something will, or will not, happen in the future.

© Stockbyte/Thinkstock

entity (organization). A person who enters into a contract with another is called a **party** to the contract.

Contract law deals with the creation and enforcement of contracts. Many attorneys' and paralegals' practices involve the practice of contract law, whether drafting contracts, reviewing contracts, or litigating disputes arising out of contracts.

There are two main sources of contract law, common law and the Uniform Commercial Code. An important source of contract law is common law, which is judge-made law coming from court opinions. State court decisions (with some federal court decisions) make up the body of the common law of contracts.

In addition, each state has enacted a commercial code, most of which are based at least in part on the Uniform Commercial Code. The **Uniform Commercial Code** (UCC) is a model code governing commercial transactions that was written by legal experts and scholars to address commercial law issues and to provide uniform guidance to jurisdictions. Every state in its own way has adopted UCC, either in whole or in part, by statute. Article 2 of UCC governs contracts for the sale of goods. Accordingly, besides the common law of contracts, each state has statutory law on contracts for the sale of goods in its commercial code. When a contract

involves subject matter other than the sale of goods, Article 2 of the state's commercial code does not apply. Where the contract involves the sale of goods, Article 2 of the state's commercial code applies. If the statute has not modified a common law principle, then the common law of contracts applies as well. In other words, sales contracts are governed both by the relevant statute (the commercial code) and by the common law of contracts. In studying Article 2 in your contract law class, you will see that UCC Article 2 provisions relax, or make easier, some of the common law rules—thus facilitating contracts for the sale of goods.

Both the common law of contracts and the states' commercial codes differ from state to state. Accordingly, while there are

A **party** is a person who enters into a contract with another.

Contract law deals with the creation and enforcement of contracts.

The **Uniform Commercial Code** (UCC) is a model code governing commercial transactions that was written by legal experts and scholars to address commercial law issues and to provide uniform guidance to jurisdictions; it has been adopted, by statute, in whole or in part by every states.

often similar general common law and statutory law principles that apply throughout the states, these laws are state-specific. In other words, both the common law and statutory law of contracts vary from state to state.

How are contracts formed? Under the common law, there are four requirements, called essential elements, of a contract. These essential elements of a contract are agreement, consideration, contractual capacity, and legality. Each of these elements is discussed in turn.

The first essential element of a contract is agreement. **Agreement** is the manifestation of assent by the parties to enter into a legally binding contract. It is often said under the law that where parties have reached an agreement, there is a "meeting of the minds." Agreement consists of two parts, offer and acceptance.

One party must make an offer to form a contract to another party. An **offer** is a promise to do or refrain from doing (not do) something at some point in the future. For there to be a valid offer, three things must be present. First, the person making the offer must intend to be bound by it. Second, the offer itself must be definite, meaning that its terms must be reasonably certain and ascertainable. Third, the offer must be communicated to the person to whom it is made. The person who makes the offer is called the **offeror**. The person to whom the offer is made is called the **offeree**. For example, Susan (the offeror) may offer to sell her diamond ring to Tony (the offeree) for $5,000.

The offeree may accept or reject the offer. If the offeree accepts the offer (in the proper form and within the time allowed under the law), then the parties have reached an agreement.

Remember that an agreement is the first essential element of a contract. For example, if Joel asks Ricky if Ricky would like Joel to wash and wax Ricky's car for $70 and Ricky responds, "Yes, that would be great," then Ricky (the offeree) accepted Joel's offer, and the two have reached an agreement pursuant to the common law of contracts.

What if Ricky's response was, "No, thank you"? In that scenario, Ricky rejected Joel's offer. Therefore, the two did not reach an agreement, the first essential element of a contract.

Remember that acceptance by an offeree is that person's indication of assent to be bound to the terms of the offer. Acceptance must be communicated to the offeree for there to be an agreement.

The second essential element of a contract is consideration. **Consideration** means something of value must be given or promised in exchange for another's promise. This element is what distinguishes contracts from gifts. In the example involving Joel and Ricky, the consideration is Joel's promise to wash and wax Ricky's car and Ricky's promise to pay Joel $70 for those services.

Consideration can be in the form of money, as indicated in the previous example. It can also be in the form of a promise to perform a service, as also indicated in that example. Consideration can be anything of value that is given or promised in exchange for another's promise, whether in the form of money,

Agreement is the manifestation of assent by the parties to enter into a legally binding contract, commonly referred to as a "meeting of the minds."

An **offer** is a promise to do or refrain from doing something at some point in the future.

An **offeror** is the person who makes an offer in the formation of a contract.

An **offeree** is the person to whom an offer to enter into a contract is made.

Consideration means something of value must be given or promised in exchange for another's promise.

other property (such as a diamond ring, computer, or shares of stock), the promise to perform an action (such as washing and waxing a car), or the promise to refrain from performing an action (such as refraining from bringing a tort lawsuit). Note that all parties to the contract must promise or give consideration for there to be a contract.

For consideration to be valid under the law, two requirements must be met. First, something of legal value must be given or promised in exchange for another's promise. To have legal value, something must be either legally detrimental to the person making the promise (such as a promise to wash and wax another's car) or legally beneficial to the person to whom the promise is made (such as a promise to pay another $70). In other words, one must promise to do something she has no legal duty to do (such as to babysit another's child) or refrain from doing something she has the legal right to do (such as refrain from bringing a validly existing legal claim against another). Second, there must be a bargained-for exchange. This means that the consideration given by one party to the contract must induce the other party's promise or performance. This is the specific part of consideration that distinguishes contracts from gifts. One party's promise or performance must induce the other party's promise or performance, and vice versa.

KEY Point

The Requirements for Valid Consideration
1. something of legal value must be given or promised in exchange for another's promise, and
2. there must be a bargained-for exchange.

To illustrate, distinguish the following examples. Lucy offers to watch Mrs. Turnball's young daughter for three hours, and Mrs. Turnball agrees to pay Lucy $10 per hour. The two have an agreement for Lucy to babysit, with the consideration being the three hours of babysitting and $30. There is a bargained-for exchange of things of legal value. What if Mrs. Turnball is talking to Lucy and other neighbors when she receives an emergency phone call asking her to immediately come to work (where she is a hospital physician). Lucy, hearing this, says to Mrs. Turnball, "Go ahead. I'll watch your daughter until you return." Upon her return, Mrs. Turnball says to Lucy, "Thank you so much for your help! I don't know what I would have done without you. Here, let me give you $30 for your trouble." In the second scenario, was Mrs. Turnball legally obligated to pay $30 to Lucy for watching her child? No. There was no

bargained-for exchange between the parties at the time Lucy agreed to watch the child. In fact, Lucy did not request payment. When Mrs. Turnball offered Lucy $30 after the fact, that compensation was a gift—not consideration that forms the basis of a contract.

What if Dennis offers to sell his Ford Mustang convertible, worth $15,000, to Samantha for $500 (because Dennis is flirting with Samantha and thinks she is really cute—plus, the car broke down last week, which really inconvenienced and angered Dennis, who is not yet over it)? If Samantha agrees to buy the car at that price, is there consideration? In other words, under the law, does it matter that Dennis is making a really bad deal? No. Generally speaking, courts will not review the adequacy of consideration exchanged between the parties so long as the consideration is both legally sufficient and bargained for. In certain extreme cases, such as where fraud or duress are present, courts may intervene, but normally they will not review adequacy of consideration—so parties are free to make bad bargains.

The third essential element of a contract is contractual capacity. **Contractual capacity** means the legal ability of a person to enter into a contractual relationship. Generally speaking, courts presume contractual capacity is present. However, some people may lack capacity to enter into contracts, depending on the circumstances. For example, minors (children) lack contractual capacity. If a minor enters into a contract, she may disaffirm (cancel) the contract at any time during her minority or within a reasonable time after reaching majority (adulthood)—thereby avoiding her legal obligations under that contract. Mentally incompetent persons may also lack contractual capacity. If a court determines (in other words, adjudicates) that a person is mentally incompetent and a legal guardian has been appointed by the court to represent that person, then that person is not capable of entering into contracts, for he lacks contractual capacity. If a person is mentally incompetent but has not been adjudicated as such by a court, he may avoid a contract he entered into when suffering from mental incompetence in the same way a minor can. Sometimes even intoxicated persons lack contractual capacity. Intoxication can result from alcohol intake or drug use, and can be voluntary or involuntary. While rare, a court may permit a person who was intoxicated at the time of entering into a contract to avoid his obligations under the contract, determining he lacked contractual capacity.

> **Contractual capacity** means the legal ability of a person to enter into a contractual relationship.

The last essential element of a contract is legality. **Legality** means the contract must be formed for a legal purpose, meaning one that is not illegal or contrary to public policy. Suppose Frank offers Vivian $1,500 if Vivian will have sex with him. Have Frank and Vivian entered into a legally enforceable agreement such that Vivian can sue Frank for breach of contract if she performs and Frank fails to pay? No, they have not entered into a legally enforceable agreement. Agreements to sell sexual services are illegal in most U.S. jurisdictions. Thus, they are not contracts at all, and promises made in that regard are not legally enforceable.

Contracts may be oral, or they may be written. All states have enacted a statute called the **Statute of Frauds**, which requires that certain types of contracts be in writing and signed by the person against whom enforcement is sought to be enforceable. While Statutes of Frauds vary from state to state, most require the following types of contracts be in writing: contracts involving interests in real property, contracts that cannot by their terms be performed within one year from their date of formation, collateral contracts (such as a contract to pay the debt of another), promises made in consideration of marriage, and contracts for the sale of goods priced at $500 or more. Even where a written contract is not required, however, and an oral contract is valid, it may be wise to reduce the contract to writing to provide clear evidence of its terms—in the event a dispute arises under the contract in the future and its terms must be proven in court.

The contracts we have just discussed are express contracts. **Express contracts** are contracts expressed in oral or written words and are voluntarily and deliberately entered into by the parties to them.

Some contracts are formed not by the voluntary agreement of the parties, however. Contracts may be implied in fact or implied in law. **Implied in fact contracts** are contracts that are inferred from the parties' conduct rather than from their words. Implied in fact contracts may be found to exist where a party provides property or services to another with the expectation of payment and the other party was given the opportunity to reject the property or services but did not do so. While no express contract was created by the parties, the courts may imply one based on the conduct of the parties. The purpose for such an implied contract is to prevent one party from being unjustly benefited to the detriment of the other party. **Implied in law contracts**, also called **quasi-contracts**, are contracts that are imposed by courts to prevent the unjust enrichment of a party to the detriment of another party. This is an equitable legal doctrine that permits a party to recover the reasonable value of property or services provided. For example, when an off-duty EMT provides emergency lifesaving services to a crime victim, that EMT may be awarded by the court the reasonable value of the services she performed to the victim.

Now that we have reviewed contract formation, we will review contract performance and contract enforcement. Most parties to contracts do what they promise to do under the terms of those contracts. Parties doing what they promise to do is the most common type of performance under contracts. Performance of a party's contractual duties terminates, or discharges, those duties because it fulfills the party's obligations, as promised under the contract. What happens when a party fails to perform his obligations under a contract, either partially or fully? For example, what happens if, when Ricky promised to pay Joel $70 for washing and waxing his car, either Ricky fails to pay Joel, or pays Joel only $20 while Joel has adequately washed and waxed Ricky's car?

KEY Point

Statute of Frauds

Most states' Statute of Frauds require the following types of contracts to be in writing:

- Contracts involving interests in real property
- Contracts that cannot by their terms be performed within one year from their date of formation
- Collateral contracts
- Promises made in consideration of marriage
- Contracts for the sale of goods priced at $500 or more

Legality means the contract must be formed for a legal purpose, meaning one that is not illegal or contrary to public policy.

The **Statute of Frauds** is a state statute that requires certain types of contracts to be in writing and signed by the person against whom enforcement is sought.

Express contracts are contracts expressed in oral or written words and are voluntarily and deliberately entered into by the parties to them.

Implied in fact contracts are contracts that are inferred from the parties' conduct rather than from their words.

Implied in law contracts are contracts that are imposed by courts to prevent the unjust enrichment of a party to the detriment of another party; they are also called **quasi-contracts**.

In such a situation, Ricky has breached the contract with Joel because he has failed to fulfill his obligations under the contract—which obligations were to pay Joel $70. **Breach of contract** is the failure of a party to a contract to completely perform under the contract. It is a type of legal claim in the civil law system. Joel would be entitled to a remedy in the event he successfully sues Ricky for breach of contract.

A **remedy** is a judicial award by which legal rights are enforced and the violations of rights are compensated. There are two types of remedies, remedies at law and remedies in equity. **Remedies at law** are money damages. In the case where Joel washed and waxed Ricky's car but Ricky only paid Joel $20, Joel would likely recovery a remedy at law, namely damages in the amount of $50, to compensate Joel for the services performed in the amount agreed on by the parties. **Remedies in equity** are all remedies other than money damages, such as injunctions, rescission, restitution, reformation, specific performance, and so on. **Injunctions** are court orders requiring a person to do, or refrain from doing, something. This type of equitable remedy is often relevant in tort claims involving trespass and in intellectual property infringement claims. **Rescission** is the termination of a contract and return of the parties to their pre-contracting positions. Based on the facts of the Joel/Ricky scenario, rescission is not possible because Joel cannot unperform the washing and waxing of Ricky's car. **Restitution** is the act of restoring a contractual party to his pre-contracting position, again not possible in the Joel/Ricky scenario. **Reformation** is the court's revision of a contract to reflect the party's true intentions, such as by correcting a typographical error in a written contract. **Specific performance** is granting the actual performance promised under the contract and is usually awarded in cases involving unique goods or real property (each parcel of real property is considered to be unique).

For breach of sale of goods contracts, Article 2 of the UCC (and related state commercial codes) sets forth sellers' and buyers' remedies appropriate for specific situations. These remedies are designed to put the injured party in as good a position as if the breaching party had fully performed under the contract.

What if Ricky paid Joel only $20 because Joel washed, but failed to wax, the car? In that case, if Joel's performance was not adequate, Joel, or both Ricky and Joel, may be in breach of contract (depending on the extent of Joel's nonperformance). Courts will consider and evaluate the extent of a party's performance when less-than-complete performance exists. They will consider whether or not a party substantially performed, and award damages or some other remedy to the injured party to the extent performance was not complete. For complete failure of performance, a court may consider remedies beyond damages, such as restitution or rescission.

Another important legal specialty area is employment law. Employment law governs the employment relationship, meaning the legal relationship existing between employers and employees. Employment and employment law are discussed next.

Breach of contract is the failure of a party to a contract to completely perform under the contract.

A **remedy** is a judicial award by which legal rights are enforced and the violations of rights are compensated.

Remedies at law are money damages.

Remedies in equity are all remedies other than money damages, such as injunctions, rescission, restitution, reformation, specific performance, and so on.

Injunctions are court orders requiring a person to do, or refrain from doing, something.

Rescission is the termination of a contract and return of the parties to their pre-contracting positions.

Restitution is the act of restoring a contractual party to his pre-contracting position.

Reformation is the court's revision of a contract to reflect the party's true intentions.

Specific performance is granting the actual performance promised under the contract, normally awarded in cases involving unique goods or real property.

EMPLOYMENT

Employment laws impact employment relationships. For employment laws to apply, an employment relationship must exist. When does an employment relationship exist?

Under the law, there is no universal definition of "employment," "employer," or "employee." That said, courts and regulatory agencies have generally defined an **employer** to be one who hires another to perform work on his behalf, and who has the right to control the details of how the work is performed. Courts, in determining whether an employment relationship exists, consider several factors, with the most important factor being the degree of control exercised by the employer over the employee. Other factors courts consider in making this determination include the skill required to perform the work; the source of the tools and instrumentalities of the work; the location where the work is performed; the duration of the relationship of the parties; the hiring party's right to assign additional projects; the worker's discretion over when and how long to work; the method of payment of the worker;

the worker's role in hiring and paying assistants; whether the work is part of the hiring party's regular business; whether the worker is in business; whether employment benefits are provided to the worker; and the tax treatment of the worker. If a worker is not an employee of the employer, she is classified as an independent contractor. This impacts not only the application of the employment laws, but also vicarious tort liability of the employer based on the conduct of the worker. Note that where employment relationships exist, employment laws apply.

Historically, employment relationships were governed by common law. The most important common law doctrine regarding employment relationships is the employment at will doctrine. The **employment at will doctrine** is a common law rule stating that when an employment relationship is of indefinite duration, it can be terminated by either the employer or the employee at any time, for any reason. In other words, employment is terminable at the will of either the employer or the employee.

Today, many federal and state statutes regulate employment and the workplace, providing many legal protections to employees. These include statutes limiting the employment at will doctrine to some extent. With the enactment of various statutes in the area of employment law, the employment at will doctrine today more narrowly provides that the employer or the employee can terminate the employment relationship at any time, for any reason *other than an illegal reason*, such as discrimination or retaliation.

KEY Point

Factors in Determining Whether an Employment Relationship Exists

The following factors are used by courts in determining whether an employment relationship exists:

- The degree of control exercised by the employer over the employee
- The skill required to perform the work
- The source of the tools and instrumentalities of the work
- The location where the work is performed
- The duration of the relationship of the parties
- The hiring party's right to assign additional projects
- The worker's discretion over when and how long to work
- The method of payment of the worker
- The worker's role in hiring and paying assistants
- Whether the work is part of the hiring party's regular business
- Whether the worker is in business
- Whether employment benefits are provided to the worker
- The tax treatment of the worker

KEY Point

The Employment at Will Doctrine

Under the common law employment at will doctrine, the employer or the employee can terminate the employment relationship at any time, for any reason.

An **employer** (generally) is one who hires another to perform work on his behalf, and who has the right to control the details of how the work is performed.

The **employment at will doctrine** is a common law rule stating that when an employment relationship is of indefinite duration, it can be terminated by either the employer or the employee at any time, for any reason.

The Occupational Safety and Health Act and Occupational Safety and Health Administration

An important federal statute in the area of employment law is the Occupational Safety and Health Act. The Occupational Safety and Health Act promotes safety in the workplace by imposing a general duty on employers to provide a work environment that is free from recognized hazards that are likely to cause or are causing death, injury, or illness to employees. The Occupational Safety and Health Act established the Occupational Safety and Health Administration (OSHA) as a federal administrative agency within the U.S. Department of Labor with authority to enforce the act. OSHA's mission is to help prevent workplace injuries, illnesses, and deaths by issuing and enforcing standards for workplace safety and health. As part of its enforcement power, OSHA inspects employment facilities for compliance, looking for safety violations and health hazards. In addition, it imposes on employers duties relating to recordkeeping and reporting of workplace deaths, injuries, and illnesses.

KEY Point

The Occupational Safety and Health Act

The Occupational Safety and Health Act is a federal statute that promotes workplace safety and established the Occupational Safety and Health Administration (OSHA) within the U.S. Department of Labor.

Workers' Compensation Statutes

State workers' compensation statutes also regulate employee safety, but in a more narrow sense—focusing on compensation. Workers' compensation statutes set forth compensation schemes for workers and families of workers who are injured or become ill on the job. The presence of workers' compensation statutes prevents employees from having to sue their employers in tort, probably for negligence, for injuries sustained by employees in the workplace. This is valuable because, before workers' compensation statutes were enacted by the states and tort lawsuits were the method used for employees to recover against their employers for workplace injuries, employers were able to successfully assert defenses to the tort of negligence and avoid liability. Workers' compensation statutes now provide an administrative procedure for workers who are injured or become ill on the job so they can receive compensation for those injuries. Compensation benefits are paid

KEY Point

Workers' Compensation

States have enacted workers' compensation statutes to make law certain administrative compensation schemes for workers and their families when a worker is injured or becomes ill on the job.

in an established amount that is set forth in the statute or a related regulation. For example, a dismembered thumb is worth a certain amount of compensation under a state's workers' compensation statute or related regulation, which amount may vary from state to state because these are state laws and regulations, not federal ones.

The Fair Labor Standards Act

The ability of children to work and the wage rates for all workers is regulated by another federal statute in the area of employment law. The Fair Labor Standards Act (FLSA) prohibits oppressive child labor, and through its regulations, restricts the employment of children.

Besides regulating child labor, the Fair Labor Standards Act also sets the federal minimum wage and overtime pay requirements. The federal minimum wage changes from time to time (at the time of the writing of this text, the last time the federal minimum wage was set was July 24, 2009, at $7.25 per hour). States also have minimum wage requirements that can be more, but not less, than the federal minimum wage. The Fair Labor Standards Act requires employers to pay nonexempt employees at least one and one-half times their regular

Child Labor Regulations

- Children under 14 years old may work only as newspaper delivery persons.
- Children who are 14 or 15 years old may work limited hours in nonhazardous employment, which is approved by the Department of Labor, such as in restaurants.
- Children who are 16 or 17 years old may work unlimited hours in nonhazardous employment.
- Children who are 18 years old or older may work in any employment, whether or not hazardous, and for unlimited hours.

There are exemptions for certain child employees, such as those who work as entertainers or in the field of agriculture.

The Fair Labor Standards Act

The Fair Labor Standards Act regulates child labor, sets the federal minimum wage rate, and regulates overtime pay.

Title VII of the Civil Rights Act

Title VII of the Civil Rights Act prohibits employment discrimination that is based on race, color, national origin, religion, or sex.

wage rate for hours worked over 40 hours per week as overtime pay. Remember our discussion from Chapter 2 regarding the debate on whether paralegals are exempt or non-exempt employees under FLSA. This determination affects whether the law requires that they be paid overtime for hours worked over 40 hours per week.

Title VII of the Civil Rights Act of 1964 and the Equal Employment Opportunity Commission

Another very important federal statute in the area of employment law is Title VII of the Civil Rights Act of 1964. Title VII of the Civil Rights Act (itself called the Fair Employment Practices Act) prohibits employment discrimination that is based on race, color, national origin, religion, or sex (gender), including sexual harassment as an additional protection made by the courts in interpreting the Title VII statute. By later amendment to Title VII, pregnancy was added to this list of categories. These categories are referred to as "protected classes." And also added was "genetics" according to Statute in Point. The Equal Employment Opportunity Commission (EEOC) is the federal agency established and given authority to enforce most of the federal employment laws prohibiting discrimination. Types of employment discrimination prohibited under Title VII include discrimination in hiring decisions, promotion or demotion decisions, decisions regarding job training, decisions regarding payment of compensation and employment benefits, and decisions regarding employment termination.

The Equal Employment Opportunity Commission

The Equal Employment Opportunity Commission (EEOC) is the federal agency established and given authority to enforce most of the employment laws prohibiting discrimination.

STATUTE *on* POINT

Genetics as a Protected Class

On November 21, 2009, a federal statute called the Genetic Information Nondisclosure Act (GINA) was enacted. This statute gives "genetic information" protected class status under Title VII of the Civil Rights Act of 1964. Genetic information includes information about a person's genetic tests and the genetic tests of a person's family members, as well as information about the manifestation of a disease or disorder in a person's family (a person's family medical history).

The statute prohibits employers from requesting, requiring, or purchasing genetic information about employees or their family members, with some limited exceptions. The statute protects employees who have suffered discrimination on the basis of their genetic information, or from retaliation for asserting their rights under this statute. A major purpose behind the passing of this statute was to prevent employers from denying certain employment benefits (like health insurance) on the basis of an employee's (or family member's) risk, even if remote, of developing a medical condition.

Sexual Orientation as a Protected Class

Note that Title VII does not include in its protected classes sexual orientation. Accordingly, federal law does not (at least not yet) prohibit employment discrimination based on sexual orientation. Some states, however, have expanded their state anti-discrimination statutes to include sexual orientation as a protected class.

The Age Discrimination in Employment Act and the Americans with Disabilities Act

Following the enactment of Title VII, further anti-discrimination statutes in the area of employment law were enacted by Congress. These include the Age Discrimination in Employment Act (ADEA) and the Americans with Disabilities Act (ADA). The Age

© INSADCO Photography/Alamy

to gender where the work requires equal skill, effort, working conditions, and the like. The federal statute requires equal pay for equal work, in essence, at least when it comes to gender.

The Family and Medical Leave Act

More recently, federal law extended employment protections for certain family and medical leave. The Family and Medical Leave Act (FMLA) provides certain workers with unpaid time off from work for important family and medical matters. There are restrictions in the types of employers and employees covered under the act, such as the number of workers employed by the employer and the length of time the employee has worked for the

Discrimination in Employment Act prohibits age discrimination in employment, which after later amendment, protects workers 40 years of age or older. The Americans with Disabilities Act prohibits discrimination against workers with disabilities, requiring employers to make reasonable accommodations for disabled workers where doing so does not create an undue hardship for the employers.

The Equal Pay Act

The Equal Pay Act, a federal statute enacted the year before Title VII of the Civil Rights Act, prohibits discrimination in compensation based on a person's gender. In other words, it protects both sexes (male or female) against pay differences due

employer. Where covered, employees may get up to 12 weeks of unpaid leave during a 12-month period for such matters as caring for a newly born or adopted child, treating a serious medical condition, or caring for a close relative with a serious health condition.

Another important legal specialty area is environmental law. In recent decades, there has been a movement to protect the Earth and its resources, for future generations. U.S. law has developed to protect the environment in certain ways. An examination of the laws protecting the environment is next.

ENVIRONMENTAL

The **environment** is the sum total of all the resources in which we live. It is important because the environment sustains all life forms, including human life. Over the last several decades, we, as a society, have begun to realize the impact, often negative, that humans have on their environment. To protect the environment from further impact and damage, at least to some extent, governments at all levels have created **environmental laws**.

Historically, tort law theories were used to bring legal actions against businesses that polluted the environment. For example, the tort of negligence could be asserted against a business for unreasonably causing environmental harm. Those injured by the abnormally dangerous activities of others, such as another's transporting of hazardous materials, could recover under the strict liability theory for the injury they suffered. Toxic torts are a special type of personal injury tort lawsuit where a plaintiff claims that exposure to a toxic chemical caused her injury or disease.

Beyond the common law tort theories of recovery, starting in the 1960s, federal, state, and local governments began to heavily regulate the environment via statutes and related rules and regulations. Governments regulated in ways to protect air and water from pollution, to protect wildlife, to make drinking water safe, and to restrict the dumping of pollutants, toxins, and hazardous wastes on land resources and into the waterways, as examples. In 1969, the statutory requirement for the preparation of an environmental impact statement (EIS), necessary when a major federal action or legislation is proposed that

will significantly impact the environment, was enacted as part of the National Environmental Policy Act (NEPA). In 1970, Congress created the Environmental Protection Agency (EPA) to oversee environmental protection on the federal level.

The Clean Air Act

The most important federal statute regulating air pollution is the Clean Air Act. This federal statute regulates air quality by monitoring pollution created both by stationary sources, such as manufacturing facilities and oil refineries, and mobile sources, such as automobiles and airplanes. These laws regulate pollution emissions in part by having EPA establish national

KEY Point

The Clean Air Act

The Clean Air Act is a federal statute that regulates air pollution.

The **environment** is the sum total of all the resources in which we live.

Environmental laws are laws created at all levels of government to protect the environment from human impact and damage.

ambient air quality standards for specific pollutants, such as for ozone and carbon monoxide (see the end-of-chapter exercise to review these pollutants and standards). Large civil damages awards can be assessed and criminal penalties imposed for violations of the Clean Air Act.

The Clean Water Act

Another significant area of federal regulation of the environment concerns water pollution. The Clean Water Act was enacted to make water bodies safe for swimming and other forms of human recreation, as well as to protect wildlife and fish. It does this by establishing water quality standards that must be achieved. The act also helps eliminate the discharge of pollutants into waterways by requiring permits before a business can discharge waste into navigable waters. It also prohibits thermal pollution, which is pollution caused by the discharge of heated water or other materials into waterways that impacts the ecological balance in those waters. Further, the act protects wetlands such as marshes and swamps, habitats for many forms of wildlife. There are other federal statutes that protect against water pollution, dealing with the safety of drinking water (the Safe Drinking Water Act), protecting waters from oil pollution (the Oil Pollution Act), and requiring a permit for dumping certain materials into the ocean and well as prohibiting ocean dumping of chemical and certain radioactive materials (the Marine Protection, Research, and Sanctuaries Act).

> ### KEY Point
>
> **The Clean Water Act**
>
> The Clean Water Act is a federal statute that regulates water pollution.

Regulation of Hazardous Waste Disposal and Toxic Substance Release

Hazardous waste disposal and toxic substance release into the environment are also regulated by federal statute today. **Hazardous waste** is waste that is generated by businesses or households whose improper disposal poses a danger to human health and the environment. Examples include dry cleaning solvents, sewage, and used motor oil. Improper hazardous waste disposal can pollute air, water, and land. Hazardous waste disposal is regulated by the Resource Conservation and Recovery Act (RCRA) and the Comprehensive Environmental Response, Compensation, and Liability Act (CERCLA, also known as "Superfund"). The main goal of these acts is to clean up contaminated disposal sites. Toxic substance release is regulated by federal statutes

including the Toxic Substances Control Act. Toxic substances refer to chemicals. Chemicals of all kinds are used by businesses or created by them for marketing and sale, and when released into the environment, they can cause adverse health effects in humans, animals, and plants. The Toxic Substances Control Act targets the release of toxic chemicals into the environment, regulating these releases and the manufacturing and sale of toxic chemicals that are a threat to the environment.

Endangered Species Protection

Nonhuman animals are also protected by federal statute. For example, the Endangered Species Act protects endangered and also threatened species of animals. This act protects the habitats in which such wildlife lives, as well as protects the wildlife from hunting and other forms of "taking" (such as capturing and collecting).

> ### KEY Point
>
> **Examples of Federal Environmental Protection Statutes**
>
> The Clean Air Act
>
> The Clean Water Act
>
> The Safe Drinking Water Act
>
> The Oil Pollution Act
>
> The Marine Protection, Research, and Sanctuaries Act
>
> The Resource Conservation and Recovery Act
>
> The Comprehensive Environmental Response, Compensation, and Liability Act
>
> The Toxic Substances Control Act
>
> The Endangered Species Act

State and Local Regulation of the Environment

Besides federal regulation of environmental protection, state and local governments also regulate in this area. Like the federal regulations, state and local regulations set forth the degree to which the environment may be polluted, limiting and prohibiting certain kinds of pollution. Similar to the federal government's establishing an agency responsible for environmental protection (EPA), states have created their own administrative agencies to oversee environmental protection within their borders.

> **Hazardous waste** is waste that is generated by businesses or households whose improper disposal poses a danger to human health and the environment.

Because of the extent of the growth of regulation of the environment at all levels of government, especially at the federal level, environmental compliance is a significant legal duty owed by businesses today and a significant expense for them.

Another important legal specialty area is intellectual property and the laws that protect it. Next we will review the different types of intellectual property and examine how intellectual property is protected by law.

INTELLECTUAL PROPERTY

Intellectual property is any product of the human mind that is protected by law. It includes certain inventive and creative works, as well as some things that help competitors in business.

Intellectual property is a form of personal property. This is so because, as discussed in the next chapter, it is property other than land and anything permanently attached to land. Intellectual property is intangible, rather than tangible, personal property because it is property that you cannot hold or touch—it does not have physical existence.

> **KEY Point**
>
> **What Kind of Property Is Intellectual Property?**
> Intellectual property is intangible personal property.

Intellectual property laws are laws that protect the different types of intellectual property. The U.S. Constitution, in Article I, Section 8, Clause 8, authorizes Congress to promote the progress of science and useful arts by giving authors and inventors, for limited periods of time, the exclusive right to their works. This clause, known as the Copyright and Patent Clause, allows Congress to make laws permitting limited monopolies to authors and inventors of copyrightable and patentable works. Besides the constitutional authorization for copyrights and patents, federal and state legislatures have enacted legislation protecting certain types of intellectual property. In addition, case law interprets these statutes, coming from both federal and state courts. These laws, together, grant intellectual property owners limited monopolies in their works to promote their development and use. In essence, intellectual property laws encourage intellectual endeavors, such as inventions and discoveries, creative works of authorship, and even unique product and service branding, as well as confidential information that gives businesses a competitive advantage.

What are the different types of intellectual property? There are four: patents, copyrights, trademarks/service marks, and trade secrets.

> **KEY Point**
>
> **The Four Main Types of Intellectual Property**
>
> - patents
> - copyrights
> - trademarks/service marks
> - trade secrets

A **patent** is a governmental grant that gives an inventor or discoverer the exclusive right to make, use, and sell his invention or discovery for a limited period of time. Examples of patents include the design for a new roller coaster, a new pharmaceutical drug, and new computer hardware technology. A patent is obtained by filing a patent application with the U.S. Patent and Trademark Office (PTO) and having that application approved and the patent issued. Because of the U.S. Constitutional grant of authority given to Congress to establish patent laws, patent laws are federal laws and the patent statute is a federal one. There are no state patent laws. While the patent statute is amended and revised from time to time, currently, the life of a patent is either 20 years from the date of the patent application or 14 years from the date of the patent's issue, depending on whether the patent is a utility patent,

> **Intellectual property** is any product of the human mind that is protected by law.
>
> **Intellectual property laws** are laws that protect the different types of intellectual property.
>
> A **patent** is a governmental grant that gives an inventor or discoverer the exclusive right to make, use, and sell his invention or discovery for a limited period of time.

a plant patent, or a design patent. Patents are not renewable, and the monopoly they provide ends when the patent expires. When a person who is not the patent owner makes, uses, or sells the invention or discovery that is the subject matter of a patent without the patent owner's permission, that person has committed patent infringement and can be held liable for damages. Further, an injunction can be issued by a court to order the infringer to stop the infringing acts.

A **copyright** is the exclusive right of an author or other creator of a copyrightable work to reproduce, publish, adapt, publicly perform, and publicly display that work for a limited time. Examples of copyright include the novel *Harry Potter and the Sorcerer's Stone,* the song "Paparazzi," and a recorded speech made by the president. Like patent law, copyright law originates in the Copyright and Patent Clause of the U.S. Constitution, where Congress was authorized to enact a copyright statute. It did so and, accordingly, copyright law, like patent law, is strictly federal law. There is no state copyright law.

Unlike patents, which protect inventions and discoveries, copyrights protect works of authorship and other creative works. There are eight categories of copyrightable works. They are literary works; dramatic works; pictorial, graphic, and sculptural works; pantomime and choreographic works; motion pictures and other audiovisual works; architectural works; musical works; and sound recordings. Like patent law, copyright law gives copyright owners a limited monopoly—the exclusive right to reproduce, publish, adapt, publicly perform, and publicly display their works. This monopoly is limited by time. The copyright statute has been revised from time to time, including amendations to change the life of a copyright. Most recently, the duration has been expanded, thanks to legislation sponsored by Sonny Bono, the late entertainer and congressman. While the duration of a copyright varies depending on its authorship (for example, whether it is the work of one known author, an anonymous author, or joint authors, or whether it is a work made for hire), a copyright acquired today may variously last for the life of the author plus 70 years, for 95 years from the date of first publication, or for 120 years from creation, whichever is shorter.

It is copyright infringement for a person to violate one or more of the exclusive rights granted to copyright owners, such as copying a work without permission.

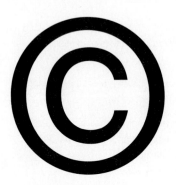

Eight Categories of Copyrightable Works

- literary works
- dramatic works
- pictorial, graphic, and sculptural works
- pantomime and choreographic works
- motion pictures and other audiovisual works
- architectural works
- musical works
- sound recordings

CASE *on* POINT

Schrock v. Learning Curve Int'l Inc., 586 F.3d 513 (7th Cir. 2009).

Discussed earlier in the text, this is a copyright infringement case. It involved a professional photographer who sued the owner of a copyright in characters on which some children's toys were based as well as the licensee that produced the toys. The legal claim asserted by the photographer alleged the infringement of the photographer's claimed copyright in the photographs the licensee hired the photographer to take. This is because the photographer's photographs of the copyrighted works (the toys) may constitute a derivative work, which may also be copyrightable (by the photographer, in this case).

Copyright infringement can entitle a copyright owner to damages and result in an injunction being issued by a court to order the infringer to stop the infringing acts. It also can result in criminal prosecution of the infringer. See the two Cases on Point involving copyright infringement. Note that the second case (*Harper*) involves a child who downloaded digital music files; beware, for this conduct may constitute copyright infringement unless a person first obtains the consent of the owner of the copyright in the music, usually gotten for a fee.

A **copyright** is the exclusive right of an author or other creator of a copyrightable work to reproduce, publish, adapt, publicly perform, and publicly display that work for a limited time.

Unlike patent law, copyright law does not require that a person apply to the government to obtain a copyright. Rather, copyright rights are acquired when a copyrightable work is created and fixed in a tangible medium of expression. However, registration of the copyright with the U.S. Copyright Office, a part of the Library of Congress, enhances a copyright owner's rights. For example, registration makes a copyright owner eligible to receive statutory damages and attorneys' fees in an infringement action, and registration within five years of publication constitutes *prima facie* (legally sufficient) evidence of the ownership and validity of a copyright.

Also, a copyright owner may provide copyright notice on its work to notify the public that a claim of copyright is made in the work. For example, an author named Hillary J. Michaud would provide notice of copyright for a work of authorship she creates in 2012 as follows: © 2012 Hillary J. Michaud. Like registration of copyrights, notice of copyrights is permissive; it is recommended because benefits flow from it, but notice is not required.

A **trademark** is a distinctive word, motto, name, symbol, or device that a person (usually a business entity) uses to distinguish its products from those from another source.

CASE *on* POINT

Harper v. Maverick Recording Co, 131 S. Ct. 590 (2010).

Discussed earlier in the text, the U.S. Supreme Court heard, and denied, this petition for *certiorari* out of the U.S. Court of Appeals for the Fifth Circuit concerning a copyright infringement claim. This case involved a 16-year-old girl who was found to have infringed the Maverick Recording Company's copyrights by downloading digital music files.

The main issue in the case was whether and how a particular section of the Copyright Act (§402(d)) applied to the case in terms of whether the infringer was an "innocent" infringer because these were digital files, which, unlike phonorecord technology, do not physically bear a copyright notice (such as "©"). The Fifth Circuit ruled that the innocent infringer defense did not apply because the recording company provided proper copyright notice on each of its works (the phonorecords from which the digital files were taken and made available through file-sharing) and the girl had access to the phonorecords. The Fifth Circuit ruled that the infringer need not actually see a material object with a copyright notice on it, but rather it is enough that the infringer could have ascertained that the work was copyrighted.

Examples include Coca-Cola, Nike, and Airtran. A **service mark** is like a trademark, but it distinguishes services, not products, from those coming from another source. Examples include Hilton hotels, Long & Foster real estate services, and Roto Rooter drain cleaning services. Both trademarks and service marks are used to indicate brand, and through their use and promotion, they generate goodwill toward their owners' products or services. **Goodwill** is the enhanced likelihood that a consumer will repurchase the company's product or service, which is an asset of a company that can be bought and sold (and quantified by accountants). Trademarks and service marks give their owners the exclusive right to use the marks in commerce in connection with similar products or services.

Copyright Notice

A copyright notice, while not required, enhances the rights of a copyright owner. Copyright notice is depicted using the internationally recognized copyright symbol (©) or the word "copyright" or an abbreviation for that word, the year the work is created or published, and the name of the copyright owner.

For example:

© 2012 Hillary J. Michaud

A **trademark** is a distinctive word, motto, name, symbol, or device that a person uses to distinguish its products from those from another source.

A **service mark** is a distinctive word, motto, name, symbol, or device that a person uses to distinguish its services from those from another source.

Goodwill is the enhanced likelihood that a consumer will repurchase the company's product or service.

**TM** Unlike patent and copyright law, trademark law did not originate from a constitutional grant. Rather, it was developed as part of a larger body of unfair competition law. Today, there are both federal and state statutes restricting unfair competition, including protecting trademarks and service marks. So trademark and service mark law consists of both federal and state law.

Also, trademark law and service mark law are substantially similar. Their main differences relate to the distinction between branding a product as opposed to branding a service. For example, where you affix a mark on a product, which is tangible, and how to use a mark in relation to a service, which has no tangible form, is an area of distinction between trademark law and service mark law.

Like copyrights, trademarks and service marks come into existence without the necessity of a government grant or filing. They come into existence when the mark is first used by its owner in commerce in connection with the goods or services. However, by registering the trademark or service mark with the government, an owner's rights are enhanced. Registration is possible with the federal government, upon successful application to the U.S. Patent and Trademark Office, for marks used (or to be used within the next six months to three years) in commerce that is regulated by the federal government—usually meaning interstate commerce. When the mark is used solely within one state, so there is *intrastate* commerce only, then registration may be possible with the state's government but not with the federal government. A mark used in interstate commerce may be registered both with the federal government and in any state where the mark is used in commerce, if such multiple registrations are desired by the mark's owner.

Unlike both patents and copyrights, trademarks and service marks may last forever, so long as a mark's owner continues to use the mark in commerce in connection with the products or services. In other words, the monopoly in them is restricted by time only if the owner abandons the mark by ceasing to use it. Further, while mark registrations expire (federal ones last for 10 years), they can be renewed. Federal registrations can be renewed every 10 years, forever, on the filing of a renewal application and fee with PTO, which filing must include a demonstration by the owner of continued use of the mark in commerce in connection with the product or service.

A person who uses an identical, or even substantially similar, mark without the owner's consent may be found liable for trademark or service mark infringement. The key issue to be decided in trademark or service mark infringement cases is whether the use of the mark by the defendant created consumer confusion. Besides an award of damages against the infringer, another common remedy in a trademark infringement case is an injunction, where a court orders an infringer to stop its infringing use of the mark.

A **trade secret** is a valuable business secret that gives the business an advantage over its competitors. Examples include secret formulas (like Coca-Cola's secret formula), secret recipes (like Colonel Sander's secret recipe for original recipe Kentucky Fried Chicken), customer lists, business practices, business plans, research and development, and manufacturing processes. The two key requirements for something to be a trade secret are (1) that the information be kept secret (confidential) and (2) that the information provides its owner with an economic advantage over its competitors, meaning that it provides a competitive advantage.

Trade secret law consists of both federal and state statutes, such as state statutes based on the Uniform Trade Secrets Act. It also includes cases interpreting and enforcing those statutes. Trade secrets come into existence when a valuable business secret is developed.

Unlike all other forms of intellectual property, trade secrets are not subject to governmental registration—either mandatory (like patents) or voluntary (like copyrights and trademarks/service marks). That is because registration with the government would defeat the secret by making it publicly known. Trade secret

KEY Point

Two Requirements of a Trade Secret

A trade secret must:

1. be kept confidential, and
2. provide its owner with a competitive advantage.

A **trade secret** is a valuable business secret that gives the business an advantage over its competitors.

owners incorporate confidentiality practices into their business practices to maintain the secrecy of their trade secrets, such as securing access to them and requiring persons with access to them to sign confidentiality and nondisclosure agreements.

Trade secrets may last indefinitely, so long as the information is kept confidential and provides the owner with a competitive advantage. However, once a trade secret is revealed—in other words, is not confidentially maintained—it is lost.

Trade secrets are protected from misappropriation on the civil side, for which damages are an appropriate remedy. They are also protected from theft on the criminal side, for which criminal prosecution and penalties are appropriate.

CHAPTER SUMMARY

- An agent is a person who agrees to act, and acts, on behalf of another person, called the principal. An agent and a principal have an agency relationship, which is a type of fiduciary relationship. An agency relationship can be formed by express oral or written agreement between the principal and the agent, implied by the conduct of the parties, created by ratification of the principal, or created by estoppel.

- Under the doctrine of *respondeat superior*, an employer can be held vicariously liable for the tortious misconduct of its employees committed within the course and scope of their employment.

- Because business organizations act through their agents, agency law is important to business organizations law.

- The four major forms of business organization are sole proprietorship, partnership, corporation, and limited liability company.

- A sole proprietorship is the simplest form of business organization where the owner of the business is the business. The owner of a sole proprietorship is a sole proprietor.

- A partnership is an association of two or more persons who carry on as co-owners of a business for profit. There are several types of partnerships, including general partnerships, limited partnerships, limited liability partnerships, and limited liability limited partnerships. Agency principles apply to partners and partnerships.

- A corporation is a legal entity, separate and distinct from its owners, that is created according to state statute to carry on a business activity. There are many types of corporations, such as public corporations, private corporations, publicly held corporations, not-for-profit corporations, professional corporations, closely held corporations, and Subchapter S corporations.

- The three groups of "players" associated with corporations are stockholders/shareholders, officers, and directors. Stockholders are the owners of a corporation. Officers are employees of the corporation who are responsible for its day-to-day operations. Directors sit on boards that are responsible for the higher-level management of the corporation.

- A limited liability company, also called a limited liability corporation, is a legal entity, separate and distinct from its owners, that is created according to state statute to carry on a business activity that combines certain advantages of both the corporate form of business organization and the partnership form of business organization. It is a hybrid form of business organization that, specifically, combines the benefits of a corporation (limited liability protection for its owners) with the benefits of a partnership (single taxation).

- Owners of limited liability companies are called members. Limited liability companies may hire officers and use boards of directors.

- Bankruptcy is the legally acknowledged inability of an individual or business organization to pay the debts it owes to its creditors. Bankruptcy law is the body of federal law that legally acknowledges the inability of an individual or business organization to pay its debts and that allows the debtor to pay certain creditors what it can while giving the debtor some relief from debts in order to make a "fresh start."

- The three main types of bankruptcy filings available under the U.S. Bankruptcy Code are Chapter 7 liquidation proceedings, Chapter 11 business reorganizations, and Chapter 13 adjustments of debts for individuals with regular income. In 2005, bankruptcy laws were significantly reformed and revised to make it harder for debtors to file for bankruptcy protection and avoid paying their debts, largely by limiting who can file under Chapter 7 and requiring more debtors to file under Chapter 13.

- A contract is a legally enforceable agreement between two or more parties. Contract law deals with the creation and enforcement of contracts. Contract law consists of the common law of contracts and state commercial statutes following Article 2 of the Uniform Commercial Code governing contracts for the sale of goods.

- Under the common law of contracts, the essential elements of a contract are agreement, consideration, contractual capacity, and legality.

- Under each state's Statute of Frauds, certain types of contracts must be in writing and signed by the person against whom enforcement is sought.

- Most contracts are express contracts, which are contracts expressed in oral or written words and that are voluntarily and deliberately entered into by the parties to them. Contracts may also be implied in fact (inferred from the conduct of the parties) and implied in law (imposed by courts to prevent unjust enrichment).

- Breach of contract is the failure of a party to a contract to completely perform under the contract. Breach of contract entitles the injured party to remedies, at law or in equity. Remedies at law are money damages. Remedies in equity are all remedies other than money damages, such as injunctions, rescission, restitution, reformation, and specific performance.

- Employment is a relationship between an employer and an employee that, among other things, triggers the application of federal, state, and local employment laws. Courts consider several factors in determining whether or not an employment relationship exists.

- The employment at will doctrine, a common law doctrine, states that an employer or an employee can terminate their employment relationship at any time, for any reason.

- The Occupational Safety and Health Act promotes workplace safety and established the Occupational Safety and Health Administration (OSHA) within the U.S. Department of Labor.

- Workers' compensation statutes are state statutes that set forth compensation schemes for workers and families of workers who are injured or become ill on the job. They set forth administrative schemes for compensation in such a way as to prevent employees from having to sue employers, in tort, for workplace injuries and illnesses.

- The Fair Labor Standards Act (FLSA) regulates child labor, sets the federal minimum wage rate, and regulates overtime pay.

- Title VII of the Civil Rights Act prohibits employment discrimination based on race, color, national origin, religion, and gender. It also prohibits sexual harassment in the workplace, as well as pregnancy discrimination. The Equal Employment Opportunity Commission (EEOC) is the federal agency established and given authority to enforce most of the employment laws prohibiting discrimination.

- The Age Discrimination in Employment Act (ADEA) prohibits age discrimination in employment, protecting workers 40 years of age or older.

- The Americans with Disabilities Act (ADA) prohibits discrimination against workers with disabilities, requiring employers to make reasonable accommodations for disabled workers where doing so does not create an undue hardship for the employers.

- The Equal Pay Act requires equal pay for equal work regardless of a worker's gender.

- The Family and Medical Leave Act (FMLA) provides many workers with unpaid time off from work for important family and medical matters.

- The environment is the sum total of all the resources in which we live. Environmental laws are laws created at all levels of government to protect the environment from human impact and damage. Environmental laws protect air quality and water quality, as well as regulate hazardous waste disposal and toxic substance release. In addition, they protect non-human animals and their habitats.

- Intellectual property is any product of the human mind that is protected by law. It is a kind of intangible personal property. Intellectual property laws are laws that protect the different types of intellectual property.

- The four main types of intellectual property are patents, copyrights, trademarks/service marks, and trade secrets. A patent is a governmental grant that gives an inventor or discoverer the exclusive right to make, use, and sell his invention or discovery for a limited time. A copyright is the exclusive right of an author or other creator of a copyrightable work to reproduce, publish, adapt, publicly perform, and publicly display that work for a limited time. A trademark is a distinctive work, motto, name, symbol, or device that a person uses to distinguish its products from those from another source. A service mark is like a trademark but it distinguishes a service, rather than a product, from the service of another. A trade secret is a valuable business secret that gives the business an advantage over its competitors.

CONCEPT REVIEW AND REINFORCEMENT

Key Terms and Concepts

Agent
Principal
Agency relationship
Doctrine of *respondeat superior*
Sole proprietorship
Sole proprietor
Partnership
Corporation
Certificate of incorporation
Corporate charter
Corporate bylaws
Stockholders
Shareholders
Officers
Boards of directors
Limited liability company
Limited liability corporation
Members
Articles of organization
Operating agreements
Bankruptcy
Bankruptcy law
Contract
Promise
Party
Contract law
Uniform Commercial Code
Agreement
Offer
Offeror
Offeree
Consideration
Contractual capacity
Legality
Statute of Frauds
Express contracts
Implied in fact contracts
Implied in law contracts
Quasi-contracts
Breach of contract
Remedy
Remedies at law
Remedies in equity
Injunctions
Rescission
Restitution
Reformation
Specific performance
Employer
Employment at will doctrine
Environment
Environmental law

Hazardous waste

Intellectual property

Intellectual property laws

Patent

Copyright

Trademark

Service mark

Goodwill

Trade secret

Questions for Review

1. What are agencies?
2. What does agency law govern?
3. What are the major forms of business organization?
4. What is business organizations law?
5. What is bankruptcy?
6. What do bankruptcy laws do?
7. What are contracts?
8. What is contract law?
9. What is employment?
10. What do employment laws do?
11. What is the environment?
12. How do environmental laws protect the environment?
13. What is intellectual property?
14. What are the main types of intellectual property?
15. How is intellectual property protected by law?

DEVELOPING YOUR PARALEGAL SKILLS

Critical Thinking Exercises

1. You and a friend want to start a business. In that business, you will provide staffing services, finding paralegals looking for employment and matching them with legal employers that have paralegal employment opportunities. You plan to charge the employers a fee, but not the paralegals seeking employment. You hope to earn a profit.

   What forms of business organizations may you use in organizing your business? Of the forms available to you, which one do you think offers you the most advantages and the fewest disadvantages? What are those advantages and disadvantages? Which form of organization will you use?

2. You are an individual (a human) who can no longer pay your debts when they become due. You lost your job as an attorney with a big law firm, but are able to set up your own practice and attract some clients. You will not, however, at least in the short term, earn anywhere near the salary you did at your former firm. You are thinking of filing for bankruptcy in order to get at least some of your debts discharged. You operate your new law practice as a sole proprietorship and you have the following debts: fixed unsecured debts of $55,552 and fixed secured debts of $826,754.

   a. Should you file for bankruptcy? What are the implications of filing for bankruptcy in terms of being able to obtain credit, such as for buying a house or car, in the next few years?

   b. Under what chapter of the U.S. Bankruptcy Code will you likely be able to file, if you decide to file for bankruptcy? What happens to your debts when you file under this chapter? What, if anything, will your creditors get paid?

3. Jackson asks Marsha if she would like him to paint the outside of her house. He says he will do it for $2,500. Marsha responds, "Great! You can start tomorrow, if it doesn't rain."

   a. Have Jackson and Marsha entered into a contract? Why or why not?

   b. If, in subpart a., a contract exists, is the contract governed by the jurisdiction's commercial code (meaning what the jurisdiction adopted based upon Article 2 of the Uniform Commercial Code)? Why or why not?

   c. What if Jackson offered to sell Marsha cocaine, rather than paint her house, for $2,500. Have they entered into a contract? Why or why not?

   d. What if Jackson, before communicating with Marsha in any way, paints Marsha's house? Before being painted, the house looked terrible. Now, the house looks wonderful! After finishing the job, then taking a shower and cleaning himself up, Jackson approaches Marsha and asks her for compensation in the amount of $2,500.

   Does Marsha have a contractual obligation to pay Jackson? Should the court step in and award Jackson recovery in quasi-contract? Why or why not?

4. Give 10 specific examples of intellectual property based on items you have in your residence. For instance, you could list the trademark "diet Coke" found on the cans of soft drinks in your refrigerator as one example if that is what you drink and have it at home.

5. Explain why you think that different types of intellectual property, namely patents, copyrights, trademarks/service marks, and trade secrets, have different durations. Some can last forever (trademarks/service marks and trade secrets), another can last for more than a century (copyrights), and another lasts just over 14 or 20 years. Why do you think there is such different treatment of these different types of intellectual property?

Assignments and Practical Applications

Research case law in your jurisdiction. Under your state's common law of contracts, what are the essential elements of a contract? Cite the case you use in answering this question.

Locate your state's commercial code. Review its Article 2 on sales of goods contracts. When you study Article 2 in your contract law course, you should review the Uniform Commercial Code provisions and your state's provisions to see if, and how, they differ.

Research to find your state's workers' compensation statute. Review that statute. What injuries does it cover? What remedy does it provide? What procedures are used to make a claim for workers' compensation?

Locate and review the workers' compensation statute in Illinois (820 Ill. Comp. Stat. Ann. 305/8 (2012)), which like other jurisdictions, schedules the amount of compensation to be paid for accidental injury not resulting in death, for injuries such as loss of a leg, arm, great toe, index finger, foot, hand, and loss of hearing in one ear.

Research to locate your state's minimum wage rate. Is it the same as the federal wage rate required by the Fair Labor Standards Act? Remember that a state rate can be higher, but not lower, than the federal minimum.

Does your state include sexual orientation as a protected class under its anti-discrimination in employment statutes? Perform legal research to answer this question.

Research to locate your state's trademark statute. Does your state also protect service marks?

Technology Resources and Internet Exercises

On bankruptcy reform, read the Internet "Nolo" article located at http://www.nolo.com/legal-encyclopedia/article-30040.html.

Review Occupational Safety and Health Act standards at the U.S. Department of Labor's website: http://www.osha.gov/comp-links.html.

Review the Environmental Protection Agency's website at http://www.epa.gov/. What information is found there?

Research to determine the name of your state's environmental protection agency. Locate its website and review the ways in which it helps to protect the environment in your state. See if it has links to state environmental statutes in your jurisdiction.

Review EPA's website page regarding national ambient air quality standards and see the pollutants regulated and standards applied. See http://www.epa.gov/air/criteria.html.

Using the Cornell University Law School website for its Legal Information Institute, found at http://www.law.cornell.edu/, find your state's legal ethics code. Use it to answer the following Ethical Applications.

Ethical Applications

Betsy Campbell is as a paralegal at the law firm of Cohen, Katz, and Berger, P.C. Working for supervising attorney Joe Silvermann on a matter, Betsy's superb legal research helps the client recover thousands of dollars in a breach of contract lawsuit against a supplier. The client is very pleased, and so is Betsy's boss, Joe.

    a. To show his appreciation, may Joe and the law firm share with Betsy the legal fee paid by the client on the matter? Why or why not?

    b. May the law firm pay Betsy a bonus for her fine work? Why or why not?

VIDEO CASE STUDIES

Video Interview of Susan Campbell

Paralegal case study videos to accompany this textbook are accessible from within both the New MyLegalStudiesLab Virtual Law Office Experience course and the Resources Website for Paralegal Studies.

13

Other Legal
Specialty Areas

Lindsay Ann Thomas

Criminal Defense Paralegal at MacVaugh and LeCompte

Lindsay works at a small law firm that specializes in criminal defense work, where she is a paralegal and office manager. She was placed at this firm for an internship through her paralegal education program and stayed afterward when offered permanent employment. Finding criminal law very exciting, Lindsay always knew that she was more interested in criminal law than civil law practice, for she enjoys talking to new clients and hearing their stories every day.

Oral communication skills are very important to Lindsay's criminal defense practice. Lindsay communicates directly with clients and prospective clients. Lindsay considers herself the "gatekeeper" at her office because she is the first person people talk with when they contact her firm.

Interviewing prospective and new clients is a daily activity for Lindsay. Because her firm does a lot of advertising of its legal services, the office receives many telephone calls each day from prospective clients. Lindsay answers all of these calls. Regularly, prospective clients ask her questions such as "Am I going to jail?" and "How much is this going to cost?" Lindsay explains that she is not a lawyer and cannot give legal advice or set a legal fee, but that the lawyer can answer those questions. Lindsay also performs all initial interviews of prospective clients. By the time a prospective client has a consultation with a lawyer at the firm, Lindsay has already gathered the information pertaining to the case and made it available to the lawyer.

Written communication skills are also critical to Lindsay's criminal defense practice. Lindsay drafts documents daily, including all of the firm's correspondence as well as legal motions. Everything Lindsay drafts she submits to a supervising lawyer for review before sending it to a client, a court, or any other third party.

The full video interview is accessible from within both the New MyLegalStudiesLab Virtual Law Office Experience course and the Resources Website for Paralegal Studies.

The chapter will answer the following questions:

- What is administrative law and government regulation?
- What is criminal law?
- What is domestic relations?
- What are estates, wills, and trusts?

- What is immigration law?
- What is property, and how is it protected by property law?
- What are torts and tort law?

CHAPTER **INTRODUCTION**

This chapter continues our examination of legal specialty areas that began in Chapter 12. In this chapter, we study several more major legal specialty areas, including administrative law and government regulation; criminal law; domestic relations; estates, wills, and trusts; immigration; property; and torts.

We begin by examining administrative law and government regulation. Next, we review the legal specialty area of criminal law, both from the prosecution and defense perspective. We study estates, wills, and trusts and the role of estate planning and estate administration in our legal system. Immigration and laws impacting immigration are examined. The topic of "property" is defined, types of property are distinguished, and property laws are examined. The chapter ends with our defining "torts" and examining the role of tort law. Our study begins with an examination of administrative law and government regulation.

ADMINISTRATIVE LAW AND GOVERNMENT REGULATION

Federal, state, and local governments, through their executive and legislative branches, create administrative agencies. There are two types of administrative agencies, executive agencies and independent regulatory agencies. **Executive agencies** are administrative agencies created under the authority of the government's chief executive (the president for federal executive agencies and the governor for state executive agencies) either as a cabinet department or as a subagency within a cabinet department. The United States Department of Commerce, the Department of Defense, the Natural Resources Conservation Service, and the National Weather Service are examples. **Independent regulatory agencies** are administrative agencies created by Congress at the federal level, and by state and local legislatures at the state and local levels. Independent regulatory agencies arise via **enabling legislation**, which are statutes that create administrative agencies. Enabling legislation authorizes not only the creation of the administrative agency but also sets forth the agency's name, the purposes for which it is created, how it is composed, and what its implementation and enforcement powers are.

Administrative agencies are created to deal with a wide variety of specific areas of law, such as environmental protection, food and drug safety, and securities regulation. Administrative agencies of the government help to administer and enforce statutes enacted by legislatures. In addition, as part of their rulemaking function, they issue rules and regulations pertaining to their areas of law. Examples of administrative agencies at the federal level include the Environmental Protection Agency (EPA), the Food and Drug Administration (FDA), and the Securities and Exchange Commission (SEC). At the state and local levels, state and local governments create agencies, many of which parallel the federal government agencies, such as in the areas of environmental protection, securities regulation, public health, and transportation.

Administrative agencies create administrative law by issuing rules and regulations pertaining to the administration and enforcement of statutes in their areas of law. In addition to establishing these substantive laws, administrative agencies also establish procedural laws to set forth the procedures that

Executive agencies are administrative agencies created under the authority of the government's chief executive either as a cabinet department or as a subagency within a cabinet department.

Independent regulatory agencies are administrative agencies created by Congress at the federal level, and by state and local legislatures at the state and local levels.

Enabling legislation are statutes that create administrative agencies.

must be followed in implementing and enforcing the substantive laws. **Administrative law** is the body of substantive and procedural law established by administrative agencies. These administrative laws established and enforced by administrative agencies are referred to as **government regulation**. Administrative law covers not only the rulemaking function and enforcement function for the agency but also its judicial function. Administrative agencies often are granted the power to adjudicate legal issues before them through the conduct of administrative proceedings before an administrative law judge. Remember from our legal ethics discussion on the unauthorized practice of law that some administrative agencies allow nonlawyers, such as paralegals, to represent parties in administrative proceedings. Also, some administrative agencies are granted licensing authority, permitting them to establish standards for issuing licenses to persons to allow those persons to do certain things (such as to operate a bank or obtain a driver's license).

Administrative law and government regulation together constitute one important legal specialty area. Another very important legal specialty area is criminal law. Here lawyers and paralegals can either represent state or federal governments in prosecuting criminals, or they can represent criminal defendants in defending against prosecutions. The legal specialty area of criminal law is examined next.

© Michael Newman/PhotoEdit

CRIMINAL LAW

In Chapter 3 of the text, we discussed the distinction between civil law and criminal law. Remember that **criminal law** is the system of law defining and governing actions that constitute crimes, as defined by statutes—mostly state statutes. Criminal law deals with wrongful actions perpetrated against society as a whole, for which society demands redress.

By way of review, either the state or federal government brings a criminal law action, called a prosecution, when a person is charged with violating a criminal law statute. See the Statute on Point for an example of a criminal law statute. At trial, the standard of proof of "beyond a reasonable doubt" is used to determine whether the criminal defendant is found guilty or not guilty (convicted of committing the crime). If found guilty, the criminal defendant can be punished, and punishment can take several forms including fines, imprisonment, probation, and in some states even death.

Because crimes are considered to be offenses against society as a whole, rather than wrongs against particular individuals (as is the case with torts, discussed later in this chapter), criminals are prosecuted by representatives of the government, such as district attorneys. In other words, they are not prosecuted by representatives of the victims; they are prosecuted by representatives of the government. Paralegals and attorneys can work in the area of criminal prosecution, working for the state or federal government.

Administrative law is the body of substantive and procedural law established by administrative agencies.

Government regulation is the establishment and enforcement of administrative laws.

Criminal law is the system of law defining and governing actions that constitute crimes, as defined by statutes.

STATUTE on POINT

Nebraska's Second Degree Murder Statute

Neb. Rev. Stat. § 28-304 (2011). Nebraska defines second degree murder as follows: A person commits second degree murder if the person causes the death of another person intentionally, but without premeditation. Second degree murder is classified as a Class 1B felony in that state.

Note that in classifying felonies into nine different categories, Nebraska's Class 1B felonies are punishable by a maximum of life imprisonment and a minimum of 20 years imprisonment.

There are two elements to criminal liability. In other words, two things must be present for criminal liability to be found, and these elements must occur together. These two elements are (1) performance of a prohibited act (the criminal act), called **actus reus**, and (2) wrongful mental state (the criminal mind), called **mens rea**. What is a prohibited act is defined by state or federal statute, such as Nebraska's second degree murder statute noted above. Most crimes are crimes of commission, meaning a person did something—such as intentionally caused the death of another person, but without premeditation. Other crimes are crimes of omission, caused by failure to act, such as by failing to file an annual income tax return when one is required to be filed. Also, there is no criminal liability if there is no wrongful state of mind. What constitutes the required wrongful state of mind varies depending on the type of action. As noted in the Nebraska second degree murder statute, the wrongful state of mind is "intent" but not "premeditation."

Crimes can be classified based on their type. Crimes are often grouped into the following five categories: violent crimes, property crimes, public order crimes, white-collar crimes, and organized crime. **Violent crimes** are crimes against people that cause them to suffer harm or death. For example, murder, the crime of assault, the crime of battery, and rape are all considered violent crimes. Violent crimes can be further subdivided by degree based on factors such as whether a weapon was used in the commission of the crime and the premeditation or intent of the perpetrator. Remember Nebraska's second degree murder statute as an example of classification of murder by degree. **Property crimes** are those crimes where the goal of the perpetrator is to damage another's property or achieve some illegal economic gain. Arson, forgery, and burglary are examples of property crimes. **Public order crimes** are prohibited acts considered to be contrary to society's morals and values. Many of these crimes are considered "victimless" crimes because they harm only the perpetrator. Examples of public order crimes are prostitution and illegal drug use. **White-collar crimes** are nonviolent commercial offenses committed by a person, public official, or business. Examples of white-collar crimes include bribery, insider trading, trade secret theft, and embezzlement. See the Case on Point for another famous example. **Organized crime** is the systematic carrying on of illegal activities by criminal organizations. Examples of organized crime include money laundering and illegal drug trafficking. Distinguish white-collar crimes from organized crime. White-collar crimes take place within legal, legitimate business activities. Organized crime, on the other hand, is the conduct of illegal, illegitimate business activities.

When a person thinks of criminal liability, he often thinks of humans committing wrongful acts. Can legal entities, such as corporations, also commit crimes? Yes, they can commit crimes, too. For example, a corporation can commit tax evasion, an antitrust violation, or make an illegal political campaign

KEY Point

Two Elements to Criminal Liability

The two elements to criminal liability are (1) *actus reus*, meaning performance of a prohibited act, and (2) *mens rea*, meaning wrongful mental state.

Actus reus means performance of a prohibited act—the criminal act.

Mens rea means wrongful mental state—the criminal mind.

Violent crimes are crimes against people that cause them to suffer harm or death.

Property crimes are those crimes where the goal of the perpetrator is to damage another's property or achieve some illegal economic gain.

Public order crimes are prohibited acts considered to be contrary to society's morals and values.

White-collar crimes are nonviolent commercial offenses committed by a person, public official, or business.

Organized crime is the systematic carrying on of illegal activities by criminal organizations.

Types of Crimes
- violent crimes
- property crimes
- public order crimes
- white-collar crimes
- organized crime

CASE *on* POINT

White-Collar Crime and Bernard "Bernie" Madoff

Bernie Madoff was an investment advisor, stockbroker, and NASDAQ chairman who operated the largest Ponzi scheme in United States history. A Ponzi scheme is a fraudulent investment operation, named by its first perpetrator Charles Ponzi, in a scam that pays early investors returns from the investments of later investors. Using such a scam, Madoff obtained $65 billion in funds from thousands of clients. He was charged with securities fraud, investment advisor fraud, mail fraud, wire fraud, money laundering, making false statements, perjury, making false filings with the Securities and Exchange Commission, and theft from an employee benefit plan. In March 2009, Madoff plead guilty to 11 federal felonies. He was sentenced to 150 years in prison, the maximum sentence allowed under the law for these crimes. Madoff's scheduled release date from the Butner Federal Correctional Facility in Butner, North Carolina, is November 14, 2139.

contribution. Corporations can be punished, such as by being fined or by being denied or losing certain privileges, like losing a business license. However, corporations cannot be imprisoned as human beings can be, so punishing corporations for crimes they commit may be different than punishing human beings.

People charged with committing crimes normally defend these actions. They are typically represented by private criminal defense attorneys, where the person charged can afford an attorney, or by a public defender, if the person charged cannot afford legal counsel—for legal counsel is provided, at the taxpayers' expense, free of charge. Both attorneys and paralegals can work in the legal specialty area of criminal defense.

How does one defend against criminal prosecution? First, he can demonstrate to the court that he did not perform the criminal act (*actus reus*) as defined by the relevant criminal statute, or that he did not possess the requisite criminal mind (*mens reus*) also as defined by the relevant criminal statute. Defendants in criminal actions may assert certain defenses to criminal liability. For example, they may assert self-defense, meaning justifiable use of force against another. For another example, they may also assert insanity, meaning that they suffered from mental illness to such an extent that they were unable to form the mental state required to commit the crime charged. Immunity, entrapment, mistake, duress, necessity, and statute of limitations are other defenses criminal defendants may assert in defending themselves during prosecution.

In addition, criminal defendants in the course of the criminal arrest and prosecution process are granted numerous safeguards and protections under the U.S. Constitution (specifically, in the Bill of Rights). They are protected against unlawful searches and seizures under the Fourth Amendment. They are entitled to due process of law under the Fifth Amendment. Also pursuant to the Fifth Amendment, they are protected from double jeopardy, meaning they cannot be tried twice for the same crime, and from self-incrimination, meaning they cannot be compelled to testify if doing so might subject them to criminal prosecution. Under the Sixth Amendment, criminal defendants are guaranteed the right to a speedy trial, the right to a trial by jury, the right to a public trial, the right to confront witnesses, and the right to legal counsel. The Eighth Amendment also protects convicted persons from cruel and unusual punishment, as well as prohibits excessive bail and fines. Further, by case law coming from a famous 1966 case called *Miranda v. Arizona*,[1] persons who are arrested must be informed of certain constitutional rights including the right to remain silent (from the Fifth Amendment) and the right to legal counsel (from the Sixth Amendment). This is often referred to today as the ***Miranda* rule**. Also, under what is called the "**exclusionary rule**," any evidence obtained in violation of the constitutional rights of the criminal defendant (from the Fourth, Fifth, and Sixth Amendments just discussed),

The ***Miranda* rule** is a common law rule that requires persons arrested be informed of certain constitutional rights including the right to remain silent and the right to legal counsel.

The **exclusionary rule** is a legal principle that prohibits the use at trial of any evidence obtained in violation of the constitutional rights of the criminal defendant, as well as any evidence *derived* from that illegally obtained evidence.

Criminal Law

as well as any evidence *derived* from that illegally obtained evidence, normally must be excluded from trial (so cannot be used against the defendant in his prosecution).

Yet another important legal specialty area is domestic relations. Domestic relations is the area of law governing family relationships. Domestic relations is covered next.

DOMESTIC RELATIONS

Domestic relations refer to family relations. **Domestic relations law**, also called **family law**, is that area of law involving premarital issues, prenuptial agreements, marriage, the dissolution of marriage, divorce, property division upon divorce, child custody, spousal and child support, adoption, and other family related legal issues.

Before two people get married, legal issues may arise. For example, one party to an engagement may decide to break off the engagement. What happens when there is a breach of a promise to marry? Historically, there was some basis for legal recovery under a breach of contract theory. Today, however, most courts will not recognize a breach of promise to marry claim, as our society's values regarding freedom in entering into and leaving marital relationships have relaxed. That said, some courts may provide relief where a party breaks off the engagement just before the wedding, when costs for the impending wedding are already paid for and are not refundable (such as deposits made for church or reception hall reservations, flowers, a cake, and the like). Who gets the engagement ring in the event of a broken engagement? Historically, a fault rule was imposed, where the party who did not break the engagement got the ring (so if the prospective groom broke off the engagement, the prospective bride could keep the ring; if the prospective bride broke off the engagement, the prospective groom was entitled to the ring's return). Today, many jurisdictions have adopted an objective rule, requiring the engagement ring to be returned to the prospective groom if the engagement is called off—no matter who calls it off.

More and more commonly today, as people marry later in life and after accumulating some assets, couples may wish to enter into prenuptial agreements prior to their marriage. A **prenuptial agreement**, also called a **premarital agreement**, is a contract that sets forth the terms and conditions of how a couple's property should be distributed on

© Andi Berger/Shutterstock

Domestic relations mean family relations.

Domestic relations law is that area of law involving premarital issues, prenuptial agreements, marriage, the dissolution of marriage, divorce, property division upon divorce, child custody, spousal and child support, adoption, and other family related legal issues; it is also called **family law**.

A **prenuptial agreement** is a contract that sets forth the terms and conditions of how a couple's property should be distributed on termination of the marriage or death of a spouse, how income will be treated during marriage, whether and how much alimony will be paid to a spouse on divorce, who will have child custody or visitation rights on divorce if minor children are involved, and what child custody and visitation rights will be; it is also called a **premarital agreement**.

termination of the marriage or death of a spouse (though a will and other estate planning devices, discussed later in this chapter, can also address the disposition of property on the death of a spouse). Prenuptial agreements can address issues regarding more than the distribution of the couple's separate and marital property, however. They can also address how income will be treated during the marriage, whether and how much alimony will be paid to a spouse on divorce, who will have child custody or visitation rights, and what child custody and visitation rights will be. Remember from our discussion of contract law that, under states' Statutes of Frauds, prenuptial agreements must be in writing and signed by the person against whom enforcement is sought.

Each state has its own marriage laws, and these laws vary from state to state. They are found in state statutes and interpreted by courts. Here are some of the marriage requirements common among states. Most states recognize only those marriages entered into between a man and a woman. A few states, however, now recognize the legal union (for it may not be called "marriage" and may be called "civil union" or something else) of two people of the same gender (see the Case on Point). Minimum age requirements are set, in most states at 18 years of age (the age of majority, meaning the age when a person becomes a legal adult), though younger people (up to a certain cutoff of usually 14 to 15 years) may be married if they have parental consent. Another requirement is that no party to a marriage can already be married to someone else—for marriage is defined by most states as a legal union between one man and one woman. Marriage between certain blood relatives, such as brothers and sisters, is prohibited, though marriage between cousins is permitted in some states.

In addition to requirements defining who can marry, states also set procedures that must be followed to wed. These procedures vary from state to state. States generally require that couples first obtain a marriage license. A **marriage license** is a legal document issued by a state that authorizes two people to marry. Many states also require that some kind of marriage ceremony be performed. This ceremony may be a religious ceremony or may be officiated by a government official, such as a justice of the peace or a mayor. Some jurisdictions require a waiting period, usually between 24 hours and 3 days, between the obtaining of a marriage license and the performance of the ceremony. After the ceremony takes place, the marriage license gets recorded, typically with the county clerk's office.

Several, but not all, states recognize common law marriage. **Common law marriage** is a marriage in which the jurisdiction's

CASE on POINT

Gay Marriage

Remember our discussion in Chapter 3 about the civil/criminal law distinction. Civil lawsuits are being filed in various states challenging bans on gay marriage. This is because some states, by law such as constitutional amendment or statute, either prohibit gay marriage or define marriage as a union between a man and a woman. Proponents of gay marriage are challenging these laws as unconstitutional. So far, they have not met with great success. However, today several states recognize same sex marriages (New York, Massachusetts, and Iowa are examples) as valid legal marriages, and some other states recognize some sort of legal union alternative (civil unions in Colorado and Vermont are examples). Challenges to gay marriage bans are being made more and more frequently, in more and more jurisdictions. The evolution of laws involving gay marriage demonstrate how laws change as our society's values and morals do.

procedures for getting married have not been met (obtaining a license and performing a ceremony), but the persons are eligible to marry (they are old enough and not brother and sister, for example), they voluntarily intend to be husband and wife, they live together, and they hold themselves out to the public as husband and wife. A common law marriage is a marriage; to terminate it, the parties to it need to obtain a divorce.

Once established, how are marriages terminated? They can be terminated in two ways: by annulment or divorce. **Annulment** is an order by a court declaring that a marriage never existed. That said, children of annulled marriages are still considered legitimate.

Annulments are rarely granted because the grounds for obtaining them are narrow. Here are some of the grounds recognized for obtaining an annulment: fraud in inducing another

A **marriage license** is a legal document issued by a state that authorizes two people to marry.

Common law marriage is a marriage in which the jurisdiction's procedures for getting married have not been met, but the persons are eligible to marry, they voluntarily intend to be husband and wife, they live together, and they hold themselves out to the public as husband and wife.

Annulment is an order by a court declaring that a marriage never existed.

to enter into the marriage (such as when the marriage was for the purpose of gaining U.S. citizenship or when one of the parties never intended to be married or sought to deceive the other through marriage); duress, force, or threats caused one party to enter into the marriage; one of the parties was already married; one of the parties lacked capacity to consent to the marriage; one of the parties was a minor who had not obtained the required parental consent; one of the parties was mentally incapacitated at the time of the marriage; temporary or permanent insanity of one of the parties to the marriage; intoxication at the time of the marriage; the parties are too closely related by blood; impotency of a party to the marriage; incest; or the marriage was never consummated. Note that a legal annulment is different from a religious annulment. For example, some religions, such as the Roman Catholic Church, do not permit a person who was married in the church to remarry in the church, even after obtaining a legal divorce, unless the earlier marriage is annulled by the church. A church's requirements and procedures for obtaining a religious annulment are different from a state's legal requirements. Legal annulments and religious annulments are separate and distinct processes.

The most common way to terminate a marriage is by divorce. **Divorce** is a legal proceeding where a court issues a decree legally terminating a marriage. Historically, a married person had to demonstrate grounds for divorce by proving that his or her spouse was at fault for creating a major problem in the marriage, such as by committing adultery or abandoning the family. Today, every state recognizes no-fault divorce, where neither party is blamed for causing the divorce. Something like "irreconcilable differences" is asserted as the grounds for a no-fault divorce. Where fault grounds for divorce are present in the case, such as where a spouse commits adultery or abandons the family, in states where fault may still be considered, those grounds may impact a spousal support award, as well as the equitable division of marital property (with perhaps more going to the injured spouse in such a case).

To commence divorce proceedings, one spouse files a petition for divorce with the relevant state court for his or her jurisdiction. Many states require a waiting period of typically from six months to two years before a court will enter a final decree of divorce terminating the marriage, imposing a period for potential reconciliation. In addition to a waiting period, some states require divorcing couples to submit their dispute to mediation to try and resolve some or all of the legal issues before trial. A decree of divorce may be issued by a court even if related issues, such as spousal support or property division, have not yet been resolved.

Where children are born of the marriage and they are still minors when a couple is divorcing, legal issues regarding child custody and visitation are among the most contentious issues presented by the divorce. Child custody must be decided. **Child custody** means the determination of what person (probably a parent) has legal responsibility for raising the minor child. Historically, sole custody was routinely granted to mothers. Today, with fathers more frequently asking for custody and perhaps taking a more active role in the parenting of their children, as well as more mothers participating in the work force, joint custody of minor children by both parents is the norm. In making child custody determinations, courts consider what is in the best interests of the child. A parent awarded legal custody of a child has the right to make the decisions concerning how the child is raised, such as where the child will go to school, in what religion the child will be brought up, what medical care the child will

Grounds for Annulment

- Fraud in inducing another to enter into the marriage
- Duress, force, or threats caused one party to enter into the marriage
- One of the parties was already married
- One of the parties lacked capacity to consent to the marriage
- One of the parties was a minor who had not obtained the required parental consent
- One of the parties was mentally incapacitated at the time of the marriage
- Temporary or permanent insanity of one of the parties to the marriage
- Intoxication at the time of the marriage
- The parties are too closely related by blood
- Impotency of a party to the marriage
- Incest
- The marriage was never consummated

Divorce is a legal proceeding where a court issues a decree legally terminating a marriage.

Child custody means the legal responsibility for raising the minor child.

receive, and so on. **Legal custody** means the custodial authority to make decisions on behalf of the child. If joint custody is awarded, divorced parents must continue to make these decisions together. They will also share joint physical custody of the child, with each parent sharing the amount of time spent with the child. **Physical custody** means the place where the child lives. Visitation must be set for a noncustodial parent if joint physical custody is not awarded, as the noncustodial parent will be awarded visitation rights with the child. **Visitation** is the right of a noncustodial parent to visit with the child. Further, child support must be awarded to the custodial parent, to be paid by the noncustodial parent, for the noncustodial parent (even if being noncustodial is not his or her preferred choice) is obligated by law to contribute to the financial support of the child during the child's minority. **Child support** is the financial support paid by a noncustodial parent to help pay the costs of the child's food, shelter, medical expenses, clothing, education, entertainment, and the like.

Another contentious issue in divorce is the division of assets. If, in divorcing, a couple cannot agree on how to divide their assets, a court will do it, ordering a division of the assets. Only marital property is divided between the parties. **Marital property** is that property acquired during the marriage. Usually this is property acquired from earnings (income) of one or both of the spouses that is earned during the marriage. Separate property is not divided between the spouses in a divorce. **Separate property** is that property owned by a spouse prior to the marriage, as well as individual gifts and inheritances received during the marriage.

Most states divide marital assets based on the equitable distribution theory. **Equitable distribution** allows a court to consider relevant factors, such as the length of the marriage, the spouses' occupations, the income of each spouse, the age and health of each spouse, the standard of living experienced during the marriage, and the child custody arrangement, in making a fair division of the marital property. Fair may or may not mean "equal" depending on the facts and circumstances of the case. A few states divide property using the doctrine of community property. **Community property** is a marital property distribution scheme where courts order that all marital property be equally divided between the divorcing spouses. This is true regardless of who earned the income from which the property was purchased.

Besides dividing assets, when divorcing, marital debts (obligations owed) must also be divided. State law and the kind of debt involved impact how these debts are divided. Normally, each spouse is responsible for any debts he or she incurred prior to the marriage, such as student loans. Where the debts are incurred during the marriage, such as a mortgage to purchase a house or buy an automobile, these are considered joint marital debts and the repayment of these is the shared responsibility of both divorcing spouses. Courts may distribute joint marital debts between the spouses as part of the division of assets and resolution of related issues. As to third parties, the spouse to whom the debt was not distributed may still be held responsible for paying the debt—the paying spouse would then have recourse against the nonpaying spouse to whom the debt was distributed.

Where one divorcing spouse earns significantly more than the other, a court may award spousal support to the lesser-earning spouse. **Spousal support**, also called **alimony**, is monthly payments made by a more affluent divorcing spouse to the other, for some period of time. Historically, spousal support was paid to wives because they either did not work outside the home or they did not earn as much as their husbands. Today, in situations where the wife earns more than the

Legal custody means the custodial authority to make decisions on behalf of the child.

Physical custody means the place where the child lives.

Visitation is the right of a noncustodial parent to visit with the child.

Child support is the financial support paid by a noncustodial parent to help pay the costs of the child's food, shelter, medical expenses, clothing, education, entertainment, and the like.

Marital property is that property acquired during the marriage.

Separate property is that property owned by a spouse prior to the marriage, as well as individual gifts and inheritances received during the marriage.

Equitable distribution allows a court to consider relevant factors, such as the length of the marriage, the spouses' occupations, the income of each spouse, the age and health of each spouse, the standard of living experienced during the marriage, and the child custody arrangement, in making a fair division of the marital property.

Community property is a marital property distribution scheme where courts order that all marital property be equally divided between the divorcing spouses.

Spousal support is monthly payments made by a more affluent divorcing spouse to the other, for some period of time; it is also called **alimony**.

husband, it is common to see the husband awarded spousal support from the wife.

Spousal support payments do not necessarily last for the life of the payee-spouse. The legal obligation to make spousal support payments terminates if the payee-spouse dies, remarries, or becomes self-sufficient such as by going back to work or getting a well-paying new job. Further, spousal support awards are often temporary, meaning that they are awarded for a limited number of years, such as half the number of years of the marriage, to allow the payee-spouse a period of time to further her education to enter the job market to obtain a job, or to allow for time until the minor children are grown and are no longer taken care of by that spouse. While more common in the past, today it is uncommon for a divorcing spouse to be awarded permanent (lifetime) alimony. When permanent alimony is awarded, the payee-spouse usually is older and was a homemaker, so without workplace skills and the ability to earn a living independently—this is especially true if the marriage was long in duration. Even in cases of permanent alimony, that, too, ends when the payee-spouse dies or if he or she remarries.

Adoption is where one person or a couple become(s) the legal parent(s) of a child who is not his, her, or their own. While preference may be given to couples by an adoption agency, single people may adopt. In addition, some states permit same-gender couples to adopt children. Each state has its own adoption laws specifying adoption requirements and procedures, and they vary from state to state. For a child to be eligible for adoption, the child's biological parents' legal rights must be terminated by death or legal decree. Once the adoption requirements and procedures are met, a court must formally approve an adoption. At that point, the child becomes the legal child of the adoptive parent(s).

Another very important legal specialty area, this one dealing with what happens to a person's property on his death, is the area of estates, wills, and trusts, which are discussed next.

> **Adoption** is where one person or a couple become the legal parent(s) of a child who is not his, her, or their own.

ESTATES, WILLS, AND TRUSTS

People, while living, may plan for what will happen to their property, called their **estate**, when they die. In doing this, a person engages in estate planning. **Estate planning** is the process of evaluating and arranging for the disposition of a person's property on his death. Through estate planning, a person can decide, while living, to whom he wants to give each article of his property and who he wants to be guardians for any dependents he may have at the time of his death (such as minor children). Further, he can maximize the value of his estate by reducing, to the extent possible, the tax consequences and other expenses (such as legal expenses) of his estate planning actions.

© EdBockStock/Shutterstock

Many different legal devices can be used in estate planning. Wills and trusts are two of the most common. Both of these devices are examined next.

> An **estate** is the property owned by a person at the time of his death.
>
> **Estate planning** is the process of evaluating and arranging for the disposition of a person's property on his death.

Wills are legal instruments through which people, called **testators**, declare how their estate (their property) will be managed and distributed on their death. For this reason, a will is sometimes referred to as **testamentary disposition of property** or a person's **last will and testament**. A testator, then, is a person who makes a will (historically, a female was referred to as a testatrix). The persons designated in the will to receive the testator's property are called **beneficiaries**. Through a will, a person may name one or more guardians that the testator desires to be granted guardianship of any dependents that may survive him, such as minor children. A personal representative, defined below, may be named in a will. Further, wills often delineate a person's desires regarding his funeral arrangements, such as whether he wants to be buried or cremated, whether he desires a ceremony of some type be performed, and so on.

Each state has its own requirements for making a valid will. These requirements vary from state to state. Generally, however, most states require that the testator have testamentary capacity, meaning be of legal age and of sound mind at the time the will is made. States also typically require that wills be in writing (typically word-processed) to be valid, with some exceptions for such things as handwritten holographic wills, deathbed wills, and nuncupative (oral) wills. States require wills to be signed by the testator. They also require that the signing of wills by testators be attested to by witnesses, though the number of witnesses and the manner of witnessing may differ from state to state. Some states require wills to be published, meaning that the testator must state before the witnesses at signing that "this is my last will and testament." Wills, once written, can be revoked or changed.

When a person has a will and dies, the process of determining the will's validity and carrying out the administration of the estate is called **probate**. Probate of wills is supervised by **probate courts**. **Probate laws** are state laws, varying from state to state, that govern the distribution of a person's property after death. Some states' probate laws are based, at least in part, on the Uniform Probate Code, a model act

Holographic Wills

Holographic wills are informal, handwritten wills that are signed by the testator but do not require witnesses. They are only recognized as valid in a few states.

Deathbed Wills

Deathbed wills are wills made by the testator, before witnesses, right before he dies, usually while he is confined to bed (hence the name). While potential for mistake or fraud exists with this type of will, some states consider a deathbed will to be valid, especially as to its disposition of personal, rather than real, property.

Noncupative Wills

Oral wills made before witnesses are called nuncupative wills. Where recognized as valid, they usually must be made during the testator's last illness; in other words, made orally at his deathbed.

A **will** is a legal instrument through which a person declares how he wants his property to be managed and distributed on his death; it is also called a **last will and testament** or a **testamentary disposition of property**.

A **testator** is a person who makes a will.

A **beneficiary** is a person designated in a will to receive a testator's property.

Probate is the process of determining a will's validity and carrying out the administration of a person's estate on his death.

Probate courts are courts having jurisdiction to probate persons' wills.

Probate laws are state laws that govern the distribution of a person's property after death.

KEY Point

Requirements for a Valid Will
- Testamentary capacity of the testator
- Written, typically word-processed (with some exceptions)
- Signed by the testator
- Attested to by witnesses
- Publication, in some states

written by experts in probate law. When a person's estate is small, the probate process may be easier, less costly, and more informal. The larger a person's estate, the more likely it is that the probate process will be more formal, time-consuming, and expensive. Note that a will becomes a public document when it is presented to a probate court for probate.

What happens if a person dies either without making a will, or with an invalid will (because it failed to meet the jurisdiction's requirements for a valid will, such as by failing to have the will attested to by the required number of witnesses)? When a person dies without a valid will, he is said to have died **intestate**. When a person dies intestate, his property does not go to the government, as is a common myth among laypersons. Instead, the property passes according to a state's intestacy statute. Every state has an **intestacy statute**. These statutes differ from state to state. All, however, set forth how the property of a person is distributed on the person's death when the person dies without a valid will. Property is distributed according to a distribution plan set forth in the intestacy statute. Generally speaking, property will pass in some way first to close relatives, such as spouses, children, parents, and siblings, and if there are no close relatives, to more distant relatives, like aunts, uncles, nieces, and nephews, then cousins. Relatives who receive property under a state's intestacy statute are called **heirs**. It is only when a person dies with no discernable relatives that his property may revert, called escheat, to the state—meaning it goes to the government.

As well as wills, trusts are effective estate planning devices. A **trust** is a legal relationship created by a person who transfers and delivers to one or more other persons his property, for the benefit of yet another person or persons. A trust itself is a separate legal entity. The person who creates the trust is called the **grantor**, **donor**, or **settlor**. The person who holds the trust property is called the **trustee**. A person for whose benefit the trust is created is called a **beneficiary**. Legal title to the property actually passes to the trust, and the trust property is called the **trust *res*** or **trust *corpus***.

Trusts can be express. An **express trust** is a trust voluntarily created by the grantor. Two important types of express trusts are *inter vivos* trusts and testamentary trusts.

Living Wills

Do not confuse a will, the estate planning tool, with a living will.

A living will is a legal document used by a person to declare her wishes regarding life-saving and life-prolonging medical treatment. In other words, it addresses deathbed considerations regarding medical treatment. It is also called an advance directive or advance health care directive because it allows a person to make her own decisions, in advance, about end-of-life medical care, including whether to save or prolong life by artificial means. A living will can be used to declare what kind of medical care the maker wishes to accept in order to sustain her life, addressing issues such as the use of life support (breathing) machines, whether she desires to be resuscitated if breathing stops, and whether she desires to be tube-fed if she cannot feed herself. She can also designate whether she wishes to donate her organs on her death. Many people have living wills and consider them important so that their wishes about end-of-life care can be known and followed in the event they are unable to speak for themselves.

In a living will or in a separate legal document called a health care directive or health care proxy, a person can name another, such as a spouse or adult child, to carry out her living will wishes or to otherwise make health care decisions for her. That designated person is called a health care agent.

The requirements for making a living will vary from state to state. Living wills are often made at the same time as wills are made.

To die **intestate** means a person died without having a valid will.

An **intestacy statute** is a state statute that sets forth how a person's property will be distributed when he dies without a valid will.

Heirs are relatives who receive property under a state's intestacy statute.

A **trust** is a legal relationship created by a person, called a grantor, donor, or settlor, who transfers and delivers to one or more other persons, called a trustee or trustees, his property for the benefit of another or others, called the beneficiary or beneficiaries.

A **grantor** is a person who creates a trust; he is also called a **donor** or **settlor**.

A **trustee** is a person who holds the trust property.

A **beneficiary** is a person for whose benefit a trust is created.

The **trust *res*** is the property held by the trust; it is also called the **trust *corpus***.

An **express trust** is a trust voluntarily created by the grantor.

An *inter vivos* trust, also called a **living trust**, is a trust that is made by a grantor and becomes effective during his lifetime. An *inter vivos* trust can be revocable, meaning that the grantor can maintain control over the trust property during his lifetime, or irrevocable, meaning that the grantor permanently gives up control over the trust property at the time he creates the trust. A **testamentary trust** is a trust that is created by a will. While it is created by a grantor during his lifetime, it does not become effective until the grantor's death. There are many different kinds of express trusts. Examples include charitable trusts, discretionary trusts, wealth trusts, and Totten trusts.

Note that while wills are public documents, trusts are not. Instead, they are private documents. Accordingly, trusts are tools that can be used in estate planning to transfer property in a private manner.

When not voluntarily created by the grantor, a trust can be implied from the conduct of the parties. A trust that is implied by the conduct of the parties is called a **resulting trust**. Further, a trust can be imposed by a court as an equitable remedy, where a trust is implied by law to rectify unjust enrichment, fraud, mistake, undue influence, or some other wrongdoing. This type of trust is called a **constructive trust**.

Besides wills and trusts, there are other kinds of estate planning tools that can be used to transfer property on a person's death as well as to care for beneficiaries such as surviving spouses and children. In terms of property transfer, two or more persons can own property together, in concurrent ownership (see the property law materials later in this chapter for a discussion of concurrent ownership and its types)—also called **co-tenancy**. With some of these types of concurrent ownership, such as joint tenancy and tenancy by the entirety, ownership of the property automatically passes to the other tenant(s) on the death of one of them. So use of co-tenancies is an estate planning tool.

Another estate planning tool is an *inter vivos* gift. An **inter vivos gift** is a gift made by a person during his lifetime. In planning for the distribution of his property on his death, a person may give away property during his life—such as by giving his granddaughter his precious jewelry or giving his son his automobile.

In terms of taking care of a person's surviving spouse, children, and other significant others, a person can purchase life insurance and name any one or more of these important individuals as the beneficiary or beneficiaries of the policy or policies. On the death of the insured, the beneficiary or beneficiaries are entitled to the insurance proceeds. So life insurance is another effective estate planning tool.

On the flip side of estate planning is estate administration. **Estate administration** is a legal process that involves the collection and disposition of a person's property on his death. Notice that estate planning occurs while a person is living and wants to control the disposition of his property and the care of his dependents upon his death. Estate administration occurs after the person's death and is the process by which the decedent's (deceased person's) property is transferred to others. If someone dies with a valid will in existence, then the person he appointed in his will (if anyone) to handle his estate administration is, in many jurisdictions, called his **personal representative**. If a person dies without a valid will in existence, or if the personal representative named in the will is unable or unwilling to serve, then in many jurisdictions the court appoints an **administrator** to oversee the administration of the decedent's estate.

Another important legal specialty area is immigration. In recent years, immigration laws have become spotlighted in the media, as social and legal issues arise regarding the number of illegal aliens entering the United States. Immigration and immigration laws are examined next.

An *inter vivos* **trust** is a trust that is made by a grantor and becomes effective during his lifetime; it is also called a **living trust**.

A **testamentary trust** is a trust that is created by a will and that does not come into existence until the grantor's death.

A **resulting trust** is a trust that is implied by the conduct of the parties.

A **constructive trust** is an equitable remedy that is imposed by the courts to rectify unjust enrichment, fraud, mistake, undue influence, or some other wrongdoing.

Co-tenancy is the concurrent ownership of property by two or more people.

An *inter vivos* **gift** is a gift made by a person during his lifetime.

Estate administration is a legal process that involves the collection and disposition of a person's property upon his death.

A **personal representative** is a person named in a will to administer a person's estate.

An **administrator** is a person appointed by the court to administer a person's estate.

IMMIGRATION

An **immigrant** is a person who comes to a country to take up permanent residence. The United States was colonized and settled largely by immigrants, and has a history defined by immigration. Today, however, with many people illegally entering the United States with the intention of staying, immigration is seen as a less positive attribute of our society. **Immigration law** is that body of law that determines who may enter this country, how long they may stay, when they must leave, and if and when they may become naturalized citizens.

© David R. Frazier Photolibrary, Inc./Alamy

Early and important federal legislation in the area of immigration law was the Immigration and Nationality Act. This act restricted immigration into the United States and established different categories of aliens, where aliens were defined as people who were not citizens or nationals of the United States. These different categories of aliens included resident, nonresident, immigrant, nonimmigrant, documented, and undocumented. This act also established the Immigration and Naturalization Service (INS), once part of the U.S. Department of Justice, to handle immigration and naturalization issues. INS was terminated in 2003, when its functions were transferred to other federal administrative agencies, including the U.S. Immigration and Customs Enforcement, a part of the U.S. Department of Homeland Security, which is the federal administrative agency charged with implementing and enforcing immigration laws.

Two federal statutes that are administered and enforced by the U.S. Immigration and Customs Enforcement, include the Immigration Reform and Control Act (IRCA) and the Immigration Act. Both of these statutes increase regulation in the area of immigration by doing such things as making the hiring of illegal immigrants unlawful and attempting to stop "sham" marriages entered into solely for the purpose of one of the spouses obtaining U.S. citizenship. Immigration and Customs Enforcement officers conduct random audits of employers to determine whether they have hired any illegal immigrants. Penalties for employers who hire illegal immigrants can be significant.

Today, employers must verify that the employees they hire are eligible and authorized to work in the United States. Further, employers must do this within three business days of an employee beginning the employment. This verification is accomplished by the prospective employee completing and filing a Form I-9 Employment Eligibility Verification with the employer. With this form, employers must verify the identity of each prospective employee and the authorization of each prospective employee to work in the United States. This is accomplished by reviewing legal documentation, including birth certificates, passports, and social security cards. Something more than a state-issued driver's license is required. Note that a worker may

KEY Point

Form I-9

This immigration-related form is called the Employment Eligibility Verification form and is used by employers to verify that prospective employees are eligible and authorized to work in the United States.

An **immigrant** is a person who comes to a country to take up permanent residence.

Immigration law is the body of law that determines who may enter this country, how long they may stay, when they must leave, and if and when they may become naturalized citizens.

2007 Arizona Immigration Law Challenged before the U.S. Supreme Court

On December 8, 2010, the U.S. Supreme Court heard oral arguments in the case of *Chamber of Commerce v. Whiting* challenging an Arizona immigration statute, the Legal Arizona Workers Act of 2007. This state law allows the government to suspend or revoke the licenses of businesses that knowingly hire illegal immigrants. Some call this a corporate death penalty imposed on any employer that violates the act's provisions. Arizona's law goes much further than federal immigration law in sanctioning employers who hire illegal workers. At issue in the case is whether federal immigration law (which is much less strict on employers) preempts (precludes) states like Arizona from passing more strict immigration laws. Specifically, those challenging the Arizona law say it violates the federal Immigration Reform and Control Act. On May 26, 2011, the Supreme Court rules that the Legal Arizona Workers Act was not preempted by federal legislation.

Arizona's Support Our Law Enforcement and Safe Neighborhoods Act

The Support Our Law Enforcement and Safe Neighborhoods Act, introduced as Arizona Senate Bill 1070 as an immigration reform statute in the year 2010, requires, among other things, that police determine the immigration status of any person reasonably suspected of being in the country illegally. Since its introduction, this broad and strict anti–illegal immigration measure has received incredible media attention and is considered very controversial.

While current federal immigration law requires certain aliens to register with the U.S. government and to have registration documents in their possession at all times, the Arizona law goes further, making it a *misdemeanor crime* for an alien to be in Arizona without carrying the required immigration documents.

In November 2010, challenges to this law were heard before the Ninth Circuit Court of Appeals. This law could end up in a challenge before the Supreme Court, like the 2007 Arizona reform discussed in the Case on Point. In April 2011, the Ninth Circuit upheld a lower court ruling blocking portions of the law from going into effect.

be eligible to work in the United States either by being a U.S. citizen or by being a foreign citizen with authorization to work in the United States.

Arizona has been a "hotbed" of immigration law issues in recent years, with both a challenge before the Supreme Court to a strict anti-immigration statute enacted in Arizona in 2007, and the promotion and passing of the most strict state immigration law statute to date in 2010. Because of its location, bordering Mexico on its southern border, Arizona is a state with great concerns regarding illegal immigration. See the above Case on Point and Statute on Point discussing these current events in immigration law.

Interestingly, Arizona adopted this controversial statute when an attempt to overhaul federal immigration law failed in 2007. Arizona Senate Bill 1070, introduced and passed in 2010, rejuvenated efforts by the Obama presidential administration and Congress to reconsider federal immigration law and its effectiveness today. Immigration reform is of particular issue to those states bordering Mexico. Immigration reform will likely remain an important current event in the law for some time.

Sometimes a foreign citizen becomes a permanent resident of the United States. A permanent resident is a person who has

KEY Point

Green Card

A green card is a Permanent Resident Card issued to a foreign citizen granted permanent residency in the United States.

been granted authorization by the United States government to live and work in the United States on a permanent basis. A permanent resident is issued a Permanent Resident Card, commonly called a green card. There are several ways in which one can become a permanent resident of the United States, including being sponsored by a family member or employer in the United States or having refugee or asylum status or some other humanitarian basis for permanent residency.

Immigration policies are implemented through the granting and denying of visas. A **visa** is an entry permit to the United States.

A **visa** is an entry permit to the United States.

There are several different kinds of visas available today, categorized as either immigrant or nonimmigrant visas. Immigrant visas allow their holders to stay in the United States permanently and to apply for citizenship. An alien who has an immigrant visa also may work in the United States. Nonimmigrant visas primarily are issued for tourists and temporary business guests, and only a few nonimmigrant visas allow their holders to work in the United States. One such visa is the H-1B visa, discussed below.

An employer who desires to employ a foreign national (a person who is a citizen of a country other than the United States) who is skilled in a specialty occupation, called a foreign guest worker, may do so if the employer is willing to sponsor that worker. To employ a foreign guest worker, the employer must apply for an H-1B visa for that worker, which is a nonimmigrant visa that allows the foreign guest worker who is skilled in a specialty occupation to work for an employer in the United States. To qualify, the foreign guest worker must have at least a bachelor's degree as a minimum level of education and must be engaged in a specialty occupation (meaning that he must be a skilled worker or professional worker), such as medicine, architecture, engineering, education, theology, computer science, arts, or mathematics. The worker may stay up to three years, with up to a three-year extension, with this H-1B visa. Further, the worker may bring along immediate family members (which include a spouse and minor children) with H-4 visas (though H-4 visas do not permit immediate family members to work in the United States). The number of H-1B visas the U.S. grants each year is limited, usually to such an extent that a year's allotment of H-1B visas is often used up within the first weeks or month of the calendar year. About 65,000 H-1B visas per year are issued by the U.S. government today.

Other types of temporary visas are available for other categories of foreign employees. For example, H-2 visas allow entry and employment of seasonal agricultural workers coming from foreign countries. H-2B visas allow temporary entry for foreign guest workers who work in areas such as maintenance and housekeeping and as hotel clerks. E visas allow certain foreign investors and entrepreneurs to enter the United States. L visas

> ## KEY Point
> **List of Major U.S. Visas**
> - H-1B visas allow foreign guest workers who are skilled in a specialty occupation to work for employers in the United States.
> - H-4 visas allow H-1B visa holders to bring along immediate family members.
> - H-2 visas allow entry and employment of seasonal agricultural workers coming from foreign countries.
> - H-2B visas allow temporary entry for foreign guest workers who work in areas such as maintenance and housekeeping and as hotel clerks.
> - E visas allow certain foreign investors and entrepreneurs to enter the United States.
> - L visas allow a business's foreign executives and managers to work within the United States.
> - O visas allow entry of workers who have extraordinary abilities in sciences, arts, education, business, or athletics, substantiated by national or international acclaim.

permit a business's foreign executives and managers to work within the United States. O visas permit entry of workers who have extraordinary abilities in sciences, arts, education, business, or athletics, substantiated by national or international acclaim.

Besides federal laws on immigration, state and local governments also have enacted immigration laws. Noted above, the immigration law in Arizona, a state with illegal immigration issues because of its geographic proximity to Mexico, has garnered much media attention, including the disapproval of President Obama. The Arizona law is considered both broad and strict in achieving its goals of identifying, prosecuting, and deporting illegal immigrants. Among other things, it allows police officers to request that people show documentation proving their immigration status, and makes the failure to carry immigration documentation a crime.

Another legal specialty area involves property law. What is property? What types of property are there? What do property laws do? These questions are considered, and answered, next.

PROPERTY

Property is something that can be owned or possessed. It can be classified into two categories, real property and personal property. **Real property** is land and anything permanently attached to it. Examples of real property include land,

> **Property** is something that can be owned or possessed.
>
> **Real property** is land and anything permanently attached to it.

houses, office buildings, silos, fences where the fence posts are embedded in the land, and crops or timber growing on the land. **Personal property** is all property that is not real property. Therefore, it is all property that is not land or anything permanently attached to the land. Personal property is also called **chattels**. Because of this definition, personal property is said to be residual because it is property that is left over when real property is defined. Examples of personal property include books, computers, clothing, crops after they have been harvested from the land or timber that has been cut from the land, tools, automobiles, stock, bonds, copyrights, and patents.

From the previous examples, consider and distinguish clothing from stock. Clothing is property with physical existence that a person can touch—and wear. Stock, on the other hand, represents ownership in a corporation. While you can touch a stock certificate, the property itself is the stock and the stock certificate merely evidences the ownership of the stock—you still own the stock even if your dog eats the stock certificate. This distinction exists because there are two kinds of personal property, tangible personal property and intangible personal property. **Tangible personal property** is personal property that has physical existence and can be seen and touched. Examples of tangible personal property include a pet, jewelry, toys, and bicycle. **Intangible personal property** is personal property that has no physical existence. Examples of intangible personal property include stocks and bonds, certificates of deposit, and the different forms of intellectual property (patents, copyrights, trademarks/service marks, and trade secrets).

Property law is the body of law that deals with ownership and transfer of property rights and interests. Ownership of property is referred to as ownership of a bundle of rights, including the right to occupy, possess, and use property; the right to sell all or part of the property; the right to bequeath the property to another in a will; the right to give the property away; the right to transfer occupancy, possession, or use of the property by contract for a limited period of time; and the right to receive the benefits derived from another's occupancy, possession, or use of the property for a period of time.

The most complete form of ownership of property is ownership in fee simple absolute. Ownership in **fee simple absolute** gives the owner of the property the entire bundle of rights relating to the property. Upon the owner's death, the land passes to the owner's beneficiaries or heirs. There are other, less-complete, forms of property ownership.

What about where only part of the bundle of rights is owned by a person? That can happen in many ways. For example, a person may have an easement in land. An **easement** is the right of a person to use the land of another for a limited purpose, such as to drive down a shared driveway to another residence or to install and maintain power, cable, or telephone lines to provide utilities to inhabitants on the real property. Another limited bundle of rights is a life estate. A person may have an interest in real property that is transferred to her for as long as she lives, but upon her death that interest either reverts back to the person who granted it or is transferred to another. This interest is called a **life estate**. Further, a person may have an interest in real property that does not legally arise until sometime in the future, such as a person who is granted an interest in property after the holder of a life estate dies. That person has a **future interest** in the property, for the interest will not legally arise until some later time. A lease is another example of ownership of only a portion of the bundle of rights relating to the property. A **lease** is a contract permitting a person to use and possess real property (such as a house or office building) or personal property (such as a car) of another for a limited period of time, usually for compensation to the property owner (called rent).

Can more than one person own property together? Sure! Think about husbands and wives owning property, as one

Personal property is all property that is not real property; it is also called **chattels**.

Tangible personal property is personal property that has physical existence and can be seen and touched.

Intangible personal property is personal property that has no physical existence.

Property law is the body of law that deals with ownership and transfer of property rights and interests.

Fee simple absolute is the most complete form of property ownership where the property owner possesses the entire bundle of rights pertaining to that ownership.

An **easement** is the right of a person to use the land of another for a limited purpose.

A **life estate** is the right of a person to use and possess the real property of another until that person dies.

A **future interest** is an interest in property that does not legally arise until sometime in the future.

A **lease** is a contract permitting a person to use and possess real or personal property of another for a limited period of time, usually upon payment of rent.

example. This is called **concurrent ownership**, when more than one person shares the bundles of rights that constitute property ownership. There are four different types of concurrent ownership, also called **co-tenancy**. One is **tenancy in common**. With this type of concurrent ownership, two or more persons own undivided interests in the property, and if one of the persons (called a tenant in common) dies, her interest in the property passes to her beneficiaries or heirs. Another type of concurrent ownership is **joint tenancy**. With this type of concurrent ownership, two or more persons own undivided interests in the property, and if one of the persons (called a joint tenant) dies, her interest automatically passes to the other remaining joint tenant(s), rather than to her beneficiaries or heirs. This is called the right of survivorship. A third type of ownership is **tenancy by the entirety**. This type of co-ownership is limited to ownership by husbands and wives jointly. With ownership in the form of tenancy by the entirety, when one of the spouses dies, the deceased spouse's interest passes to the surviving spouse. This is another example of the right of survivorship. The final type of concurrent ownership is **community property**. This type of ownership is automatic under some states' laws (in nine states today, including California and Texas). Where community property is the law, property acquired during a marriage is considered owned, in undivided one-half interests, by each spouse; on divorce each spouse is entitled to one-half of the marital property.

The government has the power to take private land for public use. The Fifth Amendment to the U.S. Constitution says that the government shall not take private property for public use without providing just compensation to the property owner. In effect, then, the U.S. Constitution allows the federal government to take the real property of private citizens, to convert that land to public use. The government must provide just compensation (which does not mean fair market value) to the property owner. For example, when the government wants to expand a road from two lanes to four, how does it acquire the additional land, which is likely owned by private citizens? Through its power of eminent domain, the government may take the land necessary to expand the public road so long as it pays just compensation to the landowner. This is called the government's power of **eminent domain**.

With the exception of the government's power of eminent domain, most property is transferred by sale. In fact, when it comes to real estate, that property is often the most valuable property a person owns. However, people may dispose of their property in any way they want, so they need not sell it. People may give away their property, or they may bequeath it in a will to a beneficiary. They may also lease their property to others, sharing the bundle of rights with the persons to whom they lease the property (called lessees), where the lessees have the right to use and possess the property during the term of the lease. Remember from our discussion of contract law that most states' Statute of Frauds require that contracts involving interests in real property, to be legally enforceable, must be in writing and signed by the person against whom enforcement is sought. This is typically evidenced in real estate transactions involving sales or leases.

The last major legal specialty area we will discuss is the area of torts. What are torts? What is tort law, and what does it protect? These questions are considered and answered in the next section.

> ## KEY Point
>
> **Types of Concurrent Ownership**
> - Tenancy in common
> - Joint tenancy
> - Tenancy by the entirety
> - Community property

> **Concurrent ownership** is co-ownership of property by two or more people; it is also called **co-tenancy**.
>
> **Tenancy in common** is a form of concurrent ownership where two or more persons own undivided interests in the property and where, if one of the persons dies, her interest passes to her beneficiaries or heirs.
>
> **Joint tenancy** is a form of concurrent ownership where two or more persons own undivided interests in the property and where, if one of the persons dies, her interest automatically passes to the other joint tenant(s).
>
> **Tenancy by the entirety** is a form of concurrent ownership where husbands and wives jointly own property and where, when one of the spouses dies, the deceased spouse's interest passes to the surviving spouse.
>
> **Community property** is a form of concurrent ownership (recognized in a minority of the states) where property acquired during a marriage is considered owned, in undivided one-half interests, by each spouse and where, on divorce, each spouse is entitled to one-half of the marital property.
>
> **Eminent domain** is the power of the government to take private land for public use, upon payment to the landowner of just compensation.

TORTS

Criminal law, discussed earlier, deals with wrongful conduct committed in violation of a criminal statute, for which the wrongdoer may be prosecuted and punished. Torts are the civil side of wrongful conduct.

A **tort** is a civil wrong, other than a breach of contract. **Tort liability** arises when a person commits such a wrongful, called tortious, act. The person who commits a tort is called a **tortfeasor**.

Through tort law, a person who suffers an injury as a result of the tortious conduct of another can receive compensation or other remedy for that injury. Where tort liability is established, a court will provide a remedy, often in the form of money damages. A **remedy** is the relief given to a party to enforce a right or to compensate for the violation of a right. **Damages** are a remedy awarded at law in the form of money.

Of the four main sources of law discussed in Chapter 3, namely constitutional law, common law, statutory law, and administrative law, tort law is derived mainly from common law. **Common law** is judge-made law, created by the courts and found in court opinions. **Case law** is another term for common law.

Torts can be classified into three main categories. These categories are intentional torts, negligence, and strict liability. Each of these classifications is discussed next.

The first main classification of torts is intentional torts. **Intentional torts** are those torts in which the tortfeasor either desired to bring about the consequences of his act or failure to act, or knew with substantial certainty that the consequences would follow from his act or failure to act. "Intent" is an essential element, meaning that it is a component part, of all intentional torts. Therefore a plaintiff must, in setting forth her case, establish that the defendant intended his act or failure to act (the defendant need not intend to cause harm or injury; it is an intent to act or not act). Because intent of the wrongdoer is an essential element of all of the intentional torts, punitive damages may be

recoverable when a tortfeasor is found liable for committing an intentional tort. This is because having requisite intent to commit the tort makes the wrongdoer's conduct, by definition, more heinous and egregious than some of the other torts where intent is not required—namely negligence and strict liability. In other words, the other tort classifications do not require intent. Examples of intentional torts include assault, battery, false imprisonment, false arrest, intentional infliction of emotional distress,

© Dedyukhin Dmitry/Shutterstock

also called **absolute liability** or **liability without fault**. Under strict liability theory, a tortfeasor is held responsible for injuries he causes to others without regard to blameworthiness. There are three typical applications of strict liability: (1) harm caused by animals, (2) harm caused by abnormally dangerous conditions or activities, and (3) products liability. An example of the application of strict liability is when a pet chimpanzee injures a guest who is visiting the owner's home. Another example of the application of strict liability is when an automobile tire malfunctions and explodes, causing the

malicious prosecution, abuse of process, trespass to land, conversion, trespass to chattels, disparagement of property, misrepresentation, tortious interference with a contractual relationship, and tortious interference with a business relationship.

Negligence is the second main classification of torts. **Negligence** is a failure to use reasonable care, resulting in harm to a person or her property. Negligence is the most common tort action. In fact, most personal injury cases are negligence cases, though personal injuries can result from intentional torts, such as battery, and strict liability torts, such as products liability. A common example of negligence is injury resulting from a car collision that is caused by the unreasonable conduct of another driver. The essential elements of the tort of negligence are duty of care, breach of the duty of care, causation, and damages.

Strict liability is the third main classification of torts. **Strict liability** is tort liability imposed without regard to fault. It is

CASE *on* POINT

Liebeck v. McDonald's Rests., P.T.S., Inc., 1995 WL 360309.

In this case, a 79-year-old woman went through a drive-thru at a McDonald's restaurant in Albuquerque, New Mexico. She was riding in the front-passenger seat of her car, which was being driven by her grandson. The grandson parked the car so that Liebeck could add cream and sugar to her coffee. Liebeck placed the cup of coffee between her knees and pulled the lid tab toward her. In the process, she spilled the entire cup of coffee in her lap. Liebeck was wearing cotton sweatpants at the time, and the coffee was absorbed and held against her skin as Liebeck sat in the spill for about ninety seconds. Liebeck suffered third-degree burns over 6 percent of her body during the coffee scalding, spent eight days in the hospital, and received numerous skin grafts. At the end of her tort trial, the jury awarded Liebeck $2.86 million for her injuries. The trial judge reduced the award to $640,000, and the parties later settled out of court for an undisclosed amount (less than the trial judge's reduced award) before judgment was rendered on McDonald's appeal. As presented in the media, this case demonstrates the point of tort reformists about excessive jury awards. Interestingly, not much media attention was paid to the fact that McDonald's had faced a large number of claims because of its scalding coffee—this was hardly the first.

vehicle to crash and damaging the vehicle, as well as injuring its driver and passengers.

Unusually large and numerous judgments handed down by juries in personal injury tort cases have some advocating for tort reform. **Tort reform** is the act of changing the rules and applications of tort law to reverse the upward trend in compensation being awarded by juries today, particularly in personal injury cases. Advocates in favor of tort reform argue that such large jury awards in some personal injury cases are exponentially disproportionate to the injury sustained, and raise insurance and health care costs for the rest of Americans. See the "McDonald's coffee" Case on Point as an example. Efforts so far in the area of tort reform have resulted in the capping of some damages awards and in limiting the number of some claims that can be brought. Not everyone favors tort reform, however. A major argument against it is that tort reform is a significant disincentive for medical practitioners, drivers, and other major categories of personal injury tortfeasors to use care in their actions. For example, it is counterintuitive to expect improved patient care by medical professionals when damages awards for medical malpractice are capped (limited).

> **Tort reform** is the act of changing the rules and applications of tort law to reverse the upward trend in compensation being awarded by juries today, particularly in personal injury cases.

Peg Hartley

Nurse Paralegal at Goodell, Devries, Leech and Dann, LLP

Peg works as a nurse paralegal at a medium-sized law firm. Before becoming a nurse paralegal, Peg worked for over 30 years as a Registered Nurse before obtaining a degree in nurse paralegal studies.

Peg was hired by her law firm after completing an internship obtained through her nurse paralegal education program. Her medical background, including her ability to perform scientific research, plus her complex litigation training obtained as part of her nurse paralegal studies program, prepared her for this employment. In her practice, Peg performs products liability defense work. Accordingly, hers is a specialized litigation practice. Peg assists with cases in both federal and state courts, mostly at the trial court level but occasionally on appeal.

Peg often conducts factual investigations, including background checks on plaintiffs and expert witnesses, performs medical records reviews, and researches medical issues. She drafts pleadings, prepares documents needed for settlement conferences or arbitration, and interviews new paralegal candidates for employment with the firm.

Technology is an integral part of Peg's practice. She regularly uses word processing, e-mail, the Internet, spreadsheets, electronic calendaring, complex litigation databases, document scanning, electronic document searching, online legal research and factual research tools, and PowerPoint for court presentations.

CHAPTER SUMMARY

- Executive agencies are administrative agencies created under the authority of the government's chief executive. Independent regulatory agencies are administrative agencies created by Congress and by state and local legislatures via enabling legislation.

- Administrative law is the body of substantive and procedural law established by administrative agencies. Similarly, government regulation is the establishment and enforcement of administrative laws.

- Criminal law is the system of law defining and governing actions that constitute crimes, as defined by statutes. The two elements to criminal liability are *actus reus* (criminal act) and *mens rea* (criminal mind).

- Crimes are often grouped into five categories: violent crimes, property crimes, public order crimes, white-collar crimes, and organized crime. Crimes may be further subdivided into degrees.

- People charged with committing crimes may defend their prosecutions by showing the court that they did not possess the *actus reus* or *mens rea* required of the relevant statute, or by asserting a defense to criminal liability such as insanity or the statute of limitations. Numerous protections and safeguards for criminal defendants are found in the U.S. Constitution, specifically the Fourth Amendment, Fifth Amendment, Sixth Amendment, and Eighth Amendment. In addition, the *Miranda* rule and the exclusionary rule provide further protections for criminal defendants.

- Domestic relations means family relations. Domestic relations law, also called family law, is the body of law involving premarital issues, prenuptial agreements, marriage, the dissolution of marriage, divorce, property division upon divorce, child custody, spousal and child support, adoption, and other family-related legal issues.

- A prenuptial agreement, also called a premarital agreement, is a contract that sets forth the terms and conditions of how a couple's property should be distributed on termination of the marriage or death of a spouse, among other things. Most states' Statutes of Frauds require prenuptial agreements to be in writing and signed by the person against whom enforcement is sought.

- Each state has its own marriage laws. Among the requirements for most states is a marriage license, which is a legal document issued by a state authorizing two people to marry, and a ceremony. Some states recognize common law marriage.

- Marriages can be dissolved by annulment or divorce. Annulment is an order by a court declaring that a marriage never existed. Divorce is a legal proceeding where a court issues a decree legally terminating a marriage. Today, all states recognize "no-fault" divorce.

- Child custody means the determination of what person has legal responsibility for raising the minor child on divorce. Legal custody means the custodial authority to make decisions on behalf of the child. Physical custody means where the child lives. Visitation is the right of a noncustodial parent to visit with the child. Child support is the financial support paid by a noncustodial parent to help pay the costs of the child's food, shelter, medical expenses, clothing, education, entertainment, and so on.

- On divorce, marital property must be divided between the spouses. Marital property is that property acquired during the marriage. Separate property is that property which is owned by a spouse prior to the marriage, as well as individual gifts and inheritances received during the marriage. Equitable distribution allows a court to consider relevant facts in making a fair division of the marital property. Community property is a marital property distribution scheme where courts order that all marital property be equally divided between divorcing spouses.

- Spousal support, also called alimony, is monthly payments made by a more affluent divorcing spouse to the other, for some period of time.

- Adoption is where a person or a couple become the legal parent(s) of a child who is not his, her, or their own.

- Estate planning is the process of evaluating and arranging for the disposition of a person's property, called his estate, on his death.

- Wills are legal instruments used in estate planning through which a person declares how he wants his property to be managed and distributed on his death. For a will to be valid, most states require testamentary capacity of the testator, that the will be in writing, the testator's signature, and attestation by witnesses. Some states require publication.

- Probate is the process of determining the validity of a will and carrying out the administration of a person's estate on his death. Probate laws govern the distribution of property upon a person's death. Probate courts have jurisdiction to probate persons' wills.

- If a person dies without a valid will, he dies intestate. Every state has an intestacy statute that sets forth how a person's property will be distributed when he dies without a valid will.

- Trusts are also used extensively in estate planning. A trust is a legal relationship created by a person, called a grantor, donor, or settlor, who transfers and delivers to one or more persons, called a trustee or trustees, property of the grantor for the benefit of another or others, called the beneficiary or beneficiaries. The property held by the trust is called the trust *res* or trust *corpus*. There are many classifications of trusts, including express trusts, *inter vivos* trusts, testamentary trusts, resulting trusts, and constructive trusts.

- Other estate planning devices include concurrent ownership of property, *inter vivos* gifts, and life insurance.

- Estate administration is the legal process that involves the collection and disposition of a person's property on his death. To handle estate administration, a testator may name a personal representative in his will, or a court may appoint an administrator.

- An immigrant is a person who comes to a country to take up permanent residence. Immigration law is the body of law that determines who may enter this country, how long they may state, when they must leave, and if and when they may become naturalized citizens. Visas are entry permits to the United States for which foreigners can apply, depending on their circumstances.

- Property is something that can be owned or possessed. The two categories of property are real property and personal property. Real property is land and anything permanently attached to it. Personal property is all property that is not real property. Personal property can be tangible or intangible depending on whether it has physical existence and can be seen and touched.

- Property law is that body of law that deals with ownership and transfer of property rights and interests. The most complete form of ownership of property is ownership in fee simple absolute. Property can be owned by one person or by two or more persons. When property is owned by two or more persons, they have concurrent ownership, which can take several forms, including tenancy in common, joint tenancy, tenancy by the entirety, and community property.

- A tort is a civil wrong, other than a breach of contract. Tort liability arises when a person commits a tortious act. That person is called a tortfeasor. A remedy, often in the form of damages, may be awarded to a person who is injured, or whose property is harmed, because of a tortfeasor's conduct.

- The three main classifications of torts are intentional torts, negligence, and strict liability. Intentional torts are those torts in which the tortfeasor either desired to bring about the consequences of his act or failure to act, or knew with substantial certainty that the consequences would follow from his act or failure to act. Negligence is a failure to use reasonable care, resulting in harm to a person or his property. Strict liability is tort liability imposed without regard to fault and is also called absolute liability or liability without fault.

- Tort reform is the act of changing the rules and applications of tort law to reverse the upward trend in compensation being awarded by juries today, particularly in personal injury cases.

CONCEPT REVIEW AND REINFORCEMENT

Key Terms and Concepts

Executive agencies
Independent regulatory agencies
Enabling legislation
Administrative law
Government regulation
Criminal law
Actus reus
Mens rea
Violent crimes

Property crimes
Public order crimes
White-collar crimes
Organized crime
Miranda rule
Exclusionary rule
Domestic relations
Domestic relations law
Family law
Prenuptial agreement
Premarital agreement
Marriage license
Common law marriage
Annulment
Divorce
Child custody
Legal custody
Physical custody
Visitation
Child support
Marital property
Separate property
Equitable distribution
Community property
Spousal support
Alimony
Adoption
Estate
Estate planning
Wills
Testators
Beneficiaries
Probate
Probate courts
Probate laws
Intestate
Intestacy statute
Heirs
Trust
Grantor
Donor
Settlor
Trustee
Beneficiary
Trust *res*
Trust *corpus*
Express trust
Inter vivos trust
Testamentary trust
Resulting trust
Constructive trust
Co-tenancy
Inter vivos gift
Estate administration
Personal representative
Administrator
Immigrant
Immigration law

Visa
Property
Real property
Personal property
Chattels
Tangible personal property
Intangible personal property
Property law
Fee simple absolute
Easement
Life estate
Future interest
Lease
Concurrent ownership
Tenancy in common
Joint tenancy
Tenancy by the entirety
Community property
Eminent domain
Tort
Tort liability
Tortfeasor
Remedy
Damages
Common law
Intentional torts
Negligence
Strict liability
Tort reform

Questions for Review

1. What is administrative law?
2. What is government regulation?
3. What are crimes?
4. What is criminal law?
5. What are domestic relations?
6. What does domestic relations law regulate?
7. What are estates?
8. What are wills?
9. What are trusts?
10. What is the legal role of wills and trusts?
11. What is immigration?
12. What do immigration laws do?
13. What is property?
14. What is the difference between real and personal property?
15. How is property protected by law?
16. What are torts?
17. What are the three main classifications of torts?
18. What is the role of tort law?

DEVELOPING YOUR PARALEGAL SKILLS

Critical Thinking Exercises

1. Erma and Ward, happily married for over 14 years, now wish to terminate their marriage. They have three children, ages 12, 10 and 4. Ward is a successful investment banker, and Erma does not work outside the home.

   What legal proceedings should they use to terminate their marriage? What legal issues will they have to resolve to terminate their marriage? List these issues.

2. What type of property is each of the following, based on what you have learned in this chapter? Your answer should be one of the following: real property, tangible personal property, intangible personal property, or intellectual property.
   a. A house.
   b. A pet rabbit.
   c. A chicken used for egg production.
   d. A chick coop to house the chicken used for egg production, which coop is on posts that are embedded in the ground and cemented there.
   e. Five hundred shares of The Coca-Cola Company stock.
   f. The copyright in this textbook.
   g. A personal computer.
   h. A yacht.
   i. Corn growing in a field.
   j. Corn harvested from a field and for sale in the grocery store.
   k. A savings bond.
   l. The building in which a law office is located.
   m. A diamond and gold Rolex watch.
   n. A stick of gum.
   o. The space shuttle *Discovery*.

3. Are cattle chattel?

Assignments and Practical Applications

Research your state's law to determine the marriage requirements for your jurisdiction. Make a list of those requirements. Does your state recognize the legal union of persons of the same gender?

Does your state recognize common law marriage? If so, what are your state's common law marriage requirements? Perform legal research to answer those questions.

Conduct legal research to determine the requirements for making a will in your state. List those requirements.

Does your state recognize the validity of holographic wills? If so, what are the requirements for making a holographic will in your jurisdiction?

Regarding green cards (Permanent Resident Cards) and immigration law, view the 1990 film *Green Card* starring Gerard Depardieu and Andie MacDowell. The film tells the story of an American woman who marries a Frenchman so that he can obtain a green card to live as a permanent resident in the United States.

Research to determine if your state is a community property state. If it is, what does that mean? Does it have a significant impact on unmarried persons? Does it have a significant impact on married persons?

Perform legal research to determine the essential elements of the tort of negligence for your jurisdiction (state). List these essential elements.

Technology Resources and Internet Exercises

Review the A to Z index of federal government agencies at http://www.usa.gov/Agencies/Federal/All_Agencies/C.shtml. How many are you already familiar with?

Remember Nebraska's second degree murder statute, presented in this chapter. Using the Internet, locate your state's second degree murder statute. Compare and contrast it with Nebraska's statute. Are they the same? If they differ, how do they differ?

The chapter discussed procedures that must be followed to get married in a jurisdiction. Some jurisdictions have waiting period requirements between the obtaining of a marriage license and the performance of the ceremony. See the following website for a review, by state, of waiting period requirements: http://marriage.about.com/cs/marriagelicenses/a/waitingtime.htm.

Using the Internet, research which states recognize the legal union of people of the same gender. What are those states' marriage requirements?

Review some of the different kinds of trusts. See http://public.findlaw.com/abaflg/flg-18-3b-1.html for some examples.

Using the Internet, review the controversial Arizona immigration statute enacted in 2010. Also review news articles describing the media frenzy it created by being more broad and strict than other states' immigration laws in effect at that time.

Using the Cornell University Law School website for its Legal Information Institute, found at http://www.law.cornell.edu/, find your state's legal ethics code. Use it to answer the following Ethical Applications.

Ethical Applications

Charles Benson works as a paralegal in a criminal defense law firm. One day, Charles's supervising attorney, Lisa Scumbath, requests Charles shred some documents relating to a client's matter. Charles asks Lisa, "What are the documents?" Lisa responds, "A one-way ticket to prison for our client if anyone ever sees them." Lisa is correct. These documents constitute evidence in a criminal prosecution against the firm's client, and are most incriminating.

    a. What should Charles do?

    b. Evaluate Lisa's actions under the advocacy rules for lawyers. Where are the bounds of "zealous" representation drawn? Has she crossed them?

VIDEO CASE STUDIES

Video Interview of Lindsay Ann Thomas

Paralegal case study videos to accompany this textbook are accessible from within both the New MyLegalStudiesLab Virtual Law Office Experience course and the Resources Website for Paralegal Studies.

ENDNOTES

[1] 384 U.S. 436 (1966).

APPENDIX

Video List

Role of the Paralegal

Administrative Agency Hearing

Confidentiality – Attorney Client Privilege

Confidentiality Issue – Disclosure of Damaging Information

Parent and Child Consult the Legal Team

Preparation for Trial – Preparing Witness for Deposition and Trial

UPL Issue – Disclosure of Status

Preparing for Arbitration

Finding Paralegal Employment

Preparing for a Job Interview – Interviewing Advice

Preparing for a Job Interview – Resume Advice

Interviewing: The Good, the Bad and the Ugly

Resume Writing Do's and Don'ts

The Court System

Jury Selection – Potential Juror Challenged for Cause

Mechanic's Deposition

A Salesman's Courtroom Testimony

Closing Argument

The Judge Instructs the Jury before Deliberations

Three Judge Appellate Review

Difference between Civil and Criminal Case

Meet the Courthouse Team

"Big Three" Legal Ethics Issues

Confidentiality Issue – Need to Know Circle

Confidentiality Issue – Family Exception

Conflict of Interest – Relationships with Clients

Conflict of Interest – Independent Paralegal

UPL Issue – Improper Supervision

UPL Issue – When Friends Ask Legal Advice

Other Legal Ethics Issues

Fees and Billing Issue – Contemporaneous Timekeeping

Fees and Billing Issue – Using Time Effectively

Solicitation in the ER – Ethical Duties of the Profession

Zealous Representation Issue – Signing Document

Zealous Representation Issue – Handling Evidence

Paralegal Skills

Legal Research – Are Books Obsolete?

UPL Issue – Interviewing a Client

Legal Specialty Areas

Altercation on the School Bus

A Corporate Officer Seeks Legal Counsel: Conflict of Interest

Lillian Harris Interview – Small Family Law Practice

GLOSSARY

A

Abuse of process The use of civil or criminal proceedings for an improper purpose or an ulterior motive.

Acquittal A "not guilty" verdict rendered at the end of a criminal prosecution.

Actus reus Performance of a prohibited act; the criminal act.

Administrative law The body of substantive and procedural law established by administrative agencies; the specialty area of law dealing with the administration and regulation of government agencies at the local, state, and federal levels.

Administrator A person appointed by the court to administer a person's estate.

Admonition A private reprimand.

Adoption Where one person or a couple become the legal parent(s) of a child who is not his, her, or their own.

Advanced fees Legal fees paid by the client at the beginning of the representation and which are usually refundable if the fees are not later earned by the attorney through the performance of legal service.

Advertising Communication designed to persuade a person to purchase a product or service.

Advocacy The act of arguing on behalf of another in a legal action.

Advocate A person who engages in advocacy.

Affirm To uphold the lower court's decision.

Affirmative defense A response to a plaintiff's claim that asserts why the defendant should not be held liable to the plaintiff.

Agency relationship A relationship between a principal and an agent.

Agent A person who agrees to act, and acts, on behalf of another person.

Agreement The manifestation of assent by the parties to enter into a legally binding contract; a "meeting of the minds."

Agreements Contracts.

Alimony Spousal support.

Alternative dispute resolution (ADR) The resolution of legal disputes in ways other than litigation.

Annulment An order by a court declaring that a marriage never existed.

Answer A defendant's response to the allegations made in the plaintiff's complaint; the initial document prepared by a party responding to a lawsuit being filed against her.

Appeal A legal proceeding undertaken to have a court's decision reviewed by a higher court.

Appellate jurisdiction The power of a court to review a decision from a lower court.

Arbitration An out-of-court process where parties submit their legal dispute to a neutral third party or parties, called an arbitrator or arbitration panel, who hears evidence and renders an award.

Arraignment The court's formal reading of a criminal complaint in the presence of the defendant.

Arrest The taking into custody of a person in response to a criminal investigation.

Articles of organization A document that is filed with the secretary of state's office to form a limited liability company.

Associate attorneys Non-owner employees of a law firm who are also attorneys.

Attorney-client privilege A rule of evidence that protects certain communications made between a client and his attorney.

Award The decision made by an arbitrator or arbitration panel.

B

Bail An amount of money that a defendant can post, the amount of which is set by the court, sufficiently high enough to ensure that the defendant will appear in court to answer a criminal charge.

Bail bondsman A person who pledges money or property as bail for a criminal defendant.

Banking law The legal specialty area involving rules and regulations governing financial institutions, such as banks, savings and loan companies, and credit unions.

Bankruptcy The legally acknowledged inability of an individual or a business organization to pay the debts it owes to its creditors.

Bankruptcy law The body of federal law that legally acknowledges the inability of an individual or organization to pay its debts and that allows the debtor to pay certain creditors what it can while giving the debtor some relief from debts in order to make a "fresh start"; the legal specialty area dealing with federal judicial proceedings commenced when an entity or individual cannot pay debts.

Bench trial A trial where a judge hears and decides the case.

Beneficiary A person designated in a will to receive a testator's property; a person for whose benefit a trust is created.

"Beyond a reasonable doubt" The standard of proof applied in a criminal case, by which the prosecution must prove the case sufficiently so that there is no reasonable doubt in the mind of any juror that the defendant committed the crime.

Bill of Rights The first 10 amendments to the U.S. Constitution.

Binding authority Legal authority that must be followed by a court in deciding a case; it is also called **mandatory authority**.

Boards of directors Groups of directors who are elected by the shareholders and are responsible for the management of a corporation.

Booking The recording of the suspect's name, offense, and time of arrival in a police blotter.

Boutique firm A small law firm that specializes in a certain practice area, such as bankruptcy law or family law.

Breach of contract The failure of a party to a contract to completely perform under the contract.

Burden of proof A party's duty to prove a disputed assertion in a lawsuit or prosecution.

Business etiquette Our society's accepted standard of social behavior in the business environment.

C

Case A written judgment of a court.

Case brief A written summary of a court case.

Case briefing The process of reading, analyzing, and summarizing a court case.

Case citations The locator references that provide information about how to find cases in the state and federal reporter systems.

Case law Common law.

Case names Identify the parties to legal actions.

Case of first impression A court case on which there is no binding precedent to base a decision.

Case on point A previous court case involving similar facts and legal issues to those being researched.

Certificate of incorporation The document issued by a state that incorporates a corporation; it is also called a **corporate charter**.

Chattels Personal property.

Chief justice The head of the U.S. Supreme Court and the highest federal judicial officer in the United States.

Child custody Legal responsibility for raising a minor child.

Child support The financial support paid by a noncustodial parent to help pay the costs of the child's food, shelter, medical expenses, clothing, education, entertainment, and the like.

Circuit courts U.S. courts of appeals.

Civil law The system of law dealing with the definition and enforcement of all private or public rights.

Civil procedure The body of procedural law that governs the process of civil litigation.

Client A party who engages an attorney as counsel in a legal matter.

Client trust accounts Bank accounts that are set up by lawyers to maintain funds that belong to one or more clients.

Closing arguments Summarizations by the attorneys of their clients' cases emphasizing their sides' strengths and the other side's weaknesses; they are also called **closing statements** and **summations**.

Closing statements Closing arguments.

Common law Law established by judges in the courts and found in court opinions; it is also called **case law**.

Common law marriage A marriage in which the jurisdiction's procedures for getting married have not been met, but the persons are eligible to marry, they voluntarily intend to be husband and wife, they live together, and they hold themselves out to the public as husband and wife.

Community property A form of concurrent ownership (recognized in a minority of the states) where property acquired during a marriage is considered owned, in undivided one-half interests, by each spouse and where, on divorce, each spouse is entitled to one-half of the marital property.

Competence The ability to successfully perform a task.

Competent representation A lawyer possesses the legal knowledge, skill, thoroughness, and preparation reasonably necessary for the client's representation in a matter.

Complaint A document that initiates a lawsuit by setting forth the plaintiff's claim, the basis for the court's jurisdiction over the matter, and a demand for a remedy; it is the initial document prepared by a party to bring a lawsuit.

Concurrent jurisdiction Where a court has shared jurisdiction with another court or other courts; more than one court has authority to adjudicate the matter.

Concurrent ownership Co-ownership of property by two or more people; it is also called **co-tenancy**.

Concurring opinion An opinion in which a judge (or judges) agrees with the court's decision but for different reasons.

Conflict of interest When the interests of a client conflict with the interests of the attorney or other clients who are or were represented by the attorney.

Conflicts check The process of evaluating a prospective client to determine if representation of the prospective client on a matter would create any conflicts of interest for the lawyer; it is also called a **conflicts of interest check**.

Consideration Something of value given or promised in exchange for another's promise.

Constitutional law Law found in the federal and state constitutions.

Constructive trust An equitable remedy that is imposed by the courts to rectify unjust enrichment, fraud, mistake, undue influence, or some other wrongdoing.

Contingency fees Fees for legal services that are based on a percentage of recovery in a civil case; they are also called **contingent fees**.

Contract A legally enforceable agreement between two or more parties; it is also called an **agreement**.

Contract attorneys Attorneys who are not employed by the law firm, but who are independent contractors hired to perform legal work on a project-by-project basis.

Contract law Law dealing with the creation and enforcement of contracts.

Contracts Legal documents that are used to evidence the terms and conditions of agreements between two or more parties; they are also called **agreements**.

Contractual capacity The legal ability of a person to enter into a contractual relationship.

Conversion The intentional exercise of dominion and control over another's personal property that seriously interferes with the owner's right to possession.

Copyright The exclusive right of an author or other creator of a copyrightable work to reproduce, publish, adapt, publicly perform, and publicly display that work for a limited time.

Corporate bylaws Rules adopted either by the incorporators or the initial board of directors that set forth how the corporation will be managed and operated.

Corporate charter Another name for certificate of incorporation.

Corporate law Transactional law dealing with the formation, financing, merger, acquisition, operation, and termination of legal entities, as well as the rights and duties of those who own and manage those entities.

Corporation A legal entity, separate and distinct from its owners, that is created according to state statute to carry on a business activity.

Co-tenancy The concurrent ownership of property by two or more people.

Counterclaim A claim initiated by the defendant in a case against the plaintiff.

Court systems The judicial branches of the federal and state governments that are charged with the application, interpretation, and enforcement of the law.

Courts of appeals The 13 U.S. circuit courts of appeals.

Cover letter Correspondence that introduces a job applicant and briefly and effectively states why she is interested in, and qualified for, the position.

Criminal complaint A legal document containing a statement of the charges that are being brought by the government against the suspect and the basis for them.

Criminal law The system of law defining and governing actions that constitute crimes as defined by statutes; it deals with public wrongs, known as wrongs against society, for which punishment may be imposed.

Criminal procedure The body of procedural law that governs the process of criminal prosecutions.

Cross-claim A claim made by a defendant against another defendant in the same case, or a claim made by a plaintiff against another plaintiff in the same case.

Cross-examination The questioning of a party or witness by the opposing side.

D

Damages A remedy awarded at law, in the form of money.

Default judgment A judgment entered by a court against a party who fails to respond to a claim brought against him.

Defendant The party being sued in a civil case, or the party being prosecuted in a criminal case.

Deliberate When the jury retires to the jury room to discuss the evidence and work toward a verdict.

Deposition The sworn testimony of a party or witness, given during a question and answer proceeding conducted before trial.

Dicta The nonlaw statements made by judges in their opinions.

Diligence Acting with steady and persistent effort.

Direct examination The questioning of a party or witness by the side that calls her to testify.

Disbarment The revocation of a lawyer's license to practice law in the state.

Discovery The process of searching for and obtaining information and evidence relevant to the case.

Disposition of the case Whether the appellate court affirmed, reversed, or remanded the case.

Dissenting opinion An opinion in which a judge (or judges) disagrees with the ruling of the court.

Diversity cases Cases that involve lawsuits between citizens of different states, between citizens and foreign countries, and between citizens and non-U.S. citizens where there is an amount in controversy of at least $75,000; they are also called **diversity of citizenship cases**.

Divorce A legal proceeding where a court issues a decree legally terminating a marriage.

Doctrine of *respondeat superior* A legal doctrine pursuant to which an employer may be held vicariously liable for certain wrongful acts of its employees.

Doctrine of *stare decisis* A legal doctrine that requires a court to follow precedent established by a higher court within that jurisdiction.

Domestic relations Family relations.

Domestic relations law The area of law involving premarital issues, prenuptial agreements, marriage, the dissolution of marriage, divorce, property division on divorce, child custody, spousal and child support, adoption, and other family related legal issues; it is also called **family law**.

E

Easement The right of a person to use the land of another for a limited purpose.

Elder law The legal specialty area dealing with laws serving the needs of elderly Americans.

Eminent domain The power of the government to take private land for public use, on payment to the landowner of just compensation.

Employer One who hires another to perform work on his behalf, and who has the right to control the details of how the work is performed.

Employment at will doctrine A common law rule stating that when an employment relationship is of indefinite duration, it can be terminated by either the employer or the employee at any time, for any reason.

Enabling legislation Statutes that create administrative agencies.

Enforce a judgment To collect the money or other property owed to the winning party by the losing party to civil litigation.

Environment The sum total of all the resources in which we live.

Environmental law The legal specialty area dealing with laws and regulations designed to protect the environment.

Environmental laws Laws created at all levels of government to protect the environment from human impact and damage.

Equitable distribution Allows a court to consider relevant factors, such as the length of the marriage, the spouses' occupations, the income of each spouse, the age and health of each spouse, the standard of living experienced during the marriage, and the child custody arrangement, in making a fair division of marital property on divorce.

Estate The property owned by a person at the time of his death.

Estate administration A legal process that involves the collection and disposition of a person's property on his death.

Estate planning The process of evaluating and arranging for the disposition of a person's property on his death.

Estate planning and probate administration The specialty area of law dealing with planning for and administering the disposition of a person's property on his death.

Etiquette Our society's accepted standard of social behavior.

Exclusionary rule A legal principle that prohibits the use at trial of any evidence obtained in violation of the constitutional rights of the criminal defendant, as well as any evidence derived from that illegally obtained evidence.

Exclusive jurisdiction Where a court has exclusive authority over a subject matter or territory, meaning it is the only court authorized to adjudicate the matter.

Execution The legal process where assets of the losing party to litigation are taken and/or sold to pay an adverse judgment.

Executive agencies Administrative agencies created under the authority of the government's chief executive either as a cabinet department or as a subagency within a cabinet department.

Expert witness A person possessing professional training or skill, advanced knowledge or education, and/or substantial experience in a specialized area who is hired to testify in court or to render an opinion on a matter related to a client's case.

Express contracts Contracts expressed in oral or written words and are voluntarily and deliberately entered into by the parties to them.

Express trust A trust voluntarily created by the grantor.

Eyewitness A person who observed an event and can testify about it.

F

Factual investigation An examination or inquiry into the facts of a legal matter.

Family law Domestic relations law.

Federal questions Cases involving, at least in part, an alleged violation of the U.S. Constitution or other law of the United States (such as a federal statute), or a treaty to which the United States is a party.

Fee simple absolute The most complete form of property ownership where the property owner possesses the entire bundle of rights pertaining to that ownership.

Felony A more serious crime than a misdemeanor, usually punishable by a fine, incarceration for more than one year, and/or death.

Fiduciary relationship A relationship between two persons that is based on trust and confidence and that gives rise to a duty to act with loyalty toward the other party to the relationship.

Fixed fees Fees for legal services of a set amount for the performance of a routine legal service; they are also called **flat fees**.

Flat fees Fixed fees.

Forum shopping Where the plaintiff in a case involving concurrent jurisdiction has the option to file suit in state or federal court, depending on which forum she feels is more beneficial to her.

Freelance paralegal A self-employed paralegal who is contractually engaged by attorneys to perform legal work, but who works for herself, typically out of a home office.

Future interest An interest in property that does not legally arise until sometime in the future.

G

General jurisdiction The power of a court to adjudicate a wide variety of types of cases, including both civil and criminal cases.

Goodwill The enhanced likelihood that a consumer will repurchase the company's product or service.

Government regulation The establishment and enforcement of administrative laws.

Grand jury A group of people who are selected, convened, and sworn in by a court to determine whether the prosecutor has sufficient evidence to support the finding that there is probable cause to prosecute a defendant.

Grantor A person who creates a trust; he is also called a **donor** or **settlor**.

Guilty A verdict that means the criminal defendant is convicted of committing the crime.

H

Hazardous waste Waste that is generated by businesses or households whose improper disposal poses a danger to human health and the environment.

Heirs Relatives who receive property under a state's intestacy statute.

Hourly fees Fees for legal services that are based on hourly rates and the amount of time actually spent performing the work.

I

Immigrant A person who comes to a country to take up permanent residence.

Immigration law The body of law that deals with citizenship, the right to be and work in the United States, naturalization, deportation, and the like.

Implied in fact contracts Contracts that are inferred from the parties' conduct rather than from their words.

Implied in law contracts Contracts that are imposed by courts to prevent the unjust enrichment of a party to the detriment of another party; they are also called **quasi-contracts**.

***In personam* jurisdiction** Jurisdiction over the person.

***In rem* jurisdiction** Jurisdiction over the property.

Independent paralegals Paralegals who offer their services directly to the public, without attorney supervision; they are also called **legal document preparers** or **legal document assistants**.

Independent regulatory agencies Administrative agencies created by Congress at the federal level, and by state and local legislatures at the state and local levels.

Indictment A formal accusation by a grand jury that a defendant has committed a crime; it is also called a **true bill**.

Information A formal accusation that takes the place of the criminal complaint and that initiates the criminal prosecution.

Initial appearance When the defendant appears before a magistrate soon after arrest to determine whether or not there is probable cause for his arrest.

Injunctions Court orders requiring a person to do, or refrain from doing, something.

Intake interview The initial client interview.

Intangible personal property Personal property that has no physical existence.

Intellectual property A product of the human mind that is protected by law.

Intellectual property law The legal specialty area covering patents, copyrights, trademarks/service marks, and trade secrets; laws that protect the different types of intellectual property.

Intentional torts Those torts in which the tortfeasor either desired to bring about the consequences of his act or failure to act, or knew with substantial certainty that the consequences would follow from his act or failure to act.

***Inter vivos* gift** A gift made by a person during his lifetime.

***Inter vivos* trust** A trust that is made by a grantor and becomes effective during his lifetime; it is also called a **living trust**.

Internship Where a student performs supervised training in her field of study.

Interrogatories Written questions prepared by a party, submitted to the other party, to be answered under oath.

Interview A meeting held for the purpose of asking questions and eliciting responses.

Intestacy statute A state statute that sets forth how a person's property will be distributed when he dies without a valid will.

Intestate When a person dies without having a valid will.

Investigation plan A list of tasks an investigator plans to perform to obtain or verify factual information about a legal matter.

J

Joint tenancy A form of concurrent ownership where two or more persons own undivided interests in the property and if one of the persons dies, her interest automatically passes to the other joint tenant(s).

Judgment creditor A litigant who has been awarded a money judgment that has not been paid.

Judgment debtor A litigant who owes a money judgment and has failed to pay it.

Jurisdiction The power of a court to hear a case.

Jurisdiction over the person The court has the power to adjudicate a matter involving this person; it is also called **personal jurisdiction** or *in personam* **jurisdiction**.

Jurisdiction over the property The court has the power to adjudicate a matter involving property located within its boundaries; it is also called *in rem* **jurisdiction**.

Jurisdiction over the subject matter of a case The court has the power to adjudicate a legal matter of this type; it is also called **subject matter jurisdiction**.

Jury instructions The rules of law given by the judge to the jury that the jury must apply to the facts in order to render a verdict in the case.

Jury selection The process of assembling a panel of jurors to hear a case.

Jury trial A trial where a jury hears and decides the case.

L

Labor and employment law The legal specialty area dealing with laws regulating the employment relationship, workplace safety, and collective bargaining.

Last will and testament A will.

Law The body of rules of conduct and procedure that are established, recognized, and enforced to govern a society.

Law clerks Summer associates.

Law firm A for-profit organization whose business is the provision of legal services.

Lawsuit A civil legal action brought by a party against another.

Lawyer advertising Communication by a lawyer designed to persuade a person to engage the lawyer's services.

Lay witness A person who can testify about factual knowledge he possesses.

Lease A contract permitting a person to use and possess real or personal property of another for a limited period of time, usually on payment of rent.

Legal assistant A paralegal.

Legal briefs Documents prepared by attorneys, advocacy organizations, or governments and submitted to the courts to present arguments in support of legal positions; they are also called **briefs**.

Legal correspondence Legal letters.

Legal custody The custodial authority to make decisions on behalf of a child.

Legal document assistants Independent paralegals.

Legal document preparers Independent paralegals.

Legal ethics The minimum standards of conduct prescribed in a jurisdiction's code of ethical conduct that govern those engaged in the practice of law.

Legal jargon Legalese.

Legal memoranda Documents that thoroughly analyze and summarize the law in a particular area, on the basis of legal research, and inform the requestor of the strengths and weaknesses of the client's legal position.

Legal research The process of locating an answer to a legal question.

Legal specialty area A separate and distinct area of law in which a lawyer or paralegal practices.

Legal writing A type of technical writing used by lawyers, judges, and legislators to communicate legal analysis and legal rights and duties.

Legalese The body of terms used by legal professionals; it is also called **legal jargon**.

Legality The requirement that a contract be formed for a legal purpose, meaning one that is not illegal or contrary to public policy.

Liability Legal responsibility.

Licensing A government's official act granting permission to a person to perform some service or use a particular title, such as practice law or hold oneself out as an attorney, which is prohibited without such permission.

Life estate The right of a person to use and possess the real property of another until that person dies.

Limited jurisdiction The power of a court to adjudicate only certain types of cases, such as tax matters or probate matters.

Limited liability company A hybrid form of business organization that permits the organization to elect to be treated like a partnership for income tax purposes while maintaining limited liability protection for its owners; it is also called a **limited liability corporation** and is abbreviated **LLC**.

Limited liability corporation A limited liability company.

Litigation The area of law that deals with the court system and the process of resolving legal disputes in the civil law system; the process of carrying on a civil lawsuit.

Living trust *Inter vivos* trust.

Long arm statutes State statutes that allow courts to exercise personal jurisdiction over nonresident defendants who have "minimum contacts" with the state.

M

Magistrate A judicial officer with limited law enforcement and administration authority.

Majority opinion An opinion in which more than half of the judges agree to it.

Malicious prosecution The initiation of a criminal prosecution or a civil lawsuit against another party with malice and without probable cause.

Malpractice Professional negligence; it is committed by a professional who breaches a duty of care owed to another, which breach causes the other person harm.

Managing partner A partner to whom management of the law firm is delegated.

Mandatory authority Binding authority.

Marital property That property acquired during a marriage.

Marriage license A legal document issued by a state that authorizes two people to marry.

Mediation A nonadversarial process where a neutral third party facilitates communications between parties to a legal dispute to help them resolve it.

Mediator A neutral third party who conducts a mediation session.

Members Owners of limited liability companies.

Mens rea Wrongful mental state; the criminal mind.

Minimum contacts A test applied under states' long arm statutes to determine if it is fair for a court to exercise jurisdiction over a nonresident defendant.

Miranda rule A common law rule that requires persons arrested be informed of certain constitutional rights including the right to remain silent and the right to legal counsel.

Misdemeanor A "lesser" crime, meaning a crime less serious than a felony and usually punishable by a fine and/or incarceration for one year or less.

Modify To change the lower court's decision.

Motion for a new trial A motion made by the losing party that asks the court to order a new trial because there were significant legal errors in the conduct of the first one.

Motion for directed verdict A motion made to the court by the defendant's counsel asking for judgment in the defendant's favor when the plaintiff has offered such insufficient evidence that no reasonable jury could rule in the plaintiff's favor.

Motion for judgment notwithstanding the verdict (JNOV) A motion brought by the losing party asking the court to enter judgment in its favor on the basis that the verdict was clearly unsupported by the evidence at trial.

Motion for judgment on the pleadings A motion filed by either the plaintiff or the defendant in an action asking the court to enter a judgment in her favor based on the information contained in all the pleadings.

Motion for summary judgment A motion filed by either the plaintiff or the defendant in an action asking the court to enter a judgment in her favor based not only on the information contained in the pleadings but also on other supporting evidence from outside the pleadings.

Motion to dismiss A request made to the court by the defendant after the filing of the complaint asking the court to dismiss the action.

N

Negligence A failure to use reasonable care, resulting in harm to a person or his property.

Negotiation A process where the parties to a legal dispute communicate, themselves or through their attorneys, to try to resolve a legal dispute.

Networking The process of making personal connections and establishing professional relationships with others in a profession, such as the paralegal profession.

O

Objective legal writing Legal writing that is neutral and unbiased.

Offer A promise to do or refrain from doing something at some point in the future.

Offeree The person to whom an offer to enter into a contract is made.

Offeror The person who makes an offer in the formation of a contract.

Officers Employees of a corporation who are charged with the responsibility of running the day-to-day operations of the corporation.

Opening statement A brief summary by an attorney of the client's position and evidence, offered at the start of a trial.

Operating agreements Contracts setting forth the rules of operation and management for limited liability companies.

Opinion The formal analysis, decision, and reasoning of the court in ruling on a case.

Ordinances Statutory laws (statutes) enacted by local governments.

Organized crime The systematic carrying on of illegal activities by criminal organizations.

Original jurisdiction The power of a court to hear a case for the first time.

P

Paralegal A person who performs certain substantive legal work for and delegated by a lawyer, under the lawyer's supervision and for which the lawyer is responsible; also called a **legal assistant**.

Paralegal registration The identification of a person as a participant in a voluntary registration program for paralegals.

Paralegal regulation The direct regulation of paralegals by the states in which they work, through licensing requirements and legal ethics rules.

Parallel citation A second (or even third) citation for a case when the case is published in more than one reporter.

Partner An owner of a partnership.

Partnership An association of two or more persons who carry on as co-owners of a business for profit.

Party A person who enters into a contract with another.

Patent A governmental grant that gives an inventor or discoverer the exclusive right to make, use, and sell his invention or discovery for a limited period of time.

Penalties What are imposed on a defendant found guilty in a criminal prosecution.

Personal jurisdiction Jurisdiction over the person.

Personal property All property that is not real property; it is also called **chattels**.

Personal representative A person named in a will to administer a person's estate.

Persuasive authority Legal authority that is not binding on a court but may be used as guidance by the court in making its decision; it is also called **persuasive precedent**.

Persuasive legal writing Legal writing that advocates your client's position.

Persuasive precedent Persuasive authority.

Petition for *certiorari* A petition brought by a party asking the U.S. Supreme Court to hear a case.

Physical custody The place where the child lives.

Plaintiff The party bringing suit in a civil case.

Plea bargain An agreement between the prosecution and the criminal defendant that the defendant plead guilty to a lesser charge or to the original charge but with the prosecution's recommendation of a sentence of less than the maximum allowed by law, and that is subject to court approval; it is also called a **plea agreement**, **plea deal**, or the **result of copping a plea**.

Pleadings The initial documents prepared by the parties in either bringing a lawsuit or in responding to the filing of a lawsuit.

Police blotter A log, or record book, of daily arrests at a police station.

Precedent An earlier court ruling that decided a case involving a similar legal issue and based on similar facts.

Preliminary hearing An evidentiary and adversarial hearing to determine whether there is enough evidence to bring a criminal defendant to trial.

Prenuptial agreement A contract that sets forth the terms and conditions of how a couple's property should be distributed on termination of the marriage or death of a spouse, how income will be treated during marriage, whether and how much alimony will be paid to a spouse on divorce, who will have child custody or visitation rights on divorce if minor children are involved, and what child custody and visitation rights will be; it is also called a **premarital agreement**.

Premarital agreement Prenuptial agreement.

"Preponderance of the evidence" The standard of proof typically applied in a civil case, by which the party must demonstrate that it is more likely than not that the allegations are true.

Pretrial conference A meeting between the attorneys and the judge, held prior to trial, to discuss possible settlement as well as trial matters.

Primary sources of law Establish the law on an issue and include such sources of law as court decisions statutes, administrative regulations, and constitutions.

Principal A person on whose behalf an agent agrees to act, and acts.

Private reprimand When an unpublished communication is sent to the attorney by the disciplinary body, admonishing the attorney for his conduct, or published to educate other attorneys, but without the lawyer's name to identify him; it is also called **admonition**.

Probable cause A reasonable suspicion that a crime was committed by the suspect.

Probate The process of determining a will's validity and carrying out the administration of a person's estate on his death.

Probate courts Courts having jurisdiction to probate persons' wills.

Probate laws State laws that govern the distribution of a person's property after death.

Probation When an attorney is permitted to practice law, subject to certain conditions.

Procedural law Law that sets forth the procedures, or methods, used to enforce a legal right by bringing a civil action or a criminal prosecution.

Professional A person who engages in an occupation that requires advanced education, training, and/or skill.

Professional corporation A corporation formed by licensed professionals, such as doctors or lawyers.

Professionalism The ability to act like a professional.

Promise An assurance by a party to a contract that something will, or will not, happen in the future.

Property Something that can be owned or possessed.

Property crimes Those crimes where the goal of the perpetrator is to damage another's property or achieve some illegal economic gain.

Property law The body of law that deals with ownership and transfer of property rights and interests.

Prosecution A legal action brought against a criminal defendant alleging the commission of a crime.

Public order crimes Prohibited acts considered to be contrary to society's morals and values.

Public reprimand When a notice about the ethics violation and admonishment of the attorney is published in a bar journal or legal newspaper, so that the public is made aware of it.

Q

Quasi-contracts Implied in law contracts.

R

Real estate law A legal specialty area dealing with transactions involving real property.

Real property Land and anything permanently attached to it.

Record on appeal Consists of the trial court transcript, the pleadings, and exhibits and is used during appellate review of a case.

Recross-examination The re-questioning of an opposing witness after the other side's redirect examination.

Redirect examination The re-questioning of a witness after the other side's cross-examination.

Reformation The court's revision of a contract to reflect the party's true intentions.

Registration The act of recording a person's identifying information in certain records.

Regulation The process of controlling something by rule or restriction.

Release A document that formally relinquishes a legal claim.

Remand To send a case back to the trial court for further proceedings.

Remedies at law Money damages.

Remedies in equity All remedies other than money damages, such as injunctions, rescission, restitution, reformation, specific performance, and so on.

Remedy A judicial award by which legal rights are enforced and the violations of rights are compensated; it is the relief given to a party to enforce a right or to compensate for the violation of a right.

Reporters Books of reported cases published in numbered, multivolume sets arranged chronologically by date of decision.

Reprimand A form of scolding that declares the lawyer's conduct to be ethically improper; it is also called **reproval**.

Reproval Reprimand.

Requests for admission Discovery requests by a party to the other party asking for admission to the truth of certain matters relating to the lawsuit.

Requests for examination Discovery requests by a party to the court asking the court to order the other party to submit to a physical or mental examination.

Requests for production Discovery requests by a party to another party for documents or other tangible things, such as written contracts, or for permission to enter on the land or other property of a party for the purpose of conducting an inspection.

Rescission The termination of a contract and return of the parties to their pre-contracting positions.

Restitution An order requiring the attorney monetarily reimburse a person he financially harmed through his misconduct; the act of restoring a contractual party to his precontracting position.

Resulting trust A trust that is implied by the conduct of the parties.

Résumé A clear and concise summary of a job applicant's employment and educational background.

Retainer fees Legal fees the client agrees to pay in advance to secure the lawyer's services and that are not normally refundable.

Reverse To overrule, or rule against, the lower court's decision.

Rule of four The requirement that at least four of the nine Supreme Court justices must approve any petition for *certiorari* for the Court to agree to hear the case.

S

Sanctions Punishments a court or state bar association may levy against an attorney for violating a legal ethics rule.

Secondary sources of law Resources that summarize or interpret the law and can be used to locate primary sources of Law and are not law themselves.

Securities law The legal specialty area dealing with the regulation of securities, such as stocks and bonds.

Sentencing The process of a court imposing penalties on a defendant found guilty of committing a crime.

Sentencing hearing A hearing held sometime after the guilty verdict is rendered when the court hears arguments and evidence from both sides of a prosecution regarding aggravating and mitigating factors the court should consider in sentencing the defendant.

Separate property That property owned by a spouse prior to the marriage, as well as individual gifts and inheritances received during the marriage.

Service mark A distinctive word, motto, name, symbol, or device that a person uses to distinguish its services from those from another source.

Service of process The act of delivering to the defendant the plaintiff's complaint and the court's summons.

Settlement agreement A contract entered into by the parties to a legal dispute that sets forth the terms and conditions of the resolution and settlement of the dispute.

Settlor A grantor.

Shareholders Stockholders.

Simultaneous representation When an attorney represents two clients whose interests are directly adverse.

Sole proprietor The owner of a sole proprietorship.

Sole proprietorship A form of business organization created when a person goes into business by herself; it is the simplest form of business organization where the owner of the business is the business.

Solicitation An attempt to gain business.

Solo practitioner The sole proprietor of a law firm sole proprietorship.

Specific performance Granting the actual performance promised under the contract, normally awarded in cases involving unique goods or real property.

Spousal support Monthly payments made by a more affluent divorcing spouse to the other, for some period of time; it is also called **alimony**.

Staff attorneys Attorneys employed by the law firm partnership but who are not on a partnership, meaning ownership, track.

Statute of Frauds A state statute that requires certain types of contracts to be in writing and signed by the person against whom enforcement is sought.

Statutes Laws enacted by legislatures, at the state and federal levels of government.

Statutory law Law enacted by legislatures at any level of government.

Statutory provisions Parts of a statute.

Statutory rules of construction Rules that courts follow in interpreting statutory provisions.

Stockholders Owners of a corporation; they are also called **shareholders**.

Strict liability Tort liability imposed without regard to fault; it is also called **absolute liability** or **liability without fault**.

Subject matter jurisdiction Jurisdiction over the subject matter of a case.

Substantive law Law that defines the rights and duties of persons.

Successive representation When an attorney represents a current client whose interests conflict with the interests of a former client.

Summations Closing arguments.

Summer associates Law school students who work for a law firm in the summer or part-time while attending law school; they are also called **law clerks**.

Summons A court order directing a defendant to appear in court and answer the complaint.

Suspension The temporary revocation of a lawyer's license to practice law.

T

Tangible personal property Personal property that has physical existence and can be seen and touched.

Tenancy by the entirety A form of concurrent ownership where husbands and wives jointly own property and when one of the spouses dies, the deceased spouse's interest passes to the surviving spouse.

Tenancy in common A form of concurrent ownership where two or more persons own undivided interests in the property and if one of the persons dies his interest passes to her beneficiaries or heirs.

Testamentary disposition of property A will.

Testamentary trust A trust that is created by a will and that does not come into existence until the grantor's death.

Testator A person who makes a will.

Tort A civil wrong, other than a breach of contract.

Tort liability Arises when a person commits a tortious act.

Tort reform The act of changing the rules and applications of tort law to reverse the upward trend in compensation being awarded by juries today, particularly in personal injury cases.

Tortfeasor A person who commits a tort.

Trade secret A valuable business secret that gives the business an advantage over its competitors.

Trademark A distinctive word, motto, name, symbol, or device that a person uses to distinguish its products from those from another source.

True bill An indictment.

Trust A legal relationship created by a person, called a grantor, donor, or settlor, who transfers and delivers to one or more other persons, called a trustee or trustees, his property for the benefit of another or others, called the beneficiary or beneficiaries.

Trust *corpus* Trust *res*.

Trust *res* The property held by the trust; it is also called the **trust *corpus*.**

Trustee A person who holds the trust property.

U

U.S. courts of appeals The 13 circuit courts of intermediate appeal within the federal court system; they are also called **circuit courts** or **U.S. circuit courts of appeals**.

U.S. district courts The federal trial courts.

U.S. Supreme Court The highest federal court in the United States.

Unanimous opinion An opinion on which all the judges agree.

Unauthorized practice of law The practice of law by a person who is not authorized, meaning the person does not have a license to practice law in the jurisdiction.

Uniform Commercial Code (UCC) A model code governing commercial transactions that was written by legal experts and scholars to address commercial law issues and to provide uniform guidance to jurisdictions; it has been adopted, by statute, in whole or in part by every state.

Unmeritorious claim or defense A legal claim or defense that is frivolous and lacks merit.

V

Verdict A jury's decision, reached on completion of a jury trial, or a judge's decision, reached on the conclusion of a bench trial.

Violent crimes Crimes against people that cause them to suffer harm or death.

Visa An entry permit to the United States.

Visitation The right of a noncustodial parent to visit with the child.

Voir dire The juror selection process where attorneys or judges question prospective jurors in the case to determine who among them might be favorable to, or biased against, a particular party.

W

White-collar crimes Nonviolent commercial offenses committed by a person, public official, or business.

Will A legal instrument through which a person declares how he wants his property to be managed and distributed on his death; it is also called a **last will and testament** or a **testamentary disposition of property**.

Witness A person who is not a party and who testifies under oath in a trial or in a deposition in a lawsuit.

Work product doctrine A rule of evidence that protects from discovery by opposing counsel materials prepared by an attorney (or her agents) in anticipation of litigation.

Writ of *certiorari* An order by the Supreme Court formally accepting a party's petition to hear a case.

Writ of execution A court order granting the judgment creditor the right to pursue the judgment debtor's assets to satisfy the monetary judgment owed.

INDEX

H

I

J

K

L